THE OXFORD HAN

AFRICAN AMERICAN THEOLOGY

THE OXFORD HANDBOOK OF

AFRICAN AMERICAN THEOLOGY

Edited by
KATIE G. CANNON
and
ANTHONY B. PINN

UNIVERSITY PRESS

Oxford University Press is a department of the University of Oxford. It furthers the University's objective of excellence in research, scholarship, and education by publishing worldwide. Oxford is a registered trade mark of Oxford University Press in the UK and certain other countries.

Published in the United States of America by Oxford University Press
198 Madison Avenue, New York, NY 10016, United States of America.

First issued as an Oxford University Press paperback, 2018

Library of Congress Cataloging-in-Publication Data
Oxford handbook of African American theology / Katie G. Cannon and Anthony B. Pinn, editors.—1 [edition].
pages cm
ISBN 978-0-19-975565-3 (hardcover)— ISBN 978-0-19-091784-5 (paperback)
ISBN 978-0-19-998310-0 (online content)
1. Black theology. I. Cannon, Katie G., editor of compilation.
BT82.7.O94 2014
230.089'96073—dc23
2013043634

Contents

SECTION IV ONGOING CHALLENGES

SECTION V PROSPECTS FOR THE FUTURE

List of Contributors

Torin Alexander is Assistant Professor of Religion at St. Olaf College.

Victor Anderson is Oberlin Theological School Professor of Ethics and Society at Vanderbilt University Divinity School. He is also Professor and Director of the Program in African American and Diaspora Studies.

Edward P. Antonio is Harvey H. Potthoff Associate Professor of Christian Theology and Social Theory, and also Associate Dean of Diversities and Director of Justice and Peace Programs at Iliff School of Theology.

Allen Dwight Callahan is a writer, translator, and independent scholar living and working in Brazil.

Katie G. Cannon is Annie Scales Rogers Professor of Christian Ethics and Director of the Womanist Institute at Union Presbyterian Seminary.

J. Kameron Carter is Associate Professor of Systematic Theology and Black Church Studies at Duke University Divinity School.

M. Shawn Copeland is Professor of Theology at Boston College.

Keri Day is Assistant Professor of Theological and Social Ethics and Black Church Studies at Brite Divinity School.

Dianne M. Stewart Diakité is Associate Professor of Religion at Emory University.

James H. Evans Jr. is Robert K. Davies Professor of Systematic Theology at Colgate Rochester Divinity School.

Stephen C. Finley is Assistant Professor of Religious Studies and African American Studies at Louisiana State University.

Juan M. Floyd-Thomas is Associate Professor of African American Religious History at Vanderbilt University Divinity School.

Lewis R. Gordon teaches in the Department of Philosophy, the Africana Studies Institute, and the Center for Judaic Studies and Jewish Life at the University of Connecticut at Storrs.

Horace Griffin is Associate Professor of Pastoral Theology at Pacific School of Religion.

Clarence E. Hardy III is Assistant Professor of the History of American Christianity at Yale University Divinity School.

Diana L. Hayes is Emerita Professor of Systematic Theology at Georgetown University.

Derek S. Hicks is Assistant Professor of Religion and Culture at Wake Forest University Divinity School.

Willie James Jennings is Associate Professor of Theology and Black Church Studies at Duke University Divinity School.

Sylvester Johnson is Associate Professor of African American Studies and Religious Studies at Northwestern University.

Terrence L. Johnson is Associate Professor of Religion at Haverford College.

Cheryl A. Kirk-Duggan is Professor of Theology and Women's Studies at Shaw University Divinity School.

Stephanie Y. Mitchem is Professor of Religious Studies and Chair of the Religious Studies Department at University of South Carolina.

Larry G. Murphy is Professor of the History of Christianity at Garrett Evangelical Theological Seminary.

Peter J. Paris is Elmer G. Homrighausen Professor of Christian Social Ethics, Emeritus at Princeton Theological Seminary.

Anthony B. Pinn is Agnes Cullen Arnold Professor of Humanities and Professor of Religious Studies at Rice University.

Anthony G. Reddie is Visiting Research Fellow at Aston University (UK).

R. Drew Smith is Professor of Urban Ministry at Pittsburgh Theological Seminary.

Josef Sorett is Assistant Professor of Religion and African American Studies at Columbia University.

Emilie M. Townes is Dean and E. Rhodes and Leona B. Carpenter Professor of Womanist Ethics and Society at Vanderbilt Divinity School.

E. Marshall Turman is Director of the Office of Black Church Studies and Assistant Research Professor of Black Church Studies at Duke University Divinity School.

Corey D. B. Walker is Dean of Arts and Sciences and John W. and Anna Hodgin Hanes Professor of the Social Sciences at Winston-Salem State University.

Jonathan L. Walton is Plummer Professor of Christian Morals and Pusey Minister in the Memorial Church and Professor of Religion and Society at Harvard University and Harvard Divinity School.

Frederick L. Ware is Associate Professor of Theology at Howard University Divinity School.

Dennis W. Wiley is pastor of Covenant Baptist United Church in Washington, DC.

THE OXFORD HANDBOOK OF

AFRICAN AMERICAN THEOLOGY

INTRODUCTION

ANTHONY B. PINN AND KATIE G. CANNON

African American theology as an academically informed enterprise began in the late 1960s through the effort of African American scholars and progressive pastors to shape the religious nature and meaning of social transformation in the years after major successes of the civil rights movement. Ministers and academics took a public stand against injustice and demanded a re-envisioning of life in the United States that took seriously the humanity of African Americans—and they found no contradiction between this demand for material advancement and the demands of the Gospel of Christ. From a *New York Times* piece proclaiming a "Black Theology" as the proper theological and religious response to injustice, to the formulation of an academic theological discourse based on the high and low points of the civil rights movement, African American theology as a theology of liberation gained voice and public attention.[1]

It went from a somewhat informal articulation of theological claims that were relatively isolated to the community of the like-minded—that is, African Americans committed to a shared agenda marked by the particular concerns of African Americans—to a systematic articulation of justice in light of religious sensibilities and a (albeit weak) social theory expressed to the world. It shifted from a primary home within religious organizations to being grounded within the structures of the academy, with trained scholars (many with church affiliations) in charge of developing and articulating its major points. Now African American theology reads the Bible and the Christian tradition through a lens of radical social change.

African American theology revolved around epistemologies, ontologies, and so on, each meant to speak theologically to the lived experience of African Americans.[2] It meant to alter the prevailing theological anthropology that positioned African Americans as "less than...." In order to do this, African American theology drew from past conversations (e.g., civil rights theology) to represent African Americans through *imago Dei* and tied to this a scripturally expressed commitment on the part of God to the transformation of social arrangements in light of this creation in the image of God. "Whiteness" became the grand narrative of oppression that had to be exposed and dismantled, and it was argued scripture, the true Christian tradition, and the cultural worlds of African Americans provided the tools for doing so.

In some instances this theology involved a blending of the social gospel orientation of figures like Martin Luther King, Jr., with the social analysis and critique of those like Malcolm X.[3] What resulted was a demand to rethink the nature and meaning of blackness over against a sense of white supremacy that had fueled religious trauma tied to political-social and economic inequality. To accomplish this, certain theological categories were put aside, and others—in particular a "blackened" Christology—were highlighted as framing the very meaning of both God's demand for justice and the importance of black humanity.[4] The cultural heritage of African Americans was drawn into this work as a way of expressing the manner in which human imagination and creativity speak to the large and pressing issues of black existence in a country preoccupied with "whiteness." Religion, culture, history, experience, and sacred texts also framed the doing of black theology of liberation and in this way grounded theological analysis and discourse not in the abstractions of faith but in the world.

Inspired by social gospel theology of the late nineteenth and early twentieth centuries, African American theology—in its two incarnations—developed into a modality of constructive theology whereby the primary consideration is the earthy impact of theology on pressing social issues. And, with this done in a way that privileges the integrity of human life over doctrine and creed, it has at times run afoul of religious (particularly conservative) communities.[5] Yet what some consider a healthy tension between a need to privilege justice and at least a mild interest in religious tradition has marked much of this discourse. The downside of this approach, however, is clear: those outside Christian communities (even Muslims and practitioners of African-derived traditions, for example, lay outside the typically recognized content of religious community for many of these theologians) have often been marginal to the normative structures of this discourse.

From the first generation of these thinkers—including an array of theologians such as James Cone, J. Deotis Roberts, Major Jones; ethicists such as Peter Paris and Preston Williams; historians like Gayraud Wilmore; philosophers such as William Jones; as well as ministers such as Albert Cleage—black theology grew to include at least two, depending on how one counts, additional generations of scholars/ministers committed to the basic framework of a theologized social agenda. These new generations have maintained a similar agenda, theological vocabulary, and grammar, but have fine-tuned certain dimensions of the discourse.[6] Examples of this include a push to theologically recognize the religious pluralism that has always marked African American communities, including the theologizing of humanism and/or atheism as intrinsic to African American experience. Furthermore, the effort initiated early in the development of black theology to engage other modalities of liberation theology for the sake of global solidarity was further advanced by those Cone and others trained. That is to say, while the first generation of scholars working on the black theology project outlined its basic structure and commitments, those following them (typically trained by them) refined this work without, in most cases, radical departures from its primary parameters. Yet there was a difficulty: the scholars tended to be men, and the work did not extend far beyond race and racism.

While this theology did heavy lifting with respect to public discourse on race, it cast the dilemma and the solution in terms of an unchallenged masculinity and maleness as normative humanity the proper lens by means of which to view life. Much of this could have been anticipated in that the theological frameworks used were drawn from the training received by this first generation—training taking place within cultural worlds that privileged men.

Their theological models—Paul Tillich and Reinhold Niebuhr among others—grew out of a deep suspicion concerning human conduct, but also a sense of hopefulness that humans could do better based upon the presence of a caring and capable God. The actors working in the world upon which they based this assessment were overwhelming men—the political figures, the economic leaders. This is not to say women weren't in positions of power, but there lingered something of the cult of domesticity that clouded the capacities and perceptions of women. At best, black theologians attempted some sensitivity by suggesting that addressing race as the dominant modality of injustice in North America would produce an environment in which other forms of injustice—vaguely defined in most cases—would have to fall. In short, get race together first.

Although places like Union Theological Seminary in New York City produced women doing liberative work from within the African American tradition, black theology through the 1970s lacked sustained response to issues beyond the socioeconomic, political, psychological, and religious impact of racism. Like the Church, Jacquelyn Grant, Katie Cannon, and Delores Williams pointed out, black theology failed to recognize the complexities of life within the United States, and truncated the nature and meaning of oppression—rendering it synonymous (only) with racism.[7]

Drawing from literature and other forms of cultural production by African American women, Grant, Cannon, Williams, and others reread the Bible and the Christian tradition in such a way as to recover the voices and perspectives of women—without which a sense of injustice and liberation are at best incomplete. Taking the name of this new approach to theologizing from Alice Walker's theory of the womanist, these scholars pushed for a more complex sense of African American religious experience, theological discourse, and ethical conduct that measured out the many ways in which African Americans are dehumanized—by sexism, racism, class, and more recently in terms of sexuality and environmental destruction.[8]

Women trained within the context of this early, academic black theological discourse provided much-needed alterations. Simply asserting a different existential arrangement of life, however, was not sufficient to turn this critique into alternate theological programs and projects. Doing so also involved the incorporation of preferred theoretical and methodological tools that made possible a healthy handling of selected source materials. Much of this theoretical grounding is drawn from Walker, whose presentation of the womanist provided different centering points for anthropology, distinct framing of social theory, and a more robust and diverse sense of ethics. Sources were used in ways that focused attention on alternate positioning of theological categories—for example, a rethinking of Christology—and new moral and ethical tools of conduct (and methodology) drawn from black women. In making these moves, womanist scholarship has been able to also expose with greater clarity and detail the "web of oppression" afflicting us.

This challenge to the metanarrative of race surfaced for the careful reader and listener a more robust theory of oppression—a sense of oppression as weblike in nature—as well as an alternate epistemology of oppression. Noteworthy in this process has been increased attention to the need for African American theology to involve a synergy of disciplines that allow the theologian to add nuance and complexity to her work by engaging research outside theology, and for that matter, outside religious studies more generally. This framework opened a way to continuously integrate theological work so as to be sensitive to the layered nature of suffering. African American theology—its form and content—has needed to evolve in order to speak a word of transformation to African Americans encountering the harshness of life in so many different and interconnected ways.

Greater and more explicit attention to postmodern thought has also served to expand both black and womanist theologies with regard to issues of sexuality, embodiment, globalization, and the dynamics of sociopolitical and economic formations. For example, explicit and implicit appeal to Michel Foucault has lent energy to issues of sexuality and embodiment, with greater complexity and in ways that challenge old notions of the subject, transcendence, and liberation among other core categories framing African American theology. The pragmatic sensibilities of others—for example, Cornel West—have helped refine theories of and engagement with history, and in this way force African American theology to move beyond romanticization of particular strategies of struggle against injustice as well as uncritical perceptions of the role of religion in the world.

This is all to say that African American theology—black and womanist theologies—has matured over the years. Its structure and content has shifted to reflect the changing existential arrangements of life for African Americans. With such changes, participants in the construction of African American theology have periodically stepped back to reflect on the work done.

Volume Structure

Self-evaluation in the form of reflection and introspection has taken place, and one finds it in published form in a variety of ways. For example, this is certainly one way of reading Cone's intellectual autobiography or his *Risks of Faith: The Emergence of a Black Theology of Liberation, 1968–1998* (2000). Or J. Deotis Roberts's review of his contributions to black theology's development in the form of *Black Religion and Black Theology: The Collected Essays of J. Deotis Roberts* (2003). More recently, theologians from the second and third generations of black and womanist theologies have contributed to this moment of introspection through a variety of Festschrift-styled volumes and other publications reflecting on the work of the first generation. We have in mind, for instance Michael Battle's *The Quest for Liberation and Reconciliation: Essays in Honor of J. Deotis Roberts* (2005) and Dwight Hopkins's *Black Faith and Public Talk: Critical Essays on James H. Cone's "Black Theology and Black Power"* (2007).[9]

In addition, Stacey Floyd-Thomas's publication, *Deeper Shades of Purple*, and Layli Phillips's *Womanist Reader* provide similar reflections on the development of womanist discourse. These projects and others like them by second-generation theologians are palimpsestic in nature, but the work of first-generation theologians not only bleeds through, but also tends to shape the tone and texture of more recent writings. The challenge entailed by this situation involves the meaning and practice of introspection—too many assumptions continue and through the years are given the weight of certainty, of "truth." Such reified thought can be difficult to alter, in spite of good intentions. Introspection, in this way, can morph into celebration and the safeguarding of tradition.

The reflective work up to this point has been highly descriptive. However, what is necessary in this historical era is an interrogation of African American theology—a self-evaluation and internal critique that lays out its structure, content, and logic, with an eye toward its future. This approach is consistent with the stated demands of African American theology.

Mindful of this need for critical engagement, this volume surveys the academic content of African American theology by highlighting in five sections, its (I) sources; (II) doctrines; (III) internal debates; (IV) current challenges; (V) future prospects, in order to present key topics related to the wider palette of black religion in a sustained scholarly format.

Every effort was made to include both Protestant and Catholic contributors so as to represent a rich sense of how the Christian faith is expressed in this discourse. In addition, we have included thinkers from outside the Christian faith who are sensitive to Africa-derived orientation as well as nontheistic orientations. Hence, both the topics covered and the range of contributors foster a volume that is layered and representative. Readers will discover that some of the essays provide more contextual information than others, and some provide more general attention to the theological, philosophical, and historical context for black and womanist theologies than others. This should not be understood as a problem, but rather as a necessity—a reflection of the manner in which African American theology borrows heavily from a larger tradition, but also that African American theology has initiated new directions and dimensions of theological inquiry. Furthermore, some of the topics within the volume required contributors to address the interdisciplinary nature of African American theology by, on some occasions, highlighting a discussion of those disciplines informing it and in other instances foregrounding the very nature of this interdisciplinarity. The goal, however, remains consistent across the essays: to provide a thick and rich description of the nature and meaning of African American theology. Finally, what we offer in this introduction provides a sense of what these sections contain and what they are meant to accomplish.

Section I

The first section describes the sources used in the development of African American theology. These eight essays constituting the lead-off division of this handbook give attention to the Christian tradition, scripture, culture/cultural production, African American history, and African American experience. In addition, however, our sense of African American theology also points to the application in both explicit and implicit ways of other categories that seem foundational to this theological discourse. In presenting these other categories—reason, theory, and methodology—the volume points out the manner in which the "how" of African American theology develops over time, and in conversation with other discourses concerned with what we know, how we know it, and how we articulate such meaningful knowledge. Some might argue these three categories better fit elsewhere in the volume, but we understand them to serve as source materials for many in African American theology. That is to say, reason, theory, and methodology do not simply constitute tools, but rather our reading of African American theology suggests they also represent the "material" used to develop this theology.

In addition, they have another function as well; hence, presenting these other three categories—reason, theory, and methodology—within the section on sources also points out the changing posture toward theological inquiry over the course of generational shifts from the first generation—for example, James Cone, J. Deotis Roberts, Katie Cannon, and Delores Williams—to more recent scholars who maintain something of the original commitment to theological inquiry premised on pressing issues of social justice, but who seek to further unpack the assumptions and fine-tune the processes by means of which African American theology is conceptualized and actualized. Through these eight categories we do not assume we capture all the various layers of source material and basic framing for the doing of African American theology; rather, we see these descriptive essays as presenting some of the foundational considerations that have informed this mode of theological discourse.

Section II

The second section presents major theological categories and concerns that define this modality of theological discourse. While they have had varying degrees of importance over the course of the contemporary presentation of African American theology, they all seem to figure into its basic vocabulary and grammar. There are eleven essays in this section that move from doctrine of God to Christology, which has often been considered the basic look of African American theology: it is in significant ways an extended articulation of the contemporary significant of the "Christ Event." From these categories, African American theology has found a way of talking about other key dimensions of theology. The second coming of Christ (the eschaton) is related to the restoration of human flourishing marked out by righteousness and justice. Salvation, primarily as a matter of social transformation over against personal spiritual renewal, draws from the commitment of God to the well-being of humanity and demands the mechanics of the Christ Event as God's "yes" to human flourishing called salvation. In this volume, salvation is treated as synonymous to liberation and social transformation. For many African American theologians, salvation in some ways resembles what Martin Luther King, Jr., understood as the Beloved Community. In certain ways, there is some overlap between the notion of salvation and that of liberation as used by African American theologians—both black liberationist and womanist theologians. As salvation is typically addressed as a corporate reality, so are evil and sin. That is to say, they are connected to moral misconduct involving the participation in various forms of injustice as opposed to notions of personal shortcomings one might find in church doctrines and creeds—for example, premarital sex and adultery.

Humans have an obligation to help bring about transformation, and for some African American theologians the Holy Spirit plays a role in gaining the insight and capacity to struggle for liberation. Heaven and hell are played out in African American theology, as the essay addressing these categories suggests; but they are not understood primarily in a literal sense. The former—heaven—more typically has something to do with transformed mundane life, and the latter representing the experience of injustice. This all takes place within the context of material life—within the basic parameters of the world.

African American theology has not been particularly clear with respect to how the world has come about, or for that matter the creation of humanity. Yet, it is safe to say, a literal reading of biblical creation accounts does not work within the context of this theological discourse. It does not seem opposed to evolution, although this explanation is not explicitly addressed by most, but there is a sense there is a divine spark or logic undergirding the unfolding of the world and the production of human life. The basic community for many, but certainly not all African American theologians, in which all of this theologizing is worked out, remains the Church. And this organization—its mechanics, intent, and capacities—has received attention (not always critical) from African American theologians.

Section III

The seven essays making up the third section highlight some of the more significant developments within African American theology, developments that challenge many of the assumptions made by African American theologians with respect to source materials and theological categories outlined in sections I and II.

While womanist theology is instrumental and discussed in the first two sections, we wanted to give it more explicit and careful attention in this section. We do this because it is a mode of African American theologizing, but also there are ways in which it has functioned as a corrective to black theology. This complexity needs to be taken into consideration. Furthermore, while most African American theologians work from an assumption of theism, from the 1970s moving forward the usefulness of this assumption has been tested and challenged. That is to say, this section also points out the ways in which African American theology has involved attention to nontheistic modes of meaning making and the emergence of a godless mode of theologizing not restricted to the "Death of God Theology." Another advancement over the past few decades has been greater attention to bodies and embodiment as the "space" in and out of which African American theology emerges. Therefore, this section gives attention to both the importance of embodiment in the doing of African American theology, as well as the possibility of African American theology as an embodied theology.

Related to this issue of embodied bodies, the growing attention to issues of sex and sexuality is serving to reshape African American theology in important ways—ways that not only change the nature and meaning of liberation but also allow for the emergence of an African American theology that addresses explicitly the voices of gay and lesbian African Americans. Such expansion of African American theology is not limited to these issues; there has also been a strong and important challenge to the Christian bias of much of this theologizing. Hence, we give attention in one of the essays to religious pluralism (but without a turn to atheism) as theological discourse—being sensitive to the decades' call for greater consideration of the diverse religious landscape of African American communities. Finally, while African American theology has involved scholarly conversation, it has also begged two important questions over the years: who is the audience for this work and how do we teach the concerns and findings of African American theology?

Section IV

The fourth section, composed of six essays, explores some of the more significant areas requiring continued attention. From its effort to think about social transformation without sustained attention to social theory, to the assumption of ontological blackness as the marker of African American identity, to the meaning of globalization for African American theology's concern with economic justice, this section points out some of the holes in African American theology's structure, while also noting ways in which these shortcomings are being addressed. In addition, other identity issues are brought into play through attention to what it means for African American theology to understand the hemispheric nature of the realities it seeks to address, as well as the basic question of how Africa and African-ness figure into the self-description of *African* American theology.

Section V

The final section presents new directions in African American theology. These are not challenges as presented in sections III and IV, but rather new and emerging areas of interest. For example, does the growth of the prosperity gospel alter African American theology in significant ways? In raising this question, the volume offers readers an opportunity to wrestle with the nature and meaning of the prosperity gospel over against the self-description of the purpose and function of the gospel message presented by many African American theologians. This section also explores more concretely the sense of public life or the public arena assumed within much African American theology as the proper arena for religious organization and theological discourse. That is to say, how and where does African American theology do its best work, and what is the public function of religious organizations, if they have one? We believe the shifts and changes within African American theology, in part stimulated by the changing nature of religion within the United States, also push for greater clarity concerning culture and the cultural context for this form of theologizing. So this topic is addressed. The three essays in this section do not provide all there is to say concerning future directions for African American theology, but they do provide readers with at least a rough sense of how its growth has nurtured a new range of questions and issues.

Purpose of the Handbook

By means of these five sections it is not our goal to provide attention to every category, every topic, and every theme that has surfaced in African American theology over the years. Based on a thematic and topical structure, this handbook provides scholars and advanced students detailed description, analysis, and constructive discussions concerning African American theology.

When this volume is taken as a whole, the nature, structures, functions, and purposes of African American theology—black and womanist theologies—become clearer. And the complexities—including a Protestant orientation and a Catholic orientation—involved in forging a new theological discourse can be better appreciated. While African American theology still remains somewhat "marginal," it is a recognized dimension of the religious landscape of the United States and is addressed as such by both African American thinkers and Euro-American thinkers alike. Its vocabulary has become part of the general makeup of theological discourse in the United States, and its proponents have held major positions within the professional societies associated with the study of religion in the United States. But it is a theological story centuries in the making and still in process. It's an ongoing effort to make theological sense of the world and what it contains—a story that requires ongoing and careful attention.

Our effort to tell this story, at this particular stage of its development, has been possible only with a great deal of help from a variety of people. Although it is common to include these remarks in a separate section titled "Acknowledgments," we want to end the introduction with an expression of gratitude as our way of indicating how central to the conceptualization and production of this volume was the assistance and encouragement we received over the years it took to bring this volume together.

We begin by thanking our editor, Theo Calderara, for his patience and good humor as the length of time necessary for completion of the project continued to grow. We would also like to thank our students who helped with a variety of tasks necessary to bring this volume to completion. Of these many students, we must express particular appreciation for the work done by Christopher Driscoll to make certain the manuscript was properly formatted and consistent with Oxford University Press style requirements. As always, we both have friends and colleagues without whom this project would have been more difficult to complete and less rich. Among them, of course, are the contributors to the volume. Finally, we offer special gratitude to those who paved the way, who provided the initial efforts that now constitute this robust discourse.

Notes

1. See the documents in James H. Cone and Gayraud Wilmore, eds., *Black Theology: A Documentary History, 1966–1979* (Maryknoll, NY: Orbis Books, 1979), parts 1–2.
2. See, for example, Cheryl Sanders, "Christian Ethics and Theology in Womanist Perspective," *Journal of Feminist Studies in Religion* 5, no. 2 (1989): 83–112. Monica Coleman has recently published a volume based on an alternate perspective on womanist thought and womanist

identity that for many is deeply problematic: *Ain't I a Womanist Too?* (Minneapolis: Fortress Press, 2013).

3. Examples include James H. Cone, *Martin, Malcolm, and America: A Dream or a Nightmare* (Maryknoll, NY: Orbis Books, 1992); J. Deotis Roberts, *Bonhoeffer and King: Speaking Truth to Power* (Louisville, KY: Westminster John Knox Press, 2004).
4. James H. Cone, *A Black Theology of Liberation* (Maryknoll, NY: Orbis Books, 1986) is a prime example, an early articulation of this structure. This strong attention to Christology filtered through African American experience is also present in Jacquelyn Grant's *White Women's Christ and Black Women's Jesus: Feminist Christology and Womanist Response* (Atlanta: Scholars Press, 1989) and Kelly Brown Douglas's *The Black Christ* (Maryknoll, NY: Orbis Books, 1993). It's important to recognize that Cone served as dissertation advisor for both Grant and Douglas.
5. See James H. Cone and Gayraud Wilmore, *Black Theology: A Documentary History, 1980–1992* (Maryknoll, NY: 1992), part 2.
6. For a sense of this development, see, for instance, Dwight Hopkins, *Introducing Black Theology* (Maryknoll, NY: Orbis Books, 1999); Hopkins, *Heart and Head: Black Theology—Past, Present, and Future* (New York: Palgrave Macmillan, 2002); Stacey Floyd-Thomas and Anthony Pinn, *Liberation Theologies in the United States: An Introduction* (New York: New York University Press, 2010), chapters 1–2; Diana L. Hayes and Cyprian Davis, *Taking Down Our Harps: Black Catholics in the United States* (Maryknoll, NY: Orbis Books, 1998).
7. Delores Williams, *Sisters in the Wilderness: The Challenge of Womanist God-Talk* (Maryknoll, NY: Orbis Books, 1993); Grant, *White Women's Christ*; Katie Cannon, *Black Womanist Ethics* (Altanta: Scholars Press, 1989). For general introductions to womanist thought see Stephanie Mitchem, *Introducing Womanist Theology* (Maryknoll, NY: Orbis Books, 2002); Stacey Floyd-Thomas, ed., *Deeper Shades of Purple: Womanism in Religion and Society* (New York: New York University Press, 2006); Katie Cannon, Emilie Townes, and Angela Sims, eds., *Womanist Theological Ethics: A Reader* (Louisville, KY: Westminster John Knox Press, 2011); Layli Phillips, *A Womanist Reader: The First Quarter Century of Womanist Thought* (New York: Routledge, 2006).
8. Alice Walker, *In Search of Our Mother's Gardens* (New York: Harvest, 1983).
9. James H. Cone, *Risks of Faith: The Emergence of Black Theology of Liberation, 1968–1998* (Boston: Beacon Press, 2000); J. Deotis Roberts, *Black Religion, Black Theology: The Collected Essays of J. Deotis Roberts*, ed. David Emmanuel Goatley (Harrisburg, PA: Trinity Press International, 2003); Michael Battles, ed. *The Quest for Liberation and Reconciliation: Essays in Honor of J. Deotis Roberts* (Nashville: Westminster John Knox Press, 2005); Dwight Hopkins, ed., *Black Faith and Public Talk: Critical Essays on James H. Cone's "Black Theology and Black Power"* (Maryknoll, NY: Orbis Books; Waco, TX: Baylor University Press, 2007).

SECTION I

SOURCES

CHAPTER 1

AFRICAN AMERICAN HISTORY AND AFRICAN AMERICAN THEOLOGY

STEPHEN C. FINLEY

African American history is one of the central issues in black theology. Not only is the chronicle of people of African descent in the United States important in the formation of black theology, since the civil rights and Black Power movements in the United States were pivotal to its development, African American history is also a crucial source of black theology.[1] The urgency and immediacy of these historical moments had implications for real human beings, concrete bodies, which meant that "African American history," as the second source in Cone's theology, served as a particular lens through which to view the world and Christian theology more generally. Such a perspective was not necessarily universal but helped to frame the task of constructing theology in terms that spoke to the historical context in which black theology appeared. Engaging James H. Cone[2] offers a good place to begin because of his position as one who initiated the formal discourse of black theology. He notes in *A Black Theology of Liberation*:

> I did not have time to do the theological and historical research needed to present a "balanced" perspective on the problems of racism in America. Black men, women, and children were being shot and imprisoned for asserting their right to a dignified existence. Others were wasting away in ghettos, dying from filth, rats, and dope, as white and black ministers preached about a blond, blue-eyed Jesus who came to make us all just like him.[3]

What Cone suggests is that the exigencies of the moment required a theology of liberation that could speak to conditions presently facing African Americans. Therefore, the history of African Americans, especially given the racism and violence that black people experienced in America, provided a source of theology that was particular to the circumstances of his community. This essay will explore both—the ways in which African American history is used to construct and justify the existence of black theology and some of the conceptual problems that its use raises.

History as a Source and Method of Theology

For Cone, history is a source of black theology since "black history refers to the way blacks were brought to this land and the way they have been treated in this land."[4] This notion of history is closely related to "the black experience,"[5] which he contends is the first source of black theology because "black theology cannot speak of God and God's involvement in contemporary America without identifying God's presence with the events of liberation in the black community."[6] Black history appears to be the acknowledgment and documentation of past experiences for the purpose of constructing a theology of liberation, while black theology seems to refer to activities that are more representative of the "present" that reveal God's work in the liberation process.

Notwithstanding the technical matters distinguishing history from experience in Cone's thought, he connects African American history to the question of black humanity, which, he argues, white people denied through the practices of chattel slavery in the United States. He does not clearly articulate why black history signifies this specific issue, but he does maintain that "the history of slavery in this country reveals how low human depravity can sink. And the fact that this country still, in many blatant ways, perpetuates the idea of the inferiority of blacks poignantly illustrates the capabilities of human evil."[7] What this may imply is that "black history" discloses slavery as a supreme example of the depths of depravity to which a black theology of liberation must speak, and it also reveals ongoing practices and discourses of black inferiority since slavery's abolition. So, Cone suggests, African American history demonstrates inhumanity committed against African Americans.[8]

African American history, as a source of theology, does more than expose whites' inhumane activities toward black people, it is also the story of black resistance.[9] For Cone, this is the most important factor that black history contributes as a source for black theology. This resistance, contrary to its exclusion in American history books, is an illustration of Black Power. Cone explains:

> More importantly black history is black persons saying no to every act of white brutality. Contrary to what whites say in *their* history books, black power is not new. It began when black mothers decided to kill their babies rather than have them grow up to be slaves. Black power is Nat Turner, Denmark Vesey, and Gabriel Prosser planning a slave revolt. It is slaves poisoning their masters, and Frederick Douglass delivering an abolitionist address. This is the history that black theology must take seriously before it can begin to speak about God and black humanity.[10]

African American history, then, becomes a theological story about black resistance to oppression and violence. It is an account of the active recalcitrance of black people in the face of the most extreme life-threatening and life-curtailing circumstances. It counters the depiction of African Americans in history books as inferior. According to Cone, this is "the" history from which black theology must draw in its formulations about God and black people.

Such a perspective is retrospective in the sense that black theological communities look at African American history as a means of determining liberating activity in the present. Of course, while African American history remains a prominent source for making such judgments, other data categories also participate the process. In other words, what God is doing and will do is thought to be gleaned from divine activity in African American history in conjunction with other sources of black theology, including the Bible, black experience, and African American culture. Perhaps Cone's strongest statement about African American history as a source of black theology is in this regard:

> Black theology focuses on black history as a source for its theological interpretation of God's work in the world because divine activity is inseparable from black history. There can be no comprehension of black theology without realizing that its existence comes from a community which looks back on its unique past, visualizes its future, and then makes decisions about possibilities in the present.[11]

In this sense, black theology is indebted to African American history, and a particular version of it, in fact. History provides the symbolic landscape by which interpretations of God's activities or absence can be made. If God is not active on behalf of black people in history, then black people can dispense with God or a particular god in lieu of a God who takes sides with African Americans against their oppressors.[12]

Moreover, Cornel West argues that, in addition to history serving as a source for black theology, it also functions as a method of historical dialectics.[13] According to West, this methodology has three movements: negation, preservation, transformation—hence the dialectic,[14] and their subject matter engages white interpretations of Christianity as well as the theological significance of black history and the black experience. West elaborates:

> The reflection by black theologians begins by negating white interpretations of the gospel, continues by preserving their own perceived truths of the biblical texts, and ends by transforming past understandings of the gospel into new ones. These three steps embody an awareness of the social context of theologizing, the need to accent the historical experiences of black people and the insights of the Bible.[15]

Regarding these theological reflections, West maintains that black theologians negate hidden agendas that they glean in given theological formulations with adverse social implications that are embedded in its symbols surreptitiously. The second step is an interpretation of black historical experience and an engagement of the biblical text in light of this experience. The biblical truth that black theologians try to preserve, West claims, is that God sides with the oppressed and is active in history on their behalf. Finally, because the gospel must speak to every age, it must be recovered and repeated.[16] The role that history plays in this methodology and in black theology generally, though provocative, is not without its problems, and the notion of African American history as a source of theology and method is itself replete with conceptual challenges.

Other forms of black theology utilize African American history as a source as well, in particular, with slavery as an entry point in theological development. That is, the subject and history of slavery become the point at which the development of black theology is initiated. This is true of nascent womanist theology, as can be seen in the work of Emilie M. Townes, Katie G. Cannon, and others, for instance.[17] Womanist theology, according to Stephanie Mitchem, is "the systematic, faith-based exploration of the many facets of African American women's religiosity,"[18] and also concerns itself with the "survival and freedom-struggles of African American women,"[19] as Delores S. Williams contends. Indeed, African American history is significant in womanist theology, but womanist readings of history privilege the experiences of African American women, especially "ordinary" black women.[20]

As such, African American history in womanist theology is often an explicit and sometimes an implicit critique of the ways in which African American history is constructed in black theology. For example, Williams contends, "Womanist analysis... suggests another kind of history to which black theology must give attention if it is to be inclusive of black women's experience."[21] What Williams has in mind, here, is attention to the "re/productive" history of African American women, by which she means the creative products of women's labor, whatever they pass on through their labor, in the interest of women's well-being and that of the family and community. This re/productive history would include black women's literary tradition, which, Cannon argues, parallels African American history, given that black women's writing was tied to the origin of black people in America.[22] This is just a sample of the ways in which womanist theologians employ African American history that is sometimes at odds with black theology, more generally understood. Other black theologians have also raised issues with black theology in particular and African American theology in general.

The Problem(s) of History in Black Theology

Most prominent among the challenges to black theology's use of African American history is William R. Jones, author of *Is God a White Racist? A Preamble to Black Theology*.[23] Originally published in 1972, Jones's engagement of the matter of history in black theology is directed toward those whom he considered the most prominent black theologians of the period—namely, Albert Cleage Jr., James H. Cone, Major Jones, J. Deotis Roberts, and Joseph Washington.[24] For Jones, these black theologians utilize history in a manner that suggests God is on the side of African Americans, that God is active in history, working on behalf of the liberation of black people, and that history indicates that liberation is not only possible but inevitable because of God's activity in the history of African American people. Black theology, then, requires a type of triumphalist interpretation of black history that views God as "good" and working on the behalf of black people to bring liberation to fruition. In Cone's black theology, this seems to be a foregone conclusion.[25] Cleage is much more explicit, concluding "that there is nothing more sacred than the liberation of Black people,"[26] and he insists that sources such as black history and the Old Testament of the Christian Bible as well as the life of Jesus. The primary indicator for the overcoming of suffering in black theology is the Christ event—the life, death, and resurrection of Jesus. And this event comes to symbolize the ways in which enduring suffering for African Americans will lead to glory as it did for Jesus.[27]

What is apparent in black theology is a unique way of constructing African American history as a primary source that demonstrates ostensibly that God, as benevolent, is working on behalf of black people and through them in service of their liberation. Jones calls this line of reasoning into question. He contends that for such claims to be valid one has to demonstrate historical evidence of God's unequal or selective activity on behalf of some and not others. Such a conclusion is untenable, he claims, since the historical record is ambiguous. Historical events could just as easily suggest a conclusion that is the opposite of those espoused by black theologians, namely, that God is a white racist. This is just as likely as any other to be the reason that black people suffer. Jones refers to this problem as "the multievidentiality of suffering."[28] He explains:

> The quickest and most effective way to execute this attack is to show that events are multievidential; specifically, the materials and events that have traditionally been

> interpreted as evidence of divine benevolence can just as easily support the opposite conclusion, of divine malevolence.[29]

Jones argues that the specific events and the multiple and cumulative events cited by black theologians indicating God's interest in the liberation of black people can also support a conclusion that is antithetical to black theology's claims. That is to say, Jones's contention is that ways of interpreting African American history that can be used to show that God takes sides with the oppressed or elects them as chosen people are faulty and can just as easily be used to support God's racism or malevolence.

How does one know what God will do on behalf of black people in the future (if God even acts on behalf of African Americans)? The question is of interest to Jones. Black theology would point to African American history as one of its sources for this answer and suggest that history provides ample illustrations of God's activity—working through individuals and communities to effectuate liberation. Related to the multievidentiality of suffering, Jones's critique would imply issues with a selective reading of "history" to support such a contention. He goes further to build on his objections by suggesting the idea that God is the sum of God's acts.[30] This would imply that God's character as good and as interested in suffering people may not be supported by African American history, since the events that could point to God's interest can also point to God's malfeasance. In short, there is no way of knowing God's character or God's activity based on African American history because what God will do in the future is based on what God has done in the past, and this proposition leaves African American history as a source of black theology ambiguous at best if not unhelpful.

In light of Jones's critique of African American history in black theology, womanist theologian Delores S. Williams suggests that God does not work actively in history to offer liberation, but rather God is active in history with humans, who must secure an outcome for themselves. What God provides, she proposes, is survival and involvement as humans struggle for quality of life.[31] Hence, Williams declares, that the "wilderness experience" is more appropriate than the black experience to describe African American existence in America.[32]

Wilderness is a much more inclusive model that can account for differences in gender and African American religious perspectives and aptly describes African Americans who are "oppressed and quasi-free"[33] and struggle to build community in uncertain circumstances.

Anthony Pinn, however, in his *Why, Lord? Suffering and Evil in Black Theology*,[34] argues that Jones does not go far enough in his criticism of black theology.[35] Implied in his work is the conclusion that only humans act in history, and that black theology's responses to the problem of theodicy do damage both to the tenets of the Christian faith and to the cause of liberation through its emphases on redemptive suffering and the notion of God's goodness. He suggests strong humanism within the African American tradition as an alternative religious perspective: "By denying the existence of God, it is free from the dangerous doctrinal and theological obligations inherent in theistic responses to suffering."[36] Jones, he says, falls into the trappings of redemptive suffering in that God is no longer accountable for human suffering. Selective reading of African American history does provide examples of people who questioned or rejected God and recognized that human agency was responsible for the destiny of individuals and communities, but this is a much more measured and realistic view of history that recognizes nothing, not even liberation, is guaranteed.[37]

Victor Anderson raises issues in his *Beyond Ontological Blackness* that pose problems for African American history as a source of black theology. Anderson sees black theology's use of history as dependent on whiteness and white supremacy, and as reactionary.[38] To explicate this point he uses Cornel West's (Nietzschean/Foucauldian) method[39] as outlined in "A Genealogy of Modern Racism,"[40] from *Prophesy Deliverance!*[41] In light of West, Anderson looks at the inception and deployment of a notion of blackness that is used to counter historic white supremacist depictions of African Americans as inferior—a "categorical racism: people of African descent were regarded as belonging to a separate species, one that was not quite human in intelligence, understanding, or cultural consciousness, and exhibited no cultural genius."[42] He suggests that much black intellectual thought, including black theology, has responded to such racial ideology through a black aesthetic that mirrors the European heroic epic in which black thinkers posit a black cultural or racial genius.[43]

While his concern is explicitly with ontology, in this case the reification of black identity as objectifiable in certain modalities of African American scholarship, African American history as a source of theology is implicated squarely. First, just as ontological blackness signifies the totality of black existence for Anderson,[44] African American history is totalizing as a source for black theology in that it signifies a unitary, linear, and shared history that is highly constructed, directed by a theological telos (or a purpose that is divinely inspired), and beyond the bounds of objectification. Second, African American history as a source of black theology functions as a racial apologetic that is always dependent on a whiteness to which it responds.[45] Therefore, it sometimes highlights and lifts up as heroic examples, as Cone does, historical figures such as "Nat Turner, Denmark Vesey, and Gabrial Prosser,"[46] who responded courageously against white supremacy. This is not true of all forms of black theology, since, for instance, womanist theology professes to democratize the experiences and theological relevance of ordinary and everyday black women, rather than simply those whom history might valorize, like Harriet Tubman, because of their great and renowned achievements.

Yet perhaps Eddie S. Glaude, Jr. has advanced the most forthright and explicit challenge to black theology's use of African American history, and he views Anderson's *Ontological Blackness* as exceedingly relevant to his concern for the topic of black theology and African American history. His chapter "'Ethiopia Shall Stretch Forth Her Hands unto God': The Problem of History in Black Theology,"[47] which appears in his book *In a Shade of Blue: Pragmatism and the Politics of Black America*" (reprinted from a previously published journal article),[48] states the problem as he sees it. Like Anderson, Glaude sees the uses of religious language at work in the construction of black identity as a response to white supremacy, which makes assumptions about allegedly shared historical experiences and vocabularies that fix frames of reference that ignore the complexity and fluidity constituting African American lives. Glaude concludes, "This is particularly true of the black theological project—that extraordinary but flawed effort on the part of theologians like James Cone to recast Christianity as essentially a religion of black liberation."[49]

Glaude suggests that the problem of history in black theology is not just an ostensible awareness of God's activity in history on behalf of black people but also a "particular historical consciousness in theological reflection."[50] Thick or detailed and longitudinal description of historical events and persons becomes a critical tool of black theology. Such a tool has to be crafted carefully so that it serves the liberatory purposes of particular forms of black theology that concern Glaude, in this case that which is represented quintessentially by Cone. Jones and Anderson have already demonstrated the problems inherent in this process (although Glaude's position holds Anderson's critique of black theology in tension), so this does not require repetition here. Nonetheless, Glaude raises other important critiques of African American history in black theology.

To this end, the primary problem with black theology as Glaude sees it is the reification of history that does not allow for the complexity of individuality and the messiness of a nonlinear notion of history.[51] That is so say, "The problem, at its root, involves the presumption of a continuous history of African Americans."[52] In other words, Glaude suggests that when black theology speaks of black history (and indeed "the" *black experience* as a variation of black history)[53] as a source of theology, it is framed as if the signifier corresponds to a real object in the world or to a linear set of objects that are progressive. Case in point: James Cone maintains that "black history refers to the way blacks were brought to this land and the way they have been treated in this land."[54] Does black history refer only to this? Glaude rejects this idea.

That is, Glaude argues that this notion of History (capital *H*) posits a "soulful" or "spiritual" event, such as slavery, "as the site for the production of an authentic black, and in this case Christian, subject."[55] Hence, apprehension of and assent to a particular form and version of African American history serves to mark authentic blackness and seemingly religious insight, since recognition of *this* History is necessary for the apprehension of God's activity in the world. Again, Glaude is concerned that—in addition to functioning as an instrument with which to police racial authenticity and racial piety in black theology in particular and other racial ideologies generally—History renders individuals unintelligible, given that History is the history of God in relation to African Americans as a *whole*.[56] Black history, in this sense, makes individuals meaningful to the extent that they identify with and are loyal to relationships that are consistent with goals of black liberation.

Glaude differs with Anderson's view that much of African American history in black theology presupposes a heroic genius that mirrors white supremacist ideology and, in fact, is dependent on whiteness as a crisis theology that is circumscribed by the notion of suffering that makes it epistemologically indebted to white oppression for its existence and legitimation. In this context, Glaude is a critic of and apologist for black theology (or a critical apologist).[57] After a lengthy response to Anderson on this point, he surmises where he and Anderson are consonant regarding black theology, which he sees as the crux of the matter. Glaude thinks that Anderson is right to worry about the views of history, culture, and identity that inform black theological formulations of what it means to be black and Christian.

In some ways, however, Glaude believes that Anderson's critique is somewhat misguided. He contends that Anderson's critique of history in black theology is too general. It should be directed more specifically at the ways in which black theology is indebted to the 1960s and 1970s for its identity. Glaude wants to focus instead on the assumptions about African American historical experience that he views as inhibiting black theology's effectiveness.[58] What Glaude seems to be suggesting is that African American history is a problem in black theology but in a more limited scope than Anderson assumes. The problem, he posits, is that a particular black historical moment—namely the Black Power movement—exerted some influence on black theology, and even then, just what he calls "classical"[59] black theology of the 1960s and 1970s. Along these lines, then, black theology was apologetic and thus beholden to historical trends in black thought and politics. In short, Anderson's critique would benefit from historical precision, according to Glaude. What the form of black history employed in black theology does, Glaude insists, is to keep the orientation in the past rather than informing the present. Here Glaude and Anderson might agree since Anderson warns of a narrative retrieval or "hermeneutics of return"[60] that keeps black theology inclined toward the past.

Conclusion

Glaude, Anderson, Williams, Jones, and others argue collectively that certain early or classical forms of black theology were limited by an orientation that makes its goal of informing black liberation difficult because it was indebted both to white supremacy and to constructions of African American history that not only keep it oriented in and to the past but require a racial piety, an assent and devotion to what is legitimately "black" and a form of African American history that itself could be seen as religious. In addition, such a construction of African American history all but guarantees an outcome of liberation, when, as Williams and Jones point out, such a position may very well be unsustainable.

Black theology is not monolithic. Neither is the subject of African American history in black theology, which is more complex and dynamic than can be represented in this limited space. What this essay does, however, is sketch some of the important issues and debates and attempts to expose some of the complexity and diversity within the discourse. In like manner, this account sheds light on some of the thinkers for whom the subject of black history within black theology has been significant. These scholars have explored the various ways in which African American history functions in black theology—as source and methodology—as well as the conceptual problems that arise when it is posited as fixed, linear, continuous, and totalizing. Views on whether black theology can or should be rescued from the problems of history also diverged, based upon philosophical and theoretical orientations of the thinkers, as did their solutions.

Notes

1. James H. Cone, *A Black Theology of Liberation*, 20th anniversary ed. (Maryknoll, NY: Orbis Books, 1990), 25–27.
2. See Albert B. Cleage Jr., *Black Christian Nationalism: New Directions for the Black Church* (Detroit, MI: Luxor Publishers of the Pan-African Orthodox Christian Church, 1987), xvii. The distinction, here, of "academic black theology" is a reference to a claim that Albert B. Cleage Jr. is the real originator of black theology outside of the academic arena and that his black theological musings antedate those of James H. Cone. Cleage suggests that Cone does black theology "within the established framework," which appears to be a reference to academic theology. See also Albert B. Cleage, Jr. *The Black Messiah* (New York: Sheed and Ward, 1968).
3. Cone, *Black Theology of Liberation*, xii.
4. Cone, *Black Theology of Liberation*, 25.
5. Cone, *Black Theology of Liberation*.
6. Cone, *Black Theology of Liberation*.
7. Cone, *Black Theology of Liberation*, 26.
8. Cone, *Black Theology of Liberation*.
9. Cone, *Black Theology of Liberation*.
10. Cone, *Black Theology of Liberation*.
11. Cone, *Black Theology of Liberation*, 26–27.
12. Cone, *Black Theology of Liberation*, 27.
13. Cornel West, *Prophesy Deliverance! An Afro-American Revolutionary Christianity* (Louisville, KY: Westminster John Knox Press, 2002), 108–9.
14. West, *Prophesy Deliverance!* 108.
15. West, *Prophesy Deliverance!* 109.
16. West, *Prophesy Deliverance!* 109–10.
17. See, for example, Katie G. Cannon, *Katie's Canon: Womanism and the Soul of the Black Community* (New York: Continuum, 1995), 38-50; Emilie M. Townes, *In a Blaze of Glory: Womanist Spirituality as Social Witness* (Nashville: Abingdon Press, 1995), 19–29.

18. Stephanie Y. Mitchem, *Introducing Womanist Theology* (Maryknoll, NY: Orbis Books, 2002), ix.
19. Delores S. Williams, *Sisters in the Wilderness: The Challenge of Womanist God-Talk* (Maryknoll, NY: Orbis Books, 1993), xiv.
20. Jacquelyn Grant, *White Women's Christ and Black Women's Jesus: Feminist Christology and Womanist Response* (Atlanta, GA: Scholars Press, 1989), 195; Mitchem, *Introducing Womanist Theology*, 46–49.
21. Williams, *Sisters in the Wilderness*, 158.
22. Cannon, *Katie's Canon*, 63.
23. William R. Jones, *Is God a White Racist? A Preamble to Black Theology* (Boston: Beacon Press, 1998).
24. Jones, *Is God a White Racist?* xxvii.
25. Cone, *Black Theology of Liberation*, 36, 38.
26. Cleage, *Black Christian Nationalism*, xxxv.
27. Jones, *Is God a White Racist?* 16.
28. Jones, *Is God a White Racist?* 6–9.
29. Jones, *Is God a White Racist?* 7.
30. Jones, *Is God a White Racist?* 10–15.
31. Williams, *Sisters in the Wilderness*, 4–5.
32. Williams, *Sisters in the Wilderness*, 159.
33. Williams, *Sisters in the Wilderness*, 161.
34. Anthony B. Pinn, *Why, Lord? Suffering and Evil in Black Theology* (New York: Continuum, 1995).
35. What Pinn means is that Jones offers black theology a way out of the problem by suggesting a "humanocentric theism," which in the end does not solve the problem, though it allows Christians to maintain the idea of a theistic deity, while making the responsibility for the amelioration of suffering both human and divine. For Pinn, this defeats Jones's own argument and threshold of the possibility of a malevolent God because it automatically preserves the notion of God's goodness and God's "limited" activity in human history. See Jones, *Is God a White Racist?* 185–97; Pinn, *Why, Lord?* 17, 95–98, 100, 145.
36. Pinn, *Why, Lord?* 157.
37. Pinn, *Why, Lord?* 113–37.
38. Victor Anderson. *Beyond Ontological Blackness: An Essay on African American Religious and Cultural Criticism* (New York: Continuum, 1999), 85–109.
39. West, *Prophesy Deliverance!* 48.
40. West, *Prophesy Deliverance!* 47–65.
41. See Anderson, *Beyond Ontological Blackness*, 121–22, for his discussion on genealogy and cognate terms.
42. Anderson, *Beyond Ontological Blackness*, 132.
43. See W. E. B. Du Bois. "The Conservation of Races," 11, accessed June 24, 2011, http://www2.hn.psu.edu/faculty/jmanis/webdubois/DuBoisNegro-ConservationRaces6x9.pdf, Penn State Electronic Classics Series Publication. Du Bois's use of "racial genius" is similar to the notion to which Anderson objects.
44. Anderson, *Beyond Ontological Blackness*, 14.
45. Anderson, *Beyond Ontological Blackness*, 51–85.
46. Cone, *Black Theology of Liberation*, 26.

47. Eddie S. Glaude Jr., *In a Shade of Blue: Pragmatism and the Politics of Black America* (Chicago: University of Chicago Press, 2007), 66–88.
48. Eddie S. Glaude Jr. "Pragmatic Historicism and the Problem of History in Black Theology," *American Journal of Theology and Philosophy* 19, no. 2 (May 1998): 173–90.
49. Glaude, *Shade of Blue*, 66–68.
50. Glaude, *Shade of Blue*, 68.
51. Glaude, *Shade of Blue.*
52. Glaude, *Shade of Blue*, 66–8.
53. Cone, *Black Theology of Liberation*, 23–5.
54. Cone, *A Black Theology of Liberation*, 25.
55. Glaude, *Shade of Blue*, 68.
56. Glaude, *Shade of Blue*, 69.
57. This seems to be the case not just in his response to Victor Anderson but in his overall intent in this essay as seen in the multiple ways and extensive attention that he gives to rescuing black theology from the problem of history, particularly using the philosophies of Dewey and Nietzsche in this endeavor. See Glaude, *Shade of Blue*, 79–88.
58. Glaude, *Shade of Blue*, 73.
59. Glaude, *Shade of Blue*, 70.
60. Anderson, *Beyond Ontological Blackness*, 93; Glaude, *Shade of Blue*, 70.

Selected Texts

Anderson, Victor. *Beyond Ontological Blackness: An Essay on African American Religious and Cultural Criticism*. New York: Continuum, 1999.

Cleage, Albert B., Jr. *The Black Messiah*. New York: Sheed and Ward, 1968.

Cleage, Albert B., Jr. *Black Christian Nationalism: New Directions for the Black Church*. Detroit, MI: Luxor Publishers of the Pan-African Orthodox Christian Church, 1987.

Cone, James H. *A Black Theology of Liberation*. 20th anniversary ed. Maryknoll, NY: Orbis Books, 1990.

Cannon, Katie G. *Katie's Canon: Womanism and the Soul of the Black Community*. New York: Continuum, 1995.

Jones, William R. *Is God a White Racist? A Preamble to Black Theology*. Boston: Beacon Press, 1998.

Mitchem, Stephanie Y. *Introducing Womanist Theology*. Maryknoll, NY: Orbis Books, 2002.

Pinn, Anthony B. *Why, Lord? Suffering and Evil in Black Theology*. New York: Continuum, 1995.

Townes, Emilie M. *In a Blaze of Glory: Womanist Spirituality as Social Witness*. Nashville: Abingdon Press, 1995.

West, Cornel. *Prophesy Deliverance! An Afro-American Revolutionary Christianity*. Louisville: Westminster John Knox Press, 2002.

Williams, Delores S. *Sisters in the Wilderness: The Challenge of Womanist God-Talk*. Maryknoll, NY: Orbis Books, 1993.

CHAPTER 2

READING AND USING SCRIPTURE IN THE AFRICAN AMERICAN TRADITION

ALLEN DWIGHT CALLAHAN

Stony the road we trod,
Bitter the chastening rod,
Felt in the days when hope unborn had died;
Yet with a steady beat,
Have not our weary feet
Come to the place
For which our fathers died?
We have come over a way that with tears have been watered,
We have come, treading our path through the blood of the slaughtered,
Out from the gloomy past,
Till now we stand at last
Where the white gleam
Of our bright star is cast.
God of our weary years,
God of our silent tears,
Thou who hast brought us thus far on the way;
Thou who hast by thy might led us into the light,
Keep us forever in the path, we pray.
Lest our feet stray from the places, our God, where we met thee;
Lest our hearts drunk with the wine of the world, we forget thee,
Shadowed beneath thy hand,
May we forever stand?
True to our God,
True to our native land.

—James Weldon Johnson, "Lift Every Voice and Sing"[1]

"Out from the Gloomy Past"

African American biblical interpretation begins with slavery. "African-American slaves, female and male," observes Delores Williams, "created an oral text from a written text (the King James Version of the Bible). They composed this oral text by extracting from the Bible or adding to biblical content those phrases, stories, biblical personalities and moral prescriptions relevant to the character of their life-situation and pertinent to the aspirations of the slave community."[2] The Bible figured prominently in the music, the folkways, and the mores of American slaves not because it was the best literature available to them but because, at the formative beginning of their American experience, it was the only literature available to them. "The imagery of the Bible plays a large role in the symbolic presentations [of the slaves]," as the historian of religion Charles Long has noted, "because it was at hand."[3] African Americans first encountered the Bible at the existential intersection of the Great Awakening and the Peculiar Institution in colonial America, where the Bible was not only the most accessible literature, but for many, slave and free, the only accessible literature.

For the slaves and their issue, the characters and events of the Bible became the functional equivalent of the ancestors and heroes that had long been celebrated in their West African homelands. An ex-slave from Kentucky, describing how he and his companions would extemporaneously compose Negro spirituals, explained, "Us old heads used to make them on the spur of the moment, after we wrestle with the Spirit and come through. But the tunes was brung from Africa by our granddaddies. They was just familiar song.... We'd all be at the prayer house the Lord's Day, and the white preacher he'd explain the word and read... and I'd jump up there and then and holler and shout and sing and pat... and they's all take it up and keep at it, and keep a-adding to it and then it would be a spiritual."[4] The musical patterns for the slaves' biblical songs were the transplanted battle anthems of their West African forebears.

African Americans began coining an idiom of biblical figures in the last quarter of the eighteenth century. The New Testament scholar Vincent Wimbush characterizes this coinage as "foundational": "All other readings to come would in some sense be built upon and judged against it. This reading is in fact the classical reading of the biblical text for African Americans; it reflects... what arguably has been so basic to the orientation of the majority of African Americans that all subsequent debates about orientation, world view, and strategies for survival and/or liberation have begun with this period and what it represents."[5] African American biblical interpretation has given pride of place to vernacular traditions; the *fons et origo* of much African American appropriation of the Bible is folk traditions of the Negro spirituals and popular folklore, and these sources have informed and legitimated subsequent interpretations.

Cheryl Kirk-Duggan has described the Negro spirituals as "an early, unique form that rereads the biblical text. These songs tailor biblical metaphors, ideas, and themes... to community use."[6] Through this canon within a canon, the slaves read their experience into and out of the Bible. The themes, interests, and concerns, to which they returned again and again in different melodies and choruses, are there in the Bible, constitutive of the biblical witness itself. The slaves did not find them as much as they found themselves in them. To say that African Americans identified with biblical figures is not quite apposite; these figures of biblical faith were not identical to African Americans, but were their intimate acquaintances, close at hand, existentially nigh unto them. They could walk in Jerusalem just like John the author of the Apocalypse, even die and be whisked away to rest in Abraham's bosom like Lazarus the humble beggar of Jesus's parable. The slaves also found that while they yet awaited complete deliverance they could be sustained against all odds and in impossible circumstances: God delivered Daniel from the mouth of the lion and from the hand of man; the slave then asked rhetorically, "Why not every man?" Saints past and present could stand together in song in a way that transgressed narrative moment and historical time: Father Abraham sits down beside the Holy Lamb, that is, Jesus, the "Lamb of God," as the Gospel of John and John of Patmos call him. And just as the slaves could look forward to deliverance, they could look back to those biblical paragons whose exemplary faith had not only enabled them to hold out until their change came, but to hold out even when it did not. The Bible bore testimony to a transcendent salvation that extended from the Red Sea to the first singers of the Negro spirituals.

It was under the American slaver regime that African Americans learned to read the Bible into their lives. They also learned to read their lives into the Bible. Former slave Robert Ellett, speaking of Harriett Tubman, testified, "Moses would come around... she would run [slaves] away and get them over near the border line... on what you call the Underground Railroad."[7] Tubman was not merely a prophet like unto Moses, as Deuteronomy 18:15 puts it; slaves and former slaves throughout the South knew Moses to be a small, wily black woman who led not one but many an "exodus" out of "Egypt," regularly outwitted pursuing armies of slave catchers, and at will repeatedly traversed the wilderness of the Mason-Dixon line.

Reading their own heroines, heroes, and heroism into the Bible was a psychic tool forged in the iron furnace of slavery that African Americans continued to wield in the construction of culture long after the fall of the slave regime. When African American politician Charlotta A. Bass accepted the nomination as candidate for vice president of the United States on the Progressive ticket in April 1952, she announced to her Socialist comrades that her campaign slogan would be the demand of Moses and Aaron in Pharaoh's court (Exodus 5:1), "Let my people go."[8] Martin Luther King Jr., who called southern segregationists "pharaohs" holding African Americans captive in "the Egypt of segregation,"[9] himself took on the mantle of Moses in his last speech, delivered the night before his assassination in

Memphis, Tennessee, in 1968; King structures his remarks with the same form that we find in Deuteronomy's report of the end of Moses's career on Mount Pisgah, and prophesied that he, like Moses, would not live to enter the Promised Land with those he had led in the wilderness of American apartheid. Annie Bell Cherry, the longtime family friend of Robert Williams, the radical NAACP leader who organized the African Americans of Union County, North Carolina, to fight against Jim Crow and the terror of the KKK in the late 1950s, said, "I believe it was God's calling, that Rob Williams was sent here to save us. God sent somebody, just like he did in the Bible."[10] The Evangelical activist John Perkins has called for a generation of "Nehemiahs" to rebuild blighted inner-city neighborhoods as the biblical Nehemiah rebuilt the walls of Jerusalem, and in the same spirit the Baptist pastor and community organizer Johnny Ray Youngblood dubbed his renowned Brooklyn redevelopment project "Nehemiah Homes." African Americans have traded in a biblical imaginary broader and deeper than creed or confession, of use even to those with no use for God. The noted humanist and antitheologian Anthony Pinn would impress the biblical figure Nimrod into this semiotic service for African American humanism: "Nimrod according to the Judeo-Christian tradition was known as a great hunter who controlled a kingdom that included Babel. Associated with the construction of the Tower of Babel... Nimrod became a cursed figure in theological-religious circles"; to "'flip' or signify earlier interpretations," writes Pinn, "the re-capturing of Nimrod provides an important icon, or central 'metaphor' for African American humanism."[11] African Americans, in part through force of a habit now over two centuries old, have tended to speak of what they do and how they do it in the image and likeness of a biblical figure.

In all these biblical appropriations we may discern several prevalent, persistent, and recurrent features that are manifest from the colonial period of American history to the present, "a priori interpretive principles through which meaning of the Bible was validated,"[12] as James Evans has called them. From the last quarter of the eighteenth century to the present, African American readings of the Bible have been contemporary, contested, and critical.

The Fierce Urgency of Now

African American biblical interpretation ever engages the contemporary moment, beginning and ending the dialectic of past and present at the pole of the present. Delores Williams, in her reading of the story of Hagar and Ishmael in Genesis, argues that it speaks of "the fabric of Hagar's and African American women's experience."[13] So construed, the ancient text, as a biblical representation of African American life, speaks with a contemporary urgency. "Hagar's and Ishmael's life-situation was like that of black female slaves and their children," writes Williams. "Like Hagar they experienced harsh treatment from slave mistresses.... Like Hagar and Ishmael when they were finally freed from the house of bondage, African-American ex-slaves were faced with making a way out of no way. They were thrown out into the world with no economic resources.... The question was and still is today, how can oppressed people develop a positive and productive quality of life in a situation where the resources for doing so are not visible?"[14]

As Vincent Wimbush has noted, this hermeneutical insistence on the present "is at odds with historical criticism as it is practiced in the theological academy": "The [modern-world practice that is the academic] study of the Bible... is about the past and about difference—the far-distant past that is radically different from the present."[15] But American slaves and their descendants came to identify biblical figures with people in their contemporary lifeworld through homologies of virtue and common elements of ultimate concern. "The interpretive move" of the slaves, observes Brian Blount, "is from experience to biblical image, not the other was around."[16]

Terrain of Contestation

These readings sighted, however distantly, a utopian horizon. "Where the Bible has been able to capture the imagination of African American women," writes Renita Weems, "it has been and continues to be able to do so because significant portions speak to the deepest aspirations of oppressed people for freedom, dignity, justice, and vindication.... And these are the passages, of oppressed readers, that stand at the center of the biblical message and, thereby, serve as a vital norm for biblical faith."[17]

But from the beginning African Americans found that norm contested. "The history and, to a great degree, the contemporary experience of African Americans' encounter with the Bible in Western culture has been a struggle for canonical control," James Evans reminds us. "The Bible has continually ignited their creative energies and sustained their understanding of themselves as creations of God."[18] The hermeneutic of African Americans is one of contestation. "The Bible in the African-American community," observes Evans, "achieved its status as 'Scripture' in the heat of a liberation struggle."[19]

That struggle was waged even within the canon itself. The Bible is a book of contradictions. In its myth of origins and subsequent rules of gender relations, the Bible has immortalized women as protagonists in a divine drama that runs from the Garden of Eden to the Garden of Gethsemane while authorizing the domination of man over woman. Though the Bible's foundational narrative is an account of God's deliverance of slaves, these same Scriptures sanction slavery and even treat of regulations for its practice. The most grandiose vision of global peace, inaugurated by the abolition of weapons of mass destruction everywhere and for all time, comes from a prophetic oracle of the Bible: "And they shall beat their swords into plowshares, and their spears into pruning hooks: nation shall not lift up sword against nation, neither shall they learn war any more" (Isaiah 2:4). Yet the Bible's instructions for the conduct of holy war give divine approbation to armed violence, genocide, and even the slaughter of noncombatants.[20] And in the geopolitical turn of the narrative of the Acts of the Apostles away from Africa and toward Europe, Cain Hope Felder has discerned a pro-European, anti-African bias canonized in the New Testament: "Luke, not unlike other New Testament writers of this period and after, seeks perhaps to assuage Rome by allowing his theological framework to be determined by the assumption of a Rome-centered world... the Lukan vision of universalism is undermined by this seeming theological emphasis on Europe."[21]

Indeed, African American biblical interpretation has been especially preoccupied with pejorative readings of Africa and Africans. In an address to Western Reserve College in 1853, Frederick Douglass argued that Negroes were builders of ancient Egypt and Ethiopia:[22] responding to the scientific turn in the anti-African racism of the mid-nineteenth century, Douglass asserted that ancient, distant African ancestors had founded Egyptian and Ethiopian civilizations that "flourished... at a time when all Europe floundered in the depths of ignorance and barbarism."[23] More than a century and a half later, Peter Nash has shown how it has only been in the past thirty years that the field of biblical studies has acknowledged that race is an anthropological and political category and not a category of the natural sciences, that racism has hindered fruitful lines of inquiry in biblical research and interpretation, and that Israelite history and culture cannot be understood properly apart from their African roots.[24]

Although African slaves and their descendants early on learned to regard Africa with contempt and shame, they found in the Bible another, altogether different and altogether glorious image of their ancestral land. The Bible knew of mighty African peoples: it makes abundant references to Ethiopia, or "Cush," as the Authorized Version, following the transliterated Hebrew, renders it. As Randall Bailey has shown, the beauty of ancient Africans' blackness, their cultural and military superiority, and their great wealth are features of their biblical profile.[25] Psalm 68:31, "Princes shall come out of Egypt; Ethiopia shall soon stretch out her hands unto God," is the most widely quoted verses of the Bible in African American letters.[26] In a 1797 address Prince Hall, founder of the African Masonic Lodge, reminded his fellow masons of the venerable African presence in both Testaments of the Bible: Moses had learned the arts of governance from his father-in-law, the Midianite Jethro, "an Ethiopian"; King Solomon had graciously received the Ethiopian queen of Sheba into his court; and in the New Testament Philip the Evangelist had readily baptized the Ethiopian eunuch.[27] "Ethiopia is one of the few nations whose destiny is spoken of in prophecy," declared Henry Highland Garnet in an 1848 address: "'Princes shall come out of Egypt, and Ethiopia shall soon stretch out her hands unto God.' It is thought by some that this divine declaration was fulfilled when Philip baptized the converted eunuch of the household of Candes, the Queen of the Ethiopians. In the transaction, a part of the prophecy may have been fulfilled, and only a part."[28] In early 1850s Frances E. W. Harper set the "plain language" of prophecy to verse in her poem "Ethiopia": "Yes! Ethiopia yet shall stretch / Her bleeding hand abroad; / Her cry of agony shall reach / The burning throne of God." In 1887 the pan-Africanist polymath Edward Wilmot Blyden argued that the story of the Ethiopian eunuch in Acts 8:26–40 shows "the instruments and the methods of Africa's evangelization. The method, the simple holding up of Jesus Christ; the instrument, the African himself."[29]

In landmark treatments of contemporary New Testament scholarship, Clarice J. Martin[30] and Abraham Smith[31] have shown the importance of the episode of the Ethiopian eunuch in the narrative of Acts, the importance of the Ethiopian's African identity in the narrative, and the various attempts on the part of modern scholarship to downplay or ignore both these key aspects in interpreting the passage. But for their part, for more than two centuries African Americans have seen Africa through the biblical figure of Ethiopia as both their heritage of a glorious past and their promise of a glorious future.[32]

Higher Criticism

African slaves early on began to question the biblical texts that they heard and what those texts meant. The Bible became the iron against which they sharpened the iron of a nascent faculty of criticism. For centuries, Western commentators had cited Noah's curse in Genesis 9:25 as a biblical condemnation of African people as the descendants of Ham. Congregational minister and former slave James W. C. Pennington identified African Americans as the distant descendants of the amalgamated lines of Cush (Ethiopia) and Misraim (Egypt), but debunked the curse of Ham by pointing out that Canaan alone was cursed, and not the entire Hamitic line from which all Africans are descended.[33] To Pauline exhortations that slaves submit to their bondage as divinely sanctioned, African Americans countered with the plain-sense Quaker reading of the Golden Rule, "Do unto others what you would have them do unto you" (Matthew 7:12), the observance of which would have rendered American slavery morally impossible. The Nigerian seaman, ex-slave, and abolitionist Olaudah Equiano, recalling the kidnapping of his sister and himself from West Africa, protested, "O, ye nominal Christians! Might not an African ask you, 'Learned you this from your God?' Who says unto you, 'Do unto all men as you would men should do unto you'? Is it not enough that we are torn from our country and friends to toil for your luxury and lust of gain? Must every tender feeling be likewise sacrificed to your avarice?"[34] And African American women summoned Scripture against Scripture to defend their calling to preach against Pauline mandates to women's silence. In 1833 the orator and political philosopher Maria Stewart, the first woman to speak in public in America whose address is extant, insisted, "St. Paul declared that it is a shame for a woman to speak in public, yet our great High Priest and Advocate did not condemn the woman for a more notorious offence than this"; had not "Mary Magdalene first declare the resurrection of Christ from the dead?... Did St. Paul but know of our wrongs and deprivations," Stewart argued, "I presume he would make no objections to our pleading in public for our rights."[35] As James Evans has observed, "The status of African Americans as outsiders within American society has shaped their perspective on the Bible. In fact, their very marginality has made them sensitive to the misuses of Scripture and has made them more open to its critical dimension."[36]

African Americans occasionally even engaged in their own brand of redaction criticism, tailoring a text from the whole cloth of the biblical canon to suit their condition. The Negro spirituals are tacitly selective in their retelling of the story of David. Anonymous folk composers celebrate David's victory over Goliath in the Negro spiritual "Little David, Play on Your Harp."

> Little David was a shepherd boy
> Killed Goliath and shouted for joy
> Little David play on your harp, hallelu
> Little David play on your harp,
> Hallelu, hallelu[37]

The "black and unknown bards," as James Weldon Johnson called them, remember David as a shepherd, a musician, and a giant-killer. His subsequent royal glory is passed over in silence. Once "Little David" is no longer little, he is no longer worth singing about. The star of David shines with a unique luster in the Bible, which luxuriates more prose and poetry on David than any other single character. The Negro spirituals, however, give that star only a cameo role: in their renderings, David is merely "Little David," the shepherd, part-time harpist, and one-time giant killer.

But just as African American readings of the Bible could reduce a star to a cameo role, they could give center stage to a bit player and give her leave to steal the show. By the middle of the nineteenth century, African American women were reading the story of Vashti, the deposed Persian queen in the opening of the book of Esther, as a tale of one woman's courageous resistance. In a remarkable reading against the grain of the text of the book of Esther, African American women have seen Vashti as a queen who loses her throne but holds on to her regal bearing. Remarkable, because the plain sense of the canonical text recounts Vashti's resistance but does not celebrate it.

In 1857 writer, educator, and activist Frances Harper rendered her admiration of the Bible's deposed queen in verse in her poem "Vashti."[38] In "Vashti" the poet once again gives voice to her strident preference for death to disgrace. The poem of the reclusive Anne Spencer (1882–1975) "Before the Feast of Shushan"[39] is a subtle exploration of sexual violence juxtaposed with a meditation on the virtue of love. Contemporary treatments by African American women continue to celebrate her,[40] and African Americans have given and continue to give the name Vashti to their daughters. African American women coined from Vashti's story of self-possession a unique interpretation that they have borne and continue to bear in the name Vashti.[41]

"Till Now We Stand at Last"

"African American women," writes Renita Weems, "have continued to read the Bible in most instances because of its vision and promise of a world where the humanity of everyone will be fully valued. They have accomplished this reading in spite of the voices from within and without that have tried to equivocate on that vision and promise."[42] The Bible—and its African American interpreters—have been only imperfectly suited to the task of fulfilling that vision, delivering on that promise. African American readings of the Bible, in the words of Hugh R. Page Jr., bear witness to "a long, and at times troubled relationship between a heterogeneous community and a body of traditions": and yet, these images and likenesses in the Bible, mediated through the Negro spirituals and other antebellum interpretations and the varied responses that have followed them in time if not in tenor, are the "enduring and emerging tropes derived from personal experience, the annals of the past, literature, music, the visual and plastic arts, and current events, by means of which Africana life is formed, sustained, queried, and at times thoroughly refashioned."[43]

That formation and sustenance, that querying and refashioning of life in relationship with Scripture, Page goes on to write, "are best derived from . . . the ebb, flow, and surprises of the 'here and now.' "[44] The appreciation of the antebellum heritage of African American biblical interpretation as "classic" and "foundational," in Wimbush's words, is descriptive, not prescriptive; these interpretations inform subsequent engagements with the Bible—they do not and cannot determine them. These "foundational" readings, as Michael Joseph Brown explains, "would serve as a point of interaction with the present."[45] In commenting on Toni Morrison's use of biblical images and language in her novel *Song of Solomon*, Abraham Smith suggests that Morrison "uses the Bible . . . to call attention to the problem of adapting traditional values wholesale in our contemporary settings. . . . Morrison's challenge affirms that . . . tradition is vital only when it speaks a word to where we are now."[46] "As life reads scripture and scripture reads life," cautions Cheryl A. Kirk-Duggan, "we must wrestle with texts from our own contexts, questioning usage and interpretation... when we engage texts for contemporary use."[47]

The African American hermeneutical circle courses from history to destiny and back through contested, critical readings. Yet it is in what Martin Luther King, Jr., called "the fierce urgency of now" that African Americans "engage texts for contemporary use"—now, "Where the white gleam / Of our bright star is cast."

Notes

1. "This anthem is promptly developing an effective history within African American biblical scholarship.... In 1991, Cain Hope Felder edited a collection of essays by African American scholars titled *Stony the Road We Trod*, words derived from the second stanza of Johnson's hymn.... 'Somehow,' Felder explained, 'these words seem to epitomize our struggle as African American scholars who have made biblical interpretation a daily vocational struggle...' In 2003, Randall Bailey selected *Yet with a Steady Beat*, also from the second stanza of Johnson's lyrics, as the title of a collection of essays from a new generation of African American scholars. This... volume represents, in Bailey's words, 'the persistent march of our people on the "Freedom Trail."' By titling our commentary *True to Our Native Land*, we recognize continuity with those who have preceded us in African American biblical scholarship.... Furthermore, this title depicts well our desire that this publication, a labor of love, may continue our struggle of interpreting the biblical texts in a way that is sensitive to our own heritage." Brian K. Blount, Cain Hope Felder, Clarice Martin, and Emerson Powery, eds., *True to Our Native Land* (Minneapolis: Fortress Press, 2007), 6–7.
2. Delores Williams, *Sisters in the Wilderness: The Challenge of Womanist God-Talk* (Maryknoll, NY: Orbis Books, 1993), 188.
3. Charles Long, "Perspectives for a Study of Afro-American Religion in the United States," *History of Religions* 11, no. 1 (August 1971), reprinted in Timothy E. Fulop and Albert J. Raboteau, eds., *African-American Religion: Interpretive Essays in History and Culture* (New York: Routledge, 1997) 29.
4. Jeanette Robinson Murphy, "The Survival of African Music in America," *Popular Science Monthly*, September 1899, 660–72, slightly modified. In James Abbington, "Biblical Themes in the R. Nathaniel Dett Collection," in *African Americans and the Bible: Sacred Texts and Social Textures*, ed. Vincent Wimbush (New York: Continuum, 2000), 282.
5. Vincent Wimbush, "The Bible and African Americans: An Outline of Interpretive History," in *Stony the Road: African American Biblical Interpretation*, ed. Cain Hope Felder (Minneapolis: Fortress Press, 1991), 89.
6. Cheryl Kirk-Duggan, "Let My People Go! Threads of Exodus in African American Narratives," in *Yet with a Steady Beat: Contemporary U.S. Afrocentric Biblical Interpretation*, ed. Randall C. Bailey (Atlanta: Society of Biblical Literature, 2003), 125.
7. Dwight N. Hopkins, "Slave Theology in the 'Invisible Institution'," in *Cut Loose Your Stammering Tongue: Black Theology in the Slave Narratives*, ed. Dwight N. Hopkins (Louisville, KY: Westminster John Knox Press, 2003), 26.

8. Charlotta Bass, "I Accept This Call," *National Guardian* 4, no. 24 (April 2, 1952), reprinted in *Black Women in White America*, ed. Gerda Lerner (New York: Vintage, 1973), 345.
9. Martin Luther King Jr., *Where Do We Go From Here: Chaos or Community* (New York: Harper & Row, 1967), 124; King, "Out of the Long Night of Segregation," *Presbyterian Outlook*, February 10, 1958, 6.
10. Cited in Timothy B. Tyson, *Radio Free Dixie: Robert F. Williams and the Roots of Black Power* (Chapel Hill: University of North Carolina Press, 1999), 81.
11. Anthony B. Pinn, *African American Humanist Principles: Living and Thinking Like the Children of Nimrod* (New York: Palgrave, 2004), 3, 7.
12. James Evans, *We Have Been Believers: African American Systematic Theology* (Minneapolis: Fortress Press, 1992), 52.
13. Williams, *Sisters in the Wilderness*, 143.
14. Williams, *Sisters in the Wilderness*, 193.
15. Vincent Wimbush, "Reading Darkness, Reading Scriptures," in Wimbush, *African Americans and the Bible*, 9–10.
16. Brian Blount, *Cultural Interpretation: Reorienting New Testament Criticism* (Minneapolis: Fortress Press, 1995), 56.
17. Renita J. Weems, "Reading Her Way through the Struggle: African American Women and the Bible," in Felder, *Stony the Road*, 70–71.
18. Evans, *We Have Been Believers*, 52.
19. Evans, *We Have Been Believers*, 52.
20. Allen Dwight Callahan, *The Talking Book: The Bible and African Americans* (New Haven: Yale University Press, 2006), 25.
21. Cain Hope Felder, *Race, Racism, and the Biblical Narratives* (Minneapolis: Fortress Press, 2002), 41.
22. Frederick Douglass, "The Claims of the Negro Ethnologically Considered (1854)," in *The Voice of Black America*, ed. Philip S. Foner (New York: Simon and Schuster, 1972), 144.
23. Frederick Douglass, "The Abilities and Possibilities of Our Race," in Foner, *Voice of Black America*, 331.
24. Peter Nash, *Reading Race, Reading the Bible* (Minneapolis: Fortress Press, 2003).
25. Randall C. Bailey, "Beyond Identification: The Use of Africans in Old Testament Poetry and Narratives," in Felder, *Stony the Road*, 165–94.
26. Albert Raboteau, "'Ethiopia Shall Soon Stretch Forth Her Hands': Black Destiny in Nineteenth-Century America," in *A Fire in the Bones: Reflections on African-American Religious History* (Boston: Beacon Press, 1995), 42.
27. Prince Hall, "A Charge, Delivered to the African Lodge, June 24, 1797, at Menotonomy," in *Early Negro Writing, 1760–1837*, ed. Dorothy Porter (Boston, 1971), 72.
28. Henry Highland Garnet, *The Past and the Present Condition, and the Destiny of the Colored Race* (Miami, FL: Mnemosyne, 1969), 6–12.
29. Edward Wilmot Blyden, "The Ethiopian Eunuch," in *Christianity, Islam, and the Negro Race* (London: W. B. Whittingham, 1887; reprinted, Chesapeake and New York: ECA Associates, 1990), 152–72, 162.
30. Clarice J. Martin, "A Chamberlain's Journey and the Challenge of Interpretation for Liberation," in *The Bible and Liberation: Political and Social Hermeneutics*, rev. ed. (Maryknoll, NY: Orbis Books, 1993), 485–503.

31. Abraham Smith, "'Do You Understand What You Are Reading?' A Literary Critical Reading of the Ethiopian (Kushite) Episode (Acts 8:26–40)," *Journal of the Interdenominational Theological Center* 22 (1994): 48–70.
32. See Callahan, *Talking Book*, 138–41.
33. See Callahan, *Talking Book*, 28–29.
34. Olaudah Equiano, *The Interesting Narrative of the Life of Olaudah Equiano, or Gustavus Vassa, the African, Written by Himself*, 2 vols. (1789; New York: Negro Universities Press, 1969), 1:87.
35. Maria Stewart, "Mrs. Stewart's Farewell Address to Her Friends in the City of Boston," in *Maria Stewart: America's First Black Woman Political Writer*, ed. Marilyn Richardson (Bloomington: Indiana University Press, 1987), 68.
36. Evans, *We Have Been Believers*, 51.
37. "Lit'le David Play On Yo' Harp," in *The Books of American Negro Spirituals*, comp. James Weldon and J. Rosamond Johnson (New York: Viking, 1925–26; reprinted New York: Da Capo, 1989), 1.65–67.
38. In *The Norton Anthology of African American Literature*, gen. ed. Henry Louis Gates and Nellie McKay (New York: Norton, 1997), 415–17.
39. Gates and McKay, *Norton Anthology*, 947–48.
40. See, e.g., LaVerne McCain Gill, *Vashti's Victory and Other Biblical Women Resisting Injustice* (Cleveland: Pilgrim Press, 2003).
41. Allen Dwight Callahan, "Vashti," in *Loving the Body: Black Religious Studies and the Erotic*, ed. Anthony B. Pinn and Dwight N. Hopkins (New York: Palgrave, 2004), 91–107.
42. Weems, "Reading Her Way," 77.
43. Hugh R. Page Jr., "Notes from a Stations Stop: An Editorial Postscript," in *The Africana Bible: Reading Israel's Scriptures from Africa and the African Diaspora*, gen. ed. Hugh R. Page Jr. (Minneapolis: Fortress Press, 2010), 339.
44. Page, "Notes from a Stations Stop," 339.
45. Michael Joseph Brown, *Blackening the Bible: The Aims of African American Biblical Scholarship* (Harrisburg, PA: Trinity Press International, 2004), 82.
46. Abraham Smith, "Toni Morrison's *Song of Solomon*: The Blues and the Bible," in *The Recovery of a Black Presence: An Interdisciplinary Exploration; Essays in Honor of Dr. Charles B. Copher*, ed. Randall C. Bailey and Jacqueline Grant (Nashville: Abingdon Press, 1995), 115.
47. Cheryl A. Kirk-Duggan, in Randall C. Bailey, Cheryl A. Kirk-Duggan, Madipoane Masenya (ngwan'a Mphahlele), and Rodney S, Sadler Jr., "African and African Diasporan Hermeneutics: Reading the Hebrew Bible as Journey, Exile, and Life through My/Our Place," in Page, *Africana Bible*, 22.

Selected Texts

Bailey, Randall C., ed. *Yet with a Steady Beat: Contemporary U.S. Afrocentric Biblical Interpretation*. Atlanta: Society of Biblical Literature, 2003.

Bailey, Randall C., and Jacqueline Grant, eds. *The Recovery of a Black Presence: An Interdisciplinary Exploration; Essays in Honor of Dr. Charles B. Copher*. Nashville: Abingdon Press, 1995.

Blount, Brian K. *Cultural Interpretation: Reorienting New Testament Criticism*. Minneapolis: Fortress, 1995.

Blount, Brian K., Cain Hope Felder, Clarice Martin, and Emerson Powery, eds. *True to Our Native Land*. Minneapolis: Fortress Press, 2007.

Brown, Michael Joseph. *Blackening the Bible: The Aims of African American Biblical Scholarship*. Harrisburg, PA: Trinity Press International, 2004.

Callahan, Allen Dwight. *The Talking Book: The Bible and African Americans*. New Haven: Yale University Press, 2006.

Felder, Cain Hope. *Race, Racism, and the Biblical Narratives*. Minneapolis: Fortress Press, 1989.

Felder, Cain Hope, ed. *Stony the Road: African American Biblical Interpretation*. Minneapolis: Fortress Press, 1991.

Gill, LaVerne McCain. *Vashti's Victory and Other Biblical Women Resisting Injustice*. Cleveland: Pilgrim Press, 2003.

Nash, Peter. *Reading Race, Reading the Bible*. Minneapolis: Fortress Press, 2003.

Page, Hugh, R., gen. ed. *The Africana Bible: Reading Israel's Scriptures from Africa and the African Diaspora*. Minneapolis: Fortress Press, 2010.

Wimbush, Vincent, ed. *African Americans and the Bible: Sacred Texts and Social Textures*. New York: Continuum, 2000.

CHAPTER 3

AFRICAN AMERICAN RELIGIOUS EXPERIENCE

M. SHAWN COPELAND

The Problematic

The phrase *African American religious experience* refers to conscious responsiveness to the holy or to divinity or to an existential sense of mystery and ultimacy expressed through sensibilities, cognitive orientations, styles, dispositions, symbols, and practices derived from reconfigurations of the religious and cultural heritages of various African peoples enslaved in the United States.[1] The roots of this consciousness and experience lie in a fertile synthesis of elements drawn from various indigenous plural and diverse African religions and their cultures. Since Africans often have been described as spiritual pragmatists, selectively incorporating or utilizing multiple religious traditions in the resolution of difficulties or the pursuit of wisdom, the Continent's centuries-old contact with Islam and Christianity ought not be excluded prima facie from this fusion.[2] And, with respect to the former, Richard Brent Turner and Michael Gomez have uncovered evidence of the "compelling presence" of enslaved African Muslims in colonial America. Moreover, members of the slave community took note of their discipline and fidelity in matters of prayer and diet (no pork) and their rigorous refusal (*jihad*) "to internalize the Christian racist significations that justified the system of exploitation."[3]

African American religious experience emerges from complex religio-cultural terrain. Several challenging and interrelated methodological, philosophical, and hermeneutical issues problematize the study of its formation. *First*, academic studies (e.g., anthropology, history, literature, and, to some extent, sociology) of African

Americans and their culture have accorded a preeminent place to religion, religious consciousness, and religious experience; indeed, religion, religious consciousness, and religious experience have come to be identified as *the* crucial mediation of African American personal and communal transformation. More than a century ago, W. E. B. Du Bois (1903) called attention to the social, psychological, and ethical role religion took as mediator of black people's "higher life."[4] Seven decades later, Gayraud Wilmore's (1973) historical interpretation of black religion reiterated its indispensable role in resistance to slavery, agitation for abolition, and engagement in postslavery struggles for freedom, emancipation, and equality, even as it exposed conserving inclinations, the exclusion of women from religious leadership, and accommodations to the political status quo.[5] *Second*, the preeminence of the religious has come to overdetermine both academic and popular representation of African Americans and their culture. Too frequently such representation relegates the religious orientation of African American cultures and peoples to the irrational, the superstitious, the premodern; alternately defines them as innately religious, then reduces their religious sensibilities, styles, dispositions, and aesthetics to stereotype; and imposes constrictive, even crippling unanimity upon their diversity. Hollywood films, television dramas, and sitcoms illustrate such misrepresentation by caricaturing African American worship styles and practices as irrational, superstitious, or comedic.[6] And the restriction of African American religious experience to forms of Protestant Christianity presents another illustration.[7]

Third, religion and religious experience occur within the contingencies of history, even as they may transcend those contingencies. For more than three centuries and across three continents, Europeans and European Americans captured, bought, sold, and enslaved African peoples. Study of African American religious experience requires coming to terms with the historical fact of the Atlantic slave trade and its historic and existential impact on peoples of African (*and* European) descent. Philip Curtin (1969), John Blassingame (1972, 1977), and David Brion Davis (1966, 1975, 1984, 2006) have produced major interdisciplinary studies that have decisively shaped scholarship on slavery in Latin and North America.[8] Both Saidiya Hartman (1997) and Marcus Rediker (2007) pursue historical and psychological concerns: Drawing on a range of sources such as diaries, slave narratives, popular theater, and legal cases, Hartman explores self-making, individuality, and freedom through uncovering the psychic insult done to slave and slaveholder—dominion and pacification, terror and deception, bodily integrity and abuse. Rediker focuses his study on the slave ship and the web of social, commercial, and mercantile relations through which the trade altered peoples and nations.

Fourth, the slave trade brought to North America various and diverse peoples from the western and central regions of the African continent. No "universal" West African cultural heritage existed, but individual and group contact and encounter through commerce, intermarriage, festivals, climatic events, or wars between villages and peoples allowed for working knowledge of different languages as well as some shared mores and beliefs. The conditions of enslavement posed difficulties as well as possibilities for cultural and religious integrity. The slave trade implied cultural and religious dispersal, disruption, and fragmentation, even collapse. Hence, African American religious thought and theology must come to terms with the loss of cultural memory as well as preservation, adaptations, and reconfigurations of cultural forms and expressions.

The mid-twentieth-century debate between anthropologist Melville Herskovits (1941) and sociologist E. Franklin Frazier (1939) forms the locus classicus of scholarly endeavors to address the roots of African American religious and cultural sensibilities and practices. Herskovits's groundbreaking research led him to contend that slavery had not stripped the enslaved people of African religious and cultural influence. African elements were discernible in worship, funeral customs, etiquette, customs, speech patterns, music, and dance. Frazier countered by arguing the weight of chattel slavery effected a decisive break with the African past, thus, stripping the slaves and their descendants of language, customs, religion, and forms of social organization. Christianity, he concluded, filled this void.[9] In *Slave Religion: The "Invisible Institution" in the Antebellum South* (1978) historian Albert Raboteau made a pioneering contribution to our understanding of the formation of African American religious life.[10] Raboteau drew on slave narratives, autobiographies, legal documents, plantation ledgers, and missionary reports to paint a vivid portrait of the "invisible" religious life of the enslaved community.[11]

Anthropologists Sidney Mintz and Richard Price (1992), on the other hand, refined and sharpened Herskovits's basic conclusions. Mintz and Price focused on the processes of cultural exchange and change. To this end, they accorded importance to the "slave sector" as a social site of autonomy, encounter, and contact between heterogeneous African peoples in the making of a "new culture [marked by] an expectation of continued dynamism, change, elaboration, and creativity."[12] Moreover, by drawing on fieldwork in the Caribbean, Peru, and Suriname, Mintz and Price locate African American culture in a comparative framework and contribute to a more nuanced understanding of black Atlantic religions and cultures. The work of Mechal Sobel and Margaret Washington offers fruitful models of research along these. Sobel traces the encounter and coalescence of various African worldviews during an early phase of slavery (ca. 1700–1730) into the formation of an Afro-Baptist worldview (ca. 1743).[13] In a study of African American culture in Georgia–South Carolina sea islands, Washington demonstrates the role of African indigenous religions in developing a cohesive "new world culture" (Gullah) among Africans from Senegambia, the Gold Coast, and Liberia.[14] Washington's meticulous research makes clear why the Gullah people represent the "*locus classicus* of African 'survivals' in the United States."[15]

Fifth, in the effort to free humanity from unblinking subservience to religious, social, and cultural authorities, the European Enlightenment promoted the exercise of human reason and personal autonomy over against revealed truth and promulgated the ideals of critique and freedom. Yet the very exercise of reason and its ideals were subordinated and corrupted in the discovery, exploration, and exploitation of the peoples and cultures of Africa and the Americas. Philosophers and critical theorists such as Cornel West (1982, 1994), Emmanuel Eze (1997, 2008), Charles Mills (1997), Susan Buck-Morss (2009), and Walter Mignolo (2011) highlight this contradiction in Enlightenment ideals.[16] Perhaps the most influential of these thinkers, West deployed a genealogical approach to explain the "discursive conditions for the possibility of the intelligibility and legitimacy of the idea of white supremacy."[17] The structure of modern discourse, he maintains, is shaped by three historical processes: the modern scientific revolution with its emphasis on observation and evidence, Cartesian philosophy's subject-object split, and the revival of Greek classical aesthetics. These interactive processes account for the emergence of those "controlling metaphors, notions, categories, and norms that shape the predominant conceptions of truth and knowledge in the modern West."[18]

Sixth, since the nineteenth century, African American religious thought presumed the significance of Christianity in the religious lives of the enslaved Africans and their descendants. Black theology, irrupting in the political and cultural tumult of the 1960s, took as its twin starting points *black experience* and Christian faith, even as it critiqued Christianity's theological and pastoral collusion with slavery and racial discrimination. With the phrase *black experience*, James Cone (1969, 1970), the progenitor and foremost exponent of black theology, sought to capture the whole of black life: Blues, beauty, extroversion, decision-making, pride, self-respect, self-love, indignant action, even rage, at injustice, and existence in a system of white racism.[19] This was a descriptive rather than explanatory definition. Black theology took "seriously the *black experience* as a life of humiliation and suffering"[20] and interpreted the gospel of Jesus Christ in light of the conditions of oppressed blacks so as to demonstrate its functions as herald and agent of black liberation. Moreover, black theology called upon the black church to revisit its historic identification with enslaved blacks and shift its emphasis from respectability and moral purity to that of concrete social liberation.[21]

Critics objected both to Cone's discussion of experience and to his confidence in the liberative potential of Christianity. Charles Long (1971) and William Jones (1973) critiqued black theology's assumptions about the role of Christianity in the formation of African American religious consciousness and in the realization of black liberation respectively.[22] A historian of religions, Long stressed phenomenological and hermeneutical method, resisted uncritical acceptance of Christianity as the dominant thread in the formation of the religious life of the enslaved people, and called for interrogation of the relation of African religious and cultural forms to African American religio-cultural life. But black theology's vibrancy and its vigorous claim on the gospel's message of justice and liberation overshadowed Long's probative proposals. In the past decade or so, scholars of African American religion, particularly Dianne Stewart Diakité, Tracey Hucks, Yvonne Chireau, and James Noel, have taken up several of Long's seminal research proposals to demonstrate the importance of anthropological tools such as ethnography and fieldwork (Chireau 2003), to reframe the response black religious experience to oppression deploying the analogy of mysticism (Noel 2009), to resituate the presumptive sway of Christianity in formative African American religious life with the term *christianisms* (Diakité and Hucks 2013). These scholars, among others, stand in the forefront of a wave of black religious scholarship that interrogates prevailing categories, definitions, vocabularies, methods, and structures in the study of religion.[23]

Jones disputed the very plausibility of black theology's claim on liberation. What had Christianity and black theology to say about the "maldistribution, negative quality, enormity, and transgenerational character of black suffering?"[24] Provocatively to some and blasphemously to others Jones asked, "Is God a white racist?" His incisive analysis provoked serious reconsideration of long-overlooked black humanism and paved the way for the work of Anthony Pinn. His aim is the articulation of an African American nontheistic humanist theology, and his productivity, originality, and wide-ranging theoretical command has begun to substantively reshape black theology and enlarge the horizon of black religion.[25]

Seventh, prior to the mid-1980s, theoretical, theological, and common-sense usage treated race as a fixed concept, a natural and immutable classification grounded on physiological characteristics with putative ontological meaning. Recent critical and theological analyses have destabilized the concept of race and problematized its ontological signification, thus calling into question black theology's use of race, and blackness in particular. The work of sociologists Michael Omi and Howard Winant (1986, 1994) has been crucial to this project. Omi and Winant formulated the theory of racial formation to explain the "sociohistorical process by which racial categories are created, inhabited, transformed, and destroyed."[26] Within this process, the notion of race pinpointed "social conflicts and interests by referring to different types of human bodies."[27] Moreover, racial formation process implicates power dynamics and the capacity of social institutions to absorb and neutralize political and social change movements, and, thereby, sustain (racial) inequality.

Theological ethicist Victor Anderson (1995) targets the notion of blackness as essentialized, totalizing identity or ontological blackness. As a philosophy of racial consciousness, he contends, ontological blackness reduces "African Americans' self-conscious perceptions of black life [to] unresolved binary dialectics of slavery and freedom, negro and citizen, insider and outsider, black and white, struggle and survival."[28] Further, Anderson argues, ontological blackness subjugates the individual's potential for self-transcendence to that of the black community. On this point, he shares with Pinn a deep concern for the flourishing of black individuality. Both these thinkers call into question black theology's propensity to limit black experience to suffering, humiliation, and struggle against white racism.[29] Thus, Anderson regards the "close connection between ontological blackness and religion"[30] with suspicion. Such proximity, he contends, risks "racial henotheism,"[31] the idolatrous temptation to make race total, absolute, even sacred.

This way of framing the problematic of study of the formation of African American religious experience neither claims to be exhaustive nor intends to be reductive. Rather, it sets out some basic recurrent issues. The following discussion (1) probes meanings of experience, religion, and religious experience; (2) deploys phenomenological method to construct a genealogy of the formation of African American religious consciousness and experience; (3) reviews two approaches to the study of African American religious experience in contemporary religious thought and theology; and (4) raises some issues for contemporary lived expressions of African American religious experience.

Contested Terms: Experience, Religion, and Religious Experience

Notoriously difficult to pin down, the term "experience" suffers from excessive generality and malleability, since experience can be made to mean nearly anything. To illustrate, consider three unsatisfactory uses of experience: In some usage, experience is synonymous with feeling or subjective emotion; it reverberates with the psychological. In other usage, experience refers to the empirical, to what can be grasped directly through the senses and, thus, rules out areas of life that do not yield to empirical verification.[32] Or, perhaps, we might consider experience as the raw, unthematized content of the stream of human consciousness. Heightened attending, questioning, understanding, and parsing the "stuff" in the stream allows a grasp and identification of several differentiated dynamic patterns that may interact or clash with one another or even break down. Rather than reductive or restrictive, the notion of patterns of experience functions as a heuristic that allows for concretizing sensation and bringing it to awareness, question, insight, and judgment. Some recognizable patterns of experience include the biological, psychological, aesthetic, social, intellectual, and religious.[33]

Still, language may demarcate experience descriptively and prescriptively, and whether verbal or signed, language emerges within culture. Heuristically, culture denotes a set of meanings and values that inform a way of life. Those meanings and values may be conveyed through language as well as intersubjective gestures (e.g., a smile or frown or touch), symbol, art, and the lives or exemplary conduct and deeds of a person or group.[34]

The slave trade thrust the captive Africans not only into literal and different geographies, but also into different cultures with their particular linguistic, intersubjective, symbolic, aesthetic, incarnate, and religious expressions of meaning and value.

The Africans met these worlds of meaning with multivalent reactions and responses that ought neither be romanticized nor maligned; the absolute human cost of chattel slavery defies rational comprehension, the consequences terrifying and terrifyingly ambiguous. That cultural carry-overs and retentions can be traced to the Akan and Ashanti of the Gold Coast, the Dahomeans, the Yoruba of western Nigeria, the Bini of eastern Nigeria, the Bakongo of west Central Africa testifies to their remarkable ingenuity and confirms the resilience of the human spirit.[35] These and other peoples remembered, misremembered, and forgot; certainly under trauma, cultural memory proves unreliable. They lost language, adapted, and improvised novel vocabularies and usage; they purged and modified and blended rites and rituals, customs, and mores. They reevaluated interpersonal relationships; they reoriented themselves. The survivors sought to make meaning afresh and to discern value; with spiritual pragmatism, they carved out a distinctive synecdochic relation between religion and culture.

Like experience (and culture), religion too is a contested term. Anthropologist Clifford Geertz considered religion as "a system of symbols which acts to establish powerful, pervasive, and longlasting moods and motivations in men by formulating conceptions of a general order of existence and clothing these conceptions with such an aura of factuality of that the moods and motivations seem uniquely realistic."[36] This definition has attracted widespread use and gains vitality from its connection to Geertz's insistence on critical interrogation of "thick description" in interpretation.[37] However, Talal Asad charges that in spelling out this conception of religion, Geertz has allowed overweening influence to Christianity with its stress on cognitive assent rather than ceremony or ritual or practices.[38] Pinn, Noel, Stewart Diakité, and Hucks, among others, concur. The interpretative control African American Christianity exerts over the praxis of black religious experience (and identity) deflects scholars and theologians from recognizing transcendence or divinity in other religions traditions, especially vodun, Santeria, and candomblé.[39] Taking Christianity as normative truncates black religious experience and ignores the dynamic spiritual pragmatism that gave rise to the plural, diverse, and varied expressive forms of African American Christianity itself.

Broadly construed, religion assumes a discernible reality or realities (perhaps sacred or holy) beyond or outside the visible world as well as various practices that may open channels of communication between believers and that reality or realities or produce certain ends. But, to paraphrase Howard Thurman, the central fact of religion is that it presupposes God.[40] Another and philosophical way of speaking about religion locates its origin in the transcendental orientation of the human spirit, in the human spirit's openness to questions and to questioning without restriction. Such openness may lead to "the exploration of life-altering questions,"[41] to discernment of the question of mystery and ultimacy, of divinity. Put more sharply, "Religion is the capacity of human consciousness to apprehend [and to signify] ultimate meaning and ultimate value symbolically."[42] In other words, the notion of religion is entwined in the structure of human consciousness, and human beings possess a natural and innate tending toward God. Appreciating that this tending is natural may help to obviate stereotyping of African Americans as the religious: *All humans are religious.* How any given individual responds to this tending must vary.

On a phenomenological approach, religious experience names the pattern of human experience that mediates an individual's encounter with or experience of that which is *beyond* the natural or empirical, an experience of what the person glimpses as mystery and ultimacy, as God, as holy, or as divinity. Human finitude dictates that religious experience occurs within spatial and temporal conditions and historical, cultural, and social circumstances. The individual comes to the experience with a personal and collective history, personal achievements and failures, ordinary and existential concerns, physical and mental qualities, and traits of personality. The individual woman or man, Thurman writes, comes "into the Presence of God [soaked in] the smell of life."[43]

Religious experience always includes "an aspect of the *extraordinary* [and] its central fact is the awareness of meeting God."[44] This meeting may be named encounter or confrontation or a sense of presence, but despite the nomenclature, in religious experience, "the individual is seen as being exposed to direct knowledge of ultimate meaning."[45] Indeed, for Thurman, the *extraordinary* denotes mystical experience of the divine. Although the person may prepare for the experience through prayer or fasting or withdrawal from the ordinary of daily life, the experience happens to the person and cannot be brought about or turned off at will. It penetrates and suffuses consciousness. At the same time, the content, meaning, and effect of the experience are available only to the person who has undergone the experience (although at times the guidance of an expert may be sought in aid of comprehending what has happened and what it might mean).

Often religious experience may generate assurance and command authoritative status in and over the person's life and conduct; yet, just as easily, the experience may upend all that an individual has, holds, believes, and lives. Religious experience may involve noetic clarity or insight, either authenticating or contravening assumed beliefs; yet the experience also may evoke confusion, "unknowing," and uncertainty. Given its intense, extraordinary, and fleeting character, religious experience eludes rationalization, propositional logic, and quantitative analysis, rendering communication of its content, meaning, and effect difficult. In the attempt to convey the ineffable, the individual may employ metaphorical or symbolic language. But should even this attempt to speak falter, the individual may resort to silence. This silence emanates not from ignorance, but from potential; thus, ironically, such silence may be a source of creative and expressive self-transformation or self-transcendence.[46] This silence may lead as well to religious eccentricity, since "personal and, hence, private religion [may become] the critical referee of what not only counts for God in experience, but also what is of social and moral worth."[47]

A Genealogy of the Formation of African American Religious Experience

The following genealogical sketch of African American religious experience takes cues from the work of Charles Long. This requires a critical move: recursive and "archaic," "crawling back"[48] through history in order to locate, excavate, and reconstruct *baseline black religious consciousness* as the fusion of elements and fragments of African indigenous or traditional religio-cultural sensibilities, rituals, cognitive and aesthetic orientations, self-understanding, meanings, and values. This section summarizes (1) the complex core of African religions, (2) the appearance of black religion, and (3) the "slave religion" that emerges in black religion's encounter with Christianity as expressed through certain practices: the spirituals, ring shout, conversion experiences, and fascination with the Bible as a "talking book."[49] But before proceeding, clarification of the use of the term "practice" in this essay is warranted.

Practice refers to the performance of certain words or actions through which something is achieved. Religious practices are complex integrative practices: linked performances (behaviors or "doings and sayings") joined by cognitive, prescriptive, and affective structures that seek certain inner dispositions (e.g., harmony) or ends (e.g., utilitarian or transcendent).[50] Religious practices are embedded in particular religions, and some, but never all, of these may translate from one religion to another. Some practices of indigenous traditional African religions include initiation rites, naming rituals, serving kola nut, pouring libations, venerating the Ancestors, dancing and drumming. Prayer, hymn singing, holy dancing, humming or moaning, and uttered responses to parts or the whole of a sermon or testimony (e.g., "Amen!" or "Teach!" or "Yes, Lord!") are some practices reflective of the experience of African American religious practitioners. Some, certainly not all, of these practices may be found in Islam or Judaism or Buddhism.

The Complex Core of African Religions

African American religious experience may be located asymmetrically within the circumference of African indigenous or traditional religion and the sacred cosmos it mediated. This sacred domain constituted a whole: religion and culture intertwined intimately and comprehensively, admitting no separation of the religious and the secular. Religion occupied the whole person and the whole of a person's living: The most mundane as well as the most important tasks and activities of daily life, human relationships, social interactions, and natural phenomena were suffused with religious meaning.

African indigenous or traditional religions, similar to Islam and Christianity, held to a kind of monotheism or belief in a supreme deity or high god, who had many names: The Yoruba referred to God as *Olódùmarè*, the Igbo called God *Chukwu*, the Akan-Ashanti designated God as *Onyame*, the Bakongo knew God as *Nzambi Mpungu*, and the Dogon named God *Amma*.[51] This deity was recognized as the originator and sustainer of all things and was considered eternal, incomprehensible, omniscient, omnipresent, omnipotent, transcendent, and immanent.[52] The indigenous or traditional sacred cosmos also included various lesser divinities and spirits. Special acknowledgment was accorded to the Ancestors, the honored dead of long ago and the deceased of more recent memory, who sustain intimate and immediate connection with their living progeny. Indeed, the Ancestors are believed capable of intervening in daily affairs and bestowing blessing or meting out punishment and must be venerated properly according to ritual custom.[53]

Whereas the Western sacred cosmos grasps time in a linear or forward motion, the African sacred cosmos mediates time in relation to rhythmic continuity and the significance of events. Traditional African thought considers time "a two-dimensional phenomenon, with a long *past*, a *present* and virtually *no future*, [while] Western thought apprehends time as an indefinite past, present, and infinite future."[54] Moreover, rather than using "numerical calendars" or fractional measurement, Africans reckon time on the basis of "phenomenal calendars" constituted by the relation of events or phenomena one to another and as they occur.[55] Significant or recurring events, rather than a fixed schedule or timetable, mark time in ordinary daily life. From the perspective of Western theology, the African sacred cosmos mediates *kairos*, that is, the interruptive or life-altering (the event or the qualitative), rather than *chronos*, that is, the sequential or fractional (the numerical or the quantitative). Human life too has a rhythm. The Bakongo believed that "[human] life has no end, that it constitutes a cycle."[56] That cycle is signified by the four moments of the sun: (1) the rising of the sun—meaning birth or beginning, (2) the sun's ascendancy—indicating maturity and responsibility (e.g., initiation, taking of titles, marriage), (3) the sun's setting—meaning death as a transition or transformation, and (4) midnight—inferring existence in the other and ancestral world and reincarnating birth.[57] So an "ontological rhythm" adheres to a rhythm of nature.[58]

African indigenous or traditional religion possessed neither scriptures to proclaim and exegete, nor dogmatic creeds requiring assent and observance. Rather, John Mbiti observes, "Religion is written not on paper but in people's hearts, minds, oral history, rituals and religious personages like priests, rainmakers, officiating elders and even kings."[59] Ritual and ceremonial practices marked initiations, funerals, births, coronations or installation of chiefs, oath taking, ordeals, purification, healing, sacrifice, and divination. Through such rituals, breaches in the social fabric were healed, and order and harmony restored. Key interconnected components of these rituals included singing, dancing, drumming, playing various musical instruments; creating and reciting poetry; and the use of ritual implements and distinctive vesture, including carved masks and figures.[60] More than twelve million men, women, and, youth carried the African sacred cosmos into the Middle Passage and onto Europe, the Caribbean, and Latin and North America.[61]

The Appearance of Black Religion

Black religion represents a creative coalescence of elements or recollections or fragments of indigenous African religions that survived the weight of the Middle Passage and New World enslavement.[62] This coalescence yielded "root paradigms"[63] that nurtured black religious consciousness and grounded a new sacred cosmos that differed decisively from that mediated by indigenous religions.[64] The notion of black religion conjectures a dynamic process of probabilities—cognitive reorientation, cultural memory, change, and transformation; it emerges in the interstices of consciousness between indigenous traditional religions and the forging of a new religio-cultural worldview.

"Slave Religion" as Encounter with Christianity

Scholars cannot pinpoint precisely the origin of efforts to Christianize the enslaved people. Early in the evolution of chattel slavery (ca. the late seventeenth and early eighteenth centuries), English planters in the American colonies were suspicious that under British law Christian baptism would compel the manumission of the Africans. Not surprisingly, many planters refused to endorse or tolerate their religious instructions. On the other hand, some masters allowed clergy to preach to the enslaved people, although in their mouths, Christian theology was put to dubious purpose. For example, Anglican minister Thomas Bacon published a sermon that exhorted the enslaved people to accept their bondage as part of a natural and divinely ordained social order in which masters were "God's overseers"; slaves were to obey masters as if they were obeying God.[65] On other plantations, the enslaved people attended white churches, sitting or standing in designated areas; but on still other plantations, they were permitted to hold independent, and sometimes, unsupervised worship services. The enslaved people distinguished their Christian praxis from that of the planter and master class, which Frederick Douglass described as "corrupt, slaveholding, women-whipping, cradle-plundering, partial and hypocritical." Planters and slave traders, he continued, donate their "blood-stained gold to support the pulpit, and the pulpit, in return, covers [their] infernal business with the garb of Christianity."[66]

The First Great Awakening (1730s and 1740s) swept through the American colonies with vivid biblically rooted preaching, insistence upon personal salvation, and the conviction that an individual could have a direct personal experience of God. This Protestant Christian movement appealed to women and men of all races and social classes who gathered at camp meetings. To be sure, such egalitarianism was confined to the meetings, but it brought enslaved people into a religious forum marked by "spiritual equality."[67] The Great Awakening also marked more direct encounter and engagement of black religion with Anglo-American Christianity. Historians and cultural anthropologists conclude religion was the sphere (the mental and physical space) in which the enslaved Africans were able to exercise some measure of autonomy in intelligence, action, and creativity.

The Pragmatic Rise of the Spirituals

In response to an act of cruelty or in order to express anguish at the loss of a beloved or joy at some event, enslaved Africans moaned and sang and, thus, gave outward expression to inner feeling. If the moan or song may have had a personal origin, it nonetheless had communal application. The folklorist Zora Neale Hurston maintained that the spirituals are "Negro religious songs, sung by a group, and a group bent on expression of feelings and not on sound effects."[68] In creation and performance, these songs were marked by flexibility, spontaneity, and improvisation. The pattern of call-response allowed for rhythmic weaving of time and tone; the chorus provided a stable foundation for the extemporized lines of a song leader. Some eyewitnesses to the creation of the spirituals insist the tunes were African in origin and involved a "wrestling with the Spirit" and a "coming through," while others held that the spirituals were "revealed by the Holy Spirit" or taught to them by "Master Jesus."[69] If the motivation for the spirituals was a response to daily events, the lyrics embellished stories, parables, and characters from the Old and New Testaments, setting the enslaved people in the middle of the biblical event, and commenting on their situation. This suggests the slaves had robust familiarity with biblical texts or, at the very least, had ongoing exposure to biblical preaching. Even minimal literacy combined with the mnemonic skill so characteristic of oral cultures would have made creative composition possible.

The ring shout was a kinetic phenomenon wherein a spiritual or other song literally was danced with the whole body. The dancers arranged themselves in a circle and moved counterclockwise, initially shuffling slowly, the foot slightly lifted from the floor, bending the knees slightly; gradually, the speed and intensity of the movement increased. Sometimes the people danced silently; most often, they sang or a community's best signers stood at one side to ground the dancers, singing and clapping.[70] On the witness of former slaves, the people sang and danced for hours in secret meetings in the "woods, gullies, ravines, and thickets,"[71] aptly called brush arbors or hush arbors. The intensity of a ring shout could evoke "an extraordinary state of mind, described as 'getting the spirit,' 'getting happy,' 'getting over,' or 'coming through.'"[72]

The phrases "getting over" or "getting through" suggest some form of trial or testing; the phrases "getting the spirit" or "getting happy" intimate descent of or possession by spirits or spiritual powers.[73] In her study of the Gullah and their practice of the ring shout, Margaret Washington infers a resonance with West African *Poro* (male) and *Sande* (female) initiation societies. The Gullah restricted the ring shout to members of the Praise House, taught the shout to their children when young, and monitored it for integrity of practice.[74]

The Second Great Awakening (1790–1840) emphasized the absolute authority of the Bible, but the literacy required for full access to this authority clashed with legal prohibitions against teaching slaves to read and write. The testimonies of former slaves give ample evidence of the fascination of enslaved Africans with the Bible or the "talking book," their surreptitious and successful literacy, and their astute biblical hermeneutics through which they collated "an oral text."[75] Biblical scholar Allen Callahan (2006) traces the first appearance of the trope of the talking book in slave narratives and memoirs as early as 1772. In each recountal the enslaved person sees a white person reading the Bible aloud, then opens the book in secret, leans an ear close to the text in expectation that it will speak, and finally, disappointedly discovers the book would not speak.[76] But, as Callahan shows, the Bible did speak to the slaves: On the one hand, the Bible sounded themes of exodus, liberation and justice; cultivated a "disposition to critical consciousness,"[77] authorized questioning of self, of others, and of the divine, and contributed to the formation of African American religious consciousness, imagination, and experience. On the other hand, the Bible resisted queries as to the meaning of black enslavement and oppression, advocated long-suffering, and encouraged a taste for the otherworldly.[78] The talking book spoke out of both sides of its mouth.

The enslaved people gained knowledge of the Bible chiefly by word of mouth, public readings, or sermons. According to biblical scholar Renita Weems, their lack of literacy released them from "allegiance to any official text, translation, or interpretation; hence once they heard biblical passages read and interpreted to them, they in turn were free to remember and repeat in accordance with their own interests and tastes."[79] These spiritual pragmatists created what theologian Delores Williams calls an "oral text"[80] and sociologist Cheryl Townsend Gilkes an "Afrocentric biblical tradition."[81] According to Gilkes, this was a communal process of critical listening designed to question, sift, winnow, and select from biblical books or passages whatever was deemed consistent with life and survival.

The experience of conversion lay at the core of the evangelical preaching of the Second Great Awakening. This experience referred to the undergoing of an intense personal emotional, even psychological, event including visions or ecstatic experiences, resulting in personal change or transformation, and accompanied by a profound reorientation and renewal of religious identity. The thirty-eight slave narratives collected in *God Struck Me Dead* open a window on African American religious consciousness and experience.[82] Sobel has identified four features that distinguish visions of African Americans from those of European Americans: (1) a notion of two selves—a "little me inside the big me," (2) detailed narration of the "little me's" journey or travel to the brink of hell, (3) the appearance of a little white man who leads the "little me" eastward to heaven, and (4) detailed descriptions of a dazzling white heaven and God robed in white.[83] To prepare for visions or other ecstatic experiences, slaves fasted, refused to sleep, spent as much time as they could alone in prayer, and, often, sought the guidance of an elder. The vision often came in dramatic form: "A light split me open from my head to my feet." "God struck me dead." "Like a flash the power of God struck me." "A hand came and struck me across the face three times."[84] After the individual has "come through" the journey to hell and the visitation to heaven, God returns her or him to life invested with a special (divine) commissions and public purpose: "Go preach my gospel to every creature and fear not, for I am with you, an everlasting prop. Amen." "Speak, and I will speak through you." "Go, wash your feet and tell the world of my undying love. Amen."[85] After the vision the individual is aware of him- or herself as transformed in body and in mind: "The next morning my hands and feet were new." "After I passed through this experience I lost all worldly cares. . . . I am a new creature in Jesus, the workmanship of his hand." "Ever since the Lord freed my soul I have been a new man."[86]

These extraordinary experiences conclude with assurance, return, and transformation for a public purpose, thereby, conferring status on natally alienated people. For centuries African indigenous religions throbbed beneath the guise of Roman Catholic saints (e.g., Shango / St. Barbara), visible and accessible to their proficients. Is it not possible these same religions vibrated (perhaps at lower register) beneath the spirituals, ring shouts, visions, and coded messages of the talking book, visible and accessible to their proficients under the guise of "slave religion"?

This genealogy serves a heuristic purpose. If, as Raboteau observes, "the majority of slaves remained only minimally touched by Christianity by the second decade of the nineteenth century,"[87] how might we explain the presumptive overidentification of African Americans with Christianity? One response is *functional*: The enslaved people, Long asserts, "used what was at hand," adapting it and investing it with their peculiar experience of chattel slavery.[88] Thus, Christianity supplied the idiom (e.g., biblical language and imagery, symbols, terms, rituals, and concepts) through which they *signified* their transformations of religious consciousness and mediated meanings and values reflective of those transformations. This process was as much an accident of geography (where the slaves were disembarked and sold) as it was of Christianity's collusion with political and economic power and its submission to ideology (making the Africans better slaves). A second response is *epistemological*: Those who watched the slaves engaged in their religious praxis assumed, looked for, and, found Christianity; they confused the message with the medium. But knowing is not a matter of taking a look and seeing what is out there already. Absent from that description of the cognitional process is questioning critically what one sees, proposing and testing probable answers, checking, testing again, weighing the evidence, judging, then deciding. In a perceptive foreword to *God Struck Me Dead*, Paul Radin warned against uncritically subordinating the religious experiences recounted therein to Christianity.[89] Conceivably, in the formative stages, Christianity served as a "surrogate"[90] or a midwife in the mediation of the religious experience of the enslaved people. Perhaps, then, it may be more appropriate, as Hucks and Stewart Diakité propose, to identify *christianisms* in African American religious practices.[91] A salutary caution lies beneath the words of this spiritual:

> I've been 'buked an' I've been scorned
> Dere is trouble all over dis worl'
> Ain' gwine lay my 'ligion down
> Ain' gwine lay my 'ligion down.

Two Contemporary Approaches to the Study of African American Religious Experience

In order to frame the problematic of the study of the formation of African American religious experience, I drew on the work of several major thinkers and theorists—historians, sociologists, philosophers, and theologians. In this section I consider two major contemporary approaches to reflection on African American religious experience—hermeneutical and womanist analysis.

Hermeneutical Approach

Since the late 1980s, African American theologians have turned to slave narratives as a source for theologizing. The early advocates of this turn were Dwight Hopkins (1991, 1993, 2000), George Cummings (1991, 1993), and Will Coleman (1999), whose interpretations stimulated a new constructive program in black theology.[92] *Cut Loose Your Stammering Tongue*, edited by Hopkins and Cummings, inaugurated a research program that has grown in quantity, sophistication, and cross-disciplinary appeal. These exponents, nearly all of whom are trained as theologians, bring black theology into contact with indigenous black historical and narrative sources that enjoy a priori authority and mine these for "insight" about the religious and cultural worldview of the enslaved people and their "theological interpretation of their experience."[93] Even as these thinkers engage "primary sources" of African American religious experience, they pursue a contemporary practical objective—providing ancestral resources for a culture in the thrall of nihilism, violence, acquisitive materialism, and narcissistic individualism. Their research demonstrates considerable methodological diversity in black theology's encounters with the slave narratives—historical, mutual critical correlational, doctrinal, functional, womanist, denominational, and pastoral or practical. Further, these theological interpreters deploy several reading or interpretative strategies—literary, linguistic, hermeneutical-phenomenological, semiotic, or structuralist. In *Tribal Talk*, Coleman comments that "the task of the sympathetic listener-reader-interpreter [is] to come to terms with the meaning(s) of their narratives through the words of their texts."[94]

Hopkins, the most influential exponent of this research, constructs a systematic black theology of liberation from spirituals, slave narratives, and folk wisdom. In both *Shoes That Fit Our Feet* and *Down, Up, and Over*, he deploys a two-part organizational and methodological strategy: The background section excavates and analyzes folk religious experiences; the foreground apprehends faith as social praxis for change, draws out exemplars (Ancestors, leaders), and indicates nourishing and corrective insights for contemporary black life. At the same time, Hopkins interrogates African American religious experience for doctrinal ends—to discern the people's thinking about God, Jesus, and human purpose and to determine what that thinking contributes to constructive development of doctrine.

Coleman, in *Tribal Talk*, argues it is "the task of the sympathetic listener-reader-interpreter to come to terms with the meaning(s) of their narratives through the words of their texts."[95] This remark intimates the epistemological stake in this research program: Whether, in the service of a *critical* reading (i.e., to demonstrate that blacks have *always* been metaphysicians) the theologian as *knower*, in fact, reads as a *conceptualist*. In other words, does a theologian interpreting slave narratives *look* for happenings or sayings that inflect Christian meanings and *find* those meanings? Anderson has been critical of this research program, putting a finger on the complex relationship between the theologian's discursive formation, interpretative strategies, and history. Efforts in theologizing slave narratives, he notes, assume the narratives not only "authentically represent religious beliefs and moral practices constitutive of slave religion [but also] exhibit a religious unity that is subject to theological formulation and moral inferences."[96] This research program, he concludes, enacts an ideological equivocation, pairing a former slave's hope for freedom and justice with black theology's demand for struggle and resistance.[97] In interpreting slave narratives, black theology of liberation, Pinn asserts, lacks a hermeneutics of suspicion.[98]

In his construction of a theology of African American religious experience, Anderson expands the notion of experience by deploying the grotesque. Experience as grotesque refers to a capacious and protean perception of apparent oppositional sensibilities (e.g., pleasure/pain), ambiguities, and enigmas that recovers and leaves the sensibilities and ambiguities and enigmas unresolved. Moreover, the grotesque resists appeals to cognitive and aesthetic syntheses and harmonizations of apparent oppositions "by highlighting the absurd and sincere, the comical and tragic, the estranged and familiar, the satirical and playful, normalcy and abnormality."[99] In Anderson's hermeneutical approach, the grotesque keeps judgments tentative, flexible, and open to creative and innovative, even disturbing, possibilities.

Womanist Approach

Katie Geneva Cannon first appropriated Alice Walker's notion of "womanist" to distinguish the intellectual work of African American female scholars (e.g., social and theological ethicists, sociologists, biblical exegetes, and theologians) from that of male black liberation theologians and female white liberation (feminist) theologians. Womanist analysis accords epistemological privilege to the experience of African American women from slavery through the present. In particular, womanist inquiry contests the biased ways in which African American women have been and are perceived in African American and other religious, cultural, and interpersonal contexts. Rather than a "school," womanist thinkers form a movement (now in its third generation) of multiple voices, cultures, theistic (Muslim and Christian) and nontheistic (humanist) perspectives and commitments in order to "shed light on the interstructuring of oppressions that affect and distort all people."[100] Thus, it may be more helpful to think of womanist inquiry in the plural—as *approaches*. Womanist approaches advance a complex paradigm of interdisciplinary critical religious reflection that breaks with traditional ethical and theological discourse and categories. Womanist language often takes poetic than doctrinal form, thematic rather than systematic, erotic than analytic. Although some critics have categorized womanist inquiry as racially essentializing, these thinkers seek to problematize not only (white) feminist or black (male) liberation hermeneutics, but also any ahistorical, amorphous, essentialist apprehension of black women and all who are excluded and despised.

Of this cohort of scholars, Cannon (1988), Delores Williams (1993), and Emilie Townes (2006) are the most prolific and prominent.[101] None of the three works discussed here focuses directly on religious experience, although religious faith as critically and humbly open to the deepest concerns of human living provides both the stimulus for these works and the objective. In *Black Womanist Ethics*, Cannon breaks with the methods and content of conventional Christian and secular ethics. The analysis outlines the historical situations during which black women are challenged to sustain dignity and live moral lives. Chattel slavery, legalized discrimination, and segregation from the postemancipation period up to the contemporary era reinscribe racial dichotomies and power dynamics to black women's detriment. Still in this murky historical and social context, black women live the promise of possibility. This conclusion is grounded in the black women's literary tradition, particularly the life and work of Zora Neale Hurston, and the theologies of Howard Thurman and Martin Luther King Jr., as resources for a constructive ethic. From her study of

Hurston's life and work, Cannon discerns three virtues: unshouted courage, invisible dignity, and quiet grace. In order to articulate the role of religious experience in ethical and moral responsibility, Cannon turned to Howard Thurman, who roots social action in "the conscious and direct exposure of the individual to God."[102] Thus, in Cannon's constructive ethic, Hurston's virtues are coupled with "mystical experience with God" in order to "provide resources which order, focus and define precepts and actions which can be used to transform socio-political structures that denigrate and inhibit the realization of wholeness that God brings to all life."[103]

Delores Williams attends to the role religion plays in black women's social oppression and their confidence in the immediacy of God's presence and promise of help. Black women insist, she maintains, that "God helped them to make a way out of no way," and, indeed, they "believe God is involved not only in their survival struggle, but that God also supports their struggle for quality of life."[104] Williams works out this folk aphorism (God can make a way out of no way) theologically by locating the biblical figure of Hagar at the center of her statement of womanist theology. The story of the slave of African descent pressed into surrogacy, brutalized by the mistress, "ravished" by the master, forced into exile, and threatened with certain death in the wilderness functions as a "route to black women's issues" of contemporary social oppression—forced motherhood, homelessness, single motherhood, poverty, and struggle for survival.[105] Moreover, this analogy telescopes African American history, especially African American women's history. This is no mere analogy and illustrates, Allen Callahan explains, why "as modernity's most thoroughly humiliated people, African Americans have taken the texts of the Bible so eagerly and earnestly."[106] At the same time, Williams discerns at least two traditions of African American biblical appropriation. One emphasized the activity and agency of men; she names this the *liberation of African American biblical appropriation*. The other focused on the activity and agency of women, she names this the *survival/quality-of-life African American biblical appropriation*.[107] For Williams, then, religious experience adverts to a *survival/quality* of life encounter with God. "In the context of much black American religious faith, survival struggle and quality of life struggle are inseparable and are associated with God's presence with the community."[108]

Womanist Ethics and the Cultural Production of Evil levels a trenchant critique of the ideological subversion of human wholeness. Here Townes demonstrates this through uncovering the ideological in the interaction of history, memory, and culture. She advances the notion of "the fantastic hegemonic imagination," a complex of ideas put forth by dominant groups in a society and positioned to secure the rule of subordinate peoples or classes: "The fantastic hegemonic imagination traffics in people's lives that are caricatured or pillaged so that the imagination that creates the fantastic can control the world in its own image. This imagination conjures up worlds and their social structures that are not based on supernatural events and phantasms, but on the ordinariness of evil"[109] Through saturating popular culture with blatant misrepresentations and negative stereotypical images (e.g., the mammy figure, the matriarch as bad mother, the welfare mother, the jezebel or whore), dominant groups disguise truth, seduce our consent, and maintain control. Moreover, the cultural production of evil deforms all of us. Townes challenges religious faith: unless it resists complicity with the dominant political powers, religion will become empty, useless, "an opiate and not a source of transformation."[110]

Issues for Contemporary Expressions of African American Religious Experience

The bulk of this essay has dealt with ways to understand the past—the formation of African American religious experience. What of the present? In the fragmentation of postmodern living, the self-indulgence of televangelists, indifference to and cognitive distancing from the poor by the affluent of all races, rampant individualism, and materialism, we can appreciate and applaud the desire "to ground contemporary black culture in a morally nurturing mythos"[111] as provided through interpretation of slave narratives. This is the longing for a common narrative that will oppose the worn and worn-out American dream. At the same time, a range of social and ethical problems such as poverty, inadequate healthcare, sexism, domestic and random violence, heterosexism, unemployment, and the extraordinarily high rates of incarceration of black males impinge upon the religious praxis of African Americans, whether they are Muslims or Jewish or Buddhists or humanists, but certainly Christians and, in particular, the black church. Moreover, each of these issues requires the church to take on thorough research, analysis, prayer, and reflection in order to formulate adequate theological ethical and pastoral responses and strategies for education and advocacy and transformation among congregants and clergy.[112] These problems are difficult, even hard, but not necessarily intractable. Their resolution (not solution) requires an approach that values modesty, openness, conflict, self-scrutiny, authentic communal and interpersonal relationships, the acceptance of difference, vulnerability, and patience, but never apathy. The resolution (not solution) of these problems requires the church to be an origin not of arbitrary or totalizing, but true value, enlarged and engaged in light of its ultimate purpose.

Notes

1. In this essay, I use the term "African American" to refer to the descendants of the enslaved Africans in the United States. Constraints of space and time limit this discussion to their

religious experience. Further, I try here, not altogether successfully, to restrict my use of the terms "black" and "blackness," reserving their meaning for a conjectural moment in the complex formation of African American religious experience. The designation "African American" may be applied as well to descendants of enslaved Africans in Latin America (e.g., Brazil, Columbia, Ecuador) and the Caribbean (e.g., Haiti, Cuba, Jamaica, Trinidad and Tobago). Within the United States, this appellation has been problematized by contemporary immigration from Africa and the Caribbean. Kobina Aidoo popularized this issue in his documentary film *The Neo-African-Americans: Black Immigrant Identities* (2008), but scholars have studied this migration and its impact on US life for some years; see, for example, Mary C. Waters, *Black Identities: West Indian Immigrant Dreams and American Realities* (New York: Russell Sage Foundation; Cambridge: Harvard University Press, 1999); Jean Muteba Rahier and Percy C. Hintzen, *Problematizing Blackness: Self-Ethnographies by Black Immigrants to the United States* (New York: Routledge, 2003); Kwadwo Konadu-Agyemand, Baffour K. Tayki, and John A. Arthur, eds., *The New African Diaspora in North America: Trends, Community Building, and Adaptation* (Lanham, MD: Rowman & Littlefield, 2006); and Yoku Shaw-Taylor and Steven A. Tuch, eds., *The Other African Americans: Contemporary African and Caribbean Immigrants* (Lanham, MD: Rowman & Littlefield, 2007).

2. See Allan D. Austin, *African Muslims in Antebellum American: Transatlantic Stories and Spiritual Struggles* (New York: Routledge, 1997); Peter B. Clarke, *West Africa and Islam: A Study of Religious Development from the 8th to the 20th Century* (London: Arnold, 1982); John K. Thornton, *Africans in the Making of the Atlantic World, 1400–1800* (New York: Cambridge University Press, 1998); Thornton, "The Development of an African Catholic Church in the Kingdom of the Kongo, 1491–1750," *Journal of African History* 25, no. 2 (1984): 147–67.
3. Richard Brent Turner, *Islam in the African-American Experience*, 2nd ed. (Bloomington: Indiana University Press, 2003), 24; Michael A. Gomez, *Black Crescent: The Experience and Legacy of African Muslims in the Americas* (New York: Cambridge University Press, 2005). The presence of African Muslims during the period of enslavement in the United States cautions against limiting African American engagement with Islam to the twentieth century—from Noble Drew Ali (1886–1929), founder of the Moorish Science Temple of America, to Mufti Muhammad Sadiq, who promoted the Ahmadiyya Movement (1872–1957) in the United States, to W. D. Fard (1893–?), who founded the Nation of Islam, to his successors Elijah Muhammad (Elijah Poole, 1897–1975) and Malcolm X (Malcolm Little, El-Hajj Malik El-Shabazz, 1925–1965), to Louis Farrakhan (Louis Wolcott 1933–), the current leader of the Nation of Islam, to Warith Deen Mohammed (Wallace D. Muhammad, 1933–2008), who founded the orthodox American Society of Muslims.
4. W. E. B. Du Bois, *The Souls of Black Folk* (New York: Modern Library, 2003), 191–96. Toward this end, the black church developed and fostered possibilities and structures of self-governance, sociality, education, and creative release—of self-transformation or self-transcendence.
5. Gayraud S. Wilmore, *Black Religion and Black Radicalism: An Interpretation of the Religious History of Afro-American People* 3rd ed. (Maryknoll, NY: Orbis Books, 1998).
6. Hollywood perversions of vodun as "voodoo" ("zombies," drums, and dolls stuck with pins) feature in *I Walked with a Zombie* (1943), *Voodoo Island* (1957), *Night of the Living Dead* (1968), and *Vodoo Lagoon* (2006). Comedic parody of black worship was a staple

of the NBC television sitcom *Amen* (produced by Carson Productions and running from 1986 to 1991). These and other distortions surface in many films including those of Tyler Perry. For some critical rejoinders to these biased depictions, see M. M. Manring, *Slave in a Box: The Strange Career of Aunt Jemima* (Charlottesville: University of Virginia Press, 1998) and Mia Mask, ed., *The Contemporary Black American Cinema: Race, Gender, and Sexuality at the Movies* (New York: Routledge, 2012). Early examples of stereotyping include Thaddeus Norris, "Negro Superstitions," *Lippincott's Magazine* 6 (1870): 90–95, http://www.southern-spirits.com/norris-negro-superstitions.html; Ulrich B. Phillips, *Life and Labor in the Old South* (Boston: Little, Brown, 1929), Newbell Niles Puckett, *Folk Beliefs of the Southern Negro* (Chapel Hill: University of North Carolina Press, 1926).

7. See Kwame Anthony Appiah and Henry Louis Gates Jr., eds., *Africana: The Encyclopedia of the African and African American Experience* (New York: Basic Books, 1999). The editors' omission of any treatment of African American Catholicism, even in the five-volume second edition (2005), is striking. Readers might profitably consult Cyprian Davis, *The History of Black Catholics in the United States* (New York: Crossroad, 1990); Kwame Bediako, *Christianity in Africa: The Renewal of Non-Western Religion* (Maryknoll, NY: Orbis Books, 1995); John K. Thornton, *The Kongolese Saint Anthony: Dona Beatriz Kimpa Vita and the Antonian Movement, 1684–1706* (Cambridge: Cambridge University Press, 1998); and Diane Batts Morrow, *Persons of Color and Religious at the Same Time: The Oblate Sisters of Providence, 1820–1860* (Chapel Hill: University of North Carolina Press, 2002).
8. Philip D. Curtin, *The Atlantic Slave Trade, a Census* (Madison: University of Wisconsin Press, 1969); David Brion Davis, *The Problem of Slavery in Western Culture* (Ithaca, NY: Cornell University Press, 1966); Davis, *The Problem of Slavery in the Age of Revolution, 1770–1823* (Ithaca, NY: Cornell University Press, 1975); Davis, *Slavery and Human Progress* (New York: Oxford University Press, 1984); and Davis, *Inhuman Bondage: The Rise and Fall of Slavery in the New World* (New York: Oxford University Press, 2006); John W. Blassingame, *The Slave Community: Plantation Life in the Antebellum South* (New York: Oxford University Press, 1979); Blassingame, ed., *Slave Testimony: Two Centuries of Letters, Speeches, Interviews, and Autobiographies* (Baton Rouge: Louisiana State University Press, 1977); Saidiya V. Hartman, *Scenes of Subjection: Terror, Slavery, and Self-Making in Nineteenth-Century America* (New York: Oxford University Press, 1997); Hartman, *Lose Your Mother: A Journey along the Atlantic Slave Route* (New York: Farrar, Straus and Giroux, 2007); and Marcus Rediker, *Slave Ship: A Human History* (New York: Viking, 2007). See also Ira Berlin, *Many Thousand Gone: The First Two Centuries of Slavery in North America* (Cambridge: Belknap Press of Harvard University, 1998), and Robert Harms, *The Diligent: A Voyage through the Worlds of the Slave Trade* (New York: Basic Books, 2002).
9. Melville J. Herskovits, *The Myth of the Negro Past* (Boston: Beacon Press, 1958); E. Franklin Frazier, *The Negro Family in the United States* (Chicago: University of Chicago Press, 1939) and *The Negro Church* (New York: Schocken, 1964), 2–19.
10. Albert J. Raboteau, *Slave Religion: The "Invisible Institution" in the Antebellum South*, updated ed. (New York: Oxford University Press, 2004). In the afterword to the 2004 edition of *Slave Religion*, Raboteau responds to various criticisms and acknowledges shortcomings, the most potent of which is his predisposition to privilege Christianity in the forging of black religious consciousness.
11. Dianne Stewart Diakité and Tracey Hucks, "Africana Religious Studies: Toward a Transdisciplinary Agenda in an Emerging Field," *Journal of Africana Religions* 1, no. 1 (2013): 38; see Raboteau's reassessment of his project, *Slave Religion*, 323–34.

12. Sidney Mintz and Richard Price, *The Birth of African-American Culture: An Anthropological Approach* (Boston: Beacon Press, 1992). See also Lawrence Levine, *Black Culture and Black Consciousness: Afro-American Folk Thought from Slavery to Freedom* (New York: Oxford University Press, 1977); Robert Farris Thompson, *Flash of the Spirit: African and Afro-American Art and Philosophy* (New York: Random House / Vintage Books, 1983); Sterling Stuckey, *Slave Culture: Nationalist Theory and the Foundations of Black America* (New York: Oxford University Press, 1987); and Joseph E. Holloway, ed., *Africanisms in American Culture* (Bloomington: Indiana University Press, 1990).
13. Mechal Sobel, *Trabelin' On: The Slave Journey to an Afro-Baptist Faith* (Westport, CT: Greenwood Press, 1979); see also Walter F. Pitts Jr., *Old Ship of Zion: The Afro-Baptist Ritual in the African Diaspora* (New York: Oxford University Press, 1993).
14. Margaret Washington, *A Peculiar People: Slave Religion and Community-Culture among the Gullahs* (New York: New York University Press, 1988); see also Michael A. Gomez, *Exchanging Our Country Marks: The Transformation of African Identities in the Colonial and Antebellum South* (Chapel Hill: University of North Carolina Press, 1998).
15. J. Lorand Matory, *Black Atlantic Religion: Tradition, Transnationalism, and Matriarchy in the Afro-Brazilian Candomblé* (Princeton, NJ: Princeton University Press, 2005), 295–98.
16. Cornel West, *Prophesy Deliverance! An Afro-American Revolutionary Christianity* (Louisville, KY: Westminster Press, 1982), and *Race Matters* (Boston: Beacon Press, 1994); Emmanuel Chukwudi Eze, ed., *Race and the Enlightenment: A Reader* (Cambridge, MA: Blackwell, 1997); Eze, *On Reason: Rationality in a World of Cultural Conflict and Racism* (Durham, NC: Duke University Press, 2008); Paul Gilroy, "Race Ends Here," *Ethnic and Racial Studies* 21, No. 5 (September 1998): 838–47; Charles W. Mills, *The Racial Contract* (Ithaca, NY: Cornell University Press, 1997), Susan Buck-Morss, *Hegel, Haiti, and Universal History* (Pittsburgh: University of Pittsburgh Press, 2009); Walter Mignolo, *The Darker Side of Western Modernity: Global Futures and Decolonial Options* (Durham, DC: Duke University Press, 2011).
17. West, *Prophesy Deliverance!* 48.
18. West, *Prophesy Deliverance!* 50.
19. James H. Cone, *Black Theology and Black Power* (Maryknoll, NY: Orbis Books, 1997); *A Black Theology of Liberation* (Maryknoll, NY: Orbis Books, 2010), 24. In this latter work, Cone lists, in no particular order, the various sources of black theology: black experience, black history, black culture, revelation, scripture, and (Christian) tradition (27–34).
20. Cone, *Black Theology of Liberation*, 24.
21. Cone, *Black Theology of Liberation*, 60–62, passim.
22. Charles H. Long, "Perspectives for a Study of Afro-American Religion in the U. S." *History of Religions* 2 (August 1972): 54–66; and *Significations: Signs, Symbols, and Images in the Interpretation of Religion* (Philadelphia: Fortress Press, 1986); William R. Jones, *Is God a White Racist? A Preamble to Black Theology* (Boston: Beacon Press, 1998).
23. Stewart Diakité and Tracey Hucks, "Africana Religious Studies: Toward a Transdisciplinary Agenda in an Emerging Field," in *Black Magic: Religion and the African American Conjuring Tradition*, ed. Yvonne P. Chireau (Berkeley: University of California Press, 2003), and James A. Noel, *Black Religion and the Imagination of Matter in the Atlantic World* (New York: Palgrave Macmillan, 2009).
24. See Jones, *Is God a White Racist?* 21–22. Jones took his title from a line in a poem written in 1906 by W. E. B. Du Bois, "Litany at Atlanta," 422–26, in *The Seventh Son: The Thought and Writings of W. E. B. Du Bois*, vol. 1, ed. Julius Lester (New York: Random House, 1971).

25. Anthony B. Pinn, *Why Lord? Suffering and Evil in Black Theology* (New York: Continuum, 1995); Pinn, *By These Hands: A Documentary History of African American Humanism* (New York: New York University, 2001); Pinn, *Terror and Triumph: The Nature of Black Religion* (Minneapolis: Fortress Press, 2003); Pinn, *The End of God-Talk: An African American Humanist Theology* (Oxford: Oxford University Press, 2012).
26. Michael Omi and Howard Winant, *Racial Formation in the United States, from the 1960s to the 1990s*, 2nd ed. (New York: Routledge, 1994), 57; cf. Joe Feagin and Sean Elias, "Rethinking Racial Formation Theory: A Systemic Racism Critique," *Ethnic and Racial Studies* 36, no. 6 (April 2012): 931–60. See also Kimberlé Crenshaw, Neil Cotanda, Gary Peller, and Kendall Thomas, eds., *Critical Race Theory: The Key Writings That Formed the Movement* (New York: New Press, 1995); Paul Gilroy, *Against Race: Imagining Political Culture beyond the Color Line* (Cambridge: Belknap Press of Harvard University Press, 2000).
27. Omi and Winant, *Racial Formation*, 55.
28. Victor Anderson, *Beyond Ontological Blackness: An Essay on African American Religious and Cultural Criticism* (New York: Continuum, 1995), 14.
29. Anderson, *Beyond Ontological Blackness*, 14.
30. Anderson, *Beyond Ontological Blackness*, 14.
31. Anderson, *Beyond Ontological Blackness*, 15. Cone, of course, would be appalled at the notion of blackness displacing God, since through the articulation of black theology he shows precisely how white racist supremacy is a form of idolatry.
32. Dermot A. Lane, *The Experience of God: An Invitation to Do Theology* (Mahwah, N J: Paulist Press, 2003), 18–23.
33. Bernard Lonergan, *Insight: A Study of Human Understanding, 5th ed., Collected Works of Bernard Lonergan*, vol. 3 (Toronto: University of Toronto Press, 1988), 204–14, 410–11.
34. Bernard Lonergan, *Method in Theology* (New York: Herder & Herder, 1972), 57. The notion of patterns might be illustrated by filling out some implications of the social: Chattel slavery nested at the core of the social (i.e., political, economic, technological) pattern of experience spawned by slaveholding southern Anglo-American culture. For *political* purposes of representation and taxation, southern delegates to the Constitutional Convention petitioned that the actual number of enslaved persons be counted and, since slaves could not vote, slaveholders would be afforded increased representation in the House and Electoral College; however, antislavery delegates objected. The result was the three-fifths compromise in which the actual numbers of slaves were reduced to three-fifths (see the US Constitution, Article 1, Section 2, Paragraph 3). For *economic* purposes, slaves were considered real estate and, as such, subject to mortgage and sale. Slaves were "deemed, sold, taken, reputed and adjudged in law to be *chattels personal*, in the hands of their owners and possessors, and their executors, administrators, and assigns, *to all intents, constructions, and purposes whatsoever*" (William Goodell, *The American Slave Code in Theory and Practice: Its Distinctive Features Shown by its Statutes, Judicial Decisions, and Illustrative Facts* (New York: Negro Universities Press, 1968), 24, 23. For *technological* purposes, slaves were tools or objects—able to be trained, useful for manual labor of all sort, production, and reproduction.
35. Herskovits, *Te Myth of the Negro Past*, 61.
36. Clifford Geertz, *The Interpretation of Cultures* (New York: Basic Books, 2000), 90.
37. Geertz, *The Interpretation of Cultures*, 3–30.
38. Talal Asad, *Genealogies of Religion: Discipline and Reasons of Power in Christianity and Islam* (Baltimore, MD: Johns Hopkins Press, 1993), especially 27–54.

39. Pinn, *Varieties*, 2; see also Matory, *Black Atlantic Religion*, 3.
40. Howard Thurman, *The Creative Encounter* (Richmond, IN: Friends United, 1954), 23.
41. Pinn, *Varieties*, 2
42. Carla Mae Streeter, "Glossary of Lonerganian Terminology: Religion," 327–28, in *Communication and Lonergan: Common Ground for Forging the New Age*, ed. Thomas J. Farrell and Paul A. Soukup (Kansas City, MO: Sheed and Ward, 1993).
43. Thurman, *The Creative Encounter*, 23.
44. Thurman, *The Creative Encounter*, 23.
45. Thurman, *The Creative Encounter*, 24.
46. This description draws insight from Wayne Proudfoot, *Religious Experience* (Berkeley: University of California Press, 1985), 152–54; see also the classic study by William James, *The Varieties of Religious Experience*, ed. Matthey Bradley (New York: Oxford University Press, 2012), 280–81; and Constance FitzGerald, "From Impasse to Prophetic Hope: Crisis of Memory," *CTSA Proceedings* 64 (2009): 21–42.
47. Victor Anderson, *Creative Exchange: A Constructive Theology of African American Religious Experience* (Minneapolis: Fortress Press, 2008), 124.
48. Long, *Significations*, 9.
49. Allen Dwight Callahan, *The Talking Book: African Americans and the Bible* (New Haven: Yale University Press, 2006), 4.
50. Theodore R. Schatzki, *Social Practices: A Wittgensteinian Approach to Human Activity and the Social* (Cambridge: Cambridge University Press, 1996), 89–90, 99–101.
51. Washington, *A Peculiar People*, 52; Thompson, *Flash of the Spirit*, 107.
52. John S. Mbiti, *African Religions and Philosophies*, 2nd ed. (London: Heinemann, 1989), 30–38.
53. Bolaji Idowu, *African Traditional Religions: A Definition* (Maryknoll, NY: Orbis Books, 1975), 184.
54. Mbiti, *African Religions and Philosophies*, 16–17.
55. Mbiti, *African Religions and Philosophies*, 17–19.
56. Thompson, *Flash of the Spirit*, 108.
57. Thompson, *Flash of the Spirit*, 108–9; Washington, *A Peculiar People*, 52–53.
58. Mbiti, *African Religions and Philosophies*, 24.
59. Mbiti, *African Religions and Philosophies*, 3, 37, 58–73.
60. Mbiti, *African Religions and Philosophies*, 74–89.
61. The Trans-Atlantic Slave Trade Data Base available online at http://www.slavevoyages.org/tast/index.faces estimates that roughly 310,000 Africans were brought to the United States.
62. Sobel, *Trabelin' On*, 39.
63. Victor Turner, *Dramas, Fields, and Metaphors: Symbolic Action in Human Society* (Ithaca, NY: Cornell University Press, 1974), 67, 163.
64. Sobel, *Trabelin' On*, 39, also, xxii–xxiv, 3–21. Sobel proposes a tripartite typology tied to the Africans' appropriation of the English language. The first groups of African captives spoke their own indigenous languages, but soon were influenced by contacts with one another and with Europeans. With the "first generation of Creole English speakers," a "quasi-African world view" was the result. In a second phase, a "black English" developed in tandem with a distinctive worldview in which Euro-American values and mores are assimilated. In a third phase, as blacks and white shared religious experiences, a new "Afro-Christian worldview" was forged (*Trabelin' On*, 38–39).

65. Thomas Bacon, "A Sermon to Maryland Slaves" (1749), 77, 83, 86, in *Religion in American History: A Reader*, ed. Jon Butler and Harry Stout (New York: Oxford University Press, 1998).
66. Frederick Douglass, "Appendix," 155, 157, in *Narrative of the Life of Frederick Douglass, An American Slave* (Cambridge: Belknap Press of Harvard University Press, 1960).
67. Callahan, *The Talking Book*, 4.
68. Zora Neale Hurston, *The Sanctified Church* (Berkeley, CA: Turtle Island, 1983), 80. For three classic discussions of the spiritual see James Weldon Johnson, ed., *The Book of American Negro Spirituals* (New York: Viking Press, 1925); John Lovell Jr., *Black Song: The Forge and the Flame—the Story of How the Afro-American Spiritual Was Hammered Out* (New York: Paragon, 1986); and Eileen Southern, *The Music of Black Americans: A History* (New York: Norton, 1983, 1997).
69. Cited in Raboteau, *Slave Religion*, 244–45.
70. Raboteau, *Slave Religion*, 70–71. The ring shout may be found in Brazil in the rituals of candomblé, the traditional religion of the West African Yoruba people.
71. Raboteau, *Slave Religion*, 215.
72. Joseph M. Murphy, *Working the Spirit: Ceremonies of the African Diaspora* (Boston: Beacon Press, 1994), 149.
73. Stuckey, *Slave Culture*, 33.
74. In "*A Peculiar People*," Margaret Washington writes, "After 1845, many [Sea Island] plantations had rude structures where the Gullah could 'hold prays' on weekday evenings and Sundays. . . . [F]or the Gullahs the Praise House was a plantation community hall where they related secular experiences, directed their religious life, openly expressed among each other their innermost frustrations, longings and expectations" (233).
75. Delores S. Williams, *Sisters in the Wilderness: The Challenge of Womanist God-Talk* (Maryknoll, NY: Orbis Books, 1994), 272.
76. Callahan, *The Talking Book*, 13–14. Theophus H. Smith interprets the Bible as a "conjure book: a kind of magical formulary for prescribing cures and curses, and for invoking extraordinary powers in order to reenvision, revise, and transform the condition of human existence" in his *Conjuring Culture: Biblical Formations of Black America* (New York: Oxford University Press, 1994), 6.
77. Callahan, *The Talking Book*, 245.
78. Callahan, *The Talking Book*, 242–45.
79. Renita J. Weems, "African American Women and the Bible" in *Stony the Road We Trod: African American Biblical Interpretation*, ed. Cain Hope Felder (Minneapolis: Fortress Press, 1991), 61.
80. Williams, *Sisters in the Wilderness*, 272.
81. Cheryl Townsend Gilkes, "'Mother to the Motherless, Father to the Fatherless': Power, Gender, and Community in an Afrocentric Biblical Tradition," *Semeia* 47 (1989): 79.
82. *God Struck Me Dead*, ed. Clifton H. Johnson (Cleveland, OH: Pilgrim Press, 1993). These interviews were conducted by Andrew Polk Watson, graduate student in anthropology at Fisk University between 1927 and 1929 and "originally published in limited circulation as *Social Science Source Documents* No. 2 by Fisk's Social Science Institute in 1945," (Raboteau, *God Struck Me Dead*, xix).
83. Sobel, *Trabelin' On*, 109; see also Riggins Earl Jr., *Dark Symbols, Obscure Signs: God, Self, and Community in the Slave Mind* (Maryknoll, NY: Orbis Books, 1993), 46–69.
84. Raboteau, *God Struck Me Dead*, 61, 45, 22.

85. Raboteau, *God Struck Me Dead*, 21, 94, 113.
86. Raboteau, *God Struck Me Dead*, 110, 111, 149.
87. Raboteau, *Slave Religion*, 149.
88. Long, *Significations*, 179.
89. Paul Radin, "Foreword: Status. Fantasy, and the Christian Dogma," viii–ix, in Raboteau, *God Struck Me Dead*.
90. Smith suggests that African Americans use the Bible "as a surrogate sacred text" in view of the absence of "indigenous texts" (*Conjuring Culture*, 250).
91. See Dianne M. Stewart, *Three Eyes for the Journey: African Dimensions of the Jamaican Religious Experience* (New York: Oxford University Press, 1994), 120–37, 162, 211–25; and Tracey E. Hucks and Dianne M. Stewart, "Authenticity and Authority in the Shaping of Trinidad Orisha Identity: Toward an African-Derived Religious Theory," *Western Journal of Black Studies* 27, no. 3 (2003): 178.
92. Dwight N. Hopkins and George Cummings, eds., *Cut Loose Your Stammering Tongue: Black Theology in the Slave Narratives*, 2nd ed. (Maryknoll, NY: Orbis Books, 2002). (this edition contains a new introduction by Will Coleman and additional essays by Joan Martin, David Emmanuel Goatley, and M. Shawn Copeland); Hopkins, *Shoes That Fit Our Feet: Sources for a Constructive Black Theology* (Maryknoll, NY: Orbis Books, 1993), and *Down, Up, and Over: Slave Religion and Black Theology* (Maryknoll, NY: Orbis Books, 2000); Will Coleman, *Tribal Talk: Black Theology, Hermeneutics, and African/American Ways of "Telling the Story"* (University Park: Pennsylvania State University Press, 2000).
93. George Cummings, "Slave Narratives, Black Theology of Liberation (USA), and the Future," 98, in Hopkins and Cummings, *Cut Loose Your Stammering Tongue*.
94. Coleman, *Tribal Talk*, 138.
95. Coleman, *Tribal Talk*, 138.
96. Anderson, *Creative Exchange*, 63.
97. Anderson, *Creative Exchange*, 68.
98. Pinn, *Varieties*, 197.
99. Anderson, *Creative Exchange*, 11. The provocative silhouette paper-cut art of Kara Walker illustrates the grotesque well; see her *Narratives of a Negress* (New York: Rizzoli International Publications, 2007).
100. Stacey M. Floyd-Thomas, "Writing for Our Lives: Womanism as an Epistemological Revolution," in *Deeper Shades of Purple: Womanism in Religion and Society*, ed. Stacey M. Floyd-Thomas (New York: New York University Press, 2006), 7; for the work of some third-generation womanists see Monica A. Coleman, *Making a Way out of No Way: A Womanist Theology* (Minneapolis: Fortress Press, 2008) and *Ain't I a Womanist Too: Third Wave Womanist Religious Thought* (Minneapolis: Fortress Press, 2013),
101. Katie G. Cannon, *Black Womanist Ethics* (Atlanta: American Academy of Religion, 1988) and *Katie's Canon: Womanism and the Soul of the Black Community* (New York: Continuum Books, 1995); Williams, *Sisters in the Wilderness*; Emilie Townes, *Womanist Ethics and the Cultural Production of Evil* (New York: Palgrave Macmillan, 2006).
102. Cited in Cannon, *Womanist Ethics*, 21.
103. Cannon, *Womanist Ethics*, 21.
104. Williams, *Sisters in the Wilderness*, 6.
105. Williams, *Sisters in the Wilderness*, 3.

106. Callahan, *The Talking Book*, xiii.
107. Williams, *Sisters in the Wilderness*, 3–6.
108. Williams, *Sisters in the Wilderness*, 3–6.
109. Townes, *Womanist Ethics*, 21.
110. Townes, *Womanist Ethics*, 136.
111. Anderson, *Creative Exchange*, 60.
112. All too often these problems penetrate one another. Consider incarceration: Legal expert Michelle Alexander argues persuasively that mass incarceration of black (and dark-skinned Latinos) has "emerged as a stunningly comprehensive and well-disguised system of racialized social control that functions in a manner strikingly similar to Jim Crow" *The New Jim Crow, Mass Incarceration in the Age of Colorblindness* (New York: New Press, 2010), 4. When these men complete their prison sentences, they are met not merely with stereotyping, but with legalized discrimination in employment, housing, education, and public health, and are blocked from voting and jury service. From such powerlessness and structural ostracism, not surprisingly, domestic and random violence occur; substance abuse and other parole violations may follow as mechanisms of escape. Hence the probability of recidivism ranks high. See also William J. Stuntz, *The Collapse of American Criminal Justice* (Cambridge: Harvard University Press, 2011).

Selected Texts

Anderson, Victor. *Creative Exchange: A Constructive Theology of African American Religious Experience*. Minneapolis: Fortress Press, 2008.

Appiah, Kwame Anthony, and Henry Louis Gates Jr., eds. *Africana: The Encyclopedia of the African and African American Experience*. New York: Basic Books, 1999.

Cannon, Katie Geneva. *Black Womanist Ethics*. Atlanta: American Academy of Religion, 1988.

Cone, James H. *A Black Theology of Liberation*. Maryknoll, NY: Orbis Books, 2010.

Du Bois, W. E. B. *The Souls of Black Folk*. New York: Modern Library, 2003.

Floyd-Thomas, Stacey, ed. *Deeper Shades of Purple: Womanism in Religion and Society*. New York: New York University Press, 2006.

Herskovits, Melville J. *The Myth of the Negro Past*. Boston: Beacon Press, 1958.

Jones, William R. *Is God a White Racist? A Preamble to Black Theology*. Boston: Beacon Press, 1998.

Long, Charles. *Significations: Signs, Symbols, and Images in the Interpretation of Religion*. Philadelphia: Fortress Press, 1986.

Mills, Charles W. *The Racial Contract*. Ithaca, NY: Cornell University Press, 1997.

Pinn, Anthony B. *Terror and Triumph: The Nature of Black Religion*. Minneapolis: Fortress Press, 2003.

Raboteau, Albert J. *Slave Religion: The "Invisible Institution" in the Antebellum South*. Updated ed. New York: Oxford University Press, 2004.

Stewart, Dianne M. *Three Eyes for the Journey: African Dimensions of the Jamaican Religious Experience*. New York: Oxford University Press, 1994.

Townes, Emilie. *Womanist Ethics and the Cultural Production of Evil*. New York: Palgrave Macmillan, 2006.

Turner, Richard Brent. *Islam in the African-American Experience*. 2nd ed. Bloomington: Indiana University Press, 2003.
Williams, Delores S. *Sisters in the Wilderness: The Challenge of Womanist God-Talk* Maryknoll, NY: Orbis Books, 1994.
Wilmore, Gayraud S. *Black Religion and Black Radicalism: An Interpretation of the Religious History of Afro-American People*. 3rd ed. Maryknoll, NY: Orbis Books, 1998.

CHAPTER 4

THE AFRICAN AMERICAN CHRISTIAN TRADITION

SYLVESTER JOHNSON

OF all that might be said of African American liberation theology, of foremost importance is its emergence within the Christian tradition. One can readily discern, in fact, that the Christian tradition has been no less influential than racial blackness for shaping the imperatives, orientations, grammatology, and modes of identification in African American liberation theology. From the earliest period of African American liberation theology in the late 1960s until fairly recently, black and womanist theologians have, with very few exceptions, literally equated African American liberation theology with *black Christian* liberation theology. The authenticating habitus of this theology, moreover, has been understood exclusively as the black church. Even in the early twenty-first century, it is still commonplace for black liberation and womanist theologians to regard Christianity as normative for black people and to equate the African American community with the black church. The normative status of the Christian tradition has raised myriad problems. But the historical reasons for this normative status, its influence, and its full implications merit explication. This essay explains how chief aspects of the Christian tradition became central to the identity, form, and content of African American liberation theology.

CIVIL RIGHTS, LIBERATION, AND THE PUBLIC MEANING OF CHRISTIANITY

African American liberation theology emerged quintessentially as a struggle over the public meaning of Christianity. At stake was the question of how black churches were to relate to racial justice activism. In this way, it boldly demonstrated a central concern with ecclesiology, the tradition of discerning the identity of the church by articulating its purpose, mission, and constituency. To make sense of this, one must understand how black liberation theology developed as a specific formation within the Christian tradition through its engagement with the particular symbolic and theoretical import of Black Power and the civil rights movement. Of special importance were the tensions created between different camps of African American Christianity about political religion—including the meaning of Black Power—and the larger tensions between white Christianity and the civil rights legacy represented by a vanguard of black churches.

The civil rights movement comprised multiple organizations like the Student Nonviolent Coordinating Committee (SNCC), the National Association for the Advancement of Colored People (NAACP), and the Southern Christian Leadership Conference (SCLC). It was SCLC, however, that became the dominant face of the civil rights movement, and this was of singular importance for shaping the movement's religious implications. When a group of African American southern clergy created SCLC in 1957, they were establishing an explicitly church-based organization to inherit the activist mantle and agenda of the Montgomery Improvement Association (MIA), which had overseen the historic bus boycott in that city. SCLC prudently selected as its chief executive Martin Luther King Jr., who had been part of a larger network of African American ministers like Gardner C. Taylor, Ralph David Abernathy, and Benjamin Mays. This group rejected evangelical fundamentalism and asserted instead that the Christian gospel mandated placing social justice at the center of ecclesiology.[1] This theology, of course, ran counter to the entrenched stance of the National Baptist Convention, USA (NBC, USA), the largest denomination of African American Christianity. Under Joseph Jackson Jr.'s leadership, the NBC, USA philosophically supported the general aim of racial justice while explicitly condemning the civil rights strategy of involving churches in politics and organized protest (particularly civil disobedience). NBC, USA impugned King's stridently political theology as a betrayal of the Christian gospel, resulting in 1961 in King's removal from the position of vice president of one division of the denomination. A bitter schism ensued, and in that same year the supporters of church-based civil rights activism walked away to create their own denomination, the Progressive National Baptist Convention (PNBC). This new denomination, unlike so many other schisms within African American Christianity, was fundamentally rooted in a deep *theological* divide over Christian identity and the church's role. Whereas the older Baptist denomination believed the church had no place in the chaotic, worldly domain of politics and civil disobedience, the PNBC was fully devoted to the social gospel understanding that only by creating social justice through political involvement could the church manifest its Christian identity.[2]

In the years that followed, a small cadre of African American theologians would respond to the urgent crisis of racial justice and the political activism of black churches by proffering what some viewed as a scandalous religious response—African

American liberation theology. As early as 1963, the year of the historic March on Washington, the rumblings of African American liberation theology were manifesting, when J. Deotis Roberts challenged the US system of apartheid as a *theological* issue, a condition he described as irreconcilable with the Christian gospel. Roberts realized he was taking sides in a fierce debate over the public meaning of Christianity. He was not attempting to launch a new field of academic theology so much as weigh in on an acrimonious debate that concerned black Christians throughout the nation.[3] The following year, the African American theologian Joseph Washington published a controversial book that identified the white church as the true locus of the Christian faith, embodying the authentic lineage of Christian theology.[4] Although his style of argument was distinctive, Washington implicitly affirmed the NBC, USA's critique of civil rights when he charged that black religion existed beyond the pale of the Christian faith to the extent that it differed from the confessional and liturgical formulations of white churches. Although he lauded the justice tradition of black churches as exemplified during the nineteenth-century antislavery movements, he claimed only their integration into white churches would render them veritably Christian. Washington would later claim that black theology itself originated as a response to antiblackness and could therefore never transcend racialism and was thus not truly Christian.[5] In this opening salvo of black liberation theology, the exchange between Roberts and Washington sharply recapitulated the fundamental divisions playing out across black churches throughout the nation. Washington, in fact, had distinctly crystallized the essential posture of Joseph Jackson Jr. and the NBC, USA. One can observe, for this reason, that the very emergence of black liberation theology was the birth of a liberationist ecclesiology because it sought to intervene at the very heart of discerning the identity of the Christian church in the crucible of a fierce struggle for racial justice.

The Black Church and Black Power

In May 1965, Adam Clayton Powell first used the term "Black Power" at a political gathering in Chicago and again when giving a commencement lecture at Howard University the following year. In the latter instance, he proclaimed that Black Power was a demand for "God-given rights" and should be taken seriously as an essential process of empowering African Americans to participate as equal members of society.[6] During the summer of 1966, Black Power became a rallying theme among SNCC activists in Mississippi. It quickly resonated throughout the nation. A firestorm of controversy erupted as many critics, among them African American Christian leaders, condemned Black Power as empty emotionalism or a dangerous, unchristian rage unfit for civil rights activism. Despite the tendency for its critics to associate Black Power almost exclusively with armed violence, the movement was far more complex. It unapologetically rejected external and internalized forms of antiblackness and instead promoted a strident embrace of racial pride and activism comprising economic, social, and political means of enabling African American to participate as power brokers in the broad social arena. Black Power's legacy included multiracial democracy (as evidenced by the activism of SNCC), the proliferation of cultural institutions, and the institutionalized scholarship of African American and Africana history, theory, and heritage.[7]

A critical mass of African American Christians were outspoken in their embrace of Black Power. Speaking as the president of the PNBC in 1968, Gardner C. Taylor argued that Black Power was a biblically sound approach to advancing the work of the church. In so doing, he offered a response from within the black church that mirrored the concerns of progressive academic theologians and insisted that liberation activism was not only compatible with the church's mission but was also demanded by the gospel.[8] In further response, African American clergy decided to form the National Committee of Negro Churchmen (later renamed the National Conference of Black Churchmen, or NCBC). This organization sought to persuade African American churches to adopt Black Power formally as a viable strategy consistent with the Christian gospel. During the summer of 1966, the NCBC issued a full-page manifesto in the *New York Times* defending the compatibility of Christianity and Black Power. The appearance of this strident, unapologetically Christian defense of Black Power evidenced an important shift in the role that liberation was to play in African American theology.

Until that time, the more integrationist themes of nonracialism had dominated civil rights. No thoroughgoing response to Black Power had emerged from Christian theologians. It was James H. Cone, a young Ph.D. trained in Barthian neo-orthodoxy, who centrally engaged the challenge that Black Power posed before African American Christianity. Cone's intellectual energies were consumed with interpreting the consternation of social and political forces of rapid change and uncertainty that marked the era. In the year following King's assassination, he published *Black Theology and Black Power*. "Black Power" was by then a common phrase, but the term "black theology" was less familiar. For those interested in learning of its meaning, Cone provided an audacious explanation in no uncertain terms. Affirming the sentiment of NCBC, he introduced black theology as the *Christian* proclamation that the central message of Jesus Christ in twentieth-century America was the Black Power movement. Cone embraced the controversy surrounding the acerbic, radical nature of Black Power. He argued that it was precisely because Black Power seemed so scandalous that it could embody the Christian revelation that Jesus as the Messiah, as one whose mission was to challenge the entrenched institutions of injustice and to identify with the most marginalized and oppressed populations. To take seriously Black Power as a Christian revelation, he further urged, required American churches to recognize that Jesus was black. And while Cone interpreted this blackness symbolically, he also emphasized that the historical Jesus of Nazareth was a person of color, not an Aryan.[9]

In the wake of the schism within the nation's largest African American Christian denomination, it was already clear that African American churches were deeply divided over the issue of ecclesiology. Cone charged that the vast majority of African American clergy and their churches had abandoned the difficult imperatives of the Christian gospel, which he identified as radical liberation, in exchange for a spiritualized theology that was perfectly compatible and complicit with racial and economic injustice. In these terms, the majority of African American churches had failed as certainly as white American churches to embody the authentic Christian gospel. Black theology also presented American theologians with a critical assessment of white social identity, long before the formal advent of whiteness studies. Because whiteness was a historical (as opposed to natural) identity with social origins rooted in imperatives of violent domination and exercising interests in power toward destructive ends, Cone urged American Christians to recognize white identity not as innocence but as the Antichrist; that is, it stood opposed to the very work that represented the demands of the Christian gospel in a white hegemonic state overwhelmingly characterized by its legal and cultural institutions of antiblack racism. By extreme contrast, Cone asserted, Jesus Christ was black (he meant this in the symbolic sense), an interpretive stance absolutely essential to grasping anew the scandalous, audacious challenge the Christian gospel posed to twentieth-century America.[10]

In response to Cone's challenge, other writers like William H. Becker drew attention to the relevance of Christology. Becker proposed that Jesus had embodied the roles of both suffering servant and righteous rebel, and he challenged black Christians to emulate both in order to advance the struggle for black freedom.[11] By contrast, the African American author William Banks published a direct critique of black liberation theology and King's social gospel theology. Writing from an evangelical viewpoint, Banks reiterated that Christianity was essentially a soul-saving religion and claimed that black churches involved in the civil rights movement were defying divine will.[12] Joseph Jackson Jr. similarly voiced deep opposition to Cone's audacious claim that Christian salvation was the work of social liberation, claiming in a 1971 address to his denomination that the divine was a spirit and that salvation was strictly spiritual. And he singled out black theology as a heretical catastrophe that undermined the Christian mission of black churches.[13]

The black theology movement, nevertheless, continued undaunted, as evidenced by Albert Cleage's sweeping Christological claims, in which he advanced that Jesus was racially black and that blacks were the chosen people whose divine mission in America lay in recognizing their identity and rejecting integration. Cleage also founded the Shrine of the Black Madonna, and he more than perhaps any other writer of the time identified the Christian tradition most thoroughly with Black Power and black people, arguing that the New Testament was literally the history of African Americans. In this way, Cleage went far beyond most black liberation theologians.

Whereas his colleagues in the movement sought to demonstrate that Black Power and racial justice were consistent with Christian meaning, Cleage argued that the Christian tradition itself was properly recognized only as the history of black people.[14]

The question of how black liberation theology was to be discerned in relationship to the Christian tradition continued to play out in myriad ways during the 1970s and 1980s. The question of blackness itself proved divisive. J. Deotis Roberts, for instance, posed an elaborate response to Cone when, in 1971, he argued that any talk of revolution and social change needed to be subordinated to racial reconciliation, which Roberts identified as more germane to the essence of the gospel. Roberts urged black theologians to take caution against investing too heavily in racial theology, although Roberts did agree with the larger aims of Black Power. At stake, he claimed, was the possibility that the black church might sever itself from mainstream (i.e., predominantly white) Christianity if racial reconciliation were not its ultimate aim.[15] Following just a few years later, the African American theologian Cecil Cone inveighed against focusing on blackness, as a threat to betray the Christian identity of the church. Although he affirmed black theology's rootedness in biblical theology, which he viewed as a corrective to patristic theology, he nevertheless urged other black theologians to subordinate their racial particularity to the universal mandates of Christianity. Only the God of the Christian faith, not the black community and not Black Power, could be the source of accountability for black theology.[16]

Black theology's unrelenting critique of whiteness as a destructive social identity, more than anything else, inspired vociferous charges that black theology promoted racism in blackface and was therefore merely paying lip service to the Christian tradition. On this score, most of black theology's critics were accustomed to conceiving race through naturalistic categories. They equated the condemnation of white social identity with the dismissal of the human beings invested in that identity. By the early 1970s, however, several white Christian theologians such as Fredrick Herzog, Peter Hodgson, Rosemary Ruether, and Glen Bucher had begun to engage substantively with black theology, some affirming its Christian character and echoing the need for white American Christians to heed its challenge to resist the theological and political aims of whiteness.[17]

In 1970, African American liberation theologians, ministers, and laity created the Society for the Study of Black Religion (SSBR). This provided the first formal arena for African American liberation theology as an academic enterprise. SSBR's significance, in contrast to that of NCBC, lay in its capacity to provide a forum outside of Christian churches for rigorous study, debate, and exchange of scholarship and analysis of theology, race, and the social justice, bearing on the most significant public issues of the times. Despite SSBR's academic focus, however, it was nevertheless clear that the organization was largely and, for the most part, unquestioningly rooted in the Christian tradition. The reason for this was not difficult to comprehend. The criticisms of black liberation theology all shared the common strategy of denying that black theology was genuinely Christian. Precisely because black liberation theology had emerged within a larger struggle over the public meaning of Christian identity, the movement functioned centrally to defend the Christian status of African American liberation theology.

One aspect of the Christian tradition had long presented a menacing challenge to African American churches: the question of suffering and the theological challenges of theodicy. Biblical theology played a tremendous role in this measure, since both the Hebrew Scriptures and the New Testament inscribed elaborate meanings to suffering through a teleological lens. Whether through the Exodus narrative, the popular legend of Job's suffering, or the persecution of saints near the end time in John's apocalypse, the Bible ascribed to the most brutal and debilitating forms of individual and social suffering a divine purpose and rendered it a presage to dividends of redemption and spiritual rewards. No act of suffering, moreover, has been of greater theological significance in the Christian tradition than Jesus's betrayal, biased trial, and brutal execution at the hands of imperial Rome. The most extreme and dominant interpretation within the Christian tradition understands Jesus as destined to become a literal human-divine sacrifice to assuage the vengeance of an omnipotent God who loved his human creation but who nevertheless insisted upon a blood sacrifice as the ineluctable price for freeing humanity from an eternal destiny of torment.[18]

It would be difficult to overestimate the deep and expansive influence this myth of redemption has exerted throughout the Christian tradition. With a naturalizing efficacy, it rendered intelligible the axiom that suffering was redemptive. And it guaranteed that the problem of innocent suffering—theodicy—would meet with a powerful rejoinder. Within the African American Christian tradition, numerous figures like David Walker and Henry McNeal Turner employed the language of redemptive suffering to explain the ravages of slavery and racism. Even Martin Luther King Jr., whose enlightened social gospel theology caused him to steer clear of evangelical fundamentalist interpretations of the faith, turned to redemptive suffering when he eulogized three young black girls killed in 1963 by white terrorists in Birmingham.[19] So it is no surprise that African American liberation theologians engaged with the issue during the 1970s and 1980s. To claim that an omnipotent being was on the side of the oppressed, however, seemed at odds with the brutal reality of black suffering. This problem was singularly crystallized in the early 1970s when the African American philosopher William R. Jones launched an elaborate critique of black liberation theology's theistic claims and Christocentric focus. Jones drew on the empirical history of blacks to challenge basic tenets of traditional theism. How could a God of unlimited power and unlimited justice, he asked, permit the extraordinary, disproportionate historical suffering of blacks? Jones offered a shocking alternative. Perhaps there did indeed exist a very powerful deity, one who was a white racist. Jones's heuristic proposal was meant as an analytical template for assessing Christian theodicy. He aimed to convince black liberation theologians to abandon the traditional formulations of theism and instead to root their theological methods in theistic humanism. Nothing less, he argued, would resolve black theology's incompatibility with the liberation it claimed to promote.[20]

Jones's work met mostly with strained silence and chafed dismissal.[21] Among those who directly engaged Jones was James H. Cone. In his *God of the Oppressed*, Cone identified the historical advance of black freedom as a manifestation of divine action in history. This demonstrated, he reasoned, that the God of Christian faith had never abandoned oppressed blacks. For the most part, however, black liberation theologians shunned Jones's work and proceeded to ignore his challenge.[22]

Emilie Townes led a team of womanist theologians to examine the linkage between theodicy and the African American historical experience of racial and gender oppression. The volume included attention to the often uncanny coexistence of theodical frameworks that invested suffering with teleological meaning while also engendering active resistance to oppression.[23] Many of these theologians observed, in other words, that theologies of suffering did not necessarily induce passivism and apathy but might instead engender more ambiguous or complex responses.[24] Also of significance were the histories of black women's social activism, which were usually allied with Christian organizations such as the National Association of Colored Women (NACW), a secular organization whose members were often religious activists.[25] Other womanist theologians reinterpreted the traditional language of servanthood and suffering that easily undermined progressive praxis and that was particularly problematic given the actual modern history of blacks as racial slaves and domestic servants.[26]

Theologians like Delores Williams dealt richly with the biblical tradition in order to respond to several concerns that African American liberationist theologians had raised through their engagement with the themes of suffering, salvation, and Christology, pivotal elements of the Christian tradition. In *Sisters in the Wilderness*, she focused on the narrative of Hagar to explain that survival, not liberation, was the frequent fate of African Americans; that Jesus was not a liberating messiah but one acting in solidarity with the oppressed; and that the Christian tradition offered rich resources for understanding and articulating black women's experiences, given a sufficient hermeneutical lens.[27] Despite this critical engagement with theodicy, it nevertheless became clear that the Christian traditional view of redemptive suffering would remain an enduring feature of most black and womanist theology, as writers like Joanne Terrell invested anew in the grammars of blood sacrifice and atonement theology to articulate an evolving framework of African American liberation. Writing in the wake of multiple critiques of atonement theology, Terrell argued that African American Christians had continually found strength in Jesus's suffering on the cross to make sense of their individual and collective suffering.[28]

African American Experience and the Christian Tradition

During the 1970s and 1980s, church historians in theological schools and divinity schools as well as secular universities began to broaden their purview of religious history beyond the realm of Anglo-American Christianity. What had been an exclusive focus on white Protestant churches and professional male theologians was steadily expanding to comprise Catholicism, African American Christianity, Judaism, Native American religions, and secular movements such as immigration reform, racial justice struggles, slavery, and politics.[29] The black cultural revolution, furthermore, had compelled a range of scholars to examine what constituted a distinctly African American culture.[30] In the context of these developments, African American liberation theologians produced several studies of individual African American historical figures, some more familiar than others, who had significantly shaped the legacy of African American Christianity's progressive resistance to social suffering. In this way, black and womanist theologians interpreted the Christian tradition through the particular lens of African American experience. Of major importance was the theological attention to figures like Ida B. Wells, whose Christian commitments became a major resource in her antilynching activism of the 1800s and early 1900s. Demonstrating Wells's role as the architect of modern civil rights strategies promoted a persuasive claim that social justice, black liberation, and the Christian tradition were of a piece and held major implications for the way contemporary African American Christians understood their faith. Martin Luther King Jr. also received renewed attention as a central historical actor in the black Christian tradition who wed religious commitment to social justice. Other figures like Maria W. Stewart, Julia Foote, Sojourner Truth, Fannie Lou Hamer, and Mary McLeod Bethune also featured in the scholarship of African American liberation theology. All served to deepen the claim that black and womanist theology was an authentic expression of the black church's legacy and thus needed to be engaged as an essential aspect of the Christian tradition. This productive phase also signaled that liberation theologians had absorbed the larger interest in validating African American history as a worthy object of serious intellectual study.[31]

Womanist Theology

Among the most enduring aspects of the Christian tradition has been its patriarchal architecture of meanings and social power. African American women soon raised a critical lens to the reinscription of this sexism in the work of black male theologians. And they did so by interpreting other aspects of the Christian tradition to challenge this patriarchy. They also linked this to interpretations of American women's history, reflections on personal spirituality, and the collectivism that marked the history of African Americans communities. Among the earliest of these womanist theologians were Katie Cannon, Renita Weems, and Kelly Brown Douglas. They examined Christology to argue that womanist theology's analysis of black women's experience was an essential element of liberation theology. Of central importance in womanist theology was the role of the communal aspect of African American experience (in contrast to black male theologians' tendency to focus on individual historical actors).[32] This typically meant examining black churches as the center of African American communal life. In this way, womanist theologians amplified the ecclesiastical dimension of the Christian tradition for articulating the liberative and empowering dimensions of African American experience. Katie Cannon demonstrated how sexism brutalized black women as individuals in their communities while undermining the vitality of their religious communities. But Cannon was also careful to explicate the multiple ways that the Christian tradition itself had been a resource for black women. And she proposed that a black feminist consciousness was historically attested in African American Christianity and needed to be engaged seriously in order to promote a liberative response.[33]

Weems examined the Bible as a resource for understanding black women's agency, thus engaging what is arguably the most authoritative symbol of the Christian tradition within black Protestantism. She emphasized the parallels between the suffering and perseverance of female characters in biblical narrative and the racial and gendered struggles of African American women in modern history.[34] Douglas's widely cited *Black Christ* interpreted the black Christian tradition in sharp distinction from white Christianity, illustrating that social power and racial imperatives were not extraneous to religion but mattered immensely in shaping the substance and content of the church. The way African American Christians conceived of Jesus, in contrast to his messianic meaning among racist whites, demonstrated that a Christology of blackness necessarily foregrounded the liberationist imperatives that had shaped black liberation theology from the start. Douglas went further, however, to argue that "the Womanist Black Christ" had a yet more fully liberating message with which black male theologians needed to reckon.[35]

In like manner, Toinette Eugene examined the legacy of womanism in the black Christian tradition, demonstrating the historical relationship between racism and sexism. Jacquelyn Grant articulated a central paradigm of womanist theology when she critiqued the racism of white feminism and advanced womanism as an urgent corrective that called white women and black men to be accountable for a just relationship with African American women. By emphasizing the legacy of racial egalitarianism in the black church, moreover, Grant demonstrated that the very identity of the church was at stake in rejecting the legacy of misogyny and antiblackness.[36]

During the late 1980s and early 1990s, at the very time black liberation and womanist theologies were establishing a veritable influence throughout progressive Christian seminaries and divinity schools, womanist theologians began to query the ways that heteropatriarchal norms of the Christian tradition were being replicated in black churches and in African American liberation theology. In a frequently cited roundtable discussion, widely held antagonism against queer sexuality was crystallized in Cheryl Sanders's argument for why the very term *womanist* and its theological framework should be rejected. Sanders identified it as an essentially secular label whose individualism was incompatible with Christianity and fundamentally at odds with the ethical norms of African American Christianity because the term *womanist* was popularized by the lesbian author Alice Walker and affirmed homosexuality. A plethora of womanist theologians responded by asserting anew the relevance of womanist theology and the potent legacy of black women that Walker's reflections sought to uplift.[37]

The challenge to this heteronormative theology was keenly articulated by Renée Hill, who emphasized the peculiar irony that womanist theologians had appropriated the terminology of Alice Walker, a non-Christian writer who affirmed same-sex love, while ignoring the massive implications for religious identity and sexuality.[38] Elias Farajaje-Jones likewise examined black liberation theology's historic silence on sexuality and its heteronormative claims that opposed gay, lesbian, bisexual, and transgendered people within the black community. His call for an "in-the-life theology" demanded central attention to sexuality and called for African American churches to jettison the destructive alienation they forced upon queer parishioners. The critiques by Hill and Farajaje-Jones anticipated other responses, including Kelly Brown Douglas's study of heterosexism in African American churches. Such writers argued that African American liberation theology would certainly have to break with these elements of biblical theology if it were to be truly liberative.[39]

By the 1990s, it was clear that African American liberation theologians were attuned to the insights of Afrocentric scholarship, Pan-Africanism, and diaspora theory that secular scholars were producing.[40] Especially significant was Josiah Young's *Pan-African Theology*, which examined the African legacy of ancestral consciousness for a constructive theology of liberation. And Diana Hayes linked African cultural and spiritual values to the more familiar African American religious history to emphasize a heritage of continuity.[41] The antithetical tensions associated with Melville Herskovits and E. Franklin Frazier were only magnified as historians who responded to the cultural turn engendered by Black Power began to concern themselves with mapping the terrain of a distinctively African American cultural history, especially that of African American Christianity.[42] Liberation theologians were inspired by this historiographical turn to interpret the history of the Christian tradition more substantially in light of the African American experience of slavery and racism. They explained that political consciousness and black resistance to oppression were not new to the era of Black Power and civil rights but instead characterized the larger history of African American Christianity. At the same time, they emphasized that black Christians had repeatedly conceived their antiracist activism and struggle for equality as a corrective critique of white Christianity. In this way, black and womanist theologians engaged with the cultural and historical dimensions of African American experience in order to interpret the black Christian tradition as liberating and accountable to black culture.[43]

In the 1990s and early 2000s, American scholars were fully engaging a range of theoretical queries into race, sexuality, and colonialism. African American liberation theologians continued to reconceive the nature of their intellectual work within this context. In an effort to emphasize the importance of racial justice as a far-reaching theological issue of continuing urgency, black and womanist theologians convened in 1997 at the Center for the Church and the Black Experience at Garrett-Evangelical Theological Seminary to consider the ways African American liberation theology in its particularity generated vital insights relevant to multiple racial and ethnic groups throughout the Christian tradition.[44] In a related fashion, African American liberation theologians during the twenty-first century began grappling with the more extensive domains of early modernity and the theological roots of European racism as well as the Iberian colonialism and racial legacy in the Americas. And they proposed, in an era of postracial claims, that a reckoning with racial justice was fundamental to reclaiming the authenticity of the Christian tradition across racial boundaries.[45] Of continuing importance has been attention to gay rights and its central relevance for African American churches. Kelly Brown Douglas issued an influential call for African American Christians to embrace the legacy of the black church as a safe space for the African American community by rejecting the antigay hatred that animated political religion of the 2000s and to align radically with the liberating struggle for gay rights.[46] By so doing, Douglas sought to recapture for the theological imagination important symbolic elements of the black church tradition.

Conclusion

Since its inception in the 1960s, African American liberation theology has continually forged a robust defense of its status as a genuinely Christian discourse. Black theology emerged as a rejoinder to divisive questions about the leadership of African American churches in civil disobedience and protest against formal apartheid, state violence, and extralegal terror. For this reason, its deep architecture has been overwhelmingly shaped by the Christian tradition. Major theological categories like Christology, ecclesiology, theodicy, and the role of scripture have continued to inform the dominant thrust of this theological tradition. As new paradigms like cultural studies, feminism, and postcolonialism have emerged, black and womanist theologians have not departed from the Christian tradition so much as they have proffered alternative interpretations of it in conversation with emerging disciplines and fields of knowledge. As liberation theology continues to engage with novel themes and challenges, there is every indication that black and womanist theologians will continue to engage closely with fundamental aspects of the Christian tradition.

Notes

1. Craig D. Atwood, Frank S. Mead, and Samuel S. Hill, *Handbook of Denominations in the United States*, 13th ed. (Nashville: Abingdon Press, 2010), s.v. "Progressive National Baptist Convention."
2. Martin Luther King Jr., *A Testament of Hope: The Essential Writings and Speeches of Martin Luther King Jr.*, ed. James M. Washington (San Francisco: HarperSanFrancisco, 1991), xii–xv; C. Eric Lincoln and Lawrence H. Mamiya, *The Black Church in the African-American Experience* (Durham, NC: Duke University Press, 1990), 36–37.
3. J. Deotis Roberts, "Christian Conscience and Legal Discrimination," *Journal of Religious Thought* 24 (1962–63): 157–61.
4. Joseph R. Washington, *Black Religion: The Negro and Christianity in the United States* (Boston: Beacon Press, 1964).
5. Joseph R. Washington, "The Religion of Anti-Blackness," *Theology Today* 38 (July 1981): 146–51.
6. Regina Jennings, "Black Power Conference of Newark, New Jersey," in *Encyclopedia of Black Studies*, ed. Molefi Kete Asante and Mambo Ama Mazama (Thousand Oaks, CA: Sage Publications, 2005), 142.
7. Peniel E. Joseph, *The Black Power Movement: Rethinking the Civil Rights–Black Power Era* (New York: Routledge, 2006).
8. Gardiner C. Taylor, "President's Message to the Progressive National Baptist Convention, Inc.," in *Black Theology: A Documentary History, 1966–1979*, ed. Gayraud S. Wilmore and James H. Cone (Maryknoll, NY: Orbis Books, 1979), 262–67. Taylor delivered this message in 1967.
9. James H. Cone, *Black Theology and Black Power* (New York: Seabury Press, 1969).
10. Cone, *Black Theology and Black Power*, chapters 1–2.
11. William H. Becker, "Black Power in Christological Perspective," *Religion in Life* 38 (Autumn 1969): 404–14.
12. William L. Banks, *The Black Church in the U.S.* (Chicago: Moody Press, 1972).
13. Joseph Jackson Jr., "The Basic Theological Position of the National Baptist Convention, USA, Inc.," in Wilmore and Cone, *Black Theology*, 257–61.
14. Albert B. Cleage, *The Black Messiah* (New York: Sheed and Ward, 1968); Cleage, *Black Christian Nationalism; New Directions for the Black Church* (New York: W. Morrow, 1972); Cleage, "The Black Messiah and the Black Revolution," in *Quest for a Black Theology*, ed. J. D. Roberts and J. Gardiner (Philadelphia: Pilgrim Press, 1971), 59–91.
15. J. Deotis Roberts, *Liberation and Reconciliation: A Black Theology* (Philadelphia: Westminster Press, 1971).
16. Cecil Wayne Cone, *The Identity Crisis in Black Theology* (Nashville: AMEC, 1975).

17. Frederick Herzog, *Liberation Theology: Liberation in the Light of the Fourth Gospel* (New York: Seabury Press, 1972). Peter Crafts Hodgson, *Children of Freedom: Black Liberation in Christian Perspective* (Philadelphia: Fortress Press, 1974). Rosemary Ruether, "Black Theology and the Black Church," *Journal of Religious Thought* 26 (Summer Supplement 1969): 26–33; Glen R. Bucher, "Liberation in the Church: Black and White," *Union Seminary Quarterly Review* 29 (Winter 1974): 91–105.
18. John Hick, *Evil and the God of Love* (New York: Macmillan, 1977); Bart Ehrman, *God's Problem: How the Bible Fails to Answer Our Most Important Question—Why We Suffer* (San Francisco: HarperOne, 2008); Gustavo Gutiérrez, *On Job: God-Talk and the Suffering of the Innocent*, trans. Matthew O'Connell (Maryknoll, NY: Orbis Books, 1987).
19. Martin Luther King Jr., *The Autobiography of Martin Luther King, Jr.*, ed. Clayborne Carson (New York: Warner Books, 1998), 229–32.
20. William R. Jones, *Is God a White Racist? A Preamble to Black Theology* (Garden City, NY: Anchor Press, 1973).
21. Jones, in retrospect, recounted that the critical reception to his work was veritably "xenophobic" and unequivocally indicated that Christian theologians regarded black humanism as a pariah and as extraneous to the historical tradition of black religion. See the 1998 edition of his text: Jones, *Is God a White Racist?* (Boston: Beacon Press, 1998), xi–xii.
22. James H. Cone, *God of the Oppressed* (New York: Seabury Press, 1975).
23. Emilie M. Townes, ed., *A Troubling in My Soul: Womanist Perspectives on Evil and Suffering* (Maryknoll, NY: Orbis Books, 1993).
24. Shawn Copeland, "Wading Through Many Sorrows: Toward a Theology of Suffering in Womanist Perspective," in Townes, *Troubling in My Soul*, 109–29.
25. Marcia Riggs, *Awake, Arise, & Act: A Womanist Call for Black Liberation* (Cleveland, OH: Pilgrim Press, 1994).
26. Jacquelyn Grant, "The Sin of Servanthood and the Deliverance of Discipleship," in Townes, *Troubling in My Soul*, 199–218.
27. Delores S. Williams, *Sisters in the Wilderness: The Challenge of Womanist God-Talk* (Maryknoll, NY Orbis Books, 1993).
28. Joanne Marie Terrell, *Power in the Blood? The Cross in the African American Experience* (Maryknoll, NY: Orbis Books, 1998).
29. Sydney E. Ahlstrom, *A Religious History of the American People* (New Haven: Yale University Press, 1972); Winthrop Still Hudson, *Religion in America: An Historical Account of the Development of American Religious Life*, 2nd ed. (New York: Scribner, 1973).
30. Eugene D. Genovese, *Roll, Jordan, Roll: The World the Slaves Made* (New York: Pantheon Books, 1974); Lawrence W. Levine, *Black Culture and Black Consciousness: Afro-American Folk Thought from Slavery to Freedom* (New York: Oxford University Press, 1977); Sterling Stuckey, *Slave Culture: Nationalist Theory and the Foundations of Black America* (New York: Oxford University Press, 1987).
31. James H. Cone, *Martin & Malcolm & America: A Dream or a Nightmare* (Maryknoll, NY: Orbis Books, 1991); Townes, *Troubling in My Soul*; Karen Baker-Fletcher, *A Singing Something: Womanist Reflections on Anna Julia Cooper* (New York: Crossroad, 1994); Marcia Riggs, *Can I Get a Witness? Prophetic Religious Voices of African American Women: An Anthology* (Maryknoll, NY: Orbis Books, 1997).
32. Katie G. Cannon, *Black Womanist Ethics* (Atlanta: Scholars Press, 1988); Renita J. Weems, *Just a Sister Away: A Womanist Vision of Women's Relationships in the Bible* (San Diego,

CA: LuraMedia, 1988); Kelly Brown Douglas, *The Black Christ* (Maryknoll, NY: Orbis Books, 1994).

33. Katie G. Cannon, "Katie Cannon Touches a Point of Pain," *Seventh Angel*, March 15, 1984, 15–16.
34. Weems, *Just a Sister Away*.
35. Kelly Brown Douglas, *The Black Christ* (Maryknoll, NY: Orbis Books, 1994), 20–30, 113–16.
36. Toinette Eugene, "Comin' to Terms: Sisterhood for Black and White Feminists," *New Women / New Church* 4 (November 1981): 3–6, and "Reflections of a Black Sistuh!" *Freeing the Spirit* 3 (Summer 1974): 10–15; Jacquelyn Grant, "A Black Response to Feminist Theology," in *Women's Spirit Bonding*, ed. J. Kalven and M. I. Buckley (New York: Pilgrim Press, 1984), 117–24, and "Black Women and the Church," in *All the Women Are White, All the Blacks Are Men, but Some of Us Are Brave*, ed. Gloria T. Hull, Patricia Bell Scott, and Barbara Smith (Old Westbury, NY: Feminist Press, 1982), 141–52.
37. See Cheryl J. Sanders Katie G. Cannon, Emilie M. Townes, M. Shawn Copeland, bell hooks, and Cheryl Townsend Gilkes, "Roundtable Discussion: Christian Ethics and Theology in Womanist Perspective," *Journal of Feminist Studies in Religion* 5 (1989), reprinted in *The Womanist Reader*, ed. Layli Phillips (New York: Routledge, 2006), 126–58. The roundtable printed in this issue featured several engaging responses to Sanders by Cheryl Townsend Gilkes, Katie Cannon, Emilie Townes, M. Shawn Copeland, and bell hooks.
38. Renee Hill, "Who Are We for Each Other? Sexism, Sexuality, and Womanist Theology," in *Black theology: A Documentary History, vol. 2, 1980–1992*, ed. James H. Cone and Gayraud S. Wilmore (Maryknoll, NY: Orbis Books, 1993), 345–51; Alice Walker, *In Search of Our Mothers' Gardens: Womanist Prose* (San Diego, CA: Harcourt Brace Jovanovich, 1983).
39. Elias Farajaje-Jones, "Breaking Silence: Toward an In-the-Life Theology," in Cone and Wilmore, *Black Theology, 1980–1992*, 139–59; Kelly Brown Douglas, *Sexuality and the Black Church: A Womanist Perspective* (Maryknoll, NY: Orbis Books, 1999).
40. Jeanne L. Noble, *Beautiful, Also, Are the Souls of My Black Sisters: A History of the Black Woman in America* (Englewood Cliffs, NJ: Prentice-Hall, 1978); Molefi K. Asante, *Afrocentricity: The Theory of Social Change* (Buffalo, NY: Amulefi, 1980); Patricia Hill Collins, *Black Feminist Thought: Knowledge, Consciousness, and the Politics of Empowerment* (Boston: Unwin Hyman, 1990).
41. Josiah U. Young, *A Pan-African Theology: Providence and the Legacies of the Ancestors* (Trenton, NJ: Africa World Press, 1992); Diana L. Hayes, *Hagar's Daughters: Womanist Ways of Being in the World* (New York: Paulist Press, 1995).
42. Melville J. Herskovits, *The Myth of the Negro Past* (New York: Harper & Brothers, 1941); Edward Franklin Frazier and C. Eric Lincoln, *The Negro Church in America* (New York: Schocken, 1974); Albert J. Raboteau, *Slave Religion: The "Invisible Institution" in the Antebellum South* (New York: Oxford University Press, 1978); Milton C. Sernett, *Black Religion and American Evangelicalism: White Protestants, Plantation Missions, and the Flowering of Negro Christianity, 1787–1865* (Metuchen, NJ: Scarecrow Press, 1975).
43. Gayraud S. Wilmore, *Black Religion and Black Radicalism: An Interpretation of the Religious History of Afro-American People*, 2nd ed. (Maryknoll, NY: Orbis Books, 1983); James H. Cone, *For My People: Black Theology and the Black Church* (Maryknoll, NY: Orbis Books, 1984).
44. This culminated in Linda E. Thomas's edited volume, *Living Stones in the Household of God: The Legacy and Future of Black Theology* (Minneapolis: Fortress Press, 2004).

45. Willie James Jennings, *The Christian Imagination: Theology and the Origins of Race* (New Haven: Yale University Press, 2010); J. Kameron Carter, *Race: A Theological Account* (New York: Oxford University Press, 2008).
46. Kelly Brown Douglas, *Black Bodies and the Black Church: A Blues Slant* (New York: Palgrave, 2012).

Selected Texts

Ahlstrom, Sydney E. *A Religious History of the American People*. New Haven: Yale University Press, 1972.

Atwood, Craig D., Frank S. Mead, and Samuel S. Hill. *Handbook of Denominations in the United States*. 13th ed. Nashville: Abingdon Press, 2010.

Baker-Fletcher, Karen. *A Singing Something: Womanist Reflections on Anna Julia Cooper*. New York: Crossroad, 1994.

Cannon, Katie G. *Black Womanist Ethics*. Atlanta: Scholars Press, 1988.

Cleage, Albert B. *Black Christian Nationalism: New Directions for the Black Church*. New York: W. Morrow, 1972.

Cleage, Albert B. *The Black Messiah*. New York: Sheed and Ward, 1968.

Cone, James H. *Black Theology and Black Power*. New York: Seabury Press, 1969.

Cone, James H. *God of the Oppressed*. New York: Seabury Press, 1975.

Douglas, Kelly Brown. *The Black Christ*. Maryknoll, NY: Orbis Books, 1994.

Frazier, Edward Franklin, and C. Eric Lincoln. *The Negro Church in America*. New York: Schocken, 1974.

Genovese, Eugene D. *Roll, Jordan, Roll: The World the Slaves Made*. New York: Pantheon Books, 1974.

Hayes, Diana L. *Hagar's Daughters: Womanist Ways of Being in the World*. New York: Paulist Press, 1995.

Hill Collins, Patricia. *Black Feminist Thought: Knowledge, Consciousness, and the Politics of Empowerment*. Boston: Unwin Hyman, 1990.

Hodgson, Peter Crafts. *Children of Freedom: Black Liberation in Christian Perspective*. Philadelphia: Fortress Press, 1974.

Joseph, Peniel E. *The Black Power Movement: Rethinking the Civil Rights–Black Power Era*. New York: Routledge, 2006.

Levine, Lawrence W. *Black Culture and Black Consciousness: Afro-American Folk Thought from Slavery to Freedom*. New York: Oxford University Press, 1977.

Noble, Jeanne L. *Beautiful, Also, Are the Souls of My Black Sisters: A History of the Black Woman in America*. Englewood Cliffs, NJ: Prentice-Hall, 1978.

Raboteau, Albert J. *Slave Religion: The "Invisible Institution" in the Antebellum South*. New York: Oxford University Press, 1978.

Riggs, Marcia. *Awake, Arise, & Act: A Womanist Call for Black Liberation*. Cleveland: Pilgrim Press, 1994.

Roberts, J. Deotis. *Liberation and Reconciliation: A Black Theology*. Philadelphia: Westminst er, 1971.

Sernett, Milton C. *Black Religion and American Evangelicalism: White Protestants, Plantation Missions, and the Flowering of Negro Christianity, 1787–1865*. Metuchen, NJ: Scarecrow Press, 1975.

Stuckey, Sterling. *Slave Culture: Nationalist Theory and the Foundations of Black America.* New York: Oxford University Press, 1987.

Washington, Joseph R. *Black Religion: The Negro and Christianity in the United States.* Boston: Beacon Press, 1964.

Weems, Renita J. *Just a Sister Away: A Womanist Vision of Women's Relationships in the Bible.* San Diego: LuraMedia, 1988.

Young, Josiah U. *A Pan-African Theology: Providence and the Legacies of the Ancestors.* Trenton, NJ: Africa World Press, 1992.

CHAPTER 5

CULTURE/CULTURAL PRODUCTION AND AFRICAN AMERICAN THEOLOGY

CLARENCE E. HARDY III

THE manner in which James Cone, then a young professor and AME minister from Arkansas teaching in a small white Michigan town, talked of God in the late 1960s inaugurated a new school of theological thought in American seminaries, and helped dominate the study and interpretation of black religious culture for a generation. From the beginning, as the always-astute historian of religion Charles Long has argued, Cone's "explicitly theological" approach shared the basic limitations of the earlier sociological studies by W. E. B. Du Bois and others, which had in turn established the modern study of black religion in the United States at the turn of the twentieth century. Scholars rooted in both methodological approaches managed to cultivate relatively fixed conceptions of Christian identity along with firm notions of what represented proper and acceptable forms for religious faith. At the same time, scholarly interpreters attached to both perspectives tended to render religious and racial identities in relatively "static terms" that seemed either "unrelated to historical experience" or at least "independent of historically contingent factors and subjective intentions."[1]

But despite their truncated and overly fixed representations of history, race, and religion, black theologians were an essential means through which the academic study of black religious culture was normalized in leading Protestant seminaries and prominent divinity schools in the United States. Even though many of these black theologians were initially committed to promoting specific conceptions of Christian faith, they ultimately helped generate the institutional and intellectual basis to interpret a much wider range of black religious expression beyond the constraints of Christian identity. Even though the most influential black theologians, at the beginning, were more interested in aiding and reflecting the social movements of the day working for justice, their increasingly self-conscious references to black culture in speaking of religion would have lasting significance in its study and deployment for political ends. As black theology's influence has declined over the last couple of decades, the embrace of culture as a frame of reference became more prominent, as various forms of cultural expression were increasingly used as crucial sites from which to make theological analysis and social critique.

Tracing these developments as they first appeared in modern black theological reflection especially in the work of James Cone is the focus of this essay. It aims to contextualize the emergence of the cultural turn in black theology and briefly assess its impact on the study of black religion while linking its development to the broader institutionalization of black religion and black studies in the nation's colleges, seminaries, and universities. The new emphasis on cultural expression evident in black theology, in fact, established an important template for future theological reflection, which helped to shape the intellectual context for the later rise of womanist theology during the 1980s. At the same time, this cultural turn redefined, animated, and propelled the analysis of black religion as a mode of social critique that could extend beyond the already established boundaries of theological discourse and leverage the space in between traditional academic disciplines. It opened up crucial rhetorical, institutional, and intellectual space for cultural critics, ethicists, and philosophers like Cornel West, Emilie Townes, and Michael Dyson to interpret and challenge a society still enthralled to various forms of hierarchical and social dominance.

But before turning to the emergence of this richly variegated but ultimately politically muted intellectual tapestry, this essay focuses on black theology's beginnings in Cone's work. I am especially interested in how Cone and his early conversation partners established the basic points of departure for the structure and what came to be emphasized in black theology, while ensuring the presence of the study of black religion as a fixture in many academic institutions after the 1970s. Dwight Hopkins, an influential student of Cone's who now teaches at the University of Chicago Divinity School, has helpfully divided the founding intellectual figures of the movement into two camps. One group, consisting of Cone and J. Deotis Roberts, saw "faith revealed" primarily "in politics," while the other, consisting most visibly of Charles Long and Gayraud Wilmore, saw "black culture," existing beyond any conception of Christian identity and norms, as the most essential context for interpreting black religious thought and practice.[2] More deliberate about establishing their work as both biblical and Christian, Cone and liked-minded scholars generally received, during the 1970s and 1980s at least, most of the attention among black religious intellectuals. Cone in particular has managed to maintain his high visibility in progressive religious circles over many decades because of his determination to claim and define Christian identity and his astounding productivity as writer and interpreter. He and Roberts became the preeminent intellectual figures in forging the basic template for black theological and religious reflection for the next several decades.

Within the basic template these "political theologians" established, however, were a set of commitments inherited from religious activists of the past, who would succeed in pushing them to engage the broader cultural and social world on its own terms and beyond the dictates of relatively insulated religious institutions. Cone and Roberts recognized, like their intellectual predecessors, that if religious speech and action were going to address the broader social concerns evident in revolutionary times, they would have to be defined in a much wider context than that of established religious institutions, dogma, or settled belief. When in 1963, Martin King famously sought in his "Letter from Birmingham Jail" to make churches "active partners in the struggle for freedom" instead of "irrelevant social clubs" supportive of the status quo, he along with activists like Fannie Lou Hamer redefined the true locus of black religious life. For them the "true *ekklesia*"—that is, the true church—could only be found among those "noble souls" who willingly "walked the streets" in protest instead of those who sequestered themselves in established churches and refused to confront the need for change.[3] Returning black veterans from overseas and an elevated awareness in black communities of the anticolonial struggles in Africa and Asia had helped create a climate where secular and religious reformers could challenge an older political order in which black Americans could not realize full and equal citizenship.

Cone and many of the black urban, intellectual, and activist communities he associated with certainly agreed with King that churches needed to respond directly to social injustice if they were going to be relevant at all. In their estimation, church leaders and members had to reject the temptations of social conformity and embrace instead the world beyond the church door. But in these efforts Cone and others pressed to adopt the much more confrontational and uncompromising style, which had become the norm of younger black activists who were rebelling against King's leadership as his civil rights coalition collapsed with the end of the 1960s. Black Power advocates represented a generational change of activists who had become less sanguine about the possibilities and wisdom of full black inclusion in a white society they increasingly saw as hopelessly corrupt. It is in this charged environment that Cone declared the Black Power movement of the late 1960s "the manifestation of God himself," defining the black theological project from the outset in ways that counter, in retrospect, the ossified academic language that would come to dominate much of the field in later years.[4] In Cone's view any "talk of God" required concrete specificity and must reckon with the divine amid the immediacy of the political struggle for freedom. From this perspective, the (white) religious establishment's continued indifference to the reality of racial injustice only confirmed for Cone and his allies among black clergy that white supremacy had infected the very core of religious institutions in the United States just as it had deformed every aspect of American life.

Given the ideologically and politically charged character of its origins, then, it is notable that black theology would become a significant vehicle for late twentieth-century efforts to conceptualize black religion as an expression of culture and as a principal basis for black identity in both personal and collective terms. Since any direct political effect from black theology was largely limited to its impact on a fading liberal Protestant establishment, this turn toward black culture as a central source for religious reflection has been a crucially important long-term legacy of Cone's generation of religious intellectuals. Of course, before the birth of James Cone's black theology, others had used black religious culture as a source for theological reflection.[5] But what most distinguished Cone from past thinkers was just how much black self-determination served as the central basis from which he (and his intellectual heirs) could interpret and define black religious culture. This emphasis would only deepen as politically involved ministers and denominational officials (sometimes in partnership with Cone) contended with the prevailing black nationalism of the streets then flourishing in urban centers especially in the Midwest and West. As the National Committee of Black Churchmen (NCBC), sharply influenced by Cone, declared in Oakland, California, during their 1969 annual convention: "Black people affirm their being [and this] affirmation is made in the whole experience of being black in the hostile American society."[6]

This "experience of being black" as revealed in history and the various forms of black cultural expression would become the center of gravity for black theological reflection produced by academics trained and teaching in American seminaries, divinity schools, and universities. But at the beginning Cone's approach focused on the immediacy of the ongoing political struggle for black freedom in the 1960s and early 1970s as a crucial point of departure for black theology. As Cone wrote in his early theological treatise, *A Black Theology of Liberation* (1970): "God-talk is not Christian-talk unless it is *directly* related to the liberation of the oppressed." Throughout his early work Cone suggested that "any other approach" amounted to nothing less than "a denial of biblical revelation."[7] In referencing "biblical revelation," of course, Cone signaled the adaptation of the Barthian perspective he had learned and written about in graduate school (his dissertation involved Barth as a central subject) to the black reality in the United States. It offered a language to condemn white supremacy as a form of idolatry in terms reminiscent of Barth's rejection of natural theology.

Whatever Barth's merits were for his time and place, Cone sensed, almost from the beginning, that his dependence on him had cramped his ability to embrace fully black cultural expression as a primary source for naming God and defining Christian faith. Even though Barth's sharp refusal to "identify" the divine with the "human" was central to the dominant Western expressions of twentieth-century Christian thought, Cone understood that he needed to find "some correlations between divine salvation and black culture" in order to address the realities of black life in the United States.[8] So even before his closest conversation partners, Wilmore and Long, criticized him for adopting white forms of religious discourse and analysis, Cone struggled to remake his theological perspective. From the outset Cone had grafted Paul Tillich's language of ontology onto Barthian thought by configuring blackness as a revolutionary state of being and defining white supremacy as the societal pressure to "dehumanize" and "make 'black being' into 'nonbeing.'" As Cone wrote in his groundbreaking *Black Theology and Black Power* (1969): "The meaning of Black Power may be found in Paul Tillich's analysis of 'the courage to be,' which is 'the ethical act in which man affirms his being in spite of those elements of his existence which conflict with his essential self-affirmation.'"[9]

Cone believed the liberal religious establishment was too preoccupied with philosophical posturing to see the "revelation" of God amid the ongoing social movement that was Black Power; instead its members offered "idle, abstract words" to mask their confusion in a revolutionary age.[10] But despite Cone's ability to convey in his God-talk the passion of his times, his promiscuous use of continental European thinkers from Barth and Tillich to the French existentialist Albert Camus left him open to criticism that he had not fully escaped the modes and habits of the theological thinking he so stridently condemned. For Wilmore and Long, as discussed earlier, Cone's work was too detached from the full complexity of black existence as exiled Africans and far too committed to the normative claims, norms, and perspectives of established forms of Christianity even as he pressed to redefine it for revolutionary times. Others (including most notably Cone's brother Cecil) feared that black theology had become too detached from the black Protestant churches theologians claimed to serve and overly reliant on a small cadre of black ministers in predominantly white denominations.[11]

Especially stung and "embarrassed" about accusations that he was using "conceptual categories that came from Europe" in his interpretation of black religious culture, Cone was eager to root his theological assertions in black sources and express his religious thinking in modes that resonated with the pulse of African American life. As he confessed in *My Soul Looks Back*: "To find out from my black colleagues that I was still held captive by the same system that I was criticizing was a bitter pill to swallow."[12] So, determined not to "deny the obvious" any longer, Cone, with the publication of *The Spirituals and the Blues* in 1972, made his first serious "effort to take seriously [this] critique,"[13] turning to black music as "the most significant creative art expression of African-Americans" for theological interpretation.[14]

Before Cone had his own cultural turn, he had already found within his study of Tillich and Camus a language and basis for asserting a black self in the face of "white power" in society, which had continually sought to "dehumanize" black people and lay waste to black potential and black being.[15] But with *The Spirituals and the Blues* he now turned to the rhythms and sounds of black culture to frame his explorations of black humanity without any of the trappings that European philosophy and theology could provide. In his analysis of black music, Cone instead found meaning in both the sacred spirituals of old and the more "secular" and modern blues of the juke joint. Within both, he saw a shared ability of African Americans to find a "measure of dignity in a society which seems bent on destroying their right to be human beings."[16] Later in his most thorough and fully articulated theological statement of the 1970s,

God of the Oppressed (1975), he turned to all types of black cultural expression as crucial sources for religious reflection, while he at the same time constructed a black sacred history of suffering and deliverance that stretched from slavery to freedom. Despite the importance Cone placed on black sacred and cultural history, at this stage of his work, he would continue, unlike Wilmore and Long, to give nearly equal credence to biblical and established Christian traditions in forging his theological perspective. Still, by adjusting to sharp criticism, Cone demonstrated just how culture would eventually supplant intense political involvement in active social movements as a primary context for religious reflection.

Cone's own cultural turn, as the Black Power movement collapsed in the early 1970s, anticipated how black theology as a whole would evolve during the 1970s and 1980s, with its influence fairly limited outside the academy as conservative and neoliberal thought became ascendant in the United States. Some twenty years after Cone had achieved international renown, he would vocally bemoan how many of his initial partners in black theology had languished in the public memory. He was amazed by just how quickly their collective "intellectual rage and spiritual energy" would be forgotten.[17] Cone warned with regularity that he did not want black theology to be "an *academic* discipline, as white theology has largely become." He wanted black theology, instead, to be a "*church* discipline" that was "validated in the context of people struggling for the freedom of the oppressed."[18] But he could see that the same black theology that had once provided him a "passionate language of commitment" had often become in the 1970s and 1980s a surprisingly sedate academic enterprise.[19] (Cone, of course, did not always acknowledge just how pronounced his own cultural turn and quest for academic legitimacy would become with his appointment as a faculty member in the fading bastion of liberal Protestantism that was Union Theological Seminary in the early 1970s.) Black theology's (and Cone's) cultural turn might have, in fact, abetted the institutionalization of black religion in the nation's leading universities and seminaries, but as C. Eric Lincoln and Lawrence Mamiya argued in 1990, the "black theological movement" only achieved "relatively limited influence" on its intended constituencies among black churches.[20] The Black Power movement might have furnished black theology's early revolutionary rhetoric, but as a "second generation" of scholars found themselves employed by wealthy and predominantly white "seminaries, universities, and colleges," black theology would become, in Cone's own estimation, "less radical and more accepting of the society."[21]

The most prominent of these younger scholars would pursue black cultural history from slavery to the modern civil rights struggle as a principal mode of theological reflection during the 1980s and 1990s.[22] The evolution of black theology during this period paralleled the development of black studies departments in leading universities and colleges. Like the integration of these programs in academic life, black theology's turn toward culture built a presence in the theological academy that represented the "limited accommodation of [the] new knowledge that emerged from the 1960s" amid a decaying liberal Protestant establishment no longer able to enact broad societal reform.[23] Political activism had inspired and shaped both forms of institutionalized knowledge, which would over time become detached from their activist roots. And indeed, by the early 1990s, Cone was nostalgic for a time when black religious activists did not have "to justify their right to do theology" and black theologians were not participating in "annual meetings of the American Academy of Religion" that would be simply "unheard of for liberation-oriented Black scholars" in the past.[24] Cone observed how the theological work of his generation had been reframed by younger scholars around the methods and concerns of cultural analysis in a mistaken quest for intellectual legitimacy that partially effaced a history of direct political engagement and struggle.

It is not surprising that during this period of relative quiescence, religious thinkers would begin to transcend older theological schools of thought and perhaps move beyond theological discourse altogether in their attempts to interpret and challenge the prevailing social order. Womanist theology, for example, would, unlike black theology, fully embrace black cultural expression from the outset while more successfully leveraging still-active social movements like Second Wave feminism in its theological affirmations. By the early 1990s, Cone himself was much more appreciative of womanist theologians than he would be of the male heirs to his theological legacy. Both men and women of this second generation of academic theologians were limited in their ability "to make much impact in the Black churches," but "in contrast to the second generation of Black male scholars," Cone argued, "womanists are clear about their [political] point of departure and the goal of their theological work."[25] And in confronting the patriarchy embedded both in biblical traditions and the broader society, womanist theologians committed to "the validity of female imagery and metaphorical language" for God, were, in fact, much more open to referencing black cultural expression than their male counterparts a generation earlier initially were.[26] There were simply "far too few positive records concerning the Black woman as moral agent" in biblical tradition, and womanist theologians were, as Katie Cannon has explained, more than willing to turn to the "Black women's literary tradition" as a "repository for understanding the ethical values Black women have created and cultivated."[27]

At the same time, the most visible black cultural critics of the 1980s and 1990s would also privilege culture in their attempts to interpret and speak against the dominant political order in a multidisciplinary fashion, which seemed well suited for a cosmopolitan age. As Cornel West declared in *Prophesy Deliverance!* (1982), the book that announced his ostentatiously eclectic Marxist-pragmatist Christian perspective to the scholarly world: "Culture is more fundamental than politics in regard to Afro-American self-understanding," and while "culture and politics are inseparable... any political consciousness of an oppressed group is shaped and molded by the group's cultural resources and resiliency."[28] In retrospect, the cultural turn in black theology, combined with its diminished prospects in the face of an ebbing social movement, can be seen as prefiguring and facilitating West's intellectual project and his inclination to root his political aspirations in cultural analysis. The wide-ranging and open nature of this new academic world West helped inaugurate might make Cone's initial efforts to define the Christian faith in the "idiom of black power" seem like a quaint and dated relic of a bygone era.[29] Still, Cone's work (along with crucial interventions from Charles Long) was among the first to illuminate how Western elites "justified and sanctified"[30] their power over others. His scholarship also anticipated recent scholarly discussions on race, which have focused on how racial thinking was linked to early theological concerns about "heathenism, the saved and the damned."[31] As Mason Stokes has memorably stated: "America's so-called 'Negro problem' has always been, at the same time, a theological problem."[32]

But by the early 1990s, as seen in his masterly *Martin and Malcolm and America* (1991), Cone had, in fact, incorporated many of the ongoing intellectual trends toward culture, cultural analysis, and cultural history within black theological and religious studies into his own work. His (thus far) last major work has, in fact, drawn on "cultural history as much as systematic theology."[33] Over many years Wilmore, Long, and others had pressed Cone to take black cultural expression much more seriously for religious reflection and scholarly analysis. Even if (or perhaps especially if) prioritizing black culture subverts the normative claims made for traditional (i.e., Western) forms of Christian expression and institutional formations, Long and Wilmore pressed scholars to make black culture and its African antecedents the primary context from which they interpreted black religion in the United States. But unlike many of his colleagues, when Cone truly began to put a true premium on cultural history, he was also able to convey a sense of the political stakes in an accessible manner unburdened with academic jargon. (No doubt he was assisted by Malcolm X's sustained popularity in hip-hop culture and among black youth and his increased mainstream acceptance as demonstrated in Spike Lee's Hollywood biopic of the black nationalist figure in 1992.) In Cone's hands, the two black saints were transformed into religious icons—that, material human representations—of political struggle and twin aspects of the black experience in America.

In Cone's latest substantial work, the drive for black identity and political inclusion are firm co-determinates in shaping the basic, broader contours of black culture in the United States. In Cone's reckoning, the "symbol systems and beliefs" that constitute black culture are not simply "abstract linguistic configurations" read in "relation to other linguistic expressions." Instead, they were viewed as "embedded within [and] reflective of... the material processes of life."[34] By focusing on the folkways and the cultural expression of the everyday, these interpreters provided conceptual space for a second generation of black theologians. More decisively, this more sophisticated (but thoroughly accessible) conception of culture meshed with nuanced and careful reflection demanded in academic work. Even though Cone might have regretted the retreat represented in black theology's cultural turn, it was really in the domain of higher education that black theology would enact its most central achievement; it "legitimated the study of black churches and black religious phenomena in academic institutions" for our contemporary times.[35]

Notes

1. Charles Long, *Significations: Signs, Symbols, and Images in the Interpretation of Religion* (Aurora, CO: Davies Group, 1995), 187–88; Victor Anderson, *Beyond Ontological Blackness* (New York: Continuum, 1995), 11–12. In many respects, Anderson and others have simply reframed Long's basic critique of the black theology movement. See a similar treatment in Eddie S. Glaude, *In a Shade of Blue* (Chicago: University of Chicago Press, 2007), 66–88.
2. For more on this division between "political theologians" and the "cultural theological trend of the first generation" of black theologians see Dwight N. Hopkins, *Introducing Black Theology of Liberation* (Maryknoll, NY: Orbis Books, 1999), 52–84.
3. Martin Luther King Jr., "Letter from Birmingham Jail," in *The Norton Anthology of African American Literature*, ed. Henry Louis Gates Jr. and Nellie Y. McKay (New York: Norton, 1997), 1864.
4. James H. Cone, *Black Theology and Black Power*, 20th anniversary ed. (San Francisco: Harper and Row, 1989), 38.
5. Perhaps the most important thinker to explicitly reference black religious culture as a source of wisdom and meaningful philosophical refection in the postwar period before Cone was Howard Thurman. As an example of his work see Howard Thurman, *Deep River and The Negro Spiritual Speaks of Life and Death* (Richmond, IN: Friends United Press, 1975).
6. "Black Theology: Statement by the National Committee of Black Churchmen, June 13, 1969," in *Black Theology: A Documentary History, 1966–1979*, ed. Gayraud S. Wilmore and James H. Cone (Maryknoll, NY: Orbis Books, 1979), 100.
7. James H. Cone, *A Black Theology of Liberation*, 20th anniversary ed. (Maryknoll, NY: Orbis Books, 1990), 60–61.
8. Cone, *Black Theology of Liberation*, 27–28.
9. Cone, *Black Theology and Black Power*, 7.
10. Cone, *Black Theology and Black Power*, 34.
11. In reality Rosemary Ruether first made this critique in her article "Crisis in Sex and Race: Black Theology versus Feminist Theology," *Christianity & Crisis*, April 15, 1974, 67–73. For a fuller critique see Cecil Wayne Cone, *The Identity Crisis in Black Theology* (Nashville: AMEC, 1975).
12. James H. Cone, *My Soul Looks Back* (Maryknoll, NY: Orbis Books, 1986), 61.
13. Cone, *My Soul Looks Back*, 61.
14. James H. Cone, *The Spirituals and the Blues: An Interpretation* (Maryknoll, NY: Orbis Books, 1972), 129.
15. Cone, *Black Theology and Black Power*, 6–7.
16. Cone, *The Spirituals and the Blues*, 130.
17. See James Cone's complaints in the general introduction to his co-edited volume with Gayraud Wilmore, *Black Theology: A Documentary History, vol. 2, 1980–1992* (Maryknoll, NY: Orbis Books, 1993), 9–10. Cone thought, quite rightly, that many of the black denominational officials and urban ministers and activists outside the academy have been largely

forgotten in most chronicles of black theology's rise. Albert Cleage and Wilmore are exceptions who proved the rule. Wilmore was a distinctive figure in black theology who served as a denominational official, urban minister, and sometime professor at New York Theological Seminary and other educational institutions. Wilmore more than any other central figure in the black theological movement was able to straddle the divide between the church and academic worlds.

18. Cone, *My Soul Looks Back*, 77.
19. Cone, *Black Theology and Black Power*, 17.
20. C. Eric Lincoln and Lawrence H. Mamiya, *The Black Church in the African American Experience* (Durham, NC: Duke University Press, 1990), 178–80. Lincoln and Mamiya found that only one-third of urban pastors acknowledged being influenced by black theology in the survey the coauthors published in 1990, reflecting "a dramatic shift" from "previous responses" that tracked "black consciousness" (179).
21. Cone and Wilmore, *Black Theology, 1980–1992*, 9.
22. Dwight Hopkins's work is perhaps the most representative of these trends. See especially his *Shoes That Fit Our Feet: Sources for a Constructive Black Theology* (Maryknoll, NY: Orbis Books, 1993) and *Down, Up, and Over: Slave Religion and Black Theology* (New York: Fortress Press, 1999).
23. Fabio Rojas, *From Black Power to Black Studies: How a Radical Social Movement Became an Academic Discipline* (Baltimore: John Hopkins University Press, 2010), 3.
24. Cone's "General Introduction," in *Black Theology, 1980–1992*, 5.
25. . See again, Cone's "General Introduction," 6–7.
26. Delores Williams, "Womanist Theology: Black Women's Voices," in Cone and Wilmore, *Black Theology, 1980–1992*, 269.
27. Katie G. Cannon, *Katie's Canon: Womanism and the Soul of the Black Community* (New York: Continuum, 1995), 61.
28. Cornel West, *Prophesy Deliverance! An Afro-American Revolutionary Christianity* (Philadelphia: Westminster Press, 1982), 71.
29. Glaude, *Shade of Blue*, 76.
30. Charles Long, "Freedom, Otherness, and Religion: Theologies Opaque," in *Significations*, 209.
31. Lee D. Baker, *From Savage to Negro: Anthropology and the Construction of Race, 1896–1954* (Berkeley: University of California Press, 1998), 12. See also Sylvester A. Johnson, *The Myth of Ham in Nineteenth-Century American Christianity: Race, Heathens, and the People of God* (New York: Palgrave Macmillan, 2004). For a review of the recent literature see Corey D. B Walker's superb review essay "'The Empire and the Garden': Race, Religion, and the (Im)Possibilities of Thinking," *Journal of the American Academy of Religion* 78, no. 1 (March 2010): 265–89.
32. Mason Stokes, "Someone's in the Garden with Eve: Race, Religion, and the American Fall," *American Quarterly* 50, no. 4 (December 1998): 718.
33. Mark Hulsether, *Building a Protestant Left: Christianity and Crisis Magazine, 1941–1993* (Knoxville: University of Tennessee Press, 1999), 195.
34. Mary McClintock Fulkerson, "Toward a Materialist Christian Social Criticism: Accommodation and Culture Reconsidered," in *Changing Conversations: Cultural Analysis and Religious Reflection* ed. Sheila Davaney and Dwight N. Hopkins (New York: Routledge, 1999), 37. Fulkerson's essay explores what a more thoroughgoing materially based analysis for culture might mean for liberation theologians.

35. Lincoln and Mamiya, *Black Church*, 178.

Selected Texts

Anderson, Victor. *Beyond Ontological Blackness: An Essay on African American Religious and Cultural Criticism*. New York: Continuum, 1995.

Baker, Lee D. *From Savage to Negro: Anthropology and the Construction of Race, 1896–1954*. Berkeley: University of California Press, 1998.

Cannon, Katie Geneva. *Katie's Canon: Womanism and the Soul of the Black Community*. New York: Continuum, 1995.

Cone, James H. *Black Theology and Black Power*. 20th anniversary ed. San Francisco: Harper and Row, 1989.

Cone, James H. *A Black Theology of Liberation*. 20th anniversary ed. Maryknoll, NY: Orbis Books, 1990.

Cone, James H. *My Soul Looks Back*. Maryknoll, NY: Orbis Books, 1986.

Glaude, Eddie S. *In a Shade of Blue*. Chicago: University of Chicago Press, 2007.

Hopkins, Dwight N. *Introducing Black Theology of Liberation*. Maryknoll, NY: Orbis Books, 1999.

Lincoln, C. Eric, and Lawrence H. Mamiya. *The Black Church in the African American Experience*. Durham, NC: Duke University Press, 1990.

Long, Charles H. *Significations: Signs, Symbols, and Images in the Interpretation of Religion*. Aurora, CO: Davies Group, 1986.

Rojas, Fabio. *From Black Power to Black Studies: How a Radical Social Movement Became an Academic Discipline*. Baltimore: John Hopkins University Press, 2010.

West, Cornel. *Prophesy Deliverance! An Afro-American Revolutionary Christianity*. Philadelp hia: Westminster, 1982.

CHAPTER 6

REASON IN AFRICAN AMERICAN THEOLOGY

TERRENCE L. JOHNSON

DAVID Walker's *Appeal to the Coloured Citizens of the World* is unusually prescient. Unlike any other oral or written literature in New England during the early nineteenth century, Walker's *Appeal* exposes the untidy relationship between religion and politics in establishing the philosophical and moral reasons that were used to justify black slavery and subjugation. In piercing language, Walker disrupts the national myth of America's chosenness, the "city on a hill," by detailing the nation's role in retrieving Christianity to establish the political, economic, and moral grounds for condoning slavery and beliefs in black inferiority. The overlap between religion and politics, according to Walker, undermines the nation's democratic aspirations, and he exposes the tradition of antiblack racism within Protestant (white) Christianity.

> I ask every man who has a heart, and is blessed with the privilege of believing—Is not God a God of justice to *all* his creatures? Do you say he is? Then if he gives peace and tranquility to tyrants, and permits them to keep our fathers, our mothers, ourselves and our children in eternal ignorance and wretchedness, to support them and their families, would he be to us a God of *justice?* I ask, O ye *Christians!!!* who hold us and our children in the most abject ignorance and degradation, that ever a people were afflicted with since the world began—I say, if God gives you peace and tranquility, and suffers you thus to go on afflicting us, and our children, who have never given you the least provocation—would he be to us *a God of justice?* If you will allow that we are MEN, who feel for each other, does not the blood of our fathers and of us their children, cry aloud to the Lord of Sabbath against you, for the cruelties and murders with which you have, and do continue to afflict us.[1]

Walker's argument is weighty, and requires heavy lifting from his readers. Indeed, Walker requires whites, and blacks for that matter, to imagine a political narrative that does not exist. He wants his readers to bracket the problem of blackness—to see the beauty in "wooly heads" and broad "noses"—and to take seriously black humanity and the epistemic viability of discourses from behind the veil of blackness. As Walker proclaims in the *Appeal*, blacks "feel," too; they love, care for, and protect their families in ways similar to whites. Walker's audacious articulation of black beauty, humanity, and intelligence is daring for a historical context in which scientific studies of Negroes in concert with the political economy were retrieved to define blacks as subhuman and well deserving of their slave status. This construction of blacks as radically "other" is what Walker aims to dismantle. He establishes the argument on two essential points: the "wretchedness" of blacks is a social construction, and not ontological; second, scripture can serve as a resource for justifying black liberty and freedom.

Walker's *Appeal* is noteworthy. While standing in a tradition of nineteenth-century black writers who retrieved scripture to protest slavery and deconstruct the limits of American democracy, Walker extends and expands the tradition. His *Appeal* moves beyond historical reflection and criticism to carve out a normative argument: justice and freedom are possible when moral agents bracket the world as they know it and examine their traditions and normative commitments through a post-white-supremacist lens. This interpretation of Walker's *Appeal* allows contemporary scholars of liberation thought to trace the emergence of what I call *emancipatory reason* within nineteenth- and twentieth-century African American religious and political thought. By appealing to the acceptable epistemic resources of his historical moment, primarily the Bible, Walker established his argument with reasons that were universal and widely accepted. The move deconstructed race as an ontological entity and more broadly introduced, at least implicitly, new approaches for exploring the extent to which reason as a cognitive response to the immediate world can adjudicate social problems without appealing to some variation of the divine or transcendent sphere. Emancipatory reason recognizes both the limits of knowledge and the employability of knowing the world beyond the historical moment. Standing in tension with history and tradition, emancipatory reason creates the epistemic conditions for extending the boundaries of human agency by appealing to, for instance, divine discourse or slave narratives as heuristic resources for reimagining and reconfiguring human agency in an effort to obtain and embody freedom.

Emancipatory reason is embedded in nineteenth- and twentieth-century discourse on the problem of blackness within black liberation thought and black theology of liberation and womanist theology. It emerges in two distinct ways: first, as a reflective hermeneutical tool for interrogating the self and society; and second, as a politico-ethical framework for imagining both the ideal and the lived experience of freedom. Emancipatory reason is primarily evident in writings that retrieve religious rhetoric and moral claims to formulate political commitments and arguments. On the one hand, emancipatory reason emerges, for instance, in *A Voice from the South* (1892) as Anna Julia Cooper investigates the binary of masculine and feminine knowledge in modern Western culture in an effort to build her case for the deployment of a revised and radical epistemology, one based on black women's epistemic resources. On the other hand, emancipatory reason is evident in James Cone's *Black Theology and Black Power* (1969) when he retrieves the problem of blackness as the primary resource for understanding God and God's liberatory hand in history. Cooper and Cone, among a range of African American philosophers and theologians, provide a framework for delimiting emancipatory reason as a central category for imagining human agents as both culturally and historically contingent *and* capable of transgressing the boundaries of traditions and narratives. Emancipatory reason, as I have formulated it, complicates Enlightenment notions of reason as simply a division between knowing and thinking. Instead, reason from the behind the veil of blackness construes reason as embodied, encumbered, *and* transcendent. Emancipatory reason unfolds in two ways: First, emancipatory reason is retrieved to raise to the level of public scrutiny arguments that are otherwise deemed irrational within a white supremacist epistemology—such as the double self within W. E. B. Du Bois's double consciousness. Second, emancipatory reason is historically contingent, but its conceptual framework leaves open the possibility of discovering ways to deepen or dismantle traditions that may impede human freedom. Human agents may choose to employ weak versions of reason when they are confronted with the questionable political practices and moral beliefs—but they are nonetheless always in possession of the requisite resources to challenge existing normative commitments.

Emancipatory reason is the cognitive faculty that enables human agents to think, know, and act in tension with their overlapping and competing traditions and narratives. Indeed, double consciousness is a prime example of the kind of critical reflection that emerges when emancipatory reason unfolds: human agents raise critical questions as to the political and moral viability of the existing narratives with the aim of discovering a "better," truer self and a more democratic tradition. This approach understands emancipatory reason as both a hermeneutical and a normative approach to grappling with the problem of blackness. More than 150 years following the publication of Walker's *Appeal*, theologian J. Deotis Roberts reminds scholars of African American religions to consider the problem of blackness as an epistemic resource for strengthening black theologies of liberation. "Blackness is far more than consciousness of a color of skin. It involves a new definition of self, a different self-understanding and a sense of worth."[2] In a rather provocative manner, Roberts understands blackness as a creative discursive tool for rethinking the prevailing categories by which scholars of liberation theology pursue their research. Charles Long describes the quest to understand black oppression in terms of hermeneutics: The oppressed must deal with both the fictive truth of their status as expressed by the oppressors, that is, their second creation, and the discovery of their own autonomy and truth—their first creation."[3] For both Roberts and Long, the problem of blackness stands as a central resource for exploring reason and examining human crisis.

Examining the category of reason from the vantage point of thinkers who were historically identified as the negation of reason, aesthetics and morality raises a number of challenges. The primary problem is that reason is rarely discussed as a distinct philosophical category among nineteenth- and twentieth-century African American scholars and writers of religion and black theology. However, I have attempted to shed light on the implicit definitions of reasons by investigating the normative grounds on which theologians and writers argue for human freedom. In Walker's *Appeal* I identify four philosophical motifs that resurface in black theology of liberation; the motifs offer a window into how African American religious thinkers imagine, implicitly or otherwise, reason and rationality: First, reason is rooted in culture, not an autonomous realm independent of history and culture. We cannot separate reason and the available epistemic resources from self-interests, desires, and motivations. As Walker suggests in his *Appeal*, white supremacist societies rely on the available epistemic resources to justify beliefs, practices, and habits that will foster white privilege and deepen black oppression. Second, the legal and moral reasons for maintaining black oppression created during Walker's era what I call the problem of blackness. The problem of blackness establishes what Victor Anderson refers to as ontological blackness, a category that fuels a discourse—especially in European and Anglo-American debates on slavery—that renders all black bodies as irrational, subhuman creatures that must be dominated and controlled. Third, the retrieval of sacred authority is common in the battle to ameliorate black oppression. Walker turns to the Bible as a resource for reimagining the reigning debates on antiblack racism. To be sure, his appropriation of the Bible for liberatory purposes was not universal. As noted by Walker, some African Americans were suspicious of scripture in light of its appropriation by slaveholders. "Thus African-Americans scorned the Christianity of whites and questioned the civil religion of the nation. Some were driven away from Christianity by race prejudice of white Christians, but most did not reject the gospel or the principles of democracy. In their critiques of American Christianity, blacks implicitly and sometimes explicitly cast themselves as the models of true Christianity in America."[4] Fourth, beliefs in black freedom within an antiblack society can be an unreasonable and unjustifiable set of expectations given the immediate social and legal context of Walker's time. However, Walker seems to suggest that history does not possess the final word in determining the fate of a people; instead, beliefs in the ontological nature of human freedom, which is defined and delimited by the cognitive ability of agents to question, deconstruct, and dismantle historical legacies that threaten to suffocate them, are crucial to sustaining human agency. Reason and rationality in Walker's *Appeal* are historically contingent and reflect, in this instance, efforts among African Americans to grapple with the physical and psychic violence against them.

Reason and the West

Reason is one of the most contested categories in Western philosophy. During the Enlightenment period, reason emerged as the cognitive faculty to adjudicate the subject's reasons for holding certain beliefs based on an acceptable epistemic framework.[5] Whether the thinking subject possessed "sufficient" reason or reasons for holding certain beliefs was critical for determining the justificatory grounds for the beliefs in question. Reason as an independent sphere of the mind alters the face of Western wo/man in general and philosophy in particular.

> Enlightenment's reign of reason had become a reign of death and destruction since the mechanistic methods of modern science, and the critical demands of modern philosophy, were leading straight toward atheism, fatalism, and anarchism. The more science advanced, the less room there seemed to be for freedom and God in the universe; and the more philosophy exercised its critical powers, the less authority could be claimed for the Bible and the old proofs of the existence of God, providence, and immortality.[6]

Understanding the place of reason in modernity is crucial. According to feminists like Genevieve Lloyd, reason is a metaphor for "man's" authority in the world. Reason is distinct from emotion, and in turn men are radically different from women. In the structural sense, the cognitive faculty of reason dethrones the universal acceptance of church authority and its religious and social power over wo/man. Reason, which for Kant was "universal and impartial,"[7] serves as a necessary tool to measure the viability and legitimacy of the "morality, religion and the state."

In the groundbreaking feminist text *The Man of Reason: "Male" and "Female" in Western Philosophy*, Genevieve Lloyd argues that reason, even when it is imagined as an autonomous sphere, emerges in Western philosophy as a gendered account of reflection and knowledge that is based on the "male" construction of the world. "Reason is taken to express the real nature of the mind, in which, as Augustine put it, there is no sex. The aspiration to a Reason common to all, transcending the contingent historical circumstances which differentiate minds from one another, lies at the very heart of our philosophical heritage."[8] But the mind is always expressed in terms that reflect the culture's sexist gender constructions. According to Lloyd, Western philosophy, as far back as Plato and extending to Nietzsche, identifies clear and coherent thought with maleness and identifies "femaleness with the vague and indeterminate."[9] In addition, reason signifies a form of dominance over nature. "The theme of the dominance of mind over body, or of intellect over inferior parts of the soul, was developed . . . in medieval versions of character ideals associated with maleness."[10] The differentiation of mind from nature is generally expressed in gendered terms that differentiate male from female in hierarchical terms. Lloyd's criticisms of Western philosophy establish the framework for reconfiguring deracialized and ahistorical accounts of reason and rationality. Black theology of liberation and especially womanist theology turn to a set of epistemic resources, narratives of knowledge otherwise ignored by whites, that indirectly respond to Lloyd's project. The retrieval of the problem of blackness as a legitimate resource for exploring, for instance, the limits of white Christianity and black male patriarchy implicitly deconstructs normative assumptions about reason and rationality.

Reason in Black Theology

In black theology of liberation, the problem of blackness is transformed into an epistemic resource that serves as an embodied form of reason for critical reflection and creative political engagement. In identifying the six stages of black theology of liberation, which I define in conversation with Cornel West's account of black theology's "evolution," I shall attempt to shed light on the fluidity with which the problem of blackness as an epistemic resource is examined and employed. In the first stage, black theology focuses on the problem of blackness within the context of slavery; in the second stage, black theology examines "institutional racism"; in the third stage, black theology turns its attention to white Protestant Christianity and illuminates its complicit role in black oppression; in the fourth stage, black theology extends its reach by investigating the relationship between black oppression and capitalism in the United States; in the fifth stage, black theology turns its attention to gender and sexuality, and womanist theology emerges; in the last stage, black theology dives into humanist and African-centered accounts of religious strivings in an attempt to shed light on the rich, albeit mostly ignored, non-Christian traditions within African American religions.[11] In the six stages of black liberation theology, the problem of blackness attempts to give an account of the reflective black subject, explore human agency, and examine the crisis of human strivings based on epistemic resources that reflect the human drama of suffering, joy, death, and despair.

Black theology of liberation brings into public conversation a set of epistemic resources based on the traditions of black nationalism, the American Jeremiad, and racial uplift ideology that reflect the religious and political strivings of a disdained people. According Dwight Hopkins, "Black theology is the interplay between the pain of oppression and the promise of liberation found in the Bible, on the one hand, and a similar existence experienced by African Americans and poor people today."[12] Black theology of liberation reimagines the Bible, Jesus, and God-talk through what James Cone calls the experience of black oppression. This overall grand narrative of the theological tradition of black theology reflects the first aspect of emancipatory reason: reflective hermeneutics.

The first two stages of black theology, examinations of slavery and institutional racism, anticipate emancipatory reason in a fundamental way: both bring attention to white supremacy's role in impeding black political agency. This move within black theology stems from a set of reflective acts, which assume blacks were legally and politically distinct from, but peculiarly woven within, the nation's political framework. For instance, in the first stage, ranging from middle of the seventeenth century to 1863, individuals like David Walker, Jarena Lee, and Gabriel Prosser attempted to build the case for black humanity by turning to scripture to validate the human nature that God inscribed within all human beings—white and black.[13] This move among the chief architects of black theology recognizes the social ontology of blackness as inferior to whites, but they spend their careers deconstructing pejorative views of blackness. By the third stage of black theology—from 1864 to 1969—we see the groundwork laid for Black Power. "This particular state was an intellectually creative one—partly in response to the spontaneous rebellion of black people in the streets, the more disciplined political praxis of Black Power groups, and the paralysis of most white North American theologians."[14] During this particular period of black theology, blacks loosen their grip on the politics of respectability and appeal to black aesthetics, black nationalism, and black literary movements to tackle the problem of blackness. In *Black Theology and Black Power*, James Cone, the architect of the academic study of black theology, writes: "In a world which has taught blacks to hate themselves, the new black man does not transcend blackness, but accepts it, loves it as a gift of the Creator. For he knows that until he accepts himself as a being of God in all of its physical blackness, he can love neither God nor neighbor"[15] The rise of the second aspect of emancipatory reason manifests itself in the effort to promote positive self-image and cultural legitimacy: the politico-ethical dimension. As human agents embrace both the beauty and the messy implications of blackness, they discover fragments of the Du Boisian "truer self" and take the necessary steps to build a framework that would promote ethical behavior and sustain a robust democracy. Blackness, then, is embraced and retrieved to expand the terrain of Christianity and the nation's political culture.

In the fourth stage, which also reflects the politico-ethical dimension of emancipatory reason, black theology examines capitalism in the United States through the lens of blackness. Cornel West in "Black Theology and Marxist Thought" argues that black theology and Marxism share similar beliefs and commitments, but they need to engage each other more seriously in order to achieve human liberation. West's criticism attempts to develop political solidarity among groups and thinkers that might not otherwise enter into a conversation.

During the fifth stage, black theology investigates gender and sexuality. This stage uses black women's interpretations of oppression as a central resource for reimagining black liberation theology and feminist theory and re-envisioning God's role in the liberation of African Americans.

> Admittedly, reconstructing knowledge is like tearing down a formidable edifice that has been built over an extensive number of years. The structure was designed by architects who had a clear vision of what the end product would be like and used only the most advanced technical devices for its erection,...The building, is, of course, our minds, and the architects are those who historically have represented patriarchal, white European cultures. A womanist, in her reconstruction of knowledge, must not only be a diligent craft person but also develop an approach using the kind of technology that can dismantle the seeming indestructibleness of the original building.[16]

As Linda Thomas aptly suggests, womanist theologians attempt to broaden the terrain on which liberation is imagined and interrogated. While the Bible remains a central resource for womanist theologians, they also bring in literature, oral traditions, and slave narratives to widen the conversation on liberation. Following Anna Julia Cooper's lead, many of the early wave of womanists, including Katie Cannon, Delores Williams, and Jacquelyn Grant, turn to black women's primary resources to shed light on the invisibility of gender and sexuality within black theology of liberation as well as to critique gendered approaches to liberation. Reason, then, is not simply knowing and reflecting; among many womanists reason is embodied insofar as it informs the normative social practices and commitments within the politico-ethical dimension of emancipatory reason.

White Women's Christ and Black Women's Jesus is a case in point. In this groundbreaking text, Jacquelyn Grant examines Christology through the lens of black women writers. Grant challenges white feminists to rethink their interpretations of Christ by expanding the category of "women's experience." "Womanist theology begins with the experiences of Black women as its point of departure. This experience includes not only Black women's activities in the larger society but also in the churches and reveals that Black women have often rejected the oppressive structure in the church as well."[17] Grant argues that the "tridimensional" nature of black women's encounter with the problem of blackness—"racism/sexism/classism"—gives them a peculiar perspective in imagining the world. The tridimensional nature provides black women with second sight—exposure to the multiple layers of oppression that are often ignored or overlooked by men.[18] By turning to the narratives of black women, especially the working class, Grant traces the degree to which historically contingent conceptual schemes inform black women's competing and overlapping interpretations of Jesus. She discovers deep differences among black and white women's interpretation of Jesus and Christ.

Womanist theologian Delores S. Williams raises to public scrutiny black theology's interpretations of biblical narratives, questions the usefulness of the Exodus to understand black suffering and oppression, and challenges black liberation theologians to clarify their analysis of the Bible's responses to slavery and oppression.

> When non-Jewish people (like many African-American women who now claim themselves to be economically enslaved) read the entire Hebrew testament... there is no clear indication that God is against their perpetual enslavement. Likewise, there is no clear opposition expressed in the Christian testament to the institution of slavery.... Womanist theologians, especially those who take their slave heritage seriously, are therefore led to question James Cone's assumption that the African-American theologian can today make paradigmatic use of the Hebrews' exodus and election experience as recorded in the Bible.[19]

Williams raises a fundamental concern: Biblical narratives do not support claims that God stands on the side of all oppressed peoples. Curiously, Williams proposes the creation of a new hermeneutical methodology—the hermeneutics of "identification-ascertainment"[20]—in an attempt to expand black theology's epistemic frameworks. The approach includes a threefold level of interpretation: subjective, communal, and objective. In sum, Williams wants black theologians (first) to identify their own social location so they can better interrogate the presuppositions and biases they bring to biblical passages. The communal component of Williams's hermeneutical methodology enables theologians to come to terms with how Christian communities interpret and appropriate the Bible. The politico-ethical dimension is subtle, but present in womanist theology: insisting on self and communal interrogation as agents explore scripture in religious traditions is a necessary procedural component of emancipatory reason as it safeguards efforts to solidify rational accounts of religion and justified beliefs as universal.

In the sixth stage, black theology dives more deeply into humanist and African-centered accounts of religious striving. Indeed, scholars during this stage of black theology, often in a more explicit way, attempt to understand epistemology in general and reason as knowing and thinking in particular within the context of African religious cultures and practices in the Americas. As theologians and humanists lift the veil to expose the degree to which non-Christian traditions shape African American religions and cultures, they begin to raise new concerns regarding the assumed disjuncture between reason and knowledge of the divine in Western theology. For instance, In *A Pan-African Theology*, Josiah Ulysses Young III establishes a normative argument concerning the necessity of appropriating African symbols for black liberation. He calls for the employment of African-centered religious discourses based on "pan-Africanization." In this context liberation requires the development of a theology based on "ancestral symbols that structure [black] humanity."[21] Traditional Christian interpretations of black liberation discourse often interpret slave religion, rhetoric, and rituals as both overt references to Christian accounts of God's liberating hand in history and covert signs of resistance and retaliation against black oppression. Such accounts are generally associated with the Exodus motif. In African-centered accounts of black religion, especially slave religion, the religious rhetoric is examined differently. The signs and symbols are imagined as extensions of the slave's memory and reconfiguration of West African religious and philosophical traditions. This characterization of slave religion takes seriously epistemic resources such as funeral rites and ritual dances as legitimating the ongoing and expanding role of African-derived religious traditions in the Americas. These epistemic resources reflect the fragments of a countertradition of epistemology and reason in African American religions and philosophy that frame the conceptual schemes within the politico-ethical dimension of emancipatory reason.

In *Three Eyes for the Journey*, Dianne Stewart Diakité offers a detailed account of the marginalization of African-derived religions during slavery in Jamaica that sheds light on the role of non-Christian traditions in the formation African American religions in the Caribbean. Stewart digs through missionary accounts of slave religion and discovers a set of epistemic resources that demonstrate the living traditions of African-derived tradition during and after slavery. "The European gaze was intrusive and untrustworthy, and Africans knew it. Much of what Africans thought and did as religious beings was safeguarded within the boundaries of African communal life. Whatever they displayed publicly before Whites, it must be assumed, was coded with the intent of generating if not tolerance, then indifference from the planters and missionaries."[22] By displacing hegemonic readings of black religion by European colonizers, Stewart uncovers rich accounts of African religious traditions in Jamaica. In fact, the African-derived religions do not emerge in Jamaican Christianity as a symbolic reminder of a dead past; instead, the African-derived religions retrieve fragments of Christianity to strengthen African-centered traditions.

Stewart's account of African religions and traditions in the Caribbean sheds light on the unique place of African-centered epistemology in sustaining life during slavery within a set of discursive practices. This characterization of epistemology expands the hermeneutical lens through which we might envision emancipatory reason within Caribbean religions. For instance, Stewart investigates the public nature of funerals in an attempt to recover the epistemic the depths of "African-Jamaican religiosity." During slavery, funeral rituals represent a "religious obligation to the Ancestors" that connect communities to the "living and the dead."[23] According to Stewart, funeral rituals point to the tension between the material and immaterial in African-derived religions. The tension, as well as the colonial efforts to criminalize conjure practices in Jamaica, introduces to public scrutiny the unexamined epistemic frameworks slaves developed to imagine themselves and life behind the veil of blackness. In this sense, the relationship between the self and the ancestors manifests itself in funeral rites, and the encounter between the material and spiritual sphere transgress traditional Western boundaries of space and time.

Expanding the Epistemic Terrain in Black Theology

The problem of blackness as an epistemic resource has produced several distinct approaches to the academic study of African American religions in general and black theology of liberation in particular. First, the scholarly study of the problem of blackness gives birth to what Katie Cannon calls the rise of black "logic." Cannon's definition of logic refers to the "cognitive maps of the logic that sets the perimeters for the intelligibility and legitimacy of race, sex, and class oppression, so that we may discern the hierarchal, mechanistic patterns of exploitation that must be altered in order for justice to occur."[24] This logic informs and instructs the reflective subject's engagement with texts and the world. In many respects, Cannon's characterization of logic extends Du Boisian double consciousness, as it assumes the black subject is involved in an ongoing interrogation of the racialized identities inscribed upon her in an antiblack society. This interrogation, the warring of ideals, creates the conditions in which emancipatory reason manifests itself.

Second, black logic unfolds into what M. Shawn Copeland calls "cognitive praxis." The category "denotes the dynamic activity of knowing: questioning patterns and the sometimes jagged-edge of experience—testing and probing answers; marshaling evidence and weighing it against cultural codes and signs, against imperious and subjugated truths; risking judgment; taking up struggle."[25] As we can see, Copeland sketches out a typology of the moral agent that is deeply reflective and committed to extending epistemic boundaries whenever they threaten to alienate marginal thinkers.[26] Copeland's typology builds a conceptual framework in which emancipatory reason can be extended in, and expanded as, a heuristic model of how human agents might deliberate on matters of deep political and religious meaning.

Third, decoding white supremacist constructions of black bodies, especially black women's bodies, is central to understanding antiblack racism in a postmodern context. According to Cannon, critical examinations of the body introduce new resources for understanding oppression: "Flesh houses memories—the color of flesh, the reproductive character of flesh and the manifold ways that the flesh of African women is the text on which androcentric patriarchy is written."[27] The body as text challenges scholars to take seriously social and theological concerns related to gender and sexuality and to explore the ways in which reason is embodied. The body as reason, for instance, might allow us to dismantle the disjuncture between knowing and feeling. It too opens the possibility of imagining the roles of conjure, prophecy, and second sight in African American religious cultures as legitimate sources of knowledge. Indeed, these practices compel us to explore the body as text and the body as reason insofar as conjure and prophecy, for instance, are often "gifted" to the human being or mounted upon him by divine forces during spirit possession. J. Lorand Matory describes spirit possession in the context of the discursive exchange between Islam and "traditional religion" in the Oyo-Yoruba Empire in Nigeria. In this instance, spirit possession illuminates the role of women "as the paradigmatic vessels of divinity, as exemplars of ritual competence" within religion.[28] Spirit possession does not displace reason or emerge as an ecstatic response to temporal circumstances; instead, it appears to work alongside reason insofar as spirit possession happens, in this instance, among women who are competent in the tradition and its practices. This competence seems to prepare the body to serve as vessel through which the divine emerges. Although Matory is focused on Nigeria, his analysis of spirit possession carries invaluable import as scholars map the various configurations African traditions in African American religions. Matory rationalizes the epistemic nature of spirit possession by illuminating the degree to which it emerges directly from preestablished discursive practices. It is not an otherworldly knowledge per se, but a reflection of deliberate traditions and ongoing engagement among a variety of religious and cultural practices.

The problem of blackness as an epistemic resource has transformed the academic study of black theology. By introducing "forgotten texts" into discourses on religion and theology, black theology of liberation has expanded the terrain on which an antiblack society might imagine human agency and developed a notion of reason as thinking, knowing, and embodiment. Emancipatory reason offers the necessary tools for imagining a robust tradition of human agency and creates the epistemic conditions in which human agents may transgress the boundaries of traditions and narratives.

Notes

1. *David Walker's Appeal to the Coloured People of the World*, ed. Peter Hinks (University Park: Pennylvania State University Press, 2000), 8.
2. J. Deotis Roberts, *Black Theology Today* (New York: Edwin Mellen Press, 1983), 91.
3. Charles Long, *Significations: Signs, Symbols, and Images in the Interpretation of Religion* (Aurora, CO: Davies Group, 1986), 170.
4. Albert Raboteau, *A Fire in the Bones* (Boston: Beacon Press, 1995), 52–53.
5. Frederick C. Beiser, *The Fate of Reason* (Cambridge: Harvard University Press, 1987), 8.
6. Beiser, *The Fate of Reason*, 2.
7. Beiser, *The Fate of Reason*, 1.
8. Genevieve Lloyd, *The Man of Reason: "Male" and "Female" in Western Philosophy* (Minneapolis: University of Minnesota Press, 1993), xviii.
9. Lloyd, *The Man of Reason*, 3.
10. Lloyd, *The Man of Reason*, 17.
11. I borrow the first four stages of the rise of black theology of liberation from Cornel West's *Prophecy Deliverance!* (Philadelphia: Westminster Press, 1982). He defines the

stages based on what he calls "the prophetic Christian tradition in the Afro-American experience" (101).

12. Dwight Hopkins, *Head and Heart* (New York: Palgrave, 2002), 7.
13. Cornel West, *Prophecy Deliverance! An Afro-American Revolutionary Christianity* (Philadelphia: Westminster Press, 1982), 102.
14. West, *Prophesy Deliverance!* 104.
15. James Cone, *Black Theology and Black Power* (New York: Seabury Press, 1969), 53.
16. Linda Thomas, *Living Stones in the Household of God* (Minneapolis: Fortress Press, 2004), 42.
17. Jacquelyn Grant, *White Women's Christ and Black Women's Jesus* (Atlanta: Scholars Press, 1989), 205.
18. Grant, *White Women's Christ*, 209.
19. Delores S. Williams, *Sisters in the Wilderness: The Challenges of Womanist God-Talk* (Maryknoll, NY: Orbis Books, 1993), 146–7.
20. Williams, *Sisters in the Wilderness*, 149.
21. Josiah Ulysses Young III, *A Pan-African Theology* (Trenton, NJ: Africa World Press, 1992), 18.
22. Dianne M. Stewart, *Three Eyes for the Journey* (New York: Oxford University Press, 2005), 30.
23. Stewart, *Three Eyes*, 33.
24. Katie Cannon, "Womanist Perspectival Discourse and Cannon Formation," *Journal of Feminist Studies in Religion* 9 (Spring–Fall 1993): 29–30.
25. M. Shaun Copeland, "A Thinking Margin: The Womanist Movement as Critical Cognitive Praxis," in *Deeper Shades of Purple*, ed. Stacey Floyd-Thomas (New York: New York University Press, 2006), 227.
26. Copeland, "A Thinking Margin," 228.
27. Cannon, "Womanist Perspectival Discourse," 36.
28. J. Lorand Matory, "Rival Empires: Islam and the Religions of Spirit Possession among the "Òyó-Yorùbá" *American Ethnologist* 21, no. 3 (1994): 505.

Selected Texts

Cannon, Katie. "Womanist Perspectival Discourse and Cannon Formation." *Journal of Feminist Studies in Religion* 9 (Spring–Fall 1993): 29–30.

Cone, James. *Black Theology and Black Power*. New York: Seabury Press, 1969.

Copeland, M. Shaun. "A Thinking Margin: The Womanist Movement as Critical Cognitive Praxis," *Deeper Shades of Purple*. Ed. Stacey Floyd-Thomas. New York: New York University Press, 2006, 226–35.

Grant, Jacquelyn. *White Women's Christ and Black Women's Jesus*. Atlanta: Scholars Press, 1989.

Lloyd, Genevieve. *The Man of Reason: "Male" and "Female" in Western Philosophy*. Minneapolis: University of Minnesota Press, 1993.

Long, Charles. *Significations: Signs, Symbols, and Images in the Interpretation of Religion*. Aurora, CO: Davies Group, 1986.

Raboteau, Albert. *A Fire in the Bones*. Boston: Beacon Press, 1995.

Roberts, J. Deotis. *Black Theology Today*. New York: Edwin Mellen Press, 1983.

Stewart, Dianne M. *Three Eyes for the Journey*. New York: Oxford University Press, 2005.
Thomas, Linda. *Living Stones in the Household of God*. Minneapolis: Fortress Press, 2004.
Walker, David. *David Walker's "Appeal to the Coloured Citizens of the World."* Ed. Peter Hinks. University Park: Pennsylvania State University Press, 2000.
West, Cornel. *Prophecy Deliverance!* Philadelphia: Westminster Press, 1982.

CHAPTER 7

THEORETICAL COMMITMENTS IN AFRICAN AMERICAN THEOLOGY

EDWARD P. ANTONIO

THEORY

MY brief is to reflect on the theoretical commitments of African American theology as they are enunciated in its treatment of "religion" and in its conceptualization of the functions and tasks of theology. This is no mean task. First of all, used in the singular, the phrase "African American theology" belies the immense variety of the forms and expression of the phenomena to which it seeks to point. Second, whatever one means by that phrase, it is not at all the case that "African American theology" has, in all its colorful diversity, been invariably explicit about its theoretical commitments. Indeed, it can be argued that there resides a general aversion to theory in many of its expressions—both popular and academic—which has tended to engender a troubling anti-intellectualism often, as in many other forms of liberation theologies, justified in the name of the importance of praxis, practice, or some form of pragmatism as though the most effective forms of political engagement must necessarily depend on the opposition between theory and practice, as though theory is necessarily depoliticized by virtue of its discursive identity.[1] If this were true, it would, of course, render inconceivable the nexus between the politics of theory and the theory of politics as constitutive of the space of both practice and "critique of ideology." Yet, as we shall see, both practice and "critique of ideology" have always been crucial to African American theology.

The suspicion against theory stems from the fact that it has often been pitted against practical everyday knowledge. Theory has a bad name in the minds of many. It is associated with speculation, abstraction, conjecture, guesswork, that which is impractical, merely cerebral, and disconnected from experience and concrete reality. The situation is compounded by the fact that the meanings of theory vary across academic disciplines (examples are its use in literature, social theory, mathematical logic, physics, and other sciences) as well as between academic and colloquial uses (in the later theory is often equated with belief, viewpoint, and opinion). A further and related problem is that theory, like ideology, which I shall invoke later, has been declared dead by some scholars.[2] Some have declared the end of theory because (*a*) of its association with the grand explanatory schemes of nineteenth- and twentieth-century modernism such as existentialism, Marxism, phenomenology, humanism, and so on; (*b*) because of its overly ambitious attempts to provide universal and prescriptively doctrinaire explanations for particular and localized events and processes; and (*c*) because, paradoxically, of its alleged abstract hairsplitting atomism.

My aim here is not to recapitulate the explanatory procedures of these theories in the name of African American theology or to arrive on a settled definition of theory in general or a theory proper to African American theology. Rather, *for the purposes of this essay*, I am interested in theory as a hermeneutical and semiotic (since it is always structured by signs) process that describes the patterns that characterize how ideas, symbols, objects, concepts, experiences, practices, and so on are represented in thinking. In other words, I take theory to be the hermeneutical framework rooted in different social and academic contexts and perspectives that generally displays regular and agreed-upon patterns or conventions of how knowledge (including practical knowledge or praxis and the life experiences it articulates) is produced, acquired, justified, processed, and used formally and informally to explain, interpret, and organize the world and information about the world. I refer to "different social and academic contexts and perspectives" in order to make visible the ineluctable location of theory in the plurivocality of the cultural politics of knowledge production. It is here that the heuristic devices, ideas, signs, theorems, and semiotics of representation are negotiated and contested. I refer to the formal and informal role of theory in explanation so as to allow space for the possibility of the differential emergence of theory in nonacademic or strictly nonformalized contexts of what Michel de Certeau calls the "practice of everyday." I take as my clue here the understanding of theory developed in the kind of postpositivism articulated by Satya Mohanty and others.[3]

My claim here is that African American theology's commitment to theory consists in the ways in which it embodies and reflects (not always consciously) the more or less determinative patterns of interpretation and understanding that are presupposed and broadly shared across the various discursive regions constitutive of its disciplinary identity. These patterns are informed by and enunciated through a persistent recourse to a repertoire of certain historical phenomena such as slavery, Jim Crow, the civil rights movement, the black church, the ghetto, the figure of the black preacher, certain prominent historical figures, lynching, race, gender, blackness, Africa, the chant and the mourn, dance and the body, the spirituals,[4] political statements, sermons, slave narratives, and the social theories of a long line of African American thinkers such W. E. B. Du Bois, Alexander Crummel, Frederick Douglass, Sojourner Truth, Harriet Tubman, Ida B. Wells, and so on. This repertoire and network of themes and topics, which is of course far from being exhaustive, can be witnessed variously and repeatedly at work in the writings of James Cone and Anthony Pinn, Delores Williams and Cornel West, Dwight Hopkins and Shawn Copeland, or again, Eddie Glaude and J. Kameron Carter, Kelly Brown Douglas, Willie James Jennings, Peter Paris, Linda Thomas, Garth Kasimu Baker-Fletcher, and many other writers.[5] We are dealing here not with epitexts, peritexts, or paratexts but with veritable markers of an African American canon that organizes and normalizes knowledge.[6] These phenomena represent "grids of specification" that derive both from the history of slavery and from each other and serve to overdetermine, amplify, instantiate, reproduce, classify, and distribute discursive practices in the field of American theology.[7] The *manner* in which and the extent to which these phenomena come up again and again in African American theology in most of its varieties has, unfortunately, never been a subject of a comprehensive comparative analysis. My contention is that far from being tendentious or merely paratextual, the recurrent way in which these and similar phenomena occur in the literature is methodologically indicative of their theoretical role(s).

Given the above, the reader would be justified to expect a discussion of the theoretical commitments of African American theology to focus on how these themes and phenomena frame and organize the field of African American theology. However, I want to approach matters somewhat differently by focusing instead on the *categories* within which the commitment to theory is carried out, that is, the categories within which these themes are invoked and discussed. These I shall claim are history, religion or the "religious," and critique of ideology. I am aware that many other forms of theoretical commitment exist. For example, one can cite the categories of gender, liberation, church, race, and so on. But I want to claim that the theoretical commitments of African American theology have, at the minimum, always been bound up with three organizing categories: history, politics (mobilizing of community, struggle for redemptive power or biopower, and critique of ideology), and religion as expressions of its own theological self-understanding. Any serious approach to African American theology (whether one is addressing race, gender, church, etc.) must take as its starting point at least these three commitments. Within this matrix of possible theory (the theoretical potential or promise of these categories as rendered in African American experience) religion has always more or less enjoyed a certain hermeneutical privilege. Thus I begin my discussion with religion and then move on to history and finally to the critique of "ideology."

Religion and the "Religious"

Clearly theology presupposes some understanding of religion, of its character and function. The connection between religion and theology is almost universally taken for granted. It is hard to imagine a theology that does not in some way require a notion of religion, however implicit, and whatever is meant by religion.[8] I want to argue here that this expectation is fulfilled in African American theology but largely indirectly and often implicitly. This is because African American theology's commitment to "religion" as an object of study and investigation is both untheorized and is theorized differently, or rather it is untheorized precisely to the extent that it is theorized differently, and is theorized differently by being left untheorized. This is because its commitment to "religion" as an object of study and investigation is, for the most part, mediated not through theorizing the category of "religion" but through *use* of the idea of the *religious*. While there are hardly any recent significant works written by African American theologians (and I am speaking principally about theologians here) that systematically address key issues in the discursive terms of the disciplinary rubric of religious studies such as the nature and function of religion, how religion is to be described and understood, and the nature of religious experience, the "religious" is routinely invoked in the titles of books, descriptions and explanations of activities, beliefs, and practices associated with religion. To make the distinction between religion and the religious methodologically significant may seem forced, if not pedantic since the second term merely modifies the first and thus seems to be semantically empty. But this can only be so if we hold, rather problematically, that adjectives add nothing to semantic content. What I want to argue is that the religious is the criterion by which to ascertain what many African American theologians mean by religion. Again, this is not because these theologians proffer anything like a theory of the "religious." What is important to notice here is that the adjective describes not an "objective theoretical entity" or concept but the "religious" as it represents and enunciates certain lifeworlds and experiences that theologians, historians, and sociologists have taken to be central to the ongoing social formation of African American history and culture. It is true this approach fuses religion and the religious in a manner somewhat parallel to how theology fuses religion and theological thought. The distinction I am making here is akin to, though not the same as, the distinction John Dewey makes in his Terry Lectures. Dewey writes, "There is a difference between religion, *a* religion and the religious; between anything that may be denoted by a noun substantive and the quality of experience that is designated by an adjective."[9] For Dewey religion pertains to specific or particular beliefs, institutions, and practices, while the religious pertains to "attitudes that may be taken toward every object and every proposed end or ideal."[10] One of the major differences between the way I use the term "religious" here and how Dewey uses it is that he is skeptical about making "religious experience" the basis of religion, while I claim that this is exactly what happens in many articulations of African American theology. There the religious is used to characterize activities, objects, processes, and so on, associated with religion. The focus is thus placed not on the categories but on what is seemingly secondary to the category. The "religious" is the discursive aura that gives certain activities their identity.

By focusing on activities, rituals, objects, experiences, and processes African American theology gives the "religious" an important ordering or methodological role. The approach here is largely phenomenological, theological, and pragmatic rather than primarily analytic. The identity of the category religion is dependent on the activities it is made to describe by its semantic relationship to the adjective, "religious," and is not prior to them. This approach avoids "analytic essentialism," according to which, tautologically, the meaning of a category comes as already defined by the category. Thus, to call the role of the "religious" in African American theology's understanding of religion phenomenological is to say that it derives its meaning from the experiences and activities it names as precisely *religious*. I am aware, as Jonathan Z. Smith has pointed out, that this begs the question of the kind or type of human experience or activity the adjective discursively modifies and how that experience or activity differs from nonreligious phenomena.[11] I have no intention of discussing this question here in any detail. Instead, I want to suggest in passing that African American theologians and religious thinkers try to address this question by positing theological and humanistic norms of description in which the claims of a non-Christian theistic humanism and the propositions of Christian faith together with the experiences they both prescribe and make possible function as the content of the religious. Thus, on the one hand, for Christian theologians, phenomena such as God, Jesus, the Church, Holy Spirit, the Bible, and so on, and how they are taken to inform life, explain the religious and thus religion. On the other hand, as Anthony Pinn has persistently argued in many of his writings, the "religious" in African American experience is characterized by a profound diversity of thought, practice, and outlook not necessarily reducible to Christian identity.[12]

The variable structure of these theological and humanistic norms of description is significant because it functions as the criterion in terms of which the field of African American religious studies is pluralistically constituted in African American theology. This can be seen in the way which, for example, Gayraud Wilmore organized his *African American Religious Studies* anthology. The book is saturated with theological matter in which church, Bible, mission, pastoral care, Christology, preaching, with "folk religion" thrown in for good measure, are all made to exemplify the content of religious studies.[13] There is at work here something like a translation of the language and vocabulary of theology into a dominant model for African American "religious studies." It is precisely this dominance of the theological model that another anthology edited by Cornel West and Eddie Glaude Jr. and entitled *African American Religious Thought*[14] invites us to transcend or to rethink. However, as just indicated above, the most concerted example of such a critical rethinking of religion and Christian theology in African American theology is the work of Anthony Pinn.

This, of course, raises the important question of just how the theological might renegotiate its Christian hegemony in the context of an open discursive space of African American experience not just in relation to the "religious" but also in relation to both black humanism (religious or otherwise) and to religious studies as a discipline (with its attempts to monopolize methodological "reflexivity," objectivity, and neutrality by disqualifying theology as confessional) in which the theological is itself a candidate for analysis and investigation. Again, I do not have the space to discuss this other than to note that this question represents a real opportunity for an African American contribution to debates on the relationship between religious studies and theology. It also opens up a space for genuine religious and theological pluralism in African American theology.

Now, it must also be said that the phenomenological and theological understanding of the religious that I have been describing is also characterized by a certain pragmatism insofar as the intentions of African American theology are directed toward intervening in the world in order to give an intelligible account of the material actions and practices, in the context of the immediacy of experience, that historically and culturally inform and shape African American lives as lived struggles for liberation from white supremacism.[15] In other words, the religious is used to described a pragmatic dimension of African American theology's approach to religion, an approach not about what religion is or what it means but what it does and how it functions historically in the struggle for freedom. As we shall see, this is in keeping with what I call in the next section of this essay the historicist imperative of African American theology.

History and Historicism

I now turn to the second dimension of African American theology's theoretical commitments, namely history. I suggest that theoretically African American theology is necessarily historical in nature, and this at different levels.[16] First, it is historical in its attention to the experience of slavery as a historical phenomenon. Second, it is historical in the sense of the connection of the slave experience to Africa and its cultures and traditions. It is for this reason that the "African" in African American must be theorized/theologized in African American theology.[17] Here the role of memory, Africanisms, and the reality of Africa for some African Americans today is crucial. To invoke Africa is not simply to invoke another history and other ways of thinking about Africa and Africans both at home and in diaspora. It is to situate African

American theology in a different register of thought about the nature as well as about the work of time.[18] Third, the commitment to history is carried out at the level of African American theology's Christian identity. Key questions here have to do with the Christianization of African slaves, with their unique appropriation of Christianity and the different ways in which this gave rise to "slave religion."[19] Slave readings of the Bible, the emergence of the black church and styles of worship, and the eventual rise of black theology all attest to a long history of how African Americans have engaged with Christianity in its political, literary, institutional, and credal forms.[20] In all of this African American theologians took on another history and made it their own. Here we might think not so much of being assimilated as of assimilating the mainstream into new and emerging forms of consciousness, essentially a different mode of social being that in time will come to be called African American Christianity and will represent a distinctive contribution to American history. Fourth, African American theology's commitment to history is articulated in its emphasis on the historicity of human experience. We might call this the "historicist" dimension of African American theology. This strand of historical understanding is the basis of the various claims at the levels of both theological content and method that give African American theology its character. Several models of describing the role of history in terms of both content and method can be ascertained not from a generalized and immediate appeal to the idea of history as such but rather from the use of a host of terms and ideas such as social location, experience, body, story, autobiography, ghetto, culture, concrete, and community. While there is little interest in the literature in formally examining how some these *terms* and *concepts* actually function as elements within a theoretical structure in African American theology, I would suggest that a phenomenological profile of their use as well as status points to an underlying historicism. These and many similar terms are crucial to understanding the historicist imperative of African American theology, that is, the appeal to the actuality of time and space through firsthand, lived knowledge of temporal reality. All these terms name and describe the properties of the actuality or existential density of time and space as experienced reality, as lived history. They are part of the "master narrative" of the meaning of African American history and the experiences mediated through it. Historicism functions at this level as an "ism" representing the interpretation and understanding of temporality and its contents. While the "ism" hints at the ever present reality of "ideology" in the makeup of historicism, it is not restricted to it but rather comes in second to, or is subsumed in the primacy of, its hermeneutical status and function. At a second level it describes what can be called a worldview or a way of looking and being existentially oriented in and toward the world that is saturated and informed by the concrete phenomena of music, dance, sport, worship, racial discrimination, sexism, class inequities, imprisonment, and a whole host of other things that are counted as part of the memory and everyday experience of African Americans. These things represent social location, the concrete, and so on. An account of historicism in African American theology that does not pay attention to the temporal actualities of language, gestures, body posture and movement, habits of eating, and sensuality will be devoid of any reference to the immediacy of culture and experience, of the earthly, and thus of history.

Fifth, African American theology shares and participates in the history of other minority groups in the United States. It participates in a kind of interhistorical solidarity in which different historical perspectives and experiences from different oppressed and racial groups entered into and contributed to the shaping of African American theology.[21] Interhistorical solidarity is not about conflating different understandings of oppression or liberation but of learning across racial, cultural, and ideological lines. These forms of what is often "unconscious" (and thus powerful, if also taken for granted) commitment to history point to a pluralism of historical understandings that precludes a unitary view of history in African American theology. A womanist view of history will look distinctively different from one governed by a black patriarchal perspective. Similarly an African American humanistic historicism might stress less interpreting experience through the constraints of religion or theology and focus more on a search for a paradigm in which the interaction between the secular and the religious is thought to provide a richer framework for a more pluralistic understanding of African American experience. It is, however, unfortunate, and this is the consequence of taking history for granted, that for all its use of that category, African American theology has not, as far as I can tell, produced its own critical historiography, its own "independent" philosophical account of what constitutes history, the methods and meanings of history. This has had a further deleterious effect on the way in which history is practiced, namely, the failure to attend to the nature and role of memory. In other words, memory and historiography have been widely neglected in African American theology.[22]

Critique of Ideology (or Is It Cultural Criticism?)

I shall now invoke an idea whose demise has been proclaimed by some thinkers. This is the idea of ideology.[23] Like Althusser, I refuse to accept that ideology can ever go away.[24] This is because human beings always produce ideas, signify the world to themselves, misrecognize the falsity and partiality of their claims, and often naturalize and attribute eternal truth to them; and throughout history they have unjustifiably imposed and rationalized their beliefs and practices on powerless members of society. Ideology never goes away also because human beings discursively question, critique, and resist oppression in and through complex systems of representation. Ideology, particularly in the United States, has been mistakenly associated with the grand and utopian political claims of socialism and Marxism. The demise of really exiting socialism in Eastern Europe in the 1990s supposedly ushered in the death of ideology. Clearly this view mistakes the end of particular totalitarian practices supported by a particular system of signification with the end of ideology or signification as such. It has a rather unsophisticated notion of ideology.[25]

African American theology has always been committed, formally and informally, to ideology and critique of ideology as part of its theoretical framework. This does not mean that African American theology has produced a fully developed theory of the nature and role of ideology or that there is one single understanding of "ideology" that is universally shared. It also does not mean that African American theology necessarily appropriates "ideology" as a label of self-identification. I shall proceed with caution here. Ideology is, of course, notoriously hard to define. Hence the quotation marks around my initial use of the term. In addition to its fundamental meaning-making (or signifying) function, I take ideology to mean the conscious and critical naming and demystification of the ideas, reasons, institutions, structures, motivations, practices, and outlooks that are, consciously or otherwise, invoked by anyone in power or victimized by power in a particular social context to explain, justify, defend, and support, on whatever grounds, creating, locating, and confining the oppressed to existentially undesirable, socially vulnerable, and politically and economically threatening and destructive social time and space. Furthermore, ideology, mutatis mutandis, entails the apparatus of critically naming and demystifying modes of corrupted resistance to oppression. Emphasizing critical naming and demystification enables us to focus on certain aspects of ideology and how they construct the terrain of ideological struggle. There is a fundamental sense in which African American theology precisely as *theology* comes into being on the terrain of ideological struggle, that is, (1) to uncover and contest the rationalizations that systemically narrate support for the oppression of African Americans, and (2) to propose new forms of Christian and human sociability.

There are at least three different ways in which the idea of "ideology" appears in African American theology. First, there is a class of use that directly invokes the notion. James Cone's early *God of the Oppressed*, for example, directly and somewhat theoretically addresses the question of ideology.[26] Second, there is a use that does not "theorize" ideology as such but makes frequent and systematic use of many of the discrete functions associated with ideology such, for example, as critique of the use of religion to justify oppression. This is sometimes mistaken for and conflated with the "hermeneutics of suspicion," and sometimes it is thought of in terms of prophetic criticism of oppressive social structures, and at other times it is assimilated to cultural criticism and deconstruction. A third approach to ideology tends to be ad hoc and rather casual and lets the concern with ideology speak from within a general critique of all discursive forms of oppression and their material consequences. Victor Anderson sometimes uses the term in this way (see his "Ontological Blackness in Theology," contained in *African American Religious Thought: An Anthology*, edited by Cornel West and Eddie S. Glaude Jr.).

Although African American theology's use of ideology is largely "negative" and thus can easily give rise to the impression that it is nothing more than a negative naming, it in fact plays a central positive, theoretical, and methodological role. Critique of ideology is its basic rule for engaging modern white and dominant theologies and thus also for clearing up a space for reimagining the theological enterprise in racist modernity. There are several levels at which the concern with ideology is theoretically operative in African American theology. The first is the analysis and uncovering of racial and racist representations of the humanity of African Americans (as inferior, slave, lazy, criminal) as a governing feature of the American imaginary. The second is, on the one hand, the analysis of the historical contexts of these representations (slavery, Jim Crow, civil rights, the prison industrial complex, the ghetto) and, on the other, critique of the *discursive* modes through which they manifested themselves. Of particular interest here are the different kinds of knowledge, both academic and popular, including "common-sense" beliefs and social and cultural practices, through which these representations occurred and were deployed. The third level at which the idea of ideology is at work in African American theology is its (admittedly uneven) attention to the systemic and multiple functions of contemporary religious, social, political, and economic institutions in reproducing and perpetuating structures of racism and other forms of oppression. The scope of this concern with the role of ideology extends beyond history and seeks to describe the structural causes and consequences of oppression as it is being experienced in African American communities.

The fourth level where critique of ideology has been at work is within African American theology itself. The example of womanism is important, as are critiques of forms of African American Christianity seen as complicit with the political and religious status quo. Womanism has persistently drawn attention to the role of patriarchy in African American Christianity (including theology) in ideologically occluding from proper recognition black women as full subjects with genuinely different and legitimate concerns about the unequal distribution of power, wealth, and other entitlements.

In all of this, critique of ideology emerges as a tool for identifying systems of oppression and their key features, for uncovering ideology as false knowledge about the humanity of blacks (this has nothing to do with false consciousness) and its inability to see beyond the social and epistemic limits of white racism.

The ensemble of the various functions of the critique of the rationalization of racist and other forms of subjugation that I have attributed to African American theology here should not be reduced to an intellectualist understanding of ideology. Critique of ideology does not mean critique of intellectual abstractions but rather critique of the concrete or material systems of social meaning and practice that organize human beings into disempowering hierarchies, which, among other things, give rise to such abstractions. Because of its interest in what I take to be the material realities of race, racism, sexism, and exclusion on the basis of social class, I want to suggest that the primary sense that critique of ideology acquires in African American theology is "materialist" and must thus be located in what I described earlier as its historicist imperative. Recall that, on my reading, history in African American theology is the actuality of the social density of time and space that narrates the reality and conditions of possibility of black situatedness and of its determinations throughout Western modernity. It is this density that I want call upon to describe as "materialist" the practice of critique of ideology in African American theology. The tension thus generated between materialism and historicism (between, for example, the materiality of human bodies and their social or historical construction in terms of race, gender, sexuality, etc.) itself becomes the locus for the possibility of interrogating ideology and its operations in all theological claims.

I have described the theoretical commitments of African American theology using three categories, of ideology, the religious, and history. These are modernist categories that have functioned within white philosophical and theological discourses to organize knowledge and practice. I have done nothing in this essay to raise the critical challenges this poses for African American theology (in terms, for example, of the uncritical reliance of some of it on modernist vocabularies to articulate the nature and goals of liberation and freedom) or to critique and analyze how these categories are actually appropriated and deployed. That is a task I reserve for another project.

Notes

1. Homi Bhabha, *The Location of Culture* (London: Routledge, 1994). See especially chapter 1 on the commitment to theory.
2. Discussions of various aspects of this can be found in the following: Terry Eagleton, *After Theory* (New York Basic Books, 2003); Frederic Jameson, *Postmodernism, or the Cultural Logic of Late Capitalism* (Durham, NC: Duke University Press, 1991), see especially chapter 7; Christopher Norris, *The Truth about Postmodernism* (Oxford: Blackwell, 1993); see especially chapter 3; W. J. T. Mitchell, *Against Theory: Literary Studies and the New Pragmatism* (Chicago: University of Chicago Press, 1985); Steven Knapp and Walter Benn Michaels, "Against Theory," *Critical Inquiry*, 8, no. 4 (Summer 1982): 723–42.
3. Satya Mohanty, "The Epistemic Status of Cultural Identity: On Beloved and the Postcolonial Condition," in *Reclaiming Identity: Realist Theory and the Predicament of Postmodernism*, ed. Paula M. Moya and Michael R. Hames-Garcia (Berkeley: University of California Press, 2000).
4. See James H. Cone, *The Spirituals and the Blues: An Interpretation* (Maryknoll, NY: Orbis Books, 1992).
5. This list of names is random and is not meant to include everyone working in the field of African American theology.
6. Gerard Genette, *Paratexts: Thresholds of Interpretation*, trans. Jane E. Lewin (Cambridge: Cambridge University Press, 1997).
7. The phrase "grids of specification" is Michel Foucault's. See Michel Foucault, *The Archeology of Knowledge* (London: Tavistock Publications, 1972), 42.

8. I am aware that some theologians think of religion as a bad thing. Recall Karl Barth's famous critique of religion. See Karl Barth, *The Word of God and the Word of Man*, trans Douglas Horton (New York: Harper and Row, 1957). Also, Emil Brunner and Karl Barth, *Natural Theology: Comprising "Nature and Grace" by Professor Dr. Emil Brunner and the Reply "NO!" by Dr. Karl Barth*, trans. Peter Fraenkel (Eugene, OR: Wipf and Stock, 2002). This book was originally published in 1946.
9. John Dewey, *A Common Faith* (New Haven: Yale University Press, 1934), 3.
10. Dewey, *A Common Faith*, 9–10.
11. Jonathan Z. Smith, "Religion, Religions, the Religious," in *Critical Terms for Religious Studies*, ed. Mark C. Taylor (Chicago: University of Chicago Press, 1998), 269–84. The religious is used to distinguish "religious activities" from nonreligious activities. If there is an African American religiosity and possibly an African theory of religion, ought we not to expect an African American theory of the "secular"?
12. Anthony B. Pinn, *The End of God-Talk: An African American Humanist Theology* (New York: Oxford University Press, 2012). See also two of his other books: *What Is African American Religion?* (Minneapolis: Fortress Press, 2011) and *Varieties of African American Religious Experience* (Minneapolis: Fortress Press, 1998).
13. Gayraud Wilmore, ed., *African American Religious Studies: An Interdisciplinary Anthology* (Durham, NC: Duke University Press, 1989).
14. Cornel West and Eddie S. Glaude Jr., eds., *African American Religious Thought* (Louisville, KY: Westminster John Knox Press, 2003). This volume includes discussion of voodoo, Islam, elements of black nationalism, alienation, etc. Yet even here the editors of this volume are unable renegotiate the theological model away.
15. Cornel West, *The Cornel West Reader* (Basic Civitas Books, 2000).
16. I do not mean by this that it is somehow sold to an idealistic view of history. Rather I mean that it takes history seriously at the level of theory, i.e., as a mode of explanation. Interesting discussion of the relevant features of historicism I draw from include the following: Pietro Rossi, "The Ideological Valences of Twentieth Century Historicism," *History and Theory* 14, no. 4, Beiheft [Supplement] 14, "Essays on Historicism" (1975): 15–29; F. R. Ankersmit, "Historicism: An Attempt at Synthesis," *History and Theory* 34, no. 3 (1995): 143–61; Delwin Brown, "Beyond 'Boundaries': Towards a Radical Historicism in Theology," *American Journal of Theology and Philosophy* 18, no. 2 (1997): 167–80; Sheila Davaney Greeve, *Pragmatic Historicism: A Theology for the Twenty-First Century* (Albany: State University of New York Press, 2000).
17. Eddie Glaude Jr., *In A Shade of Blue: Pragmatism and the Politics of Black America* (Chicago: University of Chicago Press, 2007). Glaude deals with a variety of themes pertinent to the issues I am addressing here, including pragmatism, history, and the idea of Africa.
18. J. Deotis Roberts, *Black Theology in Dialogue* (Philadelphia: Westminster Press, 1987). The chapters "African Roots of Black Theology" and "An Afro-American/African Theological Dialogue" are especially relevant. Cornel West and Eddie Glaude also make the point. See also Charles Long, *Significations: Signs, Symbols, and Images in the Interpretation of Religion*, 2nd ed. (Aurora, CO: Davies Group; 2004); Josiah U. Young, *A Pan-African Theology: Providence and the Legacies of the Ancestors* (Trenton, NJ: Africa World Press, 1992). See also Young's *Black and African Theologies: Siblings or Distant Cousins* (Maryknoll, NY: Orbis Books, 1986).

19. Albert J. Raboteau, *Slave Religion: The "Invisible Institution" in the Antebellum South* (New York: Oxford University Press, 2004).
20. See Dwight N. Hopkins, *Down, Up and Over: Slave Religion and Black Theology* (Minneapolis: Fortress Press, 1999). See also Hopkins, *Shoes That Fit Our Feet: Sources for a Constructive Black Theology* (Maryknoll, NY: Orbis Books, 1993); Gayraud S. Wilmore, *Black Religion and Black Radicalism: An Interpretation of the Religious History of African Americans*, 3rd ed. (Maryknoll, NY: Orbis Books, 1998).
21. Anthony B. Pinn and Benjamin Valentin, *Ties That Bind: African American and Hispanic American/Latino/a Theologies in Dialogue* (New York: Continuum, 2001); Shawn Copeland, "Black, Hispanic/Latino and Native American Theologies," in *The Modern Theologians: An Introduction to Christian Theology in the Twentieth Century*, ed. David Ford (Malden, MA: Blackwell, 1997).
22. Of course we need to be careful not to conclude from this that this is so in other branches of African American scholarship. I speaking here only of African American theology.
23. Daniel Bell, *The End of Ideology: On the Exhaustion of Political Ideas in the Fifties, with the "Resumption of History in the New Century"* (Cambridge: Harvard University Press, 2000); E. A. Shils, "The End of Ideology?" in *The End of Ideology Debate*, ed. Chaim I. Waxman (New York: Simon & Schuster, 1968), 49–63; R. Aron, "The end of the ideological age?" in Waxman, *The End of Ideology Debate*, 27–48; P. E. Converse, "The Nature of Belief Systems in Mass Publics," in *Ideology and Discontent*, ed. David E. Apter (New York: Free Press, 1964), 206–61; John T. Jost, "The End of the End of Ideology," *American Psychologist* 61, no. 7 (2006): 651–70.
24. Louis Althusser, *Essays on Ideology: Ideology and Ideological State Apparatuses* (London: Verso, 1984).
25. John B. Thompson, *Studies in the Theory of Ideology* (Cambridge: Polity Press, 1984) and *Ideology and Modern Culture* (Cambridge: Polity Press, 1990).
26. Harry H. Singleton III, *Black Theology and Ideology: Deideological Dimensions in the Theology of James H. Cone* (Collegeville, MN: Liturgical Press, 2002).

Selected Texts

Althusser, Louis. *Essays on Ideology: Ideology and Ideological State Apparatuses* London: Verso, 1984.

Bhabha, Homi. *The Location of Culture*. London: Routledge, 1994.

Dewey, John. *A Common Faith*. New Haven: Yale University Press, 1934.

Foucault, Michel. *The Archeology of knowledge*. London: Tavistock, 1972.

Hopkins, Dwight N. *Down, Up and Over: Slave Religion and Black Theology*. Minneapolis: Fortress Press, 1999.

Pinn, Anthony B. *The End of God-Talk: An African American Humanist Theology*. New York: Oxford University Press, 2012.

Pinn, Anthony B. *Varieties of African American Religious Experience*. Minneapolis: Fortress Press, 1998.

Pinn, Anthony B. *What Is African American Religion?* Minneapolis: Fortress Press, 2011.

Pinn, Anthony B., and Benjamin Valentin. *Ties That Bind: African American and Hispanic American/Latino/a Theologies in Dialogue*. New York: Continuum, 2001.

Smith, Jonathan Z. "Religion, Religions, the Religious." In *Critical Terms for Religious Studies*, ed. Mark C. Taylor, 269–84. University of Chicago Press, 1998.

West, Cornel. *The Cornel West Reader*. New York: Basic Civitas Books, 2000.

West, Cornel, and Eddie S. Glaude Jr., eds. *African American Religious Thought*. Louisville, KY: Westminster John Knox, 2003.

CHAPTER 8

METHODOLOGIES IN AFRICAN AMERICAN THEOLOGY

FREDERICK L. WARE

WITH respect to methodology, African American theology is quite varied and diverse. Many approaches are taken in order to construct theological interpretations. However, one thing seems to be common—the centrality of African American (or black) experience and acknowledgment that the work of theology consists of the manifold tasks of describing, analyzing, evaluating, explaining, and, when necessary, revising or rejecting religious beliefs. African American theology begins with an examination of religious knowledge that emerges from the historical and social experiences of peoples of black African descent in the United States and ends with a test of the validity of their religious beliefs, restated or amended, in social situations endangering their humanity, freedom, survival, and quality of life. This circle of interpretation is accomplished through correlation and the use of symbols and themes that structure racial consciousness, religious and cultural sources that illuminate insights of black experience, and contemporary research paradigms for the development of black constructive theology.

CORRELATION

Early in the contemporary black theological movement, James H. Cone identified correlation as a fundamental method of African American theology.[1] In following this method, African American theology is constructed by relating the corpus of Christian theology to the black experience. Cone's *A Black Theology of Liberation* (1970) weaves an interpretation of black experience into the traditional schema of Christian theology.[2] Although in Cone's early attempts to construct black theology he used the writings of major Christian theologians such as Karl Barth, Paul Tillich, Dietrich Bonhoeffer, and Rudolf Bultmann, his correlation of these theologians' works to black experience yielded interpretations of Christian doctrines radically different from those espoused by these theologians.

Presently, in African American theology, correlation is applied within a complex web of connections between religion and experience. Correlation is not a simple matter in view of there being multiple expressions of African American religion and many conceptions of blackness. The notion that correlation involves the task of relating blackness to the corpus of Christian theology must be modified to include a broader range of intellectual and religious traditions. The religious life of African Americans is not limited to Christianity or Christian thought. While the dominant tradition among African Americans is evangelical Protestant Christianity, African Americans have expressed themselves religiously in a number of ways. Other important religious traditions for correlation to blackness include Roman Catholic and Orthodox conceptions of Christianity, Islam, Judaism, African-derived religions (i.e., Santeria and vodun), eclectic spiritualist traditions, Hinduism, and Buddhism.

Not only must the meaning of religion be expanded to include non-Christian religions, the meaning of religion must encompass secular worldviews and pervasive cultural beliefs. Religion provides orientation, guides for behavior, and a core of symbols and beliefs that is foundational to, of ultimate importance or basic for, explaining and understanding all else in human experience. Modern science, political economy, and political ideology now have the quality of religion in that they present comprehensive views or conceptions of the world, define persons and peoples, and suggest how they should act and what kind of future humankind has to look forward to.

Like religion, blackness is a malleable category. There is not one but many conceptions of blackness. Blackness has never been defined definitively, once and for all times. According to W. E. B. Du Bois, the history of blacks in America is fraught with images that are not always of their making. For several generations of African Americans, their goal has been to reconcile conflicting images into "a better and truer self."[3] Toward defining this better and truer self, blackness may be, and often is, characterized by experiences of oppression, humiliation, discrimination, political disenfranchisement, and economic injustice. When these negative aspects of black people's experience are of chief concern, African American theology takes on a liberation orientation with the aim of transforming the conditions that adversely affect black people's lives. However, blackness may also refer to those positive aspects, the "beauty and joy, of African American life that are expressive of deeply held values and mores that enable African Americans' fulfillment as human beings."[4] A compelling argument for enlarging the concept of blackness is found in Victor Anderson's

Beyond Ontological Blackness: An Essay on African American Religious and Cultural Criticism (1995).[5]

Correlation is an ongoing process for African American theology. Identity as well as religion are not fixed and therefore are subject to change. As a people change, so will their religion. Blackness is constantly undergoing redefinition and renegotiation. African American religious preferences are capable of shifting. As long as race and religion circumscribe American reality, black theology will continue, and proceed using the method of correlation.

Symbols and Themes

In addition to correlation, the use of symbols and themes is vital for the construction of African American theology. Symbols may be either nonlinguistic (physical objects) or linguistic (words, phrases, and ideas). In either case, symbols focus attention on self, society, and culture. Linguistic symbols are highlighted in this essay. Themes are concepts that, when expressed in propositional form, are presumed true. Themes are foundational propositions for constructing interpretations. Symbols and themes function as "reality detectors," tools for enabling self-understanding, discernment of meanings in the contexts through which persons live, and a relationship to that which is ultimate and transcendent so that life is never restricted solely to what life happens to be at any given time. Symbols and themes are not mutually exclusive; there is much connection, intersection, and overlap between the two. Though symbols and themes are used and repeated frequently, they are subject to reformulation (modification and renegotiation) as new events and challenges emerge in African American experience, which itself is never static.

In African American religions, there are many symbols. Given the dominance of evangelical Protestant Christianity, there is a pervasiveness of biblical motifs, metaphors drawn from Christian language, and the dogmas of Trinity and Christology in African American communities.[6] However, the primary symbols, first identified by Charles H. Long, are God, race, Africa, and freedom. They are "deep symbols," words of power that constrain, guide, and become a focus of thought and action.[7] Freedom functions both as symbol (i.e., that which represents ultimacy and transcendence) and theme (i.e., something claimed to be of great value). Race, as symbol, is now expanded to include emphases on gender and sexuality.

God is a symbol for transcendence and ultimacy.[8] Among the questions revolving around God as symbol are these: What or who is the source of my value? To what or whom may I compare myself? Can I be other than what I am? What can (or will) I become?

The meaning of God is not limited to a particular doctrinal system of theism, African or Western. God is the Other. God is the One who is apart from the world. Charles Long describes Africans' encounter with God as an existential crisis finding resolution in a new locus of value. He says, "To whom does one pray from the bowels of a slave ship? to the gods of Africa? to the gods of the masters of the slave vessels? to the gods of an unknown and foreign land of enslavement? To whom does one pray? From the perspective of religious experience, this was the beginning of African American religion and culture. In the forced silence of oppression, in the half-articulate moans of desperation, in the rebellions against enslavement—from this cataclysm another world emerged."[9] God represents an altogether different reality; God is something, somewhere, or someone other than what is. Belief in God emerges from racial consciousness marked by an awareness of the power and sacredness of life (being itself) that is not restricted by the existing social order.[10] While subscribing to traditional Christian theism, African Americans have depicted God as ultimate and the locus of value over against American mores, particularly customs, policies, and laws detrimental to African Americans' well-being. For example, at the conclusion of Henry McNeal Turner's detailed analysis of the Supreme Court's decision to overturn the Civil Rights Act of 1875, he declares faith in God, the One who is ultimate and thus another source of truth and justice.[11] For both Maria Stewart and Martin Luther King Jr., God is source of authority and courage in the struggle for freedom and justice.[12] In a rather different approach to theistic faith, womanists like Zora Hurston and Alice Walker view God as the power that pervades nature, the unity that underlies as well as the spirit that animates each living thing.[13]

Race is a symbol for discernment of place. Race is used for fixing social location and for detecting and assessing the processes, historical and social, going into the formation of the world wherein African Americans live. Through the prism of race, the sorts of questions asked include these: Who am I? What is my place in the world? What is the history and experience at which I am the center?

According to Charles Long, African Americans' sense of place is perceived, for the most part, as an "involuntary presence," a condition resulting from a history of forced migration and exploitation.[14] However, in addition to the idea of involuntary presence, race may refer to color caste, minority status, ancestry, subculture, and group belonging and solidarity. The use of race is clearly beyond discussions about physical characteristics and biological classification.

Africa is a symbol for representation and reflection on origins.[15] With Africa as central focus, the sorts of questions asked are these: From where did I come? May I return? Where do I belong? When and where does my history begin? What is my past? What is my cultural heritage?

Africa is both a historical reality and mythological place. It is a historical fact that the ancestors of black Americans came from the African continent. Unfortunately, documented empirical evidence showing the specific geographical areas and ethnic groups from which these persons came is not always available. In this sense, in a vague way, Africa is seen as a point of origin lost in obscurity. Still, the general designation of "African" reminded these persons that they came to the Americas from another place. Their history began before enslavement in the Americas. The extant logs of slave ships chronicle the transport of persons from Africa to the Americas. In addition, the writings of Olaudah Equiano (Gustavus Vassa), Venture Smith (Broteer Furro), Phillis Wheatley, and Omar Ibn Said are notable recollections on life in Africa. Even when African American opinion has been mixed about African colonization (and back-to-Africa movements), African Americans have never denied their origins in Africa.[16]

Africa is not only a place of origins; it is also a place of destiny. In African American folklore, there are numerous stories about persons who, when dreaming or when expressing hopes about their status upon death, have flown back to Africa.[17] Far from being artifacts of an age past, these stories, continue to influence the production of black culture. Toni Morrison structures the ending of her popular novel *Song of Solomon* (1977) using this folktale about those Africans who claimed that they could fly back to Africa.[18] Today, African Americans are using more than dreams to get to Africa; they are using airplanes. Since the 1960s, African American travel and tourism to Africa has increased dramatically, becoming a multi-million-dollar industry. During slavery and after emancipation, in colonization and later back-to-Africa movements, Africa was perceived as a natural location for black people to settle. Then as well as now, it was believed that black Americans would find in Africa a sense of belonging, economic opportunity, and meaningful involvement in the evangelization and moral and cultural uplift of the indigenous African population. Since the 1970s, the dramatic increase of African immigrant communities in the United States has contributed as well to African American awareness and appreciation of African religion and culture. African American theology exhibits increasing interest and use of African religion and culture for theological interpretation.

Freedom is symbol of the fulfilled life. When expressed in propositional form, namely in the statement that freedom is something of great (ultimate) value, freedom functions as a theme. The importance of freedom to African Americans is expressed best in the following spiritual:

> Oh, freedom! Oh, freedom! Oh, freedom all over me!
> Before I'd be a slave,
> I'll be buried in my grave,
> And go home to my Lord and be free.

The spiritual makes clear that a life without freedom is not worth living. Death is preferable to a life of oppression. Worse than death is the mode of existence marked by bondage, injustice, and nonfulfillment.

Recurring themes, stated propositionally, include these: (1) African American Christianity is an authentic expression of Christianity; (2) African American people are special (i.e., distinct, having qualities not found in other peoples); (3) community (black solidarity) is vital for liberation, survival, and quality of life; and (4) education (literacy and knowledge) is a route to freedom.[19] These themes are found in a variety of sources. A dichotomy between "true Christianity" and American Christianity (white religion) and the association of African American Christianity with true Christianity is found in works like David Walker's *Appeal* and Frederick Douglass's *Narrative* and speeches.[20] In Frances Ellen Watkins Harper's speech "Duty to Dependent Races," she identifies as the problem with American Christianity its impotence against injustice and its not following the example of Jesus Christ.[21] In Francis Grimke's thanksgiving sermon at the close of World War I, he is hopeful that a better form of Christianity, more faithful to the teachings of Jesus, will emerge in America.[22] Black inferiority is refuted in Benjamin Banneker's personal letter to Thomas Jefferson.[23] In Maria Stewart's address to the African-American Female Intelligence Society of Boston (1832), she describes blacks as a special people with a glorious past and potential for great contribution to human civilization.[24] The importance of community (black solidarity) for liberation is emphasized in Frederick Douglass's newspaper, *The North Star*, where he wrote: "We are one . . . our cause is one, and . . . we must help each other, if we should succeed."[25] In essays and speeches by Sarah Mapps Douglass, Maria Stewart, Anna Julia Cooper, Mary Church Terrell, W. E. B. Du Bois, and Frances Ellen Watkins Harper, education is proclaimed as that which will enable blacks to fill their place in American society.[26] Through the above themes and other propositions, African American theology is construed as an alternative to dominant interpretations of Christianity in the United States. In contrast to the dominant forms of Christianity and Christian theology, usually emerging from churches of white Americans, African American theology assigns priority to addressing the suffering of black people, highly values and links freedom with equality and justice, and emphasizes the role of the church in the transformation of society.

Sources and Resources

African American theologians are at a consensus about "black religion" as the subject matter of African American theology. For the most part, black religion has meant the use of black sources, oral and written, or adoption of a perspective that emphasizes African American experience, and the functional capacity of black religious organizations for cultural critique and social change. Since the mid-1970s, through debate initiated by Cecil Cone's *The Identity Crisis in Black Theology* (1975),[27] the literature in African American theology is enriched greatly by the use of black sources.

Three methodological questions are raised about the treatment of black religion. These questions are the following: What are the sources by which African American religious beliefs are conveyed to the theologian and religion scholar? How are these sources and other resources for theology mediated through and subjected to the norm in African American experience? How are these sources distinguishable from the theological constructions produced by through the use of these sources?

Many sources have been identified as bearers of religious belief. These sources include (There shouldn't be this break between "include: and "song...") songs, sermons, ways of reading the Bible, speeches, essays, poems, art, narratives, church and community histories, folktales, institutional practices, and customary ways of behaving.

Besides conveying ideas and beliefs, black sources are methods of reflection on African American experience, and reflection on, even critique and rejection of, religious beliefs and practices. For example, in Langston Hughes's story of his experience, as a teenager, at a revival service, he both describes and critiques the idea of conversion as salvation.[28] Hughes's narrative conveys important information about religious ritual in African American churches, of the kind he knew, but also shows the inadequacy of the routinized ecstatic experience as authentic personal transformation.

The turn to black sources should not be construed to be, as Victor Anderson claims is the case, a turn to legitimization.[29] According to Anderson, legitimization amounts to attempts to make theology appear to be "black" by using black sources but without any rigorous critical scrutiny of these sources. Still the turn to black sources is appropriate for two sets of reasons: acknowledgment of (1) the general but major role of these cultural expressions in religion and (2) the essential role of cultural forms for memory, recall, and introspection. A common form of cultural expression like narrative should not be equated with legitimization because, in African American culture, not all narratives are essentially Christian or support Christian categories and themes.[30] Not all narratives are essentially about liberation or have an ethic of liberation.[31] Narrative is a fundamental cultural product, which can be said also about other black sources. In systematic theology, experience is the medium for receiving, understanding, and analyzing sources of any kind. Black sources are "markers" and "snapshots" of African American experience.

Black cultural expressions, like African Americans themselves, have not evolved in a vacuum. African Americans are citizens of the Western world. African American theologians have used a wide variety of resources that are not unique to African Americans but are deemed valuable for understanding and illuminating various aspects and insights derived from African American experience. In addition to using various academic disciplines and reliable information sources, African American theologians employ a number of intellectual traditions ranging from common-sense realism to humanism, existentialism, pragmatism, and personalism to process metaphysics.

Freedom (as the penultimate of human fulfillment) is the norm to which sources and resources as well as African American experience generally are subjected. This norm determines which sources and resources will be used and how they will be used for reflection. In African American theology, the norm (freedom) may be grounded in either a Christocentric or a theocentric conception of faith.[32] African American humanists would argue that neither form of grounding is necessary in order to justify freedom.[33]

Paradigms

In African American theology, there are several paradigms that function as research programs, models, perspectives, and theoretical frameworks for constructing African American theology. In contemporary black theology, there are three principal schools of thought: the hermeneutical school, the philosophical school, and human sciences school. These schools of thought are described and examined in Frederick Ware's *Methodologies of Black Theology* (2008).

The schools of thought have developed as a result of individual and collaborative work. The black hermeneutical school (BHS), which first emerged in clergy and seminary settings, is devoted to a quest for a "black hermeneutic"—a method of biblical and theological interpretation that recovers and is representationally accurate with respect to the earliest expression of Christian faith and struggles for liberation among African Americans in the United States. Thinkers in the BHS include Katie Cannon, Albert Cleage, Cecil Cone, James Cone, Kelly Brown Douglas, James Evans, Jacquelyn Grant, Dwight Hopkins, Major Jones, Olin Moyd, J. Deotis Roberts, Delores Williams, and Gayraud Wilmore. The BHS has been and continues to be the most prolific and popular of the three schools of academic black theology. The black philosophical school (BPS) was formed by the entry of philosophers of religion into and the use of philosophy in the field of black theology. Thinkers in the BPS include William Jones, Anthony Pinn, Alice Walker, Cornel West, and Henry Young. The human sciences school (HSS) encompasses the kinds of cultural studies of black theology conducted by historians of religion, theologians of culture, sociologists of religion, religious studies scholars, and other intellectuals adhering to prevalent canons of scholarship in college and university settings. Thinkers in the HSS include Charles Long, Cheryl Townsend Gilkes, C. Eric Lincoln, Henry Mitchell, Charles Shelby Rooks, and Theophus Smith. While the works of African American women may be classified within these schools of thought, the special emphases and themes of womanist theology warrant separate examination as a unique vantage point for African American theology.

Womanist theology is characterized by holism on several levels. On one level, womanist theology appreciates the insights and contributions of African American women regardless of the terms used for self-identification. While African American women in religious and theological studies will refer to themselves as "womanists," some prefer to be called "black feminists."[34] In addition to embracing differing women's identities, on another level womanist theology aims for a comprehensive analysis of oppression. African Americans' resistance to racism and sexism is related to opposition to classism, homophobia, and human destruction of the environment. Inspired by the writings and works of notable African American women of faith such as Jarena Lee, Harriet Tubman, Sojourner Truth, Amanda Berry Smith, Anna Julia Cooper, Maria W. Stewart, Mary Church Terrell, Ida B. Wells, Mary McLeod Bethune, and Fannie Lou Hamer, contemporary womanist theology seeks quality of life and liberation for both women and men. Womanist theologians link their work and movement to the struggles of other persons and groups seeking liberation and fulfillment. According to Anna Julia Cooper, as "black" and "Christian," African Americans cannot be indifferent about the condition of African American women.[35] The uplift of African Americans, as a whole, depends on the uplift of black women. No adequate analysis may be made of African American experience without attention to the experience and status of black women and other minority groups within African American communities. Lastly, womanist theology is conducted on a level of harmonizing scholarship and advocacy. Womanist theology develops from the use of interconnecting emphases: valuing women's experience and wisdom, identifying and preserving sources on women's experience, and disseminating theology through teaching and publication in both academic and community settings.

Conclusion

In spite of the plurality of method and interpretation in African American religious thought, there is a continuing reluctance of scholars, white and black, to address African American theology in its rich diversity and complexity. The great temptation, which is hard to resist, is to simplify African American theology by identifying one person or one type of construal as representative of African American theology. The vibrancy of African American theology seems dependent on the holism commended by womanist theology. The gift of womanist theology and African American theology's future is uniformity without conformity, solidarity without exclusion.

Notes

1. James H. Cone, *God of the Oppressed* (San Francisco: Harper & Row, Seabury Press, 1975), 16–17; James H. Cone, *A Black Theology of Liberation*, 20th anniversary ed. (Maryknoll, NY: Orbis Books, 1990, 1970), xix, 4–5, 21–23.
2. Cone, *Black Theology of Liberation.*
3. W. E. B. Du Bois, *The Souls of Black Folk* (Greenwich, CT: Fawcett Publications, 1961), 17.
4. Cone, *God of the Oppressed*, 2.
5. Victor Anderson, *Beyond Ontological Blackness: An Essay on African American Religious and Cultural Criticism* (New York: Continuum, 1995).
6. Charles H. Long, *Significations: Signs, Symbols, and Images in the Interpretation of Religion* (Philadelphia: Fortress Press, 1986), 7, 179–81.
7. Victor Anderson, *Creative Exchange: A Constructive Theology of African American Religious Experience* (Minneapolis: Fortress Press, 2008), 4, 30–31.
8. Long, *Significations*, 116, 153, 179–83; Cone, *God of the Oppressed*, 144.
9. Charles H. Long, "Passage and Prayer: The Origin of Religion in the Atlantic World," in *The Courage to Hope: From Black Suffering to Human Redemption*, ed. Quinton Hosford Dixie and Cornel West (Boston: Beacon Press, 1999), 17.
10. Long, "Passage and Prayer," 7–12, 14.
11. Thomas R. Frazier, ed., *Readings in African-American History*, 3rd ed. (Belmont, CA: Wadsworth Thompson Learning, 2001), 180–81.
12. Shirley Wilson Logan, ed., *With Pen and Voice: A Critical Anthology of Nineteenth-Century African-American Women* (Carbondale: Southern Illinois University Press, 1995), 13; Kai Wright, ed., *The African American Archive: The History of the Black Experience through Documents* (New York: Black God & Leventhal Publishers, 2001), 535.
13. Norm R. Allen, Jr., ed., *African American Humanism: An Anthology* (Buffalo, NY: Prometheus Books, 1991), 153–54; Alice Walker, *In Search of Our Mothers' Gardens* (San Diego, CA: Harcourt Brace Jovanovich, 1983), 265.
14. Long, *Significations*, 176–79.
15. Long, *Significations*, 175–76.
16. Wright, *The African American Archive*, 128–33.
17. Wendy W. Walters, "One of Dese Mornins, Bright and Fair/ Take My Wings and Cleave de Air: The Legend of the Flying Africans and Diasporic Consciousness," *Mellus* 22, no. 3 (Fall 1997): 3–27.
18. Toni Morrison, *Song of Solomon* (New York: Plume, 1987).
19. Thomas L. Webber, *Deep Like the Rivers: Education in the Slave Quarter Community, 1831–1865* (New York: Norton, 1978), 63–70, 80–101, 131–148.
20. Frazier, *Readings in African American History*, 94–100; Allen, *African American Humanism*, 109–15; Wright, *The African American Archive*, 142–50, 197–98, 213–14.
21. Logan, *With Pen and Voice*, 40–41.
22. Carter G. Woodson, ed., *Negro Orators and Their Orations* (Washington, DC: Associates Publishers, 1925), 705.
23. Wright, *The African American Archive*, 102–5.
24. Logan, *With Pen and Voice*, 12–16.
25. Wilson J. Moses, *The Golden Age of Black Nationalism, 1850–1925* (Hamden, CT: Archon Books, 1978), 85–86.

26. Logan, *With Pen and Voice*, 43–46; Wright, *The African American Archive*, 184–87, 419–20, 535.
27. Cecil W. Cone, *The Identity Crisis in Black Theology* (Nashville, TN: African Methodist Episcopal Church, 1975).
28. Allen, *African American Humanism*, 119–21.
29. Anderson, *Beyond Ontological Blackness*, 93, 99, 109–10.
30. Dwight N. Hopkins and George Cummings, ed., *Cut Loose Your Stammering Tongue: Black Theology in the Slave Narratives* (Maryknoll, NY: Orbis Books, 1991), 47–66, 67–102.
31. Hopkins and Cummings, *Cut Loose Your Stammering Tongue*, 103–36.
32. Frederick L. Ware, *Methodologies of Black Theology* (Eugene, OR: Wipf & Stock, 2008, 2002), 44–55, 84, 87–89, 94.
33. Ware, *Methodologies of Black Theology*, 99.
34. Monica A. Coleman, "Must I Be a Womanist?" *Journal of Feminist Studies in Religion* 22, no. 1 (2006): 85–96.
35. Logan, *With Pen and Voice*, 53–74.

Selected Texts

Allen, Norm R., Jr., editor. *African American Humanism: An Anthology*. Buffalo, NY: Prometheus Books, 1991.

Anderson, Victor. *Beyond Ontological Blackness: An Essay on African American Religious and Cultural Criticism*. New York: Continuum, 1995.

Anderson, Victor. *Creative Exchange: A Constructive Theology of African American Religious Experience*. Minneapolis: Fortress Press, 2008.

Cannon, Katie G., Alison P. Gise Johnson, and Angela D. Sims. "Living It Out: Womanist Works in Word." *Journal of Feminist Studies in Religion* 21, no. 2 (Fall 2005): 135–46.

Coleman, Monica A. "Must I Be a Womanist?" *Journal of Feminist Studies in Religion* 22, no. 1 (2006): 85–96.

Cone, Cecil W. *The Identity Crisis in Black Theology*. Nashville, TN: African Methodist Episcopal Church, 1975.

Cone, James H. *A Black Theology of Liberation*. 20th anniversary ed. Maryknoll, NY: Orbis Books, 1990.

Cone, James H. *God of the Oppressed*. San Francisco: Harper & Row; New York: Seabury Press, 1975.

Cone, James H., and Gayraud S. Wilmore, eds. *Black Theology: A Documentary History, 1966–1979*. Maryknoll, NY: Orbis Books, 1993.

Cone, James H., and Gayraud S. Wilmore, eds. *Black Theology: A Documentary History, 1980–1992*. Maryknoll, NY: Orbis Books, 1993.

Du Bois, W. E. B. *The Souls of Black Folk*. Greenwich, CT: Fawcett, 1961.

Floyd-Thomas, Stacey M., ed. *Deeper Shades of Purple: Womanism in Religion and Society*. New York: New York University Press, 2006.

Frazier, Thomas R., ed. *Readings in African-American History*. 3rd ed. Belmont, CA: Wadsworth Thompson Learning, 2001.

Hopkins, Dwight N. *Shoes That Fit Our Feet: Sources for a Constructive Black Theology*. Maryknoll, NY: Orbis Books, 1993.

Hopkins, Dwight N., and George Cummings, eds. *Cut Loose Your Stammering Tongue: Black Theology in the Slave Narratives*. Maryknoll, NY: Orbis Books, 1991.

Logan, Shirley Wilson, ed. *With Pen and Voice: A Critical Anthology of Nineteenth-Century African-American Women*. Carbondale: Southern Illinois University Press, 1995.

Long, Charles H. "Passage and Prayer: The Origin of Religion in the Atlantic World." In *The Courage to Hope: From Black Suffering to Human Redemption*, ed. Quinton Hosford Dixie and Cornel West, 11–21. Boston: Beacon Press, 1999.

Long, Charles H. *Significations: Signs, Symbols, and Images in the Interpretation of Religion*. Philadelphia: Fortress Press, 1986.

Moses, Wilson J. *The Golden Age of Black Nationalism, 1850–1925*. Hamden, CT: Archon Books, 1978.

Morrison, Toni. *Song of Solomon*. New York: Plume, 1987.

Pinn, Anthony B., ed. *By These Hands: A Documentary History of African American Humanism*. New York: New York University Press, 2000.

Walker, Alice. *In Search of Our Mothers' Gardens*. San Diego, CA: Harcourt Brace Jovanovich, 1983.

Walters, Wendy W. 1997. "One of Dese Mornins, Bright and Fair/ Take My Wings and Cleave de Air: The Legend of the Flying Africans and Diasporic Consciousness." *Mellus* 22, no. 3 (Fall): 3–27.

Ware, Frederick L. *Methodologies of Black Theology*. Eugene, OR: Wipf & Stock, 2008.

Webber, Thomas L. *Deep Like the Rivers: Education in the Slave Quarter Community, 1831–1865*. New York: Norton, 1978.

Woodson, Carter G., ed. *Negro Orators and Their Orations*. Washington, DC: Associates Publishers, 1925.

Wright, Kai, ed. *The African American Archive: The History of the Black Experience through Documents*. New York: Black God & Leventhal, 2001.

SECTION II

DOCTRINES

CHAPTER 9

DOCTRINE OF GOD IN AFRICAN AMERICAN THEOLOGY

KERI DAY

African American theology critiques and enhances concepts and constructions of "God" within broader theological discourse in North America. While African American theological and religious thought on "God" was present during slavery, this essay charts the historical and ideological constructions of God within African American theology from the middle of the twentieth century onward. This focus on more contemporary theological formulations of God is directly connected to the formal academic development of ideas about God over the last several decades. I have placed African American theology into four major "camps" for purpose of analysis when examining doctrines of God. These four camps include Christian personalism, black liberation and womanist theologies, atheistic humanism, and pragmatic reconstructions of African American theology. These categories provide a way to analyze central aims, questions, and tasks associated with doctrines of God within African American theology (as well as critical religious responses to these ideological viewpoints).

Before providing thick descriptions of these concepts of God as well as the possibilities and challenges such concepts present within the context of African American religious experience, a brief description of the historical, sociopolitical, cultural, and intellectual context of African Americans in the twentieth century is foregrounded. This historical context enables one to see the social milieu out of which African American theology was shaped as well as the changing patterns of its discourse in relation to its social context.

African American theology, in large part, is shaped by the historical inhumanity of racial oppression and hegemony in America. Fashioned in the crucible of slavery, blacks asserted their human worth and dignity. Enslaved Africans recognized that one's theological anthropology (being the nature of humanity in relation to God) was directly connected to one's construction of God. Because the humanity of slaves was rendered inferior through early white Christian formulations, their constructions of God were also deeply and profoundly racist. Yet slaves rejected such ideas, maintaining that they were made in the image of God, who acknowledged their humanity. Their rejection of racist Christian ideologies through oral testimonies and spiritual songs held ethical implications in terms of securing their freedom, a freedom that early America refused to grant them. Although slavery formally ended in the nineteenth century, racial apartheid was merely re-established in the form of Jim Crow laws into the twentieth century.

Jim Crow laws degraded and subjugated black people. In particular, white Christianity continued to be a primary ideological supporter of institutional racism in America, which prompted African American theologians to critically respond. A major problem within broader academic Christian theology into the twentieth century was its complete dismissal of the interconnections between theological constructions of God and projects of justice and human transcendence. As I will discuss, African American theologians, in part, write against a white theological backdrop that did not take racial equality and justice seriously in its constructions of God. White theologians tended to ignore how their "God-talk" either fostered possibilities of human liberation or impeded spaces of human flourishing. Concepts of God could either cultivate the conditions for the possibility of human equality, justice, and transcendence or frustrate these attempts altogether. Much of Christian theology remained silent on the race question and its relation to theological concepts of God, which proved to be costly for African Americans around the nation. The moral cowardice and prejudice of white theologians and ministers (and black ministers also) in the face of racial segregation was deeply felt throughout black communities, causing many African American theologians to construct more liberative concepts of God. It is against this brief backdrop that African American theology and its construction of God develops and gains voice.

Howard Thurman is a primary theologian who draws upon the first theological camp I will discuss on the doctrine of God within African American theological thought: Christian personalism. Broadly, Christian personalists, such as Borden Parker Bowne, argued that the divine personhood of God grounds and makes possible the absolute value and worth of all human persons.[1] This particular theological school of thought perceived itself as responding to various philosophical, materialist, and evolutionary theories that reduced persons to mere insignificant atoms in a larger universe. Challenging social-scientific theories into the twentieth century, Christian personalists (although in different ways) maintained that the person is "bigger" than the universe in the sense that the person is always experiencing it, which affirms the concept of a soul. Drawing from Christian personalism, Thurman proffers a concept of God that includes a critique of white racist ideas and structures that devalued human personhood, which held strong implications for African Americans who were devalued in America's legal codes, social practices, and religious doctrines. His brand of Christian personalism and doctrine of God sought to reassert a personal God who guarantees the inviolability of personhood among all people through the religious encounter. Thurman's doctrine of God is deeply embedded in an ethics of love within human community.

For Thurman, this ethics of love is deeply rooted in his vision of God. Thurman can be described as a religious mystic who grounds his understanding of God in the individual religious experience. He states, "Religious experience is interpreted to mean the conscious and direct exposure of the individual to God."[2] Thurman describes the cosmos as one in which God is the foundation of all existence, endowing every soul with a Divine Spark. For him, the "Fall" is not an abrupt obliteration of all potential for good in the individual as a result of sin, but is a turning away from God in pursuit of selfish and sensual desires.[3] The image of God, or the Spark of the Divine, is not lost in this turning away. Rather, this spark remains within the individual but is concealed. This is the source of all longing for God, and is the ultimate underlying truth of the Christian experience of salvation, which in Thurman's perspective is a process through which the image is restored, or the spark uncovered, as the soul gradually ascends to union with God. Salvation so conceived has no necessary contingency on "historical facts," objective beliefs, or "external authority." Redemption is a result of the inward movement of the soul. Redemption is "a creative act, which must be the personal act."[4]

Thurman posits that this inward movement of the soul is grounded by a foundational principle, which is the unification of all life through the common source of God. Thurman laid heavy stress upon this concept, writing at length about the interconnectedness of life throughout the entire cosmic structure, including animal and plant life. One's very consciousness is connected to that of others. Beyond this metaphysical connection, however, Thurman strongly emphasizes the importance of knowing and loving other people concretely. He is not interested in cultivating a spiritual connection that has no physical consequence.[5] In his essay "Mysticism and the Experience of Love," Thurman describes the necessity of knowing another person's "fact" in order to truly love her or him. He says, "To speak of the love for humanity is meaningless. There is no such thing as humanity. What we call humanity has a name, was born, lives on a street, gets hungry, needs all the particular things we need."[6]

For Thurman, love does require us to develop a general sphere of acceptance that will allow us to love anyone with whom we come in contact, but the emphasis is always on loving in the particulars. And this love is the grounding of community and hope. He asserts that God is the source and grounding of this experience of love, which for him is the necessary counterexperience to systems and cycles of violence and hatred in the world. Thurman's doctrine of God then calls humans to cultivate the inner life, develop character, and share the foundational belief in a call to community and harmony. This incarnation of love through the religious encounter (expressed within community) for Thurman then can confront American systems of racial oppression, violence, and dehumanization.

While Thurman's doctrine of God definitely sought to have direct ethical and social implications, some black theological scholars in the 1960s such as James Cone became more unsettled as white (as well as black) theologians often invoked "soft" discussions of love to the exclusion of wider structural and systemic explanations of racial injustice in America. These scholars, called black liberation theologians, constructed an idea of God that directly spoke to issues of structural transformation, particularly racial justice. They fashioned conceptions of God that explicitly prioritized structural transformation and systemic justice, which one might argue somewhat differs from Thurman's prioritization of the religious encounter as necessary for movement toward justice. Because white Christian ideologies and practices undergirded America's oppressive structures and institutions, such scholars questioned the liberative content of a white Christian gospel that did not directly challenge institutional destructive uses of power by elites. Specifically, many black scholars probed what it meant to be black and Christian when white Christianity fueled and buttressed institutional oppression and hegemony for black communities. Black liberation theology became preoccupied with particular questions, which included the following: Can one be black and Christian given Christianity's complicity with institutional racism in America? If white Christianity has been death-dealing for black communities, what is the meaning of the Christian gospel to oppressed black communities? How can black liberation coexist with Christianity, given its diabolic history in white America? These questions hinged upon a particular claim that a new breed of religious scholars within African American theology were asserting, namely that the *God* of Jesus, the God of the Gospels, was a God who liberates the oppressed and "least of these" from structural, social, and interpersonal oppression. Constructing a theological doctrine of God became a critical task for these scholars in cultivating a theology of liberation and holistic well-being for black people.

Theology, Cone argues, is human-talk about God. It is inseparably tied to one's historical and cultural setting and is limited by the language and experience of those espousing it. Hence, quoting Ludwig Feuerbach, Cone accents this dictum: "Theology is anthropology."[7] Accordingly, these "anthropological underpinnings" should be acknowledged by all because what "people think about God cannot be divorced from their place and time in a definite history and culture."[8] Therefore, God-talk is a human enterprise that delineates how communities come to understand God's activity in the world. Because Cone understands scripture as a witness to God's activity, he surveys both the Old and New Testaments, contending that God comes into solidarity with the oppressed or wretched of the earth. God advocates for the poor and weak of society and against those who would exploit them. From the Exodus-Sinai event to the life, death, and resurrection of Jesus, "Yahweh is the God of justice who sides with the weak against the strong."[9] For Cone, the hermeneutical principle of an exegesis of scripture is "the revelation of God in Christ as the Liberator of the oppressed from social oppression and towards political struggle, wherein the poor recognize that their fight against poverty and injustice is not only consistent with the gospel but is the gospel of Jesus Christ."[10] As a result, Cone understands the major motif of scripture to be liberation in which God advocates for the weak and oppressed, which in contemporary terms, means that God unequivocally sides with oppressed black communities. Liberation and a liberating God constitute the meaning of the Christian gospel for Cone.

In foregrounding the God of the Bible as the God of the oppressed, Cone deploys a theological method rooted in the black experience of suffering in America. Blacks are comparatively described as modern-day Jews who endure existential, social, political, and economic suffering in an "American Egyptland." Moreover, Cone points to the soteriological significance of Jesus being black or an oppressed Palestinian Jew of "dark hue." Cone writes:

> His blackness is literal in the sense that he truly becomes One with the oppressed blacks, taking their suffering as his suffering and revealing that he is found in the history of our struggle, the story of our pain.... Christ really enters into our world where the poor, the despised, and the black are, disclosing that he is with them, enduring their humiliation and pain and transforming oppressed selves into liberated servants.[11]

For Cone, it is the suffering of blacks as the "least of these" that makes black experience the correct or "true" source for doing Christian theology in that the biblical witness reveals a primary theological truth: that God liberates the outcast and weak of society.

Because God is with and for the most vulnerable and outcast within society, Cone also contends that God is "black." In a metaphorical sense, God is black because black people have been the present-day "least of these" or the weakest members of society, which means that God comes into solidarity with them. For Cone, God's blackness is ontological in the sense that God reveals Godself through Jesus's "blackness" as a poor Palestinian, Jewish man of color. However, Cone maintains that God's blackness is also symbolic because it grounds what we can say about God's liberating activity in contemporary America for black people who undergo oppression. In an American context, God is irrefutably with and for black people who have been the oppressed, which makes God black or pro-black. In the American context, this is the total meaning of Christian faith for Cone.

Womanist theology challenges the "God" of black liberation theology. While womanism found its initial expressions in black female religious scholars such as Jacquelyn Grant, Katie Cannon, and Delores Williams, Williams specifically critiques the doctrine of God that Cone's black theological discourse constructs. She argues that the God of the biblical texts is not a God who always liberates. When turning to the biblical text that Cone centers as the historical witness of God's liberating activity, Williams notes the contradictions and ambiguities of a "liberating God" within this text. While God seems to offer liberation within certain historical events (such as to the enslaved Hebrews in Exodus), God doesn't offer this same liberation within other narrative moments (such as the story of the non-Hebrew slave Hagar in Genesis).[12] In order to problematize and question black theology's bedrock presupposition on the nature of God as liberating, Williams offers the story of the servant Hagar, who is exploited both by Sarah and Abraham when she bears them a child but is forced into destructive wilderness conditions because of Sarah's insecurities and abuse. Williams points out that God "tells Hagar to go back to her owners, which is not a liberating word."[13] Her outcome is not complete freedom or liberation but survival in that a return to her owners will ensure the continued existence and survival of herself and her son, Ishmael (as she could not have survived in the wilderness).

For Williams, this Hagar narrative deeply unsettles the "liberating God" of black theology. What Cone's black liberation theology does not take into account is a God who offers survival and quality of life because it does not turn to other texts that may not be so liberating. While she primarily argues that the "contemporary Hagars," who are poor black women, are excluded from the liberation motif itself of black male liberation theology, her foundational premise undergirding this claim is that the nature of God as liberating must be questioned and destabilized in order to make possible a fuller view of a "God concept."[14] Williams insists that black liberation theology must re-envision "God" when turning to the biblical text and to poor black women's experiences (who are the contemporary Hagars). Williams critiques Cone's "God of liberation" by offering a womanist doctrinal perspective of a God who may not provide liberation from structural and systemic injustices but does provide survival and quality of life.

Williams believes Cone's doctrine of God, as developed from scripture, is uncritical and even dangerous. Williams turns to numerous other texts within the Bible that support violence against women and genocide against non-Jewish communities, which undercuts interpreting the God of the Bible as essentially liberating. For example, she points to the "conquest narratives" in Joshua and Judges in which God is seen as promoting state-sponsored violence and genocide due to religious and ethnic difference. Moreover, she questions the Christian atonement paradigm of sacrifice and surrogacy in the New Testament in which God is seen as a deity that privileges the human suffering of the innocent (Jesus) in order for redemption to be possible for all.[15] She writes, "There is nothing divine in the blood of the cross. God does not intend black women's surrogacy experience. Neither can Christian faith affirm such an idea. Jesus did not come to be a surrogate. As Christians, black women cannot forget the cross, but neither can they glorify it. To do so is to glorify suffering and to render their exploitation sacred."[16] How can black theology simply overlook these other problematic stories of God's activity, offering no critical assessment of these texts? What kind of critical hermeneutic does black liberation theology offer in relation to these oppressive texts in discussing a notion of God? These are the type of questions that Williams foregrounds.

While Williams's discourse on God remains Christocentric (although with a low Christology contrasted to Cone's high Christology), there are other womanist scholars who seek to offer a concept of God that is less Christocentric and not oriented toward traditional metaphysical notions of God. African American process theologian Monica Coleman critiques and expands womanist concepts of God in this way. In *Making a Way out of No Way: A Womanist Theology*, Coleman argues that much of womanist theological scholarship has focused on explicitly Christian motifs and has accepted without challenge "models of God that are Christocentric and given to classical metaphysical formulations of God," which may be oppressive to black women in particular and people of color in general.[17] For instance, she draws upon Alfred North Whitehead to offer an idea of God in which God is fully involved in temporal processes. God's essential character is one of "becoming" rather than "being," as God is temporal, changing, and affected by the world. This view contrasts with classical forms of theism, which holds God as both substance and Being, which is eternal (nontemporal), immutable, and unaffected by the world.

Within Coleman's process notion of God is the view that God is not omnipotent in the sense of being coercive or unilateral in power. Instead, "God has the power of persuasion rather than coercion," which suggests that God does not have unilateral and absolute control.[18] In fact, because God is changing and affected by the actions of the world, God is "changing," so to speak, over the course of time (although Coleman does implicitly hold abstract ideas of God's wisdom and goodness as eternally solid, as other process theologians have done). For Coleman, the nature of God is a radical departure from Cone's and Williams' idea of God, as her notion of God rejects God as "Being" as well as God's absolute control.[19]

Coleman's view of God also has implications on ideas of "God's will" for humankind. Because self-determination characterizes everything in the universe (not just humans), God does not have control over any series of events or processes. Instead, God influences and "persuades" human existence by offering possibilities for creative transformation. God is this universal free will that is always offering humans possibilities for justice, flourishing, and fulfillment. Therefore, God has a will in everything, but not everything is "God's will."

Coleman's idea of God provides a radical contrast to black liberation theology's doctrine of God, which understands God as "Being" and which locates absolute divine power in a God who "wills" complete liberation over history and in the coming eschaton. Cone's view of God adheres to classical metaphysical formulas, which for Coleman misses the development of creative possibilities in the nature of God as well as God's relationship to the world. Coleman's idea of God may also frustrate Cone's black liberation project, which depends on a God who absolutely wills liberation and definitely sides with the oppressed. Although Coleman would maintain these creative possibilities of God (as offering liberation with oppressed people), she would not foreground this possibility by invoking God's immutability or eternality. For Cone, such a process theological view of God might make the project of black liberation both vulnerable and relative. However, Coleman might maintain that such a view of God could strengthen the project of human liberation, as it honors the evolution and changing nature of the world's processes and foregrounds a God who relates to new emerging possibilities within the historical and material patterns of the world.

Similarly, she also questions womanist notions of God. She asks: When dealing with the religious and existential experiences of women of color, can womanists represent them solely in Christian terms and Christian-influenced classical metaphysical understandings of the divine? In other words, are womanists limiting the transformative potential of womanist theology and ethics when womanists confine their scope to such narrow Christocentric and metaphysical religious paradigms? Coleman maintains that one major problem with womanism's Christocentric paradigm is that it fails to make a distinction between the person of "Jesus" and "God." Because womanists fail to make this distinction, womanist discourse is in danger of making insufficient conceptual moves concerning how the divine influences the world. Womanist thought not only privileges (without virtually any challenge) a Christological idea of God (which confines the revelation of God to Jesus alone) but also implicitly holds that all black women adhere to and can be described within the language and praxis of Christian ontology.[20]

Coleman states that a process womanist theology "does not require belief in the person of Jesus Christ or Christianity in order to explicate a doctrine of God, but is inclusive of various religious traditions and methods of liberation" in which black women participate as equal and fellow proprietors of freedom and justice.[21] She achieves a working example of this inclusion of non-Christian religious schemas in her turn to African traditional religions, emphasizing these religions' ability to adapt to their context and serve as a means of holistic life-sustenance (such as their syncretism of the religious worldviews of the oppressors with their own religious rituals and expressions as displayed in Santeria and other African diasporic religious traditions).[22] Coleman also proposes a Whiteheadian account of spirit possession as found in African religions, which strengthens her postmodern womanist theological project as being religiously plural and multivocal in relation to constructions of God. Coleman argues that womanist discourse impedes its own transformational thrust when it does not account for plurality and mutlivocality within its models of God. Coleman calls for a "postmodern womanist theology" and a postmodern concept of God that walks away from classical metaphysical formulas of God in order to make room for emerging creative possibilities in the nature of God and God's relationship to the world, which holds profound ramifications for the plurality of black women's religious experiences.

While Coleman certainly critiques and expands black and womanist theologies, some black religious scholars find no need to include God at all in black liberation theology and black religion in general. The criticisms of William Jones and Anthony

Pinn not only focus on the inadequate ways in which black theology and womanist discourse interpret God but also question the very existence of God altogether. While Jones primarily responds to the doctrine of God within black liberation theology (God as "black" and "liberating"), Pinn responds to ideas of God within both black and womanist theologies. In different ways Jones and Pinn both offer atheistic humanist concepts of God in which God as a theological symbol is abandoned in favor of a focus on human agency in relation to human transcendence, social justice, and human fulfillment.

In *Is God a White Racist?* Jones inquires about the "definitive event of black liberation" in light of black suffering. He first begins by placing the question of theodicy at the center of all God-talk. Theodicy is not merely about justifying the goodness of God. It is also about exploring the cause(s) and nature of evil. For black liberation theology, evil is the antithesis of God's goodness, particularly evil as seen through racism. However, Jones asks, if God is inclined to unequally privilege one group's suffering over another, couldn't God be charged with divine racism? Such "in group / out group" behavior is sanctioned by God within black theology, "making God merely a member of the in-group."[23] Jones contends that privileging black experience, when marked as it is by a suffering that is not counterbalanced by white suffering, appears to stand in stark contradiction to the claim of God's love and justice for all humankind. This overtly tribal behavior, for Jones, could make God not only racist but also demonic. He concludes, "The concept of God as for the oppressed must be relinquished if this means that the oppressed are the unique object of God's activity."[24]

Faced with this fact of the disproportionate focus on black suffering, ought not black theologians raise the question: Is God a white racist? Moreover, does not raising the issue of a black messiah or black God force the black Christian to ponder whether her own picture of God and Jesus is a tribalized projection of a particular ethnic community? Jones insists that black theology must perform an internal criticism of its claims in order to avoid the logical inconsistencies that result from its theological premises regarding a "black God." Jones ultimately suggests an atheistic humanist concept of God. It is important to note that he does offer a humanocentric theism as a possible solution to theodicy for theists who want to preserve "God" as a theological symbol, arguing that theists might employ a "limiting God" who works through persuasion rather "than a God whose [absolute] goodness is brought into question by human suffering."[25] However, he ultimately sees this kind of preservation as doomed. He finds that the only solution to the theodicy question is to abandon theodicy by way of abandoning theology and its symbols such as "God." If black theology is to be liberating, it must center human agency as the focus of black liberation.

Similar to Jones, Anthony Pinn also questions black theology's foundational premise concerning the necessity of the "God" symbol in ideas of human liberation. He argues that black and womanist theologies' theistic accounts are inadequate because these accounts do not adequately explicate human responsibility in enacting liberation.[26] For Pinn, black and womanist theologies' theistic constructions of God inadequately rely on a notion of redemptive suffering as a way to justify a self-limiting God. Redemptive suffering suggests that God has divine intentions not only within the everyday activities of the world but also within instances of human suffering. Although he excludes Williams from this assessment, as she also rejects redemptive suffering, Pinn maintains that black and womanist theologies treat both God and redemptive suffering as a priori. However, Pinn sees suffering as "unquestionably and unredeemably evil."[27] If God is omnipotent and uses instances of human suffering to express divine intentions, then God is a murderer.[28] For him, where faith in God entails a justification of human suffering, he "would rather lose God than human value."[29] Pinn offers an alternative religious paradigm for liberation discourse: black humanism.

Pinn advocates a position of "strong humanism" within black religion (as an alternative to black theology and its theistic predispositions), which is a nontheistic religion that concerns itself, above all, with the ultimate role of human agency against death-dealing forces.[30] This strong humanism denies the existence of God and maintains that "there is no Being outside the human realm" who is responsible for enacting liberation.[31] Unlike Jones, Pinn does not offer a humanocentric theistic option, as it reinforces the possibility of redemptive suffering and also leads to passivism in relation to social actions of justice (God is seen as the agent of history instead of humans). Pinn finds black theologians' preoccupation with God a distraction from black suffering and alienation, as well as from the conditions under which black liberation is possible.

Jones' and Pinn's atheistic humanist concepts of God question altogether whether the theological symbol of God within black and womanist theologies holds promise. For them, the "God symbol" must die. While their criticisms are uniquely different, they do share a common rejoinder: that the "black God" of black theology remains the problem in exploring human liberation and fulfillment. For them, there is no reason to speak of God at all. These critics charge black theology and womanist thought with not only projecting a tribalized view of God but also maintaining "God" as an unnecessary theological symbol, which ends up undermining the project of human liberation altogether.

Within African American theology, one can see that there is not only contestation over whether doctrines of God should be metaphysical and/or Christocentric but also over whether blacks should speak of God at all. Religious and cultural critic Victor Anderson attempts to reconcile these tensions by offering pragmatic reconstructions of African American theology and its doctrine of God. Anderson rejects Christian doctrines of God that describe religious experience as an encounter with a personal God "who guarantees comprehensive understanding and unity of all of our experiences."[32] But he also rejects atheistic concepts of God that foreclose other possible theistic religious experiences that provide human meaning and value. Instead, he understands religious experience as the "fullness of human life and practices."[33] His pragmatic understanding of religious experience allows him to posit a pragmatic religious concept of God that names and describes the multiple, complex ways we desire to negotiate among the world's finitude, possibility, and transcendence.

Before moving to Anderson's concept of God, we should note that Anderson grounds his argument in the messiness of human realities, which are characterized by grotesqueries and ambiguities within the "unity of experience" (life as beauty and ugliness, intimacy and alienation, etc.). When speaking of the "grotesque," he means that which is found in conflict, disharmony, dichotomies, and dissonance. Since the experience of the grotesque and the ambiguous are constant realities within the unity of human experience, one must be careful not to reduce such aspects to one particular meaning, as such realities can be "read" in multiple ways within the context of varying human experiences. Anderson suggests that black and womanist theologies as well as some black religious scholars have not critically considered the conundrum of the grotesque and the concomitant ambiguity it poses.

For instance, he counters Pinn's argument on redemptive suffering because it reductively holds all suffering as "irredeemably evil." However, Anderson counters that "experience is disclosed by basic irreducible yet complexly integrating structures of physicality, temporality, spaciality [*sic*], sociality, and basic human senses and affectivities," which should leave our "interpretations of African American religious experience open to the widest ranges of our *experiencing* of the world."[34] This openness to the complexity of identities and experiences is then about "resisting interpretations of identities that are oriented towards reductivism and antithetical to ambiguity."[35] Although Anderson (similar to Pinn) would reject metaphysical concepts of God, he nevertheless remains open to the multiple ways in which people "name" and religiously experience "God" within grotesque and ambiguous realities in order to make meaning and value within the unity of experience.

Against this backdrop, Anderson sees "God" as our naming of the ways in which we as humans are able to transcend our finitude in order to be truly human as well as make meaning within tragic, temporal circumstances. Anderson understands God to be the "structure that sustains and promotes the maximization of value, that increases, enlarges, and progressively integrates human good."[36] In other words, Anderson maintains that the maximization of value and enlargement of human good can be named God but need not be named God. Rather, our naming this maximization and enlargement as "God" can give ultimate meaning and worth to the whole of human experience for individuals.[37] For Anderson, his idea of God is then pragmatic in that he supports diverse notions of God that enlarge and maximize ultimate meaning and the human good. Anderson's idea of ultimate meaning and the human good can be ascertained within the context of creative exchange. For him, creative exchange primarily involves expanding the valuing consciousness of each person, widening and deepening mutual support between individuals and peoples, and developing the unique individuality of each person.[38] For Anderson, creative exchange is then the ultimate human commitment because creative exchange is the ultimate source of community and human good. Anderson sees any pragmatic concept of God as needing to promote this ultimate value and human good that creative exchange makes possible.

Enabling spaces for the "God" symbol within the context of creative exchange could expand and enlarge human capacities for moral sympathy. If creative exchange is the way leading to the greatest good to be attained by humankind, then it "makes possible disagreement and diversity without hate or fear, without retaliation or estrangement."[39] This context of creative exchange makes room for diverse ways of meaning making, such as theistic beliefs that include the idea of God. Anderson's hope is for creative exchange to lead toward "Beloved Community," and to subsequently explore the ethical implications of how we interpret the divine. Construing God in tribalized, sectarian ways leads to division. However, understanding God as the highest value and ultimate good actualized within human community leads to love, peace, and the collective good. Through creative exchange, Anderson seeks to demonstrate that concepts of God possess ethical implications in terms of the ways in which individuals relate to each other as well as how communities treat each person.

It remains to be seen how well Anderson has held in tension the concerns of both theistic and nontheistic African American theological discourses on God. Indeed, there continues to be contestation over the doctrine of God within African American theology. However, one may be certain that African American theology and its doctrines of God hold promise in the twenty-first century if these perspectives remain open to plurality, multivocality, and difference.

Notes

1. For a broader discussion on Christian personalism, see Rufus Burrow's *Personalism: A Critical Introduction* (St. Louis: Chalice Press, 1999). Burrow delineates the contours of African American Christian personalism as expressed by Martin Luther King Jr., John Welsey Edward Bowen, and J. Deotis Roberts. He also discusses the implications of Christian personalism for doctrines of God as well as ethics.
2. Howard Thurman, *The Creative Encounter* (New York: Harper and Brothers, 1954), 20.
3. Thurman, *The Creative Encounter*, 20.
4. Howard Thurman, *The Inward Journey* (Richmond, IN: Friend United Press, 1961), 15.
5. Howard Thurman, "Mysticism and the Experience of Love," in *For the Inward Journey*, ed. Anne Spencer Thurman (New York: Harcourt Brace Jovanovich, 1984), 13. Thurman also substantively expounds on this love ethics and its impact on interpersonal relationships in *Jesus and the Disinherited* (Boston: Beacon Press, 1976), *The Creative Encounter, and The Search for Common Ground* (New York: Harper and Row, 1971).
6. Thurman, "Mysticism and the Experience of Love," 14.
7. James Cone, *God of the Oppressed* (Maryknoll, NY: Orbis Books, 1975), 37.
8. Cone, *God of the Oppressed*, 37.
9. Cone, *God of the Oppressed*, 63.
10. Cone, *God of the Oppressed*, 75.
11. Cone, *God of the Oppressed*, 125–26.

12. Delores Williams, *Sisters in the Wilderness* (Maryknoll, NY: Orbis Books, 1993), 24.
13. Williams, *Sisters in the Wilderness*, 24.
14. Williams, *Sisters in the Wilderness*, 24.
15. Williams, *Sisters in the Wilderness*, 143–50.
16. Williams, *Sisters in the Wilderness*, 167.
17. Monica Coleman, *Making A Way out of No Way: A Womanist Theology* (Minneapolis: Fortress Press, 2008), 6.
18. Coleman, *Making a Way*, xxx.
19. Coleman, *Making a Way.*
20. Coleman, *Making a Way Out of No Way*, 16.
21. Coleman, *Making a Way*, 45.
22. Coleman offers a rich description of the role of African ancestors in a process theological framework of salvation. She also explores spirit possession within African religions and how it enriches soteriological religious concepts.
23. William Jones, *Is God a White Racist?* (Boston: Beacon Press, 1973), 4.
24. Jones, *Is God a White Racist?* 201.
25. Jones, *Is God a White Racist?*
26. Anthony Pinn, *Why Lord? Suffering and Evil in Black Theology* (New York: Continuum, 1995), 17–18.
27. Pinn, *Why Lord?* 89.
28. Pinn, *Why Lord?*
29. Pinn, *Why Lord?* 142.
30. Pinn, *Why Lord?*, 148.
31. Pinn, *Why Lord?* 141.
32. Victor Anderson, *Creative Exchange: A Constructive Theology of African-American Religious Experience* (Minneapolis: Fortress Press, 2008), 17. Anderson also offers a pragmatic theological account in *Pragmatic Theology: Negotiating the Intersections of an American Philosophy of Religion and Public Theology* (Albany: State University of New York Press, 1998).
33. Anderson, *Creative Exchange.*
34. Anderson, *Creative Exchange*, 6.
35. Anderson, *Creative Exchange.*
36. Anderson, *Creative Exchange.*
37. Anderson, *Creative Exchange*, 132.
38. Anderson, *Creative Exchange*, 17.
39. Anderson, *Creative Exchange*, 18.

Selected Texts

Anderson, Victor. *Creative Exchange: A Constructive Theology of African-American Religious Experience*. Minneapolis: Fortress Press, 2008.
Burrow, Rufus. *Personalism: A Critical Introduction*. St. Louis: Chalice Press, 1999.
Coleman, Monica. *Making A Way out of No Way: A Womanist Theology*. Minneapolis: Fortress Press, 2008.
Cone, James H. *God of the Oppressed*. Maryknoll, NY: Orbis Books, 1975.
Jones, William. *Is God a White Racist?* Boston: Beacon Press, 1973.

Pinn, Anthony. *Why Lord? Suffering and Evil in Black Theology*. New York: Continuum, 1995.
Roberts, J. Deotis. *Liberation and Reconciliation: A Black Theology*. Philadelphia: Westminst er, 1971.
Thurman, Howard. *The Creative Encounter*. New York: Harper and Brothers, 1954.
Thurman, Howard. "Mysticism and the Experience of Love." In *For the Inward Journey*, ed. Anne Spencer Thurman. New York: Harcourt Brace Jovanovich Publishers, 1984, 189–98.
Williams, Delores. *Sisters in the Wilderness*. Maryknoll, NY: Orbis Books, 1993.

CHAPTER 10

CHRISTOLOGY IN AFRICAN AMERICAN THEOLOGY

DIANA L. HAYES

"BUT who do you say that I am?" (Mk 8:29). This question, asked of the disciples by Jesus himself, has echoed down through the centuries as the followers of Christ, those who believe he is God become human, have attempted to understand the significance of his life, death, and resurrection. For all Christians, the answer has been both complex and simple. Christology seeks to answer the question, "Who—according to faith—*is* Jesus, and what does it mean to name him the Christ?" The classical understanding is that of the Councils of Nicaea (325 CE) and Chalcedon (451 CE), which affirm that Jesus is the Christ, the Anointed one of God, and is both fully human and fully divine, two persons in one being, who, because of both his humanity and divinity, was able to effect salvation for all of humankind.

Through the centuries, there has been ongoing discussion and debate on the question that Peter answered so simply and succinctly: "You are the Christ" (Mk 8:29). Historically, the Christological question, "Who is this God-man Jesus the Christ?" has always been connected with the soteriological question, "What is the significance of his life, death and resurrection for humanity?" In today's Christological debates, the role of context and particularity has emerged. Traditional Western Christologies emphasized the *person* rather than the *presence* of Jesus, concentrating on how human or how divine Jesus was and emphasizing Jesus's incarnation at the expense of his incarnate Being.[1] Jesus's question is contextual and relational not abstract; it is grounded in the reality of the life and faith of the person(s) *doing* that theology. Changing times require different confessions, and each culture must rediscover Jesus for itself: "Christians have both the freedom and the obligation to confess Christ in appropriate and relevant ways in their specific context that are in continuity with the witness of the Bible and their particular experiences, needs, and hopes."[2]

All theology is contextual, emerging from the particular situations of particular peoples throughout their history. Historically, the history of African and other persons of color has been suppressed. Persons of African descent first encountered the Gospel of Jesus Christ in the first century but not until their mass forced migration to the Americas (sixteenth century) do we begin to see the emergence of a Christology that categorically conflicts with that of traditional Western Christologies. The universal theology, once mandated for all, has been revealed as equally contextual, the creation of European and Euro-American men who have made God, Jesus, and the Church into their own image and likeness. Doing so supported their interpretation of the world as one in which God condones the oppression of others, especially persons of color, and white supremacy.

However, enslaved Africans brought with them a rich and intimate religious worldview in which they actively participated, one that intimately connected them with all things and made of them a community. They initially refused to accept the teachings of Christianity especially as presented to them. Over time, they penetrated the lies and distortions being taught them and recognized the truth of the Gospel message, that God was on their side and had sent Jesus as their liberator. The encounter of the enslaved Africans with Christianity in the United States introduced a hermeneutic of suspicion that exposed the fallacy of pro-slavery readings of the gospel.

Those enslaved in the United States realized that they could not trust what they were being told by white Christians about their status or the meaning or significance of Jesus Christ for them. They developed a hermeneutic of suspicion, a way of looking at and interpreting the world around them and its alleged truths with eyes that were open to and critical of the hypocrisy of the slave owners. They wondered who this man Jesus was and why their owners were so eager to either have them believe in him or remain ignorant of him. Their growing understanding and interpretation led them to believe in a God-man radically different from that presented to them by slave masters. They knew the latter did nothing that did not benefit them regardless of its impact on those enslaved. Instead the enslaved recognized in Jesus not someone who condoned their servitude and mistreatment but one who recognized their humanity and suffered with them in their oppression. Jesus was not the great pacifier but a liberator who would in time set them free. They also applied this hermeneutic or critical interpretation to Sacred Scripture, speaking of a God who set captives free, again a very different interpretation than that of most white Christians.[3]

The Christology of the slaves was simple but profound. White Christians interpreted Christianity as God's ordination of the slaves' inferior and less than human status. The slaves rejected this understanding for one that lifted them out of the morass of slavery and dehumanization and named them as human beings, created in God's own image and likeness and therefore worthy of the respect and dignity accorded all of God's creation. They heard in Scripture of a God of freedom, one whose total identity and activity was with the poor and powerless rather than the wealthy and powerful. They discovered a God who set an enslaved people, like themselves, free and carried them to a new land where he became their God and they became his people. They believed in a God who so loved the poor and oppressed that he became one with them, a human being born into the world of the poor, condemned to death simply because of who he was, who died for their freedom. They heard and believed.

An uneducated people of the fields and kitchens, their experience of this liberating God and his compassionate love for them was more than they could fully comprehend initially. They recognized that they were being addressed by an Other and rejoiced even while not fully understanding. They had a theology, a Christology, without knowing it.[4]

Those enslaved developed an understanding of a warrior God who fought on their side, recognizing the injustice of their enslavement and dehumanization. That God sent his Son as the sign of God's expression of solidarity with the black oppressed. As a result of their encounter with God, a God both loving yet stern, they experienced a liberator, Jesus the Christ who promised to set them free. They articulated this understanding not in theological works but in song, story, prayers, and sermons, especially the spirituals, articulating a Christology and a liberating theology that healed and affirmed and encouraged their efforts to be free.[5]

Edward Blum and Paul Harvey note: "In a brilliant shift, African Americans took the Jesus presented to them (a servant of servants), attached it to themselves as servants who suffer, and then focused on how Jesus triumphed over both suffering and servitude. The suffering Jesus became their analogue and invested them (not the whites around them) with sacred value.... Jesus was their friend, mentor, guide, king, master and liberator."[6] This understanding sustained those enslaved through two hundred years and more of slavery, and was expressed in their preaching, their prayer, and in their music. Grounded in the people and events of the Bible, the spirituals were Christological statements in miniature that spoke of their longing for freedom and their belief that it would soon come from Jesus the Liberator. They "better than anything else reveal to us the spirituality of the slaves, their self-understanding, their understanding of God, their belief in Jesus, and their hope in the action of the Holy Spirit to help them stay in the race until freedom comes."[7] One song in particular, "A Balm in Gilead," reveals how those enslaved took the Old Testament question of Isaiah, "Is there no balm in Gilead?" and answered with a resounding "Yes! there is a balm in Gilead." The spirituals were not compensatory, as many believed, but revolutionary in their imagery and thought. They were subversive in nature. As the slaves sang "Steal Away, Steal Away to Jesus," they "stole away" off plantations to freedom in the North and Canada; as they sang "Swing Low Sweet Chariot," they were plotting their escapes with forged passes via trains and wagons. They sang of freedom ("Oh, Freedom"), of alienation ("Sometimes I Feel Like a Motherless Child"), and of a conquering hero, Jesus ("Ride on, King Jesus!"). They believed in and sang, prayed, and preached about a wonder-working God who made "a way out of no way" for them and all who were oppressed in this world but not in the next.[8]

That understanding was challenged, however, as their freedom, finally in reach, was snatched away by the manipulations of their former owners. Reduced to a feudal peonage little different from slavery after Reconstruction ended, blacks questioned the role of Jesus in their lives often resulting in a Christology of complacency and passivity in which many turned to an "otherworldly" perspective that counseled patience and passivity. Jesus still promised freedom, but "in glory" not in the present-day world.

Not all African Americans accepted this "pie in the sky when you die" theology but continued to speak and preach of a God active in their lives. One of the leading proponents of a radicalized Christology was Bishop Henry McNeal Turner of the AME church, who proclaimed in 1898 that "God was a Negro."[9] Turner, like W. E. B. Du Bois, believed African Americans should continue to fight against the restrictions and limitations placed on their humanity, and to do so grounded in their faith in a wonder-working God, a Jesus who was on their side, and was truly a black Messiah. He denounced their accepting a "white-skinned, blue-eyed, straight-haired, projecting-nosed, compressed-lipped and finely-robed *white* gentleman" as their God as a betrayal of their ancestors.[10] Turner urged that God has to be black because of his solidarity with the "least" among us, who, in the United States, were black. Similarly, Du Bois spoke of Jesus as black, noting that he was a "Syrian Jew" who was born and lived in an area where Asians and Africans intermingled. He saw the black Christ as critical for the self-affirmation of African Americans so that they might counter the oppression based in a racist white Christianity that continued to plague their lives. Du Bois wrote of a "black Christ (who) embodied virtue in a nation mad with sin and malevolence."[11] Du Bois's black Jesus had a black father (God) who affirmed the humanity of all oppressed, male and female. These understandings of Jesus, both passive and radical, coexisted in post-Reconstruction black churches and communities.[12]

Others also spoke of and preached a black Christ, including Marcus Garvey, who formed the Universal Negro Improvement Association in the early twentieth century in an effort to reconnect blacks with their African roots. Garvey sought "to divest Christ of his whiteness and comprehend the sacred through the eyes of black women and men."[13] At the same time, poets and writers of the Harlem Renaissance also sought to imagine a black Christ, as Countee Cullen stated: "Wishing He I served were black."[14] Yet most black Christians still professed and worshipped the holy in the image of a Nordic-appearing, blond-haired and blue-eyed white man.

In the aftermath of World War II and the massive migration of blacks, African Americans sought to take control of their own lives. Exposed to greater freedoms, economic, social, and political, in the North and West, they once again began to question their faith and its relevancy in the world of opportunity opening before them. They began to revitalize their faith in ways that reached back to their African ancestry while recontextualizing that faith in the modern era of promise and possibility. Reverend Howard Thurman began to articulate the critical questions confronting black Christians at this time, raising the question of the meaning of Christ and therefore of Christianity in a troubled world. Why, he asked, does it seem that Christianity is impotent to deal with "issues of discrimination and injustice on the bases of race, religion, and national origin?"[15] Thurman responded by noting that Jesus was a Jew, someone with a specific racial, ethnic, and religious identity; he was a poor Jew, a status that placed him in solidarity with the poor of his time and of our time today; and, lastly, he was a member of an oppressed minority. All of these factors shaped Jesus and thus shaped his religion as a "direct response to the concrete sufferings of the oppressed."[16] Thus, for Thurman, Jesus is the one who sets free those oppressed and marginalized by the powers that be of their time. He mediates the way to the kingdom of God, and he liberates those who believe in him.

Martin Luther King Jr. was another who saw Christianity and, therefore, Jesus Christ as radically present in the struggle for the civil rights of African Americans. King, a Baptist minister, was impacted by a number of influences, including the theo-ethics of Reinhold Niebuhr, the nonviolent teachings of Gandhi, and the religious and spiritual traditions of the African American church. Out of these, he forged a theology of Christian nonviolent disobedience that reradicalized the black community and the black church and, in so doing, profoundly changed the United States. King, a deeply spiritual man, believed that Jesus, the Son of God, was in solidarity with those historically oppressed and downtrodden. In the United States that meant black Americans who were confronted with racism everywhere. God was a God of the poor and meek who empowered them to fight their own battle of liberation guided by Jesus the Liberator. King rekindled black America's faith in a God who walked and talked with them and sent his Son on their behalf to guide them into the new Kingdom of God, the beloved community where all of humanity lived, worked, and played in harmony one with another.

It is in the clash between the theology of the civil rights movement and the political/sociological critique of the Black Power movement that a fully articulated black Christology emerges as part of a slowly developing black theology of liberation. Several persons were critical in this evolution including the Reverends James H. Cone, Gayraud Wilmore, Albert Cleage, and J. Deotis Roberts. As they sought to reconcile the call for political and economic empowerment of the black community that was at the heart of the call for Black Power with the teachings of Christianity, they found it necessary once again to answer the question regarding Jesus's being and salvific purpose in radically different ways: "Who is Jesus for African Americans today? Is God truly on the side of the oppressed or is he simply a white racist, siding with those who have historically oppressed blacks? What is the significance of Jesus' life, death and resurrection for African Americans? Can African Americans remain Christians in light of their ongoing situation of racist oppression or is Christianity simply a religion of whites?" For most, the response to these questions affirmed the liberative role of Jesus in their lives. Each had a different contextual perspective, which emerged as two Christological strands. The first is sociopolitical, focused on Jesus as the Messiah, the

Son of Humankind and thus the Liberator of oppressed humanity, while the second is spiritual/cultural and emphasized the understanding of Jesus as the Christ (the Son of God), Mediator between the forces of sin and evil and the forces of good.

Cone, a Methodist from the small town of Bearden, Arkansas, articulates the meaning of Jesus Christ as Liberator. Questioning the absence of the historical and religious experience of blacks in his theological studies, he sought to understand and articulate Jesus's significance for blacks. Cone argues that Jesus is the black Christ. Christ's blackness refers to both his own victimization and his victory. Blackness is the bridge between the historical first-century Jesus, and the Christ proclaimed by the faithful. The blackness of Jesus for Cone is a "comprehensive theological truth."[17] Jesus and, therefore, God are black because only as black are they in full solidarity with those who, in the United States especially, have historically been oppressed simply because they are black. As a black man, Christ "really enters into our world where the poor, the despised, and the black are, disclosing that he is with them, enduring their humiliation and pain and transforming oppressed slaves into liberated servants."[18] Jesus is ontologically black because blackness is a manifestation of God's being, revealing that neither divinity nor humanity resides in white definitions but in liberation from black captivity. In later writings as he interacted with liberation theologians from other cultural contexts and womanist theologians in the black community, Cone's understanding of Jesus's role as liberator expanded to encompass all who were oppressed because of their race, gender, class, or sexual orientation. Most recently, Cone has discussed the relevance of Jesus Christ for blacks and all who are oppressed in light of the cross and the lynching tree, connecting both to a shared experience of blacks and Jesus as humans wrongly tortured and killed.[19]

Gayraud Wilmore's understanding of Jesus is deeply grounded in the African American historical and cultural experience. Sacred Scripture, he argues, has to be contextualized and reclaimed by persons of color in order to transcend and transform the color bias inherent historically in Christianity. For Wilmore, the blackness of Jesus as the black Messiah invests blackness with religious meaning that reveals the reality of black suffering in the historical experience of black people in a racist society.[20] "The black Messiah is both a concrete incarnation of God among people of color who cannot be understood apart from their experience, and a comprehensive symbol of the divine presence whose revelatory power is available to all."[21] The black Messiah critiques the racism of biblical religion and of the political order.

J. Deotis Roberts emphasizes Jesus as Mediator whose blackness is symbolic, not ontological. His discussion of the relationship between the black Messiah and the Christ of faith reveals the former as a mythical construct necessary to counteract the negativity associated with blackness. The black Messiah is particular in light of the universal Christ of Scripture, serving as a frame of reference through which blacks can comprehend the teachings of Christianity. The black Messiah delivers a kind of psycho-cultural and experiential liberation whose ultimate goal is the reconciliation of all believers in the kingdom of Christ, which is spiritual rather than political.

Albert Cleage espoused the most radical Christology, arguing that Jesus is not simply ontologically or symbolically black, he is truly physically black, a black Jew who lived in a black nation (Israel) and who fought the status quo of Roman imperialism. Jesus "came to free a black people from the oppression of the white Gentiles."[22] Cleage founded the Shrine of the Black Madonna and Cultural Centers (Detroit, MI), which articulated the belief that Jesus was born of a black woman, was black physically, and was directly engaged in liberative action on the side of the black oppressed in the form of black nationalism.

Despite their emphasis on the black community and its needs and concerns, a glaring absence existed in the early work of these male theologians. None raised or discussed in any way the role of black women. The absence of women's voices became even more obvious as the women's movement began to expand in the 1970s and 1980s and women, of all races and ethnicities, began to enter seminaries and theologates. Just as the civil rights and Black Power movements catalyzed and mirrored the myriad liberation movements of colonized and subjected persons throughout the globe, women began to raise questions of their own position in the church.

"Who is Jesus Christ for the African American woman? How does Jesus address the plight of the marginalized and oppressed of society? Is Jesus's maleness relevant or irrelevant to his salvific purpose?" Womanist theologians have, in the last twenty-five years, sought to answer these questions from within their own historical experience. Theirs, like black theology, is a theology of, by, and for black women, one that speaks their faith into life.

The question of Jesus's role in the lives of black women has been a concern for them for decades if not centuries. Black women were not strangers to Jesus, whom they saw as brother and sister, mother and father, and beloved child, one who suffered with them in their triple oppression of race, class, and gender. Slave narratives reveal the grounding of African American women in their faith. Harriet Tubman and Sojourner Truth speak with love and pride of their relationship with the Son of God. For Sojourner, "How I found Jesus" was the only text she used to challenge the men and women of her time when they questioned her right to speak out on abolition of slavery and the rights of women. Black women were actively involved in ministry in their churches and communities, recognized and unrecognized, and saw Jesus as a model for their own lives of courage and resistance.[23]

In the 1980s with the publication of Alice Walker's *In Search of our Mother's Gardens*,[24] womanist theology emerged as the theological expression of African American Christian women who excavated the lives and experiences of black women, a hitherto unexplored source, as the foundation for their theologizing. Jacquelyn Grant, Delores Williams, and Kelly Brown Douglas were among the first to articulate a womanist Christology.

As with black male theologians, the "social context for Black Christology is the black experience of oppression and the struggle against it."[25] For black women, this means recognizing their triple (and quadruple) jeopardy as women, women of color, and women historically on the lowest rung of the economic ladder (a fourth, that of sexual orientation was not initially acknowledged even by womanists). Grant goes beyond white feminism's overriding concern with gender to acknowledge the harmful multiplicative impact of these forms of oppression for not just black women but the entire black community. Black women have always seen Jesus as one with them, the divine co-sufferer who empowers and saves blacks in situations of oppression. They ground this understanding in God's direct revelation to them as black women, as revealed and witnessed to in Sacred Scripture and in their historical experience. God/Jesus is Creator, Sustainer of life, Comforter, and Liberator, recognizing and affirming that the persons of the Trinity act interchangeably to aid and abet them in their struggle for survival and liberation. The significance of Jesus lies, therefore, not in his maleness but in his humanity. God becomes concrete not only in the man Jesus, for he was crucified, but in the lives of those who will accept the challenges of the risen Savior—the Christ.[26]

Kelly Brown Douglas provides a rich historical tracing of black Christology through slavery and the black church while questioning the absence of women's voices and experience in that theological expression. She presents both a sociopolitical and religio-cultural analysis that confronts racism, classism, sexism, and heterosexism while also lifting up aspects of black life that sustain and nurture survival and liberation. She asserts a "spirituality of resistance" resident in the lives of black women that empowered their survival and disavows the significance of Jesus's maleness for black theology, emphasizing instead the multidimensional aspect of women's oppression and the need to focus on survival and liberation for all in the black community. Christ is "sustainer, liberator, and prophet" in the face of the hegemonic oppressions confronting black women. For both Douglas and Grant, Christ, when acting on the side of the oppressed, is a "black woman."[27]

Delores Williams brings a radically different approach to black Christology, as she emphasizes that liberation is not the most critical aspect of Christ's message, survival is. What value does liberation have for a destroyed people? Her Christology is rooted in the wilderness experience of black women, who, she argues, have been instrumental in providing for the survival of the community yet have historically received little recognition for this. This wilderness experience can be traced in the story of Hagar, who was abused and cast out with her child, the son of her master, by her mistress as many slave women were. Hagar not only survived but communicated with God in her own right, and became the leader of a people, the Hagarites, from whom the Arabic peoples trace their ancestry. Williams also addresses the theory of atonement, a cornerstone of traditional Western Christology, subverting it by asking how Jesus's death on a cross could be salvific for the poor and oppressed, historically women of color, who have like Jesus been surrogates for the suffering of others. While Jesus took on his surrogacy willingly, that of black women was involuntary, forced on them by a society that did not recognize their humanity. Jesus's significance lies not in his death but his life of ministry to the poor and oppressed.

New generations of black and womanist theologians continue to respond to the question of who Jesus is for twenty-first-century African Americans. The voices of gay/lesbian/transgendered/queer African Americans are being integrated into both theologies, challenging male and heterosexual limitations historically placed on them. JoAnne Terrell critiques early womanists for their lack of inclusivity while affirming "the cross is about God's love for humankind." Those who suffer can be redeemed because of God's "with-us-ness," which means we are "already-at-one" with God.[28]

As black Catholics begin to challenge their church on a number of levels, M. Shawn Copeland has raised the question of Jesus's meaning in terms of discipleship. Discipleship serves as a starting point from which to understand Jesus of Nazareth as the "absolute meaning" of life for the world.[29] The cross thus functions epistemologically as it deepens a mystic-political consciousness of Jesus the Christ, who calls forth praxis of resistance and solidarity with the poor and oppressed. Love for Christ leads to praxis of compassionate solidarity with those in need.[30]

The issue of class oppression is becoming more of an issue as all of America is divided based on economic rather than strictly racial or gender status, with a growing underclass. Where is Christ today? If Jesus is poor with the poor, what does that mean for increasingly affluent black Christians? One response has been the emergence in the 1980s of a theology of prosperity, one that promotes material success as a sign of God's affirmation much as the Puritans saw themselves as the Elect. This is a radical shift from the Christology of black and womanist theologians, who continue to affirm Jesus as one in solidarity with the poor, marginalized, and oppressed. This theology denies the Jesus of faith proclaimed by black Christians since their first encounter with Christianity. It is a resurgence of the deradicalized black church of post-Reconstruction that sought individual gain over community survival and liberation. If this is so, what new understanding of radical Christology will emerge to counter it? Already African American male and female theologians are hard at work developing challenges to this new ideology while exploring and articulating the ongoing significance of Jesus the Christ for the black community in the United States and worldwide.[31]

Notes

1. A. Elaine Crawford, "Womanist Christology: Where Have We Come From and Where Are We Going?" *Review and Expositor* 95 (Summer 1998): 370.
2. Daniel Migliore, *Faith Seeking Understanding* (Grand Rapids, MI: Eerdmans, 1991), 143–45.
3. See chapter 2 of Diana L. Hayes, *Forged in the Fiery Furnace: African American Spirituality* (Maryknoll, NY: Orbis Books, 2012), 29–48.
4. Harold Carter notes that for African Americans, the three persons of the Trinity are interchangeable, according to need. In prayer, song, and music, they praised the Creator God

who sent his Son as Liberator to free them and the Spirit to guide and sustain them. See *The Prayer Tradition of Black People* (Valley Forge, PA: Judson Press, 1976), 50.

5. See Diana L. Hayes, *And Still We Rise: An Introduction to Black Liberation Theology* (New York: Paulist Press, 1995).
6. Edward J. Blum and Paul Harvey, *The Color of Christ: The Son of God and the Saga of Race in America* (Chapel Hill: University of North Carolina Press, 2012), 95.
7. Hayes, *Forged*, 71.
8. See Hayes, *Forged*, chapter 4, 69–88, and James H. Cone, *The Spirituals and the Blues* (Maryknoll, NY: Orbis Books, 1992).
9. In Martha Thomas and Frank A. Thomas, *Preaching with Sacred Fire: An Anthology of African American Sermons, 1750 to the Present* (New York: Norton, 2010), 347.
10. Thomas and Thomas, *Preaching with Sacred Fire*, 347.
11. Cited in Edward J. Blum, "'There Won't Be Any Rich People in Heaven': The Black Christ, White Hypocrisy, and the Gospel According to W. E. B. DuBois," *Journal of African American History* 90, no. 4 (Fall 2005): 372.
12. See Hayes, *Forged*, chapter 5, 89–109.
13. Blum and Harvey, *The Color Of Christ*, 161.
14. Hayes, *Forged*, 10, and Blum and Harvey, *The Color of Christ*, 196.
15. Howard Thurman, *Jesus and the Disinherited* (New York: Abingdon Press, 1949), 13.
16. James Evans, *We Have Been Believers* (Minneapolis: Fortress Press, 1992), 83–84.
17. Evans, *We Have Been Believers*, 89.
18. James H. Cone, *God of the Oppressed* (New York: Seabury Press, 1975), 136.
19. James H. Cone, *The Cross and the Lynching Tree* (Maryknoll, NY: Orbis Books, 2012).
20. Evans, *We Have Been Believers*, 91.
21. Evans, *We Have Been Believers*, 92.
22. Albert Cleage Jr. *The Black Messiah* (New York: Sheed and Ward, 1968), 111.
23. See Bettye Collier-Thomas, *Jesus, Jobs, and Justice: African American Women and Religion* (New York: Knopf, 2010).
24. Alice Walker, *In Search of Our Mother's Gardens* (San Diego, CA: Harcourt Brace Jovanovich, 1983).
25. Jacqueline Grant, "Subjectification as a Requirement for Christological Construction," in *Lift Every Voice: Constructing Christian Theologies from the Underside*, ed. Susan Brooks Thistlethwaite and Mary Potter Engel (Maryknoll, NY: Orbis Books, 2000), 210.
26. Thistlethwaite and Engel, *Lift Every Voice*, see 214–15.
27. Kelly Brown Douglas, *The Black Christ* (Maryknoll, NY: Orbis Books, 1994), 109–10; and Jacquelyn Grant, *White Women's Christ, Black Women's Jesus* (Atlanta: Scholars Press, 1989), 220.
28. JoAnne Marie Terrell, *Power in the Blood?* (Maryknoll, NY: Orbis Books, 1998), 124–25.
29. M. Shawn Copeland, "The Cross of Christ and Discipleship," in *Thinking of Christ: Proclamation, Explanation, Meaning*, ed. Tatha Wiley (New York: Continuum, 2003), 178.
30. Copeland, "Cross of Christ."
31. See George Yancey, *Christology and Whiteness: What Would Jesus Do?* (New York: Routledge, 2012).

Selected Texts

Cleage, Albert. *The Black Messiah*. Trenton, NJ: Africa World Press, 1989.

Cone, James H. *A Black Theology of Liberation*. Maryknoll, NY: Orbis Books, 2010.

Cone, James H. *Black Theology and Black Power*. Maryknoll, NY: Orbis Books, 1997.

Cone, James H. *God of the Oppressed*. Maryknoll, NY: Orbis Books, 1997.

Douglas, Kelly Brown. *The Black Christ*. Maryknoll, NY: Orbis Books, 1993

Evans, James H. *We Have Been Believers*. Minneapolis: Augsburg Fortress, 1993.

Grant, Jacqueline. *White Women's Christ and Black Women's Jesus*. Atlanta: Scholars Press, 1989.

Jones, William R. *Is God a White Racist?* Boston: Beacon Press, 1997.

Roberts, J. Deotis. *Liberation and Reconciliation*. Louisville, KY: Westminster John Knox, 2005.

Terrell, JoAnne Marie. "Our Mother's Gardens: Rethinking Sacrifice." In *Cross Examinations: Readings on the Meaning of the Cross Today*, ed. Marit Trelstad, 33–49. Minneapolis: Augsburg Fortress, 2006.

Terrell, JoAnne Marie. *Power in the Blood? The Cross in African American Experience*. Eugene, OR: Wipf and Stock, 2005.

Thurman, Howard. *Jesus and the Disinherited*. Boston: Beacon Press, 1996.

Williams, Delores. *Sisters in the Wilderness*. Maryknoll, NY: Orbis Books, 1995.

Wilmore, Gayraud. *Black Religion and Black Radicalism*. Maryknoll, NY: Orbis Books, 1998.

CHAPTER 11

THE HOLY SPIRIT IN AFRICAN AMERICAN THEOLOGY

JAMES H. EVANS JR.

The purpose of this essay is to engage in an analysis and constructive discussion of the essential features of Christian discourse on the Holy Spirit in African American theology, particularly in the form of black theology.

Historical Context

Discourse about the Holy Spirit in Christian theology is often referred to as pneumatology. This word connotes the idea of breathe or wind and, as such, captures the core of Christian belief about the Holy Spirit. Biblically, the Holy Spirit is associated with the breath of God, the wind. It is associated with freedom and a kind of unpredictability. In John 20:22 Jesus breathes on the disciples and they receive the Holy Spirit. In 2 Corinthians 3:17 we are told that where the Spirit of the Lord is, there also is freedom. While it is not as explicit in the Old Testament as it is in the New Testament, the Spirit of God is cited in Genesis as the creative presence of God (Genesis 1:2). The Holy Spirit is central to the identity and mission of Jesus as described in the Gospels. It is present in the form of a dove at Jesus's baptism, and elsewhere in the Gospels the

Holy Spirit is intricately connected with Jesus's embrace of his salvific mission. This tradition is carried through into the Pauline writings.[1]

In the subsequent theology of the Christian tradition the role of the Holy Spirit is critical in its development. While the Bible does not articulate a full-blown doctrine of the Holy Spirit—indeed, it does not articulate any doctrine in a full-blown, systematic manner—it does suggest, in its stories, poetry, law, legend, letters, and life stories, important aspects of the work of the Spirit among the people of God. Indeed, one could say that the manifestation of the holy among humans cannot be fully or adequately understood without attention to the role of the Spirit. The conversion of the Samaritans as recounted in Acts 8:14–17 is not held as valid among the leaders of the Jerusalem church until it is verified that they have received the Holy Spirit. It is the confirmation of the presence of the Holy Spirit among them that finally verifies that they are no longer strangers but co-heirs in the newly given covenant that exists among the believers in the Risen Christ.

In Christian traditional faith claims, the Holy Spirit is understood to be a part of the Trinitarian expression of God. The Holy Spirit is the third of the three persons of God. However, the third person is actually a person in a different way than either the first or the second person. Augustine recognized this in his classic text, *De Trinitate*,[2] as did others, like Karl Barth.[3] In the first person it is the spiritual presence (God) that of its own being (love) is drawn, compelled (in freedom) to express itself to another in life-giving and life-affirming spiritual power in the Incarnation. In the second person it is the spiritual power, present in the flesh of Jesus the Christ, that, in recognition of itself as the Son of Man, or the human one, and in obedience to another as the Son of God, or the divine one (Son of God and Son of Man), is allowed (in freedom) and compelled by love, to claim its place in this world and in the world to come. At the heart of both the presence and the power is the purpose. The Holy Spirit is a presence but not a passive presence. The Holy Spirit is a power but not a neutral power. The Holy Spirit exists with and within God and Christ in such a way as to lift up, confirm, and confess that the movement of the Trinity is always toward a loving unity. The love and unity that exists within the Trinity is always moving toward a full embrace of all that is.

African American Christians and the Holy Spirit

This biblical dimension of the Holy Spirit as that power which transcends ancient social divisions is important in understanding the development of the meaning of the Holy Spirit among African American Christians. In fact, the Bible is central to understanding this meaning, but it is only one factor in the development of a theology of the Holy Spirit.

The theological understanding of the Holy Spirit, or pneumatology, among African Americans, has taken into account the essence and existence of black religious life. This means that it acknowledges the place of the Spirit in the development of black religion (in the United States) and in the development of the black church. In his classic text *Black Religion and Black Radicalism*, Gayraud S. Wilmore argues that the Western (and modern) distinction between the human spirit and the Holy Spirit did not apply to the experience of enslaved Africans in America and elsewhere. "The traditional religions of Africa have a single overarching characteristic that survived in an attenuated form for generations—a powerful belief that the individual and the community were continuously involved with the spirit world in the practical affairs of daily life."[4] The presence and prominence of the Holy Spirit in African American Christianity has often been cited as the root of the more emotional and energetic aspects of some forms of African American Christian worship. As W. E. B. Du Bois described African American Christian worship at the beginning of the twentieth century, he noted the prominence of "the preaching, the music and the frenzy." However, not all African American worshipping communities evidence such emotion in their gatherings. Another role of the Holy Spirit is to provide counsel and guidance. As John 4:26 proclaims, the role of the Holy Spirit is more than emotional. It has a more constitutive and robust role in the life of the African American Christian community.

In African American theologies, the question of pneumatology has not received the attention given to other theological foci in theological thought, such as the doctrine of God, ecclesiology, and so on.[5] The reason for these lacunae in African American theology, in my estimation, is that the rhetoric of the Holy Spirit takes us into the realm of the supersubjective; that is, to the almost inaccessible reaches of the inner experience of the devotee. African American mystic Howard Thurman, for example, through his embrace of the deep manifestation of the Holy Spirit in the human heart as well as the cosmos, was able to connect with that deep manifestation as it was expressed in the traditions of Christianity, but also in other religious traditions such as Hinduism. After an afternoon spent conversing with a Hindu scholar, Thurman reflected on this experience and the breakthrough that occurred. "It was as if we had stepped out of social, political, cultural frames of reference, and allowed two human spirits to unite on a ground of reality that was unmarked by differences. This was a watershed experience in my life."[6] The Holy Spirit is associated with radical freedom in John 3:8, where Jesus states, "The wind blows wherever it pleases. You hear its sound, but you cannot tell where it comes from or where it is going. So it is with everyone born of the Spirit." The apostle Paul makes this point even more clearly in 2 Corinthians 3:17. "Now the Lord is the Spirit, and where the Spirit of the Lord is, there is freedom." This radical subjectivity does not always lend itself to academic scrutiny. The danger here, of course, is that this radical subjectivity regarding the Holy Spirit may easily become a detached and idiosyncratic "spirituality." While the

Bible does, in several places as noted above, associate the Holy Spirit with freedom, under the pressure of a culture where sheer "individual choice" threatens to supplant "collective responsibility," the robust commitments that life in the Spirit requires may be ignored in favor of an emotional response.

On the other hand, the Holy Spirit, and the academic rhetoric about it, can easily appear to be quite far removed from basic religious experience. An example of this kind of discourse in the history of Christian thought is the "filoque" controversy that resulted in the split between the eastern and western branches of the church.[7] At issue in this controversy was whether the Holy Spirit proceeded from the Father and the Son, or from the Son alone. What was obscured in this controversy was the deeper insight that the Holy Spirit is more than just an expression of our radical subjectivity. There is an objective dimension to life in the Spirit. The Bible speaks of these as gifts or graces of the Spirit in 1 Corinthians 12. The danger here is that the objective dimension of life in the Spirit may overshadow the personal element. It is between these two poles that the African American church has attempted to express its idea of the Holy Spirit. It has been left to theologians to give articulate voice to that idea.

There is an intimate connection between the Holy Spirit and the black church. J. Deotis Roberts observes that "the church as a creation of the Spirit is both an institution and a community. Institutions belong to the world of structures. Communities belong to the world of persons."[8] Roberts is arguing that the black church is a creation of Pentecost. Here, the church is grounded in the power of the Spirit. In its own way, the black church is the conduit for the continual and historical expression of the Holy Spirit. I am arguing that the black church does this in at least three ways. First, the black church embodies and preserves the work of the Spirit among the people. Inasmuch as the Holy Spirit is associated with freedom and liberty as noted above, the role of the church is to give shape to the work of the Holy Spirit and to provide a way for that spiritual legacy to be passed on to others. It is this Spirit that Christ promised to send to his followers as a counselor and as a guide that connects us to Christ's life, ministry, death, and resurrection. The Holy Spirit is the connection between the black church and the ancient church. Second, the Holy Spirit provided both release and order to black religious life. As noted above, the Holy Spirit is connected to liberty, and its presence announces a sign of freedom for the believer. This is why in Galatians, the apostle Paul warned his readers of the dangers of re-enslavement. "But now that you know God—or rather are known by God—how is it that you are turning back to those weak and miserable forces? Do you wish to be enslaved by them all over again?" (Galatians 4:9 NIV). These and other passages employed by African American Christians as instructive for Christian living have often come under more intense scrutiny by African American theologians. Third, the Holy Spirit provides a means for the richness of black Christian experience to be shared with and affirmed in other religious expressions.

These three affirmations regarding the work of the Holy Spirit in the black church suggest that while the black church is, in its own special way, the embodiment of the

Holy Spirit, it does not stand alone as the locus of the work of the Holy Spirit. It is possible to see creation as the primary locus of the Spirit or the ecclesia as its primary locus. The Genesis narratives support an emphasis on the connection between creation and the Spirit. Genesis 1:2 speaks of the Spirit of God brooding over the waters as the creative act begins. And the Pentecost narrative in the book of Acts, chapter 2, supports an emphasis on the connection between the ecclesia and the Spirit. That is, the reality of the divine Spirit runs throughout creation and ecclesia; church and the world. In black Christian experience, the Holy *Spirit* runs throughout its full length and breadth. James Weldon Johnson's early twentieth-century poem, "The Creation," poignantly describes a God who labors to fashion creation in all of its diversity and magnificence. But the last and most powerful words of the poem speak to the essential role of the Spirit of God in making the human, human. After the human being has been fashioned,

> Then into it He blew the breath of life, And man became a living soul. Amen. Amen.

The black church has been both embarrassed and empowered by its association with the Holy Spirit. While thinkers such as W. E. B. Du Bois celebrated the genius of the spiritually energized African American worship traditions, some black Christian communities under the gaze of a community of "cultured despisers" have eschewed those elements of its life that could be associated with the Holy Ghost. At the same time, the black church is empowered by its association with the Holy Spirit. In the context of black religious experience, the Spirit is evident as presence, power, and purpose. In an age of reason, it has been embarrassed by the expression of the work of the Holy Spirit in speaking in tongues, or "shouting." The *ring shout* is a religious ritual, first practiced by African slaves in the West Indies and the United States, in which worshippers would move in a circle while shuffling and stomping their feet and clapping their hands. Despite the name, shouting aloud is not a fundamental part of the ritual. This ritual is still evident in those communities where African retentions are strongest, such as among the Gullah people of the Sea Islands.

The Holy Spirit and Black Theology

Within black theology these three models of the Holy Spirit are clearly visible. The first is the Holy Spirit as the spirit of radicalism in black religious belief and practice. The second is the Holy Spirit as the spirit of liberation in black religious belief and practice. The third is the Holy Spirit as the spirit of survival perseverance in black religious belief and practice.

The Holy Spirit as Creator of the Cosmos and Black Radicalism

The language of the Holy Spirit provided a name for a fundamental intrinsic feature of life for people of African descent. The Holy Spirit named the conviction that they were meant to live in freedom and dignity, and that they were precious in the sight of God. This conviction could not be invalidated by the contradictory claims of their oppressors because it was rooted in their sense of themselves. It is this rootedness that funds what Gayraud Wilmore refers to as black radicalism.

Black radicalism, therefore, has been and continues to be a form of protest specific to the black community in its struggle for freedom and a more human life. Accordingly, it has been consistent, in terms of objective and style, with the intrinsic meaning of the entire history and culture of the Afro-American community. It has been an adjunct to black Christianity because it was precisely through the biblical story, the Negro spirituals, and the event of the worship of God in their own idiom that blacks knew the experience of being bound together in the family of a loving Creator and Redeemer who destined them to break the bonds of oppression, to open the doors of the prison, and let the prisoners go free.[9]

Black radicalism was the name for the breath of God that brought life to people of African descent. It affirmed that the Spirit that moved over the deep chaos of the Genesis narrative was the same Spirit that gave them life. Black radicalism does not refer, primarily, to social deviance, or incivility, but to an inescapable affirmation of life itself. And it is this affirmation that makes black social protest a spiritual practice. The assertion here is that this radicalism is at the heart of the understanding of the Holy Spirit as Creator in black theology.

The Holy Spirit as Redeemer and Black Liberation

The Holy Spirit is not just the name for that creative principle which undergirds black life. It is also the name for healing and redemptive power that limited the spatial reach and the temporal span of historical suffering. That is, the idea that love is stronger than death, and that weeping at midnight is no match for joy in the morning, connects the Holy Spirit with the notion of liberation. The theological touchstone of African American theology, Luke 4:18–19, connects Jesus's understanding of himself as being under the sway of "the Spirit of the Lord" and the liberation of oppressed humanity. The Spirit is associated with the release of captives and the setting free of the oppressed. In reference to this biblical passage, James Cone observes that "to suggest that he was speaking of a 'spiritual' liberation fails to take seriously Jesus' thoroughly Hebrew view of human nature."[10]

The Holy Spirit is redemptive in its capacity to free persons from the strictures of sin, both institutional and personal. But this liberation is also liberation from alienation. It is, as suggested by J. Deotis Roberts, also reconciliation. "For black Christians, the Holy Spirit is he who empowers. Once again, the Holy Spirit is God within the life of the individual Christian and the fellowship of believers in Christ. The Holy Spirit is giver of spiritual life. He comforts, guides, and strengthens us."[11] It is through the power of the Holy Spirit that African American Christians saw themselves as being redeemed from internal and external forms of sin. This meant that the Holy Spirit was always leading one away from those things that restricted and constrained life and toward those things that set one free to live in community with oneself and others.

The Holy Spirit as Sustainer and Black Survival

The function of the Holy Spirit is not simply to inaugurate the creative process, or to simply fix that which has been broken. The Holy Spirit also has the function of sustaining persons in the pursuit of a well-lived life. The prophet Isaiah identifies seven gifts of the Spirit.

> The Spirit of the LORD will rest on him—the Spirit of wisdom and of understanding, the Spirit of counsel and of might, the Spirit of the knowledge and fear of the LORD— and he will delight in the fear of the LORD.
>
> He will not judge by what he sees with his eyes, or decide by what he hears with his ears. (Isaiah 11:2–3 NIV)

These gifts of the Spirit clearly connect the faithful life with the presence of God. This connection is carried forth in the understanding of the church in the New Testament. They are described primarily in 1 Corinthians 12, Romans 12, and Ephesians 4; 1 Peter 4 also touches on the *spiritual gifts*. In the Corinthians passage these gifts are not only listed but are to be seen as linking the lives of each person in the community. The Holy Spirit is devoted to the maintenance of human life. For African Americans, the Holy Spirit has historically been associated with the work of survival. It is not just a historical fact, or a momentary occurrence. It is involved in the ongoing, complex tasks of survival. Up to this point we have pointed out that the Holy Spirit was a creative principle, and a liberating power. This third dimension of the Holy Spirit points to its function as a sustaining purpose. Here it works toward and for the survival of the downtrodden. This is its moral purpose. In African American theology, this dimension of the work of the Spirit has been most clearly evident in the writings of African American women theologians.

Perhaps the most eloquent and influential voice in the field of womanist theology is that of Delores S. Williams. In her classic work *Sisters in the Wilderness: The Challenges of Womanist God-Talk*, Williams lifts up the centrality of the survival motif in black women's experience. She argues that when confronted by a hostile environment—or the wilderness—black women are made privy to an often overlooked side of God's self-revelation. In this sense, the wilderness, the site of survival for enslaved Africans, becomes the place where God's sustaining presence is most clearly evident.

> The wilderness experience, as religious experience, was transforming.... So, for African-American slaves, male and female, the wilderness was a positive place conducive to uplifting the spirit and to strengthening religious life.... Yet wilderness was a place where the slave underwent intense struggle before gaining a spiritual/religious identity.... But the struggle itself was regarded as positive, leading to a greater good than the slave ordinarily realized. To the slave's way of thinking, then, the wilderness-experience was not easy. One tarried and struggled in the wilderness with oneself and finally met Jesus.[12]

The wilderness—a place normally associated with spiritual desolation—now becomes the place where divine purpose for one's life becomes clear. It is the place where the Spirit uplifts and strengthens human resolve to live life to the fullest. Theologian Dwight N. Hopkins, writing about the experience of enslaved Africans in the United States, observes,

> A primary fruit gained by the poor on their journey of freedom is the event of the Spirit of liberation speaking to them... the poor realize and feel the ever present reality of the Spirit. Jesus, as this spirit, is the divine reality with the bottom sectors of society. That is why Jesus is Emmanuel—the Spirit with us.[13]

The Gospels recount the story of the temptation of Jesus in the wilderness in which he is able to push past the challenges and temptations of the evil one, and to clearly proclaim his purpose in the world. Just as divine presence is affirmed in the creative role of the Spirit, and divine power is affirmed in the redemptive role of the Spirit, here divine purpose is affirmed in the sustaining role of the Spirit.

Conclusion

All three of the above mentioned dimensions of the Holy Spirit are rooted in a basic fundamental assumption about the nature of black existence and life. This trajectory brings us back to the assertions of Mbiti and others that in the African religious sensibility human beings and their welfare are at the center of divine concern.[14] This is why the Holy Spirit in African American experience is not confined to the ethical or ritual aspects of life. The Holy Spirit points to the aesthetic aspect of life. That is, the Holy Spirit's continual affirmation of the value of black life is at the heart of the economy of its outward expression. This means that the Holy Spirit in its radical freedom is not limited to the creative mode, or the redemptive mode or the sustenance mode. The fundamental understanding evident in African American Christian thought is that the Holy Spirit encompasses all three of these modalities. Because the Holy Spirit is always with us, our worship should know no end; our prayers should never cease, and our service should extend to the world.

Notes

1. See Romans 5:5; Romans 8:9–11; and 1 Corinthians 12:13. The Holy Spirit is central to Paul's theology, especially as he attempts to both draw distinctions between Christ and the Holy Spirit and, at the same time, to connect them.
2. In *Nicene and Post-Nicene Fathers, First Series*, vol. 3, edi. Philip Schaff (Buffalo, NY: Christian Literature Publishing, 1887), revised and edited for New Advent by Kevin Knight, http://www.newadvent.org/fathers/1301.htm.
3. See Karl Barth, *The Holy Spirit and the Christian Life: The Theological Basis of Ethics*, trans. R. Birch Boyle (Louisville, KY: Westminster John Knox Press, 1993).
4. Gayraud S. Wilmore, *Black Religion and Black Radicalism: An Interpretation of the Religious History of Afro-American People*, 2nd ed. (Maryknoll, NY: Orbis Books, 1983), 15.
5. See Barbara Finan, "The Holy Spirit: An Issue in Theology," *Spirituality Today* 38 (Spring 1986): 9–18.
6. *Howard Thurman: Essential Writings*, ed. Luther E. Smith Jr. (Maryknoll, NY: Orbis Books: 2006), 98–99.
7. See Williston Walker, *A History of the Christian Church*, 3rd ed. (New York: Charles Scribner's Sons, 1970), 164ff.
8. J. Deotis Roberts, *Black Theology in Dialogue* (Philadelphia: Westminster Press, 1987), 62.
9. Gayraud S. Wilmore, *Black Religion and Black Radicalism: An Interpretation of the Religious History of Afro-American People*, 2nd ed. (Maryknoll, NY: Orbis Books, 1983), 168–69.
10. James Cone, *A Black Theology of Liberation* (Maryknoll, NY: Orbis Books, 1986), 3.
11. J. Deotis Roberts, *Liberation and Reconciliation: A Black Theology*, rev. ed. (Maryknoll, NY: Orbis Books, 1994), 64, 67.
12. Delores S. Williams, *Sisters in the Wilderness: The Challenge of Womanist God-Talk* (Maryknoll, NY: Orbis Books, 1993), 113.
13. Dwight N. Hopkins, *Down, Up, and Over: Slave Religion and Black Theology* (Minneapolis: Fortress Press, 2000), 215.
14. See John S. Mbiti, *African Religions and Philosophy* (New York: Doubleday, 1969).

Selected Texts

Barth, Karl. *The Holy Spirit and the Christian Life: The Theological Basis of Ethics*. Trans. R. Birch Boyle. Louisville, KY: Westminster John Knox, 1993.

Cone, James H. *A Black Theology of Liberation*. 2nd ed. Maryknoll, NY: Orbis Books, 1986.

Hopkins, Dwight N. *Down, Up, and Over: Slave Religion and Black Theology*. Minneapolis: Fortress Press, 2000.

Mbiti, John S. *African Religions and Philosophy*. New York: Doubleday, 1969.

Roberts, J. Deotis. *Liberation and Reconciliation: A Black Theology*. Rev. ed. Maryknoll, NY: Orbis Books, 1994.

Roberts, J. Deotis. *Black Theology in Dialogue*. Philadelphia: Westminster, 1987.

Raboteau, Albert J. *Slave Religion: The "Invisible Institution" in the Antebellum South*. New York: Oxford University Press, 1968

Smith, Luther, Jr. *Howard Thurman: Essential Writings*. Maryknoll, NY: Orbis Books: 2006.

Walker, Williston. *A History of the Christian Church*. 3rd ed. New York: Charles Scribner's Sons, 1970.

Williams, Delores S. *Sisters in the Wilderness: The Challenge of Womanist God-Talk*. Maryknoll, NY: Orbis Books, 1993.

Wilmore, Gayraud S. *Black Religion and Black Radicalism*. 2nd ed. Maryknoll, NY: Orbis Books, 1983.

CHAPTER 12

HUMANITY IN AFRICAN AMERICAN THEOLOGY

J. KAMERON CARTER

WHAT is African American theological anthropology? What qualifies it as theological? What is its object of study? How has the field formed and subsequently developed? The following essay answers these questions and in so doing provides a general overview of the field. I begin with a consideration of the research problem animating the field, the problem that in effect called it into being. This is the problem, the myth, and indeed the invention of "man," that decidedly masculine, heterosexual, Western, and ideal overrepresentation of humanness.

ANTHROPOLOGY; OR, THE INVENTION OF MAN

Michel Foucault called attention to the fact that "man" is a nineteenth-century invention. To grasp the significance of this for African American theological anthropology requires reflection on the establishment of the modern discipline of anthropology. Anthropology, as a discipline formed in the nineteenth century and in the wake of Immanuel Kant's Enlightenment question, *Was ist der Mensch*? (What is man?), came into being as a field just as the European imperial powers were consolidating their grip on their colonies, their transformation of the planet into zones spatially structured between metropolitan centers and colonized peripheries, and temporally structured between the now of modernity, the then of those locked inside past savagery (Hegel designated Africa in this category), and the not yet of those who will eventually become fully human and civilized (Hegel put America in this one). The discipline of modern anthropology created its object—man and his Others—within these basic terms.[1] It can therefore be said that anthropology was a discourse about man that functioned at the intersection of power and knowledge in relationship to Others.[2]

As the century progressed, the relationship between man and his Others would increasingly become framed in biological terms, with the result that by the end of the century and with the work of intellectuals like Charles Darwin most notably the man-Other relationship would be cast in evolutionary terms. That is to say, the identity of man and his relationship to his Others would be represented in terms of the truth or science of race. This science would give "true" knowledge about the order of things. And this entailed nothing less than the order of the races and thus about the relationship between man and his racial Others. Such knowledge would provide a legitimating rationale for real-world power in which (European and Euro-American) man ruled the planet. This relationship of rule, the evolutionary science of man confirmed, was a life-and-death struggle of the species, what Darwin called a "survival of the fittest." But we can say, following Michel Foucault, that this was not just, as Darwin theorized, a struggle *of* the species. It was a struggle *within* the species, a life-and-death struggle between man and his Others. It was a struggle between the races. With a far-reaching grasp of these dynamics, the African American intellectual W. E. B. Du Bois announced that the twentieth century, in transitioning from economies of plantation slavery to economies of industrial capitalism with the backing of European imperialism, had inherited from the nineteenth-century understanding of (European) man "the problem of the color line." First announcing this problem at a conference in 1900 in London and then again in 1903 in *Souls of Black Folk*, Du Bois memorably observed that "the problem of the twentieth century is the problem of the color line,—the relation of the darker to the lighter races of men in Asia and Africa, in America and the islands of the sea."[3]

But this story about the nineteenth-century invention of a scientific discourse about man is only the *immediate* backdrop or context as well. Its longer-range context, the context that produced the nineteenth-century scientific invention of man. The nineteenth-century invention of man within the disciplinary field of anthropology is but the maturing of a process set in motion during the early modern Renaissance Age of Discovery, which dates back to the fifteenth and sixteenth centuries. It was during this time that there was much travel outside of Europe for purposes of territorial expansion, political conquest, and the acquisition of wealth, on the one hand, and for cultural expansion beginning with Christian missionary and socioreligious activity, on the other. Such travel involved the "discovery" and circumnavigation of the African subcontinent, journeys by sea to the subcontinent of India and the Far East, and crucially voyages to the Western Hemisphere of the Americas beginning with the Caribbean. The invention of Western man as the overrepresentation of what it means to be human is a global-spatial event. Further still, it is an event of a decidedly Western Christian sort. That is to say, coloniality/modernity—the two are bound together, with the former being the underside of the latter—is a problem of Christian theological anthropology, a mode of discourse and practice that put black and other dark bodies under duress in modernity. Indeed, a hidden and persistent theo-logic of man in relationship to his Others has been at work within modernity/coloniality.

How, more specifically, is the problem and invention of man a theological problem, a problem of the Christian imagination? In answering this, I would like to point to the issue of reason and rationality (shortly, I will link this to the issue of the body and embodiment). The Christian imagination of early modernity/coloniality is the context in which man was invented.[4] This was an imagination in which the Word or "rationality" of God (in traditional Christian thought, to speak of the Word of God is to speak of Jesus Christ as the Son of God) was ideologically collapsed into or became wholly identified with the Word of (Western) man in his so-called rational superiority over his inadequate (because less than rational) Others whom he "discovered" in other parts of the planet. The age of discovery saw the production of (European) man as an imperial God-Man. This was nothing less than the production of whiteness and white supremacy in relationship to nonwhiteness (i.e., the black, the indigenous, etc.). For man, as one scholar has put, "faith seeking understanding" mutated into "faith judging rationality versus irrationality."[5] This judging Word is the Word of Man.

Prince Henry the Navigator and Christopher Columbus were central figures in the drama of the Word of Man. It was Prince Henry the Navigator of Portugal, who in the mid-fifteenth century rounded Cape Bojador (the bulge of Africa) to explore the so-called torrid zone and supposedly uninhabitable zone of sub-Saharan Africa. In his "discovery" of people there; in making aesthetic judgments based on skin color; in deeming them demonic based on evaluations of cultural and religious practices; in making the Christian Eucharist a site of European religious and cultural superiority; and finally by inaugurating the transatlantic slave trade based on these judgments—in all of this Prince Henry was a crucial figure in the production of man and the racial but no less theological production of the human.

Something similar can be said of Christopher Columbus (whose name means literally "the one who bears Christ"). He expanded the significance of Prince Henry's actions by giving them wider, global scope. Radically challenging and altering the geo-religious rules of his time and because of his strong belief in God, his missionary ambitions, and his desire for wealth, Columbus turned the European gaze toward lands that within the established European frames of cartographic knowledge were geographically uninhabitable because geographically unimaginable. Abstracted as belonging to no one and its people as less than or insufficiently human, these lands were called *terra nullius*. As his logs show, Columbus subjected the lands to a mode of theological governmentality, eventually regulated the newly "discovered" or unimaginable lands and peoples (the *terra nullius* or lands of no one) by inscribing the lands and the peoples the Christian imaginary of man. Giving the islands such names as "the Holy Trinity" (Trinidad) and "St. Mary of the Holy Conception" (the Virgin

Islands) and by embedding the story of the discovery within the narrative of creation in the book of Genesis and lodging his voyages of discovery within an eschatological scheme, Columbus proved central to the invention of man and his human Others within a Christian theological framework, the framework of the imperial God-Man or the Word of Man.

The task of African American theological anthropology has been to interrupt and go beyond the Word of Man, which has found its "scientific" expression in traditional anthropology's analytic of man. What W. E. B. Du Bois called the problem of the color line, what Frantz Fanon interrogated under the theme of wretchedness and the need for "reconversion,"[6] or a conversion beyond this condition through revolutionary violence, and what African American theology indicted in the late 1960s as "white theology" are all targeting the problem and invention of man that I have just summarized.

But how has African American theological anthropology, in particular, carried out the task of disrupting the Word of Man? How did it emerge and how has it elaborated a different account of the theological meaning of the human? Engaging these questions will occupy the remainder of this essay.

The Emergence of African American Theological Anthropology: The Black Theology Project

The black theology project of the late 1960s and early 1970s inaugurates African American theological anthropology, and I would like to consider its emergence around James H. Cone. The decision to focus on James Cone's work does not mean that African American theological anthropology is reducible to Cone's thought, for religious and theological anthropology from an African American perspective is quite diverse—and always has been. Indeed, the late 1960s and early 1970s, which is when Cone started his work and which is also when African American religious studies (and black studies more broadly) was beginning to establish itself as an academic discipline, saw the rise of theologians and religion scholars like J. Deotis Roberts, William R. Jones, Gayraud Wilmore, and Charles Long. Each of these figures has contributed to an African Americanist discourse on theological anthropology. Yet it was James Cone, with his effort theologically to, on the one hand, inquire into the meaning of the human using the tools of Christian theology and, on the other, to bring such a disciplinary inquiry into conversation with the 1960s and 1970s Black Power movement, who would in many ways set the terms of discussion for African

American theological anthropology, a discussion that persists to this day. Thus, I begin with him.

But it is not with his seminal black theology texts—*Black Theology and Black Power* (1969) and *A Black Theology of Liberation* (1970)—that one finds the beginnings of African American theological anthropology. It is actually Cone's dissertation, which he completed at Northwestern University's Garrett Evangelical Theological Seminary in 1965, that one finds Cone working on the questions that would contribute to the rise of African American theological anthropology. The title of the dissertation was "The Doctrine of Man in the Theology of Karl Barth."

Admittedly, this is an unlikely place to discern the beginnings of African American theological anthropology, for Cone's dissertation was on the Swiss-German theologian Karl Barth's brand of revolutionary, dialectical theology (sometimes called neo-orthodox theology). Moreover, one might think—and Cone received criticism of this sort early on—that in turning to Karl Barth he was seeking to give his project white theological legitimacy. Not so.

A form of theology born in the 1920s interwar years of Germany's Weimar Republic—the journal representing the movement was titled *Zwischen den Zeit* (*Between the Times*)—around theologians like the young Karl Barth, Rudolf Bultmann, Friedrich Gogarten, and Paul Tillich among others, dialectical theology sought to do two things: (1) rethink the place of Christian theology within the intellectual architecture of Western thought given its complicity with the crises that lead to the World War I (and that would lead to World War II and Auschwitz); and (2) theologically analyze the new situation that was emerging around Western nationalism and late-modern capitalism. Eventually the dialectical theology movement of the Weimar years fragmented. But one of its lasting fruits was Karl Barth's massive theological enterprise, his *Church Dogmatics*. Barth, who died in the infamous year of world revolutionary fervor, 1968, was still working on it when Cone finished his dissertation, which dealt with how the human was conceived in Barth's thought. Why would Cone look at Barth's theology to think theologically about the question of the human, when he had his eyes on African American life, which was under assault, when cities in America were aflame, when race riots were frequent, and when blacks were fighting for their civil rights?

Cone was not seeking to do "white theology" in (Barthian) blackface. Rather, he was starting to develop a style of theology specific to this early moment of African American theological anthropology and to deal with the problem and inventions of man, for it is this invention that subalterns across the globe, including those in the United States, were revolting against. As David Walker[7] developed an appositional and not just an oppositional relationship to the Enlightenment to advance a religious critique of early Jeffersonian democracy, and as Frantz Fanon developed an appositional relationship to psychoanalytic theory (particularly, to Jacques Lacan) to address the problem of the colonization of psychic space,[8] so too Cone and early African American theological anthropology was forging an appositional relationship to theology itself in order to conceive and reframe the task of theology itself under conditions of civil rights, Black Power, and decolonization efforts around the world. This entailed stepping inside of and redirecting its rhetoric and discourse about the human in liberative directions for African Americans and other marginalized subjects in the United States. Thus, Cone transformed Barth's critique of western European man into an interrogation of man's *theological* production of his Others, particularly, his abjected black others. He turned it, in other words, into a critique of white theology, a critique launched from modernity's underside. Cone carried this out by aligning the notion of God in a positive way with black humanity. In this way, the question of the human was reopened for theological investigation.

These moves toward a new interrogation of the human become clear in Cone's immediate, postdissertation work: *Black Theology and Black Power* (1969), *A Black Theology of Liberation* (1970), *The Spiritual and the Blues* (1972), and *God of the Oppressed* (1975). In these works Cone unfolds a project engaged in a theological, aesthetic, cultural, and political struggle of life and death over the meaning of the human, and more specifically, over the prospects, possibilities, and realities of black humanity. He embarked on this through interrogations of and efforts to redirect theological method and the doctrines of revelation, God, the person and work of Jesus Christ, the church and world, eschatology and, of pivotal importance, a doctrine of the human being or theological anthropology. Arguably, African American theological anthropology has been a continuous conversation, indeed, a constructive argument with the theological anthropology or the statements made in the first stage of the articulation of African American theological anthropology in the black theology project. It has been a wrestling with the theological meanings of the human and ascribed to blackness coming out of the black theology project.

Further Developments in African American Theological Anthropology

How has African American theological anthropology developed since its late-1960s and 1970s beginnings? In this final section I summarize developments in the field that when put together indicate that post-1960s developments in African American theological anthropology have made cultural difference and especially the body itself not just additional data along side race for interrogating the meaning of the human. Rather, how we live in the body is the very basis from which to construct understanding of the human and ascribe theological meanings to human existence.

I begin with womanist theology because it represents the most important development within African American theological anthropology after its 1960s and 1970s inception. Womanist theology is related to but also distinct from black theology. It is related to black theology in its concern with the problem of race in the modern world, but it is distinct from it in that black theology emerged as a discourse articulated principally by black male theologians. As such it tended to marginalize the unique experiences of black women in theologically responding to the problem of Western man. As such, black theology proved limited in its ability to speak about how God and the divine interacted with black *women's* lives. The same can be said about womanism's relationship to feminist theology. While womanist theology is related to feminist theology in that both seek to take women's lives seriously, feminist theology was also limited in that its principal referent was the lives of white women. Feminist theology, Delores Williams, an early exponent of womanist theology, argued in *Sisters in the Wilderness* (1993), was constructed primarily to attend to the gender oppression of white women by a white male-dominated society.[9] Black women, however, have been inscribed differently within the United States and the global structures of man. They have been positioned in such a way as to receive actual and figurative violence against and domination of their bodies not just by white males but by men of any race with white women's participation. What Frantz Fanon said about Jean-Paul Sartre in his chapter on the lived experience of the black man in *Black Skin, White Masks* ("Jean-Paul Sartre forgets that the black man suffers *in his body* quite differently from the white man"), in fact was said by womanist theologians and ethicists in their own ways to both black male and white female theologians and ethicists: Black women suffer *in their bodies* in a different way. It is not only race that presses upon their bodies, causing black women to suffer differently. It is race mixed with gender and class. Womanist theology and ethics arose to account for how black women have been forced to exist in their bodies in ways that differ both from white women and black men and how they have constructed faith responses to negotiate and renegotiate the terms of their existence. In short, womanist theology sought to embed the problem of race more richly in questions of difference and the ways in which we live as bodies. Black women's experiences in the United States and in the modern world call for more robust accounts of the problem of race and the problem of man.

The seeds of how black women have uniquely suffered in the body—the lived experiences of black women, we might say in modifying Fanon—go back to the very invention of man spoken of earlier in the birth of the modern/colonial world and extended into slave plantation life. *Terra nullius* (the land of no one), coupled with *terra incognita* (unknown land), notions crucial to the invention of man, also proves crucial to how black women have been made to suffer in the body and thus suffer human existence. The point I would like to add to my earlier discussion of *terra nullius* is that this notion was from the beginning highly gendered and sexualized. Western man was conceptually invented and empirically enacted as a universal, disembodied, rational subject. That is to say, man as an overrepresentation of the human presupposed a subject distanced from all passion, which was perceived as linked to the body. This way of thinking about the mind and the body would fuel the very dichotomy at the heart of Cartesian philosophy, for example, and much of Western thought. Through mind, rationality, and thought, man could reside everywhere—but again, this can happen only because of a refusal of the passions, or because of disembodiment. But to be at a distance from the body is to be at a distance from woman insofar as woman has been thought of as bounded by her passions, which get located in her sexual organs. This means that man as universal, disembodied subject is always already gendered and normalized as male. But it also means that a woman is only her body. Or as Judith Butler has said in diagnosing and critiquing this problem, woman has been made to occupy exclusively the bodily sphere of life.[10]

Womanist theology, in effect, sharpens Butler's critique and in so doing sharpens the tasks of African American theological anthropology. In trying to think carefully through black women's lived experiences, it becomes clear that it is not enough just to say that woman is overdetermined by her gendered, sexualized body. This must be extended to say that woman has been made to function as a body *for* (disembodied) man. But if this is a statement of white women's existence in relationship to man (she is *for* [the white] man), its deepest presumption is that (white) woman does indeed *possess* a body. She is man's complement. But this is precisely what the colonial experience—and related to this, modern slavery—refused to black and similarly positioned (indigenous) women. In their situation, just as lands were deemed unknown and empty (*terra nullius* / *terra incognita*), the people of those lands (and in the case of slaves, those brought into those lands to work it) were deemed unknown and empty. They were not just reducible to their bodies as their original possessions (as in the case of white women). They lacked even this; possession of the body for them was not a possibility. Thus, there is a link, and not just a metaphorical one, between the colonization of native ("empty") lands and the colonization of native ("empty" or less than human) bodies. And there is a further link, and again not just a metaphorical one, between those dispossessed of land and those made to exist only at the level of their skin, for strictly speaking within the economy of colonization and slavery, particularly in the case of black women, they are denied possession of even the body.[11] Black women exist in the zone between dead flesh or inanimate meat and a living body; they suffer in the body as sheer utility or in being deemed rape-able flesh.[12] This rape-ability structures everyday existence.

Womanist theology has been about the task of negotiating and overcoming the legacies of this problem. It has contributed to African American theological anthropology by making black women's experiences the starting point for crafting theological meanings for their lives. Indeed, the theological enterprise is in response to black women's living conditions. It reconsiders Christian doctrines, including theological anthropology, with black women's lives, not man or black males, as the point of departure.

While there have been many robust contributions by womanist ethicists and theologians to reconceive doctrinal themes and readings of religious texts by grounding them in black women's varied experiences, theological anthropology has only recently received explicit, thematic attention. Rather, theological anthropology has been the doctrinal area around which much of womanist thought has implicitly revolved. Indeed, the implicit claim about theological anthropology in womanist thought is that the body, which was at once denied to those deemed black in the modern world and yet that which was reduced to the skin and the flesh, is the very site of what it means to be human. Thus, to stay human is to stay with and creatively reclaim the body.

This is precisely the direction the most recent work in African American theological anthropology has taken. In this most recent work the body has become thematically explicit. But before commenting on this recent work, it is worth mentioning one further development in African American theological anthropology. This concerns the importance of the theme of cultural difference. This theme emerged forcefully in the 1990s at the same time that womanist theology was coming into its own in the theological academy after its beginnings in the 1980s. The person who crystallized the importance of cultural difference perhaps more than anyone else in African American religious studies was Cornel West with his essay "The New Cultural Politics of Difference" (1990). In this essay, West describes the present task: "Black cultural workers [including scholars and those working in black religious studies] must constitute and sustain discursive and institutional networks that deconstruct earlier modern Black strategies for identity formation, demystify power relations that incorporate class, patriarchal, and homophobic biases, and construct more multivalent and multidimensional responses that articulate the complexity and diversity of Black practices in the modern and postmodern world."[13] The new cultural politics highlights the complex and diverse ways in which black folks have lived as black and continue to live the body, for the body is the sphere of life. This translated in the 1990s into critiques of interpretations within African American theological anthropology that did not allow the diverse ways in which black folks lived their lives to receive theological attention. Two important theological voices to emerge during this time were Victor Anderson and Anthony B. Pinn.

With the publication of the book *Beyond Ontological Blackness* (1999), Anderson argued that cultural difference and human flourishing must be at the forefront of interpreting the religious significance of black lives rather than isolating black lives within older frames of racial uplift and suffering, frames that did not attend to issues of sexual orientation among other things. In several texts, beginning with *Why Lord? Suffering and Evil in Black Theology* (1995), Pinn criticized the privileging of Christianity as the frame of religious reference in interpreting black lives. Instead he started developing an approach to the analysis of black lives based in black humanist traditions that could incorporate religious traditions in the analyses of black life but that do not privilege them at the outset. This has allowed Pinn to consider the religious significance of both black religious traditions and black aesthetic culture (for example, hip-hop culture) for interpreting black humanity.

I conclude by referring to two texts that exemplify the latest work in African American theological anthropology. These texts pick up on the significance of the body as the site of what it means to be human, but a site that has never been subjected to analysis. The first is from Anthony Pinn. In *Embodiment and the New Shape of Black Theological Thought* (2010), Pinn addresses this lacuna at the origins of black theology, namely, that the body as such and the black body in particular has never received theological attention in its own right. His claim is that focus on the body has been metaphorical at best. African American theology has not attended to the lived experiences of the physical, material body as such and the theological importance of those experiences. By attending to the physical body as such, Pinn has opened new interpretive possibilities for addressing issues of race, gender, and sexuality in African American theological anthropology.[14]

The second text to focus attention on the body is from Catholic womanist theologian M. Shawn Copeland: *Enfleshing Freedom: Body, Race, and Being* (2010). A landmark text of Christian theology, Copeland has rendered explicit what has been implicit to womanist theological thought from its inception, namely, the centrality of the body and the multiple ways in which we live the body.[15] A kind of theological commentary on Toni Morrison's *Beloved*, Copeland's work demonstrates how black women's historical experiences and oppressions cast light on our theological ideas about being human. Her claim is that race and how we live in the body, which is always already shot through with power relations, reframes theological anthropology. The ways in which we live, suffer, and flourish in the body around issues of race, gender, sexuality, and more open up ways of being human (and insofar as she offers a Christian theological argument, of being the body of Christ) beyond colonialism's deepest legacy: the myth and invention of man.

Notes

1. Johannes Fabian, *Time and the Other: How Anthropology Makes Its Object* (New York: Columbia University Press, 1983).
2. J. Kameron Carter. *Race: A Theological Account* (New York: Oxford University Press, 2008).
3. W. E. B. Du Bois, *The Souls of Black Folk* (Chicago: A. C. McClurg, 1903).
4. See Sylvia Wynters, "Unsettling the Coloniality of Being/Power/Truth/Freedom: Towards the Human, after Man, Its Overrepresentation—an Argument," *The New Centennial Review* 3, no. 3 (1993): 257–337. See also Willie James Jennings, *The Christian Imagination: Theology and the Origins of Race* (New Haven: Yale University Press, 2010).
5. Jennings, *The Christian Imagination*, see introduction.
6. Frantz Fanon, *Black Skin, White Masks*, trans. Richard Philcox (New York: Grove Press, 2008).
7. David Walker, *David Walker's "Appeal to the Coloured Citizens of the World"* (1829), ed. Peter Hinks (University Park: Pennsylvania State University Press, 2000).
8. Fanon, *Black Skin, White Masks.*
9. Delores Williams, *Sisters in the Wilderness: The Challenge of Womanist God-Talk* (Maryknoll, NY: Orbis Books, 1993).

10. See for example: Judith Butler, *Gender Trouble: Feminism and the Subversion of Identity* (New York: Routledge, 2006); Butler, *Bodies That Matter: On the Discursive Limits of Sex* (New York: Routledge, 1993).
11. Radhika Mohanram, *Black Body: Women, Colonialism, and Space* (Minneapolis: University of Minnesota Press, 1999).
12. Hortense Spillers, *Black, White, and in Color: Essays on American Literature and Culture* (Chicago: University of Chicago Press, 2003).
13. Cornel West, "The New Cultural Politics of Difference," in *Keeping Faith: Philosophy and Race in America* (New York: Routledge, 1993), 3–32.
14. Anthony B. Pinn, *Embodiment and the New Shape of Black Theological Thought* (New York: New York University Press, 2010).
15. M. Shawn Copeland, *Enfleshing Freedom: Body, Race, and Being* (Minneapolis: Fortress Press, 2010).

Selected Texts

Anderson, Victor. *Beyond Ontological Blackness.* New York: Continuum, 1999.

Carter, J. Kameron. *Race: A Theological Account.* New York: Oxford University Press, 2008.

Cone, James H. *God of the Oppressed.* Maryknoll, NY: Orbis Books, 1997.

Copeland, M. Shawn. *Enfleshing Freedom: Body, Race, and Being.* Minneapolis: Fortress Press, 2010.

Fabian, Johannes. *Time and the Other: How Anthropology Makes Its Object.* New York: Columbia University Press, 1983.

Fanon, Frantz. *Black Skin, White Masks.* Trans. Richard Philcox. New York: Grove Press, 2008.

Jennings, Willie James. *The Christian Imagination: Theology and the Origins of Race.* New Haven: Yale University Press, 2010.

Mohanram, Radhika. *Black Body: Women, Colonialism, and Space.* Minneapolis: University of Minnesota Press, 1999.

Pinn, Anthony B. *Embodiment and the New Shape of Black Theological Thought.* New York: New York University Press, 2010.

Pinn, Anthony B. *Why, Lord? Suffering and Evil in Black Theology* New York: Continuum, 1995.

Spillers, Hortense. *Black, White, and in Color: Essays on American Literature and Culture.* Chicago: University of Chicago Press, 2003.

West, Cornel. "The New Cultural Politics of Difference." In *Keeping Faith: Philosophy and Race in America*, 3–29. New York: Routledge, 1993.

Williams, Delores. *Sisters in the Wilderness: The Challenge of Womanist God-Talk.* Maryknoll, NY: Orbis Books, 1993.

Wynters, Sylvia. "Unsettling the Coloniality of Being/Power/Truth/Freedom: Towards the Human, after Man, Its Overrepresentation—an Argument." *New Centennial Review* 3, no. 3 (1993): 257–337.

CHAPTER 13

WORLD/CREATION IN AFRICAN AMERICAN THEOLOGY

TORIN ALEXANDER

THE objective of this essay is to present how the concepts of world and creation have been expressed within the African American theological tradition, specifically in the work of black and womanist theologians and ethicists.

Pre-Civil Rights Theological Positions

Reflections on creation and the world of an intentionally theological nature date back to at least the nineteenth century. For example, texts such as David Walker's *Appeal to the Coloured Citizens of the World* and Henry Highland Garnet's *Call to Rebellion* are more than antislavery treatises, but also construct theologically sophisticated cosmologies and anthropologies, in keeping with what I have articulated as an African American emphasis on the interconnectedness of Creator and created.

With the end of slavery and access to formal theological training, the first half of the twentieth century would see a generation of African American scholars reflecting on themes related to the concepts of creation and world. Of particular concern among such religious thinkers was the use of the Christian tradition to undergird segregation and to perpetuate race-based oppression of African Americans. Scholars such as George Kelsey, Benjamin E. Mays, and Howard Thurman accepted as central to their vocational calling the discursive resistance of racism and segregation. The proponents of a theological anthropology that emphasized "the oneness of humanity" and the "interrelatedness of life," they affirmed that the God of the universe is the creator of all human life, and thus all men and women, regardless of race or nationality, are brothers and sisters. For example, George Kelsey noted in his classic text *Racism and the Christian Understanding of Man* that segregation developed as a plan of political action to separate "inferior," "defective" black being (the out-race) from "superior," "godlike" white being (the in-race). Over against this supposedly natural hierarchy, Kelsey pointed to the Genesis creation narrative and its assertion of a singular and common ancestry of all humanity.[1] In a similar vein, Benjamin Mays asserted that the Christian tradition does not speak of one origin for the French and another for the German; not one for the English and another for the Irish; not one for the Chinese and another for the Japanese; not one for the Bantus and another for the Dutch of South Africa; and not one for the Russian and another for the American.[2]

Of this generation of pre-civil rights theological thinkers, Howard Thurman's reflection on world and creation are perhaps the most wide-ranging and extensive. As was the case with his contemporaries, Thurman's work deals with issues associated with issues of segregation and racism as they relate to the Christian tradition and witness in the world, but also goes further. For example, in *The Luminous Darkness: A Personal Interpretation of the Anatomy of Segregation and the Ground of Hope*, Thurman explores the figure of segregation in American society. It is Thurman's assertion that segregation is antithetical to *human beingness*. For Thurman, to be fully human requires being in relation, one with another (as well as with all of creation). It is only in such a context, which necessitates the dissolution of walls and barriers such as those associated with segregation, that one might experience spiritual *wholeness* and *freedom* as well as life in authentic community.

For Thurman, segregation is a churning abyss, a wall, an insidious and pernicious virus that not only separates white from black, but also does significant damage to their psyches and souls as well as being a drain upon society as a whole.[3] Thurman goes on to say that "human life is one and all men are members one of another. And this insight is spiritual and it is the hardcore of religious experience."[4] According to Thurman, to be human is to experience one's fellows as human beings. This requires one transcending fears (of the other, of harm, humiliation, loss of status, one's self) as well as notions of kinship, ethnicity, race, and nationality. It means nurturing senses of belonging to life, of being a part of existence. "It is to be alive in a living world."[5]

Being not only an eminent pastor, but also a theologian and mystic, Thurman provides a wealth of resources with respect to the understanding of the world and creation. Over the course of his numerous essays, books, prayers, and sermons, Thurman frequently references nature as a place in which he found reassurance and comfort from the psychic and spiritual assault of human society. According to Thurman, this was a relationship that "could not be affronted by the behavior of human beings."[6] The ocean, the seasons, in their ebb and flow, in their cyclical rhythms, imbued him with a sense of being a part of something much more immense and enduring.

In works such as "The Binding Unity" and "Mysticism and the Experience of Love," Thurman states that the mystic cannot escape a sense of intimacy and immediacy with all that comprises reality.[7] However, Thurman does not go as far as divinizing the world. Though central to his experience is the recognition of God as the source of life and existence, God is not coterminous with the world. God is the subject, and all existence of whatever form are predicates. However, God cannot be wholly transcendent because this would not satisfy the demands of the mystic's experience, which is a personal response to God. In the *Centering Moment*, in the section entitled "Prayer and the Search for Community," Thurman states,

> God is the Creator of Life, the Creator of the living substance, the Creator of existence, and as such expresses Himself through life. This is the meaning, essentially, of the notion that life is alive and that this is a living universe.[8]

Though tempted by pantheism, Thurman rejects it, commenting,

> There is an element of profound truth in the outlook of pantheism, which sees the work of God in the world of nature with such clarity as to identify God with His world; the temptation is hard to resist. But this is not enough. God must never be a prisoner in His creation.[9]

Thus for Thurman, God dwells within God's creation, but is not synonymous with that creation.

Post-Civil Rights Theological Positions: The Rise of Black Theology

In the wake of the civil rights movement, there arose a new theological movement that brought together some of the Christian commitments of previous generations, but was also inspired by a militant tradition at the time embodied by advocates of Black Power. This undertaking came to be known as black theology, and was most closely identified with the scholarship of James Cone. For Cone, God is the God of the oppressed and not the oppressor. God works in history to bring about the liberation of those who have been disinherited and disenfranchised. The divine disposition is evinced in the life, death, and resurrection of Jesus Christ. Jesus is known through the experience of African Americans to be the black Messiah who works to bring about God's kingdom of justice and freedom in the here and now. With respect to a doctrine of creation, Cone asserts that the liberation at the heart of black theology is not an object, but "the project of freedom wherein the oppressed realize that their fight for freedom is a divine right of creation."[10] In other words, oppression is antithetical to God's intention with respect to the creation as a whole as well as with respect to human interrelatedness. In 2001, Cone published an article that suggested the motivation behind the abuse and subjugation of certain groups of human beings was the same impetus associated with the abuse and subjugation of the planet. "People who fight against white racism but fail to connect it to the degradation of the earth are anti-ecological—whether they know it or not."[11]

Another important figure in the development of black theology, J. Deotis Roberts, also reflected on the relationship between God and creation. For Roberts, the concepts of God's providence and of God's creation are inseparable. African Americans need to know that the God of Christian faith is the God of all creation and that in spite of the evil and ugliness in their experience, creation is beautiful and good. Thus, African Americans must cultivate the ability to distinguish between disorder and human venality and God's design. Moreover, any theology that promotes a beatific existence in the hereafter while neglecting the structures of oppression and subjugation in this world is a betrayal of African Americans as well as being antithetical to the gospel. According to Roberts, creation and all its benefits have been given to all humanity for their enrichment and fulfillment.[12]

However, the embracing of creation is substantively different from vulgar materialism. Roberts asserts that Americans in general, black or white, seemed obsessed with things as ends in themselves. For many people, things are the *esse* (essence) of life rather than for the *bene esse* (well-being) of life. This, for Roberts, is the fallacy of idolatry. Steering clear of this error requires acknowledging

> God as Author of nature, as Lord and Judge of creation and history, is in the here and now. Black theology must say *yes to this* life and the order of creation which sustains it. This affirmative doctrine of creation is a sheer necessity if black men are to have a healthy approach to the goods and services which make the present life full and abundant.[13]

In addition to discourse such as that of Cone and Roberts, other African American religious scholars would deploy the concept of creation and world in a figurative manner to express particular aspects of African American experience. For example, among African American religionists, Charles H. Long has written much in the area of myth, particularly creation myths. Long asserts that myths are to be engaged as true stories in the sense that they are renderings of experiences of reality.[14] Moreover, for Long, a reliance on myth does not carry with it connotations of the illogical or irrational. Mythmaking cultures often exhibit sophisticated levels of logic and reason.[15] It is in such a context that Long introduces the idea of African Americans being the product of a "second creation." In the essay, "Conquest and Cultural Contact in the New World," Long begins to explore the myths and practices associated with and generated by the cultural contact between the West and non-Europeans. Long calls attention to European notions of pilgrimage, as well as legends and folklore, dealing with nature and the primordial. Conversely, Long also reflects on the mythic creativity of indigenous peoples, who become the colonized, the subjugated, and the oppressed.

In commenting on the theoretical and methodological basis for such a discussion, Long proffers the assertion that religion is to be understood "as the basic element in the constitution of human consciousness and human community."[16] In this context, religious experience can be seen as "a primordial experiencing of that which is considered ultimate in existence," which suggests human orientation be understood as "the meaning that human communities give to the particular stances they have assumed in their several worlds."[17] Subsequently, Long introduces the trope of second creation to describe the signification of non-Europeans by Westerners, perhaps a more poignant and expressive way of describing what he had referred to elsewhere as being othered.[18]

Likewise, in the work of the ethicist Peter J. Paris, theological and ethical reflection on African American religion and religious experience must recall that the Africans brought to the Americas were by no means tabulae rasae, especially with respect to matters of the sacred. Indeed, they were in possession of their own complex and comprehensive religious systems. As an aggregate, they represented various ethnic, cultural, and social groups in Western Africa. Yet while possessing different languages, cultural mores, and customs, they seemed to possess similar worldviews predicated on similar cosmological and cosmogonic constructs. In *Spirituality of African Peoples*, Paris asserts that most Africans brought to America subscribed to the notion of a supreme deity, or High God. This High God was mediated through lesser deities and spirits who were immanently present and active in the world. Moreover, Africans who were brought to the Western Hemisphere experienced the world without sharp lines of demarcation between the natural and the supernatural.[19] Indeed, intimate and symbiotic relationships with ancestors, spirits, and deities were unexceptional. According to Paris, African cosmologies imply "a sacramental view of life in general and of human life in particular."[20] Moreover, these cosmologies are anthropocentric and holistic to the extent that humans are ultimately responsible for maintaining good relationships with all forms of life in all realms.

Similarly, Henry Mitchell and Nicholas Cooper-Lewis note that Africans, and summarily, African Americans informed by an African-based belief system, have tended to emphasize the goodness of creation as expressed in Genesis 1:26–31.[21] However, an important distinction between most African cosmogonies and those associated with "orthodox" Christianity has to do with the idea of a "Fall," that is, Genesis 3:14–24 (the disobedience of the first parents, Adam and Eve). According to Mitchell, for the African there is no concept of original or ancestral sin by which creation and the creature are distorted.[22] Thus, concepts such as the total depravity of humanity or even the Kantian notion of radical evil do not obtain. Consequently, also absent from African religious traditions are soteriologies preoccupied with one's eternal security. In other words, Africans possessed a healthy uncertainty about life, but not some fixation about a predestined end.[23]

Returning to the work of Mitchell, it is his contention that the attributes of divinity such as the majesty, providence, and potency of God persist throughout African American vernacular culture.

> If indeed, God be God, there can be no outer limit to divine power and no entity capable of opposing it. [Thus] Nothing can exist free of the ultimate control of the Creator and Lord of the universe.... All people need to know at the core of their being that God's hand holds the whole world.[24]

While one may be at a loss to find explicit doctrinal constructions of these concepts, Mitchell invokes the "theopoetic" tradition of deacons and sisters who address God as "Thou who hast hung the stars in space" or "Thou who hast scooped out the valleys with thine almighty hand" or "O Lord, who speakest and the very waves obey..."[25]

Mitchell identifies the most "pervasive" and "persistent" divine attributes included under the rubric of God's providence, that is, God's guidance and care or God's sustaining power, with the goodness of God and creation. As noted above, enslaved Africans and their descendants drew from both African and Christian resources in comprehending the goodness of the Creator and the creation. However, Mitchell goes on to argue that the affirmation of the goodness of the Divine and creation was important to the survival of enslaved Africans in the new world.[26] Once more turning to vernacular culture, Mitchell maintains, with respect to persistence of such faith, even before such horrors of history as chattel slavery and lynching, that this particular synthesis resulting in a positive worldview is evinced in numerous spirituals, gospels, and popular hymns.

"Second Generation" Black Theology

Black theology, initiated by scholars like Cone and Roberts, was to be followed by a subsequent cohort of academics who would expand the purview of the discipline. Representing a diversity of interests as well as deploying a variety of theoretical and methodological approaches, this second wave would make significant contributions to the understanding of African American religion and religious experience. Perhaps one of the most vibrant areas of new research consists of the scholarship of African American women, many of whom came to adopt the designation of womanist. Because of the importance of their work with respect to engaging questions related to creation and world, particularly as it relates to questions of environmental and ecological nature, they will addressed in their own section.

Of this second generation of scholars informed by black theology, Theophus Smith is conspicuous for his identification and appropriation of authors within the African American religious tradition who engage in reflection and imaginative construction with respect to the relationship between God and world, a relationship that encompasses the natural and the social-historical. In the African American literary tradition, there are few works that explore the relationship between God, humanity, and the world more frequently cited than James Weldon Johnson's poem "The Creation." Johnson's imaginative retelling of the biblical story of creation as found in Genesis 1–2 is the first piece in his collections of poems that pay homage to antebellum preachers and their sermons entitled *God's Trombones*. In the introduction to the collection, Johnson notes that in form and substance the poems are reminiscent of folk sermons he had heard from his youth. In *Conjuring Culture: Biblical Formations of Black America*, Smith suggest that this sermonic heritage may evince a nascent Afro-Hebraic cosmogony.[27]

Smith, as well as others such as Steven Breck Reid, has noted that the occasion for God's creation for Johnson is divine loneliness.[28]

> And God stepped out on space, And He looked around and said, *"I'm lonely—I'll make me a world."*[29]

This is the Divine in search of community, a God who needs to be intimately connected with some "other." Smith further asserts that this is not the God of classic or orthodox Christian doctrine, a God whose aseity and perfection necessitate that God is complete, self-sufficient, and without lack. Moreover, there are other differences between Johnson's poetry and the canonical narrative. Over against Genesis 1, where God speaks light into existence, in Johnson's account, God smiles, and there is light: impersonal fiat versus the intimacy and active emotiveness of a face. Nevertheless, in both the biblical narrative and Johnson's theopoetic construction, God declares the creation good. However, Johnson continues to emphasize action as revealed in language that has God reaching, taking, rolling, and flinging the light to form the sun, moon, and stars. Subsequently, between the dark and the light, God hurls the world, and once again declares the creation good.

God continues to act intimately, tangibly, and tactilely in the formation of the world and all that resides therein, for example, mountains and valleys, seas and land, all forms of vegetation, and the myriad of beings that constitute animal life. However, as Johnson notes, though God deems all that he has made good, there is still something missing; God continues to experience a lack. God's loneliness is not quelled until he ponders for some time and decides to make a "man." God creates the human out of the soil. God's hands shape the creation of the human community. Thus, humans are made to be one with another, with the earth, and with God.

Smith goes on to note that Johnson is not alone as an African American writer who engages in reflection and imaginative construction with respect to the relation of God to the creation. Again, Smith identifies two of special note. The first is the author and anthropologist Zora Neale Hurston. For example, appearing in Hurston's *Mules and Men* as the exposition of a traveling preacher, the "poem" entitled "Behold the Rib" appears as a singular contribution in *The Book of Negro Folklore* edited by Langston Hughes and Arna Bontemps.[30] In the same anthology of Hughes and Bontemps appears another poem about God and world, this one of unattributed derivation. Entitling it "God," the unknown author imaged and imagined God as having an exceptionally intimate relationship with creation.[31]

Other African American theological discourse on creation and world with an environmental orientation includes works by Anthony B. Pinn, Dwight N. Hopkins, Theodore Smith Jr., and Mark Stoll.[32] The growth of environmental and ecological interests within African American theology can also be seen with the creation of the TheoEcology Project at the Interdenominational Theological Center (ITC), in Atlanta, Georgia. Initiated in 2005, the project reflects a commitment within ITC to stewardship of the earth as directed by God. An emergent theological voice with respect to matters of ecology and the environment is that of Tyson-Lord J. Gray. His essay "Consider This" appears in the volume *Holy Ground: A Gathering of Voices on Caring for Creation.*[33] His dissertation (Vanderbilt University) is entitled "Black Religion, Environmental Justice, and the Search for a 'Green' Community."

A rather unique approach to the theme of creation predicated on a neoclassical philosophical tradition founded by Alfred North Whitehead, and articulated by theologians such as Charles Hartshorne, John Cobb, and David Ray Griffin, can be found in the work of Theodore Walker Jr. In *Mothership Connections: A Black Atlantic Synthesis of Neoclassical Metaphysics and Black Theology*, Walker offers a synthesis of neoclassical metaphysics and black theology. In so doing, Walker proffers a distinct doctrine of God as the God of all creation and a doctrine of God as the God of the oppressed. Walker's appropriation of a neoclassical metaphysics emphasizes

> the strict metaphysical necessity of creative process and social relations. God is supremely creative and supremely social, sharing creativity with all creation.... Distinct from all others, God is the all-inclusive one, to whom all things make partly determinative differences and who makes partly determinative and wholly righteous differences to all things.[34]

It is important to note, according to Walker, that he is not deploying classical or conventional understanding of theological and philosophical terminology. Thus, God as "the all" does not extend to negative attributes or to the binaries; for example, God's being does not include the attribute of evil.

Walker maintains that his constructive project is consistent with black theology. The God of all creation is also the God of the oppressed, working in history to bring about liberation. The point of clarification that he brings to this African American theological discourse, however, is that God as the creator of all is a metaphysical necessity, that is, this is immutably and eternally the case. However, God as God of the oppressed is a "hypothetical" conditional necessity. Oppression is not necessary; it is contingent.

Environmental Racism

By the mid-1980s, various reports were being produced by the Commission for Racial Justice of the United Church of Christ, under the leadership of Ben Chavis, revealing a link between environmental issues and racial injustice.[35] As Dianne D. Glave notes in her article "Black Environmental Liberation Theology: The Theological and Historical Roots of Environmental Justice Activism by the African American Church," the efforts of the Commission for Racial Justice as well as other grassroots resistance groups to environmental racism constituted a nascent black environmental liberation theology (BELT).[36] A high point of such endeavors took place in 1993 with the National Black Church Environmental and Economic Justice Summit. At this gathering, Reverend Eugene F. Rivers III, the cofounder of the Azusa Christian Community, asserted, "What we've done in connecting the issue of environmental justice and racism is we've drawn the connection between environmental racism as an [*sic*] expression of white supremacy."[37]

Womanist Theology

As previously mentioned, among the developments within the second generation of black theologians, much innovation and vitality can be attributed to the development of womanist theology and ethics. With genealogical ties to black and feminist theologies, it emerged from female African American theologians who sought to establish the lived experience of black women as the starting point of theological and ethical discourse. Those most frequently identified with this area of discourse include the scholars Jacquelyn Grant, Katie Cannon, Kelly Brown Douglas, Delores Williams, Emilie Townes, and M. Shawn Copeland. With principal attributes of black women's experience associated with interrelatedness, wholeness, and the well-being of self and community, it is not surprising that conceptions of creation and world would find both figurative and substantive expression in their writing.

The presence of creation as a trope in the work of womanist scholars can also be associated with their use of certain literary and cultural sources that affirmed the lives of black women. Particularly influential among African American women religionists has been the work of Alice Walker. Indeed the term womanist derives from the work of Walker. In compositions such as her novel *The Color Purple*, *In Search of Our Mothers' Gardens: Womanist Prose*, and *Living by the Word: Selected Writings, 1973–1987*, a vision of a world imbued with the power and presence of the divine is depicted and venerated.

For example, while the *Color Purple* it may be read as kind of Bildungsroman for a poor black girl named Celie, one of the central motifs throughout the novel is the refiguring of the relationship between God and creation. Celie, the protagonist, progresses from imagining God as a big, white man indifferent to the plight of someone like her, to seeing God as "That Which Is Beyond Understanding But Not Beyond Loving."[38]

In other works, such as her essay "The Only Reason You Want to Go to Heaven," Walker writes about the sacred relationship her parents had with the earth as sharecroppers in Georgia as she was growing up.[39] While sharecropping was a dehumanizing system designed to dominate black people, Walker nevertheless suggests that her family's experience with the earth also transcended proximity and familiarity. According to Walker, the farming engaged in by her family was imbued with a "magical intimacy we felt with Creation."[40]

Works generated by womanist scholars addressing the plight of nature include Delores S. Williams's "Sin, Nature, and Black Women's Bodies" in 1993, Diane D. Glave's "Black Environmental Liberation Theology," Stephanie Y. Mitchem's *African American Folk Healing*, and Stephanie Y. Mitchem and Emilie Townes's, *Faith, Health, and Healing in African American Life*. In the essay "God Is Creation: Womanist Theology and the Earth," Linda Thomas reflects on why it took so long for black and womanist theologies of liberation to address environmental issues.[41] Yet connections between forms of human oppression and environmental and ecological subjugation appear to becoming more prevalent, with the most distinctive work arising among African American female scholars of religion who have adopted the appellation "ecowomanism."

The term ecowomanism appeared in scholarly discourse through the publication of Shamara Shantu Riley's essay "Ecology Is a Sistah's Issue Too: The Politics of Emergent Afrocentric EcoWomanism"[42] and Pamela Smith's essay "Green Lap, Brown Embrace, Blue Body: The Ecospirituality of Alice Walker."[43] In their reflections, ecowomanists emphasize the link between the oppression of the earth and the oppression of women of color. As noted by Riley,

> There is no use in womanists advocating liberation politics if the planet cannot support people's liberated lives, and it is equally useless to advocate saving the planet without addressing the social issues that determine the structure of human relations in the world.[44]

Other works often associated with ecowomanism include Barbara Holmes's *Race and the Cosmos: An Invitation to View the World Differently* and *Joy Unspeakable: Contemplative Practices of the Black Church*. There is also the work of Sylvia Hood Washington, which includes the essay "'We've Come This Far by Faith': Memories of Race, Religion, and Environmental Disparity," in *Echoes from the Poisoned Well: Global Memories of Environmental Injustice*.

In addition to the material listed above, perhaps *the* most complete articulations of African American reflection on creation can be found in the work of Karen Baker-Fletcher. In her seminal work *Sisters of Dust, Sisters of Spirit: Womanist Wordings on God and Creation*, Baker-Fletcher begins by alluding to the wisdom of her grandmother, who told her of "God's presence in all the lives and grows, who rejoiced in the miracle of life."[45] Calling upon the biblical tradition, she turns to scripture such as Psalm 24:1, which proclaims that the earth is the Lord's, and all that is in it. "We belong to the earth and the earth to God, who breathes through it and in every second."[46] As for the nature of the divine, she rejects gendered nomenclature, suggesting that God might better be referred to as "it," as Shug does in *The Color Purple*, or as "us." God is also spirit, as John reminds us, and as such lives in the midst of creation. Informed by a commitment to environmental justice and a creative freedom inherent in creation, Baker-Fletcher states, "Human beings require both freedom and order. Our survival requires realistic visions for a new order in which, with the rest of creation (plant, animal, soil, air, waters), we humans (black, white, brown, gold, red, rich, middle-class, and poor) can flourish in freedom."[47] Within the Christian tradition, Jesus as Christ, God incarnate, came to give us life that we might have abundantly. Abundant life includes the life of the spirit and the body. We are embodied spirits. A harmonious relationship with God, one another, and the planet is necessary for abundant life. "We are called to love God and to love our neighbors as ourselves. The earth is our nearest, dearest deeply tied to our own creation and continued life."[48] According to Baker-Fletcher, the Christian is to love all creation, material and spiritual, deeply. From such a posture, the Christian mandate to love one's neighbors includes affirming all existences, whether human or nonhuman, in a life-affirming manner.

As the title of Baker-Fletcher's book implies, if we but once more turn to the creation narrative, human beings are dust and spirit. We are earth creatures, *ha'adam* from *ha'adamah*,[49] humans from the humus. Further, Jesus Christ as God incarnate means that Jesus is God as dust. For Baker-Fletcher, this reveals God's intimate love of creation; God chooses to be one with creation. Concurrently, she contends that God as Spirit is best understood as the lovingness in creation that empowers life and aims for balance or justice.[50]

Conclusion

While it is evident that the well-being of the planet has not been completely overlooked by African American religionists, in the main, African American theological articulations tend toward the anthropological. Appeals to justice, common concern, and community are predicated on a shared humanity, the view that all persons, irrespective of race, class, gender, or sexuality, are made in the image and likeness of God. Subsequently, a comprehensive doctrine of creation or the world seems to be much more elusive.

One would be hard pressed to find within African American theology allusions to scientific theories about the origin of the universe or reflections on concepts such as deep time. Traditional theology posits God as the cause of all things. God is the progenitor of the deterministic process designed to produce certain outcomes. God is the prime mover, the Creator ex nihilo. However, as a majority of African American theologians also assert, it seems necessary for God to intercede in history and cosmos, as a corrective of nature, humanity and otherwise. Perhaps new and innovative construals of God as creativity, as emergent, and God and world as potentialities and possibilities rather than immutable and impassive actualities with definitive ends, might reveal new dimensions of beingness, human and otherwise.

Notes

1. George D. Kelsey, *Racism and the Christian Understanding of Man* (New York: Scribner, 1965).
2. Mark L. Chapman, *Christianity on Trial: African-American Religious Thought before and after Black Power* (Maryknoll, NY: Orbis Books, 1996), 28.
3. Howard Thurman, *The Luminous Darkness: A Personal Interpretation of the Anatomy of Segregation and the Ground of Hope* (New York: Harper & Row, 1965).
4. Thurman, *The Luminous Darkness*, x.
5. Thurman, *The Luminous Darkness*, 94.
6. Howard Thurman, *With Head and Heart: The Autobiography of Howard Thurman* (New York: Harcourt Brace Jovanovich, 1979), 8.
7. Howard Thurman, *For the Inward Journey: The Writings of Howard Thurman*, ed. Anne Spencer Thurman (San Diego, CA: Harcourt Brace Jovanovich, 1984), 180–81.
8. Howard Thurman, *The Centering Moment* (Richmond, IN: Friends United Press, 1984), 272.
9. Thurman, *The Centering Moment*, 278.
10. James H. Cone, *God of the Oppressed*, rev. ed. (Maryknoll, NY: Orbis Books, 1997), 138.
11. James H. Cone, "Whose Earth Is It Anyway?" in *Earth Habitat: Eco-Injustice and the Churches Response*, ed. Dieter Hessel and Larry Rasmussen (Minneapolis: Fortress Press, 2001), 23–32. See also James H. Cone, "One Earth, One Struggle," *The Other Side* (January–February 2004): 139–43; and Marguerite L. Spencer, "Environmental Racism and Black Theology: James H. Cone Instructs Us on Witness," *University of St. Thomas Law Journal* 5, no. 1 (2008): 288–311.
12. C. Eric Lincoln, *The Black Experience in Religion* (Garden City, NY: Anchor Press, 1974), 103.
13. Lincoln, *Black Experience in Religion*, 103.
14. Charles H. Long, *Alpha: The Myths of Creation* (Chico, CA: Scholars Press, American Academy of Religion, 1983), 11–12.
15. Long, *Alpha*, 18–19.

16. Charles H. Long, *Significations: Signs, Symbols, and Images in the Interpretation of Religion* (Aurora, CO: Davies Group, 1999), 107.
17. Long, *Significations*, 107.
18. Long, *Significations*, 120–21, 80, 84.
19. Peter J. Paris, *The Spirituality of African Peoples: The Search for a Common Moral Discourse* (Minneapolis: Fortress Press, 1995), 22. See also J. Omosade Awolalu's *Yoruba Beliefs and Sacrificial Rite* (New York: Athelia Henrietta Press, 1996), 3.
20. Paris, *Spirituality of African Peoples*, 131.
21. Nicholas C. Cooper-Lewter and Henry H. Mitchell, *Soul Theology: The Heart of American Black Culture* (San Francisco: Harper & Row, 1986), 142.
22. Cooper-Lewter and Mitchell, *Soul Theology*, 142.
23. Cooper-Lewter and Mitchell, *Soul Theology*, 144.
24. Cooper-Lewter and Mitchell, *Soul Theology*, 43–44.
25. Cooper-Lewter and Mitchell, *Soul Theology*, 46.
26. Cooper-Lewter and Mitchell, *Soul Theology*, 68.
27. Theophus Harold Smith, *Conjuring Culture: Biblical Formations of Black America* (New York: Oxford University Press, 1994), 22.
28. Stephen Breck Reid, *Experience and Tradition: A Primer in Black Biblical Hermeneutics* (Nashville: Abingdon Press, 1990), 27.
29. James Weldon Johnson, *God's Trombones: Seven Negro Sermons in Verse* (New York: Penguin, 1976), 3.
30. Zora Neale Hurston, *Mules and Men* (New York: Harper Perennial, 1990), 179.
31. Theophus Harold Smith, *Conjuring Culture: Biblical Formations of Black America* (New York: Oxford University Press, 1994), 25.
32. Anthony B. Pinn, "Of Money, God, and Earth: The Black Church on Economics and Environmental Racism," *Journal of Religious Thought*, 43–61 Double Issue, Vol. 56–57, No. 2–1 (Spring-Fall 2000/01): 43–61; Dwight N. Hopkins, "Holistic Health and Healing: Environmental Racism and Ecological Justice," in *Faith, Health, and Healing in African American Life*, ed. Stephanie Y. Mitchem and Emilie M. Townes (Westport, CT: Praeger, 2008); Theodore Smith Jr., "African-American Resources for a More Inclusive Liberation Theology," in *This Sacred Earth: Religion, Nature, Environment*, 2nd ed., ed. Roger S. Gottlieb (London: Routledge, 2004); and Mark Stoll, "Religion and African American Environmentalism," in *To Love the Wind and the Rain: African Americans and Environmental History*, ed. Dianne D. Graves and Mark Stoll (Pittsburg, PA: University of Pittsburg Press, 2006).
33. T. L. Gray, "Consider This," in *Holy Ground: A Gathering of Voices on Caring for Creation*, ed. Lyndsay Moseley and the staff of Sierra Club Books (San Francisco: Sierra Club Books, 2008). T. L. Gray is a minister of the National Baptist Convention and a doctoral student at Vanderbilt.
34. Theodore Walker, *Mothership Connections: A Black Atlantic Synthesis of Neoclassical Metaphysics and Black Theology* (Albany: State University of New York Press, 2004). See also Theodore Walker Jr., "African-American Resources for a More Inclusive Liberation Theology," in Gottlieb, *This Sacred Earth*.
35. United Church of Christ, *Toxic Wastes and Race in the United States* (New York: United Church of Christ Commission for Racial Justice, 1991); *The Proceedings of the First National People of Color Environmental Leadership Summit*, United Church of Christ and National Black Church Environmental and Economic Justice Summit Report (New York: National Council of Churches of Christ in the USA, 1993).

36. Dianne D. Glave, "Black Environmental Liberation Theology: The Theological and Historical Roots of Environmental Justice Activism by the African American Church," *The Griot* 23, no. 2 (Fall 2004): 61–70.
37. "National Black Church Environmental and Economic Justice Summit," National Council of Churches of Christ in the USA, Prophetic Justice Unit, Washington DC, December 1 and 2, 1993, 51.
38. Alice Walker, *The Color Purple* (New York: Harcourt, 2006), preface, xii.
39. Alice Walker, "The Only Reason You Want to Go to Heaven Is That You Have Been Driven Out of Your Mind (Off Your Land and Out of Your Lover's Arms): Clear Seeing Inherited Religion and Reclaiming the Pagan Self," in *Anything We Love Can Be Saved: A Writer's Activism* (New York: Ballantine Books, 1997), 3–27.
40. Walker, "Only Reason," 17. See also Walker, *The Cushion in the Road: Meditation and Wandering as the Whole World Awakens to Being in Harm's Way* (New York: New Press, 2013).
41. Delores S. Williams, "Sin, Nature, and Black Women's Bodies," in *Ecofeminism and the Sacred*, ed. Carol J. Adams (New York: Continuum, 1993), 24–29; Diane D. Glave, "Black Environmental Liberation Theology," in Graves and Stoll, *To Love the Wind*; Stephanie Y. Mitchem, *African American Folk Healing* (New York: New York University Press, 2007); Mitchem and Townes, *Faith, Health, and Healing*; Linda Thomas, "God Is Creation: Womanist Theology and the Earth," paper delivered at the World Forum on Theology and Liberation, 2009; Barbara Holmes, *Race and the Cosmos: An Invitation to View the World Differently* (Harrisburg, PA: Trinity International Press, 2002); Barbara Holmes, *Joy Unspeakable: Contemplative Practices of the Black Church* (Minneapolis: Augsburg Fortress, 2004).
42. Shamara Shantu Riley, "Ecology Is a Sistah's Issue Too: The Politics of Emergent Afrocentric EcoWomanism," in Gottlieb, *This Sacred Earth*, 412–27.
43. Pamela A. Smith, "Green Lap, Brown Embrace, Blue Body: The Ecospirituality of Alice Walker," *Cross Currents* 48, no. 4 (Winter 1998–99): 471–87.
44. Riley, "Ecology," 415.
45. Karen Baker-Fletcher, *Sisters of Dust, Sisters of Spirit: Womanist Wordings on God and Creation* (Minneapolis: Fortress Press, 1998), 1. See also Baker-Fletcher, "Something or Nothing: An Eco-Womanist Essay on God, Creation, and Indispensability," in Gottlieb, *This Sacred Earth*, 428–37.
46. Baker-Fletcher, *Sisters of Dust*, 1.
47. Baker-Fletcher, *Sisters of Dust*, 7.
48. Baker-Fletcher, *Sisters of Dust*, 7.
49. Reid, *Experience and Tradition*, 30.
50. Baker-Fletcher, *Sisters of Dust*, 19.

Selected Texts

Baker-Fletcher, Karen. *Sisters of Dust, Sisters of Spirit: Womanist Wordings on God and Creation*. Minneapolis: Fortress Press, 1998.

Baker-Fletcher, Karen. "Something or Nothing: An Eco-Womanist Essay on God, Creation, and Indispensability." In *This Sacred Earth: Religion, Nature, Environment*, 2nd ed., ed. Roger S. Gottlieb, 428–37. London: Routledge, 2004.

Chapman, Mark L. *Christianity on Trial: African-American Religious Thought before and after Black Power*. Maryknoll, NY: Orbis Books, 1996.

Cone, James H. *God of the Oppressed*. Rev. ed. Maryknoll, N.Y.: Orbis Books, 1997.

Cooper-Lewter, Nicholas C., and Henry H. Mitchell. *Soul Theology: The Heart of American Black Culture*. San Francisco: Harper & Row, 1986.

Johnson, James Weldon. *God's Trombones: Seven Negro Sermons in Verse*. New York: Penguin, 1976.

Kelsey, George D. *Racism and the Christian Understanding of Man*. New York: Scribner, 1965.

Lincoln, C. Eric. *The Black Experience in Religion*. Garden City, NY: Anchor Press, 1974.

Long, Charles H. *Alpha: The Myths of Creation*. Chico, CA: Scholars Press, American Academy of Religion, 1983.

Long, Charles H. *Significations: Signs, Symbols, and Images in the Interpretation of Religion*. Aurora, CO: Davies Group, 1999.

Paris, Peter J. *The Spirituality of African Peoples: The Search for a Common Moral Discourse*. Minneapolis: Fortress Press, 1995.

Reid, Stephen Breck. *Experience and Tradition*. Nashville: Abingdon Press, 1990.

Smith, Theophus Harold. *Conjuring Culture: Biblical Formations of Black America*. New York: Oxford University Press, 1994.

Thurman, Howard. *The Centering Moment*. Richmond, IN: Friends United Press, 1984.

Thurman, Howard. *The Luminous Darkness: A Personal Interpretation of the Anatomy of Segregation and the Ground of Hope*. New York: Harper & Row, 1965.

Thurman, Howard. *With Head and Heart: The Autobiography of Howard Thurman*. New York: Harcourt Brace Jovanovich, 1979.

Thurman, Howard. *For the Inward Journey: The Writings of Howard Thurman*. Ed. Anne Spencer Thurman. San Diego: Harcourt Brace Jovanovich, 1984.

Walker, Alice. *The Color Purple*. New York: Harcourt, 2006.

Walker, Theodore. *Mothership Connections: A Black Atlantic Synthesis of Neoclassical Metaphysics and Black Theology*. Albany: State University of New York Press, 2004.

CHAPTER 14

LIBERATION IN AFRICAN AMERICAN THEOLOGY

JUAN M. FLOYD-THOMAS

Definition

By strict definition, liberation is a dimension of African American experience that forms the core of the historical development of the African American theological tradition. Within the classic formulation of black theology, for instance, in its most prophetic sense, liberation is focused upon the relationship between the black experience and a faith in God as an emancipatory force in the course of human affairs. Specifically rooted in the Judeo-Christian idiom, the evidence of God's liberating power is found in the biblical imagery and stories of freedom (i.e., the Exodus narrative in the Hebrew Bible) as well as scriptural mandates by Jesus that true followers would give voice to the voiceless and uplift the downtrodden (i.e., Luke 4:18–19 in the New Testament). Therefore, from an African American Christian perspective, liberation is the positive transformation of unequal personal and societal power relations in the merger of divine and social justice in the world. The scholarly attention given to differentiating between freedom and liberation (The first deals with the absolute state of being unfettered from the sinful systems of oppression, as well as empowering the poor and debased masses to live up to their fullest potential as human beings. The second addresses the spiritual release from the bondage of sin, both structural and personal.) has hinged upon what is considered as human flourishing and fulfillment toward the well-being of God's children. This notion of freedom aligns itself with an indispensable perspective as enslaved Africans from the seventeenth to nineteenth centuries sought and fought for freedom, while the protests movements of the twentieth century highlighted liberation as the fulcrum of the black freedom struggle.

Within the purview of black theology, there is a definitive difference between liberation and freedom. On the one hand, liberation refers to the release from all forms of captivity—political, economic, sociocultural, and spiritual. On the other hand, freedom is the condition in which humans may choose their own beliefs, actions, and perspectives without external constraints or coercion. In the former case, liberation in a divine sense is marked by the salvation of humanity from sin and domination through Jesus Christ. In the case of the latter, freedom has a voluntary dimension regarding each person choosing to live an unfettered existence on the basis of Jesus Christ by the Holy Spirit giving humans liberty and inner peace even if external factors do not match that selfsame reality. In this relationship, the former makes possible the latter in the same way that liberties make possible the practice of freedom.

Liberation serves as a driving force for African Americans for several reasons. First, a liberation motif is true to the historical narrative of slave insurrections, abolitionism, and the suffrage, civil rights, and Black Power movements that mark the quintessential spirit and indestructible belief in freedom. Second, liberation, as a category abandoned after the civil rights movement, reintroduces and reasserts a much-needed conversation for this post-9/11 era filled with globalization, tribal-ethnic wars, religious fundamentalism, and terrorism about what constitutes legitimate means for ending structural oppression and systemic inequality. Third, liberation calls particular attention away from narrow perspectives of group concerns and toward a more holistic and universal understanding of human possibility wherein the struggles of oppressed and marginalized groups can find commonalty across the spectrum of race, ethnicity, gender, class, nationality, and sexuality. Fourth, the focus on liberation allows a discussion that moves beyond social description, and toward the necessity of conversation concerning ethics, practical theology, education, and pastoral care, that is, conversations that inform the mission and ministry of the church. A prime example would be critical debates concerning prophetic ministry inspired by a gospel of liberation as opposed to "profit-driven" ministry influenced by a gospel of prosperity. Liberation necessitates the interplay of theory and practice. Additionally, given the gross distortions and tragic misrepresentations about Africa and people of African descent in the popular media and scholarly literature of the late nineteenth and early twentieth centuries, philosopher Cornel West keenly observes that "the notion that black people are human beings is a relatively new discovery in the modern West."[1]

Integral to the emergence of black theology's slow but steady focus on liberation was the connection between Black Power's assault on white supremacy and the continued resonance of Christianity within the African American community. In the late 1960s, there were radical theological responses to racial discrimination and economic disenfranchisement of blacks within the United States, responses produced by the National Committee of Negro Churchmen (NCNC), Rev. James Forman's "Black Manifesto," and the formation of the Shrine of the Black Madonna by

Rev. Albert B. Cleage Jr. (aka Jaramogi Abebe Agyeman) that clearly foreshadowed the establishment of black theology as a new form of liberal theology toward liberation. Developed along lines of anger over social injustice and urgency of black consciousness, it was the seedbed for a liberationist perspective within black theology in order to challenge the demands of the Christian faith towards a vision of collective empowerment for the African American community.[2]

Historical Perspectives

Not only were the truest ideals of American democratic impulses awakened by the social and political disruptions that took place during the 1950s and 1960s but, for a generation of black religious leaders and theologians, the centrality of black liberation theology also revealed that there were much more diverse ways of interpreting the past than emphasized by earlier scholars. In the post-civil rights era, liberation as a benchmark of theological insights was brought to the fore. Without a doubt, theologian James Cone's *Black Theology and Black Power* (1969) was the first academic treatise to merge the contemporaneous struggles for racial, political, and socioeconomic equality with the critical concerns of Christian systematic theology. By offering a forcefully prophetic call for a theology rooted in black experience, this pioneering work established black liberation theology as an undeniable force within theological education and black church praxis. A year later, Cone's *A Black Theology of Liberation* (1970) advanced this proposition by developing a theological outlook in which God identified with the oppressed in general and the historical plight of black people's freedom struggle in the face of oppression. As the first work of African American systematic theology of liberation, he framed his approach around the premise that "Christian theology is a theology of liberation. It is *a rational study of the being of God in the world in light of the existential situation of an oppressed community, relating the forces of liberation to the essence of the gospel, which is Jesus Christ*."[3] By correlating the life, lessons, and legacy of Jesus's ministry to the overall experience of African Americans, one can see God's preferential option for the poor and oppressed, as epitomized in Luke 4:18–19. In this fashion, Cone's first two volumes served as the foremost works of liberation theology written in the English language. Moreover, Cone's presupposition of the ontological blackness of God, coupled with divine identification with the black oppressed, illustrated the unwillingness of normative white theology to even consider its duty to help end oppression and injustice.

Although Cone was the first of the professional black theologians to tackle the subject of liberation in a direct fashion, he was not alone in this endeavor. At various points, J. Deotis Roberts, Cecil Cone, Gayraud Wilmore, William R. Jones, and

Charles H. Long were among a constellation of African American theologians and religious scholars who provided divergent visions of liberation in theological terms. For instance, Roberts offered a counterpoint to Cone's emphasis on liberation by juxtaposing it with concerns about reconciliation. According to Roberts, "Liberation and reconciliation are the two main poles of Black Theology. They are not antithetical—one moves naturally from one to the other in the light of the Christian understanding of God and man."[4] Furthermore, he shares Cone's contention that "freedom sums up *what is*. Liberation is revolutionary—for blacks it points to *what ought to be*. Black Christians desire radical and rapid social change in America as a matter of survival. Black Theology is a theology of *liberation*. We believe that the Christian faith is avowedly revolutionary and, therefore, it may speak to this need with great force."[5] Thus, for Roberts, God's will at work in the world required a concurrent commitment to liberating African Americans and reconciling them with white Americans. Much like Cone, Roberts also focused on race, but his emphasis was guided by concerns about mutuality and dialogue among equals. Given this emphasis, Roberts effectively advances not just the prospect *for* liberation but also reconciliation as the teleological goal *of* liberation in racial matters.

In equal measures, the growing variety of perspectives on liberation as the centerpiece of black theology became quite evident in critical questions posed by the likes of Cecil Cone—James Cone's brother—and Gayraud Wilmore. For example, in their own respective ways, both scholars asserted that Cone's early writing was too indebted to Eurocentric theology, with blackness superimposed upon it. On the one hand, Cecil Cone contends that greater attention should be paid to the long history of African American protest thought that serves as the basis for black theology. In this regard, Cone agrees with his brother's early assessment by noting "the continuity between the theology of Black Power and black religion . . . the *liberation* motif of the theology of Black Power is in harmony with that aspect of the black religious tradition which is concerned with freedom and equality of all people."[6] However, Cecil Cone argues that "the problem with [James] Cone's interpretation is his failure to place liberation in its proper context. Because of the influence of the ideological concept of Black Power, he seems to view liberation primarily in political terms, thereby failing to grasp the broader meaning of liberation, defined in the black religious tradition as *the response of the people to their encounter with God*. Therefore any interpretation which does not place liberation in this context leads inevitably to a distortion."[7] On the other hand, Gayraud Wilmore argues that traditional African-centered religious practices, ethical values, and sacred beliefs had to become more central in order to understand black theology as an expression for communal concerns. Toward this end, Wilmore argues that the theology of the masses was confirmed and nourished not only in the church, but in many other institutions of the black community, oriented toward an "indestructible belief in freedom."[8] Wilmore promotes the idea that liberation within the black religious tradition was rooted in the desire and determination to survive against the ravages of slavery and segregation. By way of illustration, he contends that "Blacks could not, of course, be expected to concern themselves about liberation unless they first learned how to survive. What we shall call the liberation tradition was grounded in the will to survive, but it went beyond that. It rose above the constraining and pessimistic attitudes of slavery and established itself on the higher ground of racial improvement, moral rectitude, and benevolence."[9] In an interesting fashion, the work of Cecil Cone and Gayraud Wilmore instigated a vision of liberation that meant not only political independence or socioeconomic freedom from oppression by whites but also breaking free of epistemological indebtedness to prevailing norms and dominant theological paradigms as well.

In light of their respective challenges to the philosophical underpinnings and cultural origins of liberation within his scholarship, James Cone eventually shifted his focus. It is with his landmark text *God of the Oppressed* (1975) that Cone outlines a hermeneutic method for doing black liberation theology effectively.[10] In order to constructively engage the sources for doing relevant black theology, Cone notes that "the sources include Scripture and [African American cultural] tradition as they bear witness to the higher source of revelation as particularized and universalized in Jesus Christ. But also with equal and sometimes greater weight, the sources must include the history and culture of oppressed peoples."[11] In short order, Cone states that the sources—"the places to go for answers"—consisted largely of sermons, songs, prayers, and stories drawn from black experience. Most importantly, Cone made a critical, if in retrospect seemingly self-evident, discovery by insisting that the interpretive methods employed in analyzing these elements must arise organically from the sources themselves, as opposed to the classical Western religious tradition.

As articulated by Cone, liberation theology is invested in fostering a religious sensibility based in and responsive to the demands of the Black community. One needs only read Cone's 1982 memoir, *My Soul Looks Back*, to see how even he grappled with what precisely makes black liberation theology "black" per se. As he recalls, he had been seeking ways to incorporate black experience and culture into the articulation of a theological framework. In order to achieve this goal, he began focusing upon African American cultural resources as well as those found among other similarly oppressed people."[12] Central to James Cone's evolving theological approach to liberation is the realization that utilization of these conceptual tools involves viewing blackness as the epistemological core of theology wherein theology, community, and history cannot be severed from one another.

Unlike contemporaries such as James Cone, J. Deotis Roberts, Cecil Cone, and Gayraud Wilmore who, despite their own fervent debates, did not question the primacy of liberation as the core premise of black Christianity, philosopher William R. Jones and historian of religion Charles H. Long posed fundamental challenges to some of the most basic assumptions of black theology. To illustrate this point, Jones's *Is God a White Racist? A Preamble to Black Theology* (1973) overturned the intrinsic belief among black liberation theologians that God inherently sided with the oppressed by asking the simple yet provocative query: what is the empirical evidence—either historically or currently—for such a God? From this critical perspective, while the historic black church tradition may have helped black women, men, and children survive the plights of slavery and segregation, achieving the goal of liberation was going to involve more drastic measures than permitted by their strict adherence to theism. According to Jones, liberation theology, by its very nature, should be committed to the end of oppression and suffering at the core of unjust living conditions. Following this logic, Jones contends that engagement with the concept of theodicy has to be central to the work of anyone focused upon the annihilation of oppression with the objective goal "to eliminate the suffering that is the heart of oppression.... The theologian or philosopher of liberation, in short, *must* engage in the enterprise of theodicy if [he or she] is to accomplish [his or her] task."[13]

In light of black Christian theology's dominance within black religious discourse, Jones's contention that divine racism might have been the greatest obstacle to the liberation of black people was an undeniably bold articulation. Likewise, historian of religion Charles Long's emphasis on non-Christian (or "extra-church" in his own terms) expressions of liberating praxis within the African American experience, as a means of bringing forth a "theology of black freedom," has been a particularly slow and awkward turn within black theology. Long introduces the term *oppugnancy* into theological discourse by referring to the inordinate cruelty, animosity and carnage characterized by the enslavement of people of African descent as a constitutive element of the black religious experience and historical reality. In other words, oppugnancy addresses the "hardness of life" by confronting the harsh conditions that brought such a devastating situation into being. Moreover, Long's definition of the term reflects the sense that said reality was opaque and opposed to the well-being of the enslaved and oppressed, thereby provoking oppositional response to such hardship.[14] Without question, Jones and Long advance more incisive levels of theological thinking and historical consciousness in hopes of fully comprehending the nature of liberation. The challenge they put forth presaged the looming fear that liberation theology would become watered down by a loss of focus or diminished by a lack of a culturally centered perspective.

Second Generation of Liberationist God-Talk

During the 1980s and 1990s, the pioneering works of black theologians and religious scholars eventually gave rise to a new generation of self-identified black intellectuals focused upon advancing the cause of liberation in a variety of new directions. Whereas this younger cohort of black theologians surely built upon the framework established by their predecessors, they also heeded the emerging voices of their contemporaries who pushed the liberative discourse in new ways that had been previously underdeveloped. The emergence of the second wave of liberationist viewpoints within black theology was signaled by three separate strands. First, the groundbreaking essay "Black Theology and Black Woman" (1979) by systematic theologian Jacquelyn Grant offers a strong critique as well as a necessary corrective to the work of black male theologians who promoted a narrow definition of liberation that utterly ignored the gender discrimination and misogyny suffered by black women in a wholesale fashion. Grant's article served as a necessary spark that would eventually ignite the theological imagination and intellectual vitality that would later coalesce into the womanist movement (more to follow later). Second, philosopher of religion Cornel West's "Black Theology and Marxist Thought" (1979) wholeheartedly affirmed the vital need for black theology but implied its imminent irrelevance if it failed to meet the needs of the growing masses of poor and working-class people through a radical redistribution of wealth. West's genius in this regard was illustrating that black Christian principles and democratic socialist praxis were not antagonistic realities but actually were much more closely linked than previously acknowledged. Third, driven by the theologian John S. Mbiti's groundbreaking text *African Religions and Philosophy* (1969), a rising tide of contemporary African theologians such as Mercy Oduyoye, Bishop Desmond Tutu, Englebert Mveng, Patrick Klailombe, and others were sharing theological insights gleaned from the freedom struggles undertaken on the African continent. The promise of a transatlantic black theological project that envisions the decolonization of mind, body, spirit, and land as a ubiquitous objective of liberation was an undeniable contribution of African theologians.

In this fashion, the second generation of black male liberation theologians has developed a varied array of approaches. For instance, Josiah Young's *Pan-African Theology* (1992) attempts to bridge the perceived gaps between African and African American theological perspectives. James Evans's *We Have Been Believers* (1992) was a systematic theology fueled by his dual commitments to theology and literary criticism. Noel Erskine's *Decolonizing Theology* (1981) added the Afro-Caribbean dimension to the liberationist discourse. Likewise, George Cummings's *A Common Journey: Black Theology and Latin American Liberation Theology* (1989) sought to illustrate the synergy between the two most widely regarded yet least understood strands of liberation theology. Without question, as the most prolific liberation theologian of his generational cohort, Dwight Hopkins in works such as *Black Theology USA and South Africa* (1989), *Shoes That Fit Our Feet* (1993), *Down, Up and Over* (1999), *Heart and Head: Black Theology—Past, Present, and Future* (2002), and *Being Human* (2005) demonstrated the far-reaching possibilities of forging a constructive black theology of liberation attentive to race, class, gender, and sexuality in both historical and global contexts.

Current Perspectives

There are two current theological perspectives that stand to influence the future trajectory of how we understand and envision liberation within black theology, namely womanist theology and humanist theology. Over twenty-five years ago, the rise of womanist theology and ethics has revolutionized the interpretation of African American religion with the need to include gender within the purview of liberation. The cause of providing a corrective to the invisibility imposed upon race is superseded only by the obfuscation of the centrality and value of black women's presence and activity in religious experience. Alice Walker's *In Search of Our Mothers' Gardens* (1983) provided the definitive criteria and basis for womanism. In Walker's definition of "womanist" as both individual and movement, there are a number of guidelines that must be dealt with in order to understand womanism as a movement and ideology.[15] By arguing that ending sexual oppression must be as essential to liberation struggles as dismantling racial discrimination, womanist scholars such as Katie Cannon, Jacquelyn Grant, Delores Williams, Emilie Townes, Kelly Brown Douglas, and others were able to contend that the burden of the cross was best symbolized by the historic exploitation of black women along lines of race, class, and gender. It should be noted that womanism is not merely adding gender to the equation but rather is the wholesale expansion of theological discourse to include the entirety of humankind.

Womanism finds its basis in notions inherent in African American ethics such as a sense of community, a longing for justice, and a deep and personal love of oneself, of others, and of God. In combination, these elements not only make a complete and fully realized womanist but also a holistic and integrated woman of color. Taken individually, these elements of the womanist definition involve an epistemology and vocation that are both challenging and affirmative. Offering the prospects for extensive research of black women's activities within the black Protestant tradition, Jualyne Dodson and Cheryl Townsend Gilkes contend that "if anything characterizes the role of black women in religion in America, it is the successful extension of their individual sense of regeneration, release, redemption and spiritual liberation to a collective ethos of struggle for and with the black community."[16]

In light of this situation, womanism as both a movement and an ideology will be a model to other oppressed peoples to look internally, toward their own culture, institutions, and concerns, in order to improve their external conditions. In their constant quest for liberatory knowledge, Emilie Townes asserts, "Womanists in the religious academy make great use of and have ongoing conversations with other academic disciplines."[17] Such interdisciplinary discourse and analysis will, in turn, provide the means for the edification and quickening of all oppressed peoples. The inclusion of black lesbians, the elderly, the physically/mentally disadvantaged, and the poor is also present in Alice Walker's vision of womanism, but it still remains to be seen if the actual embodiment of her vision will do the same within the auspices of the black church tradition and the broader African American community. Kelly Brown Douglas astutely illustrates how womanist theology as "a social-political analysis of wholeness" confronts racism, sexism, classism, and heterosexism that impact the black community and black institutions—that is, church, schools—and perpetuate black oppression.[18]

Based on the sense of communal commitments and accountability that emerges from womanist ethics and theology, womanists will not allow the same kind of oversights that occurred in feminism such heterosexism, ageism, or classism. In her essay "The Emergence of Black Feminist Consciousness," ethicist Katie Cannon asserts that the moral agency of black women cannot be comprehended separate and apart from the historical and contemporaneous contexts of their social reality.[19] Cannon's distinctive hermeneutical turn is indicated by her declaration that "throughout the history of the United States, the interrelationship of White supremacy and Black patriarchal sexism has characterized Black women's reality as a situation of struggle—a struggle to survive in two contradictory worlds simultaneously, one White, privileged, and oppressive, the other Black, exploited, and oppressed. Thus, an untangling of the Black religious heritage sheds light on the feminist consciousness that guides Black women in their ongoing struggle for survival."[20] In describing a key transition from a black, male-dominated theology of liberation to womanist theological perspectives, Delores Williams explains that womanist scholarship has been intentional about reconstructing and redeeming the worldviews of African American women from invisibility.[21]

The work of womanist scholars and their grasp of the complex interconnection of race, class, gender, and sexuality offer a considerable wealth of insight about the growing edge of liberation. As a means of addressing black women's religious experience, Jacquelyn Grant asserts that "womanist theology begins with the experiences of Black women as its point of departure.... These experiences provide a context which is significant for doing theology. Those experiences had been and continue to be defined by racism, sexism and classism and therefore offer a unique opportunity and a new challenge for developing a relevant perspective in the theological enterprise."[22] Taken collectively, womanist theology has the potential to provide substantial inroads into how gender relations operate within the collective experiences of African Americans. Furthermore, moving forward, the reevaluation and reinterpretation of religious history that readily bespeaks a sacred tradition of black women's sense and celebration of their relationship with the divine, their community, and themselves is in and of itself a radical hermeneutical act that intrinsically redefines the historical enterprise.

Conversely, the articulation of humanist theology has developed greatly since the initial considerations made by William R. Jones over four decades ago. Building upon the theological foundations established in works such as *Why, Lord? Suffering and Evil in Black Theology* (1995), *Varieties of African American Religious Experience* (1999), *Terror and Triumph: The Nature of Black Religion* (2003), Anthony B. Pinn's most recent work, *The End of God-Talk: African American Humanist Theology* (2012), challenges the idea that African American liberation theology is unequivocally theistic in nature. Arguing that this long-held assumption has undermined African American theological discourse and excluded a rapidly growing segment of the African American population who self-identify as humanists, Pinn poses a crucial question: What is a nontheistic theology?

Drawing examples from Frederick Douglass, Harriet Tubman, and Alice Walker, Pinn's *End of God-Talk* outlines the first systematic African American nontheistic theology. Pinn offers a new center for theological inquiry, grounded in a more scientific notion of the human than the concept of *imago Dei* that dominates African American theistic theologies. He proposes an exploration of ethical conduct as well as the religious significance of ordinary spaces and activities as settings for humanist theological engagement. Through an innovative turn toward the study of human embodiment and ordinary life as the proper arena and content of theologizing, Pinn opens up new theological perspectives with important implications for future discussions of liberation in theological terms. In essence, Pinn forces us to recognize the limits of liberation in contemporary theological discourse by demanding a sharper focus on what black theology has to say about the evolving nature of moral evil and enduring signs of oppression given its steadfast commitment to redemptive suffering. By this token, Pinn's work raises a vital realization that the form, function, and fruition of liberation in any real sense within the black Christian perspective have to either be affirmed or abandoned.

In the final analysis, if the wellspring of liberation theological classification is strictly defined by a culture of black struggle and heroic ingenuity in response to suffering and oppression wrought by white supremacy, does that mean that the realization of liberation qua the end of white supremacy also marks the end of black theology? Instead, one might argue that these new theological perspectives were more about liberalization than liberation. Put another way, to an extent, the latter-day expression of the black freedom struggle shifted from the opportunity to make choices to specific choices themselves. And it is freeing, this expansion of self-defined and self-determined liberation into spaces visual as well as sonic, instinctual as well as intellectual, structural as well as spiritual, and performed as well as lived. Indeed, if liberation is the key concern of black religion writ large, it must ultimately focus on how black women, men, and children encounter that which they deem most sacred in their existence in the depths of their struggle to be fully and freely human.

Notes

1. Cornel West, *Prophesy Deliverance: An Afro-American Revolutionary Christianity* (Louisville, KY: Westminster John Knox Press, 1982), 47. See *Prophesy Deliverance*, 15–24 on sources of black thought, 27–36 on the black predicament in the United States, and 69–91 on the variety of black responses to white supremacy.
2. Anthony B. Pinn, "Black Theology," in *Liberation Theology in the United States*, ed. Stacey Floyd-Thomas and Anthony Pinn (New York: New York University Press, 2010), 19.
3. James H. Cone, *A Black Theology of Liberation*, 20th anniversary ed. (Maryknoll, NY: Orbis Books, 2004), 1.
4. J. Deotis Roberts, *Liberation and Reconciliation: A Black Theology* (Philadelphia: Westminster Press, 1971), 26.
5. Roberts, *Liberation and Reconciliation*, 27.
6. Cecil Cone, *The Identity Crisis in Black Theology* (Nashville, TN: African Methodist Episcopal Church, 1975), 97.
7. Cone, *Identity Crisis in Black Theology*, 118.
8. Gayraud S. Wilmore, *Black Religion and Black Radicalism: An Interpretation of the Religious History of Afro-American People*, 2nd ed. (Maryknoll, NY: Orbis Books, 1983), 219.
9. Wilmore, *Black Religion and Black Radicalism*, 228.
10. Cone asserts that "the theologian is before all else an exegete, simultaneously of Scripture and of existence." James H. Cone, *God of the Oppressed* (Maryknoll, NY: Orbis Books, 1975), 8.
11. Cone, *God of the Oppressed*, 9.
12. James H. Cone, *My Soul Looks Back*, 103.
13. William R. Jones, *Is God a White Racist? A Preamble to Black Theology* (Garden City, NY: Anchor Press / Doubleday, 1973), xix–xx.
14. Jones, *Is God a White Racist?* 211.
15. Alice Walker's classic definition of womanism is as follows:

> 1. From womanish. (Opp. of "girlish," i.e., frivolous, irresponsible, not serious.) A Black feminist or feminist of color. From the Black folk expression of mothers to female children, "You acting womanish", i.e. like a woman. Usually referring to outrageous, audacious, courageous, or willful behavior. Wanting to know more and in greater depth than is considered "good" for one. Acting grown up. Being grown up. Interchangeable with another Black folk expression: "You trying to be grown." Responsible. In charge. Serious.
>
> 2. Also: A woman who loves other women, sexually and/or nonsexually. Appreciates and prefers women's culture, women's emotional flexibility (values tears as natural and counterbalance of laughter), and women's strength. Sometimes loves individual men, sexually and/or nonsexually. Committed to survival and wholeness of the entire people, male and female. Not a separatist, except periodically, for health. Traditionally universalist, as in: "Mama why are we brown, pink, and yellow, and our cousins are white, beige and black?" Ans.: "Well, you know the colored race is just like a flower garden, with every color flower represented." Traditionally capable, as in: "Mama, I'm walking to Canada and I'm taking you and a bunch of slaves with me." Replay: "It wouldn't be the first time."

3. Loves music. Loves dance. Loves the moon. *Loves* the Spirit. Loves love and food and roundness. Loves the struggle. Loves the Folk. Loves herself. Regardless.

4. Womanist is to feminist as purple is to lavender. (Alice Walker, *In Search of My Mothers' Gardens* [San Diego, CA: Harcourt, 1983], xi–xii.)

16. Jualyne Dodson and Cheryl Townsend Gilkes, "Something Within: Social Change and Collective Endurance in the Sacred World of Black Christian Women," in *Women and Religion in America*, ed. Rosemary Radford Ruether and Rosemary Skinner, vol. 3 (San Francisco: Harper and Row, 1986), 80–130. This examination of black women's roles within church and society is later advanced in Cheryl Townsend Gilkes, *If It Wasn't for the Women . . . : Black Women's Experience and Womanist Culture in Church and Community* (Maryknoll, NY: Orbis Books, 2000).
17. Emilie M. Townes, "Voices of the Spirit: Womanist Methodologies in the Theological Disciplines," *The Womanist* 1, no. 1 (Summer 1994): 1.
18. Kelly Brown Douglas, *The Black Christ* (Maryknoll, NY: Orbis Books, 1994), 99.
19. Katie G. Cannon, *Katie's Canon: Womanism and the Soul of the Black Community* (New York: Continuum, 1995), 47.
20. Cannon, *Katie's Canon*, 47.
21. Delores S. Williams, *Sisters in the Wilderness: The Challenge of Womanist God-Talk*, (Maryknoll, NY: Orbis Books, 1993), 175.
22. Jacquelyn Grant, "Womanist Theology: Black Women's Experience as a Source for Doing Theology, with Special Reference to Christology," in *Black Theology: A Documentary History*, vol. 2, *1980–1992*, ed. James H. Cone and Gayraud S. Wilmore (Maryknoll, NY: Orbis Books, 1993), 278.

Selected Texts

Cone, James H. *A Black Theology of Liberation*. 20th anniversary ed. Maryknoll, NY: Orbis Books, 2004.

Floyd-Thomas, Stacey and Anthony Pinn, eds. *Liberation Theology in the United States* New York: New York University Press, 2010.

Gilkes, Cheryl Townsend. *If It Wasn't for the Women . . . : Black Women's Experience and Womanist Culture in Church and Community*. Maryknoll, NY: Orbis Books, 2000.

Jones, William R. *Is God a White Racist? A Preamble to Black Theology*. Garden City, NY: Anchor Press/Doubleday, 1973.

Roberts, J. Deotis. *Liberation and Reconciliation: A Black Theology*. Philadelphia: Westminster, 1971.

West, Cornel. *Prophesy Deliverance! An Afro-American Revolutionary Christianity*. Louisville, KY: Westminster John Knox, 1982.

Williams, Delores. *Sisters in the Wilderness: The Challenge of Womanist God-Talk*. Maryknoll, NY: Orbis Books, 1993.

Wilmore, Gayraud. *Black Religion and Black Radicalism: An Interpretation of the Religious History of Afro-American People*. 2nd ed. Maryknoll, NY: Orbis Books, 1983.

CHAPTER 15

EVIL AND SIN IN AFRICAN AMERICAN THEOLOGY

LARRY G. MURPHY

POPULAR Christian understandings of evil, among clergy and laity, typically have cast it as a cosmic force, personal or impersonal, that perpetrated unmerited pain, suffering, and misfortune on humans and/or on the created order. Often this cosmic force was named as Satan or the devil. The negative experiences that were evil's fruit were also commonly referred to as evil. The negative cosmic force was understood to be operating contrary to the will and positive intentions of a divine, benevolent being. Sin, correspondingly, was understood as those human actions that served evil's ends and as human actions that were in violation of the divinity's prescriptions for right behavior in the divine/human relationship or in human community. But the depth of oppression and suffering pervasively experienced by black people across the span of their residence in the United States caused black and womanist theological reflections on evil and sin almost invariably to come to focus on the relationship of those concepts to the historical black social condition.

Thus, one finds that the discussion among black and womanist theologians typically addresses evil and sin in terms of their contemporary *social construction*, that is, exploring the ways in which they seemingly emerge from human will, rather than from a transhuman, cosmic force, even if there lingers implicitly in the background of the conversation an inchoate assumption of a transcendent existence of evil. This emphasis on *social evil* and *social sin* centralizes the negative impact of these constructs on human and environmental well-being, rather than on violation of divine sanctity. This, says black theologian Stephen Ray, distinguishes black theology's treatment of evil and sin from that rendered by traditional Evangelical theology in North America. The latter almost exclusively casts the issue as something between the individual and God. Evil is essentially located in the heart, so one can be evil apart from one's actions. But in black theology, says Ray, "Evil is not what is in your heart but what you are doing to your neighbor." Thus, black theology focuses on the horizontal, social meanings of evil, rather than its personal and vertical vectors. The critical pertinence of this is that if evil is *only* a matter of the heart, one can be convinced that one's heart is right with God and hence go forth to engage in actions that are destructive to human and ecological well-being but feel vindicated and exonerated from any culpability. Alternatively, for black theology the proof is in the consequences of action for the social order and the larger terrestrial ecology.[1]

Early Black Theological Treatments Evil, Sin, and Suffering

In his 1968 collection of sermons, *The Black Messiah*, the Reverend Albert Cleage[2] claimed that God, Jesus, and the biblical Israelites were *black*, in ontology and biology, as fully and in the same way as oppressed African Americans are biologically black. This total identification of God as black, along with the assertion that God had acted in history to liberate a black people, the Israelites, through the Exodus event, is the validation of God's intention to liberate black people through the "revolutionary" ministry of the black Jesus. A white God and white Jesus logically would not, argues Cleage, intervene in history to undermine the interests of their own people—white people—for the sake of black people. Extrapolating from this theological and hermeneutical premise, Cleage articulated a construct of black *suffering* as a deserved consequence of black people's *sin*, which he defines as their quietism in the face of black oppression. In Cleage's own words,

> The people who accept oppression, who permit themselves to be downtrodden, those people are faithless because God did not make men to be oppressed and to be downtrodden.[3]

Cleage offers no definition of evil, nor makes any reference to it, but the concept of sin is directly connected in social behavioral terms to historical black suffering. It is framed as both acting outside of one's divinely intended identity and, correspondingly, refusing to act in ways that uphold God's will for how human community is to function. Specifically, God intends human freedom, and so to tolerate subjugation is to commit sin.

Then, in 1969, seminary professor James Cone published his landmark *Black Theology and Black Power*. This volume, commonly cited as the launching point of the contemporary black theology movement, channels Cleage's general notions of blackness and God's identity, as well as sin being definitionally connected to the social/

historical situation of black people and their response to it. While Cleage's God is ontologically black, God in Cone's thought is black insofar as God radically identifies with blackness due to black people's iconic role as oppressed, suffering humanity. The Christ event, culminating in the cross and the Resurrection, is God's liberative response.

For Cone, the black experience, historically framed by unmerited oppression and suffering, epitomizes *evil* and *sin*. Furthermore, evil in US history has become synonymous with whiteness, and sin is what whiteness perpetrates in the world. Indeed, says Cone, whiteness is "the source of human misery in the world, whether Amerindian reservations, or black concentrations camps, or the rape of Viet Nam." More particularly, it is the taking away of black people's humanity. "The sin of whites is the definition of their existence in terms of whiteness." By this, Cone seems to mean that whites have made ontological whiteness a norm for human existence, an idol to which obeisance is to be given, a value center around which social privilege coalesces. It arrogates to itself the power and prerogative to possess the world and to orchestrate the world's business. One may see an illustration of Cone's claim in the 1900 assertion of Indiana senator Albert Beveridge defending the US annexation of the Philippines:

> We will not renounce our part in the mission of the race, trustee, under God, of the civilization of the world. . . . He has made us the master organizers of the world to establish system where chaos reigns. . . . The judgment of the Master is upon us: "Ye have been faithful over a few things; I will make you ruler over many things."[4]

Whiteness, then, is, in effect, asserted as the *imago Dei*. This confusion of divine and human identity results in the arrogance of power that, in turn, translates into the oppression of those whose very being stands beyond the pale of white identity.

Cone's definitions allow for blacks, as full participants in the human enterprise, to be participants, also, in evil/sin. To the degree that black people become conscripted into "whiteness" or aid and abet its intentions, they, too, are sinners. Indeed, in black people's efforts to negotiate their existence in the US context of white cultural normativity and empowerment, this does occur. But the hegemonic historical agency of white people in their idolatrous self-assertion has essentially confined black people to the position of being victims of, rather than co-conspirators in, evil and sin. And the urgency of the resultant existential dilemma for black people makes whites and whiteness the focus of Cone's theologizing on evil and sin.

In his second book on black theology, *A Black Theology of Liberation*, Cone discusses at greater length the matter of sin in relationship to blacks. In Cone's view, sin for the black community is the loss of identity and a corresponding condition of estrangement from the source of one's being. This view is consistent with the many black conversion narratives in which even those persons thoroughly nurtured into and active within the life of the church nonetheless labor under what they name as the weight of *sin*, until that metanoiac event in which intimate connection is made with the source and giver of life and one assumes a new sense of self as a child of God.[5] But Cone seems to be saying something more. For the normal process of identity formation and connection to transcendent reality is problematized for blacks by whites' purposeful manipulation of black *and* white identities, in the service of white interests. This was evidenced in whites' common hermeneutical distortion of the Ephesians 6 passage in the New Testament when used as a text for sermons delivered to the enslaved. "Servants be obedient unto your masters as unto Christ" was homiletically explained as the mandate to see the white master and the deity as interchangeable entities, to whom blacks, as the modern counterparts to the scriptural "servants," were bound to submit. This is further evidenced in whites' consistent pictorial imaging of Jesus as a blond-haired northern European. Thus, Cone seems to suggest that there emerged among some blacks an inadvertent idolatrous confusion of terrestrial whiteness with the cosmic, divine value center and, consequently, the seduction into a desire to be white. Therefore black sin is "a refusal to be what we are"; it is "saying yes to the white absurdity"—accepting the world as is, structured on white terms, and conceding to whites the power and prerogative to define black existence. To be in sin is to be contented with white solutions for the "black problem" and not rebel against every infringement of white being on black being.[6]

As aforementioned, Cone does not speak directly to the origin or nature of evil as an ideational construct. He seems simply to grant evil's existence, as that which generates what he terms "negative suffering," suffering that is unmerited and unrelated to any precipitating act on the part of the sufferer. The negative suffering that blacks historically have experienced is the consequence of the evil of whiteness extant in the world. The exploration of the metaphysical origin or nature of evil must not become a diversion from working to eradicate its manifestations in the world. In so doing, though, one will meet with what Cone terms "positive suffering," which is the unavoidable experience of those who, like Christ, engage themselves in the fight against the evils of the world. The distinction between these two types of suffering lies only in the fact that positive suffering *is* precipitated by the actions of the sufferer; it is the retaliation against efforts to counter evil and achieve justice and caring mutuality in human social relationships. Christians, in general, and black Christians, in particular, are called to oppose the negative suffering that evil perpetrates and, as co-laborers with God for liberation, to embrace their positive suffering as the emblem and inevitable price of their struggle to bring about a world that is as God intended.

Cone Critiqued

In *Redemption in Black Theology*, published in 1979, Olin P. Moyd offered what he thought to be a constructive critique of Cone's position on sin. He argued that "in

Black theology sin is understood to be the fallout of the initial distortion of human nature...the lust for omnipotence which the Creator has reserved for himself."[7] Further, says Moyd, "Black theology assumes that *all persons* are sinners before God and stand in need of redemption." Moyd does not make reference to evil or other sources of sin, but he sees the concept of sin as primordial and applicable across the human family and across human behaviors, essentially in keeping with traditional Christian theology. Thus he takes some exception to Cone's assertion that "sin is whiteness—white people's desire to be God in human relations." While he concurs with much of the premise of Cone's definitional understanding of sin, he says it is not properly limited to whites, because other groups, including blacks, try to be what they are not, and there are instances of both blacks and whites asserting themselves as God in relations with other people. In regards to the historical oppression of African Americans, he sees the naming of this as sin, as asserted by Cone, to be but a particularized manifestation of what sin definitionally is. Moyd wants to guard against a notion of sin that is too closely tied to whites' negative behavior; he wants one that allows that others can sin, that is, can act oppressively and outside of their divinely established identity. But Cone's work, in fact, admits of this, while focusing upon what for him is historically the primary and most problematic instantiation of sin, white hegemony.

In another critique of Cone, and similar to Moyd, theologian-ethicist Riggins Earl points to what he sees as Cone's too narrowly confining the black understanding of sin to whites' perpetration of slavery, social abuse, and its consequent suffering. While granting this to be included in the understanding, Earl contended that at least for enslaved black people, the encounter with God also yielded "an existential and ontological understanding of sin as...the fear of 'being-in-general,'" that is, as "the lack of courage to be in the face of being, itself." The state of sin was not, according to Earl, defined by commission of such behavioral violations as drinking and dancing but by being in alienation from one's true selfhood, thus from God and one another; it was blacks' lack of courage to challenge their historical/social victimization and reclaim their original creative selfhood, as endowed by God. Redemption from this state of sin came in the experience of conversion.[8] Interestingly, though, both Earl and Cone locate sin, for blacks and whites, in the matter of living in a misconstrual of one's divinely ordained identity in the context of white oppression. Both include in black sin the acquiescence in whites' idolatrous self-distortion. Thus it would seem that, as with Moyd, Earl is asserting a distinction from Cone that is without an essential difference.

One notes, then, the continuity of theological definitions of black people's sin:

- Cleage's notion of black sin as failure to fight ferociously against one's oppression, in fulfillment of one's true selfhood as made in the image of God
- Cone's assertion of black sin as "refusal to be what we are," as created by God, expressed as refusal to rebel against the infringement of whites on black being

- Moyd's view that black sin includes "capitulating to white power" and failure to join in God's activity of black social historical redemption from oppression
- Earl's contention that black sin is "the lack of courage to be in the face of being itself," that is, the failure to challenge historical black victimization, thereby reclaiming the original, divinely endowed black selfhood

One also notices that neither the origin nor nature of evil, per se, is explored, nor is the human capacity and propensity to sin. The discussion focuses, on the one hand, upon evil and sin, used somewhat interchangeably, as the perpetration of harm and suffering upon black people and, on the other hand, upon sin in terms of black people's deficit behavior in response to their subjugation.

Variations on the Early Expositions of Evil and Sin

Furthering and nuancing the conversation, Stephen Ray offers a definition of evil as "that which causes, and whose presence is seen in, human suffering."[9] It manifests in three primary expressions: racial/cultural oppression; patriarchy; and the maldistribution of the goods of creation, which leads, in turn, to intergenerational poverty and destitution. These modalities of evil are, says Ray, "the predicate" for other, collateral evils that generate suffering and negatively impact the well-being of the human community and the planetary order.

Sin, for Ray, is human participation in the workings of evil, either through willful action or through a "cultivated naivete." By the latter term, Ray means a refusal to see or acknowledge what is demonstrably an evil reality; a willingness to refuse to name an evil reality for what it is; a disposition to displace accountability for evil by attributing it to something not transparently the source. He cites as an example the displacement of blame for the degradation of black communities onto such factors as black intellectual deficiency, or black moral lassitude, or the Moynihanian "defective black family," as opposed to naming the racial animus that has systematically stymied black individual and communal flourishing.

Ray grants that blacks can participate in the social production of evil and the commission of sin so defined. But with *rare* exceptions, they, either as individuals or as a group, have not had the social, cultural, or economic power to assert and enforce the widespread, systemic suffering that is black theology's urgent concern.

As to the source or origin of the impulse to evil, Ray points to "the predatory, parasitic nature of all life within creation." Every life form, in order to sustain itself, must impose upon the existence of other elements in creation. This given propensity, facilitated by the human imagination, is the entry point for evil, that is, for the initiation of acts that result in the continuing modes of suffering in the world. But though such acts are built into the order of creation, Ray contends that they are not, thereby, outside of the definition of sin. Ray thus imputes to humans an Augustinian vision of "original sin." But, avers Ray, "The Christian faith says that through the work of the Holy Spirit, while Christians are not, and will never be, fully liberated from human propensities, we are able to *see* their fruits as *evil*, and are motivated to work against them."[10]

Thus, for Ray, if evil has to do with human's imposition of suffering on other humans and other acts that negate the well-being of the larger created order, the initiation of evil is built into the created order of things. The resultant seeming inevitability of evil is addressed in Christian theology, says Ray, by the action of the Holy Spirit, which motivates humans to work to moderate and counteract the negative consequences of their inherent predispositions.

Sharing essentially this same position on the created human disposition to predation, and thus, in consequence, to the generation of suffering, the late William Jones, humanist theologian, once wrote,

> We are born into a world where, in order to survive, everything has to feed on something else. Thus, we have only two ontological options, as defined by God's creation: suicide or homicide. If I choose not to feed on something else, my only choice is to nibble on myself, which soon exhausts the food supply (suicide). If I reject suicide—which is the demonstrated choice of all those still living—I am convicted of choosing to feed on something else (homicide).... this scenario defines ontological or original oppression.[11]

Jones's position seems to be that what humans name as evil is the unearned oppression and suffering that they experience, but that this is actually the result of the natural working out of the inherent will to survive and flourish. However circumstantially it comes about, certain groups acquire the capacity to oppress others, that is, to assert their will to survive and flourish—to "feed on" others—subjugating them to their needs and desires. This dynamic is not racially based but rather is universal and self-referential, whatever the identity of the self and its group extensions.

However, Jones's particular concern is with the historic subjugation of black people by whites, buttressed by theological claims that privilege white survival over black, justifying and obfuscating the reality of black suffering. This has happened in a manner that has made black suffering maldistributed, enormous, dehumanizing, and transgenerational. The magnitude and endurance of black suffering leads Jones to query if their subjugation is owing to *God's* privileging of whites because God, Godself, is, in fact, *white*. Thus, Jones sees issues of theodicy as the very heart of the matter. Jones's humanist theological solution to this seemingly divinely established, endemic, but maldistributed assertion of evil is, similar to Ray's: *acknowledgment* of human realities and *action* to counteract them. Ray's Christian faith offers the assistance of the Holy Spirit in this effort. But Jones's effort to navigate the multiple issues of theodicy leads to the conclusion that the suffering that black people have experienced under a supposedly benevolent *and* omnipotent God is not evidence that God is a white racist. Rather, Jones chooses the option that God does not coerce humans toward given social and historical outcomes. Instead, God created humans with the capacity to exercise freedom. Humans, thereby, act in "functional ultimacy," that is, with the authority and capacity in their freedom to negotiate the conditions of their existence, including the consequences of their parasitical nature. Thus, upon *humans* falls the responsibility to effect those personal and systemic modes of communal governance and interaction that avoid oppression and provide for mutual well-being.[12]

Resonant with this conclusion of Jones is the work of humanist theologian Anthony Pinn. Pinn, who has published widely on this subject, says, "Humanists resolve the problem of evil through an appeal to human accountability. Humans have created the problems presently encountered and humans are responsible for changing those conditions."[13]

Womanist Reflections on Evil and Sin

Womanist theology emerged as a critique of both feminist theology, which subsumed black women's experience under that of white women, if it considered it at all, and early black theology, which it saw as being guilty of similar omissions, that is, assuming that the category "black" covered male and female perspectives, or that black womanhood added no critical dimensions to the black theological project.

One of the progenitors of womanist theology, Delores Williams, centers her treatment of sin upon its social manifestations, particularly in regards to black women. Williams says that the womanist concept of social sin is drawn from the historical "devaluation of black women's humanity and 'defilement' of their bodies as the social sin American patriarchy and demonarchy have committed against black women and their children."[14] Womanism derives the validation of this both from classical European traditions against bodily defilement, as well as from biblical treatments of the issue of defilement, which suggest the gravity of the sin of this defilement of women's bodies and of women's spirits and self-esteem.[15] Her reference is to what was the recurrent rape and domestic violence visited upon black women's bodies by white slaveholders and overseers, as well as the abuse of their labor through overwork and consignment to the most onerous of labor tasks, during slavery and beyond. But to the degree that black men participate in rape and violence against women, they, too, share in the guilt of this social sin.

Womanist theology extends this conception of social sin as defilement of the body to the twentieth-century American defilement of nature—of *earth's* body, its spirit and self-esteem—through the profit-driven pursuit of industrial and technological advances that result, for example, in oil spills, chemical dumping into rivers and streams, urban smog, and other modes of pollution of earth's land, air, and water.

Notwithstanding this notion of sin as social/corporate, womanist theology does also recognize *individual* sin, from which black women are not exempt. Says Williams,

> Individual sin has to do with participating in society's systems that devalue black women's womanhood (humanity) through a process of invisibilization—that is, invisibilizing the womanist character of black women's experience and emphasizing the stereotypical images of black women that prevail and are perpetuated in the larger society. These stereotypes image black women as having "child-like mentality," as being "girlish" in their actions, and as being "frivolous and loose" in character. . . . black women also participate in sin when they do not challenge the patriarchal and demonarchal systems in society defiling black women's bodies through physical violence, sexual abuse, and exploited labor.[16]

Womanist analysis, then, goes beyond racial abuse and suffering in its consideration of sin. It recognizes the particular ways that suffering devolves upon women, especially black women. Womanist theology further incorporates larger justice/ethical concerns, for example, sexual orientation and the sustainability of the ecosystem. Since, therefore, the sin that engages Williams's attention is socially derived, the remedy must be also, a point womanist theology shares with black theology. It lies in cooperative efforts to oppose defilement and devaluation of human and material creation.

But if Williams sees the issues of defilement and devaluation as the social challenge of black women, for Emilie Townes it is *domination.* Among the prominent voices in the continuing advancement of womanist social ethical and theological discourse, Townes names domination as systemic evil, which seems to define evil as the arrogant imposition of control over others. This, in turn, leads to their suffering. Drawing insights from Audre Lorde, Townes speaks of suffering as a stagnant accommodation to human-imposed disabilities, which becomes the entering point for the institutionalizing and routinizing of those disabilities as *structures of oppression. Pain*, on the other hand, occasions the recognition and naming of one's constrictions and social disabilities and serves as the energizing point for opposing them and transforming one's situation toward justice.

In Townes view, suffering is not in the will of God. Indeed, "It is an outrage that there is suffering at all." The removal of suffering is "God's redeeming purpose."[17] Through God's intervention in history, specifically in the work of Jesus and his Resurrection, "God has spoken against evil and injustice." Through the empty cross and tomb, God has taken the initiative "to transform suffering into wholeness—to move the person from victim to change agent."[18] What is implied is that the work of God through Christ, signified by God's power to effect the *empty* cross and tomb, is to reassert the proper paradigm of power relationships, with God as determinative authority in human relations, not humans over humans in oppressive control—dominance, the essence of "evil."

Townes challenges African Americans to work collaboratively to move past the suffering that dominance brings, to pain, thereby saying no to their oppressive conditions and freeing them to bring creative change.

Employing Literary/Cultural Sources for Reflection on Evil and Sin

Ethicist-theologian Katie G. Cannon plumbs the traditions of African American preaching, incorporated in black women's literary productions, as resources for her take on questions of theodicy and her definitions of evil and sin. She is particularly informed by the sermons found in the works of famed cultural anthropologist and folklorist Zora Neale Hurston. Cannon distinguishes between "ills suffered because of physical and natural calamities" (natural evil) and the suffering brought on by "transgressions that proceed directly from human sin—structures of domination, subordination, and constraints that reinforce and reproduce hierarchies based on race, sex, class, and sexual orientation."[19] Cannon identifies these transgressions as "moral evils that take such forms as chattel slavery, economic impoverishment, wars and the atrocities they involve."[20] She declines a speculative exploration of evil's provenance and, instead, implies a popular understanding of moral offense, hence moral evil, as egregiously initiated pain, oppression, and suffering visited by humans both upon other humans and on the broader created order. And the perpetration of such morally offensive human acts seems to be traceable to "God's gift of freedom to act rightly or wrongly."[21] Cannon asserts as one womanist liberative response to the presence of evil in the world the bringing to bear of a womanist critique of African American sermonic texts to counter their traditional patriarchy but then to draw from their rich spiritual legacy the energizing affirmation of God's sustaining presence as the resource to resist evil.

Catholic Womanist Perspectives on Evil and Sin

Theologian Sister Jamie Phelps, O.P., speaks of two kinds of evil: natural and moral. The former results from catastrophic acts of nature; the latter results from humans acting out of their free will, which she says results in socially constructed evil, or moral evil. Note that in Phelps's framing of the terms, evil is not equated either with the natural or the human acts but, rather, with what "results from" these, namely, harm and suffering. She indicates that while investigations of the source of evil and how it could exist given the reality of a benevolent and omnipotent God would be "interesting and . . . intellectually stimulating," she instead focuses upon the manifestation of socially constructed, moral evil in the world. She says,

> Socially constructed evil involves patterns of relationships that are directed toward the denial of the human dignity and value of some human beings for the benefit of other human beings. Such dehumanization is the source of existential and physical suffering, including death.[22]

Phelps is particularly concerned with the socially constructed evil that centers upon race, as that has been so consequential for the well-being of African Americans. She asserts that "racism is a sin. . . . [But] not merely one sin among many; it is a radical evil that divides the human family and denies the new creation of a redeemed world."[23] Yet, as generally with womanist theologians, she does not disaggregate racial oppression from what is seen as the triumvirate of interlocking oppressions: race, gender, and class.

Again, then, one sees Phelps's concern over the *social, systemic* instantiations of evil, with the corrective being a collaborative effort on the part of benevolent-minded persons to achieve an "intellectual and moral conversion" of their acquired oppressive beliefs and attitudes. They could, in turn, infuse and transform the prevailing oppressive systemic structures of church and society.

Another Catholic womanist take on evil is offered by theologian M. Shawn Copeland. She relates suffering and evil as two essentially endemic aspects of the order of things. On the one hand, she asserts that suffering is the universal, unavoidable condition of human existence. Like the rain, it falls indiscriminately upon the just and the unjust. Suffering is "the disturbance of our inner tranquility caused by physical, mental, emotional, and spiritual forces that we grasp as jeopardizing our lives, our very existence."[24] At the same time, she defines evil as "the negation and deprivation of good," as well as "the condition or experience of negated good."[25] Evil is, thereby, one of those forces of which suffering is a consequence and manifestation. Indeed, it is of the nature of evil to precipitate suffering.

Given her definition of evil as the negation of good, Copeland speaks of slavery and institutional racism as "monstrous evil." And she speaks of human oppressors as the *agents* of negated good, of evil, through the personal degradation and affliction that their actions bring about. Copeland acknowledges that the suffering that persons and groups of all identities experience is an essential concern of theology. Hence it is simply as a particularization of this larger concern that her womanist theologizing focuses upon what theologian William Jones referred to as the maldistribution, negative quality, enormity, and transgenerational character of black suffering,[26] but especially focusing on that suffering as experienced by black women. This theologizing directs itself to evil and its consequent suffering by highlighting the counterpoint to evil, namely, freedom. She asserts that though they invariably occur in tandem, evil and suffering are not identical. For the pursuit of freedom also may eventuate in suffering, but this suffering is "redemptive" in that black women have willingly endured suffering as the price of the liberation struggle. It is "resistant" in that it has been taken on in defiance of the personal degradation the oppressor intends for it to accomplish. Womanist theologians, says Copeland, employ a self-defensive attitude of self-definition, a dismissal of the oppressor's attempt to define their lives and their being.

And so, as with other black and womanist theologians, Copeland focuses upon evil as an outcome of human initiative, with its remedy also coming from the agency of humans to counteract evil's negative consequences.

Conclusion

One rarely finds among black and womanist theologians metaphysical, speculative reflections toward defining evil and sin or toward identifying their ultimate, ontological source. These theologians have tended to point, instead, to what they term the *social production of evil*, that is, to the perpetration of harm and suffering on black people in general, and black women in particular, growing out of human motivations and institutionalized into prevailing social systems, structures, and practices. For instance, black theologian J. Deotis Roberts credits the efforts of theologians and philosophers over the ages to plumb the mysteries of evil's nature and origins, but he concludes, "The question, From whence comes evil? remains an intellectual puzzle."[27] And so, rather than reflect upon evil in abstract, cognitive terms, he chooses to focus his attention upon what he understands as the expression of evil represented in "the suffering that human beings inflict upon each other," a task he assesses to be "important and urgent," since it relates to the predicament of the oppressed.[28] Similarly, womanist theologian Jaime Phelps dispensed with such inquiries into evil's nature and origin as "interesting and intellectually stimulating" but not to be taken as focal. Instead, she, Roberts, and other black and womanist theologians consistently have opted to center their critical attention upon the ways in which the categories of evil and sin have related to the enormous historical suffering of black men and women. With variations and nuances, they have essentially defined evil as human harm and suffering and sin as its willful perpetration. Thus, they have posited human predatory willfulness as the relevant source of evil and black suffering. That self-interested willfulness is said to be asserted by identity groups that confuse their privileged social and economic identity with God status and who articulate their oppressive will into social systems that enforce and perpetuate their privilege and domination.

Virtually all black Christian theological expressions have assumed and asserted that the Bible gives witness to the divine opposition to the evil of human suffering and to the divine mandate for human liberation, with God actively working through and beyond human efforts to bring it about. Thus, they focus their writings on canonical theological mandates for addressing evil conditions and opposing its sinful manifestations. And they challenge black people to act assertively, aggressively, under divine authority and with divine assistance, in countering their oppression. As Roberts says, "Evil... is transmuted spiritually. It is faced and conquered... by the sufficiency of God's grace to enable and sanctify." In their God-endowed freedom, "Human beings can be agents of good as well as evil."[29]

Internal critique among black and womanist theologians has primarily been on the matter of whether, or how, the attention to *social* sin disallowed adequate attention to sin as a broader category of the faith, applicable to all believers, beyond white oppressors, and including dimensions of *individual* moral/ethical behavior. The Christian faith speaks of humanity as existing in sin and in need of redemption. If evil and sin are only racialized, societally instantiated realities, can blacks, individually or collectively, be "sinners?" The responses typically provided have been in the affirmative, though they have trended, nonetheless, toward the social framing of sin, rather than being concerned with violations of traditional religious proscriptions against "worldly" behaviors, for example, gambling, alcohol consumption, dancing, and so on. They have asserted black sin as various modes of acquiescing in white domination; or as declining to assert divinely endowed black ontological integrity and agency; or as participating in aspects of patriarchy, classism, environmental degradation, or other forms of social oppression.

In the face of the conundrum of an omnipotent, benevolent God and perduring evil, most black and womanist theologies have either explicitly or implicitly exonerated God from responsibility for evil and suffering, though some push the envelope of the theodicy issue, as in William Jones's challenging inquiry "Is God a white racist?" This was not a rhetorical question for Jones. In his and other black and womanist theologies, the resolution of the issue is shifted to human agency, locating evil's relevant, effective origination in the *human* choice that divinely endowed free will enables. And the suffering that evil causes has been interpreted by various black and womanist theologians as "redemptive" or fruitful in some fashion, for instance as the spur to the development of the character traits (patience, endurance, courage, etc.) that could underwrite a liberation thrust or as the consequence of their solidarity in struggle with the God who, by faith tradition, also suffered, for the sake of humanity's ultimate redemption and liberation.

Perhaps the most notable divergence from the foregoing approaches to evil, sin, and their remedy has been forms of black humanism, which does not accept the notion of a transcendent deity active determinatively in historical events. This, thereby, revises concerns with why a benevolent, omnipotent deity allows the suffering resulting from evil to persist. Humanism attributes evil simply to misbegotten human behavior, thus directing its corrective efforts to humans finding ways to foster better behavior. This actually does not diverge from the main postures of black and womanist theologies, in terms of locating evil's source and correction in human initiative. The main difference is found in that these theologies appeal to various theistic resources to inspire, motivate, and empower human opposition to evil. For instance, Ray points to the work of the Holy Spirit. Humanism, however, relies fully upon the initiative of humans, whether acting in a wholly nontheistic conception or in Jones's construct of human "functional ultimacy."

Notes

1. Stephen Ray, interview with author. May 9, 2013, Evanston, IL.
2. Albert Cleage was the pastor of a United Church of Christ congregation in Detroit, MI, who renamed his local church The Shrine of the Black Madonna, in keeping with his founding of a black liberationist movement by the same name.
3. For this treatment of Cleage's theology, see William R. Jones, *Is God a White Racist? A Preamble to Black Theology* (Boston: Beacon Press, 1973), 127–28.
4. See George C. Bedell, Leo Sandon Jr., and Charles T. Wellborn, *Religion in America* (New York: Macmillan, 1975), 56.
5. See, for example, Larry Murphy, "'God's Got You Now': Religious Formation and Black Christians," unpublished manuscript, in the collection of the Institute for Black Religious Research, Garrett-Evangelical Theological Seminary, Evanston, IL.
6. See James H. Cone, *A Black Theology of Liberation* (New York: Orbis Books, 1986), 107–9, 190.
7. This and the following Moyd material is taken from Olin P. Moyd, *Redemption in Black Theology* (Valley Forge, PA.: Judson Press, 1979), 97–100.
8. See Riggins Earl Jr., *Dark Symbols, Obscure Signs: God, Self, and Community in the Slave Mind* (New York: Orbis Books, 1993), 168–69.
9. For this and the following material on Ray, see Ray, interview.
10. Ray, interview.
11. Jones, *Is God a White Racist?* 248–49.
12. Jones, *Is God a White Racist?*, chapter 12.
13. Anthony B. Pinn, *Varieties of African American Religious Experience* (Minneapolis: Fortress Press, 1998), 185. See also Anthony B. Pinn, *Why, Lord? Suffering and Evil in Black Theology* (New York: Continuum Books, 1995).
14. Delores S. Williams, "A Womanist Perspective on Sin," in *A Troubling in My Soul: Womanist Perspectives on Evil and Suffering*, ed. Emilie Townes (Maryknoll, NY: Orbis Books, 1993), 144.
15. Williams, "Womanist Perspective on Sin." Williams cites as examples the anger of the Greek gods in Homer's *Iliad* over Achilles's defilement of the slain Hector's body; the retribution reaped on a prince in Genesis (Hebrew scriptures) who raped (defiled) a woman, and the Christian gospel narratives about the wrath directed toward Jesus for contradicting Jewish laws concerning women's ritual cleanliness and defilement.

16. Williams, "Womanist Perspective on Sin," 146.
17. Williams, "Womanist Perspective on Sin," 84.
18. Williams, "Womanist Perspective on Sin." 85.
19. Katie G. Cannon, "'The Wounds of Jesus': Justification of Goodness in the Face of Manifold Evil," in Townes, *Troubling in My Soul*, 219.
20. Cannon, "The Wounds of Jesus." 220.
21. Cannon, "The Wounds of Jesus," 222.
22. Cannon, "The Wounds of Jesus," 48–49.
23. Cannon, "The Wounds of Jesus," 54.
24. Cannon, "The Wounds of Jesus," 109.
25. Cannon, "The Wounds of Jesus." 110.
26. See Jones, *Is God a White Racist?* 74.
27. J. Deotis Roberts, *Black Theology in Dialogue* (Philadelphia: Westminster Press, 1987), 95.
28. Roberts, *Black Theology in Dialogue*, 97.
29. Roberts, *Black Theology in Dialogue*, 98.

Selected Texts

Bridges, Flora Wilson. *Resurrection Song: African American Spirituality*. Maryknoll, NY: Orbis Books, 2001.

Bruce, Calvin E., and William R. Jones. *Black Theology: Essays on the Formation and Outreach of Contemporary Black Theology*. Lewisburg, PA: Bucknell University Press, 1978.

Cone, Cecil. *The Identity Crisis in Black Theology*. Nashville: African Methodist Episcopal Church, 1975.

Cone, James H. *Black Theology and Black Power*. New York: Seabury Press, 1969.

Cone, James H. *A Black Theology of Liberation*. New York: Orbis Books, 1986.

Cone, James H., and Gayraud Wilmore, eds. *Black Theology: A Documentary History*. Volume 1, *1966–1979*. Maryknoll, NY: Orbis Books, 1979.

Cone, James H. and Gayraud Wilmore, eds. *Black Theology: A Documentary History*. Volume 2, *1980–1992*. Maryknoll, NY: Orbis Books, 1993.

Earl, Riggins. *Dark Symbols, Obscure Signs: God, Self, and Community in the Slave Mind*. New York: Orbis Books, 1993.

Erskine, Noel. *Decolonizing Theology: A Caribbean Perspective*. Maryknoll, NY: Orbis Books, 1981.

Evans, James. *We Have Been Believers: An African American Systematic Theology*. Minneapolis: Fortress Press, 1992.

Hayes, Diana. *And Still We Rise: An Introduction to Black Liberation Theology*. New York: Paulist Press, 1996.

Jones, William R. *Is God a White Racist? A Preamble to Black Theology*. Boston: Beacon Press, 1973.

Moyd, Olin P. *Redemption in Black Theology*. Valley Forge, PA: Judson Press, 1979.

Phelps, Jamie T., ed. *Black and Catholic: The Challenge and Gift of Black Folk*. Milwaukee: Marquette University Press, 1997.

Pinn, Anthony B., ed. *Moral Evil and Redemptive Suffering: A History of Theodicy in African American Religious Thought*. Gainesville: University Press of Florida, 2002.

Pinn, Anthony B. *Why, Lord? Suffering and Evil in Black Theology*. New York: Continuum Books, 1995.

Ray, Stephen G. *Do No Harm: Social Sin and Christian Responsibility*. Minneapolis: Fortress Press, 2003.

Roberts, J. Deotis. *Black Theology in Dialogue*. Philadelphia: Westminster, 1987.

Townes, Emilie, ed. *A Troubling in My Soul: Womanist Perspectives on Evil and Suffering*. Maryknoll, NY: Orbis Books, 1993.

CHAPTER 16

THE CHURCH IN AFRICAN AMERICAN THEOLOGY

R. DREW SMITH

AFRICAN American church life has been a topic of much discussion and has been approached from many angles. Perspectives from practitioners about the value of black church life are quite diverse, as captured in surveys on American religious practice, where consistently 80 percent or more of African American respondents report attending church, and within a wide cultural and doctrinal assortment of (mainly) Protestant contexts. With African Americans designated as one of the most religious populations on earth,[1] African American religiosity has generated considerable scholarly attention, including a theoretically diverse body of scholarship exploring the religious and social significance of African American churches.

Cutting across these various theoretical trajectories have been certain commonly encountered theoretical constructions and critiques of black church life. Approaching black church life from various interpretive and empirical vantage points, scholarship on black churches has often described them as (1) spiritual springboards; (2) refuges; and (3) social resources. Scholars have also drawn attention to aspects of black church spiritual and socio-structural positioning that have been deemed problematic, especially with reference to (1) biblical grounding; (2) cultural inclusiveness; and (3) social productivity.

Although African American church life has been explored from various theoretical perspectives, not all of this scholarship speaks directly to or for black churches. This is partly a matter of the evidence on which scholarship on black churches has been based, but it also has to do with what sociologist Peter Berger refers to as the "socio-historical presuppositions" that sometime underlie sociological, theological, and historical scholarship on religion and society.[2] Diverse theoretical vantage points opening out on frequently reiterated suppositions about social standards by which black church life should be measured will be evident in the scholarly renderings of black churches examined here.

Church as Spiritual Springboard

The Christian religious experiences of African American slaves serve as starting points in historical (and in some instances theological and sociological) understandings of African American Christianity. Albert Raboteau's seminal study of slave religion provides a complex, multidimensional analysis of the priorities, practices, and sociopolitical effects of the Christianity of African American slaves. Raboteau points out that in African American slave exposures to Christianity, as conveyed to them through the mostly distorted teachings and practices of white slaveholders and missionaries, slaves embraced those dimensions with which they resonated (including the suffering savior principle at Christianity's core and the deliverance of the ancient Hebrew people from their earthly captivity). Raboteau traces the centrality of these thematic motifs within the Christianity of African American slaves while also documenting the many ways that slaves' sense of Christianity, sense of self, and sense of sociocultural wholeness were infused with and informed by a rich and vibrant spirituality. He writes: "Prayer, preaching, song, communal support, and especially 'feeling the spirit' refreshed the slaves and consoled them in their times of distress. By imagining their lives in the context of a different future they gained hope in the present." Raboteau makes clear throughout his analysis that a reimagined future and even an alternative present for the slaves took on sociopolitical forms at times, but Christianity's transformational thrust for slaves was founded mainly upon an individual conversion experience consisting of "a feeling of sinfulness, then a vision of damnation, and finally an experience of acceptance by God and being reborn or made new."[3]

While Raboteau stresses conceptual aspects here of slave religiosity, W. E. B. Du Bois details the spirituality of slaves as expressed in their worship practices. For Du Bois, the centrality and vibrancy of slave spirituality was manifest most clearly in the practice of "shouting" or being seized by the Spirit, which "made [the devotee] mad with supernatural joy" and which constituted "the last essential of Negro religion and the one more devoutly believed in than all the rest."[4] James Baldwin's classic novel *Go Tell It on the Mountain*, drawing from Raboteau's pietistic aspects of slave religion and Du Bois's ecstatic aspects, narrates the experience of mid-twentieth-century black urban dwellers immersed in a church life with deeply southern cultural tones and a distinctly spiritual quality. In a juxtaposition of "saints" and "sinners," the family of Baldwin's protagonist strolls to church on Sunday morning past "sinners along the avenue [who] watched them—men still wearing their Saturday night clothes . . . and women with harsh voices and tight, bright dresses." Upon arriving at their church, the protagonist's family enters a space filled with spiritual expectancy, where "the white caps of the women seeming to glow in the charged air like crowns, the kinky, gleaming heads of the men seeming to be lifted up . . . [t]hey sang with all the joy that was in them, and clapped their hands for joy. . . . Something happened to their faces and their voices, the rhythm of their bodies, and to the air they breathed; it was as though wherever they might be became the upper room, and the Holy Ghost were riding on the air."[5] Baldwin's depiction here popularizes in more than one way the common characterization within pre-1960s scholarship of black church life as mystical, emotional, and pietistic.

Other rich articulations of black churches as contexts for pursuits of saintliness and spiritual communion with God can be found in the writings of scholars speaking from or about African American holiness, Pentecostal, or evangelical churches. For example, in an important study on Holiness-Pentecostal churches, Cheryl Sanders identifies a number of key characteristics to these churches, including an "emphasis on the experience of Spirit baptism [and on] sanctification, or personal holiness." Sanders also points out: "Historically, these churches have been known to preach and promote an ascetic ethic forbidding the use of alcohol, tobacco, and other addictive substances, gambling, secular dancing, and the wearing of immodest apparel."[6]

A focus on pursuits of holiness is found also in the writings of evangelical scholars, such as theologian Thabiti Anyabwile, who notes that African American Christianity during the slavery era was characterized by Bible centeredness, an emphasis on spiritual conversion, and a reliance on the sovereignty of God. Anyabwile argues that this emphasis must be maintained by the black church if it is to remain true to the Christianity of its forebears, and if it is to "effectively address both the spiritual needs of its communicants and the social and political aspirations of its community."[7] Anyabwile builds on a previous generation of black evangelical prescriptive analysis of black churches that characterized the core purposes of African American churches mainly in spiritual transformational terms. Howard O. Jones, an influential mid-twentieth-century black evangelist with the Billy Graham Evangelistic Association, states in a 1966 book that a standard by which African American churches are most appropriately defined is that they are intentional "fellowship[s] of born-again believers" that are centered in scripture and in a "ministry of prayer" that reflect "the holiness of God" and that moves in the power, "control," and "discipline" of the Holy Spirit.[8]

Church as Refuge

Another formulation of black church priorities encountered frequently in scholarly writings casts black churches in terms of spiritual or social refuge. Mid-twentieth-century sociologist E. Franklin Frazier succinctly summarizes this view:

> In providing a structured social life in which the Negro could give expression to his deepest feeling and at the same time achieve status and find a meaningful existence, the Negro church provided a refuge in a hostile white world. For the slaves who worked and suffered in an alien world, religion offered a means of catharsis for their pent-up emotions and frustrations. Moreover, it turned their minds from the sufferings and privations of this world to a world after death where the weary would find rest and the victims of injustice would be compensated.[9]

The spiritual dimensions of black church refuge Frazier alludes to can be found in scholarly accounts as far back as Du Bois's 1903 publication, *The Souls of Black Folk.* Du Bois here discusses the "plaintive" melodies that Christian slaves wove through their religious music: "Sprung from the African forests [and] intensified by the tragic soul-life of the slave,... under the stress of law and whip, it became the one true expression of a people's sorrow, despair, and hope."[10]

The religious music of African American Christians, and especially the Negro spirituals that were central expressions of faith and spirituality on the part of African American slaves, have also provided the primary source material successive generations of scholars have used in interpretations of black church life. In a 1933 study of black church life, Benjamin E. Mays and Joseph W. Nicholson state that Negro spirituals represented for slaves "the joy and sorrow, the hope and despair, the pathos and aspirations of the newly transplanted people; and through them the race was able to endure suffering and survive.[11] Book-length studies of Negro spirituals as interpretive resources were produced by theologian Howard Thurman in 1945 and by theologian James Cone in 1972, and spirituals have been at the center of theologian Dwight Hopkins's analysis of black church life as well.[12] These theologians attributed varying degrees of political intentionality to Negro spirituals, with each arguing that spirituals evidence a use of religious language and concepts that convey a consciousness of Christianity as a spiritual refuge and as a basis for envisioning and pursuing a future of political freedom and social empowerment. Thurman, for example, views slave religion, as communicated through the spirituals, as "a source of consolation" and as "one of the most striking instances on record in which a people forged a weapon of offense and defense out of a psychological shackle."[13] Cone sees in the slave spirituals a theological content pointing to the "divine *liberation* of the oppressed from slavery [as] the central theological concept."[14]

Black churches served as spiritual refuges, but black churches, on several levels, have also provided psychic and social refuge from the dehumanizing and destructive forces of white racism. In a context that hammered away at African American identity and self-worth, black churches were often places where African Americans were invested with individual and collective dignity, authority, and respect. Mays and Nicholson speak to this where they write: "The opportunity found in the Negro church to be recognized and to be 'somebody,' has stimulated the pride and preserved the self-respect of many Negroes who would have been entirely beaten by life, and possibly completely submerged."[15] Evelyn Brooks Higginbotham's 1993 study of black Baptist women reiterates the role black churches have played in providing recognition and respectability, noting that this dates back to the days of slavery: "As the 'invisible institution' of the slaves, the church had long promoted a sense of individual and collective worth and perpetuated a belief in human dignity that countered the racist preachings of the master class."[16] Martin Luther King Jr. voiced concerns about assaults on black self-worth and celebrated the affirmations of African American humanity (or "somebodiness") resulting from black church spiritualities. He remarked:

> We must maintain a sense of somebodiness and self-respect. One of the great tragedies of the system of segregation is that it so often robs its victims of a sense of dignity and worth. It tends to develop a false sense of inferiority in the segregated. But despite the existence of a system that denies our essential worth, we must have the spiritual audacity to assert our somebodiness.[17]

James Cone also advanced this analysis of black "somebodiness," with some additional nuances: "The essence of ante-bellum black religion was the emphasis on the *somebodiness* of black slaves.... Because religion defined the *somebodiness* of their being, black slaves could retain a sense of the dignity of their person even though they were treated as things."[18]

Church as Social Resource

In addition to their many spiritual and theological dimensions, black churches are also social institutions that fulfill many social needs and concerns. Although referring mainly to roles played by black churches during the civil rights movement, sociologist Aldon Morris lists a number of important ways black churches have served as social resources that can be applied to black churches in a broad sense:

> Churches provided... an organized mass base; a leadership of clergymen largely economically independent of the larger white society and skilled in the art of managing people and resources; an institutionalized financial base [and] meeting places where the masses planned tactics and strategies.... [Moreover, churches have] furnished outlets for social and artistic expression; a forum for the discussion of important issues; a social environment that developed, trained, and disciplined potential leaders from all walks of life; and meaningful symbols to engender hope, enthusiasm, and a resilient group spirit.[19]

C. Eric Lincoln and Lawrence Mamiya place an even stronger emphasis on this point:

> The Black Church has no challenger as the cultural womb of the black community. Not only did it give birth to new institutions such as schools, banks, insurance companies, and low income housing, it also provided an academy and an arena for political activities, and it nurtured young talent for musical, dramatic, and artistic development.[20]

These descriptions by Morris and by Lincoln and Mamiya capture several primary ways black churches have served as social resources, including their responsiveness to communal, cultural, economic development, and political organizing needs and considerations.

As many scholars have pointed out, black churches often fulfilled these various social roles and purposes by default, due to the fact that institutions responding to the same range of social needs and purposes within the broader society withheld their services from African Americans. Du Bois, for example, in describing black churches of the late nineteenth and early twentieth centuries in terms of alternative communities, observes: "One can see in the Negro church to-day, reproduced in microcosm, all that great world from which the Negro is cut off by color-prejudice and social condition."[21] In a more detailed enumeration of this dynamic, Du Bois writes: "Perhaps the pleasantest and most interesting social intercourse [for blacks] takes place on Sunday [after] the weary week's work is done.... [T]he social life of the Negro centres in his church—baptism, wedding and burial, gossip and courtship, friendship and intrigue—all lie in these walls."[22] Sociologist George E. Haynes makes roughly the same assessment of black churches in 1928: "All his leisure-time activities that condition intellectual development and emotional motivation under present conditions of segregated Negro life must find their channel mainly through the principal community agency the Negro has—his church."[23] This characterization of black churches as an alternative to mainstream or secular social contexts can be found in scholarship on black churches through the 1980s, including E. Franklin Frazier and Arthur Paris's analysis of internal black church politics as a political arena paralleling and competing with a broader secular politics.[24]

More recent scholarship has also explored a different range of rationales and more outwardly directed trajectories for black church educational, economic development, social service, and political involvements. Black churches have been shown to sponsor schools and to facilitate social services ministries based upon their commitments to making such services more readily available to African Americans at an improved level of quality,[25] concerns with integrating faith-based and values-related components into standard educational or social services approaches,[26] or interest in emerging opportunities for channeling government and philanthropic monies into these church-based initiatives.[27] Black church economic development motives detailed by scholars have included explanations of such activities as intentional challenges to economic structures and practices that continue to marginalize and oppress black communities,[28] and also as logical expressions of a doctrine of stewardship.[29] Black church political activism has been discussed by scholars as engaging and often directly challenging political power structures through protest, electoral action, and public policy advocacy.[30]

Black Church Distributions by Typology

In many respects, all historically black denominations are known for an emphasis on spiritual development and refuge. These priorities within black churches, as well as a priority on personal salvation, are typically associated with evangelical churches, so it is not surprising that historically black denominations tend to be categorized as evangelical in orientation. According to 1990 estimates, more than 85 percent of African American Christians were affiliated with historically black denominations (as opposed to predominantly white Protestant and Roman Catholic "mainline" denominations), with approximately 60 percent of the historically black church sector being comprised of Baptists, 23 percent comprised of Methodists, and the remaining 17 percent comprised of Pentecostal, charismatic, and nondenominational churches.[31] Statistical data from 2012 assigns somewhat different percentages to historically black denominational groupings, with Baptists constituting 63 percent, Methodists constituting 9 percent, and Pentecostal, charismatic, Holiness, and nondenominational churches constituting 29 percent.[32] While each of these historically black denominational groupings have been strongly associated with an emphasis on spirituality-oriented and refuge-oriented faith expressions, a smaller portion of black church expressions have placed a priority on addressing social needs and concerns.

Where churches place a priority on social engagement, the way this commitment is most frequently expressed is through social service provision, and, as sociologist Mark Chaves reports, theologically liberal congregations perform more social services than theologically conservative congregations.[33] Theological liberalism within African American Christianity is associated most strongly with blacks within mainline Protestant and Catholic denominations as well as with blacks in larger or more affluent congregations in general. Black Christian political advocacy also correlates strongly with affiliation with those same types of liberal-leaning congregations, although the frequency of political advocacy (with the exception of voting) is less than the frequency of social service provision.[34]

Concerns about Biblical Grounding

Although historically there has been a noticeable reverence for scripture within African American church life, there has been debate as to whether black church attention to scripture has been (or should be) driven more by theological or by sociocultural instincts and imperatives. One line of argument within this debate has been that African American church life has drawn too literally and uncritically on a biblical content containing cultural dimensions not always as germane to African American contexts as they were to the ancient Near Eastern contexts in which they originated, or even as they were to the white church whose racially oppressive interpretations were consistently reinforced within the American context. There has been a substantial body of scholarship on black church life pursuing analysis along these lines, quite comprehensively by scholars such as Vincent Wimbush, who notes that black slave salvationism took cues from white evangelicals' "sacralization of the Bible" even as slaves' liberationist approaches to scripture found reinforcement in the interpretive freedoms evident in white evangelicals' approaches to scripture. Renita Weems makes a similar assessment of black women slaves, whose distorted exposures to the Bible through slave owners still allowed possibilities for women to "remember and repeat in accordance with their own interests and tastes."[35] A concern expressed frequently by evangelical writers, however, has been that black churches are not systematic enough in their use of scripture. Howard O. Jones argues that the "Negro church has failed, and is spiritually weak and deficient" because of a loss of "vision as to the purpose of the church" and through drifting "far from the divine pattern and program of the church."[36] Similarly, Thabiti Anyabwile observes that essential attributes of an orthodox Christianity ironically became less evident within African American Christianity after "God intervened in history to prove his goodness" by delivering African Americans from chattel slavery.[37] Theologian Anthony Bradley outlines the need for a black theology with "a correctly biblical understanding of sin in its personal and structural dimensions" that "will be able to develop an ecclesiology that fits with the Scripture's witness" pertaining to Christ and that is sound in "its articulation of social justice." His assessment of most contemporary academic versions of black theology is that they "will remain useless to the black church and to black communities unless [they embrace] biblical teachings on the fact and implications of the Fall."[38]

Concerns about Cultural Inclusiveness

Among the strongest and most systematic critiques of black church cultural boundaries have been critiques by womanist scholars. In an incisive analysis of black churches, womanist theologian Delores Williams calls for a women's movement within black churches and beyond that frees "women's minds and lives of the androcentric indoctrination and the exploitative emotional commitments that cause many women to be tools of their own oppression... [an oppression] tied to the male-dominated and androcentric character of the liturgy and to the thoroughly masculine character assigned to the deity the church women have been taught to worship and celebrate."[39] Williams and other womanist scholars focus not only on matters of consciousness but also on matters of black church practice that bear on the lives of black women, including "sexism that denies black women equal opportunity in the churches' major leadership roles"; "collusion between some black male preachers and the political forces... oppressing black women"; and "sexual exploitation of black women... by some preachers."[40]

Black church attitudes toward persons who are gay, lesbian, bisexual, and transgender (GLBT) have increasingly been challenged as well. Theologian Kelly Brown Douglas provided one of the first systematic theological critiques of the religious and cultural basis of black church treatment of GLBT persons, arguing that such treatment lacks scriptural authority inasmuch as such authority derives "in large measure [from] whether or not a text supports the life and freedom of the Black community." Douglas opposes the scripture-based antagonisms by many black churches toward GLBT persons, pointing out that these antagonisms have contributed to lethargic black church responses to the growing problem of black HIV/AIDS infection and have in other ways abetted forces contrary to black well-being.[41] Theologian Horace Griffin's comprehensive analysis of black church responses to GLBT persons interrogates various scriptural and philosophical arguments invoked by black churches against homosexuality, and classifies black church responses as "oppressive and duplicitous" and in contradiction to black church promotion of justice and liberation in other areas. Griffin contests black church perspectives on homosexuality on hermeneutical and pragmatic grounds.[42]

Black church cultural space has also been viewed as generationally constricted due to its entrenchment in ecclesiastical, organizational, ideological, communicational, and artistic approaches inherited largely intact from past generations. Paradigmatic shifts occurred at an organizational level in the transition from slavery-era to postslavery-era churches and at an ideological level with the authentication through the civil rights movement of black church activism. Scholars such as Cornel West, Michael Eric Dyson, and Anthony Pinn, however, have also been calling for shifts that allow black churches to more effectively reflect latter-twentieth-century and twenty-first-century generational priorities, styles, and worldviews—especially from the perspectives of youth and young adults.[43] Scholars such as Shayne Lee and Jonathan Walton have also shed light on ways black megachurches embody desires for generationally relevant approaches to black church life.[44]

Concerns about Social Productivity

Although scholars have acknowledged both quietist and activist postures within African American church life, a great deal of scholarly emphasis prior to the 1960s was on the quietist inclinations of these churches. For example, Mays and Nicholson suggest a strong "otherworldly" disposition among black churches, where, "seeing little hope in this world," black Christians have "projected [their] hopes in a heaven above."[45] Referring to black churches in the period up through the mid-1900s, Frazier described black religion as "other-worldly in its outlook, dismissing the privations and sufferings and injustices of this world as temporary and transient" and concluded that it functioned often as a compensatory refuge from a hostile society.[46] This view of black churches persisted even after the civil rights movement, including such political scientists as Manning Marable, who criticized black ministers that "emphasize prayer over politics, salvation over suffrage, [and] the study of Ecclesiastes over the construction of economic cooperatives," and Adolph Reed Jr., who characterized black churches as "fundamentally antiparticipatory and antidemocratic."[47]

Much of this pre-1960s scholarship traced low levels of black church social activism to a lack of institutional capacity as much as to a lack of theological inclination. Mays and Nicholson argued, for example, that smaller churches lacked the capacity to effectively serve community needs and should consider merging into larger, more socially resourceful institutions.[48] Similarly, Frazier makes the case that it was the larger black churches in northern cities during the 1900s that tended to lose "their predominantly other-worldly outlook and... to focus attention upon the Negro's condition in this world," as demonstrated by their increased involvement in organizations such as the National Urban League and the NAACP.[49] More recently, Lincoln and Mamiya emphasize the correlation between church size and outreach programs, noting "larger black churches tend to have more financial resources and facilities, a more educated leadership, and more people available to staff their programs."[50] Likewise, Andrew Billingsley shows that black churches with large memberships and college-educated pastors are more likely to sponsor outreach programs.[51] Scholars have also pointed to clergy leadership attributes and the educational attainment levels of congregants as factors influencing the social activism of churches.[52]

Conclusion

Black church life has been constructed, deconstructed, celebrated, and criticized from many vantage points. Black churches may be much of what scholars say they are, but they are undoubtedly much more than that as well—especially as viewed by the many congregants and clergy who have sustained and been sustained by these institutions over the centuries and who may bring fewer social presuppositions than scholars sometimes do to their perspectives on churches.[53] Black church life is informed by a rich mixture of social and religious factors requiring analysis capable of accounting with increasing accuracy for each of these factors and, thereby, advancing a field of study that is gaining in importance and scope with each decade.

Notes

1. See, for example, George Gallup and Jim Castelli, *The People's Religion: American Faith in the 90's* (New York: Macmillan, 1989).
2. Peter Berger, *The Sacred Canopy: Elements of a Sociological Theory of Religion* (New York: Anchor Books, 1969), 181.
3. Albert Raboteau, *Slave Religion: The "Invisible Institution" in the Antebellum South* (New York: Oxford University Press, 1978), 218, 268.
4. W. E. B. Du Bois, *The Souls of Black Folks* (Chicago: A. C. McClurg, 1903), 136.
5. James Baldwin, *Go Tell It on the Mountain* (New York: Doubleday, 1952), 10, 12.
6. Cheryl J. Sanders, *Saints in Exile: The Holiness-Pentecostal Experience in African American Religion and Culture* (New York: Oxford University Press, 1996), 5. See also Cheryl Townsend Gilkes, "The Role of Women in Sanctified Churches," *Journal of Religious Thought* 43, no. 1 (Spring–Summer 1986): 24–41; and Leonard Lovett, "Black Holiness-Pentecostalism: Implications for Ethical and Social Transformation," Ph.D. dissertation, Emory University, 1978.
7. Thabiti Anyabwile, *The Decline of African American Theology: From Biblical Faith to Cultural Captivity* (Downers Grove, IL: Intervarsity Press Academic, 2007), 19.
8. Howard O. Jones, *For This Time: A Challenge to Black and White Christians* (Chicago: Moody Press, 1966), 31, 32, 35, 40–44.
9. E. Franklin Frazier, *The Negro Church in America* (New York: Schocken Books, 1964), 50.
10. Du Bois, *Souls of Black Folks*, 135–36.
11. Benjamin E. Mays and Joseph W. Nicholson, *The Negro's Church* (New York: Institute of Social and Religious Research, 1933), 2.
12. See for example, Dwight Hopkins, *Down, Up, and Over: Slave Religion and Black Theology* (Minneapolis: Fortress Press, 2000).
13. Howard Thurman, *Deep River: Reflections on the Religious Insight of Certain of the Negro Spirituals* (New York: Harper & Brothers, 1945), 27, 36.
14. James Cone, *The Spirituals and the Blues: An Interpretation* (New York: Seabury Press, 1972), 34.
15. Mays and Nicholson, *The Negro's Church*, 281.
16. Evelyn Brooks Higginbotham, *Righteous Discontent: The Women's Movement in the Black Baptist Church, 1880–1920* (Cambridge: Harvard University Press, 1993), 5. See also Daphne Wiggins, *Righteous Content: Black Women's Perspectives of Church and Faith* (New York: New York University Press, 2006).
17. Martin Luther King Jr., "Address at Public Meeting of the Southern Christian Ministers Conference of Mississippi," Jackson, MS, September 23, 1959.
18. James Cone, *The Spirituals and the Blues* (New York: Seabury Press, 1972), 34, 17.
19. Aldon Morris, *The Origins of the Civil Rights Movement: Black Communities Organizing for Change* (New York: Free Press, 1984), 4, 5.
20. C. Eric Lincoln and Lawrence Mamiya, *The Black Church in the African American Tradition* (Durham, NC: Duke University Press, 1990), 8.

21. Du Bois, *Souls of Black Folks*, 137.
22. W. E. B. Du Bois, *The Philadelphia Negro: A Social Study* (Philadelphia: Published for the University, 1899), 145–46.
23. George E. Haynes, "The Church and Negro Progress," *Annals of the American Academy of Political and Social Sciences*, November 1928.
24. Frazier, *Negro Church in America*, 47–51; and Arthur Paris, *Black Pentecostalism: Southern Religion in an Urban World* (Amherst: University of Massachusetts Press, 1982), 117–37.
25. Desiree Pedescleaux, "African American Clergy and School Reform," in *Long March Ahead: African American Churches and Public Policy in Post-Civil Rights America*, ed. R. Drew Smith (Durham, NC: Duke University Press, 2004).
26. Mark Chaves, *Congregations in America* (Cambridge: Harvard University Press, 2004).
27. Michael Leo Owens, *God and Government in the Ghetto: The Politics of Church-State Collaboration in Black America* (Chicago: University of Chicago Press, 2007).
28. Leon Sullivan and Clarence Taylor, *The Black Churches of Brooklyn* (New York: Columbia University Press, 1994).
29. Shayne Lee, *T. D. Jakes: America's New Preacher* (New York: New York University Press, 2007).
30. The literature on black church protest activities, especially as part of the civil rights movement, is vast, with key examples including Taylor Branch, *Parting the Waters: America in the King Years, 1954–1963* (New York: Simon & Schuster, 1988); Vincent Harding, *There Is a River: The Black Struggle for Freedom in America* (New York: Vintage Books, 1981); Adam Fairclough, *To Redeem the Soul of America: The Southern Christian Leadership Conference and Martin Luther King, Jr.* (Athens: University of Georgia Press, 1987); and Rosetta Ross, *Witnessing and Testifying: Black Women, Religion and Civil Rights* (Minneapolis: Fortress Press, 2003). Key sources on black church electoral and public policy activism include Adolph Reed Jr., *The Jesse Jackson Phenomenon: The Crisis of Purpose in Afro-American Politics* (New Haven: Yale University Press, 1986); Lincoln and Mamiya, *Black Church; Allen Hertzke, Echoes of Discontent: Jesse Jackson, Pat Robertson, and the Resurgence of Populism* (Washington, DC: CQ Press, 1993); Fredrick Harris, *Something Within: Religion in African American Political Activism* (New York: Oxford University Press, 2001); R. Drew Smith, ed., *New Day Begun: African American Churches and Civic Culture in Post-Civil Rights America* (Durham, NC: Duke University Press, 2003); and Smith, *Long March Ahead.*
31. Lincoln and Mamiya, *Black Church*, 407.
32. See the 2012 U.S. Religious Landscape Survey conducted by the Pew Forum on Religion and Public Life.
33. Mark Chaves, *Congregations in America* (Cambridge: Harvard University Press, 2004), 53.
34. See, for example, R. Drew Smith and Corwin Smidt, "System Confidence, Congregational Characteristics, and Black Church Civic Engagement," in Smith *New Day Begun*; and Tamelyn Tucker-Worgs, *The Black Megachurch: Theology, Gender, and the Politics of Public Engagement* (Waco, TX: Baylor University Press, 2011).
35. Vincent Wimbush, *The Bible and African Americans: A Brief History* (Minneapolis: Augsburg Press, 2003), 22–23; and Renita Weems, "Reading Her Way Through the Struggle: African American Women and the Bible," in *Stony the Road We Trod: African American Biblical Interpretation*, ed. Cain Hope Felder (Minneapolis: Augsburg Press, 1991), 61.
36. Jones, *For This Time*, 27–28.

37. Anyabwile, *Decline*, 242–43.
38. Anthony B. Bradley, *Liberating Black Theology: The Bible and the Black Experience in America* (Wheaton, IL: Crossway Books, 2010), 188.
39. Delores S. Williams, *Sisters in the Wilderness: The Challenge of Womanist God-Talk* (Maryknoll, NY: Orbis Books, 1993), 215.
40. Williams, *Sisters in the Wilderness*, 206, 208; Womanist theologian Marcia Riggs approaches these matters systematically as well in *Plenty Good Room: Women versus Male Power in the Black Church* (Eugene, OR: Wipf and Stock, 2008), as does Anthony Pinn in *The Black Church in the Post-Civil Rights Era* (Maryknoll, NY: Orbis Books, 2002). Also see accounts of black women's empowerment struggles within specific black denominations, including Higginbotham, *Righteous Discontent*; Sanders, *Saints in Exile*; and Cheryl Townsend Gilkes, *If It Wasn't for the Women: Black Women's Experience and Womanist Culture in Church and Community* (Maryknoll, NY: Orbis Boos, 2001).
41. Kelly Brown Douglas, *Sexuality and the Black Church: A Womanist Perspective* (Maryknoll, NY: Orbis Books, 1999), 106–7.
42. Horace Griffin, *Their Own Receive Them Not: African American Lesbians and Gays in Black Churches* (Cleveland: Pilgrim Press, 2006), vii, *passim*.
43. Cornel West, "On Afro-American Popular Music: From Bebop to Rap," *Prophetic Fragments* (Grand Rapids, MI: Eerdmans Publishing, 1988); Michael Eric Dyson, *Between God and Gangsta Rap: Bearing Witness to Black Culture* (New York: Oxford University Press, 1996); Pinn, *Black Church*.
44. Lee, *T. D. Jakes*; Jonathan Walton, *Watch This! The Ethics and Aesthetics of Black Televangelism* (New York: New York University Press, 2009).
45. Mays and Nicholson, *The Negro's Church*, 93.
46. Frazier, *Negro Church in America*, 51.
47. Manning Marable, *How Capitalism Underdeveloped Black America: Problems in Race, Political Economy, and Society* (Boston: South End Press, 1983), 213; Reed, *The Jesse Jackson Phenomenon*, 56; see also James Cone, *A Black Theology of Liberation* (Philadelphia: Lippencott, 1970); Robert Franklin, *Liberating Visions: Human Fulfillment and Social Justice in African-American Thought* (Minneapolis: Fortress Press, 1985); Dwight Hopkins, *Heart and Head: Black Theology—Past, Present, and Future* (New York: Palgrave, 2002); Hertzke, *Echoes of Discontent*.
48. Mays and Nicholson, *The Negro's Church*, 19, 227.
49. Frazier, *Negro Church in America*, 56.
50. Lincoln and Mamiya, *Black Church*, 188.
51. Andrew Billingsley, *Mighty Like a River: The Black Church and Social Reform* (Oxford: Oxford University Press, 1999), 204–5.
52. For example, Harris, *Something Within*; Allison Calhoun-Brown, "African-American Churches and Political Mobilization: The Psychological Impact of Organizational Resources," *Journal of Politics* 58, no. 4 (November 1996): 935–53; Clarence Taylor, *Black Churches of Brooklyn* (New York: Columbia University Press, 1994); Smith and Smidt, "System Confidence"; Michael Leo Owens, *God and Government in the Ghetto: The Politics of Church-State Collaboration in America* (Chicago: University of Chicago Press, 2007).
53. Peter Paris writes in the closing section of his book on African spiritualities: "Though dependent throughout on the findings of many scholars principally in anthropology, ethnography, and history, I have taken great care not to become captive to their social-functionalist methodologies." *The Spirituality of African Peoples* (Minneapolis: Fortress Press, 1994).

Social-functionalism refers to a well-established sociological approach to religion that validates religion in relation to its social usefulness more than by its religious claims or purposes. Social-functionalist approaches to black church studies are even more systematically challenged by Barbara D. Savage in *Your Spirits Walk beside Us: The Politics of Black Religion* (Cambridge: Belknap Press of Harvard University Press, 2008).

Selected Texts

Baldwin, James. *Go Tell It on the Mountain*. New York: Doubleday, 1952.

Berger, Peter. *The Sacred Canopy: Elements of a Sociological Theory of Religion*. New York: Anchor Books, 1969.

Du Bois, W. E. B. *The Souls of Black Folk*. Chicago: A. C. McClurg, 1903.

Frazier, E. Franklin. *The Negro Church in America*. New York: Schocken, 1964.

Higginbotham, Evelyn Brooks. *Righteous Discontent: The Women's Movement in the Black Baptist Church, 1880–1920*. Cambridge: Harvard University Press, 1993.

Lee, Shayne. *T. D. Jakes: America's New Preacher*. New York: New York University Press, 2005.

Owens, Michael Leo. *God and Government in the Ghetto: The Politics of Church-State Collaboration in Black America*. Chicago: University of Chicago Press, 2007.

Raboteau, Albert. *Slave Religion: The "Invisible Institution" in the Antebellum South*. New York: Oxford University Press, 1978.

Riggs, Marcia. *Plenty Good Room: Women versus Male Power in the Black Church*. Eugene, OR: Wipf and Stock, 2008.

Sanders, Cheryl J. *Saints in Exile: The Holiness-Pentecostal Experience in African American Religion and Culture*. New York: Oxford University Press, 1996.

Walton, Jonathan. *Watch This! The Ethics and Aesthetics of Black Televangelism*. New York: New York University Press, 2009.

CHAPTER 17

ESCHATOLOGY IN AFRICAN AMERICAN THEOLOGY

DEREK S. HICKS

The Wonder of the "End Times"

Questions abound about the "end times." What will become of us? What unseen things lie ahead in our future? Within the Christian tradition, the question of ultimate things is invariably wed to the study of eschatology. What becomes of this world and what happens when we die fill many a Christian cup of concern. The culmination of the world is an essential focus as people stir about where they fit within God's eternal plan. Jesus and the finished work on the cross set for many a discourse centered on hope for the future. For them the "other side of the Jordan" holds the promise that God, through Jesus Christ, will make all things right for the believer. In truth, eschatology is not merely an issue of what happens next, or even what happens in eternity. Eschatology is unique in that it fuses many theological perspectives into the broader discussion of politics, sociology, history, anthropology, and philosophy. It colors the very language of Christianity and encourages people to "take sides," hoping that they are on God's chosen side.

African Americans have sought answers to many questions about God's ultimate plan for the world. Reflecting on their experiences in enslavement, Jim Crow, and segregation, and within every struggle for civil rights, blacks have fought to be considered among God's chosen. Eschatology is not merely a notion connected to African American Christian faith. Rather, considerations about the end times and eternity take on prominence in black culture as African Americans make sense of their social and political experiences in a society of domination. The importance and symbolism of heaven does not extinguish a desire for African Americans to come to grips with God's eternal plan for them in the "here and now." In short, God's eschatological plan must, for blacks historically struggling for human dignity, include a component where their earthly needs are addressed.

What Is Eschatology?

Eschatology is the study of "last things" or the "end times." Within theological studies it is the study of the culmination of humanity and the earth according to God's plan. Some scholars identify eschatological study as the task of giving believers a reason to hope for an uncertain future. The study of eschatology includes issues of the Rapture, the Tribulation, and the Millennium. All of these variations are aimed at explaining the way God will bring the world to an end, especially in relationship to the Christian Church. As a component of theological study, eschatology is not limited to a consideration of things to come, such as the Tribulation, heaven, or the new earth. Rather, it is a study that covers the entire existence of the world and humankind in order to uncover what God intends by this entire project, and how those future events fit within it. The study of eschatology is fundamental to uncovering the significance of the Christian connection to God through the Christ Event, or Jesus's finished work on the cross. Eschatology identifies God's redemptive plan and the program through which God will carry out that plan.

The major themes associated with eschatology are the world's end, the return of Jesus Christ, the resurrection of the dead, heaven, and God's final judgment. Some Christians approach these themes with anxiety as they reflect on an uncertain future, in this world or in eternity. Eschatological hope in God's future plan is therefore sustained not solely through doctrine or appealing to the formal authority of the Bible. Rather, it begins with a general belief in God's eternal plan for the world, and that such a plan benefits the believer. Glorified by an eternal connection with God through Christ, the Christian believes that Jesus will return at an unknown time to receive the church and ultimately restore order to the world. Exactly how or what method God uses to bring a climactic end to the world is debated by theologians. As a result, several perspectives about eschatology are available.

Evangelical Perspectives on the "Last Things"

As with other theological positions, perspectives about eschatology are varied. Several theological sources of eschatology are systematic in that they attempt to arrange a set of ideas about God's redemptive and culminating work into a fixed plan. In part, what one finds in evangelical forms of eschatology are rewards based ideas about God's plans for the world. In short, those who live obediently to God's desire for pious Christian living can expect great things in eternity. The *saved* and *sanctified* are guaranteed to live forever with God through their declaration of faith in Jesus Christ. The question becomes how God intends to work out this eschatological program.

Millennialism in Eschatological Study

Millennialism is a part of eschatological study identifying a period of time when Christ will physically reign on earth. Millennial views about eschatology consist of *amillennialism, postmillennialism*, and *premillennialism*. Each of these perspectives of eschatology offers a picture of God's final work in bringing this world to a close, as well as what is offered to "the church" in eternity once the world ends.

Amillennialism sees the church age (contemporary times) as the millennial age. That means there will be no separate millennial period of worldwide peace. Technically there will also be no forthcoming millennial period where God brings all things to order. Conversely, amillennialism teaches that a parallel reckoning of good over evil—wherein God's kingdom is overtaking Satan's kingdom—is currently underway in this world. The struggle between these kingdoms will continue until the return of Jesus Christ for the church. Arguments against this view hold that amillennialism seems to ignore the first six verses of Revelation 20, which speaks about a separate millennial reign of Christ. While this would not be a totally accurate characterization of their perspective, it is true that they do not believe that there will be a literal thousand-year period when Christ reigns on a peaceful earth. For them, no future "golden age" of Christ exists. They read Revelation 20 as pointing to a prior age or the church age in its entirety. In either case, God's redemptive plan is unfolding now, not in an age to come.

Postmillennialism holds that the Kingdom of God is currently being extended throughout the world through the preaching of the Gospel and the conversion of people to the Christian faith. For the *postmil* the world will eventually be Christianized and Christ will return after the end of a period of peace called the Millennium. Hence,

Christ will return *post* or *after* millennial conditions on earth. Immediately following Christ's return will be a resurrection of fallen believers, final Divine judgment of evil, and the induction of the new heaven. This position discloses continuity between the current age and the millennial age to come.

Premillennialism holds that we are currently in the church age. This is a time of hope for the Christian because the church is in a position to at any time be "raptured" into the clouds to be with Christ upon his initial return to earth. Following the Rapture will be a seven-year period understood as the Tribulation, where those remaining on earth will be judged. It is important to note that other premillennialists believe that Christ will not return to rapture the church until the middle or end of the tribulation. In either case, after the seven-year tribulation is completed, Christ will *again* return (this time *with* the church) for those who converted during the tribulation and commence the millennial dispensation. The Millennium will be a time of peace, as Satan will be bound. At the close of this one-thousand-year period the Day of the Lord (final reckoning) will take place. On that day Satan will be defeated finally and eternally by Christ. The emphasis of this Day of Judgment is on sin. In the culmination of this millennial reign, sin, evil and death will be stamped out for eternity and the Kingdom of God will transition into its final, eternal state of perfection in the form of a new heaven and new earth.

Dispensationalism in Eschatological Study

Dispensationalism is a system of biblical interpretation that sees God's redemptive plan in light of God's dealings with humanity within distinct periods of time (dispensations). This idea fits, for example, within the premillennialist schema as the current church age is seen as a dispensation in God's unfolding historical/eschatological plan. Dispensationalists separate the covenantal promises God made to Israel from those eschatological promises directed at the Church. They hold to a literal millennial period. It holds that God unfolds the world's redemptive plan in dispensations or segments of time to fulfill promises of that age. *Classical* dispensationalism sees Judaism and Christianity as separate religions with separate eschatologies but drawing from one sacred text, the Bible. *Revised* dispensationalism sees two converging eschatologies between Judaism and Christianity. In this way, both sides draw from the biblical covenants. *Progressive* dispensationalism sees both convergence and points of separation between the eschatological blessings of God's chosen people Israel and the Church. For instance, the Abrahamic covenant of "land and seed" with its sign of male circumcision is set aside for Israel. Also, God's eschatological work on earth will not be completed until the regions promised to the twelve tribes of Israel have finally been acquired in some future time. Yet the ultimate blessings of the Abrahamic covenant are extended to the church in that gentile believers are grafted into the community of the chosen seed by way of faith. For the church, Abraham's faith becomes their central connection to God's chosen people.

A Covenantal Eschatological Perspective

A primary example of the convergence of God's promises to Israel and the church is exhibited in the Davidic Covenant. In this covenant, God promises that a representative of the house of David (or Davidic line) will reign on the throne of Israel forever. Jesus fulfills this covenantal promise to Israel because he is a part of the Davidic familial line. To be seated at the right hand of a king is to be anointed king. Therefore, the fact that Jesus now sits at the right hand of God (Acts 2:33; Col 1:13) means that Jesus is currently exalted with all kingly privileges. Accordingly, Jesus is currently King and thus fulfills the covenantal promise. Here lies the central convergence of God's eschatological and covenantal promises to Israel and the church. While Jesus already fills the kingly role in heaven (in relation to the church), he is not yet physically sitting on the throne of David here on earth (as connected to Israel). This principle is what has been termed the "already, not yet" eschatological promises of God. Jesus will physically sit on the throne of David during the Millennium. In the end, Jesus sits on both the physical and eternal throne of David, carrying out justice for all believing saints.

Blacks and Evangelicalism: Eschatology in Transition

The term "evangelical" reflects a certain Christian orientation. It is Christian expression concerned first with winning souls to saving faith in Jesus Christ. Contemporary religious scholar Glenn Shuck reveals certain tenets of evangelicalism: a conservative position about the Bible as authority; the necessity of a saving faith experience in Christ; evangelizing or "witnessing" to the lost (unbeliever) as a requirement of every believer; and the belief that Christ will return soon to establish his literal, millennial kingdom on earth.[1] There is no question that evangelicalism fosters norms and values that impact culture and society. But how impactful are evangelical perspectives of eschatology when they are funneled through the African American experience? One way to get at this question is to consider the interesting relationship between predominantly black churches and evangelicalism.

The black church can be puzzling to the onlooker because it simultaneously conforms to certain ideas of conservative private morality and a prophetic social gospel. Are black Christians liberal or conservative? To be sure, some black pastors will publicly declare conservative theology from the pulpit, encouraging appropriate Christian behavior. Yet that same church will support and promote what would be considered liberal programs that advance the community of people it serves. In this light, African Americans are only partially served by an eschatology connected to evangelical ideas of future eternal reward in Christ based on saving faith. For them, a component that identifies the needs and values of the community must also affect any eschatology.

African Americans and Eschatology

On the eve of his assassination, Martin Luther King Jr. made the following declarative eschatological statement:

> It's all right to talk about "long white robes over yonder," in all of its symbolism. But ultimately people want some suits and dresses and shoes to wear down here! It's all right to talk about "streets flowing with milk and honey," but God has commanded us to be concerned about the slums down here, and his children who can't eat three square meals a day. It's all right to talk about the new Jerusalem, but one day, God's preacher must talk about the new New York, the new Atlanta, the new Philadelphia, the new Los Angeles, the new Memphis, Tennessee. This is what we have to do.

Speaking at a rally in support of Memphis sanitation workers, King eloquently framed a shared eschatological discourse among African Americans. At its core lies not solely a future hope tied to end times. Also infused within this eschatological thought is a desire for a future time of justice for historically maltreated blacks in America. King's words underscore an augmented eschatological emphasis on faith in eternal things and in God's redemptive plan to improve things here on earth for the least of these. An eschatology of justice also brings into focus an inner impulse among God's people, triggered by their faith, to engage in the struggle to bring about needed social and political change.

In his essay "Of Our Spiritual Strivings" W. E. B. Du Bois highlights an inner feeling shared by many African Americans of being a problem. This "strange experience" of *being* forces blacks in the United States to confront the potentially stifling issue of double consciousness. Whether or not double consciousness is a permanent state and simply has historical and temporal import, it has been a state of being that black people have wrestled with for centuries. To understand this form of reckoning as a stagnant condition of living within the world would be a misreading of the term. Double consciousness is an active wrestling with the way things are, a seeking for clarity about the worth of life, and an articulation of eschatological striving within a culture of domination. As a basis for a black eschatological faith, double consciousness deals with the current state of things in the world, wrestles with history to understand how we got here, and moves toward a new understanding of freedom and human fullness.

Turning the evangelical constructions of eschatology on their heads, theologian James Cone pushes for a countersystematic eschatology for oppressed blacks.[2] Of course, this does not mean that African American theologians and religious scholars have not thought of or offered a systematic configuration of eschatology. The question for some within black theological camps ultimately is whose side is God on in the divine finale of the world. Moving toward a greater future for African American life, eschatology consistently tackles the issue of impending ceasing of life. While those Christians who have lived a life of plenty await rewards for their earthly piety, blacks in America have been constantly reminded of death. The spectrum of imminent death functions both as a social and physical reality in African American life. Thus, blacks sought an eschatological hope to counter the stifling ill effects of a deathly sociopolitical reality.

In black life, death is always a current reality, not something far off or in the future. In communities where there are substandard living conditions, poor public schools, few employment options, and where a majority of a given community isworking poor or living on or below the poverty line, death runs rampant. Thoughts of future glory "on the other side of the Jordan," where all believers will "walk all over God's heaven," do little to mitigate the social reality of death in everyday African American life. Therefore, systematic formulations of eschatology for blacks are infused with an intolerance of injustice. Their eschatological hope seeks a new articulation of God's final plan, as they have grown tired of "pie in the sky" status quo notions of future glory bankrupt of social justice. Eschatology within this model must challenge the present reality of social inequity. Eschatology is therefore concerned with the existential situation oppressed peoples find themselves in. Never separated from the present historical moment, this eschatology progressively moves throughout time and space, identifying reference points for God's ultimate work of establishing justice for all.

Internal considerations of the meaning and worth of black life motivate actions to bring about social change. Black biblical scholars such as Cain Hope Felder have revealed an eschatological justice laced within the biblical narrative. In this case, God's work through Jesus Christ in the culminating Day of Judgment will be a decisive day of reward or punishment in response to one's earthly deeds. Here eschatological justice casts its attention forward to pinpoint those instances where God, before bringing an end to all things and making way for the new heaven and earth, brings oppressors and abusers to justice along with sinners (1 Cor 3:13; Rom 14:10–12; Matt 12:36). As Felder points out, eschatological justice is not an emphasis on punishment of evil, but rather in the hope for justice and the reward that accompanies repentance and carrying out of justice by people on earth.[3] While the "deeds" of justice are sought, the biblical emphasis is on God's mercy through the effort to reconcile all people as one human family.

Apocalyptic Notions

African American reflections on eschatology include perspectives on the Apocalypse. Some scholars have missed this point by evaluating black Christianity in terms of practices and experiences, detached from Judgment Day considerations. Yet the central feature of the Apocalypse is God's divine judgment. Ethicist and womanist scholar Emilie Townes gives prominent space to what she calls an "Apocalyptic vision" in womanist work that is ultimately useful for black eschatological thought generally.[4] Such a vision is rooted in the history of African American women and men. In addition to issues of racial oppression, Townes casts this vision as a concern for issues of class, gender, sexuality, age, militarism, death, and the poor. This vision fires the souls of suffering people to get involved with social movements to secure equal justice for oppressed people. People are thusly encouraged to hope as they put apocalyptic vision into action in the midst of inhumane treatment.

The question for some is how one might biblically ground an apocalyptic vision and social action. To what can blacks anchor their hope and inner power to bring about the change they seek? New Testament professor Brian Blount gives us insight through his analysis of Revelation. Placing black Christians in action, Blount shows that they are driven by notions of divine apocalyptic judgment of evil.[5] Reading the book of Revelation through African American experience, Blount expresses the book as a call to active resistance. This form of resistance falls squarely within John's message as a component of God's intended eschatological plan. Blount does not consider this a call for black counterviolence to oppression, but rather as perpetual active nonviolent resistance. Blacks are encouraged against inactive compliance.

Religious scholar and clergyman Theophus Smith introduces an irony in black eschatology. For him this irony comes in the form of the *warrior/Lamb* model in black Christian thought.[6] A "wrathful Lamb" would seem a paradox. However, this constellation of attributes works within the context of African Americans' struggles for humanity. In this case, dreams of a beloved community combat black Christian's thoughts of Christ's return and physical reign being marked by catastrophe. This apocalyptic subplot calls for the church to come together with Jesus Christ for a revolution. During this revolutionary period injustice is rooted out and defeated, and oppressors are given what is due them for their part in harming others. Actions associated with black eschatology are nurtured by the reality of black displacement and experience in the diaspora. A nomadic state of existing in the world brings focus to Du Bois's double consciousness and its effect on African American life. As Smith sees it, diaspora for African Americans represents not only a form of sociocultural and historical existence, but also a transhistorical experience wherein eschatology is of primary concern. Eschatological hope is therefore tied to the power of God to transform citizenship. Transformed, African Americans hope as they work toward a day where their humanity is fully valued.

From Exodus to Ethiopia: A Hopeful Black Nation

The perpetuation of violence against African Americans has also necessitated an eschatology of hope as drawn from the Exodus narrative. The Exodus story places the theme of liberation at the forefront of black eschatological thought. Theirs is a hope against hope that the violence perpetuated on them will be rooted out through God's deliverance, as with the Israelites. But transforming self-consciousness from a broken community to a nation of people worthy of esteem is no small feat. Eschatologically, the Exodus storyline encourages suffering black Christians to press for greater socio-political positioning in the face of a dominant society. But where the Exodus story offered hope for eventual equality, the Ethiopia model turned African Americans toward a fuller expression of life as part of God's family. Psalms 68:31 places Ethiopia, read as all of the African race, at the center of eschatological hope. If suffering was the destiny for African Americans, then too Ethiopia's connection to God sheds light on God's ultimate plan for the black race. The notion that Ethiopia, the African nation, and all black people could command God's divine attention was a primary ingredient in changing black social consciousness. Hope not only in God's divine justice for their suffering, but also in God's biblically "stated" love and plan for the black race, created a new posture of strength as African American Christians looked to the future.

Conclusions on Blacks and Eschatology

Taken together, African American Christians and theological thinkers have created a unique eschatology. This eschatology is woven together by thoughts of future glory in heaven *and* future justice on earth. Make no mistake, the scales tilt toward restorative justice. African American Christians cannot see the significance of eschatology without an emphasis on this latter component. Through eschatology black believers seek satisfactory answers for the nature of God's love and care for the least of society. It functions as a way toward divine reconciliation of faith with experience. Evangelical constructions of eschatology give an account of God's program in the biblical-supernatural-heavenly-eternal spheres in connection to personal faith and piety. But an eschatology based in individual rewards falls flat for African Americans, many of whom seek answers that explain why other Christians have for so long challenged their humanity. They seek a community-based eschatology. African American theology critiques evangelical eschatology for its failure to capture the existential plight of believers as well. For it, African American theology, eschatological analysis must also be grounded in the historical present, and must challenge present circumstances that stand in contrast to God's desire for justice and equality for all people.

Notes

1. Glenn W. Shuck, *Marks of the Beast: The "Left Behind" Novels and the Struggle for Evangelical Identity* (New York: New York University Press, 2004).
2. James H. Cone, *A Black Theology of Liberation*, 20th anniversary ed. (Maryknoll, NY: Orbis Books, 2004).
3. Cain Hope Felder, *Troubling Biblical Waters: Race, Class, and Family* (Maryknoll, NY: Orbis Books, 1989).
4. Emilie M. Townes, *In a Blaze of Glory: Womanist Spirituality as Social Witness* (Nashville: Abingdon Press, 1995).
5. Brian K. Blount, *Can I Get a Witness? Reading Revelation through African American Culture* (Louisville, KY: Westminster John Knox Press, 2005).
6. Theophus H. Smith, *Conjuring Culture: Biblical Formations of Black America* (New York: Oxford University Press, 1994).

Selected Texts

Blount, Brian K. *Can I Get a Witness? Reading Revelation through African American Culture.* Louisville, KY: Westminster John Knox Press, 2005.

Bock, Darrell L., editor. *Three Views on the Millennium and Beyond.* Grand Rapids: Zondervan, 1999.

Braaten, Carl E., and Robert W. Jenson, eds. *The Last Things: Biblical and Theological Perspectives on Eschatology*. Grand Rapids: William B. Eerdmans, 2002.

Callahan, Allen Dwight. *The Talking Book: African Americans and the Bible*. New Haven: Yale University Press, 2006.

Cone, James H. *A Black Theology of Liberation*. 20th anniversary ed. Maryknoll, NY: Orbis Books, 2004.

Felder, Cain Hope. *Troubling Biblical Waters: Race, Class, and Family*. Maryknoll, NY: Orbis Books, 1989.

Glaude, Jr., Eddie S. *Exodus! Religion, Race, and Nation in Early Nineteenth-Century Black America*. Chicago: University of Chicago Press, 2000.

Raboteau, Albert J. *A Fire In the Bones: Reflections on African-American Religious History*. Boston: Beacon Press, 1995.

Saucy, Robert L. *The Case for Progressive Dispensationalism: The Interface between Dispensational and Non-dispensational Theology*. Grand Rapids: Zondervan, 1993.

Shuck, Glenn W. *Marks of the Beast: The "Left Behind" Novels and the Struggle for Evangelical Identity*. New York: New York University Press, 2004.

Smith, Theophus H. *Conjuring Culture: Biblical Formations of Black America*. New York: Oxford University Press, 1994.

Terrell, JoAnne Marie. *Power in the Blood? The Cross in the African American Experience*. Maryknoll, NY: Orbis Books, 1998.

Townes, Emilie M. *In a Blaze of Glory: Womanist Spirituality as Social Witness*. Nashville: Abingdon Press, 1995.

CHAPTER 18

HEAVEN AND HELL IN AFRICAN AMERICAN THEOLOGY

E. MARSHALL TURMAN

> Black Theology refuses to embrace an interpretation of eschatology which would turn our eyes from injustice now. It will not be deceived by images of pearly gates and golden streets, because too many earthly streets are covered with black blood.
>
> —James H. Cone, *Black Theology and Black Power*

CRITICAL consideration of heaven and hell in African American theology resists the singularity of normative eschatological inquiry that limits its discursive scope to the *eschatos*; namely, those "last things" that most commonly refer to the Second Coming of Christ, the resurrection of the body, final judgment, and everlasting life. Given the palpability of the flesh-and-blood realities of black suffering, it appears that the urge to privilege a redemptive otherworldly landscape functions as a tool of appeasement meant to sedate the fury of the oppressed with the certain promise of a heavenly hereafter for the meek and mild, and eternal damnation for the hellion. While it is the case that many black churches have been corrupted by the "white lie" that suggests that the Christian reality of an otherworld recompenses the oppressed for their present sufferings, the varieties of African American theological reflection on heaven and hell categorically reject this compensatory contention.[1]

Black theologian James Cone surmises that the contemplation of heaven and hell as otherworldly milieu is constituent of the heretical act of white supremacy that denies the veracity of the Jesus event.[2] Taking his cue from the historicity of God in Christ's active presence in the world as "suffering slave" (*doulos*, Phil 2:7) and God's incarnate victory over suffering in the world as the "resurrected Christ," Cone leverages the historicity of God in Christ in order to assert the primacy of "present things" as the determinative substance of that which is "not yet." In other words, the "now" realities of black suffering that are born from the cruel inheritance of American enslavement, Jim Crow segregation, and the more dubious postmodern emergence of a *new* Jim Crow, necessarily provide the groundwork for the primary eschatological motifs that propel the African American apocalyptic imagination; namely, heaven and hell as *historical happening, benevolent promise*, and *cultural mechanism of hope.*

Here and Now: Heaven as Historical Happening

The historical significance of heaven and hell in African American theology begins with the inescapable peculiarity of death that is always, and simultaneously, "past," "present," and "not yet" in the lives of the black oppressed.[3] For blacks, death is not a future reality that may be indefinitely postponed as a consequence of political, social, and economic power, and the lavish recreation that the will to power engenders. To the contrary, death is an ever-present existential threat to black life, especially in relation to white life and the unjust societal structures of white dominance that preclude the possibility of black escape from the dread of this present life and the anxiety of imminent death.[4]

Cone's *The Cross and the Lynching Tree* correlates the historicity of the hanging of Jesus upon a tree by the Roman Empire with the red record of black death at the hands of white American lynch mobs, in order to demonstrate how the past and present sufferings of the oppressed, though estranged by the transition of time, are irrevocably linked to each other and to an approximating future victory that is almost always "not yet." This constant theological negotiation of what is *past*, what is *present*, and what is *to come* is the impetus toward a distinctly African American crafting of eschatological vision that privileges the import and significance of historical continuity. Consequently, heaven and hell as *historical happening* cannot be conceived apart from God in Christ's historical activity on the side of the oppressed and victory over suffering and death in the world as gospeled. For Cone, if theological ideas of heaven and hell are not primarily and immediately responsive to the historical condemnation of the oppressed, then the pearly gates of the otherworld should be torn down, the golden streets torn up, and the leaves on the trees that are good for the healing of the nations might as well wither and die:

> To be sure, we may "walk in Jerusalem jus' like John" and "there may be a great camp meeting in the Promised Land," but we want to walk in *this* land.... We want to know why Harlem cannot become Jerusalem and Chicago the Promised Land? What good

> are golden crowns, slippers, white robes, or even eternal life, if it means that we have to turn our backs on the pain and suffering of our own children?[5]

Staunchly rejecting an otherworldly ethos that passively concedes black oppression for the hope of the next life, Cone's historical consideration of the "last things" adopts a reactionary blend of Rudolf Bultmann and Jürgen Moltmann's theological eschatologies in order to further emphasize the significance of black historicity in the *now* unfolding eschaton. Informed by Heideggerian phenomenology, which contends that in the pursuit of genuine selfhood, *Dasein* or being must always be "mine," that is, that authentic human existence is always and solely determined by the facticity of the subject, Bultmann's eschatological perspective decries apocalyptic speculation that rejects one's existential circumstances.[6] Alternatively, Bultmann claims reciprocity between the present and the future, arguing that eschatology "cannot be separated from being-in-the-present," but must always emerge from the *now* historical moment of the subject.[7] In his *Theology of Hope*, Moltmann presses this dynamic relationality between present realities and future possibilities to the imperative of present action and transformation. He concedes that while the salvific work of God in Christ is once and for all, salvation is not all at once. Thus, contrary to the opinions of the arbiters of white supremacy, the lived realities of the black oppressed are not congruent with God's intention for humanity and therefore must be resisted at all costs.[8]

Holding Bultmann's and Moltmann's eschatological visions in tension with black suffering, Cone surmises that the promise of *what is to come* must always serve as a theoethical mechanism that forthwith transforms the present circumstances of oppressed communities into communities of presently actualized and actualizing liberation. To be sure, the development of Cone's theology recognizes the perimetric value of heaven as a transcendental place. However, his historical eschatology posits heaven as much more than this evangelical-pietistic vision of an otherworldly locale that has been promised and prepared by Christ. Above all, heaven is a revolutionary happening now that disrupts the circularity of black oppression. Heaven empowers African Americans to live in spite of their suffering precisely because of the revaluation of the oppressed in light of God's victory over suffering in the flesh and blood of Jesus Christ. In short, heaven demands that African Americans confront and dismantle the hell that troubles black flesh and demands black blood on earth *right now*, as it is dismantled in heaven. It opposes a world of racism and discrimination and is the realization of the "eschatological hope of justice, the humanizing of man [*sic*], the socializing of humanity, [and] peace for all creation."[9]

Nowhere is this exposition of heaven and hell, as a distinctly African American affirmation of the "terrible right to live" in the historical *now* in binding relationship with *what is to come*, more prevalent than in the Negro spirituals, those sorrow songs that emerged from the belly of black suffering, and adroitly witnessed and testified to the aspirations of black life and the complexity of black death in the Americas.

Accordingly, heaven emerges within black spirituals as the predominant theme of African American religious experience.[10]

Although overwhelmingly identified with a transcendent reality beyond time and space, heaven as thematic referential simultaneously refers to subversive activity in the historical present that defies the social conditions of the oppressed. This is the primary significance of heaven. To insinuate escape in the antebellum South by intoning,

> Steal away, steal away,
> Steal away to Jesus;
> I ain't got long to stay here

or by asserting the righteous and prolonged battle to the death against the enmity of black freedom with the confession,

> O Freedom! O Freedom!
> Oh Freedom, I love thee;
> And before I'll be a slave,
> I'll be buried in my grave,
> And go home to my Lord and be free

not only affirms the eschatological promise of God's future for the oppressed that endures in "bright mansions above," but more importantly for African American historical eschatology, legitimates the immediacy of struggle, survival, and radical liberation, in light of the acrid palpability of black oppression in the here and now.

Now and Then: Heaven as Benevolent Promise

Heaven as *benevolent promise* emerges from black theologian J. Deotis Roberts's evaluation of the intersection of black suffering and "messianic humanism" as outlined in Rubem Alves's *A Theology of Hope*. Echoing Dietrich Bonhoeffer's *Ethics*, Alves's "messianic humanism" prioritizes God's incarnate humanity in Christ as the fullness of human liberation. Although the ideals, consciences, and experiences of the oppressed mirror the ideals and sufferings of God in Christ to such an extent that Alves concedes that God may be found among those who suffer and "participates in the weakness and the suffering of the slave," Alves's "messianic humanism" asserts that God alone initiates human deliverance and thus exclusively governs the potential for eschatological promise.[11]

Contrary to the historical eschatology of James Cone, contemplation of the "last things" from the perspective of God's benevolent promise eschews the material immediacy of revolution as the primary criterion of heaven as a meaningful response to the cross of black suffering. Instead the *benevolent promise* of God posits the resurrected Christ as the ultimate condition for eschatological vision. For Roberts, the future is not the future if it is left up to the cross, that is, the cross of the present sufferings of African Americans as a result of white racist society. In this regard, the future is always overtaken by the past and present realities and consequences of legal chattel enslavement and segregation. The *eschatos* necessarily loses its hopeful quality of an afterward, insofar as *what is to come* merely exists as an approximating regurgitation of *what already is*. Because suffering is a shared human phenomenon to which God's promise is fully responsive, not bifurcated according to a normative and uniquely American racialized hierarchy of black and white, African American eschatological vision must rebel against preoccupation with the material conditions of black misery and suffering.

Privileging African American victimization in the conceptualization of the eschaton as *benevolent promise* disregards the commonality of human suffering and compromises the reconciling integrity of divine response. Thus, in the development of his African American ethics and eschatology dialectic, Roberts embraces the theocentric thrust of the messianic humanist principle and its dependence on divine agency as the ultimate horizon that initiates justice, peace, and solidarity in love. Accordingly, for Roberts the promise of the future is always and simultaneously God-initiated and God-fulfilled. *What is to come* is never dependent on the disparaged predicament and oscillating virtue of humankind.

At the same time, Roberts's dialectic argues in opposition to Alves's urge to privilege *what God will do in the future that is to come*, precisely because "black theologians must be concerned about their present."[12] For Roberts, "No future God is adequate for [African American] hope." Instead, "The God of the consummation must also be the 'God of our weary years' and the 'God of our silent tears' "; and yet while held in tension with African American oppression, divine consummation is never determined by or dependent on human weariness or tears.[13] *Historical eschatology* similarly holds the past and present realities of African American suffering in tension with eschatological promise, but differs in its assertion of the future as relevant to black people only insofar as it is determined by and actualized in immediate liberation. Roberts's *benevolent eschatology* inverts the materiality of Cone's eschatological claim by holding the future in tension with the present toward the end of hope for humanity's moral and spiritual transformation that equally corresponds with the liberating and reconciling work of God in Jesus Christ.

Heaven does not happen as a result of the rebellious efforts of the black oppressed to radically transform the world from its present condition. Despite the vivid contours of human endeavor to oppress on the one hand and revolt on the other, God's promise of being raised with Christ for all those who "know the Christian experience of forgiveness, who have been sanctified . . . and who have been led by the Spirit into a life of social concern and action " has the last word.[14] Therefore, while faithful interpretation of heaven as *benevolent promise* seriously accounts for the materiality of the cross, namely, the verity of black pain and suffering, African American eschatological vision necessarily transcends the cross by regarding the Resurrection as the divine act that binds the promise of a future "for all nations" to a present ethical imperative that is grounded in the eternal morality and benevolence of God's hereafter, rather than the quantifiable material gains of human striving here and now.[15]

As symbolic and emblematic of the anticipated fulfillment of human potential, heaven is neither a revolutionary happening nor a locale, but according to God's promise in Christ, heaven "is a quality of life" that mirrors the best of human potential.[16] Ungraspable by human effort, this quality of blessedness that emerges from God's benevolence toward humanity is that quality of existence which humankind must constantly reach for and aspire to. In other words, although for Roberts heaven will never be proximate as an actualized place, African Americans may approximate the quality and timelessness of heaven's blessedness, not through defiant and rebellious acts that place an immediate demand on the present and fortuitously gamble with black life and death through a precarious "teleological suspension of the ethical," but by reaching for the promise of black liberation and human reconciliation consummated in the One who has already died and been raised for all.

Roberts juxtaposes the eternal blessedness of heaven as a quality of life with hell as a state of estrangement; the experience of eternal separation from God's love, mercy, and grace.[17] Hell is the absence of reach for the ungraspable benevolence of God. Like heaven, hell is not a place constructed by the whims of white supremacy or black power, but it is an internal quality that manifests when one's reach toward the promise of God is compromised by a fallen and perverted will. Forasmuch as racial discrimination reflects hell for the oppressed, insofar as it proceeds as the offspring of a distorted will to power, Roberts provocatively concedes that the oppressed have capacity to actively and equally participate in their experience of hell by compounding the initial hell of white racism with the estrangement that emanates from the will to power inherent in revolt, and which explicitly deviates from *what ought to be* according to the ethical imperative of divine benevolence. Consequently, in his *A Black Political Theology* Roberts offers a scathing critique of Cone's "reckless and despairing" eschatological position that reinforces hell with its potential yield of black suicide and black-on-black homicide, precisely because black suffering has not been eliminated by the liberating God who is on the side of the oppressed.[18] Roberts brazenly contends that the "here and now" compulsion of African American eschatology as *historical happening* is exceptionally dangerous insofar as it rejects the benevolent promise of God and thus self-inaugurates the estrangement that inevitably regenerates hell in blackface.

Hell No! The Hope of Heaven

To be sure, many enslaved blacks were convinced that they had tasted the depths of hell for themselves. Uncle George, a black slave, "believed that hell was the plantation that he had been born on in South Carolina, and that the devils there had been the white people."[19] In *The Negro Spiritual Speaks of Life and Death*, Howard Thurman claims that the gross evil of white masters and mistresses cast them so far beyond the pale of moral and ethical responsibility that the designation of hell lacked the moral capacity to fully capture the contours and consequences of white depravity. The physical and moral vicissitudes of hell on earth and hell as moral estrangement from God notwithstanding, the hope of heaven and the certainty of hell have endured in African American theology as the eschatological vision that invariably disrupts what Mircea Eliade identified in his *Myth of the Eternal Return* as the "terror of history."[20] Constituted by the cultural remnants of those who have been most objectified by the dehumanization and demoralization that attends the inheritance of American enslavement, heaven and hell as both the ethical rectification and the apocalyptic consummation of history are inseparable from the protracted struggle for black freedom that persists as a consequence of the hope of the oppressed.

The very determination to survive and prosper under the weight of slavery and Jim Crow compelled African American Christians to envision a "new order," and thus to reconceive the eschatological missionary preaching of the masters of hegemony in ways that made sense of black oppression, that accorded with the impoverishment of slave life, and that reconciled with the promise of abundant life in Christ. Therefore, as indicated by slave narratives and black spirituals, heaven was apprehended by the enslaved as both the eternal dwelling place of God and as a mediating ethic that did not disregard the historicity of black oppression or the benevolence and justice of the "coming Christ." To the contrary, heaven as the abode of a kindly and compassionate God who paradoxically acts in the terror of history necessarily implied a "both/and" negotiation of place and personality that allowed for the reversal of the present order through both the "radical transformation of the world . . . and [human] relationships." Heaven therefore recasts the social and political valuation of black flesh, in light of the assumption of freedom and benevolence as constitutive characteristics of God's reign.[21]

While attesting to the fact that enslaved blacks responded to the conflict that arose from the irreconcilable intersection of black enslavement and Christian faith in various ways—including unmitigated rejection of the gospel as espoused by white Christians and the more "immediatist" presumption that the reign of God was already at hand—black historian Gayraud Wilmore also outlines the delicate eschatological balance of black historicity and black hope that led many enslaved Africans to embrace a vision of Christianity's heaven and hell as the "model for and judgment upon the present order."[22] In accord with Cone and Roberts, Wilmore's cultural eschatology similarly emphasizes heaven's inseparability from the material condition of black historicity. However, for Wilmore the hope of the eschaton is grounded in the facts of black culture and history; thus, the *last* things are not determined by history as in James Cone's *historical eschatology* or determinative of history per J. Deotis Roberts's *benevolent eschatology*, but rather are incontrovertibly bound to those existentially determined *first* things that are embedded in the cultural experiences, physical needs, and spiritual hunger of the oppressed. Wilmore peremptorily explains at the outset of his eschatological consideration:

> Perhaps the most important consequence of our exploration will be the discovery that what Christians believe about the "last things" may be *first* in terms of influence upon their behavior in the world.[23]

Wilmore's prioritizing of cultural experience in the black religious imagination makes sense out of the socially, politically, and economically indigent African Americans' sacred contemplation of shoes, robes, and bright mansions. In light of the facts of black cultural reality, which more often prescribed shoeless and ragged existence confined to slave quarters, rural shacks, or, more contemporarily, urban ghettos, to proclaim "I got shoes, you got shoes; all God's children got trav'lin shoes," or "I wanna be ready to put on my long white robe," or "When you hear me prayin, I'm buildin' me a home," meant that among other things God must be a worldly God who understands the needs and social predicaments of God's people; and, similarly, God's heaven must be relevant to the cultural sensibilities and lived realities of the oppressed.

Moreover, the African Americans' bold intonation, "When we all get to heaven what a day of rejoicing it will be," alludes to the traditional communal solidarity that is characteristic of African and African diasporic cultures. The cruel institutionalization of the auction block and the propensity for white lethal violence against African Americans fragmented black families and attempted to thwart black cultural compulsion toward the communal. However, heaven, as the reversal of the status quo, signifies the blessedness of community as an African cultural norm, and reifies the opportunity to reconstitute community among those who share the experience of suffering in the world. This is what is meant when the Negro spiritual speaks:

> I'll meet you in de mornin',
> When you reach de promised land;
> On de oder side of Jordan,
> For I'm boun' for de promised land.[24]

Heaven affirms the black cultural norms that are ordinarily reviled by white racism. Whether interpreted as a historically grounded call for escape to the "promised land" of the North or escape to a heavenly hereafter, the mediating nature of heaven as *present transcendence*, that is, as actively breaking into the historicity of the oppressed and as the ever-approximating ungraspable, reorders the present disorder of black life, black community, and black culture by disrupting and transforming the normative order of things. This divine transformative activity necessarily substantiates and impels hope in an *other* reality that actively defies the apparent material defeat of the present world.

This hope in an *other* reality conjures an *eschatology of place* that is essential for understanding the breadth of African American theological consideration of the "last things." James Cone concedes that for African American Christians, "the concept of heaven was not exhausted by historical reality or present existence."[25] Thus, hope for God's future, as opposed to a future dictated by white supremacy, necessarily forecasts *heaven as a place* where "the mourner, the despised, the rejected, and the black" would find eternal rest and peace from the pain and suffering of the world. This is why amid the torturous legacy and experience of African enslavement, Jim Crow segregation, mass incarceration, and political disenfranchisement blacks can deliberately and uninterruptedly declare Good News: "I've got a crown up in a dat Kingdom; ain't a dat Good News?"[26]

However, although good news is presently evident, it is clear that the divine attributes of justice and judgment are equally significant in African American theology. Whereas heaven signifies the place of eternal reward for the righteous, hell is similarly conceptualized as the place where the wicked are eternally punished. Hell is the natural counterbalance to the virtue of God that ushers in the coming Kingdom; thus, heaven and hell are eschatological visions of divine justice. Forasmuch as heaven signals the "final" rupture of the the yoke of black suffering and death, hell is the *not yet place* that signals the judgment of a just God according to the theological orthodoxy that maintains in the face of evil and suffering, "You shall reap what you sow."[27]

Conclusion

Although often misread in light of its apparent otherworldly focus, African American theologians generally maintain that the assertion of an otherworld—as largely attested to in the black church, black preaching, Negro spirituals, and slave narratives—does not limit African American eschatology to an inconsequential otherworldliness, that compensatory theological framework which is more concerned with "saving souls than saving bodies." The mulattic intersection of black faith and ingenuity with the sadistic practices of white racism that circumscribed being black in America gave birth to the claim and anticipation of heaven and hell as *historical happening, benevolent promise*, and a *cultural mechanism of hope*, all of which in their varied intensities rebelled against the oppressive schemes of the "key masters and mistresses of hegemony."[28] African American theological conceptualization of heaven and hell continues to propel the black religious imagination beyond the finite terror of degradation and suffering. This is African American apocalyptic vision; and it is this eschatological hope of terror's defeat that doggedly revisions black humanity in spite of oppression, and casts divine identity and culturally relevant divine activity in history as the *first and last* assurance that what is not yet, is yet coming; that is, that the last will indeed be first (Mark 10:31).

Notes

1. James H. Cone, *Black Theology and Black Power* (New York: Orbis Books, 1997), 121.
2. Cone, *Black Theology and Black Power*, 125. See also James H. Cone, *God of the Oppressed* (New York: Orbis Books, 1997), 176–77.
3. For further treatment on the inescapability of black death see Howard Thurman, *Deep River and The Negro Spiritual Speaks of Life and Death* (Richmond, IN: Friends United, 1990), 13.
4. James H. Cone, *A Black Theology of Liberation* (New York: Orbis Books, 2008), 136.
5. Cone, *Black Theology of Liberation*, 137.
6. See Martin Heidegger, *Being and Time*, trans. John Macquarrie and Edward Robinson (New York: Harper & Row, 1962), 236–311.
7. Cone, *Black Theology of Liberation*, 138. See also Rudolf Bultmann, *History and Eschatology* (Edinburgh: University Press, 1957).
8. Adapted from class notes. Christopher Morse, "Heaven and Hell," Union Theological Seminary, 2005–6. See Christopher Morse, *The Difference Heaven Makes: Rehearing the Gospel as News* (New York: T&T Clark, 2012). See also Cone, *Black Theology of Liberation*, 139.
9. Cone, *Black Theology and Black Power*, 126.
10. James H. Cone, *The Spirituals and the Blues: An Interpretation* (New York: Orbis Books, 1972).
11. J. Deotis Roberts, *Liberation and Reconciliation: A Black Theology* (Louisville, KY: Westminster John Knox Press, 2005), 85.
12. Roberts, *Liberation and Reconciliation*, 85.
13. Roberts, *Liberation and Reconciliation*.
14. Roberts, *Liberation and Reconciliation*, 91.
15. Roberts, *Liberation and Reconciliation*.
16. Roberts, *Liberation and Reconciliation*, 92. See also James H. Evans Jr., *We Have Been Believers: An African American Systematic Theology* (Minneapolis: Fortress, 2012), 176.
17. Roberts, *Liberation and Reconciliation*, 92.
18. J. Deotis Roberts, *A Black Political Theology* (Philadelphia: Westminster, 1974), 182.
19. Dwight N. Hopkins and George C. L. Cummings, eds., *Cut Loose Your Stammering Tongue: Black Theology in the Slave Narrative* (Louisville, KY: Westminster John Knox Press, 2003), 40.

20. See Mircea Eliade, *Myth of the Eternal Return* (New York: Pantheon, 1954).
21. Evans, *We Have Been Believers*, 177. See also Hopkins and Cummings, *Cut Loose Your Stammering Tongue*, 40.
22. Evans, *We Have Been Believers*, 177.
23. Gayraud S. Wilmore, *Last Things First* (Philadelphia: Westminster, 1982), 11.
24. Cone, *The Spirituals and the Blues*, 80.
25. Cone, *The Spirituals and the Blues*, 87.
26. Cone, *The Spirituals and the Blues*, 89.
27. Hopkins and Cummings, *Cut Loose Your Stammering Tongue*, 41.
28. Emilie M. Townes, *In a Blaze of Glory: Womanist Spirituality as Social Witness* (Nashville: Abingdon, 1995), 121.

Selected Texts

Bonhoeffer, Dietrich. *Ethics*. Ed. Clifford J. Greene. Trans. Reinhard Krauss, Charles C. West, and Douglas W. Stott. Minneapolis: Fortress Press, 2005.

Bultmann, Rudolf. *History and Eschatology*. Edinburgh: University Press, 1957.

Bultmann, Rudolf. *Jesus Christ and Mythology*. New York: Scribner, 1958.

Bultmann, Rudolf. *Kerygma and Myth*. New York: Harper & Row, 1961.

Cone, James H. *Black Theology and Black Power*. New York: Orbis Books, 1999.

Cone, James H. *A Black Theology of Liberation*. 20th anniversary ed. Maryknoll, NY: Orbis Books, 2008.

Cone, James H. *God of the Oppressed*. New York: Orbis Books, 1997.

Cone, James H. *The Spirituals and the Blues*. New York: Orbis Books, 1991.

Eliade, Mircea. *Myth of the Eternal Return*. New York: Pantheon, 1954.

Evans, James H., Jr. *We Have Been Believers: An African American Systematic Theology*. 2nd ed. Minneapolis: Fortress, 2012.

Heidegger, Martin. *Being and Time*. Trans. John Macquarrie and Edward Robinson. New York: Harper & Row, 1962.

Hopkins, Dwight N., and George C. L. Cummings, eds. *Cut Loose Your Stammering Tongue: Black Theology in the Slave Narrative*. 2nd ed. Louisville, KY: Westminster John Knox Press, 2003.

Moltmann, Jürgen. *Theology of Hope: On the Ground and Implications of a Christian Eschatology*. New York: Harper & Row, 1967.

Morse, Christopher. *The Difference Heaven Makes: Rehearing the Gospel as News*. New York: T&T Clark, 2010.

Roberts, J. Deotis. *A Black Political Theology*. Philadelphia: Westminster, 1974.

Roberts, J. Deotis. *Liberation and Reconciliation: A Black Theology*. 2nd ed. Louisville, KY: Westminster John Knox Press, 2005.

Thurman, Howard. *Deep River and The Negro Spiritual Speaks of Life and Death* Richmond, IN: Friends United Press, 1990.

Townes, Emilie M. *In a Blaze of Glory: Womanist Spirituality as Social Witness*. Nashville: Abingdon, 1995.

Townes, Emilie, ed. *A Troubling in My Soul: Womanist Perspectives on Evil and Suffering*. New York: Orbis Books, 1993.

Washington, Joseph. *Black Religion*. Boston: Beacon Press, 1964.
Wilmore, Gayraud S. *Last Things First*. Philadelphia: Westminster, 1982.
Wilmore, Gayraud S. *Black Religion and Black Radicalism*. Garden City, NY: Anchor/Doubleday, 1973.

SECTION III

INTERNAL DEBATES

CHAPTER 19

WOMANIST THEOLOGY AS A CORRECTIVE TO AFRICAN AMERICAN THEOLOGY

CHERYL A. KIRK-DUGGAN

WOMANIST theology emerged as a corrective discipline during the 1980s, concerned about the plight of black women in the United States, of global African diasporan women, ultimately the wholeness of all persons across gender, race, class, age, and ability. Black women have lived the ontologies, existential realities, and subversive strategies that undergird womanist thought. Alice Walker—poet, novelist, activist—coined the term and explored it in her 1983 collection, *In Search of Our Mother's Gardens: Womanist Prose*. Her four-part definition examines relationality steeped in love; qualifies womanist strength, maturity, willfulness, and audacious spirit; explores the sexual and nonsexual experiences of committed womanist love; reflects on the aesthetics and politics of womanist love; and ends with a comparative view of womanism, in conjunction with black feminism. Womanist thought became a discipline when scholar-activist Katie G. Cannon adapted Walker's definition as an analytical rubric. She recognized that neither traditional feminist theology, which problematized gender, nor traditional black theology, which problematized race, provided all the categories needed for her world, which included poor black women, "the least of these." Initially, Cannon and others like Delores Williams, Jacqueline Grant, Cheryl Townsend Gilkes, and Emilie Townes began to use this term to expose oppression and to correct some of the systemic and personal challenges to black people worldwide. The inclusive nature of womanist thought ultimately organizes toward the love, justice-making, and transformation of all people. This essay follows with selected themes, concepts, and categories womanists have used, from an interdisciplinary perspective, as a corrective toward love as activism, to affect transformation and sociocultural, political, physical, mental, spiritual, personal, and communal wholeness.

While most indicate that Alice Walker first coined the term "womanist" in her aforementioned 1983 volume, she first used it in 1979, in her short story "Coming Apart," placing women's realities in everyday situations. Two other scholars served as catalysts for nurturing womanist thought, publishing an article and a book, respectively: Chikwenye Okonjo Ogunyemi published "Womanism: The Dynamics of the Contemporary Black Female Novel in English" (1985); Clenora Hudson-Weems published *Africana Womanism: Reclaiming Ourselves* (1983). These scholars gave voice to a previously existing entity in the academy and social activism. Layli Philips defined this named thing of womanism as a social change perspective grounded in black women's and other women of color's daily experiences and methods of problem solving in everyday spaces, committed to ending oppression for everyone, restoring balance between humanity and creation, and reconciling human life with the spiritual dimension. Womanism exists in Africa, North America, Europe, Latin America, and Asia. Staying within yet beyond political and intellectual structures, womanism has remained accessible for many across diverse sociocultural locations. Philips posits that womanists work to orchestrate, manage, and engage difference, where it does not become conflictual and dissolve into violent devastation. Womanist thought has five elements: it works against oppression, for liberation; is vernacular or of everyday realities; is nonideological, abhorring rigid lines of demarcation toward decentralization; is communitarian, where collective well-being is the goal of social change; and is spiritualized: it acknowledges a spiritual/transcendental realm where humanity, creation, and matter interconnect. Womanist theologians have related to Walker's definition of womanism, expanded it, and not been confined to her parameters.

Two seminal moments helped galvanize womanist theology: Delores S. Williams's 1987 article, "Womanist Theology: Black Women's Voices," where she acknowledges the infancy of womanist thought, examines part of Walker's definition, recognizes cultural code usage and the place of freedom fighters, and delineates womanist theology and method. She posits four intents needed to inform womanist methodology: multidialogical, liturgical, didactic, and a commitment to reason and the validity of female imagery and metaphorical language in constructing theological statements.[1]

The second moment was the 1989 "Roundtable Discussion: Christian Ethics and Theology in Womanist Perspective," with Cheryl J. Sanders, Katie G. Cannon, Emilie M. Townes, M. Shawn Copeland, bell hooks, and Cheryl Townsend Gilkes.[2] Sanders's essay led the discussion, providing an overview of womanist thought and questioned whether womanism, which she views as a secular cultural category, can critically and meaningfully engage theology and ethics. Sanders argued that Walker's definition pays too little attention to the divine, and affirms/advocates homosexual practice, which she views as antithetical to ethics and values of black families and black churches. For Sanders, that Walker's definition does not explicitly mention God or Christ smacks of entrapment regarding Christian virtue practices. She called for critique and celebration. The other scholars responded in kind. Cannon moved to engage the radical work of love, instead of anger, suggesting that the term womanist is an accurate context of engagement for creating a liberation theo-ethical framework, which supports black women's moral agency. As such, a womanist paradigm critiques all human-generated domination. Womanist Christian ethical praxis involves black women's commitments to understand and change oppressive, systemic structures and alienating experiences. Townes noted Sanders's move to raise critical, constructive questions was solid, yet found them problematic, rooted in conceptual error. Where Sanders did not see the sacred, Townes noted that Walker clearly articulates her understanding of the Spirit, the divine; and that womanist thought has tremendous promise for theological and ethical reflection for the black community, and engages human equality and the powerful, sustaining, ever present, judging, redeeming presence of God. Copeland noted the import of Sanders's critique, yet finds missing references to works womanists use in their analysis and creativity of Christian thinkers who have incorporated secular feasts, fables, and festivals for Christian purposes. Copeland sees the self-defining womanist project as one that loves her traditions, people, culture, and people's struggle, which can reshape and help black theology expand. Bell hooks notes that womanist thought affords black women scholars options to engage feminist thinking, inclusive of race and survival of the folk. She contends that Sanders's focus on varied sexual practices forges a paradigm that posits a womanist view antithetical to Christian praxis. Hooks counters that Walker's term helps women affirm their connections to black traditions, and it helps black women scholars expand their grasp of relevant theological ethical discourse. Gilkes finds Walker's notion of womanist liberating and refreshing, engaging significant aspects of religious experience: Spirit manifesting God in daily life, rooted in love. In response, Sanders insists on standing for differences between the sacred and secular, and her deep passion for the moral import of sexual ethics praxis comes out of her commitment to her holiness tradition. She does, however, commend her sister scholars in using the work of black women, whose material is worthy of celebration.

Since these two watershed publications over the last three decades, many womanist scholars have used this discourse to forge new ways of constructing religious discourse, epistemologies, and social-justice-based praxis. While not all womanist theologians are Christians, this essay primarily focuses on their contributions to this discipline and praxis. Some scholars focus globally, some domestically on the African American context.

Katie Cannon, in works of critique and celebration, challenges, cautions, and gives witness to black women's moral agency. Her correctives become emancipatory songs of pedagogy and praxis that prod one to consciousness.[3] She embodies and features an epistemological privilege of the oppressed, focusing on the dynamic dualities of double consciousness, from a prophetic vantage point as master pedagogue who wants humanity to know wholeness. She views womanist theory as a "balm in Gilead," healing opportunities that expose the muddles and messes of sexism, racism, and classism via the lived experience of the "least of these," poor black working women. Problematizing issues of power, renewal, and regeneration, she views life as challenging, but not hopeless. Womanist thought offers a corrective for the distortions of white hegemony and black inferiority. Cannon exposes erroneous lies, misuse of biblical interpretation, and fairy tales of African depravity and misconstrued divine sanction that attempt to legitimate oppression. Expressing moral reasoning and ethical praxis, womanist thought signifies wisdom of elderly black folk who have survived Jim Crow. Such thought tackles historical and personal dynamics of injustice and white hegemonic hypocrisy apparent in the wake of poverty and unemployment. The corrective is paradoxical, simultaneously exposing injustice while nurturing and witnessing womanist consciousness. Cannon uses black women's experiences via black women's literary works that relay their quality of moral good and their moral virtues, central to black life, notably expressed in the life of Zora Neale Hurston. Such resources provide a corrective as a constructive, liberationist, womanist ethic to expose the range and profusion of human sin, including constructions of domination, subordination, and constraints that reinforce and reproduce systemic hierarchies of oppression based on class, race, age, sex, and sexual orientation. She questions skewed idolatries in the classroom, in church life, within the liturgics of homiletics. Cannon commends and excavates the mother lode of God-sanctioned freedom over against lies and incongruities of oppression, particularly amid social constructs that misuse biblical symbols to justify cruelty and corruption. Cannon's corrective is a womanist, constructive, liberationist pedagogy, where liberationist ethics require that one takes action, framed by a knowing that results from the doing. That one is not in charge does not hinder one's capacity for resistance and making a difference.

Resisting evil and embracing survival, for the chaplain Rosita deAnn Mathews, involves exercising power from the periphery. Here one refuses to use violence or aggressive methods, and offers corrective resistance by maintaining ethical principles and moral standards. Such a location is often dangerous regarding systemic oppression, particularly in corporate politics. Maintaining power from the periphery requires thinking carefully through all strategies and actions, and allows one response with dignity, out of love of neighbor. Such a stance affords one a prophetic posture to name and criticize the dynamics of an action, and the capacity to set limits around interacting within the system. In the process, one gains strength from other spaces to exist and flourish. Using this position as a seat of justice, rather than abuse, one helps transform reality and creates a new spirit. Exercising power from the periphery involves practicing integrity, abstaining from destructive options, and recognizing the prophetic nature of this position, so that one helps transform the system through careful observation, offering critique, being creative, and energizing the system toward new possibilities. Such action often meets with resistance from those in authority.

Resistance and challenges to healthy access to power and community building include social stratification due to competitive individualism versus internal, communal engagement of social responsibility. Marcia Riggs observes the black women's club movement and notes that black people continue to struggle due to matters related to systemic oppression rooted in sociocultural, economic experiences and oppressions due to class/race/gender realities.[4] Those reformers engaged in the black women's club movement practiced collective solidarity. As a corrective, they saw one's personal autonomy as interdependent with the collective of blacks globally. An experience of liberation involved embodying an ethic of responsibility, accountability, and commitment. Such an ethic in the black women's club movement fostered three elements: renunciation, where elite black women see their connections with women of other classes and renounce the advantage of difference; inclusivity, the intention to connect with women from different life experiences and classes; and a moral vision of religious and social responsibility, based on their vision of God's justice and divinely willed justice for the black community. Such community building provides opportunity for engagement in social witness.

To begin to correct social ills, social ethicist Emilie Townes reminds us that gender, race, class, age, ability, and heterosexist ideas are part of our cultural system.[5] Where white femininity and hegemonic masculinity exist, black bodies and souls are frequently battle grounds. Dominant culture tends to objectify and sensationalize these bodies. As a corrective, black folk must work for or live into justice; otherwise there can be no self-respect and communal connectivity. Justice-based life with spirituality as social witness appreciates traditions, remembers and shares its stories, offers witness to communal heritage, and endeavors to create a community of accountability. That community accountability involves connectedness to God and intergenerational exchange of ideas.

Part of being in community is the intergenerational sharing of spiritual values and belief systems: theological ethics in action. Prophetic homiletician Teresa Fry Brown argues that enslavement produced a subjugation that black folk had to counter with a corrective to enable them to face systemic oppression as they affirmed universal humanity.[6] African diasporan women worked to instill concepts they believed God bequeathed: justice, freedom, and equality both personally and socially—which have political, judicial, economic, and spiritual ramifications. Black women worked in the arenas of black family, black community, and black church to inspire and instill moral values, the same arenas where black women experience liberation and oppression. One adage black families use to indicate moral imperative is "God don't like ugly."[7] Fry Brown notes this proverb means that God wants us to behave in Christ-like ways, and not misbehave. We must be accountable to God for all of our actions. God's grace and mercy stand in concert with God's judgment. One is ugly if not living authentically, thus denying one's God-given life as gift and one's family roots. Some of that denial inevitably emerges when dealing with issues of sexuality.

Kelly Brown Douglas, womanist theologian, notes that if humanity is created in God's image, then authentic humanity emerges in the incarnated Jesus.[8] When people, motivated by God's love, enter into relations with divine creation, their humanity is actualized. Knowledge of God's love moves us to share love with other persons, realizing one's own divinity. When people opt to reflect God's image in the world, they exist as agents of love. While God's love is in every person, every human being does not necessarily manifest this love. God's love manifested in Jesus is *agape*: active love where one gives of her- or himself toward justice and authentic communal life without expecting anything in return. As a corrective move, Douglas views sexuality as God's gift to humanity.[9] Sexuality is important to *agape*, allowing people to engage relationally with others toward authentic humanity. While some tend to view Jesus in an abstract, docetic, disembodied manner not really, fully human, it is critical that we view God as embodied in human actions throughout history. Such a spiritual reading corrects our negation and repulsion of our physical body and helps us to appreciate the human body. In the process, one comes to be like Jesus, living lives of liberating, empowering, healing, life-sustaining, loving relationships. As such, we see God and ourselves as relational. Relationality connects with salvation and suffering.

Womanist theologian Stephanie Mitchem reminds us that the question of salvation must deal with suffering for black women, where women engage Jesus midst active, empowering love.[10] Some womanist scholars root their analysis in suffering to name the memory of past wrongs. Such memory language shields identity and religion, where black women connect with God to redeem the souls of black folk. Womanist salvific theology involves a response to pain consisting of agency toward resisting dehumanization. One corrective posits that suffering is not salvific, though it may invoke analytical, critical rethinking about community, responsibility, and sin. Mitchem, who posits a corrective of a holistic Christology, notes that Delores S. Williams's concept of personal and social sin, where any devaluation and abuse of black women, created *imago Dei*, is indeed sin.[11] The corrective involves embracing Williams's ministerial vision of Jesus, which is redemptive as it involves self-care and right relationships. Jacquelyn Grant argues that sin occurs when black women do too much service, as society devalues their servanthood, as evinced in the novel and subsequent film *The Help*, which examines lies of southern black female domestic workers employed in white households. Her corrective is to suggest discipleship as paradigm. Conversation regarding salvation, servanthood, and ministerial vision are critical correctives, because the mindset related to such concepts permeates the mental, spiritual, and physical realities of black women, including that of work.

Womanist ethicist Joan M. Martin reminds us of the valuable resources of enslaved women's work ethic and the impact it had on community building. Their work ethic embraced a relationality grounded in a theological ethics where God, giver of life, also gives freedom and protection.[12] With this divine framing, enslaved women crafted an intergenerational moral teaching, authority, and action that produced empowerment and solidarity. They advocated struggle for self-reliance and determination regarding the use of their own labor, and that same self-reliance garnered them confidence in their skills and crafts. Such an embodied cosmology moved the women to view work as that which helped them assist other people and communities throughout their life cycles. These cultural, communal midwives understood the parameters of their society and knew how to work within and against cultural mores for the survival of their people. Work becomes the site of a womanist ethical corrective as it connects their moral authority and work to foster well-being in their daily lives, as whole persons. Martin posits that the characteristics and significance of work occur in the dialectic search for real freedom and human wholeness amid socially constructed, systemic subjugation and evil. Dynamics related to work affect our moral agency. When we work and see change, we experience hope.

Womanist theologian A. Elaine Brown Crawford uses "hope in the holler" as a corrective to elevate the import of hope in helping African American women to transcend historical oppression in society and church, where it has been permissible for them to be scapegoated.[13] The holler is the space of recognition, renunciation, and refusal. Such a space unfolds where the one and the many viscerally cry out against oppression, honor their own humanity, and say no to cyclical intergenerational terror and violence. They have deep desire for new possibilities, transcending survival, toward transformation. Crawford examines the context of multidimensional oppressions, particular texts or story content, and the intent of how hope works in black women's lives to move beyond the holler toward communal and self-actualization. Her review of various ways womanist thinkers have envisioned hope reflects Christological, eschatological, paradoxical, prophetic, and faith-based analysis. Transgenerational abuse and faith as content and context for multiple generations of black women reflect maldistribution of hope, forging a sociopolitical, communal resistance to abuse. Hope is not static. The focus of hope shifts from quest for freedom and humane treatment, to gaining voice, autonomy, and equality. The focus changed as dynamics of oppression changed. In assessing womanist theological treatments of hope, Crawford sees a limited focus on hope. She posits that we need to explore actual black women's voices to ascertain their notions of hope as a theological and psychosocial enterprise to affect the black church, while remaining inclusive. A womanist theology of hope must be embodied. This theology cannot allow stereotypes, scripture, or systems to maintain abuse and violence, or rob one of spiritual, sexual, psychological integrity: such is the voice of wisdom.

Womanist wisdom, an accumulated knowledge or erudition and experience framed by common sense and insight learned by women of African descent, involves courage to embody and share life's lessons and experiential truths for life's journey. The late womanist pastoral theologian Linda Hollies noted that womanists learn this wisdom from foremothers and sisters via their quilting bees, sewing circles, and cookouts.[14] These communal experiences involved socializing, networking, caring, and sharing that helped them bond in sisterhood and spiritual reinforcement. They spoke into existence the future they hoped would be, and might never see. These sister friends embodied the adage "making a way out of no way," as they made beautiful quilts from scraps. The process of quilting, sewing, and cooking provided sacred time together to fashion beauty, offer encouragement, and strategize for each other and the community. Without the accoutrements of modern technology, these foremothers supported each other toward a life of honor, dignity, self-respect, self-fulfillment, and significant relationships of mutuality. Womanist wisdom was a safety net of inspiration that provided time and space to work toward wholeness. Amid systemic oppression, paradoxes, and hard times, womanist wisdom provided coalitions where community women offered nurturing, pastoral care, as love correctives of all the isms that oppress, internally and externally. Such wisdom affords a profound understanding of life, empowering womanists to choose or act consistently, effectively, and efficiently.

The work, presence, and ministries of women of wisdom helped to provide leadership and inspiration to churches and other groups and organizations that supported and transformed the survival of people and community. Women exist and are engaged in all levels of sociocultural interactions and production, despite disrespect and objectification from dominant culture. To understand the experience and functions of black women, one must explore communal connections. Even with mostly patriarchal and male-centered religious structures, if it were not for women, sociologist of religion Cheryl Townsend Gilkes indicates, the church could not exist.[15] Womanist ethicist Marcia Riggs's corrective explores sexism, sexual ethics, clergy/ministerial ethics, and ecclesial practices. She challenges the misuse of power and the resulting institutional sexism that produces tokenism based on gender as opposed to change that would create a gender-inclusive church. Riggs problematizes the distortions between the church's stated theological and ethical beliefs and its oral practices.[16] She believes that a womanist liberationist, Christian ethical analysis begins with the historical, political, religious/spiritual, familial, woman-centered, woman-identified lived experiences of actual black women, oriented toward sexual-gender justice, at the core of the church's identity and practices—anthropological concerns.

Linda E. Thomas's corrective suggests a womanist theological anthropology that embraces survival and liberation.[17] With self-reflection, one becomes mindful of sociocultural, historical factors that precipitate the construction of political economy and its influence on marginalized African diasporan women. By intentionally including working-class and poor women's voices, so they speak for themselves, we see how everyday activities shape the ways black women make choices and live. As a womanist interdisciplinary scholar, Cheryl Kirk-Duggan studies these women's lives to expose the violence in them. Here the corrective involves critical examination where one sees and confesses one's complicity, denial, or acceptance of abuse and violence.[18] The prevalence of global, personal, and institutional violence is horrific. The proliferation of violence in culture, legal systems, neighborhoods, and homes has reached pandemic proportions. Violence is often dressed in polite language, ingrained by supremacist patriarchy, and camouflaged in subtle, frightening feminist privilege: male domination on the one hand, and on the other women so inculcated with this pathological system that they engage privilege while firmly believing they are liberationist. The tragedy is the loss of a fullness of life for everyone. Many women, regardless of class or race, are often so wounded that they cannot help themselves. Many so-called white liberals never see the violence of their own prejudices. The pretense of collaboration and solidarity vanish. The patriarchal feminist and the good-old-boy liberal fail to see their hypocrisy. Kirk-Duggan uses the metaphor of "misbegotten anguish" as a corrective to name and expose the dynamics, depths, and communal complicity of violence in lives, texts, and actions globally. We cannot correct that which we do not admit. In this context, society and individuals need conscientization around abuse of power and authority, the cowardice of feigning ignorance, and the ultimate betrayal of God, others, and self. The body, particularly the female body, is often the site of violence and abuse.

Womanist educator Nancy Lynne Westfield connects perceptions, traditions, and practices of African American church worship and the black female body, to offer a corrective around sexism, misogyny, and aesthetics in the black church. Critical to the corrective is awareness.[19] First, to survive, black women had to embrace self-hatred, while loving everyone else: all children, black and white men and white women. Second, egregious sexism in black churches produced internalized sexism within black Christian women, supporting gross, unexamined schizophrenic stereotypes that pit black women against other black women. Third, the worship event involving preaching, teaching, praying amid liturgical drama can implicitly and explicitly miseducate God's people. Rooted in these three scenarios, many black churches participate in systemic gender oppression, as they ignore sexuality, the body, and the beauty of the body. Consequently, many black churches fail to ordain women or elevate them to prominent position; and black church women often uphold a supermoral decorum of decency that involves self-denial and repression. Westfield contends that we must engage in the tradition of "meddling" where one becomes intentional and prescriptive about congregational lives and behaviors and cease being hypocrites or naive by avoiding discussing multiple sexisms, sexuality, and the black body aesthetic. Her corrective calls for ceasing the silence and sinning against God that turns our beautiful bodies and minds away from God. One profound reality is the various ways/methods womanist theologians approach God.

Monica E. Coleman engages lived reality, intellectual thought, and transformative hope to construct a postmodern womanist theology. Using the folk adage "making a way out of no way," Coleman builds on faith, social responsibility, and truth telling amid autobiographical, contextual experiences, to explore soteriological scholarship of selected womanist theologians and process thinkers.[20] Her corrective is to construct a communal, soteriological theology. Coleman uses philosophical metaphysics to explore how the world operates, how God and world relate in reality, and to account for all nature: constant change, human freedom, evil and suffering as loss. God's activity and nature call us toward beauty and justice: human becoming, and valuing all creation. Creative transformation produces empowering change when people create teaching, healing communities of God; challenge the present circumstances; decenter Christ and Jesus; engage human agency toward holistic justice; and pursue salvation as a process of change. For Coleman, dialogical engagement is an ethical imperative fostering world salvific transformation. Using case studies, she constructs a salvific womanist postmodern theology that embodies communal and theological change, to engage a diverse womanist theology that can address black women's lives.

Framed with the metaphorical folk adage "standing in the shoes my mother made," Diana Hayes uses a womanist commitment in Christian tradition as a critical lens for assessing Christianity, which often flourished at expense of African Americans.[21] She honors the historical moves of womanist thought and signals the particularity of being a Catholic, lay, celibate womanist, who is a theologian and attorney: one called to refute the invisibility of black Catholics. She views womanist thought as a challenge to love framed by a subversive faith to critique domination and oppression, toward making an open, inclusive community. Thematically, one moves into embodiment of womanist Catholicism by engaging faith and worship, yoking ministry and social justice, viewing the public face of faith, challenging church and world to embrace God's hope, and working toward inclusive engagement that moves toward peace. How one understands the work of faith can press a reconfiguring of one's spiritual praxis.

Barbara A. Holmes focuses on moving the black church from congregational, individualistic piety and denominational limits, as a corrective toward a mystical, communal spirituality: prophetic contemplative discourse.[22] She invites a contemplative life amid crisis. One can engage interdisciplinary, autobiographical, poetic, prophetic, political, socioeconomic, historical, liturgical, and biblical strategies to create a provocative discourse through persuasive argument. Questions of attitude, virtue, commitment, and behavior signal her accomplishments respectively as litigant and ethicist. Questions of paradox, incongruities, and physics engage process thought, science, technology, and theology. Her corrective of "joy unspeakable" is a black aesthetic that calls for justice, sanity, and faithful, living actualization. Her call is to remember and embrace contemplative practices—ranging from prayers or moans in the bowels of slave ships and shouts to tap dancing and rap—as praxis to keep the community safe during crisis. Such crisis emerges from communal oppression and individual anxiety. Her corrective exposes pathologies of desolation black folk experience, crafting an invisible spirituality. Prophetically, Holmes asks if and when the current generation can pass on the rich legacy of diversity and complexity of the historical, nonmonolithic, creative black church. Stories of migration, survival, and overcoming, amid indigenous contemporary practices and Africana monastic traditions, provide tools of contemplation and empowerment. Afrocentric Midrashic biblical interpretation and the study of black contemplative saints whose inner life fueled their commitment to social activism and justice reveal intergenerational contemplative practices. Contemplative practices enable one to appreciate diversity, chaos, and incongruity, beyond malaise, pessimism, and denial about African diasporan realities. Joy unspeakable warns us not to sell out our legacy, our joy, for we can lose our abiding spiritual ethos. To know one's joy is to know one's legacy.

Stacey Floyd-Thomas reminds us that womanist discourse follows the legacy of innovative muses of the African diaspora who embraced struggle, survival, and celebration, who affirm the black community, themselves, and their relationship with the Spirit and the divine. This discourse is interdisciplinary, engaging substance from art, black literature, music, film, and sacred witness to address systemic and personal oppressions.[23] These oppressions span the gamut from sexism and racism to classism, heterosexism, and anti-intellectualism, amid the black church tradition and other related faith communities. This discourse involves town and gown, faith communities, and the academy. Historically, then, the corrective exposes dualisms that divide black women from women, and black women from black men. The division beetween women, couched in feminism, takes black women out of their sociohistorical context, denying them total agency and disregards their accomplishments, which fail to fit the feminist perspective. The division between black men and black women, rooted in systemic, patriarchal realities, denies the oppression of black women. Womanist thought becomes the corrective that provides African diasporan women opportunities to honor black women's virtues that provide agency, an actualized view of black womanhood. Such agency affords communal and self-actualization, self-determination, and an epistemology that honors her with options to improve her own reality, in communal, redemptive, critical, healthy ways toward human flourishing. In sum, womanist discourse as corrective investigates, interrogates, and exposes historical and contemporary systemic oppression toward liberation. Within this paradigm, African diasporan moral wisdom is foundational for the transformation of all people. Floyd-Thomas methodologically gleans four tenets of womanist thought: radical subjectivity, traditional communalism, redemptive self-love, and critical engagement, expanding womanist theology to a larger field of inquiry. Womanist thought as corrective is open to all people who work for justice and liberate the oppressed, toward transforming persons and systems in the academy, society, and faith communities.

Notes

1. Delores S. Williams, "Womanist Theology: Black Women's Voices," *Christianity and Crisis* 47, no. 3 (March 2, 1987), reprinted in *Black Theology: A Documentary History*, vol. 2, *1980–1992*, ed. James H. Cone and Gayraud S. Wilmore (Maryknoll, NY: Orbis Books, 1993), 265, 266, 267, 271.
2. Cheryl J. Sanders, Katie G. Cannon, Emilie M. Townes, M. Shawn Copeland, bell hooks, and Cheryl Townsend Gilkes, "Roundtable Discussion: Christian Ethics and

Theology in Womanist Perspective (1989), in *The Womanist Reader*, ed. Layli Phillips (New York: Routledge, 2006), 126–58.

3. Katie G. Cannon, *Katie's Canon: Womanism and the Soul of the Black Community* (New York: Continuum, 1995).
4. Marcia Y. Riggs, *Awake, Arise, Act: A Womanist Call for Black Liberation* (Cleveland, OH: Pilgrim Press, 1994).
5. Emilie M. Townes, *Womanist Ethics and the Cultural Production of Evil* (New York: Palgrave Macmillan, 2006).
6. Teresa Fry Brown. *God Don't Like Ugly: African American Women Handing on Spiritual Values* (Nashville: Abingdon, 2000).
7. Brown, *God Don't Like Ugly.*
8. Kelly Brown Douglas, *Sexuality and the Black Church* (Maryknoll, NY: Orbis Books, 1999).
9. Douglas, *Sexuality.*
10. Stephanie Y. Mitchem, *Introducing Womanist Theology* (Maryknoll, NY: Orbis Books, 2002).
11. Mitchem, *Introducing Womanist Theology.*
12. Joan M. Martin, *More Than Chains and Toil: A Christian Work Ethic of Enslaved Women* (Louisville, KY: Westminster John Knox, 2000).
13. A. Elaine Brown. *Hope in the Holler: A Womanist Theology* (Louisville, KY: Westminster John Knox, 2002).
14. Linda H. Hollies, *Bodacious Womanist Wisdom* (Cleveland, OH: Pilgrim Press, 2003).
15. Cheryl Townsend Gilkes, *If It Wasn't for the Women: Black Women's Experience and Womanist Culture in Church and Community* (Maryknoll, NY: Orbis Books, 2001).
16. Riggs, *Awake, Arise, Act.*
17. Linda E. Thomas, *Living Stones in the Household of God: The Legacy and Future of Black Theology* (Minneapolis: Fortress Press, 2004).
18. Cheryl A. Kirk-Duggan, *Misbegotten Anguish: A Theology and Ethics of Violence* (Louisville, KY: Chalice Press, 2001).
19. Nancy Lynne Westfield, "The Foolish Woman Grows Angry Because They Teach Her: Influences of Sexism in Black Church Worship," in *Black Religion and Aesthetics: Religious Thought and Life in Africa and the African Diaspora*, ed. Anthony B. Pinn (New York: Palgrave Macmillan, 2009), 37–52.
20. Monica Coleman, *Making a Way out of No Way: A Womanist Theology* (Minneapolis: Fortress Press, 2008).
21. Diana L. Hayes, *Standing in the Shoes My Mother Made: A Womanist Theology* (Minneapolis: Fortress Press, 2011).
22. Barbara A. Holmes, *Joy Unspeakable: Contemplative Practices of the Black Church* (Minneapolis: Augsburg/Fortress, 2004).
23. Stacey M. Floyd-Thomas, "Womanist Theology," in *Liberation Theologies in the United States*, ed. Stacey M. Floyd-Thomas and Anthony Pinn (New York: New York University Press, 2010), 37–60.

Selected Texts

Brown, Teresa Fry. *God Don't Like Ugly: African American Women Handing on Spiritual Values*. Nashville: Abingdon, 2000.

Cannon, Katie Geneva. *Katie's Canon: Womanism and the Soul of the Black Community*. New York: Continuum, 1995.

Coleman, Monica. *Making a Way out of No Way: A Womanist Theology*. Minneapolis: Fortress, 2008.

Crawford, A. Elaine Brown. *Hope in the Holler: A Womanist Theology*. Louisville, KY: Westminster John Knox, 2002.

Douglas, Kelly Brown. *Sexuality and the Black Church*. Maryknoll, NY: Orbis Books, 1999.

Floyd-Thomas, Stacey M. "Womanist Theology." In *Liberation Theologies in the United States*, ed. Stacey M. Floyd-Thomas and Anthony B. Pinn, 37–60. New York: New York University Press, 2010.

Gilkes, Cheryl Townsend. *If It Wasn't for the Women: Black Women's Experience and Womanist Culture in Church and Community*. Maryknoll, NY: Orbis Books, 2001.

Hayes, Diana L. *Standing in the Shoes My Mother Made: A Womanist Theology*. Minneapolis: Fortress Press, 2011.

Hollies, Linda H. *Bodacious Womanist Wisdom*. Cleveland, OH: Pilgrim Press, 2003.

Holmes, Barbara A. *Joy Unspeakable: Contemplative Practices of the Black Church*. Minneapolis: Augsburg/Fortress, 2004.

Kirk-Duggan, Cheryl A. *Misbegotten Anguish: A Theology and Ethics of Violence*. Louisville, KY: Chalice Press, 2001.

Martin, Joan M. *More Than Chains and Toil: A Christian Work Ethic of Enslaved Women*. Louisville, KY: Westminster John Knox, 2000.

Mitchem, Stephanie Y. *Introducing Womanist Theology*. Maryknoll, NY: Orbis Books, 2002.

Riggs, Marcia Y. *Plenty Good Room: Women versus Male Power in the Black Church*. Cleveland, OH: Pilgrim Press, 2003.

Riggs, Marcia Y. *Awake, Arise, Act: A Womanist Call for Black Liberation*. Cleveland, OH: Pilgrim Press, 1994.

Thomas, Linda E. "Womanist Theology, Epistemology, and a New Anthropology Paradigm." In *Living Stones in the Household of God: The Legacy and Future of Black Theology*, ed. Linda E. Thomas, 37–48. Minneapolis: Fortress, 2004.

Westfield, Nancy Lynne. "The Foolish Woman Grows Angry Because They Teach Her: Influences of Sexism in Black Church Worship." In *Black Religion and Aesthetics: Religious Thought and Life in Africa and the African Diaspora*, ed. Anthony B. Pinn, 37–52. New York: Palgrave MacMillan, 2009.

Williams, Delores S. *Sisters in the Wilderness: The Challenge of Womanist God-Talk*. Maryknoll, NY: Orbis Books, 1995.

CHAPTER 20

HUMANISM IN AFRICAN AMERICAN THEOLOGY

ANTHONY B. PINN

African American theology, in the form of black and womanist discourses, has been described at times as an extended Christology based on the importance given to the Christ Event as the dominant logic of its self-understanding and liberation agenda. Whether this is the case or not, it is accurate to suggest African American theology has been primarily undertaken from the vantage point of black Christianity as both conceptual paradigm and personal faith stance. In this regard, connections between African American theology and African American communities have been projected as based on a shared Christianity (theistic) sensibility. The vocabulary and grammar of African American theology has been overwhelming drawn from the Christian faith, thereby constructing a vision of the world based on Christian imaginaries. Source materials have been selected and unpacked based on a Christian hermeneutic, and conversation partners have been tested based on their proximity to the basic parameters of the Christian faith. Furthermore, the agenda/shape of African American theological discourse in particular and African American religious studies in general has been organized in line with the function and form of the black church tradition as primary framing of praxis. In the words of Gayraud Wilmore, one of the early and significant figures in the twentieth-century study of African American religion:

> We want to subject the academic conceptualization of the student to both the authority of the Christian message and the priority of the valid religious and cultural experiences of the people. In this view theological education will have failed, despite having expertly decoded the Black experience by means of an interdisciplinary theory, if there is no faith-decision, no new and enriching sentiment embraced by the student.[1]

One might wonder if Wilmore's stated interest in the seminary context (i.e., the training of ministers) indicates a preoccupation with the Christian faith that is not present in the defining of African American theological studies more generally. However, the available literature suggests this preoccupation is not bound to particular institutional types—those explicitly training students for ordained ministry—but is rather the general posture of many within the study of African American religion.[2]

African American Theology's Theism

In general terms, the initial framing of a twentieth-century academic black theology urges this very Christocentric paradigm. "When I began to write *A Black Theology of Liberation*," James Cone states, "I was deeply involved in the black struggle for justice and was still searching for a perspective on Christian theology that would help African-Americans recognize that the gospel of Jesus is not only consistent with their fight for liberation but is its central meaning for twentieth-century America."[3] The second generation of black theologians, as represented by James Evans's systematic theology, for instance, makes a similar assumption concerning the logic and structure of African American theology in the form of a black (Christian) theology. He writes, "Black theology reflects the passion, feeling, and expressiveness of African-American Christianity. It must be in touch with the 'guts' of black religion.... Black theology is also a formal, self-conscious, systematic attempt to interpret the faith of the church."[4] Furthermore, a similar perspective on African American theology seems present in the work of womanist theologians as well. As Delores Williams notes, "The appropriateness of womanist theological language will ultimately reside in its ability to bring black women's history, culture, and religious experience into the interpretive circle of Christian theology and into the liturgical life of the church. Womanist theological language must, in this sense, be an instrument for social and theological change in church and society."[5] Even when outlining distinctions between womanist theology and black theology, a shared assumption of theism, if not Christianity, is apparent. While pointing out the manner in which black theology's take on African American experience has privileged the male, and womanist theology has given overdue attention to the experience and struggles of black women, Kelly Brown Douglas posits this corrective work within a framework whereby womanist theology "also affirms Black women's faith that God supports them in their fight for survival and liberation. This means that a womanist theology engages a social-political analysis of wholeness and a religio-cultural analysis."[6] In short, according to dominant wisdom, African American theology is not always gendered in such a way to privilege males, but it *is* theistically framed and somewhat confessional in tone.

African American theology is most often constructed based on a short and deeply theistic definition. Theology is God-talk. The assumption is this: theology can be done from a variety of religious perspectives—although in African American communities this is decidedly a Christian (and Protestant) orientation—but it holds to a basic litmus test of theistic commitment. The structuring of both modalities of African American theology—black and womanist—hence, entails a commitment to theological inquiry premised on revelation and metaphysical underpinning. This, it has been argued, is the way to do black and womanist theologies because it is consistent with the basic claims of African Americans throughout their presence in North America. Such is the perspective advanced in their cultural production, and it is the dominant orientation expressed in their systemic structural arrangements of collective life. The counterpoint to this logic, while widespread in African American culture (e.g., the blues, folktales, Harlem Renaissance literature), was interpreted in ways that rendered it not a critique of theistic assumptions, but rather a more focused attack on white supremacy. The controlling hermeneutic privileged theism. It was not until the late twentieth century that strands of theological discourse within African American communities would begin to challenge in a systematic fashion these theistic assumptions.

Challenging Theism and Its Ramifications

The most notable of these early academic challenges to the theistic take on African American theology was presented in the work of William R. Jones—particularly his 1973 book titled *Is God a White Racist?*[7] Using the theological trope of black suffering, Jones's text achieves a variety of ends including (1) demonstration of key limitations of theistic theologizing; and (2) presentation of humanistic orientations as viable theological models. It is arguably the first text within academic African American theological discourse to provide a significant apologetic for humanism as African American life orientation and as the basis for theological thinking. In this regard, it introduced to African American theology the possibility of nontheistic theologizing as organic to African American praxis.

Moving from the early blues forward, an argument has been made that humanism is as inherent to African American thought and practice as any other orientation. From the robust anthropology of African American folktales, through the work and personal commitments of numerous leaders within African American life and letters—such as Richard Wright, Lorraine Hansberry, James Weldon Johnson, and so on—it has been argued that African American humanism is not a turn away from "the" African American tradition; but rather it is an underappreciated but nonetheless vital dimension of this tradition. Sociological work such as Benjamin May's *The Negro's God* points out the presence of nonbelief within African American communities, but this work has been read largely as a particular take on a nonreligious orientation, a secular presence, as opposed to entailing a nontheistic religious commitment.[8]

Jones argues with great insight that black theology—represented by leading figures such as Albert Cleage, James Cone, Major Jones, J. Deotis Roberts, and Joseph Washington—has promoted an unsubstantiated perspective on the intersections of divine intent and African American history that begs the question of God's relationship to the disproportionate suffering encountered by African Americans. Hence, *Is God a White Racist?* urges the theodical dilemma embedded in black theological discourse. While this catchy phrase garnered a great deal of attention and was the focus of a great deal of heated debate, Jones's larger concern was the presentation of an alternate to the "logical potholes, theological washouts, and elaborate but unsound detours" hampering the black theological enterprise and its rhetoric of liberation.[9] Black theology's flaws were exposed to the extent that assumptions undergirding its response to "ethnic suffering" left without substantive historical evidence the argument that God sides with the oppressed and is concerned with their welfare. This is a basic assumption of liberation theology—God's preferential option for the poor—and it is restated in black theology through the argument, for example, that God is ontologically black and thereby intimately connected to the project of liberation for oppressed African Americans.[10] Such a challenge to the doctrine of God (and by extension the Christ Event) upon which black theology is built fostered a need to rethink its fundamental claims and its hermeneutic; and, more importantly it opened conversation concerning the significance of a nontheistic humanist orientation.[11] This is not to suggest Jones is the first to promote humanism as a viable alternative to black Christianity. As scholars Juan Floyd-Thomas and Mark Morrison-Reed have detailed, figures such as Reverend Ethelred Brown and Reverend Lewis McGee promoted humanism much earlier in the twentieth century as their mission within what would become the Unitarian Universalist Association (UUA), and this organization continues to have some importance for African American humanists. What these figures in particular and the UUA in general did not do, however, is attempt the formulation of an African American humanist theology as the companion to their religious humanism.[12]

The assumption that black religion must be theistic was shown faulty—thereby requiring an alternate theory of black religion. And by extension, theology was presented by Jones as having no required doctrine of God. While not embracing "Death of God" theology, Jones offered African American religious studies a theological platform that extended anthropology and pushed a postmodern sense of the divine as an unnecessary trope. Religion could be atheistic, and theology could revolve around the stories associated with this atheistic orientation. Secular humanism is Jones's preferred system for resolving the issue of divine racism and ethnic suffering; it in fact is the basis for a new black theology he promotes. However, up until the time of his death, he had not provided amore robust theological system, but instead had offered pieces of a corrective. For example, in his book he offers a fill-gap, an alternate view of the God/human relationship as a modality of humanism. By means of this effort, Jones highlights the *humanocentric theism* undergirding much of African American religious thought, whereby humanity obtains a type of functional ultimacy and significance in the outcome of human history. Yet, as Jones notes, to the extent this is a modality of theism, humanity has its status as "a codetermining power" as part of God's will and "by virtue" of God's creative act.[13] This turn to the human on Jones's part counters strong claims concerning the workings of the divine through revelation, and so on, and entails an effort on Jones's part to "make this humanistic wing of black religion the norm for contemporary black theology, thereby providing a more realistic interpretation of the meaning of black experience."[14] Humanocentrism was meant to explain certain elements of black theology, but also push black theologians beyond unjustifiable claims. Yet any appeal to humanism only goes so far, as Linda Thomas and Dwight Hopkins remark: "Though William R. Jones's *Is God a White Racist?* (1973) awakened the intellectual lethargy of his peer scholars in the foundation generation of the 1960s, his academic assault on the mainstream black church and its theology failed to cause a significant ripple. None of the second generation of (male) black theologians (1980–1995) took seriously the humanistic and philosophical claims of Jones."[15] Black theologians by and large have not taken on an explicit and nontheistic humanism as part of the black theological discourse; but this is not to suggest humanism has had no impact on black theological thinking. Those who suggest this are incorrect. Nor is it to suggest Jones's critique has gone unnoticed. Although James Evans, for example, understands Jones's critique as a "philosophical treatise" rather than having any real theological weight, his proposed framing of the "ungiven God" certainly seeks to address Jones's charge regarding doctrine of God by repositioning the nature and meaning of moral evil over against our capacity to "know" the mind of God. In Evans's words: "God's 'ungiven' character in African-American theology refers to the fact that one can never fully apprehend God, no matter how intimately the Divine manifests itself in human experience. At the same time, it refers to the fact that the reality of God is hidden in the experience and history of oppressed and marginalized peoples. In essence, the ungivenness of God suggests that we can only follow God, whose wake leads us through the labyrinth of life."[16]

The Humanism of African American Theology

Of primary importance here is the manner in which Jones's attention to humanocentric theism introduces to black theology a more robust attention to anthropology and the existential arrangements of human life as the necessary verification of theological claims. To the extent certain elements of humanocentric theism are present in the work of the first generation of black theologians (e.g., modified omnipotence), it is safe to suggest that elements of humanism shadow the anthropological dimensions of black theology. (This sense of modified omnipotence and increased concern with the historical and embodied nature of life are also given some expression in womanist scholarship) That is to say, the functional ultimacy of humanity plays out in much black theology and womanist theology, and notions of God's omnipotence are modified so as to support a more robust attention to the activities of humans and the impact of these activities on human history. Present is a humanist impulse lodged to a large extent in the nature/meaning of moral evil as evidenced in acts of racism, sexism, and so on; as well as being present in the implications of the Christ Event. Human accountability with respect to moral evil and the historical significance of current human liberative activity as the "embodiment" of God's work in the world suggest a sense of anthropology that gives a certain type of power to human thought and activity. This does not displace God for black theologians and womanist theologians, but it does entail a deeper regard for human history shaped by the details of an "earthy" and "fleshy" theological anthropology. Furthermore, embedded in this is a sense of ethics that is tied to biblical tradition but also premised on a type of functional ultimacy for humans: people act in the world, and these actions have ongoing meaning and consequence that is not overridden by divine maneuvers. This "freedom" to act can be for good or ill, as Kelly Brown Douglas notes with respect to manipulations of the Christian faith: "What is it about Christianity that has allowed it to be both a bane and a blessing for black people? Clearly it has played a significant sanctioning role in the white assault on the black body. Christianity has conspired with white supremacy not simply in the horror of enslaving black people but also in the odious deed of lynching them. It has provided theological legitimation for the overall dehumanizing denigration of black bodies. Yet it has also sustained black people in their struggle against white dehumanization. It has provide them with the strength and courage to resist white assaults on their bodies."[17] Throughout all this speculation is the underlying assumption of human agency—again, a type of functional ultimacy.

Humanism's hold on black and womanist theologies is limited to the extent black theologians continue to claim God's preferential option for the oppressed. Furthermore, a nebulous appeal to the inner workings of the Christian tradition, particularly the Christ Event, as adequate response to ethnic suffering pushes against an ultimate embrace of the humanist perspective shadowing certain dimensions of black and womanist theologies. Cone's response to William Jones in *God of the Oppressed* (one of the few, direct responses to Jones) puts the theism of black theology in perspective. "Black humanism from the slave seculars to William Jones," writes Cone, "represents an appealing tradition. However, not all blacks accepted this perspective. Although many blacks rejected the claims of Christianity, they did not reject religion. Some substituted Allah for Yahweh, Mohammed for Jesus, Islam for Christianity."[18] Yet, more to the point and with greater force, Cone says,

> In responding to Jones, Christian theologians have to admit that their logic is not the same as other forms of rational discourse. The coming of God in Jesus breaks open history and thereby creates an experience of truth-encounter that makes us talk in ways often not understandable to those who have not had the experience. This statement is not meant to exclude my theological perspective from philosophical criticism. Rather, it is an honest attempt to give an account of black faith in the social context of a world that seems to contradict it. There is the experience of suffering in the world, and no amount of theological argument can explain away the pain of our suffering in a white racist society. But in the experience of the cross and resurrection, we know not only that black suffering is wrong but that it has been overcome in Jesus Christ. This faith in Jesus' victory over suffering is a once-for-all event of liberation.[19]

Black theology goes afield of humanism in part because of how source materials are read through a hermeneutic of revelation. Yet one might think womanist scholarship, to the extent it draws from Alice Walker's definition of womanist, would be more open to elements of humanist sensibilities. While Walker's orientation is described in a variety of ways, she did accept an award from the American Humanist Association ("Humanist of the Year," 1997) and there is little about her work that excludes basic elements of a humanist (or freethought) stance. With few exceptions, however, Walker-indebted womanist theology is typically described in theistic terms. Efforts toward a womanist humanism, based on a misreading of humanism as presented by Jones and Anthony Pinn, typically collapse into an uncertain and unfocused Christian humanism indistinguishable from the dominant framings of black and womanist theologies. In this regard efforts toward an explicit womanist humanism illicit an apologetics for Christianity to the extent such moves really entail an effort to make humanism acceptable to theists—a theological sleight of hand, or "Can't we all get along" pronouncement.[20] Such efforts to formulate a womanist humanism tend to limit the reconstruction of theological presentation to religious pluralism, while leaving intact the challenges to basic theological categories advanced by Jones and later by Pinn. As a result, the unique contributions of humanism to African American theological discourse are lost. Even when not explicitly described as such, there are modalities of womanist thought that speak to the humanocentric theistic concern with human will. As Karen Baker Fletcher remarks concerning ethics and ecology: "We must literally re-member ourselves. We have become disembodied. We are disembodied from community. We are disembodied from self. We are disembodied from God. We are disembodied from earth. To become whole is to re-member. It is to become part of the body of God. We are God's body."[21] A womanist nontheistic theological platform is yet to be developed. And while both black theology and womanist theology have embraced particular elements of humanist thought and practice, attention to a systematic approach to a humanist theological orientation is more limited.

Although initially questioned, over the past several decades, recognition of humanism within African American thought and practice has marked the work of womanist and black theologies. A recently initiated book series speaks to this growth: "The series [Black Religion / Womanist Thought / Social Justice Series with Palgrave Macmillan] will include a variety of African American religious expressions. By this we mean traditions such as Protestant and Catholic Christianity, Islam, Judaism, Humanism, African diasporic practices, religion and gender, religion and black gays/lesbians, ecological justice issues."[22] This move proved fairly easy to the extent black and womanist theologians could view humanism either as humanocentric theism (and in this way an effort to give anthropology greater weight without a firm denial of God) or as a philosophical pronouncement with little to do with theological concerns. More difficult, however, has been the acceptance of humanism as a separate and competing religious orientation—one devoid of God. African American scholarship throughout the twentieth century sought to explore the religious terrain of African American communities—noting along the way the various theistic orientations—for example, black churches, Nation of Islam, Moorish Science Temple, black Jews, and so on. Underlying this work has been the assumption that African American religion is present in various incarnations, but each points to a theistic base.

Humanist Theology as African American Theology

Whereas Jones's writings pointed out the shadow of humanist sensibilities in certain dimensions of black theology (and I would add womanist theology), his work while important did not extend much beyond apologetics for secular humanism and brief explications of its meaning and presence in African American culture. More recent work such as Anthony Pinn's *The End of God-Talk: An African American Humanist Theology*, the first presentation of an African American humanist theology, however, builds on Jones's earlier efforts in ways meant to (1) further demonstrate the humanist strands of thought and practice within African American history; (2) more precisely present humanism as a modality of religious orientation in African American communities through an alternate theory of African American religion; and (3) promote an alternate theological discourse based on African American nontheistic humanism.[23]

Much of the earlier work centered on critique of and challenge to doctrine of God (and the characteristics and intent of the divine). While this remains in place, current effort to forge an African American humanist theology extends beyond this critique or negation and is more concerned with a constructive agenda. It offers a theory of African American religion that takes as its starting point a quest for meaning firmly lodged in human activity and human history.[24] It does not assume divine revelation, nor does it assume the workings of god(s). Instead, religion becomes a way of interrogating human experience as opposed to being assumed to constitute a unique modality of human experience. (This involves an implicit push against sui generis framings of religion/religious.) Connected to this, recent work suggesting humanism is a religion has tied to it a nontheistic theology that troubles old definitions of theology that mandate a god-center. Instead, this thinking positions theology as the description and interrogation of human stories of meaning making and draws from a rich array of source materials that point to a nontheistic framing of life. Although some object to the labeling of this "theology," doing so is meant to push beyond narrow understandings that seek to privilege theology as a mode of discourse and to disassociate it from other methodologies for studying human experience. To counter this, African American humanist theology claims the label, but alters the categories used in its systematic presentation. Most obviously, the god concept is replaced with a centering idea that does not involve traditional notions of revelation and transcendence. In this case the centering trope serves to connect humans to a larger, yet historically arranged and nonspiritualized sense of more expansive meaning and purpose. And, over against the centrality of Christology in black and womanist theologies, African American humanist theology promotes a robust anthropology grounded not in *imago Dei* but rather in science (e.g., evolutionary processes) and culture (the creative power of discourse—signs, symbols, tropes, and so on—and the constructive dimensions of aesthetics). The source material for nontheistic theology so conceived amounts to the ordinary moments and occurrences in life. Put differently, because the religious does not involve a unique form of experience and has nothing to do with transcendence and revelation, everything humans do and experience says something about religion as a quest for life meaning. Hence, this modality of theology takes a full range of human experience and cultural creations as proper material for the development of theology.

Ethics has remained a vital dimension of this theological conversation; yet here it has nothing to do with the biblically outlined and divinely sanctioned practices of liberation discussed in black and womanist theologies. Rather, ethics for the humanist theologian has to do with human conduct toward fuller life meaning—but this isn't guaranteed movement, nor is it safe to assume a certain normative structuring of the "good."[25]

Humanism as a force within African American theology, and as the source for a unique African American nontheistic humanist theology is relatively young. It does not have the long legacy and list of students associated with more traditional modalities of African American theology—black and womanist theologies. Yet it is gaining greater attention and is represented by a growing corpus of descriptive and constructive materials.

Notes

1. Gayraud Wilmore, *African American Religious Studies: An Interdisciplinary Anthology* (Durham, NC: Duke University Press, 1989), xvii.
2. For example: liberal arts college—Coby College: Cheryl Townsend Gilkes's work on subtle forms of power within black churches assumes this framing (*If It Wasn't for the Women* [Maryknoll, NY: Orbis Books, 1999]), as does Goucher College's Kelly Brown Douglas, with work on sexuality (and embodiment) within black religion (*Sexuality and the Black Church* [Maryknoll, NY: Orbis Books, 1999] and *What's Faith Got to Do with It?* [Maryknoll, NY: Orbis Books, 2007]). University—Diana Hayes's work, from a perspective of personal faith, on liberation theology in the Catholic context takes place at Georgetown University, which is a Ph.D.-granting institution (Hayes, *And Still We Rise: An Introduction to Black Liberation Theology* [Boston: Paulist Press, 1996] and *Standing in the Shoes My Mother Made: A Womanist Theology* [Minneapolis: Fortress Press, 2010]).
3. James H. Cone, *A Black Theology of Liberation*, 20th anniversary ed. (Maryknoll, NY: Orbis Books, 1986), xi–xii.
4. James H. Evans, Jr., *We Have Been Believers: An African-American Systematic Theology* (Minneapolis: Fortress Press, 1992), 2.
5. Delores Williams, "Womanist Theology: Black Women's Voices," in *Black Theology: A Documentary History*, vol. 2, *1980–1992*, ed. James H. Cone and Gayraud S. Wilmore (Maryknoll, NY: Orbis Books, 1993), 270–71.
6. Kelly Brown Douglass, "Womanist Theology: What Is Its Relationship to Black Theology?" in J. Cone and Wilmore, *Black Theology, 1980–1992*, 292.
7. William R. Jones, *Is God a White Racist? Prolegomenon to Black Theology*, 2nd ed. (Boston: Beacon Press, 1997).
8. Benjamin E. Mays, *The Negro's God as Reflected in His Literature* (New York: Russell & Russell, 1968).
9. Jones, *Is God a White Racist?* xiii.
10. See Cone, *Black Theology of Liberation.*
11. Jones provides a rationale for why he does not develop a secular humanism derived theology: (1) black theologians should first seek a theistic model that is adequate to the task; (2) discussion of plausible theistic models "paves the way" for a nontheistic alternative; (3) the secular humanism alternative is beyond the scope of the book (Jones, *Is God a White Racist?* 172).
12. Juan Floyd-Thomas, *The Origins of Black Humanism in America: Reverend Ethelred Brown and the Unitarian Church* (New York: Palgrave Macmillan, 2008); Mark Morrison-Reed, *Black Pioneers in a White Denomination*, 3rd ed. (Boston: Skinner House Books, 1994). Beyond these texts, there are organizations such as African Americans for Humanism and African American atheists who are interested in the spread of humanism. However, many of these African American atheists tend to be antireligious in a way that does not allow consideration of nontheistic humanism as a religious orientation.
13. Jones, *Is God a White Racist?* part 3 (188).
14. Jones, *Is God a White Racist?* xv.

15. Dwight Hopkins and Linda Thomas, "Series Editors' Preface," in Anthony B. Pinn, *African American Humanist Principles: Living and Thinking Like the Children of Nimrod* (New York: Palgrave Macmillan, 2004), xi.
16. Evans, *We Have Been Believers*, 76.
17. Kelly Brown Douglas, *What's Faith Got to Do with It? Black Bodies / Christian Souls* (Maryknoll, NY: Orbis Books, 2005), xiii. This human capacity for action is also a running theme in the work of Dwight Hopkins. See for example, *Being Human: Race, Culture, and Religion* (Minneapolis: Fortress Press, 2005).
18. Jones, *Is God a White Racist?* 201; James Cone, *God of the Oppressed* (New York: Harper & Row, Publishers, 1975), 187.
19. Cone, *God of the Oppressed*, 191–92.
20. Melanie L. Harris, "Womanist Humanism: A New Hermeneutic," Cross Currents, Vol. 57, Issues 3 (Fall, 2007): 391–401.
21. Karen Baker-Fletcher, *Sisters of Dust, Sisters of Spirit: Womanist Wordings on God and Creation* (Minneapolis: Fortress Press, 1998), 57.
22. http://us.macmillan.com/series/BlackReligionWomanistThoughtSocialJustice.
23. Anthony Pinn, *The End of God-Talk: An African American Humanist Theology* (New York: Oxford University Press, 2012).
24. Pinn, *African American Humanist Principles.*
25. The first, full African American humanist theology: Anthony B. Pinn, *The End of God Talk* (New York: Oxford University Press, 2012).

Selected Texts

Allen, Norm, ed. *African American Humanism: An Anthology*. Amherst, NY: Prometheus Books, 1992.

Allen, Norm, ed. *Personal Paths to Humanism*. Amherst, NY: Prometheus Books, 2003.

Floyd-Thomas, Juan. *The Origins of Black Humanism in America: Reverend Ethelred Brown and the Unitarian Church*. New York: Palgrave Macmillan, 2008.

Harris, Trudier. "Three Black Writers and Humanism: A Folk Perspective." In *African-American Literature and Humanism*, ed. R. Baxter Miller, 50–74. Lexington, KY: University Press of Kentucky, 1981.

Jones, William R. "The Case for Black Humanism." In *Black Theology II: Essays on the Formation and Outreach of Contemporary Black Theology*, ed. William Jones and Calvin Bruce, 149–61. Lewisburg, PA: Bucknell University Press, 1978.

Jones, William R. *Is God a White Racist? A Preamble to Black Theology*. Boston: Beacon Press, 1996.

Jones, William R. "Religious Humanism: Its Problems and Prospects in Black Religion and Culture." *Journal of Religious Thought* 7, no. 2 (Spring 1980), 175–80.

Jones, William R. "Theism and Religious Humanism: The Chasm Narrows." *Christian Century* 92 (May 21, 1975): 520–25.

Jones, William R. "Theodicy: The Controlling Category for Black Theology." *Journal of Religious Thought* 30, no. 1 (Summer 1973): 28–38.

Jones, William R. "Theodicy and Methodology in Black Theology: A Critique of Washington, Cone and Cleage." *Harvard Theological Review* 64 (October 1971): 541–57.

Jones, William R. "Toward an Interim Assessment of Black Theology." *Christian Century* 89 (May 3, 1972): 513–17.

Mays, Benjamin E. *The Negro's God as Reflected in His Literature.* New York: Russell & Russell, 1968.

Mitchell, Mozella G. "Howard Thurman: Literary/Humanist Theologian." *Journal of the Interdenominational Theological Center* 9, no. 2 (Spring 1984): 31–56.

Morrison-Reed, Mark. *Black Pioneers in a White Denomination.* 3rd ed. Boston: Skinner House Books, 1994.

Pinn, Anthony B. *African American Humanist Principles: Living and Thinking Like the Children of Nimrod.* New York: Palgrave Macmillan, 2004.

Pinn, Anthony B., ed. *By These Hands: A Documentary History of African American Humanism.* New York: New York University Press, 2001.

Pinn, Anthony B. *Why, Lord? Suffering and Evil in Black Theology.* New York: Continuum, 1995.

Walker, Alice. "The Only Reason You Want to Go to Heaven Is That You Have Been Driven out of Your Mind (off Your Land and out of Your Lover's Arms): Clear Seeing, Inherited Religion and Reclaiming the Pagan Self." *On the Issues* 6, no. 2 (Spring 1997). http://www.ontheissuesmagazine.com/1997spring/sp97walker.php. Accessed January 11, 2014.

CHAPTER 21

AUDIENCES OF ACCOUNTABILITY IN AFRICAN AMERICAN THEOLOGY

DENNIS W. WILEY

AFRICAN American theology has come a long way since the emergence of contemporary black theology in 1966.[1] Historical black theological reflection was no novelty at the time, but its systematic and conscious development as a written, academic discipline was a new phenomenon. It is no accident that black theology surfaced in response to socio-political events. With the winding down of the civil rights movement, the rise of "Black Power," and the eruption of urban unrest prior to and immediately following the 1968 assassination of the Reverend Dr. Martin Luther King Jr., black theology initially unfolded as a raw, defiant, and passionate expression of solidarity by mainstream African American clergy in the church and academy with their secular and religious grassroots brothers and sisters in the streets. It was one of those *kairos* moments[2] in which the black church[3] and African American theologians were compelled to choose sides. Were they on the side of the continued racist oppression of black people in America, along with the gradual, integrationist/assimilationist method of addressing it, or were they on the side of liberation, along with a radical, more immediate process of bringing it about?

The response of African American theologians to practical events reflecting the "spirit of the times" is consistent with what later, Latin American liberation theologians would identify as "critical reflection on praxis."[4] According to this understanding, in which there is no such thing as "theology for theology's sake," praxis is the *first* step and reflection is the *second* step in the theological enterprise.[5] In other words, theology is never done in a vacuum, but always in a particular social, political, and historical context. Practical experiences lead to theological conclusions, and theological concepts yield practical consequences. Furthermore, theology "does not stop with reflecting on the world, but rather tries to be part of the process through which the world is transformed."[6] This alternating rhythm between theological reflection and theological praxis implies an *interdependent* relationship between the two whereby neither can be separated nor isolated from the other. Generally speaking, African American theology, or *any* theology for that matter, should not and, indeed, *cannot* be disconnected from African American praxis.

It is from this concept of interdependence that the notion of *accountability* arises. Accountability has to do with a sense of responsibility, answerability, and obligation. Consequently, if one accepts the premise that theology is not done in a vacuum but in a context, and that theology and praxis are interdependent, it follows that responsible African American theologians are obligated to be accountable *to* and *for* the audiences whom their theology represents. The purpose of this essay, then, is to explore ways in which African American theologians define and justify specific audiences *to* whom and *for* whom they write and are accountable. I propose to do this (1) by sharing my personal pilgrimage, as an African American theologian, to theological accountability; (2) by revisiting an early debate among black religious scholars regarding the issue of accountability; (3) by discussing some of the challenges of twenty-first-century audience accountability; and (4) by examining three essential components of accountability.

My Pilgrimage to Theological Accountability

Accountability has been an important aspect of my personal sense of mission and purpose ever since my undergraduate days at Harvard University. On April 4, 1968, during the spring semester of my senior year in high school, Martin Luther King Jr. was assassinated in Memphis, Tennessee. Here was a man who could have easily enjoyed the comfort and security of a tenured professor or the prestige and privilege of a prominent pastor who chose, instead, to give his life serving his people in the nonviolent struggle for freedom, justice, and equality. It was against this backdrop that I began my freshman year in college that fall.

Joining a handful of other black students who were either entering or already matriculating at this elite, predominantly white, Ivy League institution, I soon discovered that the air was thick, not only with the spirit of King, but also with the spirit of another political activist who, just three years earlier, had also been shot down in the prime of his life—Malcolm X. As we found ourselves engaged in campus protests and demonstrations demanding that the university establish an African American Studies Department and Cultural Center, divest from apartheid South Africa, and withdraw support for the war in Vietnam, the spirits of Martin and Malcolm marched with us. As a result, we realized that we were not at Harvard simply to pursue our own individualistic, self-centered ambitions and aspirations. We were there on behalf of our people. We were there *on account of* the communities from which we came, in particular, and the African American community, in general.

This sense of *accountability* was an integral ingredient of the ethos and spirit of the times. Accountability recognizes the interconnectedness and interdependence of human achievement, that is, that I did not arrive at where I am on my own and that, as I climb the ladder of success and stand on the shoulders of those who paved the way for me, I have a responsibility not only to remember where I came from, but to reach back and extend a hand to help lift those I left behind. This is what Black Power and black pride were all about—"Power to the *people!*" not "Power to *me!*" The emphasis was not on the Cartesian principle, "I *think*, therefore I *am*," but on the African proverb, "I *am* because we *are*."

In light of this emphasis on accountability, there was much talk among black students about returning home to serve our communities once we left Harvard. We were not there to get caught up in the Harvard mystique. We were not there to become "sellouts," to get bought off, or to forget where we came from. We were there on a mission: to prepare ourselves so that we, like Martin and Malcolm, might go back better equipped to serve our people and our respective communities. Of course, I later learned that the *rhetoric* of accountability did not always translate into the *reality* of accountability. To paraphrase an old, Negro spiritual, I discovered that "everybody talkin' 'bout community ain't goin' there."[7]

In his 1933 classic, *The Mis-Education of the Negro*, Carter G. Woodson wrote,

> One of the most striking evidences of the failure of higher education among Negroes is their estrangement from the masses, the very people upon whom they must eventually count for carrying out a program of progress. Of this the Negro churches supply the most striking example.[8]

Therefore, with my Harvard degree, I returned to Washington, DC, to work in a community arts program and to assist my father in an urban church he pastored in the heart of the African American community.

After several years, I entered Howard University School of Divinity, where I met James Cone, a visiting professor, during the first semester of my final year in the Master of Divinity program. After I took his course, Introduction to Black Theology, he invited me to come to Union Theological Seminary in New York City to pursue a Ph.D. degree in systematic theology. Upon accepting his invitation, I made it clear that I did not feel called to serve exclusively in the ivory tower of the academy, but to help bridge the gap between the church and the academy from the vantage point of pastoral ministry in a local congregation. Cone vigorously argued against my pursuing this course of action because he felt that I had a gift for writing, that I might become consumed by pastoral responsibilities, and that the black church already had enough preachers, but not enough theologians.[9] Nonetheless, I remained resolutely committed to this "call" on my life.

One might infer from Cone's resistance to my plans that he opposed a relationship of accountability between black theology and the black church. Early debates among members of the Society for the Study of Black Religion (SSBR) prove just the opposite.

Accountability Debated among Black Religious Scholars

In 1970, the first annual meeting of the SSBR was convened by Charles Shelby Rooks, a distinguished minister then serving as executive director of the Fund for Theological Education. Conceived by Rooks as a "place for African American teachers in religion to relate to each other,"[10] some in this elite guild, in which membership was by invitation only, were concerned about the *accountability* of black religious scholars to the black church and the African American community. According to Rooks,

> One expectation was that the Society would be a forum whose principal purpose would be to connect research about and study of African American religion with the freedom struggle. It was a dramatic vision of a hopeful new union between church and academy. Gayraud S. Wilmore... pushed hard for this idea of what the SSBR should be about.[11]

Rooks respected Wilmore for being one who "embodied the vision he espoused" and who "set a very important example for action and reflection."[12]

Despite Wilmore's insistence, however, the SSBR never became what he envisioned. In fact, he lamented that during this period, black theology "was becoming more of an academic affair among a relatively small group of schoolmen," and he wryly observed that the SSBR gave it "a rather decorous respectability."[13] A similar disappointment was expressed by Cone:

> Not everyone was pleased with the new focus of black theology, because its prophetic thrust was being blunted, and the SSBR... was becoming too much of an academic society, like the American Academy of Religion, with little focus on practical and urgent issues in the black community. "Scholarship for the sake of scholarship" seemed to define most SSBR activity, and some of its members wondered how such an approach differed from white scholarship. As I saw the issue then and now (although

> not so clearly *then*), the problem... was not the academic focus of black theology, but rather the *accountability* of black theologians: for *what purpose*, and for *whom*, did they do theology? We did not explore these questions in sufficient depth and with adequate care.[14]

Rooks took issue with Cone's suggestion that black theologians must be "accountable." According to Rooks,

> The true accountability, or obligation, of any scholar, African American or white, is always to the pursuit of truth, wherever it leads. No accountability to persons or organizations dictates or intrudes upon that quest.[15]

He suggested that his distaste for the concept of accountability, as opposed to Cone's affinity for it, might have had something to do with their dissimilar church backgrounds. Since Cone, an African Methodist Episcopal minister, was a product of a "connectional tradition" headed by bishops, and Rooks, first a Baptist and then a Congregationalist, was a product of a "free church tradition," he contended that Cone may have been more inclined to entertain "strong concepts about the obedience of clergy that no one in a free church tradition would maintain." Although he acknowledged that Cone never employed the word "obedience," Rooks felt that the concept of accountability implied notions of obligation and obedience that he found repulsive.[16]

He claimed that the issue for him was not *accountability*, but *relevance*, that is, "the relationship of scholarship to the life of African American churches." He firmly believed that if African American religious scholars were committed to "intellectual engagement" and the pursuit of truth, their work would inevitably impact the preparation of future "ordained" church leaders and, in turn, the development of the black church.[17] In other words, he was convinced that relevance was a natural byproduct of genuine academic inquiry, dialogue, and debate.[18]

There were at least two problems with Rooks's argument concerning accountability. First, his juxtaposition of accountability versus relevance appeared to set up a false dichotomy between these two integrally related concepts. Instead of negating each other, they complement each other; and, instead of being mutually exclusive, they are interdependent. He was right that black theology must be relevant to the black church and community. What he failed to see is that there can be no guarantee of relevance without accountability. Accountability monitors relevance. Where there is no accountability, there can be no assurance of relevance.

Second, while Rooks was correct in suggesting that accountability implied obligation, he was incorrect in suggesting that it entailed obedience. Cone would doubtless be the last person to propose that black theology should be *obedient* to the black church, based on his negative experience with AME bishops who demanded unquestioning *obedience* and submission from their ministerial subordinates.[19] In fact, Cone so adamantly opposed this kind of obsequious obedience that he declared

> the problem of lack of accountability of episcopal power was pervasive enough for me to conclude that there was no way that I could be a critical theologian and also be controlled by AME bishops.[20]

Perhaps this helps explain how Cone could be such a strong advocate for the accountability of black theology to the black church and community while also fervently resisting the aspiration of some of his students to become both pastors and theologians at the same time.

Challenges of Twenty-First-Century Audience Accountability

Almost twenty years ago, I wrote an essay exploring the issue of accountability in relation to black theology, the black church, and the African American community.[21] As the twentieth century was rapidly concluding, I was concerned that an extended white backlash in retaliation for the gains of the civil rights movement had resulted in a "double assault" on the African American community. This right-wing, conservative assault that began in 1968 with the assassination of the Rev. Dr. Martin Luther King Jr., and the subsequent election of President Richard Milhous Nixon, continued all the way through the presidential administrations of Ronald Reagan and George H. W. Bush. It included the familiar, *external* displays of overt racism as well as a subtle, *internal* attack fostered by a climate "in which racist attitudes became not only acceptable, but respectable."[22] Manifestations of this attack within the African American community included the excessive spread of HIV/AIDS and other health threats, the inundation of drugs, the preponderance of black-on-black violence, and the disproportionate rate of incarceration.

It was in this atmosphere that I concluded that contemporary black theology had been deficient (1) in helping the black church develop an internal, "on-going process of self-critique," and (2) in empowering the black church not simply to *receive* theology taught by academic theologians "from the top down," but to *do* theology as grassroots theologians "from the bottom up." In other words, I challenged black theology and, more specifically, black theologians to be *accountable* for the salvation and empowerment of the black church, and I charged the black church, both clergy and laity, to be accountable for the salvation and liberation of the African American community.[23]

I also concluded that since the presumption that the black church and the African American community were identical was a thing of the past,[24] the latter faced "a severe crisis of spirituality":

> No longer can it be assumed that African Americans—particularly of the younger generations—have any affinity for the Black Church, or that they know anything about it. Indeed, we are living in a time when a generation of our young people has grown up knowing nothing about the Black Church, nothing about Jesus Christ, and nothing about God.[25]

In 1999, on the thirtieth anniversary of the publication of James Cone's *Black Theology and Black Power*,[26] Gayraud Wilmore confirmed some of my concerns about black theology's negligible impact on the black church and the black church's increasing irrelevance to African American young people.[27] Essentially, he proposed three steps to help black theology and the black church mend their strained relationship and form an effective partnership for the twenty-first century. First, he recommended "a new institutional base" for black theology that would foster the relation between practical theological issues and action-oriented public policy advocacy. Second, he recommended the development of age-appropriate curricula and Christian education materials that would provide the "biblical and theological foundations for black religious thought," and help black people apply their faith to political, economic, and cultural activity. Finally, he recommended that this 'base' incorporate a "new African-centered pluralism" that would embrace a wide spectrum of beliefs... and that would foster a new bonding with blacks in the diaspora."[28]

His proposals, outlined on the eve of the twenty-first century, were designed, as was my earlier article, to challenge black and womanist theologies to become more accountable to the black church and the black church to become more accountable to the African American community. Despite the prophetic prescience of his recommendations, little did he know that September 11, 2001, would literally *change everything*. The terrorist attacks against the United States on that fateful day (1) provided a rationale for government to divert resources away from social programs and toward military objectives; (2) gave license to xenophobia as expressed in ostentatious American "patriotism" and the demonization of individuals and organizations who dared question US domestic and/or foreign policy; (3) created a climate of increasing intolerance and suspicion of individuals perceived to be "different" racially, ethnically, sexually, theologically, ideologically, or otherwise; (4) justified an increased invasion of personal privacy; and (5) legitimized religious intolerance, hate speech, and a growing lack of civility in both public and private discourse. Despite the historic election of the nation's first black president in November 2008, if there ever was a time when the black community needed an *accountable* black church, and the black church needed *accountable* African American theologians, it was during the first decade of the twenty-first century.

Unfortunately, this was not the case. African American theologians, both black and womanist, continued to talk to each other more than to the people in the pulpits, pews, and streets, and the black church continued its post-civil rights tendency of becoming an increasingly reactionary, apolitical, and socially conservative institution driven more by the quest for individual prosperity than by the pursuit of collective liberation. At the same time, however, there were black and womanist theological voices "crying in the wilderness" in anticipation of the crucial need to broaden the theological understanding of oppression beyond the evils of racism, sexism, and classism.

Much of the groundwork for constructing this broader understanding of oppression was laid in the early stages of black theology. From an initial preoccupation with external oppression alone, especially in the form of racism, black men eventually opened their eyes, at the behest of their black sisters, to the reality of *internalized* oppression, especially in the form of sexism. And although black theology, from the very beginning, has emphasized the need to liberate the poor, it has not always included a social or economic analysis, of which the insights of Latin American liberation theologians have been particularly helpful.[29] But as we move deeper into the twenty-first century, African American theologians, again largely with the aid of our womanist sisters, are continuing to gain a deeper appreciation for the interconnectedness of oppression, wherever it occurs and whomever it affects.

Two issues that have been a part of the conversation among African American theologians ever since the inception of black theology, on the one hand, and womanist theology, on the other, demand our attention today with a new sense of urgency. These issues are Christocentrism and heterosexism. They were provocatively raised a few years ago by African American theologian Monica Coleman in her essay "Must I Be Womanist?"[30] While Coleman specifically addressed womanist theologians, these issues are critical to the projects of *all* African American theologians in this multicultural society.

From Howard Thurman to Albert Cleage to Charles Long to Gayraud Wilmore to Delores Williams to Kelly Brown Douglas to Anthony Pinn to Joanne Terrell and others, the Christocentric focus of African American theology has been a major concern. The problem is not that there is anything inherently wrong with being a follower of Jesus Christ. The problem is how Christianity, as an organized religion, has been used so brazenly to support the oppression, discrimination, and persecution of marginalized people. The concern also is how Christo-normativity tends to disregard or berate other religions or faith expressions and insists not only that the Christian God is the only God, but also that the Christian way is the only way. Christianity has left a trail of blood, tears, and devastation wherever imperialistic crusaders have conquered, massacred, colonized, enslaved, whipped, tortured, and lynched innocent human beings, all "in the name of Jesus." In this world that has grown smaller and smaller through the advances of information technology and high-speed transportation, African American theologians are struggling to take seriously Rodney King's question, "Can we all get along?"[31] and Martin Luther King Jr.'s mandate: "We must learn to live together as brothers [and sisters] or perish together as fools."[32]

An issue related to Christocentrism is the problem many African American theologians have with the Christian symbol of the cross and the doctrine of atonement. Because of the surrogacy experiences of black women, Delores Williams rejects the imagery of the cross and argues, "There is nothing divine in the blood of the cross."[33] On the other hand, while James Cone also rejects the atonement theory, he does not reject the cross. Instead, as he compares it with "the lynching tree" that was the fate of untold numbers of black people in the days following slavery, he contends, "The cross is the most empowering symbol of God's loving solidarity with the 'least of these,' the unwanted in society who suffer daily from great injustices."[34]

Another issue that demanded our attention in the first decade of the twenty-first century is heterosexism—the systematic discrimination and oppression of persons based on their sexual orientation. Coleman not only critiqued womanism for its Christocentrism, but she also critiqued its often subtle heterosexism. Openly lesbian theologians like Renee Hill and Irene Monroe have also challenged their "lesbian, bisexual, transgender and queer" womanist sisters concerning this very issue. According to Monroe,

> When these Christian womanist scholars do not openly write, teach, and preach from their social locations, they...silence LGBTQ voices by maintaining a tacit "don't ask, don't tell" policy. Despite their appending heterosexism to their litanies of interrelated oppressions in their writings and homilies, cheering from the sidelines us openly African American LGBTQ scholars, they collude with the status quo, because our queer voices become subsumed by a heteronormative universality that renders us not only invisible but also speechless.[35]

If nothing else, the first decade of the twenty-first century has taught African American theologians that oppression takes many forms and if we are serious about overcoming the oppression we experience because we are black men and women, then we must be just as serious about helping others overcome the oppression they experience simply because they are whoever they are. As Howard Thurman once said, "I have always wanted to be *me* without making it difficult for you to be *you*."[36]

Three Primary Components of Accountability

Several factors determine audiences of accountability for African American theologians. Here I will only mention three of the more important ones. The first factor is the *context* in which one's theological views are formed. It has already been established that not just African American theology, but *all* theology is contextual. This means that one's context or social location plays a critical role in determining one's audience of accountability.

However, while social location is a major factor in making this determination, it does not strictly or uniformly lead to consistent results. In fact, two people can come from what appears to be the exact same context and hold radically different views on the same issues because no two people are exactly alike. No one can predict, with any degree of certainty, how one's social location will ultimately influence the determination of one's audience of accountability.

Womanist theologian Kelly Brown Douglas makes an important observation along these lines when she says,

> If who we are—that is, our life experiences—helps us to determine our theological questions and concerns, then who we are also circumscribes those questions and concerns. Our particular social, historical, cultural, and political actualities can free us to address certain topics, and at other times those very same actualities can hinder us from doing so.[37]

Another important element in understanding *to* whom and *for* whom African American theologians write is what might be called "evolutionary accountability." By that I simply mean that one's audience does not always necessarily remain the same, but may change or *evolve* as the theologian in question, and his or her context, evolve. Over the years, many theologians have written essays titled "How My Mind Has Changed." This reminds us that the doing of theology is a fluid exercise that is constantly in flux. Because of this reality, *accountable* theologians are not hesitant to confess previous weaknesses in their work or areas where their thinking has matured.

While womanist theologians have helped black theologians mature in the area of recognizing *internalized* oppression within the African American community, they have also revealed that, as important as context is in determining one's audience of accountability, it should never imprison us to the point where we forget that "injustice anywhere is a threat to justice everywhere."[38] Only when oppressed people appreciate what Kelly Brown Douglas calls "multidimensional oppression"[39] will the black church and the African American community fully understand that none of us is free until all of us are free.

The second component that African American theologians must possess in order to determine their audience(s) of accountability is a general sense of responsibility to and for *community*. As I mentioned earlier in this essay, accountability is not about individualism. It is about community and it is based on the answers to the following questions: Do African American theologians write for themselves or do they write on behalf of, and in the interest of, a larger audience? Is their intention simply to raise their own voices, or to speak on behalf of the voiceless? And, finally, do they write solely to advance their personal agendas, or do they write to empower, elevate, and liberate the communities they represent?

Dale Andrews, in his important book *Practical Theology for Black Churches*, contends that the failure of black churches to embrace black theology is due to "an invasive influence of American individualism in African American religious folk life, which disrupts corporate solidarity and contributes greatly to both the displacement of black churches and the fragmentation of the black community."[40] As Andrews would agree, however, the failure of black theology to take root in the black church is not solely the fault of the black church. Black theologians must also bear a share of the blame. With just a tinge of humor, Wilmore explains, "Most of us have become so old, middle-class, tenured, and disoriented by personal greed and the irresponsible use of power, that we have permitted the radical tradition in African American culture and religion to become weakened and trivialized."[41] Albert Cleage, the most radical voice in the early stages of contemporary black theology, succinctly makes a similar point when he declares, "The group concept is historic Christianity. Individualism is slave Christianity."[42]

I would like to share two examples of what accountability in relation to community means. The first example is in reference to Kelly Brown Douglas's dedication of and introduction to *Sexuality and the Black Church*. She dedicates the book to Lloyd James Miller and, in her introduction, explains that as a gay man who eventually died of AIDS, he "was quite simply one of the best human beings I had ever had the pleasure of knowing." She went on to say that she could "no longer sit quietly by and let him be ridiculed or castigated."[43]

When Douglas and I were at Union Theological Seminary together, I had the pleasure of meeting and getting to know Lloyd. He was truly a wonderful person. Douglas and I used to think it was somewhat amusing that Lloyd thought if he dressed in a certain way and behaved in a certain manner, he could hide his gay identity. But in reality, no matter how hard Lloyd tried to conceal his true identity, his efforts were usually in vain. What is unfortunate is not that he was unsuccessful in disguising himself, but that he lived in a world that failed to appreciate him for the incredible human being that he was.

In her acknowledgments, Douglas credits "a great cloud of witnesses"—including other friends of hers who have also died—for their spiritual presence that helped her to finish writing the book. I share all of this simply to say that this is what it means to be accountable. It is to understand that, as African American theologians, we write not simply for ourselves, but for untold others who are unable to speak for themselves.

Last, but not least, I am reminded of my friend, Cornel West. In his memoir titled *Brother West: Living and Loving Out Loud*,[44] he recounts how Lawrence Summers, the former president of Harvard University, where West was a Distinguished University Professor, reprimanded him for being the "organic intellectual" that he is. Instead of encouraging West to continue to alternate theory and praxis through a brilliant balancing of his academic assignments with his active engagement in the religious, political, and cultural life of the African American community, Summers wanted to reign him in so he would conform to the more traditional profile of an Ivy League professor. Finally, when West had had enough of Summers's insults, he told the president, "You've messed with the wrong brother,"[45] made his departure, and soon afterward resigned his position at Harvard University. As much as he appreciated his coveted position at Harvard, West was clear that he was not about to compromise his integrity or his accountability to the African American community, no matter how high the cost.

The third factor that enables African American theologians to determine their audience(s) of accountability is the sense of a higher *calling*. In the African American religious experience, it is not unusual to find that African American theologians understand the particular scope and focus of their work and commitment not simply as something they *chose* to do, but as something God *called* them to do. Hence, the theologian's audience of accountability is actually greater than the community one represents. It is also the God whom one serves, or whatever the theologian considers "ultimate" or the source of meaning. Ultimate accountability, therefore, grows out of a sense of mission, purpose, and calling whereby one must answer to that Source to which one's "call" responds. In the final analysis, however, the Source motivating the call and the beneficiaries of the call (i.e., the human audiences of accountability) cannot be radically separated. It is this sense of calling that propelled Kelly Brown Douglas to break her silence on the issue of sexuality and the black church. As she recalls, one day in the midst of giving a lecture and addressing the issue of homophobia and heterosexism in a relatively safe manner, it suddenly dawned upon her that she needed to go deeper. If she was going to be true to the memory of Lloyd and other departed friends and colleagues whom she dearly loved and who had touched her life so profoundly, she had to struggle with the complexities of sexuality and help others struggle as well. She remembers,

> It was then that I felt the call of God. What, I wondered, might the God of Jesus Christ be saying to me, a Black female, a womanist theologian, and the rest of the Black community about matters of sexuality, especially that of Black women and men?[46]

Her experience is not radically different from the experience of Martin Luther King Jr. when, late one night in the middle of the Montgomery bus boycott, he received a hate call from a white racist threatening him and his family if he did not get out of town immediately. King got up out of bed, made a cup of coffee, and sat down at the kitchen table to pray. He confesses he was weak, afraid, and ready to give up. And then, he says,

> At that moment I experienced the presence of the Divine as I had never experienced [God] before. It seemed as though I could hear the quiet assurance of an inner voice saying: "Stand up for righteousness, stand up for truth; and God will be at your side forever."[47]

In other words, King began to understand that his sense of accountability to the black community of Montgomery was in response to a Power greater than himself.

J. Deotis Roberts recounts how, at the completion of his Ph.D. dissertation at Edinburgh University in May 1957, he was torn between accepting a call to pastor a church in Glasgow, Scotland, or returning to the United States to be closer to King and the civil rights movement:

> There was a strong feeling that I belonged in the struggle of my people to be free. After prayerful consideration of the Glasgow offer, I confidently decided that my ministry should be in my country, especially among black people.[48]

It is this same sense of calling that led him to conclude that black theology, at its best, is "church theology," "practicing" theology, "a theology for active witnessing in the world" among black people and others.[49]

It was a sense of context, community, *and* calling that inspired Old Testament scholar Renita Weems to write user-friendly books like *Just a Sister Way* so that black women would have an accessible "resource tool and study guide" reminding them that they "are not an afterthought to salvation."[50] It was this same sense that motivated theologian Dwight Hopkins to uncover rich "sources for a constructive Black Theology" in *Shoes That Fit Our Feet*;[51] sociologist Cheryl Townsend Gilkes to remind us that *If It Wasn't for the Women*,[52] there would be no such thing as a black church *or* a black community; ethicists Katie Cannon and Emilie Townes to explore *Black Womanist Ethics*[53] and *Womanist Justice, Womanist Hope*;[54] theologian Jacquelyn Grant to help us differentiate between *White Women's Christ and Black Women's Jesus*;[55] and humanist Anthony Pinn to dare ask the question, *Why, Lord?* in the face of black suffering and evil.[56] The sense of human and divine accountability that prompted mystic Howard Thurman to write Mordecai Wyatt Johnson in 1918, declaring, "My people need me,"[57] also inspired theologian James Cone to publish a volume in 1984 with the message "This book is 'for my people.'"[58]

Notes

1. The publication of "Black Power: Statement by the National Committee of Negro Churchmen, July 31, 1966," in the *New York Times* marks the official beginning of contemporary black theology. The document is included in James H. Cone and Gayraud S. Wilmore, eds., *Black Theology: A Documentary History*, vol. 1, *1966–1979* (Maryknoll, NY: Orbis Books, 1993).
2. *Kairos* is a Greek word that means "a propitious moment for decision or action." *The New Oxford American Dictionary*, 2nd ed. (2005).
3. I am aware that, as several scholars have made clear, there is no such thing as "the black church" in a monolithic sense. However, for this essay, I have chosen to use the term as the simplest way of referring to the general institutional and historical concept to which

this designation refers. This usage is in no way intended to ignore the broad diversity that characterizes specific black churches.

4. See Gustavo Gutiérrez, *A Theology of Liberation: History, Politics, and Salvation*, trans. and ed. Sister Caridad Inda and John Eagleson (Maryknoll, NY: Orbis Books, 1973), 6ff.
5. For a further discussion of this concept, see Robert McAfee Brown, *Theology in a New Key* (Philadelphia: Westminster Press, 1978), 72ff.
6. Gutiérrez, *A Theology of Liberation*, 15.
7. The actual words are "Everybody talkin' 'bout *heaven* ain't goin' there."
8. Carter G. Woodson, *The Mis-Education of the Negro* (Washington, DC: Associated Publishers, 1933), and *The Negro Church* (Washington, DC: Associated Publishers, 1921), 52.
9. To further understand Cone's position on this issue, see his essay "Loving God with Our Heart, Soul and Mind," in *Blow the Trumpet in Zion! Global Vision and Action for the 21st Century*, ed. Iva Carruthers, Frederick D. Haynes III, and Jeremiah A. Wright Jr. (Minneapolis: Fortress Press, 2005).
10. Charles Shelby Rooks, *Revolution in Zion: Reshaping African American Ministry: 1960–1974* (New York: Pilgrim Press, 1990), 134.
11. Rooks, *Revolution in Zion*, 136.
12. Rooks, *Revolution in Zion*, 136.
13. Gayraud S. Wilmore and James H. Cone, *Black Theology and the Black Church* (Maryknoll, NY: Orbis Books, 1979), 5.
14. James H. Cone, *For My People: Black Theology and the Black Church* (Maryknoll, NY: Orbis Books, 1984), 26.
15. Rooks, *Revolution in Zion*, 138.
16. Rooks, *Revolution in Zion*, 138. In all fairness to Rooks, he also believed that the SSBR should be "both activist and scholarly." But because there were many arenas for action and few for reflection within the context of the black church, he was convinced that the SSBR should focus on the latter. As he observed, "Members of the SSBR were called to be scholars, not pastors or civil rights activists" (Rooks, 137). He further observed that "not everyone can or should be on the front lines of any battle. There is a legitimate role for those who also research, reflect upon and record the struggle of human beings to live abundantly and free (Rooks, 139).
17. Rooks, *Revolution in Zion*, 138–39.
18. Rooks, *Revolution in Zion*, 137.
19. See James H. Cone, *My Soul Looks Back* (Nashville: Abingdon Press, 1982), 71.
20. Cone, *My Soul Looks Back*, 71.
21. Dennis W. Wiley, "Black Theology, the Black Church, and the African American Community," in *Black Theology: A Documentary History*, vol. 2, *1980–1992*, ed. James H. Cone and Gayraud S. Wilmore (Maryknoll, NY: Orbis Books), 127–38.
22. Wiley, "Black Theology," 128.
23. Wiley, "Black Theology," 129, 134.
24. C. Eric Lincoln and Lawrence H. Mamiya, *The Black Church in the African American Experience* (Durham, NC: Duke University Press, 1990), 7–10.
25. Wiley, "Black Theology," 135.
26. James H. Cone, *Black Theology and Black Power* (Maryknoll, NY: Orbis Books, 1989).
27. Gayraud S. Wilmore, "Black Theology at the Turn of the Century: Some Unmet Needs and Challenges," in *Black Faith and Public Talk*, ed. Dwight Hopkins (Maryknoll, NY: Orbis Books), 232–45.

28. Wilmore, *Black Faith and Public Talk*, 236ff.
29. Cone, *For My People*, 86–98.
30. Monica A. Coleman, "Must I Be Womanist?" *Journal of Feminist Studies in Religion* 22, no. 1(Spring 2006): 85–96.
31. Rodney King was the African American victim of a police brutality beating that was caught on video tape in the Watts section of Los Angeles in 1992. The acquittal of the four white police officers who beat him sparked a riot and prompted King to plead through the media, "Can't we all get along?"
32. From a speech by Martin Luther King Jr. in St. Louis, Missouri, March 22, 1964.
33. Delores S. Williams, *Sisters in the Wilderness: The Challenge of Womanist God-Talk* (Maryknoll, NY: Orbis Books, 1993), 167.
34. James H. Cone, "The Cross and the Lynching Tree," in *Walk Together Children: Black and Womanist Theologies, Church, and Theological Education*, ed. Dwight N. Hopkins and Linda E. Thomas (Eugene, OR: Cascade Books, 2010), 324.
35. Irene Monroe, "Response" [to Monica A. Coleman, "Must I Be A Womanist?"] in *Journal of Feminist Studies in Religion* 22, no. 1(Spring 2006): 112.
36. Howard Thurman, *The Search for Common Ground: An Inquiry into the Basis of Man's Experience of Community* (New York: Harper & Row, 1971), xi.
37. Kelly Brown Douglas, *Sexuality and the Black Church: A Womanist Perspective* (Maryknoll, NY: Orbis Books, 1999), 5.
38. Martin Luther King Jr. "Letter from the Birmingham Jail," in *Why We Can't Wait* (Boston: Beacon Press, 2011).
39. Kelly Delaine Brown, "God Is as Christ Does: Toward a Womanist Theology," *Journal of Religious Thought* 46, no. 1 (Summer–Fall 1989): 8.
40. Dale P. Andrews, *Practical Theology for Black Churches* (Louisville, KY: Westminster John Knox Press, 2002), 10.
41. Wilmore, "Black Theology at the Turn of the Century," 239.
42. Albert B. Cleage Jr., *The Black Messiah* (New York: Sheed and Ward, 1968), 43.
43. Douglas, *Sexuality*, 3.
44. Cornel West with David Ritz, *Brother West: Living and Loving Out Loud, a Memoir* (New York City: Smiley Books, 2009).
45. West, *Brother West*, 221.
46. Douglas, *Sexuality*, 4.
47. Martin Luther King Jr., *Stride Toward Freedom: The Montgomery Story* (New York: Harper & Row, 1958), 134–35.
48. J. Deotis Roberts, *The Seasons of Life* (Largo, MD: Charp Communications, 2007), 30.
49. J. Deotis Roberts, *The Prophethood of Black Believers* (Louisville, KY: Westminster John Knox Press, 1994), 138.
50. Renita J. Weems, *Just a Sister Away: A Womanist Vision of Women's Relationships in the Bible* (San Diego, CA: LuraMedia, 1988), ix–x.
51. Dwight N. Hopkins, *Shoes That Fit Our Feet: Sources for a Constructive Black Theology* (Maryknoll, NY: Orbis Books, 1993).
52. Cheryl Townsend Gilkes, *If It Wasn't for the Women* (Maryknoll, NY: Orbis Books, 2001).
53. Katie G. Cannon, *Black Womanist Ethics* (Atlanta: Scholars Press, 1988).
54. Emilie M. Townes, *Womanist Justice, Womanist Hope* (Atlanta: Scholars Press, 1993).
55. Jacquelyn Grant, *White Women's Christ and Black Women's Jesus: Feminist Christology and Womanist Response* (Atlanta: Scholars Press, 1989).

56. Anthony B. Pinn, *Why, Lord? Suffering and Evil in Black Theology* (New York: Continuum, 1995).
57. Walter L. Fluker, senior ed., *The Papers of Howard Washington Thurman*, vol. 1, *My People Need Me, June 1918—March 1936* (Columbia: University of South Carolina Press, 2009), 2.
58. Cone, *For My People*, 3.

Selected Texts

Brown, Robert McAfee. *Theology in a New Key*. Philadelphia: Westminster, 1978.

Carruthers, Iva E., Frederick D. Haynes III, and Jeremiah A. Wright Jr. *Blow the Trumpet in Zion! Global Vision and Action for the 21st Century Black Church*. Minneapolis: Fortress Press, 2005.

Coleman, Monica. "Must I Be Womanist?" *Journal of Feminist Studies in Religion* 22, no. 1 (Spring 2006): 85–96.

Cone, James H. *My Soul Looks Back*. Nashville: Abingdon, 1982.

Cone, James H., and Gayraud S. Wilmore, eds. *Black Theology: A Documentary History*. Volume 1 *1966–1979*. Maryknoll, NY: Orbis Books, 1993.

Douglas, Kelly Brown. *Sexuality and the Black Church: A Womanist Perspective*. Maryknoll, NY: Orbis Books, 1999.

Gilkes, Cheryl Townsend. *If It Wasn't for the Women*. Maryknoll, NY: Orbis Books, 2001.

Gutiérrez, Gustavo. *A Theology of Liberation: History, Politics, and Salvation*. Trans. and ed. Sister Caridad Inda and John Eagleson. Maryknoll, NY: Orbis Books, 1973.

Lincoln, C. Eric, and Lawrence H. Mamiya. *The Black Church in the African American Experience*. Durham, NC: Duke University Press, 1990.

Roberts, J. Deotis. *The Prophethood of Black Believers*. Louisville, KY: Westminster John Knox Press, 1994.

Roberts, J. Deotis. *The Seasons of Life*. Largo, MD: Charp Communications, 2007.

Rooks, Charles Shelby. *Revolution in Zion: Reshaping African American Ministry, 1960–1974*. New York: Pilgrim Press, 1990.

Thurman, Howard. *The Search for Common Ground: An Inquiry into the Basis of Man's Experience of Community*. New York: Harper & Row, 1971.

Williams, Delores. *Sisters in the Wilderness: The Challenge of Womanist God-Talk*. Maryknoll, NY: Orbis Books, 1993.

Woodson, Carter G. *The Mis-Education of the Negro*. Washington, DC: Associated Publishers, 1933.

Woodson. Carter G. *The Negro Church*. Washington, DC: Associated Publishers, 1921.

CHAPTER 22

EMBODIMENT IN AFRICAN AMERICAN THEOLOGY

STEPHANIE Y. MITCHEM

AFRICAN American theologians and ethicists have been exploring questions of black bodies within theo-ethical constructions in some specific form since the 1970s. The idea of "bodied" experiences of being raced in the United States is not simply a rhetorical construction, or simply discursive. The experiences of being bodied and raced have real and material consequences. The use of embodiment as a frame for research has some important implications for future theological scholarship and especially African American scholars. A working definition of embodiment begins this discussion.

Embodiment is a route to considering the material conditions of a particular group of people. The human person, grounded in a given community, becomes the subject of study, integral to the work, rather than the reified object. Embodiment changes the focus of theological reflection because it is centered on the experiences of particular people rather than dogma or church polity, both of which are sometimes accepted as universal despite human experiences. However, when the material experiences of human groups are the foci, the cultural narrowness of some church rules can be addressed; as an example, some Christian churches during the 1960s began to portray Jesus as a modern black man and to challenge the blond-haired, blue-eyed, historically inaccurate version—with one that met the needs of the congregants. Embodiment, then, requires attention to physical realities, even as it changes the nature of discourse from high-minded theory toward the practical implications of human meaning.

Before turning to embodiment in African American theologies, this essay will consider components of scholarly discussions, beginning with some historical foundations of the concept. A brief consideration of some aspects of racial constructions and deconstructions of black bodies across disciplines will provide the turn to consider embodiment in African American theologies.

Racism and Black Bodies

The constructions of black bodies begin in the histories of enslavement, from the Middle Passage throughout the black slave-owning nations such as England, France, and Belgium that took root in what became the countries of Brazil, Cuba, Jamaica, Dominican Republic, Haiti, and the United States. Global economies were built around enslavement as colonies used many resources, including humans, to build up the conquering country's wealth. In the development of enslavement, legal justifications gave way to moralized and pseudoscientific arguments for the capture and control of black bodies. White racism against black bodies was integral to the development of enslavement across nations: how else could centuries-long, dehumanizing mistreatment of one group of people by another be justified?

Brutal and systematic processes were used to "season" captured Africans to their new enslaved status and tasks in foreign lands. One author stated: "From an early age slaves' bodies were shaped to their slavery. Their growth was tracked against their value; outside the market as well as in it, they were taught to see themselves as commodities.... From an early age, enslaved children learned to view their own bodies through two different lenses, one belonging to their masters, the other belonging to themselves."[1]

The controlled shaping of black bodies included beatings, threats, seeming rewards, rapes, and lynching, and were all justified by accompanying white interpretations of those bodies. A black body "language" developed over the centuries. A "one-drop rule" decreed that even one "drop" of black blood, that is, the discovery of the most distant black ancestor, thereby would render a person as fully black and qualified to be excluded from white society. Light-skinned black people learned to "pass" for white. Children of black and white parentage could be defined by some degree of colored-ness: quadroon, octoroon, mustee, or yellow. Fear of the "mongrelization" of white people, through cross-racial marriages led to laws against miscegenation and inheritance. There were no black body parts considered private from the slave owners, including and especially sexuality. Perhaps the most infamous overlapping of these ideas can be seen in Sarah Baartman, the so-called Hottentot Venus. She was born in South Africa in 1789, but captured and exhibited in Britain and France from 1810. The exhibitions were showings that centered on her genitalia as freakish and inhuman. Baartman died in captivity in 1815; but it was not until 2000 that her body parts, preserved in formaldehyde and still exhibited for some years after her death, were returned to South Africa for burial.

Legal enslavement ended for the colonizing countries at different times throughout the mid- to late 1800s. Despite ending legal enslavement, white constructions of black bodies did not stop but continued unabated. In the United States, the systematic construction of black bodies as laboring, inferior, and disposable continued through the era of Jim Crow, which was the legal segregation of races in the United States during the remainder of the nineteenth and through the mid-twentieth centuries. While much Jim Crow law was based in the South, the attitude and concept of "separate but equal" infected the entire country.

Laws and customs enforced separated societies claiming equality between white and black worlds until 1954. In reality, access to services such as education and health care were never equal. The possibilities of black success or survival were constrained by white definitions, often violently. Robert F. Williams, a former marine, helped to organize his town of Monroe, North Carolina, in 1962 to fight against the violence of the local Ku Klux Klan. Williams wrote of the meaning of white violence to black bodies. "The majority of white people in the United States have literally no idea of the violence with which Negroes in the South are treated daily... deliberate, conscious, condoned by authorities.... Negro existence in the South has been one long travail."[2]

After Emancipation, many black Americans migrated from the South, the historic center of enslavement, in search of greater opportunities to improve their lives; yet they met the definitions of black bodies that were detrimental to their health and well-being: lazy, unless forced to work by industrious white people; hypersexualized, unless under white moral superiority; stupid, with need for white genius. Fables of white southern graciousness, gentle plantation life, and benevolent care of black bodies were exported throughout the country. The layers of segregation were maintained with law, custom, and embedded interpretations of blackness continually reinforced through such cultural representations as minstrel shows, radio, movies, and eventually television. The texture of hair, shapes of noses and lips, the size of buttocks, in contrast with those of white people, were pointed to as scientific evidences of an evolutionary hierarchy. The measurements of black head circumferences "proved" smaller brains, while black speech patterns were given as further evidence of lower intelligence. The construction of black bodies in the framework of the white imaginary is evident in white-written black dialect like that in radio and television portrayals in the *Amos 'n Andy* show, the actions of the black actors, such as the often critically vaunted *Gone with the Wind*, and in interactions with white actors in such movies as D. W. Griffiths's silent film *Birth of a Nation*. These ideas were culturally ingrained in the fabric of the United States and exported around the globe.

Two historic incidents in West and North provide a glimpse into the difficulties beyond the southern United States. One of the most affluent black communities was in the West, in Tulsa, Oklahoma, in the early 1900s. Because of that affluence, it was nicknamed "black Wall Street." In June 1921, the area was bombed and burned by white people who were resentful of the success of the black community; this was the original meaning of "race riot." In this confrontation, black people died, their families and wealth broken. They have never been granted restitution for that act, and that community has never recovered.

The northern city of Boston, as a response to the Civil Rights Act of 1964, bused black children to white schools in an attempt to address racially segregated schools. In 1974, white riots against the plan and the children in the buses, under a "Restore our Alienated Rights" movement, added fuel to the flight of white citizens from Boston as well as other northern urban areas to white enclave suburbs. The presence and success of black folks was not welcome in Boston or Tulsa.

The white views of black bodies over history are not discrete but linked across time. Analyzing the meaning of Sarah Baartman, one author points to links between past to the present:

> As evidenced in the life of Baartman, the "black" body is a lived hyper-corporeal abstract representation framed within external systems.... The exhibition of "primitive" peoples in the context of the "culture of abundance" and pleasure has had lasting influence in the spatial location of the "other" within the dominant order.[3]

Across the continuum of physical degradation such as Sarah Baartman's, the resistance to black success, and other experiences of violence as pointed out by Robert Williams, black activist-scholars defended the bodies of black people. Throughout enslavement through the present, these scholarly analyses provide a range of arguments. David Walker was a self-educated, free man who critiqued the enslavement of black bodies as anti-Christian and inhumane in the early 1800s.[4] Ida B. Wells's antilynching campaigns brought global attention to American black bodies in the late 1800s.[5] W. E. B. Du Bois's analysis of black conditions of life provided an analytical lens over his decades of work from the late 1800s to the mid-1960s.[6] These three thinkers are a few examples of black analyses of the care of black bodies. These and others provide important connections from history to the present that serve as bases for contemporary theological analyses that include embodiment.

At the same time, the wider range of scholars working through racial constructions—and deconstructions—provides another context for the questions of black and womanist theologians and ethicists. To be clear, however, none of these analyses are easy, since there was and is pushback from those scholars who want to maintain the traditional status quo based on canons that centered white, European scholarship and cultural superiority over against all other peoples.

Embodiment begins with analysis of the lived, material conditions of *this* person in *this* group and time in history. Several general theoretical frames became part of scholarly thinking in the mid-twentieth century that admitted embodiment as a legitimate route for analysis.

The concept of historicity, for example, provided awareness of the limits and time boundaries of human knowing; in general, scholarship no longer seeks to establish some kind of universal standards for all humanity. Awareness of the social location of the researcher is another example, and the scholar should no longer solely arbitrate meaning for any group. The shift in focus toward the lived realities of a particular group is central to studies that incorporate embodiment; in such ways, embodiment also becomes a discursive framework for contemporary scholars. For black people around the world, a focus on embodiment must incorporate the lived realities of race and racism. Explorations of race and bodies and materiality became more intense, heightened and speeded by the shifts in wider scholarship: other fields, such as history and sociology, provided new analyses available to many black scholars. Some scholars were deconstructing and revisioning human meaning, using theoretical approaches like postmodernism or structuralism.

Theories from many disciplines aided the analyses of raced bodies. Despite such developments, some scholars held fast to concepts of universals based on whites as normative and a belief in the superiority of Western (read, white) thought. Pseudosciences such as eugenics and sociobiology grew in the late nineteenth century and sought to prove black people lacked intelligence, had a proclivity to violence, but were athletic and strong and thereby uniquely suited as unthinking laborers. Whether or not there was such a thing as black culture became an argument among some scholars through the nineteenth and most of the twentieth centuries. Black men and women as hypersexualized beings became the focus of some research. Ultimately, such scholarly views are not benign and could influence policy and popular culture as lynch mobs and prisons reinforced laws supporting segregation and disenfranchisement.

The majority of mainstream research prior to the mid-1960s had excluded black voices while bringing white researchers' culturally developed biases into the conclusions of their studies. Often the material they produced misrepresented the realities of black life but was widely accepted in white society. So ideas of black people who were more than servants, who might become, say, an astronaut or president of the United States, were completely far-fetched to many people based on their expectations of racial limits.

Black people were not immune to the constructions of themselves by those in power and recognized the efficacy of not looking or acting "black" if they wanted to be somewhat socially mobile. Therefore, colorism grew among black people that set them as judges of their own bodies in this white framework. The history of black consumerism is a story of product development that defines whiteness as normative, such as straightening combs and skin whiteners. From a children's rhyme—"If you're black get back"—to churches with paper bag tests—a person darker than a paper bag was not welcome—black folks' self-critical judgments in light of white standards became brutal. The late 1960s and early 1970s began to see a trickle of black scholars enter mainstream academia, and new contributions to scholarship began to be added. Many of these additions challenged the canons. In like manner, black discussions of embodiment challenged theological scholarship as new scholars brought other ideas into the conversations.

Embodiment and African American Theologies and Ethics

Embodiment took particular shape when considered by black theologians and ethicists. Earlier analyses of black bodies' conditions whether from David Walker in the 1800s or W. E. B. Du Bois a hundred years later provided one basis for later theologians. Yet this was not easy; the centuries of constructing black bodies to fit white fantasies required black scholars to spend time explaining, justifying, or excusing black people, even as their scholarship was ignored. As an added complication for black theologians, the more socially prevalent ideas of the negative black body had been supported and advanced through the poor theologies of white supremacists.

The bad biology, cultural constructions, and political power reinforced ideas of some natural hierarchy and separation of races in Christianity particularly. Such race-based distinctions became components of some Christian theologies. For example, the "curse of Ham" theory developed during enslavement, looking at a Genesis story of Noah and his sons in which the son who laughed at Noah's drunkenness was cursed. White apologists for enslavement identified the curse, theologically, as black skin, handed from generation to generation, the continued sign of God's disfavor.[7] Ham's curse and other such theologically developed ideas became religious bases for enforcing segregation, long after enslavement ended. The history of the fights for integration and civil rights are filled with the arguments from white Christians about the God-designed, embodied inferiority of black people.

Black bodies were imagined by white people so as to construct idealized white bodies; eventually such ideas were given the blessings of white theologies. So, for example, if the curse of Ham, mentioned above, decreed that black skin equaled enslavement, it simultaneously identified their necessary enslavement to the divinely selected white people. Therefore, black theologians had to work against long-standing prejudgments of black people's morals that were embedded into myths of black bodies. These prejudgments included a generalization of black people's incapacity for honesty and integrity, maturation, and intellectual excellence. Sexuality was an inherent part of the erroneous generalizations, and black people were viewed as licentious children, like Sarah Baartman, without sexual boundaries and readily available for sexual activity. Therefore, black women were viewed as unable to be raped and black men as predisposed to rape of white women.

However, like David Walker and Ida B. Wells of past centuries, black theologians and ethicists could see the effects of racism and the concept of race on black bodies, especially when understood through the lens of religions. The material effects of violence, threats, disenfranchisement, poverty, overwork, undereducation, and social exclusion became a strong base for religious analysis, despite the lack of honest historical records.

With the growth of the Black Power movement in the 1960s, new questions were raised with the statement that black is beautiful. One of the new questions was critical for theologians to address: is Christianity incompatible with being black? After all, Black Power challenged unquestioned acceptance of views now deemed as benefiting only white people. James Cone began to tackle the question in late 1960s, fueled by his studies, conversations with black ministers, and growing social unrest among black communities. His groundbreaking first book brought these ideas together and began to speak to black religious expression while developing the field of black theology.[8] Yet it was a later book, *God of the Oppressed*, wherein Cone addressed painful black experiences of oppression and how authentic Christian experiences could become liberatory; black bodies and their experiences were given religious meanings.[9] Cone firmly connected social existence to the tasks of theology as a valid context for thinking about liberation.

The 1980s saw the publication of two books that took discussions of black bodies into greater depth. Charles Long deconstructed cultural, social, and symbolic worlds used in the construction of black religions. As a result he was able to emphasize the agency of black Americans in the matters of religion.

> If one is oppressed, unable to mold a meaning about oneself that can become cultural coin, one must nevertheless deal critically with the language about oneself. This language is itself contradictory, and many of the struggles of Afro-Americans have taken place within this language game. It has been an attempt to verify, act upon, and come to terms with a language created *about* them. . . . The situation of the cultures of black peoples in the United States afforded a religious experience of radical *otherness*, a resourceful and critical moment that allowed these communities to undertake radical internal criticisms of themselves, their situation, and the situation of the majority culture.[10]

Long challenged underlying philosophies of racism while defining black religious thought as a fully human activity within the wider conversation of religious studies.

The second book brought black women into discussions of embodiment and theology with the first significant statement of womanist theology by Jacquelyn Grant. Grant's work situates black women by considering who Jesus is for them; their life experiences craft religious meanings reflected in their own physical beings. By her womanist explorations, the focus of gender as a component of embodiment began as a significant strand of black intellectual life.[11]

From these beginnings to the present, the concept of embodiment continues to be explored in black theologies and ethics. The concept has been expanded in new directions, continuing to draw on interdisciplinary research in order to understand embodiment. Theologians and ethicists continue to deconstruct old ideas of black bodies in connection with religious thought while aiming for new understandings that demand more research for the twenty-first century. Only a sampling of these thinkers is possible in this essay; by no means is this an exhaustive listing. However, the range of those including embodiment within current black theological and ethical writing can be seen.

Kelly Brown Douglas engages the topic of black sexuality and black religious life. She writes of the embodied realities of black sexuality, bounded by historical and present white sexual assault and church experiences in support of homophobia and heterosexism. Instead, she calls for "a sexual discourse of resistance... needed to help Black men and women recognize how the White cultural exploitation of Black sexuality has corrupted Black people's concepts of themselves, one another and their God."[12]

Roger Sneed brings a sharp focus on gender by analyzing black male homosexuality and black religious life. The very exclusion of black men and women who are same-sex loving from many black churches establishes lines of oppression. These forms of oppression based on disapproval of nonconforming bodies, Sneed challenges us, require liberatory action on the part of black communities.[13]

The issue of the humanity of black people developed in times past but still lingers in the present. Dwight Hopkins uses anthropology to address the flaws in the arguments as well as to show how black Americans have used cultural tools to construct views of self and community in order to survive and thrive across history.[14] The question of black humanness becomes a focus for Stephanie Mitchem as she considers folk healing practices, particularly those with spiritual sources.[15] Despite negative constructions of their bodies over time by white people, black people have found ways to care for themselves and their communities with the resources at hand, including religion, and to construct identities despite oppression. But a different take on the same issue—humanity—finds Victor Anderson "rather suspicious about the ways African American experience is typified in black and womanist theologies." He cautions against falling into essentialist constructions of black people. Drawing from his own understandings of black family, home, church, and value, Anderson then constructs a theology of religious experience.[16]

Yet questions from the negative constructions of black bodies continue into the twenty-first century, sometimes overtaking the constructions of positive identities. Emilie Townes tackles some images of Mammy, Sapphire, and Aunt Jemima that still remain and the challenges that black people face as she asks: "How do we grasp a hold of our identity and truly name ourselves instead of constantly looking into some strategically placed funhouse mirror of distortions and innuendos and mass marketing that smacks its lips and rolls its eyes while chanting 'mmmm mmmm good'?"[17]

M. Shawn Copeland addresses embodiment through the lens of Christianity, for "no Christian teaching has been more desecrated by slavery than the doctrine of the human person or theological anthropology."[18] She uses multiple disciplines with a solid grounding in Christian theology in order to turn to sacramentality and sacrifice as a way to undo the wounds at the heart of Christianity.

Anthony Pinn takes a different route in thinking through embodiment using interdisciplinary constructive theology. The body is an incomplete knowledge base, under construction both as metaphor and as material. Engaging postmodernist theories with the movement of rap music, Pinn states: "The shape of new black theological thought shifts away from preoccupation with Christology and theodicy as the proper framing for discussions of natural disasters.... We begin to recognize the nature and meaning of our existence in flesh as part of a vulnerable earth."[19]

In conclusion, the concept of embodiment is not limited to an analysis of the experiences of black people's oppressions. The social constructions of black bodies are tied to the development of white racism and control of those bodies. But as black scholars including theologians and ethicists have wrestled with the results of those constructions, something else becomes clear: many black people and communities materially participate in their own constructions even as they resist demeaning limits imposed by others. The tasks of researching black embodiment in theology has moved far beyond providing explanations of who black people are. To return to Charles Long's words, coming to terms with language *about* black people is one set of tasks and only the first. The study of embodiment cannot stay there. The next set of tasks is to analyze the "religious experience of radical *otherness*, a resourceful and critical moment that allowed these communities to undertake radical internal criticisms of themselves, their situation, and the situation of the majority culture."[20] To state this in another way, an ongoing exploration of the past of black bodies takes new meaning when theologians and ethicists turn toward the concept of embodiment.

NOTES

1. Walter Johnson, *Soul by Soul: Life inside the Antebellum Slave Market* (Cambridge: Harvard University Press 1999), 20, 21.
2. Robert F. Williams, *Negroes with Guns* (New York: Marzani and Munsell, 1962), 41.
3. Yolande Daniels, "Exhibit A: Private Life without a Narrative," in *Black Venus 2010: They Called Her "Hottentot,"* ed. Deborah Willis (Philadelphia: Temple University Press, 2010), 66.
4. David Walker's *Appeal to the Coloured Citizens of the World*, ed. Charles M. Wiltse (New York: Hill and Wang, 1965).
5. Ida Wells was a respected journalist who turned her attention to antilynching efforts after the lynching of her friend Thomas Moss, writing in 1892 in the black Memphis newspaper *Free Speech*: "The city of Memphis has demonstrated that neither character nor standing avails the Negro if he dares to protect himself against the white man or become his rival." Cited in Paula Giddings, *When and Where I Enter* (New York: Bantam Books, 1984), 19.

6. W. E. B. Du Bois's first book was *The Philadelphia Negro*, published in 1899, a sociological study. Over the next decades, he wrote books, essays, and managed the publication, *The Crisis*, of the National Association for the Advancement of Colored People, an organization that he helped to found.
7. See, for example, Thornton Stringfellow "A Scriptural View of Slavery," written in 1856, republished in Slave*ry Defended*, ed. Eric McKittrick (Englewood Cliffs, NJ: Prentice Hall, 1963), 86–98.
8. James H. Cone, *Black Power and Black Theology* (New York: Seabury Press, 1969).
9. James H. Cone, *God of the Oppressed* (New York: Seabury Press, 1975).
10. Charles H. Long, *Significations: Signs, Symbols, and Images in the Interpretation of Religion* (Aurora, CO: Davies Group, 2004), 8, 9.
11. Jacquelyn Grant, *White Women's Christ, Black Women's Jesus: Feminist Christology and Womanist Response* (New York: Scholars Press, 1989).
12. Kelly Brown Douglas, *Sexuality and the Black Church: A Womanist Perspective* (Maryknoll, NY: Orbis Books, 1999), 142.
13. Roger Sneed, *Representations of Homosexuality: Black Liberation Theology and Cultural Criticism* (New York: Palgrave Macmillan, 2010).
14. Dwight N. Hopkins, *Being Human: Race, Culture, and Religion* (Minneapolis: Fortress Press, 2005).
15. Stephanie Y. Mitchem, *African American Folk Healing* (New York: New York University Press, 2007).
16. Victor Anderson, *Creative Exchange: A Constructive Theology of African American Religious Experience* (Minneapolis: Fortress Press, 2008).
17. Emilie M. Townes, *Womanist Ethics and the Cultural Production of Evil* (New York: Palgrave Macmillan, 2006), 45.
18. M. Shawn Copeland, *Enfleshing Freedom: Body, Race, and Being* (Minneapolis: Fortress Press, 2010), 23.
19. Anthony B. Pinn, *Embodiment and the New Shape of Black Theological Thought* (New York: New York University Press, 2010), 156, 157.
20. Long, *Significations*, 9.

Selected Texts

Cone, James H. *God of the Oppressed*. New York: Seabury Press, 1975.

Cone, James H. *Black Power and Black Theology*. New York: Seabury Press, 1969.

Copeland, M. Shawn. *Enfleshing Freedom: Body, Race, and Being*. Minneapolis: Fortress Press, 2010.

Grant, Jacqueline. *White Women's Christ, Black Women's Jesus: Feminist Christology and Womanist Response*. New York: Scholars Press, 1989.

Hopkins, Dwight N. *Being Human: Race, Culture, and Religion*. Minneapolis: Fortress Press, 2005.

Johnson, Walter. *Soul by Soul: Life inside the Antebellum Slave Market*. Cambridge: Harvard University Press, 1999.

Long, Charles. *Significations: Signs, Symbols, and Images in the Interpretation of Religion*. Aurora, CO: Davies Group, 1985.

Pinn, Anthony B. *Embodiment and the New Shape of Black Theological Thought.* New York: New York University Press, 2010.

Townes, Emilie. *Womanist Ethics and the Cultural Production of Evil.* New York: Palgrave, 2006.

Williams, Robert F. *Negroes with Guns.* New York: Marzani and Munsell, 1962.

CHAPTER 23

PEDAGOGICAL PRAXIS IN AFRICAN AMERICAN THEOLOGY

KATIE G. CANNON

Over the past two and a half decades, an alternative pedagogy has been evolving in the United States.[1] It can be found in all the disciplines of religious study where African American women, once locked out, have been able to enter. The notion of womanist pedagogy can probably be traced to those moments in black women's seminary training when a few of those enrolled in theological education gathered to share observations of classroom dynamics, to question the weighty authority of male canonized texts and interpretations, and to contemplate meaningful research projects of their own design. These women, of whom I was one, dreamed of inscribing what black women really think, see, and do upon a small section of the large tabula rasa of genuine inclusivity in the academy of learned societies.[2]

Some twenty-five years ago there were fewer than thirty-five African American women enrolled in master of divinity programs and only one African American woman registered in a doctoral program in the two hundred accredited seminaries in North America.[3] As black women choosing to pursue advanced theological degrees in a predominantly male setting, alienation, isolation, and marginalization became daily fare. Even with the requisite credentials for matriculation in hand, black women were constantly barraged with arrogance and insults, suspicion and insensitivity, backhand compliments and tongue-incheek naiveté. For instance, an expression of encouragement from a male professor for scoring the highest grade on examinations quickly turned to a thrashing lambasting of male classmates for allowing a woman to earn the highest grade. Again for instance, acts of civility and respect often spiraled down to persistent teasing about facial features and female anatomy. And still again, the vast majority of black women theologians share the common testimony of being told that we are conspicuously too attractive, or our legs too shapely, or our bosoms too buxom for anyone to hear our intelligent treatises and well-reasoned commentaries. The worlds of divinity school, denominational headquarters, regional judicatory offices, and local parishes that black women negotiated demanded different and often wrenching allegiances.[4] But they continued to study, struggling for their rightful places in the church and in the academy.

From time to time the paths of African American women seminarians crossed, and a sisterly solidarity started to form. On such occasions, they talked about how they walked into every situation knowing that they were "the sister outsider."[5] They entered every class discussion with a developing awareness that the indisputable norms of established orthodox truth[6] would not be the norms of their daily existence.[7] Black women engaged with others across all kinds of barriers, and most of those with whom we dialogued were not even aware such obstacles existed. In order to crack open the patriarchal traditions that underlie and generate oppressive Christian practices, particularly against women of color, they worked with their sleeves rolled up, busily sharpening their oyster knife.[8]

In 1978, Dr. Delores Williams published an essay that identifies the foundational underpinning of womanist pedagogy. In it, she says:

> If I were asked what we black women students need to make the Union Theological Seminary experience meaningful, I would say we need what every other student needs. We need role models. We need competent scholars who are black women. We need black women to provide input into selection processes.... We need to select our own voices to represent us in those processes. We need mature black women scholars who are actively committed to the task of welding together the theological and the ethical, the theoretical and the practical dimensions of the theological enterprise. We need black women in the support and counseling areas.... We need spiritual, community and financial support to structure whatever it takes to make our academic experience here compatible with our vocational objectives and with our personal needs as students. We need the facilities to enter into those self definition processes which help us understand more fully our ministry to the world.[9]

What I want to suggest by highlighting these remarks is how womanist pedagogy emerged out of this lived context where black women have been challenging conventional and outmoded dominant religious resources so as to deconstruct those ideologies that lead into complicity with their own oppression.

Seminary-trained African American women began inventing opposable-thumb processes by problematizing the "obvious" to create alternative ways of conceptualizing the "natural." Illuminating the connections between how students learn and the subjects we teach, womanist scholars created new modes of rigorous inquiry for dealing critically with the tradition, structure, and praxis of our fields of study in order to invite women and men of contemporary faith communities to a more serious encounter with the contribution African American women have made and continue to make to the study of religion. The imperatives suggested by this pedagogy call for engaged theological scholarship organized around three major concepts: historical ethos, embodied pathos, and communal logos—these three concepts help us to live more faithfully the radicality of the Gospel.[10]

Historical Ethos

"Historical ethos" is a liberating term applied to politically and socially aware members of the African American intelligentsia who embrace the spirit, standards, and ideals that characterize our rich educational heritage. In other words, *historical ethos* is a conventional device used to critique the cultural context and the political climate that prevail in formally structured learning environments. The long and conflictive history of African Americans in the United States of America lies at the heart of such vigilant affirmation—rallying around this black educational heritage, safeguarding its everyday wisdom, and proclaiming its diversified depth as an invaluable asset to civilization.[11]

Several African American writers have produced works that address historical memory as cultural resistance. Michelle Cliff and Toni Morrison are two of several women writers who have written narratives in which memory is central. In her novel, *Free Enterprise*, Michelle Cliff successfully argues women of African descent carry within themselves complex fundamental values that underlie, permeate, and actuate major African patterns and retentions. Cliff's narrative strategy is predicated on the notion that if their lips, their hips, their skin color, and their bone structure are passed on from their ancestors, then why, why not memory?[12] Toni Morrison marks this distinct kind of conceptual memory as journeying to a site to see what remains have been left behind and reconstructing the world that these remains imply.[13]

The foregoing considerations lead back to cultural memories functioning as *historical ethos*. Beginning in 1793, black women, in relatively small, albeit significant numbers, toiled day and night constructing a legacy as educators. The dominant society makes little reference to the contributions of the "freed intelligentsia" among African Americans.[14] Steadily increasing in numbers throughout the nineteenth and twentieth centuries, black women taught reading, writing, and arithmetic in overcrowded one-teacher schools.[15] Despite a paucity of funds, multiple obstacles, deplorable learning environments, even when the much-needed material resources were nonexistent, teacher after teacher said to African American students in run-down, dilapidated Jim Crow buildings, "I will give you the best I got and I want you to be even better."[16]

Womanist scholars have found it surprising to teach students of affluence who question with suspicion such commitment to African American pedagogical tradition—"to give each student the best that I got because I want them to be even better." It is safe to say that womanist scholars are familiar with office hours discussions with students worrying whether or not the womanist's constructive feedback in the margins of their papers is no more than wolf tickets, wooden nickels, academic pennies with holes in them.[17]

The invisible imbalance of cognitive imperialism gets played out in the culture of education in very visible expectations. The ubiquitous assumption of many scholars as well as students in the womanist classroom is that they are not learning, that they are not participating in the rigor of academic excellence, that they are not getting the biggest bang for their educational buck if they are not beaten up, if they are not being told repeatedly how they got it wrong, how they messed up, if their papers are not bleeding with red ink from nonstop nitpicking of minor flaws.

Due to the collective power of educational convention, womanist pedagogy will neither jeopardize nor lower the "core" value of academic currency. What joins most educational institutions whose claim-to-fame is training "the talented tenth" is that the deliberate policies and repeated practices of white and male hegemony will continue to enforce the norms of cognitive imperialism as legitimate. In fact, what emerges from this example is that the traditional, normative classroom in dominant institutions of higher learning in this country is dictated by "knowledge capitalism." The market value of academic currency is determined by the ability to deconstruct, to tear a work apart, and to rip an idea limb from limb, to chew up the data and spit it out as a negative raw product.[18] Womanist pedagogy, and the pedagogical commitments of others in theological discourse in line with womanist sensibilities, says otherwise.

Womanist pedagogy, and the theological discourse it supports, is rooted in a particular historical ethos. Therefore, it will not allow the classroom nor professional personhood as a self-defined womanist scholar be made into anybody else's image. Based on this pedagogy womanists (and those aligned with this approach) refuse to participate in the imposing presence, the enshrined perpetuation and the sometimes subtle, subliminal legitimatizion of androcentric patriarchy. To put it succinctly, the protective arena of historical ethos operative in the womanist classroom bears witness to the ancestral gifts from my foreparents. The particular educational tradition I inherited demands that the influence of history cannot be ignored.[19]

Embodied Pathos

For the second concept, womanist pedagogy claims the phrase *embodied pathos*. Linking "historical ethos" with "embodied pathos" centralizes personal experience in teaching for justice-making transformation. Embodied pathos means that requirements for the course are designed to facilitate students in teaching themselves what they need to know. In addition to past history, it is important to unmask the truth of life circumstances as identifiable referents. Hence, womanist liberation ethics is very much like what the prophet Ezekiel talked about—"wheels in the middle of wheels way up in the middle of the air."[20]

One wheel deals with the intellectual predisposition of traditional male thinkers, usually dead or of European ancestry whose very language of objective universality masks our existence, forces persistence in the binary opposition of either-or, and looks askance at black women as superfluous appendages, saddled with odd concerns about race, sex, and class oppression.[21] The second wheel focuses on the specificity of African American Christian culture, systematic accounts of the history and achievements, perspectives and experiences of members of the black church community. The third wheel explores the experiential dimensions of women's texts and interpretations. This is the part of each course—theological and otherwise—wherein students listen to women of the African diaspora speaking their mother's tongue, as black women refine and critique their own realities across time and space through the written word.[22]

Now underlying this womanist pedagogy imaged as wheels in the middle of wheels is the comprehensive definition of liberation ethics created in 1981. I, Katie Cannon, was a tutor in Introduction to Christian Ethics with Dr. Beverly Harrison at Union Theological Seminary in New York. Asked by students what, then, is the special nature of "liberation ethics?" I wrote on the chalkboard:

> Liberation ethics is debunking, unmasking and disentangling the ideologies, theologies and systems of value operative in a particular society.
>
> "How" is it done? By analyzing the established power relationships that determine the cultural, political and economic presuppositions and by evaluating the legitimating myths which sanction the enforcement of such values.
>
> "Why" is it worth doing? So that we may become responsible decision-makers who envision structural and systemic alternatives that embrace the well-being of us all.

The "what" and thereby the "how" and the "why" give perspectives for how best to design a syllabus, select required texts, compile bibliographies, prepare instructional strategies, choose reference materials, organize the sequence of assignments, and create pre- and postassessment questionnaires.

In light of such a creative agenda for embodied pathos, womanist pedagogy makes it possible to begin each course by introducing the syllabus as the "covenant-of-intention." The principle of personal accountability of intellectual inquiry is crucial. In order for participants to move in the same direction, they, many womanists argue, must mutually own the course of study. Under this model, there is always time during the first class session to walk through the requirements collaboratively, actually doing a facsimile of the assignment that is due the next class period.

Yet if this educational endeavor is not to miscarry, the scholar, womanist or otherwise, must be clear in the introductory session to name straight up, front and center, the discombobulation that most students will experience. The majority of students enter a different world when they walk into the classroom. Their cultural reality of order is no longer the basic, core scholarship of study. Womanism is the backdrop for this new experience, the upside-downness of meaning.

Over the years, embodied pathos has enabled some to become even more cognizant of what is required for students to move into another culture, another context, another country, one that is the womanist's home. Sometimes students read and reread required texts because the books transport them across unfamiliar space and time. The contextual nature of learning means that one must cross with care new boundaries. Womanists, and others committed to this pedagogical approach, work at staying sensitive to the slowness of the majority of students who feel alienated by the reality of poor, black women as the point of departure. Even the most capable students can lose a lot of time hunting, digging, and rooting up some semblance of the familiar.

Far too many students in today's world enter the womanist classroom armed with ferocious mythologies derived from past experiences wherein African American women are stereotyped either as hostile villains or as subservient mammies. For students who are members of the dominant race, the African American woman intellectual in the role of authority is "the embodiment of inferiority whether we are inside or outside particular institutions and regardless of how we perform."[23] A large number of students are trapped, locked into previous interpretations of experiences drawn from the powerful, distorted interplay of negative stereotypes of race, gender, and class. These students test, retest, and still test again the paradigm shifts occurring in the womanist classroom.

What then, would womanists or anyone say after such brutal, unrestrained disrespect? What are the options in dealing with this type of contempt? What structural recourse is in place for handling and dealing with these types of indignities? There are still occasions, occasions too numerous to count, when womanists and those committed to womanist pedagogy for teaching theology and other areas of African American religious studies are rendered dumbfounded, completely stunned on a regular basis by the rude arrogance and low-down despicable audacity of a handful of students who believe that their white-skinness or their materially privileged backgrounds or their male genitalia give them licenses to make the most offensive, bludgeoning comments and to pose gross abominable questions in any course taught by women of color. The simple common courtesy granted to other professors is nowhere to be found.

Communal Logos

The third and final concept of *communal logos* distinguishes the womanist classroom as a place where dialectic-dialogic conversations can happen. What is important to point out is that discussions are organized so that questions and answers are continually reformulated. A key feature in the womanist classroom is reciprocity; all parties must participate. In a learning environment of wide differences and sharp contrast, communal logic conveys the irreducible character of our common language, as well as the tension that besets our conflicting realities.

This points to the heuristic nature of womanist pedagogy wherein students use cognitive, self-educating exploratory processes to discern mechanisms of exploitation in order to identify what patterns must be altered in order for justice to occur.

The students generate the energy that translates pedagogy into praxis by actively seeking and naming the cognitive dissonance they experience in their belief systems, lifestyles, and behavior. This type of educational process is designed to get students to become self-conscious and deliberate learners who continually confront the inherent contestability of life's contradictions. The emancipatory historiography requirements (wherein students question whose experience is validated, what groups are left out, what ideology accompanies the analysis, and what is the framework that provides meaning and holds conflicting elements together) sharpen their analytical skills as to how particular death-dealing situations came to be what they are and how they affect our lives and the life of our communities. By consistently applying an ever-developing liberationist rationale to classroom discussions, time is not wasted on rehashing what is already known. Areas beyond the classroom of the college, university, or seminary setting are alive with the hum of "erons"[24] as students reflect on their work of demystifying the ever-present dominating and chauvinistic Christian heritage, in order to act more effectively as empowered doers of justice.

It is essential that class discussions be structured so that the dialectic of historical ethos, embodied pathos, and communal logos can be apprehended. For example, data gathered in the assessment questionnaires and in the race, sex, class inventories can be used to design lectures and to facilitate class discussions. The knack is to encourage a certain movement toward conscientization without seeming to squelch others. Like Ann Berthoff,[25] a philosophy professor at the University of Massachusetts, some womanists, and those influenced by this womanist pedagogy, have learned to come to class, not thinking of a territory to be covered but with a compass, so as to determine the metalogical direction among a community of critically conscious ethicists.

Womanist teaching is interactive—reading students' papers the way letters are read, to learn more, especially more about the person. This includes, furthermore, conducting a running dialogue in the margins of each paper, informing students of supplemental readings and challenging them to find their ethical voice so that they can develop a method of moral reasoning that will stand them in good stead in any situation. The chief pedagogical value of weekly community announcements, lecture-note handouts (which the students have coined as "opaque transparencies"), conscientization exercises, written course requirements, and an-end-of-each-course annunciation/celebration ceremony is to encourage students to see how they can embrace what Professor Beverly Harrison called a faith praxis that transforms life in the direction of nonalienating experience.[26] The overall objective of this work implies moral notions about obligations, values, and virtues characterized by benevolent co-humanity and sacred power.

In addition, this pedagogical approach requires self-referential, social class inventories. Each student applies a fundamental inquiry of economic anatomy to her or his bio text. In order to assess the functioning dimensions of social class, students critique patterns of distribution in capitalist political economy and the different stratifications of political power that have been studied in the course. Besides the systemic analyses, students wrestle with authoritative, legitimate interpretations of subtle as well as highly theoretical concepts and consequences of social origins and mobility within our collective consciousness. This perspective of individual subjectivity, oftentimes shaped by excruciatingly painful experiences that students coined as a *class attack*, takes into consideration categories of cultural dispositions of class.

It is not surprising, therefore, that these inventories of social genealogy emerge carrying deep implications, endowed with profound power-shift dynamics in the womanist classroom and other classrooms—theological or not—that are influenced by this particular pedagogical orientation. Social class identification tends not to follow a straight line but rather the contours, detours, and byroads within a minimum time period of three generations. Many students, in writing their socioreligious autobiographies, have found something within themselves that links their lives to others, according to the communal logic that shapes the human condition. So understood, class is a mandatory tool in justice-making transformation.

In using their own experiences as data, students in successive stages of development sharpen their skills in moral reasoning. Gradually, they grasp the fundamental objective, which is that long-range, justice-making internal resolutions are more important than quick, end-of-the-semester, grade-point-average external solutions. In short, the major merit of "communal logos" is that there is no value-free space, no color-blank space, no apolitical space, and no mathematically regulated spatiotemporal dispassionate space of so-called neutral, detached objectivity.

Conclusion

Regardless of the differences between *historical ethos, embodied pathos*, and *communal logos*, they retain a common characteristic within the womanist classroom, which is the interactive engagement of both professor and students. A question implicit in what has been the translating of womanism into pedagogical praxis is "Why?" In fact, some womanists may argue that if the power dynamics in the classroom are so oppressive, why don't women of color leave, why don't they simply fold up their tents, shake the dust off our feet, and go teach somewhere else? Others may wonder as to the overall significance of what African American women teach. A few may question as to whether or not all the time and effort we put into our teaching is worth it. One or two may ask, does any of this really matter?

This work by womanists has also generated the "So what?" question. One response as to why every institution of learning needs womanist classrooms is that these are the spaces/places where students and faculty critique epistemological assumptions. What one knows, how one knows, and the way one goes about knowing is reconstructed. A further answer to the question "So what?" is that as justice-making moral agents, people committed to this pedagogical orientation, we have the responsibility to identify the so-called normative aspects of social, political, cultural, and economic typologies that have minimized African American women's experiences or totally erased African American women's contributions as liabilities to civilization. And, a final answer to the question "so what?" argues that the omission of womanist traditions results in education that is unbalanced, knowledge that is incomplete, and a worldview that is distorted.

In essence, translating womanism into pedagogical praxis is something womanists have done; epistemology is accepting the findings one comes to know; womanist pedagogy is the process by which one brings this kind of knowing about African American women into relation with a justice-praxis for members of our species and the wider environment in which we are situated, in order to resist conditions that thwart life, arriving at new understandings of our doing, knowing, and being.

NOTES

1. This essay was first presented on April 2, 1997, as the thirteenth annual Loy H. Witherspoon Lecture in Religious Studies at the University of North Carolina–Charlotte.
2. For discussions of pedagogy in the theological academy see Helmut Richard Niebuhr, Daniel Day Williams, and James M. Gustafson, *The Advancement of Theological Education* (New York: Harper & Row, 1956); Ed Farley, *The Fragility of Knowledge: Theological Education in the Church and University* (Minneapolis: Fortress Press, 1988); Joseph C. Hough Jr. and John B. Cobb Jr., *Christian Identity and Theological Education* (Atlanta: Scholars Press, 1985); The Mud Flower Collective, *God's Fierce Whimsy: Christian Feminism and Theological Education* (New York: Pilgrim Press, 1989); and Barbara G. Wheeler and Edward Farley, eds., *Shifting Boundaries: Contextual Approaches to the Study of Theological Education* (Louisville, KY: Westminster John Knox Press, 1992).
3. Toinette M. Eugene, "Under-represented Constituencies: Minorities and Majorities in the Seminary," *Christianity and Crisis* 49, nos. 5–6, (April 1989): 110–13.

4. Yolanda T. Moses, "Black Women in Academe: Issues and Strategies," a paper for the Project on the Status and Education of Women: Association of American Colleges, August 1989.
5. Audre Lorde, *Sister Outsider* (New York: Crossing Press, 1984).
6. Katie G. Cannon, *Katie's Canon: Womanism and the Soul of the Black Community*. (New York: Continuum, 1995).
7. Elisabeth Schussler Fiorenza, "Feminist Theology as Critical Theology of Liberation," *Theological Studies* 36, no. 4 (December 1975): 605–26.
8. Zora Neale Hurston, "How It Feels to Be Colored Me," *World Tomorrow*, May 1928, 17.
9. Delores Williams, "One Black Woman Reflects on Union," *Union Dues* 2, no. 1 (November 8, 1978): 4.
10. Don S. Browning, David Polk, and Ian S. Evison, ed., *The Education of the Practical Theologian: Responses to Joseph Hough and John Cobb's Christian Identity and Theological Education* (Atlanta: Scholars Press, 1989).
11. Other references that support this viewpoint include Darlene Clark Hine, ed., *Black Women in America: An Historical Encyclopedia*, 2 vols. (Brooklyn: Carlson Publishing, 1993); Bert James Loewenberg and Ruth Bogin, eds., *Black Women in Nineteenth-Century American Life* (University Park: Pennsylvania State University Press, 1976); Henry Louis Gates Jr., *Colored People* (New York: Knopf, 1994); Tricia Rose, *Black Noise: Rap Music and Black Culture in Contemporary America* (Hanover, NH: University Press of New England, 1994).
12. Michelle Cliff, *Free Enterprise* (New York: Dutton, 1993), 144. Cliff's work on epic memory has resonance in the works of many others. See, for example, Kariamu Welsh Asante, *The African Aesthetic: Keeper of the Traditions*. (Westport, CT: Greenwood Press, 1993); *The Woman That I Am: The Literary Culture of Contemporary Women of Color*, ed. D. Soyina Madison (New York: St. Martin's Press, 1993); and Chester Hedgepeth Jr. *Theories of Social Action in Black Literature* (New York: Lang, 1986).
13. Wilfred D. Samuels and Clenora Hudson-Weems, *Toni Morrison* (Boston: Twayne, 1990).
14. Catherine Ferguson is known in the formal history records as the first African American teacher. Ferguson purchased her freedom, and in 1793 opened the Kathy Ferguson's School for the Poor in New York City, with forty-eight children. Gerda Lerner, *Black Women in White America* (New York: Vintage Books, 1972); Micheline R. Malson et al., eds., *Black Women in America: Social Science Perspectives* (Chicago: University of Chicago Press, 1990); Paula Giddings, *When and Where I Enter: The Impact of Black Women on Race and Sex in America* (New York: Bantam Books, 1984); Roseann P. Bell, Bettye J. Parker, and Beverly Guy-Sheftall, eds., *Sturdy Black Bridges: Visions of Black Women in Literature* (New York: Doubleday, 1979).
15. For historical overviews with invaluable bibliography see "Contributions of Black Women in Education," in *Contributions of Black Women to America*, ed. Marianna W. Davis, vol. 2 (Columbia, SC: Kenday Press, 1982), 261–356. Also, *The Jeanes Story: A Chapter in the History of American Education, 1908–1968*, Prepared by the NASC Interim History Writing Committee (Jackson, MS: Southern Education Foundation, 1979) and Carol V. R. George, ed., *"Remember the Ladies": New Perspectives on Women in American History* (Syracuse, NY: Syracuse University Press, 1975).
16. From 1945 to 1967, this statement, offering limitless encouragement of students' potentialities, was a verbal recitation repeated often by African American teachers at George

Washington Carver School, the one and only public school for black children in Kannapolis, NC.

17. Each of the following expressions: wolf tickets, wooden nickels, and pennies-with-holes refer to situations where one is cheated, ripped off, or receives as the real thing an object with no value.
18. Gloria Joseph and Jill Lewis, *Common Differences: Conflicts in Black and White Feminist Perspectives* (Garden City, NY: Anchor Press, 1981).
19. Johnnella E. Butler, *Black Studies: Pedagogy and Revolution—a Study of Afro-American Studies and the Liberal Arts Tradition through the Discipline of African American Literature* (Washington, D.C.: University Press of America, 1981); C. Peter Ripley, ed., *Witness for Freedom: African American Voices on Race, Slavery, and Emancipation* (Chapel Hill: University of North Carolina Press, 1993); Patricia Hill Collins, *Black Feminist Thought: Knowledge, Consciousness and the Politics of Empowerment* (Boston: Unwin Hyman, 1990).
20. The Spiritual "'Zekiel Saw de Wheel Way up in the Middle of de Air" was inspired by the biblical writings in the book of Ezekiel, the sixth-century B.C.E. Hebrew prophet who called those exiled in Babylon to return to godliness. Ezekiel 1: 15–16 (NRSV) says, "As I looked at the living creatures, I saw a wheel on the earth beside the living creatures, one for each of the four of them. As for the appearance of the wheels and their constructions: their appearance was like a gleaming of beryl; and the four had the same form, their construction being something like a wheel within a wheel."
21. Michele Russell, "An Open Letter to the Academy," *Quest* 3 (1977): 70–80.
22. See Elsa Barkley Brown, "Mothers of Mind," *Sage Magazine: A Scholarly Journal on Black Women–Black Women's Studies* 6, no. 1 (Summer 1989): 4–11.
23. Patricia A. Williams, *The Rooster's Egg: On the Persistence of Prejudice* (Cambridge: Harvard University Press, 1995), 105.
24. "Erons" is a phrase coined by Wynn Legerton in May 1989 to describe the erotic particles emitted into the air whenever we are doing the work our souls must have. For a fuller discussion see the Work in Progress Paper, "Alienation and Anger: A Black and a White Woman's Struggle for Mutuality in an Unjust World," by Katie G. Cannon and Carter Heyward, with a Response by Sung Min Kim, No. 54, Stone Center, Wellesley College, 1992.
25. Ann E. Berthoff, *Forming/Thinking/Writing: The Composing Imagination* (Rochelle Park, NY: Hayden, 1978).
26. Beverly W. Harrison, "Toward a Christian Feminist Liberation Hermeneutic for Demystifying Class Reality in Local Congregations," in *Beyond Clericalism*, ed. Joseph C. Hough Jr. and Barbara G. Wheeler (Atlanta: Scholars Press, 1988), 137–51.

Selected Texts

Ann E. Berthoff. *Forming/Thinking/Writing: The Composing Imagination*. Rochelle Park, NY: Hayden, 1978.

Cannon, Katie G. *Katie's Canon: Womanism and the Soul of the Black Community*. New York: Continuum, 1995.

Gates, Jr., Henry Louis. *Colored People*. New York: Knopf, 1994.

Hine, Darlene Clark, ed. *Black Women in America: An Historical Encyclopedia*. 2 vols. Brooklyn: Carlson, 1993.

Hurston, Zora Neale. "How It Feels to Be Colored Me." *World Tomorrow*, May 1928.

Joseph, Gloria, and Jill Lewis. *Common Differences: Conflicts in Black and White Feminist Perspectives*. Garden City, NY: Anchor Press, 1981.

Mud Flower Collective. *God's Fierce Whimsy: Christian Feminism and Theological Education*. New York: Pilgrim Press, 1989.

Lorde, Audre. *Sister Outsider*. New York: Crossing Press, 1984.

Niebuhr, H. Richard, Daniel Day Williams, and James M. Gustafson. *The Advancement of Theological Education*. New York: Harper & Row, 1956.

Samuels, Wilfred D., and Clenora Hudson-Weems. *Toni Morrison*. Boston: Twayne, 1990.

Wheeler, Barbara G., and Edward Farley, eds. *Shifting Boundaries: Contextual Approaches to the Study of Theological Education*. Louisville, KY: Westminster John Knox Press, 1992.

Williams, Delores. "One Black Woman Reflects on Union." *Union Dues* 2, no. 1 (Nov. 8, 1978).

CHAPTER 24

RELIGIOUS PLURALISM AND AFRICAN AMERICAN THEOLOGY

DIANNE M. STEWART DIAKITÉ

> The black cultural revival, especially my concern for the role of religious experience in it, led me to Afro-Arab Islam and then to the religions of tropical Africa. The task of writing a black theology has caused me to read history backwards in search of the faith of my fathers.[1]
>
> —J. Deotis Roberts

SINCE its inception as a discipline of critical intellection, African American[2] theology—most commonly appreciated as black and womanist theology—has developed lines of inquiry related to three major sources of knowledge production: (1) a significant corpus of religious thought gleaned from scripts of public figures in African American religious history; (2) the field of African American studies and, in particular, African American religious studies, whose foundational methodologies and conceptual frameworks emerged from the pioneering scholarship of W. E. B. Du Bois; and (3) the school of liberation theology within the discipline of systematic theology. As a result, seminal discussions in African American theology have addressed the dehumanization and oppression of US African Americans and prophetic dimensions of US African American Christian thought and practice.

The reality of Africa as an originary locus and heritage symbol for US African Americans has received attention in each of these arenas of thought. In addition, scholarly studies of US African Americans involved with Islamic, Hebraic, and indigenous African religions document a diverse landscape of religious affiliation and devotion beyond the walls of Christian churches. However, social scientists and historians remain in the forefront of the search for the multiple faiths of black fathers and mothers. Over the past forty years of its existence, African American theology has developed no substantial discourse on the subject of religious pluralism. Instead, the dominant strategy embraced by most black/womanist theologians has privileged Christianity as the distinct source of religiously inspired social activism in US African American history. Discussions about African American religious diversity or religious pluralism in general are negligible, as few theologians have produced scholarship premised upon non-Christian religions. Only Josiah Young, Anthony Pinn, Will Coleman, Dianne Stewart Diakité, and Monica Coleman[3] have demonstrated a commitment to theological analysis and reflection grounded upon Old and New World African religious cultures or—in the case of Pinn—humanist philosophies. These minority voices are accented, nonetheless, by a softer conversation among pioneering scholars during the earliest phase in the development of black liberation theology.

The Contributions of Pioneering Scholars

During the early 1970s, discussions about Africa's significance to a developing black theology introduced the imperative to ground the new school of thought in the rich symbols and idioms of black folk culture and spirituality as well as indigenous African religions. Among the founding contributors to black theology, J. Deotis Roberts provided the most sustained treatment of indigenous African religions, authoring a number of essays that (1) examine common philosophical, ethical, and theological features across varied religious traditions; and (2) explore resonances between African American and African religious traditions. As the above epigraph indicates, he also investigated Islamic influences in black nationalist and ethnic religious cultures and acknowledged African retentions in the US African American Christian heritage.[4] Roberts's research, relative to other pioneering architects of black theology, is distinguished by the fact that he appears to be the only scholar among his cohort (James Cone, Gayraud Wilmore, Cecil Cone, Albert Cleage, and Major Jones) to actually interrogate continental African religious cultures, in and of themselves, as an essential starting point in theological reflection. Furthermore, he specifically argued for the development of African and black theologies that access African *indigenous* religions as sources of revelation and theological insight.

Roberts was meticulous in framing possibilities for dialogue across lived religious and reflective theological communities in Africa and African America. In one of his most substantial essays on the subject he confessed, "I have even discovered that there are 'theologians' of the traditional African religions as well as African Christian scholars who are 'Africanizing' Christianity."[5] Roberts's careful review of the established scholarship on African religions and their cultural contexts led him to conclude that "African religions embrace the total life of the individual and the community. God consciousness and social consciousness are one. To belong to a community is to accept the divinity that gives sanction to the laws and customs undergirding the life and activities of the group."[6] Without diminishing the value of outside perspectives, he also called for more expansive studies of African religions from continental African scholars who have intimate firsthand exposure to the social contexts of lived religion and intuitive access to the nuances of Africa's indigenous languages and symbolic material cultures.[7]

In other essays Roberts "assumed the task of looking at traditional African religion and lifting out elements that might contribute to Christian theology."[8] The significance of such a move in the context of formal theological reflection is that it detribalizes African religions and debunks the Western tendency to interpret them reductively through the lens of cultural relativity. Most of all, his approach mirrors comparative and pluralistic leanings in the vernacular theological imagination and praxes of engagement with the religious Other so pronounced among the oppressed communities of the African diaspora.[9] Clearly no scholar should attempt to deny the theme of particularity evident in any local ethnic or pan-ethnic "African cultural theology."[10] However, often overlooked by Western-trained theologians who desire to engage indigenous African religions are translatable principles that remain compatible with Christian principles or that address deficiencies in Western Christian thought. In addition to underscoring the fact that African thought generally transcends the kind of dichotomous conceptualization and the dualistic partitioning of sacred and secular reality common in many branches of Western Christianity, Roberts appeals to the "high esteem for humanity and interpersonal relationships" expressed through the concept of familyhood/*Ujamaa* as critical in "overcom[ing] the dehumanizing effects of technology" and "developing a doctrine of the church."[11] Though he does not state the point directly, these concepts and relational dispositions that link entities and phenomena in the visible and invisible worlds signal the universal relevance of African religions and their derivative cultural theologies for cosmos and creation beyond African and African diaspora contexts.[12]

Roberts's "desire to see blacks representing the various disciplines of religious knowledge working as a team with African religious scholars to excavate and interpret this rich [African] religious heritage for all humankind"[13] did not derail his search for resonances between African and African American religions. In "An Afro-American Theological Dialogue," he specifically identifies, for example, how African concepts of the individual, community, kinship, family, and ancestors correspond with "a sustained belief in the reunion of families beyond death" among US African Americans: "This common cultural aspect of the Afro-American connection," Roberts contended, "could be a building block of a relevant doctrine of church and sacraments" and "also provides a rich suggestion for the doctrine of last things."[14] Roberts's move in the direction of doctrinal construction is, perhaps, one avenue Gayraud Wilmore hoped black theology would take soon after its emergence. In

1972 Wilmore put forth methodological criteria for black theological reflection that anticipated much of Roberts's emphasis upon African religions. Among Wilmore's sources for black theology were "the existing black community, where the tradition of black folk religion is still extant and continues to stand over and against the institutional church... the writings and addresses of the Black preacher and the public men of the past...[and] the traditional religions of Africa."[15]

Wilmore's comprehensive study and his published articles, however, do not develop a conceptual theology that one might classify as systematic or constructive. His scholarship corresponds with the imperatives of black theology by tracing the motif of black radicalism in the religious thought and activisms of US African Americans. In this endeavor, he analyzes what conceptual black theologians would identify as the legacy of prophetic or social justice commitments in the beliefs and praxes of Christian and non-Christian religious cultures across conventional boundaries of sacred and secular, ecclesial and political. Wilmore's scholarship reinforces the declaration in conceptual black theology that US African American Christians have identified with a God who favors the oppressed and wills their material and spiritual liberation in human history. As Wilmore explores religious dimensions of pivotal black radical thinkers and activists, the scholarly convention of "black religion" appears to offer the most accurate classification of the pluralistic contexts in which "black radicalism" found expression over the centuries of African presence in the United States. From the religiously inspired slave revolt of Nat Turner to the rise of black independent denominations; from the protest literature of David Walker to that of Alexander Crummell; from the emergence of Marcus Garvey's United Negro Improvement Association to the appearance of black ethnic and nationalist religions; or from the prophetic leadership of Martin Luther King Jr. to the aesthetic appeal of Black Power within sacred and secular institutions, including its impact upon the very formation of the discipline of black liberation theology, Wilmore's volume offers a concise yet broad historical portrait of the pluralism that cannot be ignored if one is to treat the motif of liberation in the religious heritage of the collective body of African descendants in the United States.

If Wilmore's text had never been released, the scene portrayed by conceptual black theologians would have given the impression that black Christianity alone gave birth to black radicalism in the African American experience. Certainly no conceptual black theologian would ever state such a claim. However, confessional commitments position most black theologians within a vulnerable and distortive discursive space of collapsing blackness and Christian-ness. *Black* religion then is *Christian* religion and *black* radicalism is *Christian* radicalism in the majority of works produced by African American professional theologians. Wilmore's *Black Religion and Black Radicalism*, though not a conceptual theology, disrupted this pattern among the first generation of black theological scholars and, as a result, holds a unique place in the canon of black theological discourse.

Pan-African Religious Cultures and Theological Reflection

In the mid-1980s Roberts cautioned that "the exclusive christocentrism of [James] Cone is inadequate for the contextualization of black and African theologies." He went on to pose a critical question that should have inspired theological scholarship attentive to religious pluralism and diverse religious heritages of African descendants in the United States if properly addressed by second-generation black and womanist theologians. Roberts inquired whether Cone's "program allows for a non-Christian faith in its encounter with non-Western and non-Christian religious expression to be at the center of both African and black theological reflection." Roberts remained unconvinced by Cone's Christological norm and instead insisted that "as process theologians such as John Cobb are attempting to reconceive Christology in dialogue with Buddhists, black theologians will need to participate in 'Africanization' of Christian theology at its Christological center."[16]

One theologian did seem to understand the significance of Roberts's call for "Africanization." Josiah Young's conceptualization of a pan-African theology was the first theological project that carried preliminary investigation among first-generation black theologians to its logical systematic conclusion. In appealing to indigenous African religions, nineteenth-century pan-Africanists, black folk religion, jazz, blues, and other musical legacies, Young developed a constructive pan-African Christian theology that built upon the seminal contributions of J. Deotis Roberts, Gayraud Wilmore, James Cone, and Charles Long. For the first time in the history of the field, a US African American theologian went beyond the nascent stage of merely acknowledging the need for this type of theological reflection to actually producing it.

As a Conian-trained scholar, Young's theology assumes a systematic framework that conceptualizes the doctrines of revelation, incarnation, Christology, pneumatology, providence, creation, sin, redemption, and eschatology for postcolonial pan-African contexts. Young premises his constructive theological insights upon an impressive array of sources, including indigenous religions of Africa, African social and political movements, and postcolonial African thought. Young is deliberate in linking symbolic thought and ritual practices of specific regions of Africa with expressions of the same in the US American slave community. For example, he appeals to the works of established Africanists and African Americanists, such as Wyatt MacGaffey and Sterling Stuckey, to theorize important spiritual connections between the Kongo cosmogram from Central African religious cultures and the ring shout as it emerged among US African Americans. Under subheadings such as "African Traditional and Slave Religions and Pan-Africanization," "Black Religion," and "Jazz: Inseminating Spirits of Meaning and Power," Young situates his theological project within the religious culture and vernacular theological imagination of the "lowest strata" among US African Americans—the "less fortunate slaves." Young's project discloses how James Cone's identification with the faith of Richard Allen, James Varick, and Daniel Alexander Payne ignores a nuance in the class and cultural distinctions between black church fathers (and mothers) and the masses they endeavored to uplift. Young maintains that

> if there is a tension *which presupposes a cultural continuity* between the slaves of Allen's day and the black underclass today, the faith of Allen may be distinct from the religion of the masses—then and now. Ancestors such as Richard Allen take us away, in a certain sense, from the religion of the "lowest strata." Like Crummell, AME clergy such as Daniel Alexander Payne devalued the religion of slaves whose Christianity was quite different from that of AME clergy. Although Allen had been a slave undoubtedly in touch with the spirituality of "less fortunate" slaves, he, like Crummell, went in the wrong direction in his understanding of Providence, thus heightening his alienation from the masses who shuffled counterclockwise in ringshouts. The ecclesiology of Allen, though opposed to slavery and reflecting the African heritage, is rooted in Great Britain rather than the African-American masses.[17]

Young's appreciation for Charles Long's phenomenological research is evident in his contention that black religion is not reducible to Christianity[18] and in his rejection of Cone's Christological norm as too narrow to reflect the spiritual inheritance that informed the lived religion of enslaved persons of African descent in the United States. "If Sterling Stuckey is correct," says Young,

> the "norm" of slave religion was not Jesus Christ, but "the ancestors and elders." Indeed Jesus himself tended to be interpreted in terms of the religiosity of ancestors. Thus the "Christian faith answered to African religious imperatives." Drawing together the visible and the invisible—the seen and unseen matrices of the sky, earth and all these things—the hermeneutical center is an "Africanness," from which the matrix of black religion is diffused in time and space.[19]

Young's central objective compels a candid and critical analysis of the Eurocentric values and colonialist imperatives of celebrated pan-Africanists whose collective footprint upon West African soil casts a shameful shadow above relations between the elite descendants of African diaspora settlers and indigenous populations. Thus, he debunks the distorted and oppressive doctrine of providence that guided the missionary operations of Alexander Crummell and Edward Blyden in Liberia. Instead, Young wants to argue that "in the providence of God, African people have resisted totalization in an ancestral spirituality that renews, reforms, recreates and restores African people to the integrity of their persons."[20] For Young, the *imago Dei* preserves creation and "liberates the African people through the redemptive actions of popular culture.... Failure to probe the meaning of ancestral legacies is an exercise in alienation from the image of God made flesh and blood in the Pan-African experience."[21]

Through his probing Young also addresses J. Deotis Roberts's stated concern for accessing the meanings that inhere within African symbolic thought.[22] In Young's pan-African theology, sacred symbols and ritual processes that have sustained linkages between Africa and African America in the lived religions of the black/African poor and oppressed are excavated and explored for their enduring value to the personal and communal integrity and regeneration of pan-Africa. In distilling from African religious cultures "a philosophical element" and "transcontextual symbols of Pan-African theology,"[23] Young provides a substantive conceptual foundation for later works that would advance the search for the faiths of the fathers and mothers among liberation theologians of the African diaspora.

A New Era in African American Theology: Explorations in Black Religious Pluralism

The new millennium saw the emergence of theological scholars and the publication of several texts committed to research on African American / diaspora theologies and religious pluralism. If Young's work helped to "unlock" *symbolic* structures in pan-African religious experience, Will Coleman's *Tribal Talk: Black Theology, Hermeneutics, and African/American Ways of "Telling the Story"* also addressed Roberts's concern in its attempt to "unlock" the *mythical* dimensions of African oral narratives while juxtaposing them with African American spiritual narratives.[24] Coleman explores cosmological and ontological Dahomean myths, accessing the sophisticated level of reasoning associated with the Vodun (Divine Community) who govern the invisible world. One does not develop overnight the ornate bodies of thought attributed to the various deities and phenomena of lived experience in vodun theology. Coleman explains, for example,

> The term "Da" signifies movement and therefore life itself. It is associated with the particular movement of a serpent, but much more is signified here. Da is the source of all that is dynamic and living in its resistance against stagnation and death. Da was present with Mawu-Lisa at the creation of the earth. She-he was carried in the mouth of Aido Hwedo who is represented in a giant rainbow serpent.... As an archetype, Da... represents the cycle of creation and destruction, genesis and apocalypse. Through the image of the serpent devouring its own tail, the narrative suggests that Da force is essential, not only for the genesis of earth life but also for its maintenance.[25]

Coleman draws parallels between African religious cultures and the religious experiences of enslaved African Americans, underscoring their appreciation for the invisible world of spirits and the powers of roots and mystical technologies (charms, hands) to transform the human condition. In so doing, he reinterprets their vernacular (speech and religious culture) as sites of subversive and playful theological and philosophical expression, noting how "through... manipulation of phonetic words, [they encourage] a contemporary form of theological conjure through the process of writing in a style different from that of dogmatic categories and traditional modes of expression."[26] Like Young, Coleman takes a step back from the symbols of blackness and gestures of resistance, as elaborated by Cone, to probe more deeply the hidden transcripts embedded in the figurative speech and coded comportment of enslaved African Americans. In the end, Coleman concludes that African American narrative strategies "serve as the basis for an emerging black 'story' or 'tribal talk' theology—that is, a theology that is rooted in a uniquely metaphorical and poly-voiced African American way of speaking about religious experiences."[27]

Embedded within Will Coleman's promotion of "tribal talk" among black and womanist theologians is an invitation to produce theologies that will reflect the pluralistic and syncretic religious traditions of African Americans.[28] In 2008 Monica Coleman's *Making a Way out of No Way: A Womanist Theology* gave new emphasis to this "tribal talk" objective among black and womanist theologians: Her text is the first to construct a process womanist theology of salvation attentive to diverse US African American religious traditions. In this endeavor she privileges black feminist literature, the African tradition of honoring ancestors, and Yoruba goddesses/Orisha. Naming her work a "postmodern womanist theology,"[29] Coleman establishes early on that "in order to speak to today's realities, a womanist theology cannot require a belief in Jesus Christ for salvation, and it must uphold a religious framework that can discuss the relationship between God and the world for more than one single religious tradition."[30] Her shift away from the systematic-dogmatic framing of theology so common among black and womanist theologians suggests that alternative approaches to theological construction might be more compatible with the goal of developing African American theologies that reflect religious diversity. She locates an ideal narrative context from which to draw redemptive womanist parables in the science fiction literature of Octavia Butler. Butler's 1993 *Parable of the Sower* is saturated with the symbols and metaphors of Orisha-based traditions. In fact, the goddess Oya—who manifests in the character of the chief protagonist, Lauren Oya Olamina, and across the entire range of experiences felt by the "Earthseed community" Lauren leads—becomes the metaphor for salvation as a process that involves creative transformation in "building a community of diverse, disenfranchised people with a common yearning for a better life."[31]

Coleman's distinct contribution to the theological quest for the faiths of US African Americans is twofold. First, her creative postmodern adoption of womanist resources within Orisha-based spiritualities contests the tendency toward anachronistic interpretations of "African traditional religions" and the assumption that the wisdoms they contain belong to an archaic age of primitive timelessness. Second, in elaborating a nonconfessional vision of salvation, she jettisons confining dogmatic features in search of pan-religious relevance across the diverse US African American communities. Coleman, then, liberates womanist/black theology from its dogmatic attachment to systematic frameworks that privilege Christian revelation as the entrance to theological reflection.

African Caribbean Theologies and Religious Pluralism: Straddling a Shared Heritage with US African American Theologies

While Monica Coleman perceives a US African American community as her primary audience, Dianne Stewart Diakité's front-row audience has been the Anglophone African Caribbean world. At the same time, she hopes to find US African Americans among her wider audience and invites theologians and communities of African descent across Latin America and the wider Africana world to eavesdrop on her conversation given its broader implications for liberation theological perspectives among Africana communities. Trained by Josiah Young at the undergraduate level, and by James Cone and Delores Williams at the doctoral level, Stewart Diakité pioneered the move away from Christian dogmatics in Africana womanist theology and religious thought. Indeed, she was the first theologian to do constructive theology based upon African religious cultures in the New World with no teleological commitments to Christianity. All previous conceptual theological projects that considered any dimension of African religiosity either flirted with the theme of an African heritage or explored that heritage toward the end goal of Christian theological reflection.

Stewart Diakité's most sustained theological conversation on the subject of African diaspora religious cultures is found in her 2005 text, *Three Eyes for the Journey: African Dimensions of the Jamaican Religious Experience*. Therein she offers a historically and ethnographically grounded theological analysis of the motif of liberation in vernacular religious cultures of Jamaica from the eighteenth to the twenty-first centuries. Stewart Diakité contends that African heritage religions provided the translational structures—institutional, metaphorical, and conceptual—for organized political and cultural resistance to the Western Christian project of slavery and colonialism in Jamaica. She interrogates the six major religious contexts in which those translational structures exhibited enough flexibility to reject, absorb, and/or negotiate with dominant expressions of Christianity in the formation of an African-Jamaican spiritual heritage. As a result, she contests the assumption that the Afro-Protestant diaspora suffers disproportionately (relative to the Afro-Catholic diaspora) from an impoverished and diluted African religious heritage. Stewart Diakité theorizes African Jamaican religions not primarily as black expressions of Christianity lightly peppered with Africanisms (à la Herskovits) but principally as ethnic and pan-ethnic African-derived traditions that adopted "christianisms"[32] both as an intuitive strategy for confronting worlds of new ideas and experiences and as a survival strategy for coping with multiple levels of exile and the foreboding prospect of annihilation. In terms of her conceptual theological work, Stewart Diakité develops a distinct womanist perspective on the cross through comparative theological analysis of the Kongo-based Kumina ritual of spirit manifestation and US African American womanist doctrines of soteriology/redemption. As a result, she describes an African cross of recurring incarnation "that promotes the holistic liberation of Black women and Black communities."[33] Stewart Diakité's prediction that "the next phase of the theological enterprise in the African diaspora will be saturated with conversations about Black religious pluralism"[34] might well be true, especially if we consider the scholarly contributions of those discussed above alongside the insights of humanists like Anthony Pinn.

Black Humanist Religion and Theology

Due to Anthony Pinn's interventions in black and womanist theology, discussions of US African American theology in the twenty-first century must include black humanist religion. Pinn's 1995 text, *Why Lord? Suffering and Evil in Black Theology*, was his first comprehensive statement on black humanism as the most ethical and pragmatic response to evil and suffering in the US African American experience. While Pinn did not go as far as categorizing humanism as a religion in his first text, he later clarified his working definition of religion, which fits squarely within the scope of perspectives leading scholars tend to support. Since "religion is the 'underlying resources of meaning and ritual that inform and fund the ongoing living and dying in a culture as a whole,'" for Pinn, black humanism is not a theistic religion but a "praxis oriented religion," nonetheless, that provides "one way to gain orientation and motivation toward the framing of human life through useful goals and agendas."[35]

In claiming a space for humanism at the desk of theological reasoning, Pinn aims "to broaden the possibilities, the religious terrain, and to foster conversation concerning liberating ways of addressing the problem of evil."[36] Pinn brings to the surface primary source materials that witness to a continuum of nontheistic (often anti-Christian) positions (from speculative disbelief to radical rejection) embraced by celebrated, ordinary, and anonymous persons in the US African American experience. These perspectives are found in reports about enslaved communities' dismissal of Christianity, agnostic and humanist literatures of the Harlem Renaissance, as well as the published opinions of black communists and nationalists.

Pinn's research into black humanism and his presence among the black theological community compel a reassessment of the pluralistic elements of black religion. Moreover, he contributes significantly to the legacy of internal criticism in the black/womanist theological tradition when he offers reinterpretations of sources conventionally adduced to support confessional Christian theological projects. Born during the black revolution of the 1960s, black theology had always recognized some of the non-Christian religious platforms that spawned many to black consciousness and political action. Leading black theologians made some mention of Islamic, Hebraic, and secular Afrocentric or black nationalist religions[37] in their analyses of the spiritual moods and motivations characterizing the ethos of the day. Humanist leanings within US African American religious thought and culture, however, were either ignored or eclipsed by Christian theological agendas. In addition, humanist arguments forwarded by predecessors like William Jones, and even Pinn, were collapsed with Eurocentric rationalism and politely dismissed as an irrelevant polemic that, if left to fester, would only frustrate the triumphal theistic vision of the black/womanist liberation theological project. With Pinn's spotlight on the pragmatic ethic guiding much of humanist thought in black oral, musical, literary, and philosophical canons, it is no longer possible or even desirable to dismiss as cynical or hopeless vernacular and elite perspectives that choose a humanist vision over a Christian theistic one in response to suffering and evil in the African American experience.[38]

On the Horizon: Religious Pluralism and the Future of African American Theology

What should the future hold for African American theology if it is to reflect the rich variety of religious cultures now nourishing persons of African descent in the United

States and the wider American and Caribbean diasporas? As a preliminary response, I aim to address in a concise manner two topics that invite further attention if the field of African American theology is to mature into an authentically inclusive intellectual school of thought: (1) the problem of audience and receptive arenas for African American/diaspora theologies that reflect non-Christian traditions; and (2) the need for collaborative research and publications across US African American, Latino/a, and Caribbean contexts.

Audiences for Non-Christian and Pluralistic African American Theologies

If there is a central problem plaguing the rise of pluralistic African American theologies, it is the problem of audience reception. Who in the world of lived Africana religions is actually interested in or listening to Josiah Young, Anthony Pinn, Will Coleman, Dianne Stewart Diakité, Monica Coleman, and others following in their paths? Are there suitable popular or academic audiences for their theological scholarship? These are pressing questions that reveal an underlying problem for theologians with commitments to religious pluralism in the African diaspora: Most of their academic projects are guided by a quest to resolve scholastic dilemmas that emerged within their research discipline. Yet they engaged their scholarly peers while simultaneously appealing to popular audiences. And here lies the rub: popular audiences are often alienated from and disinterested in the disciplinary problems that generated their original research questions in the first place.[39]

It is clear that to be effectively heard these academic theologians cannot "perform their *ebo* and eat it too."[40] Now that they have identified conceptual limitations and methodological flaws in conventional expressions and modes of black, womanist, and Caribbean theological construction, they must take a more accurate pulse of the communities they hope to engage to discover the theological issues and agendas of relevance for them. In so doing, they might encounter novel styles of, and objectives for, liberation theological discourse that will diversify the idioms and intonations of theological "tribal talk" in the African diaspora. Additionally, they must make a stronger case for why Christian-identified persons with confessional orthodox commitments should pay attention to black religious pluralism and the theological insights of Africana traditions beyond their own familiar theological worlds.

The Collaborative Imperative

The agendas outlined above also register the urgency of developing comparative and collaborative African American / diaspora / Africana theologies that reflect the trans-ethnic and religious exchanges occurring among US African Americans, Latino/as, and Caribbeans within the United States and within transnational contexts.[41] Latina theologian Michelle Gonzales's contention that "somehow Latino/a and black theologians have to find a way to dialogue about their contexts, take seriously each other's identity constructions, yet not attempt to fold one into the other"[42] should not go unaddressed in the future of African American theological construction. To be sure, Gonzales feels the weight of this collaborative responsibility in her primary Latino/a theological community and confesses:

> When one examines the importance of slave religion and slave narratives in black theology, for example, I am, as a Latina, often perplexed as to how to enter into this conversation. And yet it is a conversation I should enter, for as Luis Pedraja notes, Latino/as share in the legacy of slavery, "both as slaves and as enslavers."[43]

Here Gonzales opens a little wider the theological door perhaps first cracked by J. Deotis Roberts, who called for collaborative efforts among theologians of Africa and the African diaspora over twenty-five years ago. In "An Afro-American Theological Dialogue," Roberts penned the following closing remarks:

> The context of black theology is temporally and spatially distinct from African theology. A common ancestry links them remarkably. Here one can claim too much and one can claim too little. What is important is to affirm what we have in common that is mutually enriching and together develop meaningful statements of doctrine for our people through critical yet positive dialogue. To this conversation we invite all people of African descent—those in the West Indies and Latin America as well as blacks and Africans.[44]

The future of US African American theology will indeed be contingent upon its ability to sustain new and relevant poly-voiced conversations not only with its internal academic and vernacular communities but also with global partners in Africa, Latin America, the Caribbean, and elsewhere.[45] Global dialogue among theologians of Africa, the Caribbean, Europe, the Pacific nations, and the Americas will necessarily invite critical analysis of our global condition(s) in this new millennium. Advances in today's technologies allow us to experience more immediately the positive and adverse effects of globalization, which encourages mutual and stratified flows of interaction and influence across Africa and the African diaspora.[46] This fact of our common existence as citizens of the twenty-first-century world, in my view, justifies all the more the search for common ground—including economic and political parity, and a sharing in the dignity of life—among disparate peoples of African heritage.

It is not accidental that, in an era marked by the postmodern deconstruction of essentialisms, identity politics, and the concomitant awareness of identity as socially constructed, the African Union declared that the African diaspora is a sixth region of Africa.[47] This gesture toward unification should signal new and more equally rewarding possibilities for solidarity and collaboration among theologians of African heritage today. The balancing act required to not "claim too much" yet not "claim too little" can only be achieved if we enter one another's narratives attentive to the idiosyncrasies and absurdities of the degrees of suffering that touch us all.

Notes

1. J. Deotis Roberts, "African Religion and Social Consciousness," in *Black Religion, Black Theology: The Collected Essays of J. Deotis Roberts*, ed. David Emmanuel Goatley (New York: Trinity Press International, 2003), 98. Originally published in *Journal of Religious Thought* 28 (Fall–Winter 1971): 95–111.
2. This essay examines the field of "African American" theology produced by African descendants in the United States of America whose experience of racial blackness is a foundational source of their collective identity. I often employ the term "US African American(s)" throughout the essay in order to distinguish this group from persons of African descent in other regions of the Americas, for example, Canada, Brazil, Columbia, Mexico, Belize, etc.
3. This essay addresses the body of scholarship produced by formally trained professional theologians. Since the principal task of this essay is to focus on the development of African American *theology*, it will not treat contributions from ethicists, historians, textualists, phenomenologists, and others trained in religious and theological studies broadly speaking. Also unaddressed are the works of important emergent theological scholars contributing to discussions of religious pluralism. By the time this essay is released, readers should be able to locate relevant book publications from Jawanza Clark and Adam Clark and article publications from Marcus Harvey and Shani Settles.
4. See especially J. Deotis Roberts, "Afro-Arab Islam and the Black Revolution," *Journal of Black Religious Thought* 28, no. 2 (Autumn–Winter 1971): 95–111, and "Africanisms and Spiritual Strivings," in Goatley, *Black Religion, Black Theology, 97, originally published in Journal of Religious Thought* 30 (Spring–Summer 1971): 16–27.
5. J. Deotis Roberts, "African Religion and Social Consciousness," in Goatley, *Black Religion, Black Theology, 97, originally published in Journal of Religious Thought* 28 (Fall–Winter 1971): 95–111.
6. Roberts, "African Religion and Social Consciousness," 113.
7. J. Deotis Roberts, "Traditional African Religion and Christian Theology," in Goatley, *Black Religion, Black Theology*. See especially 136, 142–44. Originally published in *Studia Africana* 1 (Fall 1979): 206–18.
8. Roberts, "Traditional African Religion and Christian Theology," 128.
9. In other words, I am arguing that Roberts attempted to undertake in the scholastic arena what practitioners of African-inspired diaspora religions have accomplished over the centuries in the arena of vernacular theological reasoning and religious practice. I employ the term "vernacular" to distinguish lived religion and popular beliefs from institutional religion and orthodox theologies. Joyce Flueckiger's notion of "vernacular Islam" has been most influential here. See her book *In Amma's Healing Room: Gender and Vernacular Islam in South India* (Bloomington: Indiana University Press, 2006).
10. Roberts uses this term to distinguish theologies of indigenous African religions from Christian African theologies. See J. Deotis Roberts, "An Afro-American Theological

Dialogue," in Goatley, *Black Religion, Black Theology*, 152. Originally published in *Toronto Journal of Theology* 2 (Fall 1986): 172–87.

11. Roberts, "Traditional African Religion and Christian Theology," 40.
12. Roberts, "Traditional African Religion and Christian Theology, 140–42.
13. Roberts, "Traditional African Religion and Christian Theology, 144.
14. Roberts, "Afro-American Theological Dialogue," 162.
15. Gayraud Wilmore, *Black Religion and Black Radicalism* (Garden City, NY: Doubleday, 1972), 298–300.
16. Roberts, "Afro-American Theological Dialogue," 163.
17. Josiah U. Young, *A Pan-African Theology: Providence and the Legacies of the Ancestors* (Trenton, NJ: Africa World Press, 1992), 113–14.
18. Young, *A Pan-African Theology*, 107. Also see the following essays by Charles Long: "Perspectives for a Study of African-American Religion in the United States," *History of Religions* 11 (August 1971): 54–66; "Oppressive Elements in Religion and Religions of the Oppressed," *Harvard Theological Review* 69, nos. 3–4 (1976): 397–412; "Freedom, Otherness and Religion: Theologies Opaque," *Chicago Theological Seminary Register* 73, no. 1 (Winter 1983): 13–24; "Assessment and New Departures for a Study of Black Religion in the United States of America," in *African American Religious Studies*, ed. Gayraud S. Wilmore (Durham, NC: Duke University Press, 1989), 34–49.
19. Young, *A Pan-African Theology*, 108.
20. Young, *A Pan-African Theology*, 152.
21. Young, *A Pan-African Theology*, 152–54.
22. Roberts expressed it this way: "Thus far few African scholars have done serious work in either the history of religion or comparative religion. This makes the work of black scholars such as Charles Long doubly important. We need to know that literalness and logic do not necessarily equal truth, that mythic and/or symbolic ways of thinking are up to date and that they touch life at a profound level of meaning. This understanding would unlock for us the context in [which] much of African traditional religious experience is expressed." See Roberts, "Traditional African Religion and Christian Theology," 136.
23. Young, *A Pan-African Theology*, 106.
24. Coleman specifically acknowledges the connection between his theological "tribal talk" and Roberts's quest for the faith of his fathers when he writes: "J. Deotis Roberts contends that black theology should develop its own metaphysics as distinct from a traditional, Eurocentric one. In other words, it should address questions of ultimate reality beyond historical understandings of oppression and liberation from a uniquely African American perspective. Such could be rooted, for example, in a West African cosmology and/or metaphysics instead of a Greek one. For Roberts the roots to an Afrocentric metaphysics could be found through the study of such materials as West African and African American folklore and African American sermons. I have taken this challenge seriously throughout this book." See Will Coleman, *Tribal Talk: Black Theology, Hermeneutics, and African/American Ways of "Telling the Story"* (University Park: Pennsylvania State University Press, 2000), 183–84.
25. Coleman, *Tribal Talk*, 12–13.
26. Coleman, *Tribal Talk*, 113.
27. Coleman, *Tribal Talk*, 162–63.
28. Coleman, *Tribal Talk*, 194.

29. Monica Coleman, *Making a Way Out of No Way: A Womanist Theology* (Minneapolis: Fortress Press, 2008), 12.
30. Coleman, *Making a Way*, 36.
31. Coleman, *Making a Way*, 147.
32. Dianne M. Stewart, *Three Eyes for the Journey: African Dimensions of the Jamaican Religious Experience* (New York: Oxford University Press, 2005), 128.
33. Stewart, *Three Eyes*, 158.
34. Stewart, *Three Eyes*, 241.
35. Anthony B. Pinn, "Anybody There? Reflections on African American Humanism," *Religious Humanism* 31, nos. 3–4 (Summer–Fall 1997): 63.
36. Pinn, "Anybody There?" 62.
37. In addition to sources cited in earlier sections of this essay, see, for example, James Cone and Gayraud Wilmore's article "Black Theology and African Theology: Considerations for Dialogue, Critique, and Integration," which was first published in 1972 and republished several times later, including in *Black Theology: A Documentary History, 1966–1979*, ed. Gayraud S. Wilmore and James H. Cone (Maryknoll, NY: Orbis Books, 1979), 463–91.
38. Readers can follow Pinn's developing argument for a humanist theology in his recent publication, *The End of God-Talk: An African American Humanist Theology* (New York: Oxford University Press, 2012).
39. This problem plagues much of academic discourse and certainly poses major challenges to classic black and womanist Christian liberation theologies. It becomes much more acute, however, for theologians reflecting on non-Christian traditions.
40. *Ebo* is a Yoruba term for ritual sacrifices and offerings to deities and ancestors. *Ebo* are often cooked and consumed by worshipping communities during great festivals and celebrations and are considered sacred nourishment partaken by those in the visible human and invisible Divine Community.
41. For a recent study of transnationalism in the formation of a neo-African Yoruba religious community, see Kamari Clarke, *Mapping Yoruba Networks: Power and Agency in the Making of Transnational Communities* (Durham, NC: Duke University Press, 2004).
42. Michelle Gonzales, *Afro-Cuban Theology* (Gainesville: University Press of Florida, 2006), 9.
43. Gonzales, *Afro-Cuban Theology*, 9–10.
44. JRoberts, "Afro-American Theological Dialogue," 164.
45. We must include in the dialogue blacks in Europe and others who broaden our understanding of Africana experiences. For example, see Anthony G. Reddie, *Dramatizing Theologies: A Participative Approach to Black God-Talk* (Sheffield, UK: Equinox Publishing, 2006); Robert Beckford, *Jesus Is Dread: Black Theology and Black Culture in Britain* (London: DLT Publishers, 1998); Beckford, *Dread and Pentecostal: A Political Theology for the Black Church in Britain* (London: SPCK, 2000); Beckford, *Jesus Dub: Theology, Music and Social Change* (New York: Routledge, 2006); and Delroy A. Reid-Salmon, *Home Away from Home: The Caribbean Diasporan Church in the Black Atlantic Tradition* (Sheffield, UK: Equinox Publishing, 2008), for leading examples of how black theology is being articulated in Britain. Also see Gary W. Trompf, *The Gospel Is Not Western: Black Theologies from the Southwest Pacific* (Maryknoll, NY: Orbis Books, 1986) for black theological perspectives from Pacific nations.
46. Though often referenced as an oppressive phenomenon, I understand globalization as a phenomenon with the capacity to operationalize oppressive and asymmetrical as well as

symmetrical and liberating structures of encounter and exchange among diverse global cultures, polities, and economies. I agree, for example, with Forte's claim: "Globalization itself can no longer be seen as merely Western expansionism and Western cultural homogenization—it contains multiple currents of counter-Westernization and is the framework for many cultural revitalizations whereby diasporas are now more solidly structured and integrated, homelands' revivals are felt globally, local revivals structured globally, where the ethos of community can now be understood as an international phenomenon." See his *Against the Trinity: An Insurgent Imam Tells His Story* (Binghamton, NY: Polaris–Australis Publishing, 1996), 271.

47. The declaration was preceded by important and sometimes contentious discussions about the various African diaspora communities now living outside Africa, including descendants of enslaved Africans in the West and more recent waves of African immigrants now residing in Western countries. The official inclusion of the African diaspora as a sixth African region with the right to participate in the African Union's agenda took place in 2006. See the official website of the African Union at http://www.au.int/en/.

Selected Texts

Abimbola, Kola. *Yoruba Culture: A Philosophical Account*. Birmingham, UK: IAP Publishers, 2006.

Anderson, Victor. *Beyond Ontological Blackness: African American Religious and Cultural Criticism*. New York: Continuum, 1995.

Beckford, Robert. *Dread and Pentecostal: A Political Theology for the Black Church in Britain*. London: SPCK, 2000.

Beckford, Robert. *Jesus Dub: Theology, Music and Social Change*. New York: Routledge, 2006.

Beckford, Robert. *Jesus Is Dread: Black Theology and Black Culture in Britain*. London: DLT Publishers, 1998.

Clark, Adam. L. "Honoring the Ancestors: Toward an Afrocentric Approach to Christian Theology." Ph.D. diss., Union Theological Seminary, 2007.

Clark, Jawanza. "The Dead Are Not Dead: A Constructive, African-Centered Theological Anthropology." Ph.D. diss., Emory University, 2008.

Clark, Jawanza. "Reconceiving the Doctrine of Jesus as Savior in Terms of the African Understanding of an Ancestor: A Model for the Black Church." *Black Theology* 8, no. 2 (August 2010): 140–59.

Clarke, Kamari. *Mapping Yoruba Networks: Power and Agency in the Making of Transnational Communities*. Durham, NC: Duke University Press, 2004.

Coleman, Monica. *Making a Way out of No Way: A Womanist Theology*. Minneapolis: Fortress Press, 2008.

Coleman, Will. *Tribal Talk: Black Theology, Hermeneutics, and African/American Ways of "Telling the Story."* University Park: Pennsylvania State University Press, 2000.

Cone, James H., and Gayraud S. Wilmore. "Black Theology and African Theology: Considerations for Dialogue, Critique, and Integration." In *Black Theology: A Documentary History, 1966–1979*, ed. Gayraud Wilmore and James Cone, 463–91 Maryknoll, NY: Orbis Books, 1979.

Curry, Mary Cuthrell. *Making the Gods in New York: The Yoruba Religion in the African American Community*. New York: Routledge, 1997.

Du Bois, W. E. B. *The Souls of Black Folk*. Greenwich, CT: Fawcett Premier Book, 1968.

Duncan, Carol. *This Spot of Ground: Spiritual Baptists in Toronto*. Waterloo, ON: Wilfred Laurier Press, 2008.

Faraji, Salim. "Walking Back to Go Forward." In *Black Religion After the Million Man March*, ed. Garth Baker-Fletcher. Maryknoll, NY: Orbis Books, 1998, 68–78.

Forte, Maximillian. *Against the Trinity: An Insurgent Imam Tells His Story*. Binghamton, NY: Australis, 1996.

Gonzales, Michelle. *Afro-Cuban Theology: Religion, Race, Culture and Identity*. Gainesville: University Press of Florida, 2006.

Hardy, Clarence. *Baldwin's God: Sex, Hope, and the Crisis in Black Holiness Culture*. Knoxville: University of Tennessee Press, 2003.

Harris, Melanie. *Gifts of Virtue: Alice Walker and Womanist Ethics*. New York: Palgrave Macmillan, 2010.

Harris, Melanie. "Womanist Humanism: A Deeper Look." *Cross Currents* 57, no. 3 (Fall 2007): 391–403.

Harris, Melanie. "Womanist Humanism: A New Hermeneutic." In *Deeper Shades of Purple: Womanism in Religion and Society*, ed. Stacey Floyd-Thomas, 211–25. New York: New York University Press, 2006.

Harvey, Marcus. "Engaging the Orisa: An Exploration of the Yoruba Concepts of Ibeji and Olokun as Theoretical Principles in Black Theology." *Black Theology* 6, no. 1 (January 2008): 61–82.

Hucks, Tracey. *Approaching the African God: Yoruba Traditions and African American Religious Nationalism*. Albuquerque: University of New Mexico Press, 2013.

Hucks, Tracey. "'Burning with a Flame in America': African American Women in African-Derived Traditions." *Journal of Feminist Studies in Religion* 17, no. 2 (Fall 2001): 89–106.

Hucks, Tracey. "From Cuban Santería to African Yoruba: Evolutions in African American Orisha History, 1959–1970." In *Orisa Devotion as World Religion: The Globalization of Yoruba Religious Culture*, ed. Jacob Olupona and Terry Rey, 337–54. Madison: University of Wisconsin Press, 2008.

Hucks, Tracey. "I Smoothed the Way, I Opened Doors: Women in the Yoruba-Orisha Tradition of Trinidad." In *Women and Religion in the African Diaspora*, ed. Ruth Marie Griffith and Barbara Savage, 19–36. Baltimore: Johns Hopkins University Press, 2009.

Johnson, Sylvester. "Religion Proper and Proper Religion: Arthur Fauset and the Study of African American Religions." In *The New Black Gods: Arthur Huff Fauset and the Study of African American Religions*, ed. Edward Curtis, 145–70. Bloomington: Indiana University Press, 2009.

Johnson, Sylvester. "The Rise of Black Ethnics: The Ethnic Turn in African American Religions, 1916–1945." *Religion and American Culture: A Journal of Interpretation* 20, no. 2 (Summer 2010): 125–63.

Long, Charles. "Assessment and New Departures for a Study of Black Religion in the United States of America." In *African American Religious Studies*, ed. Gayraud Wilmore, 34–49. Durham, NC: Duke University Press, 1989.

Long, Charles. "Freedom, Otherness and Religion: Theologies Opaque." *Chicago Theological Seminary Register* 73, no. 1 (Winter 1983): 13–24.

Long, Charles. "Oppressive Elements in Religion and Religions of the Oppressed." *Harvard Theological Review* 69, nos. 3–4 (1976): 397–412.

Long, Charles. "Perspectives for a Study of African-American Religion in the United States." *History of Religions* 11 (August 1971): 54–66.

Love, Velma. "Casting the Sacred Reading of the Self: Material Culture and Storied Environment of Ifa Divination and the Holy Odu." *Postscripts* 4, no. 2 (2008): 217–31.

Majeed, Debra. "Clara Evans Muhammad: Pioneering Social Activism in the Original Nation of Islam." *Union Seminary Quarterly Review* 57, nos. 3–4 (2003): 217–29.

Majeed, Debra. *Encounters of Intimate Sisterhood? Polygyny in the World of African American Muslims*. Gainesville: University Press of Florida, forthcoming.

Majeed, Debra. "Womanism Encounters Islam: A Muslim Scholar Considers the Efficacy of a Method Rooted in the Academy and the Church." In *Deeper Shades of Purple: Womanism in Religion and Society*, ed. Stacey Floyd-Thomas, 38–53. New York: New York University Press, 2006.

Mitchem, Stephanie. *Faith, Health, and Healing in African American Life*. Westport, CT: Praeger, 2008.

Mitchem, Stephanie. *African American Folk Healing*. New York: New York University Press, 2007.

Mitchem, Stephanie. *African American Women Tapping Power and Spiritual Wellness*. Cleveland, OH: Pilgrim Press, 2004.

Mulrain, George. *Theology in Folk Culture: The Theological Significance of Haitian Folk Religion*. Frankfurt am Main: Peter Lang, 1984.

Noel, James. *Black Religion and the Imagination of Matter*. New York: Palgrave Macmillan, 2009.

Paris, Peter. *The Spirituality of African Peoples: The Search for a Common Moral Discourse*. Minneapolis: Fortress Press, 1995.

Pinn, Anthony B. *The End of God-Talk: An African American Humanist Theology*. New York: Oxford University Press, 2012.

Pinn, Anthony B. "Anybody There? Reflections on African American Humanism." *Religious Humanism* 31, nos. 3–4 (Summer–Fall 1997): 61–78.

Pinn, Anthony B. *Why Lord? Suffering and Evil in Black Theology*. New York: Continuum, 1995.

Reddie, Anthony G. *Dramatizing Theologies: A Participative Approach to Black God-Talk*. Sheffield, UK: Equinox, 2006.

Reid-Salmon, Delroy A. *Home Away from Home: The Caribbean Diasporan Church in the Black Atlantic Tradition*. Sheffield, UK: Equinox, 2008.

Roberts, J. Deotis. *Black Religion, Black Theology: The Collected Essays of J. Deotis Roberts*. Ed. Emmanuel Goatley. New York: Trinity Press International, 2003.

Roberts, J. Deotis. "Afro-Arab Islam and the Black Revolution." *Journal of Black Religious Thought* 28, no. 2 (Autumn–Winter 1971): 95–111.

Settles, Shani. "The Sweet Fire of Honey: Womanist Visions of Osun as a Methodology of Emancipation." In *Deeper Shades of Purple: Womanism in Religion and Society*, ed. Stacey Floyd-Thomas, 191–206. New York: New York University Press, 2006.

Stewart, Dianne M. "Orisha Traditions in the West." In *The Hope of Liberation in World Religions*, ed. Miguel De La Torre, 239–56. Waco, TX: Baylor University Press, 2008.

Stewart, Dianne M. *Three Eyes for the Journey: African Dimensions of the Jamaican Religious Experience*. New York: Oxford University Press, 2005.

Thomas, Linda. *Under the Canopy: and Ritual Process and Spiritual Resilience in South Africa*. Columbia: University of South Carolina Press, 1999.

Trompf, Gary W. *The Gospel Is Not Western: Black Theologies from the Southwest Pacific*. Maryknoll, NY: Orbis Books, 1986.

Vega, Marta. *The Altar of My Soul: The Living Traditions of Santería*. New York: One World / Ballantine Books, 2001.

Wilmore, Gayraud S. *Black Religion and Black Radicalism*. Garden City, NY: Doubleday, 1972.

Young, Josiah. *Dogged Strength within the Veil: Africana Spirituality and the Mysterious Love of God*. New York: Trinity Press International, 2003.

Young, Josiah. *A Pan-African Theology: Providence and the Legacies of the Ancestors* Trenton, NJ: Africa World Press, 1992.

CHAPTER 25

SEXUALITY IN AFRICAN AMERICAN THEOLOGY

HORACE GRIFFIN

> Sexuality is that dimension of humanity that urges relationship. Sexuality is a gift from God that, if properly appreciated, helps women and men to become more fully human by entering into loving relationships.... A sexual discourse of resistance signals that it is time for change. It demands a transformation in the way the Black Church community, especially its leaders, has conducted itself in terms of women and gay and lesbian persons.
>
> —Kelly Brown Douglas

In 1999, womanist theologian Kelly Brown Douglas offered a major contribution to the sacred canon of black theology by publishing her groundbreaking *Sexuality and the Black Church.* In the above statement, she put into words what many black Christians think about sexuality in the academy and black church but dare not say for fear of reprisal or a dismissal of their work and worth from fellow black colleagues and church folks. In terms of black theology and sexuality, a few black theologians give passing references to the issue, but still fewer write articles or book chapters on the subject (Douglas's *Sexuality and the Black Church* remains one of few African American theology books on the subject).

It is a striking phenomenon that African American theologians are so reticent about sexuality and the construction of a sexual theology, much more so than their white counterparts, James Nelson, Carter Heyward, and Robert Goss, to name a few. It is easy to conclude that such reticence about sexual discourse in black theology stems from black theology's primary task in tackling racist US structures that adversely affect black people. Or one might conclude that—despite the frequent sexual comments, references, and sermons in black churches—sexual expressions outside of a heterosexual marriage are considered taboo. Since many black theologians are products of black churches, remain active within those churches, and write for and teach black people in those churches, these theologians resist offering the much-needed critique of the gender and sexual proscriptions given by black pastors to black people for fear of losing support. Thus, expansive work on African American theology and sexuality has yet to be realized.

The dawn of academic responses to Negro religion and black Christianity included few black religious voices. In the mid-twentieth century, Howard Thurman and Benjamin Elijah Mays wrote about black religion and the evils of segregation facing black people during this time. C. Eric Lincoln wrote decades later about the historical significance of the black church and its moral teachings to black people. The black church eventually rose in the 1960s as a force opposing the racist evils of this period. Drawing from the race consciousness of the 1960s civil rights movement, "The idea of 'black theology' emerged when a small group of radical black clergy began to reinterpret the meaning of Christian faith from the standpoint of the black struggle for liberation in the United States during the second half of the 1960's."[1] In July 1966, the National Committee of Negro Churchmen crafted what became known as the "Black Power Statement" for the church. It stated,

> All people need power, whether black or white. We regard it as sheer hypocrisy or as a blind and dangerous illusion that opposes love to power. Love must be the controlling element in power, not power itself. So long as white churchmen continue to moralize and misinterpret Christian love, so long will justice continue to be subverted in this land.[2]

Inspired by this new liberating voice in the black church and the Afrocentric theology of Albert Cleage (Shrine of the Black Madonna, 1967), in 1969, the Reverend Dr. James Cone, Charles A. Briggs Professor of Systematic Theology, Union Theological Seminary, introduced black liberation theology in his *Black Theology and Black Power* followed the next year by *A Black Theology of Liberation*.[3] As its progenitor, Cone asserted "black liberation theology must take seriously the reality of black people—their life of suffering and humiliation."[4]

Throughout the 1970s, Cone and other black male theologians, for example, Gayraud Wilmore, Joseph Washington, and J. Deotis Roberts, addressed the social and ecclesial racism encountered by black people and challenged white religious and political leaders to participate in dismantling the evil structures of racism. While Cone's writing asserts that black theology must address black suffering, he identifies racism and the common byproduct of poverty as *the* cause of black suffering and only considers black suffering in the context of white racism. African American theology remained so focused until the 1980s.

In 1979, the Reverend Dr. Jacqueline Grant (*White Woman's Christ, Black Woman's Jesus*), Callaway Professor of Systematic Theology at the Interdenominational Theological Center (ITC) in Atlanta, raised questions as to how far black liberation theology went in terms of the pain and suffering of black women in churches and beyond. Although appreciative of Cone's compelling challenge of white racist structures in the church and society, she calls Cone—and other black churchmen—to task for not putting forth the same liberation ethic of equality and justice for African American women in the black churches that they demanded of white people for themselves. In her piece "Black Theology and the Black Woman," Grant exposes the sexism of black male church leaders and the need for black theology to critique itself within black circles, arguing "if the black church does not share in the liberation struggle of black women, its liberation struggle is not authentic."[5]

Other African American women theologians and ethicists, who framed early womanist theology and ethics, such as Katie Cannon (*Black Womanist Ethics*), Delores Williams (*Sisters in the Wilderness*), Kelly Brown Douglas (*Sexuality and the Black Church: A Womanist Perspective*), and Linda Thomas (*Living Stones in the Household of God: The Legacy and Future of Black Theology*), quickly joined Grant's voice in pointing out the striking irony of Cone's grand claims about racial injustice while remaining silent about similar offenses committed by black male clergy and church leaders against black church women.

Cone later expressed regret for not taking sexism more seriously and "confessed what must have already been clear to many African American women: sexism was not a part of [his] theological consciousness when he began writing black theology and that he rejected women's liberation as a 'joke,' 'an intrusion' and a 'white trick' to distract from the injustice being committed by whites against blacks."[6] It is also worth pointing out that despite Cone's eventual acknowledgment of oppressive sexist structures, he initially resisted conversion to this perspective from the challenge raised by black women. In *Christianity on Trial: African American Religious Thought before and after Black Power*, Mark Chapman, a former student of Cone, notes that "when Cone did become fully aware of the evil of sexism in 1975, it was not the result of his sensitivity to the plight of African American women, but rather in the context of responding to Korean Christian women who objected to their subordination in the church."[7]

Despite Cone's confession of his shortcomings about gender oppression and Grant's and other womanists' efforts to be heard throughout this period of the 1980s, they all remained virtually silent about sexuality, especially regarding black homophobia and the acute oppression encountered by African American lesbians and gays. It was ironic, noted Episcopal priest and womanist theologian the Reverend Dr. Renee Hill, that womanist theologians remained silent about lesbian and gay oppression (and in the case of Cheryl Sanders, opposing black lesbian and gay equality and liberation) while appropriating the term "womanist" coined by the nonheterosexual Alice Walker (*In Search of Our Mothers' Gardens: Womanist Prose*). Hill, also a product of the black liberation theology mecca Union Theological Seminary, challenged her womanist sisters in her 1993 essay "Who Are We for Each Other? Sexism, Sexuality and Womanist Theology" in James Cone and Gayraud Wilmore's *Black Theology: A Documentary History*, volume 2.[8] In this piece, Hill asserts that

> the lesbian voice is silenced in Christian womanist theology. Heterosexism and homophobia are nonissues in the Christian womanist paradigm for liberation. There is no widespread discussion of sexuality in African-American Christian theology in general. Christian womanists, like their male counterparts, focus for the most part on the impact of racism on the Black community. The Christian womanist focus on gender is to a great degree a focus on the retrieval of Black women's stories, words and perspectives. There is no great emphasis on the impact of sexism on the black community. This may be a key to the lack of discourse on sexuality.[9]

As Grant challenged Cone nearly a decade earlier, Hill compelled black and womanist liberationist scholars to engage in the reckoning of yet another oppressive practice within black religious and social communities: Homophobia.

In her appeal to liberation theology, Hill argues that "womanists have failed to recognize heterosexism and homophobia as points of oppression that need to be resisted if *all* Black women (straight, lesbian and bisexual) are to have liberation and a sense of their own power."[10] Hill's writing proved effective. Womanist scholars admitted that they had been far too silent on issues related to sexuality, homosexuality, and gay justice. Womanist ethicist Emile Townes emerged as one of the first voices responding to Hill's challenge, and like Hill "has also been vocal about the need to address matters of sexuality."[11] Womanist theologian Karen Baker-Fletcher recognizes that black cultural responses—especially as they relate to black churches—stymied even the more liberal womanist thinkers from "confront[ing] the potentially divisive issue of homosexuality." She says, "I sometimes wonder why womanists, myself included, are not more forthright about this particular subject. I suspect that for many it is for the same reason that many gays and lesbians hesitate to come out of the closet: fear of losing a job, of being thrown out of Church, ostracized in community."[12]

Reminding them of Walker's definition of womanism and what they represent, Hill commented that a "womanist is a woman who loves other women, sexually and/or nonsexually. Appreciates and prefers women's culture, women's emotional flexibility (values tears as a natural counterbalance of laughter)... women's strength... includes the lesbian voice, [and] the voice of black women in relationship with each other."[13] Other womanists also demonstrated that they understood Hill's frustration, and several committed themselves to the work of liberation in all its forms.

This commitment did not come, however, without challenges within its ranks. The Reverend Dr. Cheryl Sanders, professor of Christian Ethics at Howard Divinity School and Church of God pastor, had been a part of the womanist roundtable prior to Hill's challenge and expressed her discomfort with the homosexual component of Walker's term, identifying such inclusion as necessarily inconsistent with Christian theology and black family values. In this respect, Sanders argued, womanist nomenclature is derived from a secular enterprise without reflecting "God or revelation" apparently found in scripture.[14]

In Sanders view, "There is a fundamental discrepancy between the womanist criteria that would affirm and/or advocate homosexual practice, and the ethical norms the black church might employ to promote the survival and wholeness of black families."[15] She further argues that a womanist perspective in this regard is at odds with Christianity and, if such a position is supported, "conveys a sexual ethics that is ambivalent at best with respect to the value of heterosexual monogamy within the black community."[16] And while Sanders is correct that Walker does not provide a systematic theology of God's "relation to the plight of the oppressed, as blacks and/or women," in her advocacy for an exclusive heterosexual paradigm in black communities Sanders surrenders black lesbians and gays, their relationships and children to further discrimination, inequality, ridicule, and other forms of injustice at the hands of heterosexual supremacists in black churches and communities.[17]

Throughout her work, Sanders does not offer any support for her claim that lesbians and gays threaten the survival or wholeness of black families. Since Walker neither advocates for all women to be lesbian nor demeans heterosexual women, it remains unclear as to why Sanders does not support the womanist concept and a black church liberation that affirms and celebrates lesbian/gay members and their love relationships as well as heterosexual ones. Sanders's response rang hollow, however, in the circles of black and womanist liberation quite familiar with the Bible and Christian theology and tradition having been used as support for their own racial and gender oppression. They found this perspective antithetical to their work and a gospel of liberation. Ironically, Sanders's own pastoral role is a violation of the very moral teachings and black church tradition that she upholds regarding lesbian and gay Christians and gay members of black communities. Sanders's cry notwithstanding, the response of womanists to consider lesbian and gay issues and encourage the larger body of black liberation theology to do likewise, along with women's issues, provided an opportunity for black theologians to participate in a constructive theology of sexuality.

In his 1996 *Xodus: An African American Male Journey*, African American ethicist Garth Baker-Fletcher expresses an evolving perspective on sexuality and homosexuality. Although Baker-Fletcher brings a liberative voice regarding gender and rightfully challenges sexist structures, he, nonetheless, is not as clear in making a claim regarding gay equality. On the one hand, he is moved by Hill's voice and argues that "we must listen to *all* the sisters, including lesbians," while on the other hand, as a Jamaican American, "raised in a traditional community, [he] admit[s] that [he has] struggled at times with ways in which we can affirm homosexuals and yet be obedient to the biblical injunctions concerning homosexuality."[18] As a heterosexual, Baker-Fletcher moves the conversation from black liberation silence and typical black church condemnation to a place where black heterosexuals must confront the injustice they impose on black lesbians and gays. Baker-Fletcher states that "both condemnation and avoidance fail to listen to the pain, the promise, and the hopes of flesh-and-blood lesbians and gay men."[19]

As Baker-Fletcher and other authors addressed particular issues related to sexuality, the need for a constructive black theological response to sexuality became apparent. It is precisely this recognition that prompted one of those black theologians to write a book on sexuality, long avoided by her cohorts in the field. As mentioned earlier, in 1999, the Reverend Dr. Kelly Brown Douglas, an Episcopal priest and then associate professor of theology at Howard University Divinity School, published the much-needed work on black sexuality and religion, *Sexuality and the Black Church.*

This comprehensive study of black theology and sexuality, thirty years after Cone's introduction to black theology, finally provided a thoughtful, critical analysis for the many conversations that had emerged in the last few decades about sexuality in general and black sexuality in particular. More importantly, it provided an alternative to the moralistic and unhelpful responses about sexuality that had long dominated black churches. For the many black Christian scholars and others who did not share such shortsighted views, this work received much praise. Perhaps Princeton scholar and Christian ethicist Peter Paris summarized it best: "This book is one of the most important works by an African American theologian in the past decade.... One wonders why we have waited so long for such a helpful treatise on this crucial subject."

Paris's query is a good one. Although the fear of and resistance to this topic were noted earlier, it is worth exploring why the resistance seems especially strong among African Americans. In a postsexual revolution United States, this reality might appear strange until one examines black culture—especially black religion and the church. In a description of Douglas's book by the publisher, Orbis Books, there is recognition of black culture's peculiar response about sexuality:

> This book tackles the "taboo" subject of sexuality that has long been avoided by the Black church and community. Douglas argues that this view of Black sexuality has interfered with constructive responses to the AIDS crisis and teenage pregnancies, fostered intolerance of sexual diversity, frustrated healthy male/female relationships, and rendered Black and womanist theologians silent on sexual issues.

In this context, African American scholars often do not see the issue as paramount and central to the lives of black people. Even Douglas expressed surprise in the fact that she would be leading the charge in addressing sexuality and black theology. At the time of its publication, she said, "If someone had told me five years ago that I would be writing a book on Black Sexuality, I would have replied, you're crazy." She further states, "At that time in my theological journey I simply had not given any thought to such a topic."[20]

Douglas does a masterful job in explaining why sexuality continues to be such a difficult topic for black people. In this work, she explains that it is not only the sex-negative Christian tradition, laden with puritanical mores, imposed on black people, but the racist attacks on black sexuality and black bodies internalized by them. Black people carry a history of sexual violence directed toward them largely by the many white men who saw no contradiction in violating the bodies and minds of black women, in keeping black mistresses and in patronizing black-run houses of prostitution.... Black men were regarded, like their female counterparts as highly sexualized, passionate beings. They were considered lewd, lascivious, and also quite sexually proficient."[21] In this portrayal of black women and men, white males sought justification in their rape of wanton black women, and both white men and women experienced a warped sense of justice in lynching black men "for protection against such a passionate animal" and maintaining a respectable reputation, respectively.[22]

Douglas argues that sexual discourse in the context of black liberation theology can begin the unraveling of the psychic pain harbored by all black people, heterosexual and nonheterosexual, alike. She asserts that this study and dialogue will not only begin the much-needed healing for black people but can identify the ways that black people participate unwittingly in forms of oppression often created by larger oppressive structures. She especially challenges black churches to address the sexism and homophobia in the black church and black community and laments the recent failings of the black religious summit on sexuality to "address the interrelationship between the exploitation of Black sexuality and racist, sexist, classist and heterosexist structures of oppression."[23] Like Hill, Douglas is especially strong in challenging African Americans to move beyond a homophobic disposition. She invites black people to be mindful of how they use the Bible by stating that if they "find themselves utilizing the Bible in a way that terrorizes other human beings, then they should disavow such usage."[24]

Douglas is not the only black theologian raising sexuality issues for the field of black liberation theology. Although he has not written a book on sexuality, the Reverend Dr. Dwight Hopkins, theology professor at the University of Chicago Divinity School, has perhaps devoted more attention to the issue of sexuality, especially homosexuality, than his other heterosexual colleagues. His writing offers promise and may be indicative of the future of black liberation theology. In addition to viewing womanist issues as central to black liberation theology (see *Introducing Black Theology of Liberation*), in *Heart and Head: Black Theology Past, Present and Future* Hopkins continues a liberal, inclusive approach to sexuality and repudiates the pervasive homophobia in black settings:

> One of the greatest points of unity that black heterosexuals have is their agreement to oppress and discriminate against black lesbians and gays in the church, family and larger society. Although black heterosexuals suffer from class exploitation...racial oppression relative to whites, and male supremacy especially for women, one of the few negative things heterosexuals can hold onto as a group is to oppress lesbians and gays. The tragedy of African Americans heterosexuals is that they continue a system of oppression using some of the same arguments that whites have used against blacks and men have used against women.[25]

Hopkins and Douglas understand that it will take a more progressive theological approach for black people in order for them to make progress, not only on homosexuality but sexuality in general. In 2004, Hopkins joined Dr. Anthony Pinn (*Why Lord? Suffering and Evil in Black Theology*) in editing *Loving the Body: Black Religious*

Studies and the Erotic. Here they provide a valuable contribution to progressive black sexuality in the context of black religious studies and faith communities.

As black liberation theology moves toward its fiftieth year, it has remained self-critical enough to include those black voices that have experienced more oppression than racism. In its consideration of how it moves forward, black liberation theology brings to bear such voices in an effort to create a true liberation theology for black people. Addressing the very issue of the future of black liberation theology, Linda Thomas and Dwight Hopkins organized and led the 2005 conference "Black Theology and Womanist Theology in Dialogue: Which Way Forward for the Church and Academy?" This meeting of leading African American theologians and clergy engaged all of the above issues, especially offering progressive approaches for the future of African American theology and sexuality. This gathering, like the gathering in 1966 of radical clergy, proves—as much as anything—black liberation theology's efforts to remain relevant in the lives of African American people and others.

Notes

1. James H. Cone, *For My People: Black Theology and the Black Church* (Maryknoll, NY: Orbis Books, 1984), 5.
2. Cone, *For My People*, 5.
3. M. Chapman, *Christianity on Trial: African-American Religious Thought before and after Black Power* (Maryknoll, NY: Orbis Books, 1996), 111.
4. James H. Cone, *Black Theology and Black Power* (New York: Seabury Press, 1969), 137–38.
5. James H. Cone and Gayraud S. Wilmore, *Black Theology: A Documentary History, vol. 1, 1966–1979* (Maryknoll, NY: Orbis Books, 1979), 423.
6. Chapman, *Christianity on Trial*, 147–48.
7. Chapman, *Christianity on Trial*, 148.
8. In the second volume of *Black Theology: A Documentary History*, Cone expresses an understanding for a more expansive black liberation theology addressing sexism, to be sure, but also the rampant oppression encountered by black lesbians, gays, bisexual, and transgendered persons in particular. As part of expanding black liberation theology, he includes the writings of Hill and the compelling work of black bisexual Elias Farajaje-Jones ("Breaking Silence: Toward an In-the-Life Theology"). Cone is unequivocal in his stand that "black theology and the Black Church . . . must also come out of the closet and take a stand with human beings who are struggling for liberation." See James H. Cone and Gayraud S. Wilmore *Black Theology: A Documentary History, vol. 2, 1980–1992* (Maryknoll, NY: Orbis Books, 1993), 3.
9. Cone and Wilmore, *Black Thelogy, 1980–1992*, 346.
10. Renee. Hill, "Who Are We for Each Other? Sexism, Sexuality and Womanist Theology," in Cone and Wilmore, *Black Theology, 1980–1992*, 346.
11. Douglas, *Sexuality*, 4.
12. Douglas, *Sexuality*, 5.
13. Cone and Wilmore, *Black Theology, 1980–1992*, 346.
14. Cone and Wilmore, *Black Theology, 1980–1992*, 339; Douglas, *Sexuality*, 101.

15. Sanders, "Christian Ethics and Theology in Womanist Perspective," in Cone and Wilmore, *Black Theology, 1980–1992*, 342.
16. Sanders, "Christian Ethics and Theology," 342.
17. Womanist theologians Linda Thomas and Emilie Townes recognize that the ethnographic approach to black women's stories, including the stories of the many black Christian churchwomen and other religious women, reveal God's presence in their lives and a theology from their experiences. In her *A Troubling in My Soul: Womanist Perspectives on Evil and Suffering*, Townes identifies "the anchor for womanist thought [as] the African American church and its people." See Emilie M. Townes, *A Troubling in My Soul: Womanist Perspectives on Evil and Suffering* (Maryknoll, NY: Orbis Books, 1993), 2.
18. Garth Baker-Fletcher. *Xodus: An African American Male Journey* (Minneapolis: ortress Press, 1996), 35.
19. Baker-Fletcher, *Xodus*, 36.
20. Douglas, *Sexuality*, 1.
21. Douglas, *Sexuality*, 39, 45.
22. Douglas, *Sexuality*, 48.
23. Douglas, *Sexuality*, 141.
24. Douglas, *Sexuality*, 96.
25. Dwight Hopkins, *Heart and Head: Black Theology Past, Present and Future* (New York: Palgrave, 2002), 187. As a gay African American pastoral theologian, I have offered a similar challenge for black liberation theology to advocate for gay equality in the chapter "Toward a True Black Liberation Theology for Pastoral Caregivers," in my book *Their Own Receive Them Not: African American Lesbians and Gays in Black Churches* (Cleveland, OH: Pilgrim Press, 2006).

Selected Texts

Baker-Fletcher, Garth. *Xodus: An African American Male Journey*. Minneapolis: Fortress Press, 1996.

Chapman, M. *Christianity on Trial: African-American Religious Thought before and after Black Power*. Maryknoll, NY: Orbis Books, 1996.

Cone, James H., and Gayraud Wilmore. *Black Theology: A Documentary History. Volume 2: 1980–1992*. Maryknoll, NY: Orbis Books, 1993.

Cone, James H. *For My People: Black Theology and the Black Church*. Maryknoll, NY: Orbis Books, 1984.

Cone, James H., and Gayraud Wilmore. *Black Theology: A Documentary History. Volume 1: 1966–1979*. Maryknoll, NY: Orbis Books, 1979.

Cone, James H. *Black Theology and Black Power*. New York: Seabury Press, 1969.

Douglas, Kelly Brown. *Sexuality and the Black Church*. Maryknoll, NY: Orbis Books, 1999.

Hill, Renee. "Who Are We for Each Other? Sexism, Sexuality and Womanist Theology." In *Black Theology: A Documentary History*, volume 2: *1980–1992*, ed. Jame H. Cone and Gayraud Wilmore, 345–51. Maryknoll, NY: Orbis Books, 1993.

Hopkins, Dwight. *Heart and Head: Black Theology Past, Present and Future*. New York: Palgrave, 2002.

Townes, Emilie M. *A Troubling in My Soul: Womanist Perspectives on Evil and Suffering*. Maryknoll, NY: Orbis Books, 1993.

SECTION IV

ONGOING CHALLENGES

CHAPTER 26

THE PROBLEM OF HISTORY IN AFRICAN AMERICAN THEOLOGY

LEWIS R. GORDON

In this essay, I will examine the ways in which African American history is understood and framed in terms of the development of African American religious identities within the context of the US nation-state. A difficulty of achieving this task, however, is that history, African Americans, and the US nation-state are all modern developments, and religious identities—indeed, religion itself—while correctly applied to the context of these modern convergences are also at times done so through a fallacious retroactive ascription to past groups from which these modern ones are formed. Moreover, the expression "US nation-state" is one to which "nation-state" worked best during a period of a presumed racial integrity of the nation. Without that notion, the United States is properly a post-nation-state, by which is meant a state not premised on a single ethnic or racial nationality. A US citizen or resident could, in other words, be anybody. This discussion will therefore proceed through interrogating each layer before offering a discussion of their synthesis.

History

One of the conundrums of history is that the concept itself is historical. There is, in other words, a "history of history," so to speak, and that involves realizing that people did not always think in such terms about the past. As antiquated time was often cyclical, this meant a greater tendency across human communities to imagine frameworks of eternal returns instead of linear movements or radical breaks.[1] The shift required, first, the move to eschatological conceptions of time, where people such as the ancient Israelites thought in terms of a completion of divine tasks. This model was not, however, premised on a principle of rational order but instead an ethical demand. Its fusion with the Greek concept of logos or rational principle created a shift to an *explanation* of unfolding events. In the thought of St. Augustine, this consideration posed the problem of the relationship of reason to faith, and much of medieval thought addressed this challenge with another fusion—namely, the fusion of *theos* and *logos* into theology.[2]

The fusion of reason and faith raised the question, as well, of the relationship of the natural to the miraculous. This concern led to at least two areas of medieval investigation: (1) theonaturalism and (2) theodicy. The first involves the question of the status of that which deviates, in monotheism, from the omnipotent Deity. The natural, in other words, was simply that which is divinely created. It is also the definition of the miraculous. The unnatural, by contrast, is that which deviates from divine creation. As theonaturalism is also normative, such deviation was also a mark of immorality and evil. Thus, as in Dante's *Inferno*, the center of hell, where the incarnation of evil stood frozen with hatred, was cold and the farthest point from the radiance of all holy. The theodicean problem emerged from the omnipotence, omniscience, and goodness of the Deity. How, with such reach, could deviation be possible? Would not such a Deity be responsible for all events? If so, would not the responsibility for evil also rest on such a being?[3]

The theodicean question required an interpretation of past events in a way that questioned future actions. Resolutions to the challenge of theodicy often took at least two forms: (1) demonstrating that the Deity's will exceeded human finitude and comprehension, which, in effect, amounted to saying that perhaps evil and injustice doesn't ultimately exist or at least simply appear to be features of the world or (2) showing that the benevolence of such a being requires human freedom, which, if properly understood, requires human responsibility for human actions. The first eliminates deviation; the second permits deviation. The second also raises the question of the human capacity to initiate that which stands outside of the actions of the Deity but that which, as sanctioned by such a Deity's commitment to human freedom, is compatible with its or his will paradoxically even when incompatible with the laws of that will.[4] The great German scholar Hans Blumenberg considered this development the birth of modern history and the modern age. It requires a story of the past in which the genuinely new came into birth and a conception of the future governed by the possibilities of human agency.[5]

Religion and History

Religion emerged in antiquity, whereas theology was a feature of medieval thought. The former was more properly a concept from ancient Roman society, where the empire permitted allegiance to a variety of gods and practices in its territories so long as there was adherence to the Roman legal system, especially regarding taxation. The term *religion* referred, at least in its etymological links to *religere* and *religare*, to practices in which, especially through ritual and text, one becomes bound. This binding took sacred form. It should be borne in mind that not all of the Roman colonies regarded their practices under such a rubric. The people of Judah, for example, regarded themselves as a people living under their set of laws and practices of sacrifice. Thus, in the famous challenge posed to Jesus of following the laws of Cesar (Rome) or G-d/Torah (Judah) through the payment of taxes, the subtext is also one of binding, which was an imposition onto the Judean people. The response of paying Cesar his taxes and offering in the Temple of Jerusalem what belonged to G-d reflected a temporary response that set the stage for what was to come, for the people of Judah faced annihilation as an ethnic group in the midst of an empire. The adoption of various dimensions of Roman law eventually took the form of incorporating the Roman notion of religion, and this led to the transformation of Judeanism (the practices of the ethnic group of Judea) into Judaism (the religion created out of the fusion of that group and Roman laws).[6]

The Romanizing of Judah created two important fusions. The first was rabbinic Judaism. The second was Christianity. The latter became the Roman religion by the fourth century ACE, which transformed Rome into the Holy Roman Empire. The struggle, however, between the nonreligious conception of pre-Roman Judeanism and similar kinds of struggles for many groups across the empire, such as those in North Africa, East Africa, and West Asia, led to the rise of different movements, among which was Islam. As a reassertion of pre-Roman laws in West Asia, Islam at first offered itself as beyond religion or Rome. Yet, as Islam means "submission," its significance was quickly, and continues to be, absorbed under the rubric of religion, even though it was a movement that was at first against and perhaps beyond religion in the Roman sense through its attesting to Muhammad as the Last Prophet. Sharia, Islamic law, was supposed to stand not as a law permitted within the framework of the greater legal system and thus a religion that bounded, say, Arabs and the various other ethnicities that adopted it, but instead as the law of laws.[7] As the latter, it would transcend religion.

Several considerations thus immediately arise. The first is the status of laws and practices through which different peoples' identities are forged but are not genealogically or culturally linked to the lines from Rome—namely, Christianity and Judaism.

Second, if those within the framework and genealogy of Rome have embraced the theodicean resolution of deviation creating the genuinely new, what are they? One difficulty is that these questions are already framed by the concepts of religion and history. Thus, the answer to the first is, simply, paganism, and for the second: secularism.

Africans in America

Our discussion of history and religion sets the context for the framework of meaning into which Africans were forced in the modern world. To consider their situation, we should bear in mind first that there was no reason for most of the people of the continent of Africa even to have considered themselves African. Most lived according to the cosmologies and laws of what today could be called their ethnic groups. As the continent was also traversed by vast systems of trade routes, this meant that various groups interacted not only with their neighbors but also with those who traded far away. The foreign and distant included Christians, Jews, and Muslims. For the first, non-Christian groups were either pagans or heathens. For the second, *goyim* (non-Jews). And for the third, infidels. We should additionally bear in mind, however, that Christianity was in Africa since its early formation in the Roman Empire, which included its northern and eastern regions; the same was the case for Judaism, especially along the trade routes; and larger numbers in the case of Islam as caliphates spread in those regions from the seventh century onward.

The period of what could be called Afro-Islamic rule in North Africa spread into the southern parts of Europe that was known in the Middle Ages as Christendom. The Iberian Peninsula became Andalusia until Isabella and Ferdinand overthrew the Muslim rulers, also known as "Moors," in Grenada in 1492 in what was called "the Reconquest." That year is crucial in the transformations that were to come. In addition to the Reconquest in January of that year, there was the intensification of the Inquisition in March, wherein those outside of the framework of Christianity faced elimination or conversion (which, for many, was the same), and the extension of these conflicts to the seas through which Columbus landed in the Bahamas by October of that year and inaugurated the notion of the New World.[8]

The Age of Exploration, which characterized the period of the expansion of Christendom into a global force and the emergence of global Europe, was not the only kind of expansion going on during that period. The Ottomans rose to power but opted to maintain control over the eastern Mediterranean and focused their energy increasingly eastward. In East Africa, the Solomonid Empire emerged in Abyssinia and staked its terrain into the twentieth century, and varieties of expansion occurred across West Asia and eastern Asia without much concern for the rapid changes going on in the Atlantic. There were varieties of expansion across different parts of the continent, as wars in what is today the Congo, Cameroon, and parts of Nigeria, such as Igbo Land and Yoruba Land, attest.

The expansion of Christendom across the Atlantic was accompanied by what could be called a theo-anthropology, wherein "man" was properly Christian and those who deviated from that normative center, such as Jews and Moors (designated under the category *raza*, which became race), became part of the less human. This order had catastrophic consequences in the New World, where the first-dubbed "Indians," originally misconceived of as lost Israelites (to be accounted for within the scheme of an all-encompassing Bible), were eventually realized outside of the biblical organization of divine concern. The result, in many instances, was genocide, which posed problems under a system offering conversion and salvation. The priest Bartholomé de las Casas realized this contradiction, and his efforts inaugurated the debates leading not only to modern questions of the human being but also the framework, theologically and historically understood, for the question of responsibility for the future.[9] Concerns about Amero-Indian genocide matched with the prize of rapidly growing wealth that was transforming Christendom into modern Europe demanded a large supply of cheap labor. Africans, rationalized as deviations from the theonatural center, became the objects of such exploitation. The transatlantic slave trade was born. This trade also joined those in the Indian Ocean as colonies began to spring up around the African coasts. The north was still governed by the Islamic trades.

The Middle Passage and Indian Ocean passages transformed many of the various captured ethnic groups on the continent into Africans and eventually "Negroes" and "blacks." These captives had to negotiate their understanding of reality with those of their captures. As none were of a singular cosmological schema, translations and transformations became the order for some, and in others, as they were already either Christian, Jew, or Muslim, there was confusion since they found themselves in both the familiar and the radically different because of the shifting anthropology from religious membership to racial designation. In short, a *black* Christian was not equal to what was by that point a Christian, who was presumed white. These shifts took time to occur as well among Jews and Muslims. The African in the New World, now the Negro or the black, faced a world of white supremacy, black inferiority, and a retroactive realignment of the past in terms of a presumed future in which she or he is expected no longer to exist. This new being, born of the modern world, needed explanations.

Black Religions and Theology

The many non-Christian, non-Jewish, and non-Muslim Africans who survived the Middle Passage into the Americas came from ethnic groups with cosmologies and normative schemes with similarities to those of their capturers except for their normative conceptions of time. Those who were Akan, for instance, regarded themselves and the world as such as in declining value according to their distance from the creating Deity. They also, as Kwame Gyekye and Paget Henry have shown, took their lot as indication of being off course from their promised purpose in relation to the originating Deity.[10] This meant that there was a sense, always, that there was something they needed *to do* about their circumstances. Thus, Christianity and the minority Judaism were not simply adopted by these groups but were, as Jane Anna Gordon and others have argued, *creolized* or brought into a living synthesis with explanatory and critical force.[11] In many instances, this took the form of rebellion, often with the blessings of a theologically critical leadership. In other instances, it took the form of innovations among the enslaved, movements among those who were freedmen and women, and theological reflection.

As the focus of this essay is the problem of history, the question of how the various denominations, sects, and entirely different religious communities were formed will only be summarized in what follows so as to move on to the problems of history they pose.[12]

Among the Christians, those who were Catholics and the variety of Protestant denominations were formed under the influences of where they were enslaved and also the abolition movements that joined their liberation struggles. Others, however, engaged the contradictions of the proposed Christian denominations and formed their own in stream with antislavery efforts being formed, especially in relation to Africa, such as the African Methodist Church (founded in 1816). Although there were enslaved Africans who were Jews and Muslims, they were forced throughout the Americas to be in predominantly Christian environments.[13] The minority of Jewish enslavers, if they were maintaining Jewish law (Halacha) created conditions similar to their Christian counterparts, which offered Afro-Jewish possibilities.[14] In some parts of the Americas, the story of religious membership was complicated by the conditions for baptism and conversion. A child could be baptized Catholic, for example, but the Protestant groups required consent from the petitioned convert. In places such as Curaçao, this meant that some masters sought out Catholic priests to convert newly born enslaved babies. The situation was complicated, however, in instances where Halacha required those enslaved on Jewish plantations to become Jewish upon manumission. One problem of African American history is thus already framed here—namely, that the African enters modernity *as black* primarily through the framework of Christianity.

The emergence of African American Christians raised the question of their relation to white Christians. If white Christians were the "in" group with regard to conceptions of the Christ, this meant that nonwhites were the deviating or "out" group, although by virtue of religion "in" Christianity. Antiblack Christian tracts supporting this in effect theodicy of black exclusion were written by white theologians and religious leaders, for whom there was no problem of history: blacks, simply, were not agents of that phenomenon.[15] The unfolding truth, the creative potential of history in the modern age, as Blumenberg asserted, was not, for white supremacists—worse, *could not*—be for blacks.

There were, however, critical responses from black theologians and religious leaders. The upshot of their position was simply that white Christians were not being, in a word, Christian.[16] Black Christological critique emerged, in other words, through the articulation of an eschatology of black presence instead of black elimination. Since Central and South America were primarily Catholic, where the framework of protest and debates were more in the hands of priests beholden to a rich system, with the exception of the thought of las Casas, of hierarchical relations, the focus will here turn to North America, where Protestantism afforded accountability and critique from a fluid set of anointed and lay ministers.

The theology that unfolded as black theology began with a focus on several themes: the evils of enslavement and racism, the significance of equality, the meaning of freedom, the symbolic significance of *imago Dei*, and theodicean problems of justification of theological accounts. At the core of these foci is the central one of a philosophical anthropology of black worth, for the equality of blacks rested in the (denied) humanity of black people. Inequality, in other words, was pernicious because it shifted from earlier models of individuated divine devotion to preordained human membership. In no instance is this more present than in the adage of judgment by content of character instead of skin color.

The American Revolutionary War veteran and Calvinist minister Lemuel Haynes (1753–1833) offered such a critique in the New England region through theonaturalistic appeals to natural rights, although a more systematic articulation of theology and the problem of history came from his contemporary Ottobah Cugoano (c. 1757–c. 1803) in England. Writing on the slave trade, slavery in the Americas, and its rationalization in the work of European philosophers that included David Hume, Cugoanao articulated the problem of slavery in the colonies in terms also of a theodicy that brought the question of the idolatry of enslavers and colonizers to the fore. No one is a natural slave, Cugoano argued; people are *forced* into slavery, which challenges the character of enslavers. Cugoano, however, understood that the question of force, pushed to its farthest point, raises the theodicean problem of deific omnipotence. As theonaturalism makes the Deity the force also of nature, Cugoano posed the question of the intelligibility of historical events as the expression or language of the Divine: reality and its historical unfolding is, in other words, the language of the Deity thinking, speaking, expressing. Cugoano thus creatively asserted the first theodicean response in which there is no intrinsic nature in the natural order of things, which, in this case, is also the theological order. He argued, however, that there is spiritual meaning in events. Thus, the enslavement of blacks transcends the enslaved into a message of sin—namely, *slavery*. As an expression of sin, slavery must be fought in this view as an imposition *onto* reality (the Deity's language). As that which is not intrinsic to the language, it is *outside*. But meaning properly emerges *inside* the divine language. Thus, to become meaningful, slavery must enter that language, but in doing so, it would encounter the contradiction of being inside-outside. In effect, Cugoano turned the white supremacist's schema on its head and reveals it as idolatrous. His theodicy is in effect to undermine the effort to justify slavery in theodicean terms. In other words, he effected a theodicy of theodicy. This extraordinary insight anticipated many to come in the nineteenth and twentieth centuries.

The immediate problem becomes the legitimacy of freedom as the conclusion of theodicean reflection. We have already seen a similar argument in the move from theology to secularism, from eschatology to modern history, and from idolatrous inequality of human beings (treating some groups as gods) to equality (all human beings as human beings). The message, so to speak, that became prevalent from all this in the succeeding nineteenth century became that redemptive suffering in which there was only one acceptable conclusion: liberation. This expectation took at least two forms. The first was the specificity and meaning of *black* suffering. David Walker's famous *Appeal* is one instance of this, and Anna Julia Cooper (1858–1964) expanded this reasoning in terms of *black female* suffering. The second form, related to the first, is in terms of the symbolic significance of blackness. Could not, if redemptive, blackness also be a virtue and, further, the personification of beauty and goodness? Martin Delany (1812–1885), as well as to some extent the Trinidadian Edward Blyden (1832–1912) and the Jamaican Robert Campbell (1829–1884) explored this consideration, especially with an eye on continental Africans as exemplars.[17] Together, these considerations led to the reading of history in terms of the significance blackness in ways that reverberated to this day; what, in other words, is to be learned from black suffering?[18]

Consider, for example, the Episcopalian minister and scholar Alexander Crummell (1818–1898), whose version of redemptive blackness was premised on the adaptability of blacks. Crummell turned social Darwinism on its head by making the case for the sustainability and survivability of blacks because of the hybrid potential of black identity. In his days, the familiar "Negro X" or "Negro Y" meant that any version amounted to "Negro + something." The "Negro" was always in the equation.[19] The "fitness" of whites should not be judged by the period of white supremacy, which, in the larger scheme of history, is only a moment in the unfolding path of time wherein birth and decay are constants. Purification is an unsustainable project, and since mixture for whites constitute their disappearance, the future appears brighter for those who could sustain their identity in the midst of mixture—namely, blacks.

The problem of history thus returns as a twofold one of appearance: a place for blacks in the future meant a retroactive accounting for blacks in the present and the past. As Christology offered the model of redemptive history, the question of black presence inevitably raised the question of redemptive blackness in terms of salvation *in black*—namely, the blackness of Christ. Such reflections emerged at the end of the nineteenth century into the early twentieth century in theological reflections from an odd constellation of thinkers such as Marcus Garvey (1887–1940), whose prophetic ruminations led to a pan-African Zionism that was a major impetus to the formation of Rastafari in Jamaica; W. E. B. Du Bois, especially in terms of his poetic and literary formulations of the returning savior as a man of color; and the poet Countee Cullen (1903–1946), whose "The Black Christ" brought this dialectic to its poetic conclusion.[20]

The theodicean problem was thus transformed in the Christian framework into the Christological question of symbolic incarnation. The meaning of black presence—and by extension black historicality—became one in which the meaning of black suffering was the symbolic role of redemptive blackness retroactively placed into Christ as colored embodiment. The history of black theology as a liberating one of redemptive blackness thus took several paths with repercussions to this day. One was primarily through symbolic incarnation. Jaramogi Abebe Agyeman (1911–2000), formerly known as Albert Cleage Jr., presented a revolutionary savior in *The Black Messiah*.[21] A similar path was taken by James Cone in his powerful series of books *Black Theology and Black Power* (1969), *Black Theology of Liberation* (1970), and *God of the Oppressed* (1975), and by several of his students, including Jacquelyn Grant, whose *White Women's Christ, Black Women's Jesus: Feminist Theology and Womanist Response*, pushed the formulation of symbolic identification to its conclusion with redemptive incarnation in terms of black female embodiment.[22] There were, as well, integrationist lines with foundations in the eighteenth century, as seen in the earlier reference to Haynes, in the nineteenth century primarily through the activism and thought of Frederick Douglass (1818–1895), and most acutely manifested in the twentieth-century thought of Martin Luther King Jr., where the historical problem was not resolved in terms of embodied redemption but, akin to the Jewish model of the ethical face of the *imago Dei*, the historical path of ethical and political action. The influence of Howard Thurman (1899–April 10, 1981) is evident in King's theology of history, where resolution becomes the universalist model of ameliorating human suffering. This makes the actions in which King was involved at his death—fighting a struggle for the rights of sanitation workers in Memphis, Tennessee, in addition to his stand against the war in Vietnam—consistent. It should be borne in mind that El-Hajj Malik El-Shabazz (1925–1965), born Malcolm Little and most known as Malcolm X, although eventually endorsing a model of historical redemption through political action, stressed the importance of *human rights* over civil rights, which was a point of convergence with King in spite of his rejection of King's integrationist model.[23] Then there is the paradoxical response of Afrocentricity, which rejects the Christological framework while endorsing the underlying logic of historical resolution through the recognition of African peoples' historical agency.[24]

Redemptive suffering did not resolve the theodicean challenge, however. William R. Jones's *Is God a White Racist?* made this problem clear through challenging the *evidentiality* of the meaning of redemption in suffering.[25] While suffering is clear, interpreting it as theological purpose or teleology begs the question of the legitimacy of theological approaches to the problem. The point of theodicy, after all, was about the legitimacy, in ethical and existential terms, of the Deity. If the actions of human beings are necessary conditions for that resolution, the possible directions in which they could go are contingent. This meant putting the question of agency squarely back into the actions of human beings, Jones argued, which brought forth a peculiarly humanistic conception of agency. The debate stimulated by Jones led to more radical reflections on secular humanism and historical agency in the thought of such scholars as Anthony Pinn and (with regard to the specificity of alternatives in Islam) Sherman Jackson. For our purposes, the basic and continued expectation round the African diaspora's relationship to history persists: religious affiliation offered redemptive expectations, and in each instance, *the meaning of blackness* and black people's relation to America (broadly defined through to the Americas) was fundamental.

Concluding Considerations on Historical Redemption and Contingency

That the transformation of African peoples into blacks was a modern phenomenon of colonization and enslavement brought the question of redemptive suffering to the fore and raised important considerations on the meaning of history as a portrait of challenged and fought-for freedom. This is peculiar narrative of modern thought, for it was not only the enslaved who saw freedom as a beacon of redemptive significance but also those who enslaved them. The contradictions, perhaps irony, of the white rebels of the American colonies formulating themselves as fighting for freedom, couched in predominantly Protestant language mixed with Enlightenment notions of reason, were apparent in the concluding protections of the newly founded United States as a nation of slavery. As the historian Gerald Horne recently demonstrated, another interpretation of the American Revolution was that of a *counterrevolution*—namely, the protection of slavery.[26] This counterrevolutionary history took form in the United States' role in undermining the Haitian Revolution (1791–1804) and its subsequent historical significance through the policies the consequence of which has been structural dependency not only for Haiti but also for the region. Struggles against enslavement in the region thus meant fundamentally doing so against the United States, a country with an explicit white supremacist national identity well into the twentieth century from which it is reluctantly departing in the twenty-first.

A similar story about the meaning of history unfolded, as well, with Marxism, which offered a conception of redemptive history under the auspices of scientific interpretations of the material unsustainability of slavery and its transformation into class stratification. Although a rewriting of Christian eschatology into a dialectical materialist model of history, Marxism, however, faced the problem of erasing its own theological roots as ideological critique. There is not enough space to detail that debate here.[27] What should be evident, however, is that Marxism's significance in the US context led to its fusion with liberation theologies and conflicts with religious, primarily Protestant, movements that sought historical redemption through the accumulation of material capital. What was at stake, in other words, was the meaning of freedom.

Where, as in Rastafari, the United States represented biblical Babylon, history means ultimately returning to Zion. The meaning of the latter, however, is more complicated than a place such as Ethiopia or Israel.[28] It is also a form of memory, namely, of what it means to live as free human being, one with high self-esteem and self-love. The dreadlocks, for example, signify embodying Babylon/US dreads: blacks no longer enslaved to whites as standards or measurements of self-worth. Where the United States represents ancient Egypt, the Exodus narrative of seeking a Promised Land emerges. And then there are models of healing the earth, of repair and transformation. The United States is simply part of a larger problem of imperialism and colonization against which humanity must build alternative models for a redemptive future.

These narratives of redemption amount to a consistent portrait of African Americans as paradoxically inside outsiders of the modern world. It is paradoxical because African Americans are, *as blacks*, indigenous to the modern world that rejects them. The problem of history as also that of freedom means, then, that membership also becomes central: blacks are homeless in the epoch to which they belong. The various strategies of addressing this problem included problematizing history itself and facing the contingency not only of blacks in the future or the latter in black but also a multitude of possibilities not hitherto thought of. The paradox of all this, however, is that contingency in the present is nothing short of the dark reminder of reason when it seeks its own necessity across time. In Du Boisian language, it is the potentiated double consciousness of the contradictions by which and through which humanity attempts to move forward.

Notes

1. Although Nietzsche articulated this aspect of Greek chronology, Hannah Arendt offers a rich discussion in her classic *The Human Condition* (Chicago: University of Chicago Press, 1958).
2. For discussion and development, see, e.g., Ernst Cassirer, *An Essay on Man: An Introduction to a Philosophy of Human Culture* (New Haven: Yale University Press, 1962); cf.

also his *The Individual and the Cosmos in Renaissance Philosophy*, trans. Mario Domand (Mineola, NY: Dover, 2000).

3. For more on theodicy, see John Hick, *Evil and the God of Love*, reissued (New York: Palgrave Macmillan, 2010). And for discussions most relevant to the African American context see Anthony B. Pinn, *Why, Lord? Suffering and Evil in Black Theology* (New York: Continuum, 1999) and Sherman A. Jackson, *Islam and Black Suffering* (New York: Oxford University Press, 2009). Cf. also Kwame Gyekye's *An Essay on African Philosophical Thought: The Akan Conceptual Scheme*, rev. ed. (Philadelphia: Temple University Press, 1995).
4. This is an argument explored in the thought of the classic German idealists, especially F. W. J. Schelling; see his *Philosophical Investigation into the Essence of Human Freedom*, trans. Jeff Love and Johannes Schmidt (Albany: State University of New York Press, 2006). For discussion, see Markus Gabriel, Markus Gabriel, *Transcendental Ontology: Essays on German Idealism* (New York: Continuum, 2011).
5. Hans Blumenberg, *The Legitimacy of the Modern Age*, trans. Robert M. Wallace (Cambridge: MIT Press, 1985). It should be borne in mind that Blumenberg was also responding to Karl Löwith's *Meaning in History: The Theological Implications of the Philosophy of History* (Chicago: University of Chicago Press, 1957), which he regarded as an overdetermined conception. The discussion that unfolds in this essay will culminate in that tension between theological necessity and existential contingency.
6. For a detailed history and critical discussion of this process, see Shaye J. D. Cohen, *The Beginnings of Jewishness: Boundaries, Varieties, Uncertainties* (Berkeley: University of California Press, 1999).
7. See Jackson, *Islam and Black Suffering.*
8. For discussion, see, e.g., Margaret R. Greer, Walter D. Mignolo, and Maureen Quilligan, eds., *Rereading the Black Legend: The Discourses of Religious and Racial Difference in the Renaissance Empires* (Chicago: University of Chicago Press, 2007).
9. See, e.g., Lewis Hanke, *All Mankind Is One: A Study of the Disputation between Bartolomé De Las Casas and Juan Gines De Sepulveda in* 1550 *on the Intellectual and Religious Capacity* (Dekalb: Northern Illinois University Press, 1974).
10. See Gyekye, *African Philosophical Thought*, and Paget Henry, *Caliban's Reason: Introducing Afro-Caribbean Philosophy* (New York: Routledge, 2000), introduction and chapter 1.
11. See Jane Anna Gordon, *Creolizing Political Theory: Reading Rousseau through Fanon* (New York: Fordham University Press, 2013).
12. Historical studies of the formation of the formation of religious groups across the African diaspora are many. For a comprehensive studies incorporating problems of history and historiography, see, e.g., Anthony B. Pinn, *The African American Religious Experience in America* (Westport, CT: Greenwood Press, 2005), Pinn, *Introducing African American Religion* (New York: Routledge, 2012), and Gayraud Wilmore, ed., *African American Religious Studies: An Interdisciplinary Reader* (Durham, NC: Duke University Press, 1989). Cf. also Walter Isaac, *"Beyond Ontological Jewishness: A Philosophical Reflection on the Study of African American Jews and the Social Problems of the Jewish Human Sciences,"* Ph.D. diss., Temple University, 2011.
13. In addition to the previously cited work by Isaac and Pinn, see also Allan Austin, *African Muslims in Antebellum America: Transatlantic Stories and Spiritual Struggles* (New York: Routledge, 1997).
14. See Isaac, "Beyond Ontological Jewishness."

15. For critical engagement with some of this literature, see Eulalio Baltazar, *The Dark Center: A Process Theology of Blackness* (New York: Paulist Press, 1973). This view of blacks in history—and, indeed, with regard to civilization—isn't peculiar to religion. It was, and to some extent continues to be, an obstacle in the social sciences. See Vernon J. Williams Jr., *Rethinking Race: Franz Boas and His Contemporaries* (Lexington: University of Kentucky Press, 1996), chapter 1.
16. See, e.g., Quobna Ottobah Cugoano, *"Thoughts and Sentiments on the Evil of Slavery" and Other Writings*, ed. Vincent Carretta (New York: Penguin, 1999). This eighteenth-century text outlined many of the theodicean and rhetorical responses to come, as nineteenth-century writers ranging from David Walker to Anna Julia Cooper demonstrated.
17. See Lewis R. Gordon, *An Introduction to Africana Philosophy* (Cambridge: Cambridge University Press, 2008) for discussions of Blyden and Crummell. See also Josiah Ulysses Young III, *A Pan-African Theology: Providence and the Legacies of the Ancestors* (Trenton, NJ: Africa World Press, 1992), and for a detailed discussion of Robert Campbell, see Anthony Williams, *"Caliban's Victorian Children: The Poetics and Politics of Black Victorian Prose, 1850–1900,"* Ph.D. diss., Temple University, 2013.
18. See William R. Jones, *Is God a White Racist? A Preamble to Black Theology*, 2nd ed. (Boston: Beacon Press, 1997); Jackson, *Islam and Black Suffering*; and Pinn, op. cit. Cf. also, Lewis R. Gordon, *Existentia Africana: Introducing Africana Philosophy* (NY: Routledge, 2000), chapter 1.
19. See Alexander Crummell, "The Destined Superiority of the Negro," in Wilson Jeremiah Moses (ed.), *Destiny and Race: Selected Writings, 1840–1898* (Amherst, MA: University of Massachusetts Press, 1992), 194–205.
20. Garvey's influence on Rastafari has received many studies. See, e.g., Leonard Barrett's classic, *The Rastafarians* (Boston, MA: Beacon Press, 1997) as well as Tony Martin, *Race First: The Ideological and Organizational Struggles of Marcus Garvey and the Universal Negro Improvement Association* (Dover, MA: Majority Press, 1986) and Rupert Lewis, *Marcus Garvey: Anti-Colonial Champion* (Trenton, NJ: Africa World Press, 1988); for Du Bois, see, e.g., Terrence L. Johnson, *Tragic Soul-Life: W.E.B. Du Bois and the Moral Crisis Facing American Democracy* (New York: Oxford University Press, 2012). And for Cullen, see his *The Black Christ and Other Poems* (New York: Harper & Brothers, 1929).
21. Albert Cleage, Jr., *The Black Messiah* (New York: Sheed and Ward, 1968).
22. James Cone, *Black Theology and Black Power* (New York: Seabury Press, 1969), *Black Theology of Liberation* (Philadelphia: Lippincott 1970), and *God of the Oppressed* (New York: Seabury Press 1975); Jacquelyn Grant, *White Women's Christ and Black Women's Jesus: Feminist Christology and Womanist Response* (Atlanta, GA: Scholars Press, 1989).
23. See *Malcolm X Speaks* (New York: Merit Publishers, 1965). See also his reflections on the same in Alex Haley, *The Autobiography of Malcolm X* (NY: Grove Press, 1965).
24. See, e.g., Molefi Asante, *The Afrocentric Idea* (Philadelphia: Temple University Press).
25. Jones, *Is God a White Racist?*. For critical commentary, see Pinn, *Why, Lord?*
26. Gerald Horne, *Negro Comrades of the Crown: African Americans and the British Empire Fight the U.S. Before Emancipation* (New York: New York University Press, 2012) and *The Counter-Revolution of 1776 Slave Resistance and the Origins of the United States of America* (New York: New York University Press, 2013). Cf. also W. E. B. Du Bois's critique of racist historiography and his analysis of US counterrevolutionary efforts in *Black*

Reconstruction in America: 1860–1880 (New York: Atheneum, 1992), which was originally published in 1935.

27. For discussion, see, e.g., Cornel West, *Prophesy, Deliverance! An Afro-American Revolutionary Christianity*, anniversary ed. (Louisville, KY: Westminster John Knox Press, 2002), 72–80, and *The Ethical Dimensions of Marxist Thought* (New York: Monthly Review Press, 1991), and cf. also C. L. R. James, *Notes on Dialectics: Hegel, Marx, Lenin* (Westport, CT: Lawrence Hill, 1980); Jean-Paul Sartre, *Critique of Dialectical Reason*, trans. Alan Sheridan-Smith, new ed. (London: Verso, 2004), and Cedric Robinson, *An Anthropology of Marxism* (Aldershot, Hampshire: Ashgate, 2001).
28. See, e.g., Michael Barnett, ed., *Rastafari in the New Millennium: A Rastafari Reader* (Syracuse, NY: Syracuse University Press, 2012) for portraits of the creative symbolic representation of Zion in Rastafari across the globe.

Selected Texts

Arendt, Hannah. *The Human Condition*. Chicago, IL: University of Chicago Press, 1958.

Blumenberg, Hans. *The Legitimacy of the Modern Age*. Trans. Robert M. Wallace Cambridge: MIT Press, 1985.

Cohen, Shaye J. D. *The Beginnings of Jewishness: Boundaries, Varieties, Uncertainties*. Berkley: University of California Press, 1999.

Gordon, Lewis R. *An Introduction to Africana Philosophy*. Cambridge: Cambridge University Press, 2008.

Henry, Paget. *Caliban's Reason: Introducing Afro-Caribbean Philosophy*. New York: Routledge, 2000.

Jackson, Sherman A. *Islam and Black Suffering*. New York: Oxford University Press, 2009.

Jones, William R. *Is God a White Racist? A Preamble to Black Theology*. 2nd ed. Boston: Beacon Press, 1997.

Moses, Wilson Jeremiah, ed. *Destiny and Race: Selected Writings, 1840–1898*. Amherst: University of Massachusetts Press, 1992.

Pinn, Anthony B. *Introducing African American Religion*. New York: Routledge, 2012.

Pinn, Anthony B. *The African American Religious Experience in America*. Westport, CT: Greenwood Press, 2005.

Pinn, Anthony B. *Why, Lord? Suffering and Evil in Black Theology*. New York: Continuum, 1995.

Wilmore, Gayraud. *African American Religious Studies: An Interdisciplinary Reader*. Durham, NC: Duke University Press, 1989.

CHAPTER 27

SOCIAL THEORY AND AFRICAN AMERICAN THEOLOGY

COREY D. B. WALKER

> The theological and ideological languages of conquest and pilgrimage formed the lens through which the reality of other non-European traditions were refracted, as through a glass darkly; they were obscured.
>
> Charles H. Long

> All religious developments are, in one sense, parochial cultural responses. And, the theology which arises from black culture is equal in authenticity to other such responses.
>
> —Roy D. Morrison II

> Even a critical social theory cannot avoid an "ultimate" in which its criticism is rooted because reason itself is rooted therein.
>
> —Paul Tillich

African American theology must not only *critically* engage the Christian theological tradition, but the modern social and cultural context in and through which this tradition expresses itself. The task for African American theology is thus dialectical—it must not only attend to matters that can be termed properly theological, that is, the doctrine and dogma of the faith that renders it intelligible to the Christian faith community, but also the major questions, issues, and problems that arise from the experiential context of its adherents in the American polity. In order to adequately articulate the norms, concepts, and methods that form and inform African American theological reflection in light of this dialectical challenge, theologians and scholars of religion have developed a requisite range of responses that have sought to give expression to this multiply determined, and at times contradictory, task. This essay highlights some of the dominant trends in African American theological thinking that confronts this dialectical challenge in elaborating a viable theologically resonant form of thought responsive to the social, cultural, and political concerns and contexts of African American people. By adopting the language of theological thinking in this respect, we are better attuned to the subtle nuances of African American thought that while deploying the language of theology is better understood through the register of critical thought that *poaches* the theological yet is not and cannot be fully accounted for within the history of theological discourse proper, thus expanding the horizon of possibility for a more historicist and materialist critical social theory of society.[1]

Confronting the multiplex of issues in the American social and political order is a necessary first step when attempting to fashion a theology that renders explicit the principles of the faith that New World Africans adopted. Indeed, analogous to Lucius Outlaw's understanding of the task of philosophy—"Efforts to elaborate a critical, global, theoretical view of social, political, economic, and cultural life in general, and of a particular people within the social order, are instances of the endeavor of philosophizing at its very best"—African American theology's perennial attempt to wrestle with the deep and complex nature of social and political life in the United States is the very nature of theology.[2] Since the founding of the American Republic, African American theological thinking has needed to exhibit a critical dexterity to navigate the turbulent waters of a theological stream that was consistently influenced by domestic and international theological movements as well as the highly contested American social milieu. The responses ranging from theological acquiescence in the face of manifest social injustice to radical theological thinking that caused other theologians and scholars to question the very idea of African American theology are but two key nodes in this protean discursive terrain. Thus, the task inevitably is reflexive in that African American theological thinking not only must render legible the social and political challenges that inform its faith utterance, there is also a corollary task that impinges on the very discourse of theology itself. That is, theology as the theoretical discourse that renders intelligible the claims and commitments of religious life and ritual practice must enter a continual rethinking in order to remain faithful to its intellectual task.

African American Theological Normativity and the Secular Society

With the establishment of the United States, American society has continually presented African American theological thinkers with a host of challenges that frustrate the claims of a theologically informed social theory to speak effectively to the place and position of African Americans in the polity. The invocation of the political sovereignty as established by "the people" and not by God sought to resolve the contamination of the political by the theological and inaugurate a political space free from of religious influence and interference. The American founding fathers, Thomas Jefferson and Thomas Paine foremost among them, were intent on the establishment of a social and political order grounded in the inviolability of a secular government that eschewed appeals for authority in a transcendent God.[3] While popular sovereignty came to serve as the legitimate and authorizing foundation for politics in the American nation, it was not able to absolutely restrict the usage and deployment of religious language, metaphors, and ideas in the cause of politics. Scholars such as Harry Stout, Jon Butler, and Patricia Bonomi have convincingly demonstrated the lasting influence of religion on American politics from the colonial period into the opening decades of the early Republic.[4] Puritan beliefs, New Divinity theology, covenant theologians, and moral law teachers had a profound impact on the development and usage of particular political ideas and languages in America's evolving experiment with democracy. If the political principle of "the people" could not create a conflict-free political grammar devoid of all vestiges of religion, then the principle itself was equally exposed to being contested. Indeed, those peoples not included within the circle of "the people" developed critical strategies to expand the scope and meaning of the political principles in an effort to reestablish the grounds of political community on a logic of explicit inclusion rather than a logic of implicit exclusion. In so doing, new political actors fashioned political languages that did not adhere to the neat and clean divides between the theological and the political that statesmen like Jefferson sought to maintain. Instead, they would tarry on the boundaries of the theological and the political in advancing their claims and commitments for political inclusion in the service of expanding the framework of the political and redefining such key principles as freedom, liberty, and citizenship. As J. G. A. Pocock so presciently reminds us:

> We should beware of supposing that whenever in the study of Christian politics we meet with apocalyptic, eschatological and even millennial concepts, we are necessarily dealing with those chiliastic "religious of the oppressed" which are so much and so rightly studied. Concepts of this order formed a vital and powerful element in the vocabulary of Christian society, one just as likely to be employed by members of the established power structure as by rebels against it; they were used to explain events and justify claims too dramatic and unprecedented to be dealt with in any other way, and the powerful as well as the powerless might find themselves needing to do this.[5]

Thus, the appeal to a modern democratic polity as signified by "the people" that became the repository of power for the new nation-state was transformed into a space for contesting the formal languages of politics and the very definition of the political in and through a theological register.

In this emerging and evolving modern political community, African Americans created elaborate theological frameworks to challenge their formal exclusion from membership in the American polity. These political theologies exhibited a broad social theoretic vision that took into account the social, cultural, and political struts of white supremacy in supporting and maintaining American democratic governance while also challenging the supremacy of the state to adjudicate all matters properly political. The challenge to state sovereignty occurred through appeals to the moral, ethical, and theological languages of a transformed African American Christianity that grounded appeals to the transcendent within the realm of the historical. Navigating the space between transcendence and history enabled African American theological thinkers to fashion a critical political language that animated their new political identity while registering a critique of the exclusionary principle that lay at the heart of democracy in America. The ability to deploy a *heterodox* political language that freely borrowed theological ideas, concepts, and themes and pressed them into political service empowered individuals like Richard Allen, Lemuel Haynes, Jarena Lee, John Marrant, Maria Stewart, and others to construct a variety of theo-political responses in confronting the contradictory discourses of rights, liberty, freedom, and equality that excluded African American men and women from these discourses. Moreover, these theological actors effected a virtual theological revolution in pressing this discourse to respond to political claims that grounded and authorized citizenship in the polity while simultaneously supporting the regime of antiblack racist chattel slavery. These political actors fashioned a panoply of socially responsive theologies—from the "Africanist Calvinism" of John Marrant to the politically charged Christian egalitarianism of David Walker—to challenge the formal domains of secular American society, which denied the very humanity and political presence of African Americans in its political doctrines and dogma, and to appeal to a higher law in order to transform the secular order of things.[6]

In their response to the question captured in the title of the West African Jacobus Elisa Johannes Capitein's 1742 published thesis, *Political-Theological Dissertation Examining the Question: Is Slavery Compatible with Christian Freedom or Not?* African American theological thinkers not only answered in the negative, but also offered alternative visions for political community inspired by their theological dreams.[7] In many ways, African American theology offered a framework to begin to articulate a "holy black Zion community."[8] Whether through establishing independent continental and New World African Christian communities or challenging the chattel slave and white supremacist regimes in the abolitionist movement or fashioning new political subjectivities through the African American convention movement of the mid-nineteenth century, African American theology provided a malleable and flexible discourse to meet the challenges of an antiblack social order while articulating new visions of an inclusive community. Recently, Eddie S. Glaude Jr. has directed our attention to the manifold ways in which African Americans employed the biblical Exodus narrative as "a source for a particular use of nation language among African

Americans as well as a metaphorical framework for understanding the middle passage, enslavement, and quests for emancipation."[9] Glaude's *Exodus! Religion, Race, and Nation in Early Nineteenth-Century Black America*, along with the work of scholars like Valerie Cooper, John Saillant, and Joanna Brooks, reminds us of how African Americans engaged the realm of the theological in forming an alternative conception of the political, one that included African Americans as proper political subjects. It is within the interstices of the theologico-political—a highly contested and contradictory terrain—where African Americans fashioned a political useful and socially resonant language that poached the theological in advancing a broader conception of freedom and citizenship to underwrite American secular society.

African American Theological Thinking and the Challenge of Reason

In his powerfully instructive collection of essays *Significations: Signs, Symbols, and Images in the Interpretation of Religion*, Charles Long writes, "While the reformist structure of the Enlightenment had mounted a polemic against the divisive meaning of religion in Western culture and set forth alternate meanings for the understanding of the human, the same ideological structures through various intellectual strategies paved the ground for historical and evolutionary thinking, racial theories, and forms of color symbolism that made the economic and military conquest of various cultures and peoples justifiable and defensible."[10] Long highlights the ways in which the twin economic and political projects of chattel slavery and colonialism were at one and the same time critical theological projects. That is, these material efforts received intellectual justification and moral affirmation in and through the registers of theology proper. In so doing, the political architecture of the New World was supported in and through appeals to that which is considered ultimate. Thus, African American theology confronted not only the political challenges of a secular political regime, but also a theological imagination tethered—however tenuously—to a rationalizing project that provided ultimate intellectual legitimation of antiblack racism and discrimination.

The imbrication of the racialist and racist Western imagination and the project of reason created the theoretical conditions of possibility for the elaboration of African American theological thinking that, by necessity, exhibited a critical social theory. To be sure, there were elaborations of theology by African American thinkers and religious figures that were within the discursive context established by Western reason and held fidelity to the theoretical and theological prerequisites of race and reason. One only needs to examine certain theological articulations by such nineteenth-century luminaries as Alexander Crummell and Jarena Lee to witness that contesting the racial logic of the project of reason was suffused with biases and prejudices that were part and parcel of African American theological thought.[11] However, the principle of a racialized reason forced open the boundaries of theology to incorporate a critical social theory of society that sought to unravel the fundamental logics underpinning American democracy and its attendant social order.

In responding to the question, "What does the Negro want in our democracy?" posed at the 1919 National Conference of Social Work, the African American churchman who was one of the first of a generation of African Americans to earn a Ph.D. from the University of Chicago, Richard R. Wright Jr., stated plaintively, "The Negroes' wants in 'our democracy' are simple and fundamental. The Negro wants a democracy and not a 'whiteocracy.'"[12] Wright's response elegantly captures a key dimension of the critical social theory of African American theological thinking—the critique of the theoretical and material conditions that maintain white supremacy within American democratic politics and cultural practices. Wright thus becomes one within a stream of African American theological thinkers who creatively and critically wedded a theologically informed political ethic with a critique of actually existing political democracy. Such a nexus of thinking would include the gender critique undergirding the reform efforts of Nannie Helen Boroughs, the moral philosophy that informed the theological imagination the Yale-educated Thomas Nelson Baker, who earned his Ph.D. in philosophy in 1903, and the institutional and intellectual challenge issued by the socialist scholar and minister Reverdy C. Ransom.[13] Indeed, instead of thinking critical social theory and theological thinking as *necessarily* opposed, African American theological thinkers remind us of the imperative to think through the multiple ways in which the critique of society is intimately bound up with a theologically informed ethic of society.

African American theological thinking has keenly demonstrated the significance of formulating a critical social theory with its theology in order to challenge the racial logic of reason and its instantiation within the social and political registers of society. To recognize this crucial dimension of African American theology forces us to rethink such eighteenth- and nineteenth-century formations as the abolitionist movement, the colonization movement, and the Negro convention movement, as well as articulations of black nationalism and Christian socialism as theoretical complexes in which a critical social theory of society reflexively forms and informs theology. In other words, African American theological thinking can be productively read as a *critical* theory of American society inasmuch as it can profitably be read as a rereading and renewing of the Christian theological tradition. As a critical theory of American society, it attempts, in keeping to the thought advanced by Lucius Outlaw, "to reconstruct, through reflective understanding, the development of historical forms of understanding, and their groundings in the social order, to reveal how they misrepresent actual social relations and thus justify forms of oppression that are in reality historical."[14] In such a vein, moral and ethical underpinnings of the antilynching movement can be read not just through the lens of social movement theory or through the biography of one of its towering figures, Ida B. Wells, but as a theologically inflected critique of actually existing society as well as the normative underpinnings of the construction of what it means to be human in the modern world.[15] The systematic theologian James Cone's recent examination of the symbolic meaning of the cross and the lynching tree in African American and American life and thought can be viewed as the latest installment in tradition that would most certainly include Howard Thurman's *Jesus and the Disinherited* and *The Luminous Darkness: A Personal Interpretation of Segregation and the Ground of Hope*, as well as the often understudied theological efforts of Howard University scholar and dean of the Divinity School William Stuart Nelson.[16] Indeed, to think the example of William Stuart Nelson is to engage the theological significance underpinning the social and political philosophies informing the African American political presence in post–World War I Europe, the global imagination inspiring African American theo-political engagements with India, and the post–World War II nonviolent black freedom struggle.[17] In all, a critical stream of African American theological thinking cannot be read and thoroughly understood without being critically attentive to the social theory that operates in and through the languages of theology as well as social theory.

African American Theological Thinking and the Challenges of Postsegregation America

"To be sure," Charles Long writes, "the recognition of the visibility of the black community in America will prompt many to confront the new situation as simply an ethical-moral problem. It is certainly this, but it is much more. The visibility of this community raises critical and constructive issues on the intellectual and theological levels of our work."[18] The challenge that Long highlights gains acute resonance in the wake of the global black freedom struggle of the mid-twentieth century. Along with the political liberation of continental and diasporic Africans came a renewed thrust for intellectual liberation that included the discursive space of the Christian theological tradition. Texts like the classic collection edited by Joyce Ladner, *The Death of White Sociology*, formally and forcefully highlighted the theoretical inadequacies of traditional academic disciplines in providing robust frameworks and conceptual criteria to account for the social reality of a racialized and antiblack racist modern world.[19] The theological thus becomes an analogous space of contestation due to the cognitive frameworks, conceptual vocabularies, and material registers of thought that give expression to the meaning of human existence in the world. In this respect, it too is subject to critique as a result of this political and theoretical revolution advanced by the "visibility of the black community."

In this regard, African American theological thinking represents a particular critique of American society, and to understand it just within a dominant register of academic theology is to misrepresent its intellectual aim and trajectory. James Cone's classic text *Black Theology and Black Power* exemplifies how and in what ways the modern black freedom struggle forced a renewed and critical form of African American theological thinking to frontally confront not only the white supremacist foundation of American society, but also the ways in which a normative whiteness has conditioned dominant expressions of Christian theology in the modern moment. "In this new era of Black Power," Cone argues, "the era in which blacks are sick of white power and are prepared to do anything and give everything for freedom now, theology cannot afford to be silent. Not to speak, not to 'do theology' around this critical problem, is to say that the black predicament is not crucial to Christian faith."[20] Cone's statement can be most critically understood as a manifesto calling thinkers to act. This text spearheaded a movement of new critical theological works that aimed at nothing less than a foundational and immanent critique of the dominant class, gender, and sexual hierarchies in society and in the life of the mind that marginalized the lives and life chances of African Americans. African American theological thinkers undertook the crucial work of moving beyond a discourse of theology *proper* in advancing theological projects informed by the latest theoretical and methodological advancements in womanist and black feminist thought, black studies, queer studies, process, existential, and pragmatic philosophy, and new currents in cultural studies and postmodern thought. In addition, a diverse array of theological thinkers including M. Shawn Copeland, Clarence Hardy, and Anthony Pinn, just to name a few, embrace critical interdisciplinary movements within the traditional academic disciplines with the effect of providing a more textured and nuanced understanding of African American theological thought in conversation with the social and political situation of African Americans across space and time.[21]

African American theological thinking in the wake of the global black freedom struggle reminds us that the place and position of African Americans in society and in discourses of theology can no longer be treated simply as a byproduct, at best, or as an invisible component, at worst, of the dominant discourses of society and theology. In other words, theology, if it is to construct thinking appropriate to lives and thought of African American people, must articulate a critical social theory of society that takes into account these epochal political and intellectual shifts in the modern world. In the words of Long, "I am saying that the hegemony of Western Christian categories and thought models has come to an end. Notice that I did not say that they were invalid or useless; I am here making the relativity argument. I am saying that the kind of provincialism stemming from the aforementioned hegemony might be overcome if we take seriously the otherness manifested through and in the visibility of the black community." The kinds of provincialism to which Long directs our attention are those intellectual discourses—even discourses that attempt to critique what is taken as African American theology—which fail to recognize the imbrication of a critical social theory in and through the theological languages and categories and prematurely arrests the development and elaboration of African American theological thinking in its most critical elaboration.[22]

The conditions of possibility for the expression and elaboration of African American theology in the modern Western world force a reexamination of the norms and methods that inform its articulation. To this end, what is needed to fully grapple with the depth of the theological impulse is a differential kind of thinking that confronts the twin challenges of critically thinking theology and society. Such thinking inhabits the gaps between *a* history and the im/possible transcendence of history and exposes the false necessity of thinking theology over and against the critique of society. Given the dynamics surrounding the historical and theoretical construction of dominant (and dominating) formulations of the theology in the modern world, African American theological thinking constructs a social theory not as dogma but as an intellectual initiative whose prospects and possibilities have not, indeed cannot, be accounted for in the calculus of reigning paradigms of theology proper. In other words, by recasting African American theological thinking in such a manner, we are reminded of the limit conditions of the discourse of theology itself in accounting for the protean language and categories of African American religious thought. Moreover, we are better positioned to understand how and in what ways an accounting of the social reflexively conditions perceptions of life and thought. It is only by a theological thinking—critical thinking that *poaches* the theological yet is not and cannot be fully accounted for within the history of theological discourse—that we are able to mark the limit of the categories of critical thought as well as expand the horizon of possibility for a fully historical and materialist critique of religion. As Walter Benjamin aphoristically put it, "The tradition of the oppressed teaches us that the 'state of emergency' in which we live is not the exception but the rule. We must attain to a conception of history that is in keeping with this insight." It is therefore an imperative to critically mine those forms of African American theology forged in a constant "state of emergency" in an effort to theologically think a critique of society that resists the organizing code of dominant registers of thought while not reinscribing the *aporia* that leads to failure in the very recognition of the innovation that is constitutive of these intellectual efforts.[23]

Notes

1. See Michel de Certeau, "Reading as Poaching," in *The Practice of Everyday Life*, trans. Steven Rendall (Berkeley: University of California Press, 1984), 165–76. For further

elaboration of theological thinking, see Corey D. B. Walker, "The Infinite Rehearsals of the Critique of Religion: Theological Thinking after Humanism," *boundary 2* 35, no. 3 (2008): 189–212.

2. Lucius Outlaw, *Critical Social Theory in the Interests of Black Folks* (Lanham, MD: Rowman and Littlefield, 2005), 2.
3. See Matthew Harris and Thomas S. Kidd, eds., *The Founding Fathers and the Debate over Religion in Revolutionary America* (New York: Oxford University Press, 2011).
4. See Harry S. Stout, *The New England Soul: Preaching and Religious Culture in Colonial New England* (New York: Oxford University Press, 1986), Jon Butler, *Awash in a Sea of Faith: Christianizing the American People* (Cambridge: Harvard University Press, 1992), and Patricia U. Bonomi, *Under the Cope of Heaven: Religion, Society, and Politics in Colonial America*, updated ed. (New York: Oxford University Press, 2003). See also E. Brooks Holifield, *Theology in America: Christian Thought from the Age of Puritans to the Civil War* (New Haven: Yale University Press, 2003).
5. J. G. A. Pocock, *Politics, Language and Time: Essays on Political Thought and History* (New York: Atheneum, 1971), 83–84. See also John Howe, *Language and Political Meaning in Revolutionary America* (Amherst: University of Massachusetts Press, 2004).
6. On the protean political thought of African Americans in this era, see Bernard Boxill, "Populism and Elitism in African American Political Thought," *Journal of Ethics* 1, no. 3 (1997): 209–38, and, more recently, Robert Gooding-Williams, *In the Shadow of Du Bois: Afro-Modern Political Thought in America* (Cambridge: Harvard University Press, 2009).
7. See Jacobus Elisa Johans Capitein, *The Agony of Asar: A Thesis on Slavery by the Former Slave, Jacobus Elisa Johannes Capitein, 1717–1747*, trans. Grant Parker (Princeton, NJ: Markus Wiener, 2001).
8. Joanna Brooks and John Saillant, eds., *"Facing Zion Forward": First Writers of the Black Atlantic, 1785–1798* (Boston: Northeastern University Press, 2002).
9. Eddie S. Glaude Jr., *Exodus! Religion, Race, and Nation in Early Nineteenth-Century Black America* (Chicago: University of Chicago Press, 2000), 3.
10. Charles H. Long, *Significations: Signs, Symbols, and Images in the Interpretation of Religion* (1986; Aurora, CO: Davies Group, 1995), 4.
11. See William L. Andrews, ed., *Sisters of the Spirit: Three Black Women's Autobiographies of the Nineteenth Century* (Bloomington: Indiana University Press, 1986), and J. R. Orfield, ed., *Civilization and Black Progress: Selected Writings of Alexander Crummell on the South* (Charlottesville: University of Virginia Press, 1995).
12. *Proceedings of the National Conference of Social Work* (Chicago: Rogers and Hall, Company, 1920), 538.
13. See Evelyn Brooks Higginbotham, *Righteous Discontent: The Women's Movement in the Black Baptist Church 1880–1920* (Cambridge: Harvard University Press, 1993); Anthony Pinn, ed., *Making the Gospel Plain: The Writings of Bishop Reverdy C. Ransom* (Harrisburg: Trinity Press International, 1999); and George Yancy, "On the Power of Black Aesthetic Ideals: Thomas Nelson Baker as Preacher and Philosopher," *AME Church Review* 107, no. 234 (2001).
14. Outlaw, *Critical Social Theory*, 17.
15. See Anthony Bogues, *Black Heretics: Black Prophets: Radical Political Intellectuals* (New York: Routledge University Press, 2003).
16. James H. Cone, *The Cross and the Lynching Tree* (Maryknoll, NY: Orbis Books, 2011).

17. See Clayborne Carson, ed., *The Papers of Martin Luther King, Jr.*, vol. 5, *Threshold of a New Decade, January 1959–December 1960* (Berkeley: University of California Press, 2005); Gerald C. Horne, *The End of Empires: African Americans and India* (Philadelphia: Temple University Press, 2009); William Stuart Nelson, ed., *The Christian Way in Race Relations* (New York: Harper & Brothers, 1948); Nico Slate, *Colored Cosmopolitanism: The Shared Struggle from Freedom in the United States and India* (Cambridge: Harvard University Press, 2012); Chad Louis Williams, *Torchbearers of Democracy: African American Soldiers in World War I Era* (Chapel Hill: University of North Carolina Press, 2010).
18. Long, *Significations*, 135.
19. Joyce Ladner, ed., *The Death of White Sociology: Essays on Race and Culture* (Baltimore: Black Classic Press, 1998).
20. James H. Cone, *Black Theology and Black Power* (New York: Orbis Books, 1989), 88.
21. See for example, M. Shawn Copeland, *Enfleshing Freedom: Body, Race, and Being* (Minneapolis: Fortress Press, 2009); Clarence Hardy III, *James Baldwin's God: Sex, Hope, and Crisis in Black Holiness Culture* (Knoxville: University of Tennessee Press, 2003); and Anthony Pinn, *Embodiment and the New Shape of Black Theological Thought* (New York: New York University Press, 2010).
22. See, for example, Alistar Kee, *The Rise and Demise of Black Theology* (Burlington, VT: Ashgate, 2006).
23. Walter Benjamin, "Theses on the Philosophy of History," in *Illuminations*, ed. Hannah Arendt, trans. Harry Zohn (New York: Knopf Doubleday, 1968), 257.

Selected Texts

Anderson, Victor. *Beyond Ontological Blackness: An Essay on African American Religious and Cultural Criticism*. New York: Continuum, 1999.

Baer, Hans A. *The Black Spiritual Movement: A Religious Response to Racism*. Knoxville: University of Tennessee Press, 2001.

Baer, Hans A., and Merrill Singer. *African American Religion: Varieties of Protest and Accommodation*. University of Tennessee Press, 2002.

Brooks, Joanna. *American Lazarus: Religion and the Rise of African-American and Native American Literatures*. New York: Oxford University Press, 2003.

Cannon, Katie G. *Katie's Canon: Womanism and the Soul of the Black Community*. New York: Continuum, 1996.

Cleage, Albert, Jr. *Black Christian Nationalism: New Directions for the Black Church*. New York: William Morrow, 1972.

Collier-Thomas, Bettye. *Jesus, Jobs, and Justice: African American Women and Religion*. New York: Random House, 2010.

Cone, James H. *Black Theology and Black Power*. New York: Harper and Row, 1969.

Cooper, Valerie C. *Word, Like Fire: Maria Stewart, the Bible, and the Rights of African Americans*. Charlottesville: University of Virginia Press, 2011.

Dickerson, Dennis C. *African American Preachers and Politics: The Careys of Chicago*. Jackson: University Press of Mississippi, 2010.

Dillard, Angela D. *Faith in the City: Preaching Radical Social Change in Detroit*. Ann Arbor: University of Michigan Press, 2007.

Frazier, E. Franklin. *The Negro Church in America*. New York: Schocken, 1963.

Frederick, Marla Faye. *Between Sundays: Black Women and Everyday Struggles of Faith.* Berkeley: University of California Press, 2003.

Glaude, Eddie S., Jr. *Exodus! Religion, Race, and Nation in Early Nineteenth-Century Black America.* Chicago: University of Chicago Press, 2000.

Grant, Jacquelyn. *White Women's Christ and Black Women's Jesus: Feminist Christology and Womanist Response.* Atlanta: Scholars Press, 1989.

Harris, Fredrick C. *Something Within: Religion in African-American Political Activism.* New York: Oxford University Press, 1999.

Higginbotham, Evelyn Brooks. *Righteous Discontent: The Women's Movement in the Black Baptist Church, 1880–1920.* Cambridge: Harvard University Press, 1993.

Jones, William R. *Is God a White Racist? A Preamble to Black Theology.* Boston: Beacon Press, 1998.

Long, Charles H. *Significations: Signs, Symbols, and Images in the Interpretation of Religion.* Minneapolis: Fortress Press, 1986.

Lincoln, C. Eric, and Lawrence H. Mamiya. *The Black Church in the African American Experience.* Durham, NC: Duke University Press, 1990.

McRoberts, Omar M. *Streets of Glory: Church and Community in a Black Urban Neighborhood.* Chicago: University of Chicago Press, 2005.

Nelson, William Stuart, ed. *The Christian Way in Race Relations.* New York: Harper and Brothers, 1948.

Newman, Richard S. *Freedom's Prophet: Bishop Richard Allen, the AME Church, and the Black Founding Fathers.* New York: New York University Press, 2008.

Oltman, Adele. *Sacred Mission Worldly Ambition: Black Christian Nationalism in the Age of Jim Crow.* Athens: University of Georgia Press, 2008.

Owens, Michael Leo. *God and Government in the Ghetto: Politics of Church-State Collaboration in Black America.* Chicago: University of Chicago Press, 2007.

Paris, Peter J. *The Social Teaching of the Black Churches.* Minneapolis: Fortress Press, 1998.

Pinn, Anthony B. *Why Lord? Suffering and Evil in Black Theology.* New York: Continuum, 1999.

Raboteau, Albert J. *Slave Religion: The Invisible Institution in the Antebellum South.* New York: Oxford University Press, 1978.

Roberts, J. Deotis. *A Black Political Theology.* Louisville, KY: Westminster, 1974.

Saliant, John. *Black Puritan, Black Republican: The Life and Thought of Lemeul Haynes.* New York: Oxford University Press, 2003.

Savage, Barbara Dianne. *Your Spirits Walk Beside Us: The Politics of Black Religion.* Cambridge: Harvard University Press, 2008.

Smith, R. Drew, ed. *Long March Ahead: African American Churches and Public Policy in Post-Civil Rights America.* Durham, NC: Duke University Press, 2004.

Smith, R. Drew, ed. *New Day Begun: African American Churches and Civic Culture in Post-Civil Rights America.* Durham, NC: Duke University Press, 2003.

Smith, R. Drew, and Fredrick C. Harris, eds. *Black Churches and Local Politics: Clergy Influence, Organizational Partnerships and Civic Empowerment.* Lanham, MD: Rowman and Littlefield, 2005.

Thurman, Howard. *Jesus and the Disinherited.* Abingdon: Abingdon Press, 1949.

Townes, Emilie. *Womanist Ethics and the Cultural Production of Evil.* New York: Palgrave, 2006.

Washington, Joseph R., Jr. *Black Religion: The Negro and Christianity in the United States.* Boston: Beacon Press, 1972.

West, Cornel. *Prophesy Deliverance! An Afro-American Revolutionary Christianity*. Louisville, KY: Westminster, 1982.

West, Cornel, and Eddie S. Glaude Jr., eds. *African American Religious Thought: An Anthology*. Louisville, KY: Westminster John Knox, 2003.

Wilmore, Gayraud S. *Black Religion and Black Radicalism: An Interpretation of the Religious History of African Americans*. New York: Doubleday, 1973.

Williams, Delores. *Sisters in the Wilderness: The Challenge of Womanist God-Talk*. Maryknoll, NY: Orbis Books, 2002.

Woodson, Carter G. *The Negro Church*. Washington, DC: Associated Publishers, 1921.

CHAPTER 28

BLACK ONTOLOGY AND THEOLOGY

VICTOR ANDERSON

ONTOLOGY is philosophical reflection on the nature and meaning of *Being* (*ontos*). Significant philosophical shifts mark its history in the West away from classical metaphysical epistemologies and hierarchical dualisms to black existentialism, which has fundamentally shaped mid-twentieth-century African American theologies of black existence and continues to do so in the present.

METAPHYSICAL EPISTEMOLOGIES

Martin Heidegger begins *Being and Time* (1962) with these words: "For manifestly you have long been aware of what you mean when you use the expression 'being.' We, however, who used to think we understood it, have now become perplexed."[1] The question of the meaning of being is anticipated in every assertion, proposition, or statement operating in typical sentential forms: (*a*) "This *is* a P," (*b*) "That is Q," or (*c*) "These are R and S." It matters little what signs stand in for P, Q, or R and S. The meaning of each sign is settled by reference to its definition, which constitutes the sign's meaning. The ontological question, Heidegger insists, is "not just any question. It is one which provided a stimulus for the researches of Plato and Aristotle, only to subside from then on *as a thematic question of actual investigation*."[2]

When examining the meanings of names, words, or signs in relation to their referents, Aristotle demonstrates how confusing the whole matter can be. He says: "We must not forget that sometimes it is not clear whether a name means the composite substance, 'a covering consisting of bricks and stones laid thus and thus,' or the actuality or form. . . . For soul and to be soul are the same, but to be man and man are not the same, unless indeed the soul is to be called man; and thus on one interpretation the thing is the same as its essence, and on another it is not."[3] This confusion has produced a history in which the question of the meaning of Being escalated into all manner of hierarchical dualisms.

These dualisms stipulate the rational order of things, and their effects continue to distort our understandings of human relations. Such dualisms include *nature* over reality, *essence* over existence, *substance* over thought, *higher* over lower, *human* over animal, *species* over genus, *soul* over body, *same* over different, *mind* over matter, *civilized* over barbarian, *West* over *East*, and *white* over black. Aristotle thought of such ontological hierarchies as the work of nature. Thus, they constitute the natural order of things. He argues, "That one should command and another obey is both necessary and expedient. Indeed some things are so divided right from birth, some to rule, some to be ruled."[4]

While seventeenth-century British empiricism exorcised any future for this prior metaphysical ontology from its experimental methods, Descartes strategically consigned ontological reflection to the self-introspection of human conscious life, to the world of "thought-thinking-itself," which is summarized in his famous dictum: "*cogito ergo sum* / I think therefore I am." Although experience, mind, and forms of consciousness became new grounds for ontological inquiry, classical metaphysical hierarchies remained, reconstituted themselves, and reproduced modern forms of the alterity between the civilized and conquered and the superiority of white over the black. If the ontological question was to have new or contemporary significance, as Heidegger insisted, it required a *destructuring* of its reception in Western thought; it required a deconstruction of what Franz von Brentano calls "thought-content" or "thought-matter."[5] In African American philosophy and theology, the ontological question, its thought content or matter, reconstitutes itself as the existential question of the meaning of black existence.

Black Existential Hope and Tragic Soul-Life as Ontological Schemes

Philosopher Lewis Gordon has argued "any theory that fails to address the existential phenomenological dimensions of racism suffers from a failure to address the situational dimensions, what Fanon called *l'expérience vénue* (lived experience) of race."[6] Ontological reflection on the existential meaning of blackness requires attention to the concrete actuality of the situated moments of black suffering. This concern always stands against the impinging threat of nothingness, of nonbeing, which, says Gordon, "exposes a world that will ultimately be better off without blacks. Blacks from such a standpoint 'must' provide justification for their continued presence."[7]

W. E. B. Du Bois describes this situation as "the Negro Problem." When blackness is raised as the ontological question, Gordon says, "It usually takes the form of another question: What is to be done in a world of nearly a universal sense of superiority to, if not universal hatred of black folk? Or, to paraphrase W. E. B. Du Bois from *Darkwater*; What is to be understood by black suffering?"[8] Gordon continues: "It is this question that animates a great deal of the theoretical dimension of black intellectual productions. It is what signals the question of liberation, on one level, and the critique of traditional, read 'European,' ontological claims on the other."[9]

Black existence is situated, concretely determined, and already known as the problem within the existential situation. The word "problem" ought to be understood as designating neither a puzzlement nor a quandary as in sentential logic. In fact, the "problem" of blackness does not beg for an answer at all. It requires only recognition of situational moments of black lived existence. When the ontological question shifts from the meaning of being itself to the meaning of black lived experience, Fanon insists, all ontological explanation is cut off. "In the weltanschauung of a colonized people, there is an impurity or a flaw that prohibits any ontological explanation. Ontology does not allow us to understand the being of the black man, since it ignores the lived experience."[10] The word-sign "black" presented here by Fanon is an abstract noun that qualitatively modifies neither a person nor a place but a "thing!": situated flesh. It articulates what the philosopher of existence understands as meaning (*bedeutung*) within the *determinate situation* of lived experience (*l'expérience venue*). Blackness therefore encodes situational moments of black lived experience, moments of freedom, anguish, responsibility, embodied agency, sociality, and liberation, says Gordon.[11]

I describe such clustering of existentially situated moments as an economy of black existential hope. According to Gordon, "Philosophy of existence is marked by a centering of what is often known as the 'situation' of questioning or inquiry itself. Another term for situation is the lived- or meaning-context of concern. Implicit in the existential demand for recognizing the situation or lived-context of Africana peoples' being-in-the-world is the question of value raised by people who live the situation." Gordon explains: "A slave's situation can only be understood, for instance, through recognizing the fact that a slave experiences it. It is to regard the slave as a value-laden perspective in the world."[12] Such value-laden presentations of black lived experience come to expression as a plenitude of being within a multiplicity of African American forms: slave tales, prayers, letters, journals, sermons, autobiographies, spirituals, blues, jazz, gospel music, literature, fine arts, political treatises, social activism, and theological discourse.

When speaking of an economy of black existential hope, it operates as a heuristic devise for gathering up clusters of existential, situated moments that symbolically qualify blackness as consciously lived experience. Within this economy of black conscious life, which is a plenitude of being, no situated moment is reducible into another. Each marks off distinction within a unity of lived experience. Thereby, ontological hierarchies are subverted by difference within identity. Each situated moment of the economy of existential hope is, moreover, infinitely possible, that is, potentially repeatable, even as the conditions for its possibilities persist in situated moments of black suffering, oppression, anguish, closure, freedom, responsibility, community, liberation, and more.

Political theologian Terrence L. Johnson uses the trope black "tragic soul-life" to describe just how such an economy of existential hope constituted the moral center in the life of W. E. B. Du Bois. More importantly, however, he argues that this ontological signifier goes a long ways toward making sense of enduring situated moments of oppression in black lived experience. In *Tragic Soul-Life* (2012), Johnson uses this trope heuristically for gathering up—in a synthetic manner—aspects of Du Bois's widely dispersive life. Although Du Bois's was a rather traveling life, Johnson insists that tragic soul-life operated at the center of Du Bois's moral disposition and philosophy and that it has continuing ontological significance. Tragic soul-life operates as a moral thread spun from black existential suffering and sorrow to form an economy of faith, hope, and democratic fulfillment among black people, for whom American realities make actualization of freedom, solidarity, and liberation far-off ideals.

Tragic soul-life connects "the spiritual striving of ancestors" and predecessors to contemporaries who struggle, resist, and survive while articulating freedom, hope, faith, and joy. As a trope of ontological significance, tragic soul-life travels throughout fields of black expressive culture toward a moral philosophy that centers blacks' struggle for liberation and what Johnson calls "human fulfillment" within a democratic society fractured by antiblack racism, homophobia, sexism, and class alienation. Tragic soul-life is Johnson's way of ontologically framing an economy of black existential hope in the situated moments of black existence: "confronting a haunting racial past for the purpose of expanding individual and collective imaginations of justice, freedom, and what allows humanity to flourish." Tragic soul-life, moreover, "provides a new ethical imagination, a process for reconstituting our racially constructed selves into flourishing and thriving souls." As an economy of black existential hope, tragic soul-life "calls into question what is familiar and easily taken for granted, and beckons us to step into forgotten narratives that shed light on the complex and rich history of American democracy."[13]

The clustering of situated moments of black lived experience and tragic soul-life form an economy of black existential hope that represent a plenitude of being within a unity of lived experience, which is often signified as "the black experience." Thus, whether one speaks of the black experience, black existence, black culture, the black community, black religion, the black church, or black theology, such identifiers operate as gathering terms. Ontologically, they signify economies of black existential situated moments that entail multiplicity within identity or plenitude within unity. As an ontologizing scheme, this plenitude of being is manifest in the tragic soul-life of folktales and prayers, letters and journals, sorrow songs and sermons, autobiographies and manifestos, worship and political activism, and more. The challenge of ontological reflection on black existence for contemporary African American theology is to imagine, articulate, cultivate, and reproduce the conditions of possibility for this plenitude of being within religious and morally situated moments of black existential hope.

Black Religion and the Ontological Problem

African American theology has contributed powerfully toward constructing economies of black existential hope within the study of black religion and black religious and moral experience. In *Terror and Triumph* (2003), Anthony Pinn relates black religion to such economies. Black religion is Pinn's gathering term for what he calls in black religious experience the quest for "complex subjectivity." This quest pushes against histories, systems, and technologies of power by which black existence is dehumanized by terrors of antiblack racism, white supremacy, and global economic capitalism from the transatlantic slave trade to present-day global economic oppressions. "This subjectivity, Pinn says, "is understood as complex in that it seeks to hold in tension many ontological possibilities, a way of existing in numerous spaces of identification as opposed to reified notions of identity that mark dehumanization."[14]

This quest for complex subjectivity rejects ontological dualisms such as the Cartesian mind/body dualisms. It resists such dualisms in favor of the multidimensionality of subjectivity. "This quest is not achieved in one act or in one moment in which a new status is secured, nor does it depict a separate or distinctive element of reality," says Pinn. Rather, "it involves an unfolding, a continuous yearning and pushing for more, an expanding range of life options and movements."[15] The quest is at the core of black religion and black religious experience, Pinn argues, and operates much like Johnson's tragic soul-life trope. This quest for complex subjectivity is black insofar as it is "shaped by and within the context of black historical realities and cultural creations," and it is religious in that it "addresses the search for ultimate meaning."[16] It operates as a religiously determined center of existential hope, signifying a plenitude of being in social, moral, and spiritual transformations in black religious experience. The quest for complex subjectivity is the core of black religion, motivating blacks' yearning, push, desire, or impulse for fullness.[17] It is agential, directing blacks' agency toward ever enlarging liberative ends of fulfillment and fullness of life. Although the quest for complex subjectivity in black religious experience "may not result in sustained sociopolitical and cultural transformation," says Pinn, "it does involve a new life meaning that encourages continued struggle for a more liberated existence."[18]

In *Dark Symbols, Obscure Signs* (1993), Riggins Earl Jr. describes how slaves gave expression to their lived experience with moral and religious significance through his analysis of slave songs, conversion narratives, autobiographies, journals, and folklore. From these they produced and reproduced an economy of existential hope within the religio-moral universe of slave culture. "Each genre of the folk sources produces its own conceptual paradigm for looking at the fundamental ideas of *self, God*, and *community*," says Earl.[19] These sources provide three insights: (1) they collectively and individually form African Americans' identity; (2) they help to understand how slaves navigated their ethical duties; and (3) they exhibit complexity among slaves in their understanding of self, God, and community.

Slaves' religion produced a remarkably resilient moral universe of deep spiritual and ethical significance that sustained them against the death-dealing effects of the transatlantic slave trade and dehumanizing plantation systems. Slaves' culture offered an economy of existential hope, spirituality, conjuring practices, and folk wisdom that Earl maintains are articulated in black folk-cultural productions of spirituals, conversion narratives, preaching, journals, folktales, and more. In these cultural products, not only did slaves emphasize their ambiguous and contradictory relation to white Christianity, as Earl has argued, but slave religion centered slaves' confidence that divine justice and freedom would triumph over oppression.

The economy of black existential hope that Earl discovers in the moral universe of slave religion and culture is given theological interpretation in *Cut Loose Your Stammering Tongues: Black Theology in Slave Narrative* (2003).[20] Slave religion produced "an organic syncretism that enabled slaves to combine their Afrocentric religious beliefs with the Eurocentric ones of their masters. The consequence of this merger was their unique form of African American Christianity," says Will Coleman.[21] From this spiritual and moral economy, collaborators construct a theological and moral economy of black existential hope from which today's generations of blacks may find enough faith and hope for liberation praxis against the effects of white oppression. "Enslaved Africans realized that God had created them originally with a free soul, heart, and mind. Yet white American Christians had re-created them in the demonic image of a distorted Christianity," says Hopkins. He surmises: "For the slave, the purpose of humanity was to show fully the spark of God's created equality implanted deep within black breasts. To return to original creation, then, African American slaves pursued a resistance of politics and a culture of resistance."[22] The spiritual and moral economies of back existential hope discovered and interpreted by Earl and the slave narrative theologians offer rich depositories of human creativity and moral wisdom that, even while antecedent to the black church, continue to exert spiritual and moral influence within this tradition, argue C. Eric Lincoln and Peter J. Paris.

The Ontological Problem as the Theological Concern in the Black Church

As a center of black existential hope, the black church is ontologically thematized as a "Sacred Cosmos" and "Surrogate World." In *The Black Church in African American Experience* (1990), sociologists C. Eric Lincoln and Lawrence Mamiya interpret the black church tradition in terms of the black sacred cosmos. Although the tradition is identified mostly by Protestant denominations, Lincoln and Mamiya also see conceptual and moral connections between the black church and traditional African religions. For them, "The Black sacred cosmos or the religious worldview of African Americans is related both to their African heritage, which envisaged the whole universe as sacred, and to their conversion to Christianity during slavery and its aftermath."[23] Moreover, it designates black people's "unique and distinctive forms of culture and worldviews as parallels rather than replications of the culture in which they were involuntary guests."[24]

The black sacred cosmos signifies an economy of black existential hope in which "core values of black culture like freedom, justice, equality, an African heritage, and racial parity at all levels of human intercourse, are raised to ultimate levels and legitimated."[25] In this sacred cosmos, the Incarnation stresses God's and Christ's immanent presence in black people's lives and in the world; the Resurrection symbolizes black people's triumph or transcendence over death so that fatalism is no option for blacks' orientation to the world; universal egalitarianism and freedom are norms of interhuman relations in which all are God's children; and ecstatic worship displays realized eschatological hope and fulfillment of union with God, Christ, and ancestors through the Spirit. As an ontological scheme, the black sacred cosmos "reflects the deepest values of African Americans, giving primal consideration to the necessity of freedom as an expression of complete belonging and allegiance to God."[26]

Peter Paris ontologically construes the black church as "surrogate world." It is a parallel sacred and moral universe to the world of white Christianity. As a surrogate, black churches aim "at socializing their members into creative forms of coping along with the development of imaginative styles of social and political protest, both grounded in a religious hope for an eschatological victory."[27] Its absolute moral norm of black moral agency, says Paris, is the biblical view that all people are equal under God, and this proposition is the final authority for all matters pertaining to faith, thought, and practice.[28] It was from such ontological schemes of the black church as sacred cosmos and surrogate world that black theology offered perhaps the most pervasive and determinate theological reflection on the ontological problem of the meaning of black existence and black existential hope from the late 1960s even to the present, but not without progressive interventions of subsequent theologians and ethics.[29] James Cone's *A Black Theology of Liberation* (1970) remains a classic statement of the ontological problem of the meaning of black existence for black theologies of liberation.

The Ontological Problem in Black and Womanist Theology

For Cone, the culture of black survival and black revolutionary consciousness constitute ontological schemes for interpreting the existential meaning of blackness.[30] "Black theology is a theology of survival," says Cone, "because it seeks to interpret the theological significance of the being of a community whose existence is threatened by the power of non-being."[31] Second, black self-assertion is "an event of liberation taking place in the black community in which blacks recognize that it is incumbent upon them to throw off the chains of white oppression by whatever means they regard as necessary."[32] Black theology articulates the existential religious and theological meaning of these situated moments in light of the black experience, black history, and black culture. By defining black existence by black experience, Cone thereby constituted for subsequent theologies of black existence the ontological problem of the being of blackness: "The black experience is existence in a system of white racism."[33] Blackness is an "ontological symbol and visible reality which best describes what oppression means in America."[34]

Cone does not describe the ontological problem of the meaning of black existence in terms of an economy of existential hope. Nevertheless, he comes close. Blackness expresses "the power to love oneself precisely because one is black and a readiness to die if whites try to make one behave otherwise." It ushers in cultural demands for black pride, respect, and loving "the spirit of blackness." "It is hearing black preachers speak of God's love in spite of the filthy ghetto, and black congregations responding Amen, which means that they realize that ghetto existence is not the result of divine decree but of white inhumanity."[35] Cone's economy of black existential hope is symbolically rendered black soul. "Black soul is not learned," says Cone, but "comes from the totality of black experience, the experience of carving out an existence in a society that says you do not belong."[36] For Cone, the answer to the ontological problem is the ontological blackness of black experience, black expressive culture, black history, and the black messiah.

Cone's answer to the ontological problem of the existential meaning of blackness has posed considerable challenges for subsequent generations of African American theologians and ethicists including womanist theologians and ethicists. According to Stephanie Mitchem, womanist theologians and ethicists such as Jacqueline Grant,

Katie G. Cannon, and Delores S. Williams, among others, contextualize the ontological problem theologically in terms of black women's experience. "Womanist approaches to theology aim to develop a variety of theological constructions in which black women are the main subject," says Mitchem.[37] Cannon's *Black Womanist Ethics* (1989), says Mitchem, "signaled new beginnings in several ways. She launched her work from the perspective of black women's truths, long overlooked as a location from which to begin an ethical study. By valuing black women's experience, she challenged the basic assumptions of white, male, Christian ethics about individual, personal and communal power, and acts of choice."[38] From sources of black women's literature, spirituality, and experience, womanist theology and ethics construct an economy of black existential hope that sustains black women and the whole community from systemic assaults or oppressions of racism, classism, sexism, and heterosexism. From black sources of novelists, poets, autobiographers, ex-slave interviewers, journalists, and black women essayists, womanist theologians and ethicists construct an economy of black existential hope. "Black women have created and cultivated a set of ethical values that allow them to prevail against the odds, with moral integrity, in their ongoing participation in the white-male-capitalist value system," says Cannon.[39] She continues: "The best available literary repository for this underground treasury of values is the Black women's literary tradition."[40]

Mitchem identifies the ontological scheme of a womanist's economy of black existential hope by five themes: (1) it attends to the ordinary theologies of black women's lives, Christian and non-Christian; (2) it stresses the communal aspects of black women's experiences that include social activism and their creation of safe spaces; (3) it insists on being interdisciplinary, while keeping all aspects of black women's lives central; (4) it is the starting point for womanist theology and critical social analysis; and (5) it includes dialogue and openness, which are essential for keeping womanist theology and ethics connected to other liberation theologies, particularly black and feminist, sometimes serving even as a corrective.[41]

This ontological scheme gathers up the histories, social constructions, activism, and faith of black women as theological and ethical responses "to the unique realities of black women," says Mitchem.[42] Womanist theologian Delores Williams articulates this economy of black woman's existential hope as an economy of struggle, survival, resistance, and quality of life. The power of this economy is that situated moments of black women's lived experience appear enduring for sustaining black women against the perpetual threat of nonbeing, which threatens their quality of life and the life of the whole community.[43] When reflecting on Hagar's and black women's wilderness experience and the ministerial vision of Jesus, Williams theologically concludes that God cares, meets them through their life of prayer and struggles, and provides the resources and support for ongoing resistance against black women's oppression.[44] In Williams's womanist economy of black existential hope and Johnson's tragic soul-life, God does not liberate; liberation must be the work of black women themselves for themselves.[45]

Conclusion

African American theological and moral ontological reflection on black existence is a counterdiscourse to a prior Western classical metaphysical ontology, its episteme, and dualisms. For Fanon and Gordon, following Heidegger's insistence, ontological inquiry required a destructuring of the thought-content of this prior ontology, away from defining the *Being* of being to describing black lived experience of suffering. Ontology and black existence highlight black lived experience as a plenitude of being derived from situated moments of black lived experience and constitute economies of black existential hope. Such situated moments include survival, struggle, anguish, and resistance as well as responsibility, embodied agency, community, liberation, human flourishing, and more. The ongoing challenge of ontological reflection on black existence for contemporary African American theology is imagining, articulating, cultivating, and reproducing the conditions of possibility for this plenitude of being.

Notes

1. Martin Heidegger, *Being and Time*, trans. John Macquarrie and Edward Robinson (New York: Harper Collins, 1962), 1.
2. Heidegger, *Being and Time*, 42.
3. Aristotle, "Metaphysics" Bk. VII.3, §1043b, in *A New Aristotle Reader*, ed. J. L. Ackrill (Princeton, NJ: Princeton University Press, 1987), 316.
4. Aristotle, *Politics*, Bk. I.5, §1254a, 20, 512.
5. Franz von Brentano, "Letter to Anton Marty, 17 March 1905," in *The Phenomenology Reader*, ed. Dermot Moran and Timothy Mooney (New York: Routledge, 2006), 55–56.
6. Lewis R. Gordon, ed., *Existence in Black: An Anthology of Black Existential Philosophy* (New York: Routledge, 1997), 70.
7. Gordon, *Existence in Black*, 6.
8. Gordon, *Existence in Black*, 1.
9. Gordon, *Existence in Black*.
10. Franz Fanon, *Black Skin, White Masks*, trans. Richard Philcox (New York: Grove Press, 2008), 89–90.
11. Gordon, *Existence in Black*, 3.
12. Gordon, *Existence in Black*, 4.
13. Terrence L. Johnson, *Tragic Soul-Life: W.E.B. Du Bois and the Moral Crisis Facing American Democracy* (New York: Oxford University Press, 2012), 13.
14. Anthony B. Pinn, *Terror and Triumph: The Nature of Black Religion* (Minneapolis: Fortress Press, 2003), 158.
15. Pinn, *Terror and Triumph*, 159.
16. Pinn, *Terror and Triumph*.
17. Pinn, *Terror and Triumph*, 173.

18. Pinn, *Terror and Triumph*, 175.
19. Riggins R. Earl Jr., *Dark Symbols, Obscure Signs: God, Self, and Community in the Slave Mind* (Maryknoll, NY: Orbis Books, 1993), 8.
20. Dwight N. Hopkins and George C. L. Cummings, eds., *Cut Loose Your Stammering Tongue: Black Theology in Slave Narrative*, 2nd ed. (Louisville, KY: Westminster John Knox Press, 2003); other contributors are Will Coleman, Cheryl J. Sanders, Joan Martin, David Emmanuel Goatley, and M. Shawn Copeland.
21. Will Coleman, "Legions," in Dwight N. Hopkins and George C. L. Cummings, eds., Cut Loose Your Stammering Tongue, 2003, 48.
22. Dwight N. Hopkins, *Shoes That Fit Our Feet: Sources for a Constructive Black Theology* (Maryknowl, NY: Orbis Books,1993), 47.
23. C. Eric Lincoln and Lawrence Mamiya, *The Black Church in African American Expereince* (Durham, NC: Duke University Press, 1990), 7.
24. Lincoln and Mamiya, *Black Church*, 2.
25. Lincoln and Mamiya, *Black Church* , 7.
26. Lincoln and Mamiya, *Black Church*, 7.
27. Peter J. Paris, *The Social Teaching of the Black Church* (Philadelphia: Fortress Press, 1985), 6.
28. Paris, *Social Teachings*, 10.
29. Dwight N. Hopkins, *Black Theology of Liberation* (Maryknoll, NY: Orbis Books, 1999), 7–13.
30. James H. Cone, *A Black Theology of Liberation*, 20th anniversary ed. (Maryknoll, NY: Orbis Press, 1991), 16–17.
31. Cone, *Black Theology of Liberation*, 16.
32. Cone, *Black Theology of Liberation*, 5.
33. Cone, *Black 'Iheology of Liberation*, 24.
34. Cone, *Black Theology of Liberation*, 7.
35. Cone, *Black Theology of Liberation*, 25.
36. Cone, *Black Theology of Liberation*,70.
37. Stephanie Mitchem, *Introducing Womanist Theology* (Maryknoll, NY: Orbis Books, 2006), 46.
38. Mitchem, *Introducing Womanist Theology*, 69.
39. Katie G. Cannon, *Black Womanist Ethics* (Atlanta: Scholars Press, 1988), 75.
40. Cannon, *Black Womanist Ethics*, 75.
41. Mitchem, *Introducing Womanist Theology*, 64.
42. Mitchem, *Introducing Womanist Theology*, 22.
43. Delores S. William, *Sisters in the Wilderness: The Challenge of Womanist God-Talk* (Maryknoll, NY: Orbis Books, 1993), 175.
44. Williams, *Sisters in the Wilderness*, 175.
45. Williams, *Sisters in the Wilderness*, 238–39.

Selected Texts

Cannon, Katie G. *Black Womanist Ethics*. Atlanta: Scholars Press, 1988.

Cone, James H. *A Black Theology of Liberation*. 20th anniversary ed. Maryknoll, NY: Orbis Books, 1991.

Earl, Jr., Riggins R. *Dark Symbols, Obscure Signs: God, Self, and Community in the Slave Mind*. Maryknoll, NY: Orbis Books, 1993.

Fanon, Franz. *Black Skin, White Masks*. New York: Grove Press, 2008.

Gordon, Lewis R. *Existence in Black: An Anthology of Black Existential Philosophy*. New York: Routledge, 1997.

Hopkins, Dwight N. *Black Theology of Liberation*. Maryknoll, NY: Orbis Books, 1999.

Johnson, Terrence L. *Tragic Soul-Life: W.E.B. Du Bois and the Moral Crisis Facing American Democracy*. New York: Oxford University Press, 2012.

Lincoln, Eric C., and Mamiya, Lawrence. *The Black Church in African Amerfican Expereince*. Durham: Duke University Press, 1990.

Mitchem, Stephanie. *Introducing Womanist Theology*. Maryknoll, NY: Orbis Books, 2006.

Paris, Peter J. *The Social Teaching of the Black Church*. Philadelphia: Fortress Press, 1985.

Pinn, Anthony B. *Terror and Triumph: The Nature of Black Religion*. Minneapolis: Fortress Press, 2003.

Williams, Delores S. *Sisters in the Wilderness: The Challenge of Womaniust God-Talk*. Maryknoll, NY: Orbis Books, 1993.

CHAPTER 29

AFRICAN AMERICAN THEOLOGY AND THE GLOBAL ECONOMY

ANTHONY G. REDDIE

It can be argued that African American theology in the shape of black and womanist theologies has played a pivotal role in calling into question the workings and ethics of the "global economy." In using the term "global economy," I am concerned with the interconnected means by which nation-states undertake their economic activity and the ways in which multi- and transnational companies, operating from within seemingly all-enveloping global markets, seek to maximise their profits, under the aegis of techno-capitalism.[1]

The global economy was one of the hallmarks of the age of modernity, although there is no doubting that in our present postmodern epoch, the characteristics of this phenomenon have been refined and, indeed, extended. It is now, in many respects, an archetypal postmodern phenomenon. As the boundaries of so-called sovereign nations have been traversed by the entrepreneurial ingenuity of those firmly committed to the process of profit maximization,[2] we are now witnessing the demise of fixed identities predicated on the parameters of national identity.[3] This global economy often works hand in hand with neoliberal models of political ideology, which assert the inviolate nature of the market, the necessity of free and unfettered trade and minimal governmental intervention, and the harm done by centralized planning or the collectivist control of the means of production.

I want to look at the contribution that black and womanist theologies have made to critiquing the global economy, as I have just defined it.

The Implacable, Prophetic Opponents of the Global Economy

Perhaps the tradition within African American theology that has become almost emblematic of the critique of the present global economy is that of black theology. Black theology burst into academic life[4] within the crucible of the Black Power movement in 1960s America. Black theology and its developmental sibling, womanist theology, represent the radical, politicized wing of African American theology. It is the polemical and politically charged, standpoint-epistemological framing of black and womanist theologies that has garnered them the sobriquet of "lacking theological legitimacy" in some quarters.[5] The strength of black and womanist theologies has been their engagement with broader hinterland of "Third World theologies" or theologies from the "Underside" of history,[6] as detailed in the work of EATWOT.[7]

From an early point of departure in the movement, African American black theologians have addressed their concerns to the wider issues of global poverty. As we will see, a number of black and womanist theologians argue that endemic poverty has emerged from the machinations of the fundamentalist free market capitalist system of world trade. It is simply not the case that black and womanist theologies have reified the internal contradictions of American religion and so divorced themselves from the concerns of the global poor.[8]

I have identified a three-part movement in the theological analysis provided by African American black and womanist theologies with respect to the global economy. I make no claims for this analysis to be a definitive rendering of this subject. Like any form of historical heuristic, the semantic framing of movements and countermovements between differing scholars and their ideas is one that is always fraught with danger. One person's chronological and epistemological demarcations between differing paradigms in black theology might well be contested by others.[9]

In choosing to highlight the following scholars and their differing approaches to engaging with and critiquing the global economy, it is imperative that I stress that this work is descriptive as opposed constructive; nor is it in anyway polemical, which is often the preferred mode in which my scholarly work is often couched.[10]

The Racialization of the Problem: The Probing of James H. Cone

In his early work, Cone identified Marxism as offering a helpful framework for articulating the central tenets of black theology, as a theology of liberation that was committed to challenging and supplanting the poisonous tentacles of the white hegemonic power structure.[11] Cone, in aligning black theology to the biblical revelation of God, argues clearly for a qualitative difference between the Kingdom of God that is inaugurated in the life, death, and resurrection of Jesus and that of the global economy.[12] While Cone's work has often invoked a nascent articulation of Marxist social thought as an interlocutor for his critique of Euro-American, white hegemony, I think it is a basic truth that the normative methodological point of departure for his work has been Christian theological hermeneutics.

Cone's biblical theology provides a robust theological rationale for outlining the qualitative difference between the characteristics of the Kingdom of God and that of the global economy. His neo-Barthian-influenced, Christocentric approach to liberation for black people is one that seeks to mine African American history and biblical models of justice and equity in order to create a theological paradigm that critiques the contours of the present world order; one based on white privilege.[13] Cone has largely eschewed class analysis of capitalism in the direct fashion one often finds in Latin American liberation theologians, for a more trenchant critique of the symbolic power of whiteness, as a category of epistemological privilege.[14] For Cone, it is no coincidence that the residue of the fallout from the iniquities of the global economy is black people and other people of color.[15] For Cone, poverty has a color, and it is his contextualized and particularized reading of oppression that separates him from the more generic approaches to the subject that one often finds in Latin American liberation theologians, for example.[16]

Free market proponents of the global economy will assert the largesse of the efficiency of choice that accrues to all persons across the globe. Cone, conversely, is clear that this is an evasive smokescreen that seeks to mask the intentionality of the greed and myopic gaze of white self-interest in the so-called democratic nations of the West.[17] Cone's critique of the global economy is more elliptical than obviously encircled, meaning that there are not many finely thought through treatises on the global economy and its macro effects upon all people of color across the world. This does not mean that Cone is ignorant of or deafened to their plight.

Rather, as a contextual theologian, the immediate purview of his gaze is the historical experience of suffering of African Americans. Nevertheless, his racialized theological reflections make clear the incongruity that exists between the global economical world of white privilege and the gospel of Jesus Christ. The latter is one of equity, justice, and liberation, for all marginalized and economically dispossessed people of color. Cone's critique is essentially a theological one. By focusing his critique of white hegemony through the lens of "race," one could argue that Cone has failed to identify the key cause for black poverty, both in the United States and across the world. As far back as the nineteenth century and the ideas of Marx and Engels,[18] through to the iconic work of Caribbean anti-imperial historian Eric Williams in the 1940s, scholars on the political left have argued that the despairing corruptions of the global economy and its deleterious impact on the poor across the globe have arisen through the role of pernicious economics and not racialized forms of human negation.[19]

How Cone's critique of white supremacist economic power sits alongside the bourgeoning growth of China and India—nonwhite countries—is a critical question to be addressed by succeeding generation of Cone scholars. To what extent has the tilt in the axis of power in the world economy rendered the majority of Cone's more trenchant polemics vis-à-vis black suffering at the hands of white power a form of sociotheological anachronism?

Will the changing geopolitical landscape offer greater degrees of equity for the largely poor people of the global South, as the new masters (who are also people of color) take command of a more inclusive and less rampant form of economic system, one predicated less on profit maximization at all costs? Or is this an illusory dream? I think it unfair to place such scholarly burdens on the shoulder of a seasoned scholar like Cone.[20]

Dwight Hopkins and the Religion of Globalization

While Cone has offered a trenchant and oblique critique of the global economy, from within the parameters of African American black theology, one could argue that a more consistent gaze on the workings of this phenomenon has been enacted by Dwight Hopkins. While Hopkins's early work seeks to build on the theological legacy of Cone, particularly in the use of African American religio-cultural history, often in the form of an exploration of the historiography of slave writings,[21] one can also detect a broader internationalist perspective in this early work.[22]

Hopkins's later work has sought to provide a more refined and sustained intellectual gaze on the global economy from within the parameters of Christian hermeneutical perspectives on black theology. Whereas Cone's gaze was primarily filtered through the refining optics of a polemical charge against white supremacy, Hopkins has adopted a more eclectic set of interlocutors for his more macro theo-cultural analysis of global monopoly capitalism.

In using the latter term, a key critical insight in his social analysis, Hopkins is speaking to the accumulation of capital and the private possession and ownership of the means of production within the oligarchy of those who would be defined as the superrich.[23] Monopoly capitalism seems be an oxymoron, as the proponents of the laissez-faire, free market economics will point to such inviolate religio-political tenets as "competition" and "democracy" as being characteristics that sit as polar opposites to the repressive regimes of the eastern Communist bloc, where such facets were conspicuous in their absence. So, in notionally free societies in the West, there is a surfeit of choice and yet, this system is underpinned by a closed and elitist form of dogma that is every bit as inflexible and coercive as the communism it sought to critique and oppose in the East.[24]

Hopkins's work has not paid the same kind of attention to Marxist frameworks as West's oeuvre, particularly that which emerged in the early phase of the latter's work. Instead, Hopkins has reflected more critically on the very nature of globalization as a form of religious orientation in its own right, one that is possessed of its own conceptual models of doctrine and concomitant theological articulations.[25]

Hopkins's analysis of the global economy entails a theological reframing of the anti-Christian basis of this phenomenon, where the basic rubrics of the Christian faith, he argues, are replaced by that of an alternative, parallel religion.[26] In this classic expression of the prophetic element within African American black theology, Hopkins seeks to unmask the alternative epistemological frameworks that govern the postmodern project that is globalization, critiquing it for its pseudo-Christian rhetoric. Hopkins writes

> The god of the religion of globalization is the concentration of monopoly, finance capitalistic wealth. The god of globalization, in this sense, is not merely a belief in the accumulation of capital for private possession by owners operating inside one country, a signification of the lower stage of in the development of capitalism. On the contrary, the god of globalization embodies the ultimate concern or ground of being, where there is a fierce belief in the intense concentration, in a few hands, of monopoly, finance capitalist wealth on the world stage.[27]

Writing from within a committed black theology hermeneutical[28] purview, Hopkins is arguing for a clear delineation between the liberative dimension of the Christian Gospel and the false consciousness of the globalization project and its pretensions to progress and beneficence for all.

The black theological scholarly mode of attack that Hopkins adopts is a multifaceted one. In the first instance, he explores the relationship between the African American experience, which provides the critical underscoring for the developmental progress of black theology in the United States, and the comparative theological movements of the so-called Third World.[29] Hopkins, a longtime dialogue partner with the World Council of Churches and EATWOT, assesses the ways in which a more plural, interfaith model of African American black theology[30] can speak in solidarity with those who have been consigned to the marginal spaces of the world due to the fundamentalism of the free market, monopoly capitalist paradigm that is the global economy. It is worth quoting Hopkins at length here:

> Interfaith dialogue is crucial because the international economy of monopoly capitalism, the destruction of indigenous cultures, racial discrimination against darker-skinned peoples around the world, the oppression of women, and the attack on the earth's ecology are global dynamics that do not limit themselves to the Christian community. When American monopoly capitalist corporations seek cheap labor in Asia, particularly among Asian women, these companies are not concerned about whether the workers are Buddhist or Christian. The bottom line is using their labour power in order to make profit. When American monopoly capitalist corporations pursue investments in Nigerian oil, they ate not concerned if the workers are Muslim, indigenous religious practitioners or Christians.[31]

The second major tenet of Hopkins's black theological riposte to the workings of the global economy is to locate its epicenter, indeed the beating heart of its globalized identity, in the immanent life of the United States. Like Cone, but perhaps with a greater attention to theological minutiae of American corporate religious life, Hopkins argues that the global economy takes it cue from the neoconservative moorings of mainstream America.[32]

The theological assessment pertaining to the revelatory theism inherent within the global economy can be expressed in two central characteristics. First, the burgeoning growth of the postmodern character of globalization that is synonymous with the global economy should be seen as a form of religion itself. In effect, corporate America is not so much Christian as worshipping the theism of globalized, free market, monopoly capitalism, whose rapacious intent is concealed within the veneer of civic Christianity.

Second, the major characteristic of Hopkins's theological analysis is to identify African Americans within the United States as being in solidarity with the poor and marginalized of color across the globe.[33] The aberrant theological paradigm that links African Americans and the poor of color across the globe is that of prosperity teaching,[34] in which the central tenets of the aforementioned religion of globalization is writ large. Although Hopkins is addressing an expansive, global context in his work, like Cone, he remains at heart a contextual, African American black theologian. Juxtaposed with his black theology critique of the macro processes of the global economy, his work continues to hold the micro experiences of black people in America as central to his theo-ethical concerns. Consistent with his Christian hermeneutical approach, the heart of Hopkins's theological critique can be found in the scriptures, with a key "proof-text" being Matthew 25, 31–46. The claims of salvation that are declared by Jesus,[35] argues Hopkins, can found in the type of liberative praxis that places priority in engaging with needs of the poor and the marginalized.[36] The aforementioned characteristics of liberative black theology stand in contradistinction to the impersonal workings of the global economy. Neither are they reflected in the alleged Christian discipleship of Pat Robertson and his seemingly callous theological remarks regarding the disaster that was Hurricane Katrina within the United States and its impact on predominantly poor African Americans.[37]

While Hopkins provides a more thorough interlocking analysis of the theological flaws exposed within the workings of the global economy, it can be argued that he, like Cone, has missed an important dimension in his black theology-led critique. Scholars such as Ivan Petrella have argued that the apparent ineffectual rhetorical bombast of African American black theology's critique of the global world order arises from its lack of critical engagement with alternative epistemological and methodological approaches to analyzing the complexities of the postmodern globalized epoch in which we presently live.[38] In both models that have been examined in this essay, one sees an overreliance on theology. Neither Cone nor Hopkins can offer an alternative form of praxis by which the economic exchange between human persons can be effected. The likes of Petrella, Jung Mo Sung,[39] and Wilf Wilde[40] have all argued that theologians need to become increasingly conversant with and comfortable utilizing the insights of economics and the broader social sciences in order to create a more praxiological critique of the global economy. Whether one will witness this form of epistemological and methodological turn to other disciplines in the future work of African American black theologians is a question for future debate.

The Contribution of Womanist Theologians

This critical stance within the prophetic tradition of African American theology has also possessed a female dimension. African American womanist ethicists such as Katie Cannon and Emilie Townes have reflected theologically on the sociocultural machinations of the global economy and its deleterious effects upon black women and other poor people of color in the United States and across the world.[41]

Cannon and Townes have added an important gender critique to the ideological attack against the worst iniquities of global economy that has been launched from the prophetic wing of African American womanist theology. Namely, it is imperative that we need to move from an amorphous deductive analysis of the poor as the fallout from the intrigues of the global economy. Just as Cone and more latterly Hopkins would argue that global poverty has color—black (people of African descent)—then equally, it also has a gendered complexion to it; namely, it is the face of the African woman that is recipient of the unfortunate sobriquet of "least of the least.[42]

At the time of writing, the younger generation of African American womanist ethics, in the shape of Keri Day, has joined the fray and has sought to extend the prophetic tradition exemplified by Cone, West, Hopkins, and others.[43] The importance of Day's emerging work in the context of this essay is that she has, in an almost prescient way, begun to address some of the challenges and limitations identified by leftist liberation theologians regarding existing black and womanist approaches to addressing the global economy.

Day argues that previous African American theologians who have addressed the area of the global economy have not offered a practical economic framework for exploring the dialectical interplay between the need for the structural transformation of the global economy and the markers that might explicate what human flourishing and full life looks like for the poor of the world. Day's work sits within a broader tradition of African American prophetic theological work that has sought to challenge and appraise the workings of the global economic system from within the rubric of a liberative model of Christianity.

Day's work explores how black and womanist liberation theologies can respond to the chronic poverty experienced by communities of color around the world. Day argues that while black liberation theologies have performed the theological task of reframing the global economy by rereading the Gospels from the margins of society, these theologies would do well to couple that hermeneutical work with the political task of offering practical guidance toward a more preferable future for poor communities of color. Day's work seeks to provide a more nuanced and detailed articulation of human flourishing and liberation for the poor and marginalized across the world, who are struggling within the context of a global political economy.

The emerging thesis of Day begins by acknowledging the debt she owes to the two major womanist ethicists of their generation, Katie Cannon and Emilie Townes. From Cannon, she acknowledges the distinctive contours of racism and how they frame the underlying economic structure that renders the exploitation of black people within a capitalistic construct a material reality.[44] Alternatively, from Townes, she draws insights regarding the manner in which public policies reinforce the socioeconomic deprivation of the poor in America.[45]

A central thesis of Day's argument is that black and womanist theologies need to provide a theoretical paradigm for imaging an "economy of hope." Day writes,

> Black liberation and Womanist theologies need a social critique that not only spells out the roots of advanced capitalist crisis but also provides possibilities [beyond] this mode of economic activity. This social critique, which provides the roots and possibilities of capitalist crisis, might enable Black liberation and Womanist discourses to offer more insightful theological reflection on what liberation for the global poor might look like within such arrangements.[46]

As a means of theorizing around what an economy of hope might look like for the global poor people of color, Day argues for the construction of a set of contextual indices that might embody the lived realities of human rights and social justice.[47]

These concepts are not merely abstract utopian propositions; for they can also be contextualized in differing religio-cultural and sociopolitical milieus, depending upon the historical narratives and constructs that impinge on the subjectivities of the poor in any particular country or nation-state.

The hermeneutical optics through which Day seeks to articulate the contextual indices for assessing appropriate paradigms for human rights and social justice is the *imago Dei*. Invoking the *imago Dei*, Day pushes black and womanist theologies to begin to articulate a broader range of concepts that might assist the global poor (predominantly women people of color) to envision what shape or form communal thriving might take for them. The theological framing of the *imago Dei* is juxtaposed with Martha Nussbaum's articulation of the call for "universal values"[48] in order to create a platform for elucidating the concrete materiality of communal thriving, particularly for poor women of color, from within the existing economic system.

In effect, Day is calling for African American black and womanist theologies to assist in apprehending the contours of what liberation might look like for predominantly poor women of color across the globe, living within the aegis of the dominant, free market paradigm of the global economy. She is clear, however, that while black and womanist theologians might still want to claim dogmatic universal theological truths for such notions of liberation, built largely on theological reflections drawn from the Christian scriptures and their concomitant traditions, these nevertheless need to be nuanced and explicated contextually.[49] That is, it would be wrong and self-defeating, not to mention neoimperialistic, to seek to prescribe the necessary developmental standards for what constitutes human flourishing for the poor in their differing contexts across the globe.

Day's articulation of the theological challenges that confront African American black and womanist theologies vis-à-vis the global economy can be seen as the latest addition to the continuum of radical, prophetic thought that has emerged since the inceptions of Cone's biting polemics in the early 1970s. The underlying challenge that confronts Day's penetrating analysis is the potential danger that she ends up reinscribing the very model of US neoimperial, homogeneous notions of normativity that she and many of her intellectual forebears have accused the global economy of imposing on the "Third World."

Day, in all fairness, is careful not to prescribe any specific models or standards pertaining to notions of human flourishing. But it is fair to speculate, however, whether invoking the Christian concept of the *imago Dei* and linking that to the universality of liberation is but a short step from *actually* imposing an American-centered normative standard by which others will be judged and to which they should aspire. Some black theologians from outside of America have already accused African American scholarship as being complicit in this form of religio-cultural hegemony to which I have just drawn attention.[50]

These concerns notwithstanding, there is no doubting the penetrating power of the prophetic stream of African American theology that is represented in the black and womanist traditions. Long may it continue!

Notes

1. I am indebted to Keri Day for this helpful shorthand descriptor for "global economy" in an essay published in *Black Theology*. See Keri Day, "Global Economics & U.S. Public Policy: Human Liberation for the Global Poor," *Black Theology: An International Journal* 9, no. 1 (2011): 9–33.
2. See Eric Williams, *Capitalism and Slavery* (London: Andre Deutsch, 1983).
3. This issue is addressed with great alacrity by the renowned Sri Lankan liberation theologian Tissa Balasuriya. See Tissa Balasuriya, "Liberation of the Affluent," *Black Theology: An International Journal* 1, no. 1, 2001: 83–113.
4. Some African American black theologians have argued that prior to academic conceptualization of black theology one could detect elements of this nascent practice in the actions and writings of enslaved Africans living in the United States. Slave narratives, in particular, are seen as a foundational source for determining the historical trajectory of black theology in the United States, from the eighteenth and nineteenth centuries through to the present day. For further information see Dwight N. Hopkins, *Down, Up and Over: Slave Religion and Black Theology* (Minneapolis: Fortress Press, 2000).
5. See Thabita M. Anyabwile, *The Decline of African American Theology: From Biblical Faith to Cultural Captivity* (Downers Grove, IL: IVP Academic, 2007), where the author questions the "orthodox" theological credibility of black theology, along with other paradigms of African American theology. See also the more recent Anthony B. Bradley, *Liberating Black Theology: The Bible and the Black Experience in America* (Wheaton, IL: Crossway, 2010).
6. Both terms represent the bourgeoning consciousness of theologians and critical scholars whose work has emerged from nations and contexts that have been marginalised by the twin threats of colonialism and neocolonialism and the economic rapacity of free market economic globalization. See Marcella Althaus-Reid, Ivan Petrella, and Luiz Carlos Susin, eds., *Another Possible World* (London: SCM Press, 2007), R. S. Sugirtharajah, ed., *Voices from the Margin: Interpreting the Bible in the Third World* (London: SPCK; Maryknoll, NY: Orbis Books, 1997), John Parratt, ed., *An Introduction to Third World Theologies* (London: Cambridge University Press, 2004), and Virginia Fabella and R. S. Sugirtharajah, eds., *Dictionary of Third World Theologies* (Maryknoll, NY: Orbis Books, 2000).
7. EATWOT stands for the Ecumenical Association of Third World Theologians, which was founded in 1976. A helpful summary of the formation, identity, and character of the organization can be found in Fabella and Sugirtharajah, *Dictionary of Third World Theologies*, 70–72.
8. See Alistair Kee, *The Rise and Demise of Black Theology* (Aldershot: Ashgate, 2006), vii–x.
9. While greatly admiring Frederick Ware's work in outlining differing methodological approaches to black theology, I have nevertheless, offered a relatively mild critique of the African American–centric focus of the work, not withstanding any substantive critique one might make of the efficacy of the three categories he identifies in this work. See

Frederick L. Ware, *Methodologies of Black Theology* (Cleveland, OH: Pilgrim Press, 2002). For my mild critique, see Anthony G. Reddie, *Black Theology in Transatlantic Dialogue* (New York: Palgrave Macmillan, 2006), 40–41.

10. This latter point can be seen in one of my more recent books. See Anthony G. Reddie, *Working against the Grain: Re-imaging Black Theology in the 21st Century* (London: Equinox, 2008).
11. James H. Cone, *God of the Oppressed* (1975; Maryknoll, NY: Orbis Books, 1997), 156.
12. Cone, *God of the Oppressed*, 39–114.
13. See James H. Cone, "Theology's Great Sin: Silence in the Face of White Supremacy," *Black Theology: An International Journal* 2, no. 2 (July 2004): 139–52.
14. See Cone, *God of the Oppressed*, 108–37.
15. See Cone, "Theology's Great Sin," 142–45.
16. See James H. Cone, *My Soul Looks Back* (Maryknoll, NY: Orbis Books, 1986), 114–38.
17. See James H. Cone, "Looking Back, Going Forward: Black Theology as Public Theology," *Black Faith and Public Talk: Critical Essays on James H Cone's "Black Theology and Black Power,"* ed. Dwight N. Hopkins (Maryknoll, NY: Orbis Books, 1999), 246–59.
18. Alistair Kee has repeated the claim of the alleged failure of black theology to seriously engage with the legacy of Marx and Engels, in his polemical attack on the movement, in what is a highly contentious and often controversial book. See *Rise and Demise*, 90–94, 180–87.
19. See Eric Williams, *Slavery and Capitalism* (1944; Chapel Hill: University of North Carolina Press, 1994). See more recently Ivan Petrella, *The Future of Liberation Theology: An Argument and Manifesto* (London: SCM Press, 2006)
20. While Cone's engagement with the class-based analysis of Marxist thought has been relatively peripheral to his overall corpus of work, the same cannot be said of the stellar career of Cornel West. West analyses the nexus between black theology and Marxism, outlining how a comprehensive critique of capitalism can expose the hegemonic tendencies of the market, which often give rise to interlocking systems of poverty and oppression for poor and underclass people across the world. The theological perspective outlined by this particular dimension of African American black theology has been to indict the global economic system, dominated as it is by laissez-faire, liberal capitalism; as aberrant and contrary to the theology of hope that has been a central plank of European political theology, for example, since the Second World War. See Cornel West, "Black Theology of Liberation as Critique of Capitalist Civilisation," in *Black Theology: A Documentary History*, vol. 2, *1980–1992*, ed. James H. Cone and Gayraud S. Wilmore (Maryknoll, NY: Orbis Books, 1993), 410–25. The most substantive articulation of West's prophetic conceptualization of African American Christianity and its concomitant theology can be found in Cornel West, *Prophecy Deliverance! An Afro-American Revolutionary Christianity* (Philadelphia: Westminster Press, 2003). Given the semantic challenge of West's work—is he a theologian or a philosopher?—his immense contributions to the many fields of academic endeavor have been summarized in the above in order to provide greater attention to those scholars whose work sits centrally within the arena of African American black and womanist theologies.
21. See Dwight N. Hopkins and George C. L. Cummings, eds., *Cut Loose Your Stammering Tongue: Black Theology in the Slave Narrative* (Louisville, KY: Westminster John Knox Press, 2003), and Hopkins *Down, Up and Over.*
22. See Dwight N. Hopkins, *Black Theology—USA and South Africa: Politics, Culture and Liberation* (Maryknoll, NY: Orbis Books, 1989).

23. Dwight N. Hopkins, "Theologies in the USA," in Althaus-Reid, Petrella, and Susin, *Another Possible World*, 98–100.
24. Hopkins, "Theologies in the USA," 94–98.
25. See Dwight N. Hopkins, "The Religion of Globalization," in *Religions/Globalizations: Theories and Cases*, ed. Dwight N. Hopkins, Lois Ann Lorentzen, Eduardo Mendieta, and David Batstone (Durham, NC: Duke University Press, 2001), 7–32.
26. Hopkins, "The Religion of Globalization."
27. Hopkins, "The Religion of Globalization," 9.
28. Frederick Ware outlines three schools or methods for undertaking black theology. The first and perhaps most visible is the "hermeneutical school." This approach is one that seeks to ground God-talk within the revelatory framework that emerges from the Bible and the Judeo-Christian tradition. The Christ Event represents the center of this model of black theology, and liberation is the theological norm of its modus operandi. See *Methodologies of Black Theology*, 28–65.
29. See Dwight N. Hopkins, *Heart and Head: Black Theology, Past, Present and Future* (New York: Palgrave, 2002), 109–25, 127–29.
30. As opposed to the more Christocentric framework often adopted by James Cone.
31. Hopkins, *Head and Heart*, 113–14.
32. Hopkins, "The Religion of Globalization," 10–29.
33. See Dwight N. Hopkins, "New Orleans Is America," *The Sky Is Crying: Race, Class and Natural Disaster*, ed. Cheryl A. Kirk-Duggan (Nashville, TN: Abingdon, 2006), 59–68.
34. See Dwight N. Hopkins, "Black Christian Worship: Theological and Biblical Foundations," *Another World Is Possible: Spiritualities and Religions of Global Darker Peoples*, ed. Dwight N. Hopkins and Marjorie Lewis (London: Equinox, 2009), 338–40.
35. This is one of the few occasions when he offers clear instructions on the means by which people will enter heaven.
36. Hopkins, "Black Christian Worship," 340–42.
37. See Cheryl A. Kirk-Duggan, "Pimping Jesus for Political Gain: Casting Stones at Our Neighbours (Luke 10: 25–28)," in Kirk-Duggan, *The Sky Is Crying*, 210–19.
38. See Ivan Petrella, *The Future of Liberation Theology: An Argument and Manifesto* (London: SCM Press, 2006), 123–37.
39. See Jung Mo Sung, "Economics and Theology: Reflections on the Market, Globalization, and The Kingdom of God," in *Global Capitalism, Liberation Theology and The Social Sciences*, ed. A. Muller, A. Tausch, and P. Zulehner (New York: Nova Sciences Publishers, 2000).
40. See Wilf Wilde, *Crossing the River of Fire: Mark's Gospel and Global Capitalism* (Peterborough: Epworth Press, 2006).
41. With regard to this work, see Katie G. Cannon, *Katie's Canon: Womanism and the Soul of the Black Community* (New York: Continuum, 1995), 144–61, and Emilie Townes, *Womanist Ethics and the Cultural Production of Evil* (New York: Palgrave Macmillan, 2006), 111–38.
42. See Elaine E. Thomas, "Macroeconomy, Apartheid and the Rituals of Healing in an African Indigenous Church," in Hopkins et al., *Religions/Globalizations*, 135–60, where the author identifies the subjectivity of the likely victims of the global economy and the means by which African Christians are seeking to survive against this neo-imperialistic backdrop.
43. See Day, "Global Economics & U.S. Public Policy."
44. See Cannon, *Katie's Canon*, 160.
45. See Townes, *Womanist Ethics*, 126.
46. Day, "Global Economics & U.S. Public Policy," 24.

47. Day, "Global Economics & U.S. Public Policy," 24–29.
48. Martha Nussbaum, *Women and Human Development: The Capabilities Approach* (Cambridge: Cambridge University Press, 2000).
49. Day, "Global Economics & U.S. Public Policy," 27–29.
50. See Delroy A. Reid-Salmon, "A Sin of Black Theology: The Omission of the Caribbean Diasporan Experience from Black Theological Discourse," *Black Theology: An International Journal* 6, no. 2, 2008): 154–73.

Selected Texts

Anyabwile, Thabita M. *The Decline of African American Theology: From Biblical Faith to Cultural Captivity*. Downers Grove, IL: IVP Academic, 2007.

Bradley, Anthony B. *Liberating Black Theology: The Bible and the Black Experience in America*. Wheaton, IL: Crossway, 2010.

Cannon, Katie G. *Katie's Canon: Womanism and the Soul of the Black Community*. New York: Continuum, 1995.

Cone, James H. *God of the Oppressed*. Maryknoll, NY: Orbis Books, 1997.

Cone, James H. *My Soul Looks Back*. Maryknoll, NY: Orbis Books, 1986.

Cone, James H. "Theology's Great Sin: Silence in the Face of White Supremacy." *Black Theology: An International Journal* 2, no. 2 (July 2004): 139–52.

Cone, James H., and Gayraud S. Wilmore, eds. *Black Theology: A Documentary History. Volume 2: 1980–1992*. 2nd ed. Maryknoll, NY: Orbis Books, 1993.

Day, Keri. "Global Economics & U.S. Public Policy: Human Liberation for the Global Poor." *Black Theology: An International Journal* 9, no. 1 (2011): 9–33.

Hopkins, Dwight, and Marjorie Lewis, ed. *Another World Is Possible: Spiritualities and Religions of Global Darker Peoples*. London: Equinox, 2009.

Hopkins, Dwight N. *Heart and Head: Black Theology, Past, Present and Future*. New York: Palgrave, 2002.

Hopkins, Dwight N., Lois Ann Lorentzen, Eduardo Mendieta, and David Batstone, eds. *Religions/Globalizations: Theories and Cases*. Durham, NC: Duke University Press, 2001.

Hopkins, Dwight N. *Down, Up and Over: Slave Religion and Black Theology*. Minneapolis: Fortress Press, 2000.

Hopkins, Dwight N. *Black Theology—USA and South Africa: Politics, Culture and Liberation*. Maryknoll, NY: Orbis Books, 1989.

Kee, Alistair. *The Rise and Demise of Black Theology*. Aldershot: Ashgate, 2006.

Kirk-Duggan, Cheryl A., ed. *The Sky Is Crying: Race, Class and Natural Disaster*. Nashville, TN: Abingdon, 2006.

Marcella, Althaus-Reid, Ivan Petrella, and Luiz Carlos Susin, eds. *Another Possible World*. London: SCM Press, 2007.

Townes, Emilie. *Womanist Ethics and the Cultural Production of Evil*. New York: Palgrave Macmillan, 2006.

Ware, Frederick L. *Methodologies of Black Theology*. Cleveland, OH: Pilgrim Press, 2002.

West, Cornel. *Prophecy Deliverance! An Afro-American Revolutionary Christianity*. Philadelp hia: Westminster, 2003.

Williams, Eric. *Slavery and Capitalism*. Chapel Hill: University of North Carolina Press, 1994.

CHAPTER 30

AFRICAN AMERICAN THEOLOGY AND THE AMERICAN HEMISPHERE

JOSEF SORETT

> But in order to deal with the untapped and dormant force of the previously subjugated, in order to survive as a human, moving, moral weight in the world, America and all the Western nations will be forced to reëxamine themselves and release themselves from many things that are now taken to be sacred.... The struggle, therefore, that now begins in the world is extremely complex, involving the historical role of Christianity in the realm of power—that is, politics—and in the realm of morals.
>
> —James Baldwin, *The Fire Next Time* (1962)

JAMES Baldwin's premise that Christianity and colonialism are inseparably linked in the institutional marginalization of black and brown people around the globe remains, if nothing else, provocative. Yet his claim that the discourses of religion, race, and nation coalesced in the formation of the Americas is well founded. While a number of scholars have advanced related arguments in recent years, Henry Goldschmidt captures the matter quite poignantly. Discussions of Christianity, he writes, "must account for the complex relationships between religious rituals and symbols, the economics of chattel slavery, and the politics of national and racial identity. These seemingly 'nonreligious' social forces are, in fact, intrinsic to the history of American Christianity."[1] While Baldwin sought to locate Christian theology within its colonial context in the Americas, the social upheaval of the decade in which he wrote also facilitated the emergence of a novel theological discourse in the academy; namely, black liberation theology. By 1970, James Cone's first two books—*Black Theology and Black Power* and *A Black Theology of Liberation*—were published. Together these texts effectively inaugurated a new school of Christian theology that began with the African American experience of enslavement and oppression in the United States and resonated with the militant ethos of Black Power, which crystallized at precisely the moment in which Cone delivered his manuscripts.

Whereas James Cone's work began with the black-white binary that set the terms of racial discourse in the United States and which ordered his upbringing in the segregated South, other theologians extended this liberation motif to elsewhere in the Americas.[2] And while Baldwin shared Cone's particular southern US past, his claims in *The Fire Next Time* anticipated these respective liberation trajectories in the form of a comprehensive critique of colonial Christianity as an ordering social and spiritual force in the West. To be sure, discourses on race and religion take on particular meanings within the context of specific nation-states. However, the distinctiveness of respective nations developed as part of an emerging New World complex identified as the Americas. In this regard, Baldwin's arguments are especially pertinent to this essay's effort to examine black theology from a hemispheric perspective. For even as the language of globalization grows increasingly popular, contemporary discussions of black theology often remain bound by a historical memory that maps neatly onto a particular moment in space and time; that is, the United States at precisely the moment that Baldwin penned his prescient words. Otherwise put, conversations about black theology continue to conjure a particular iconography and narrative of African American religious history—namely, of Martin Luther King Jr. and the modern civil rights movement of the 1960s.[3] To this day, practically speaking, King serves as an exemplary model of progressive spirituality for aspiring religious leaders; across lines of race and nation, both within and beyond Christian churches. However, for scholars, King's image often works to constrain an intellectual vision of the field such that black liberal Protestantism continues to be taken for granted as normative. Thus, as an academic field initiated by James Cone still finds itself in the shadows of figures such as King—the black Baptist preacher who stands in as proxy for a North American-centered Afro-Protestant Christianity—a hemispheric approach to black theology, and the African American religious experience it aims to interpret and embolden, is both timely and necessary.

More generally, an account of how race and religion mediate asymmetries of power both within and across national borders is paramount. Indeed, Baldwin's 1962 clarion call to national reflection on the colonial politics of Christianity in the Americas remains relevant for interpreting the present state of affairs. Yet it is equally compelling as a historiographical question. Black theology, as a field, has for some time been preoccupied with what might be called "the problem of Christianity," that is, its historic ties to colonialism and white supremacy in the shaping of social life in the Americas. Indeed, shortly after their publication, James Cone's first books were met with vigorous debate. Like Baldwin, Cone rightfully took white Christian churches to task for their racism. Yet some argued that in his indebtedness to white theologians before him the father of black theology in effect reinscribed the logics of white supremacy. In this view, Cone's racial critique did not go far enough; black sources and methods were required to sustain the aims of a theology of Black Power.[4] However, others argued that black theology's limitations could not solely be attributed to race matters. Rather, Cone's recasting of theology on the premise that "authentic" Christianity must privilege the oppressed failed to sufficiently account for a more complicated matrix of relationships that made Christianity in the modern world. In fact, the making of new worlds (i.e., the Americas) produced Christianity anew, alongside a set of other novel social formations, including race and nation—to name just two.[5] Thus, under the sign of modernity, Christianity is as much a matter of power, place, and practice, as it of race, doctrine, or dogma. Rather, it is all of these and, perhaps, more, as the discourses of religion, race, and nation are co-constitutive and always part of a shared geopolitical terrain.[6] Thus, the Americas emerged as a novel historical complex in which a number of people groups, organized by multiple competing forces, interests, and institutional arrangements, came into *contact* with one another under particular historical circumstances; and the categories of religion, race, and nation figured as primary interpretive and ordering discourses.

This essay is, in part, a response to James Baldwin's provocation. Too many Americans, he diagnosed, mistakenly took a peculiar coalescence of race, nation, and religion to be gospel; and it was this fundamental (mis)formulation that required re-examination. In particular, I take up the international scope of Baldwin's critique and follow it as frame for tracing the development of black theology as an academic enterprise. Thus far I have suggested that a hemispheric approach to black theology more helpfully captures the role of Christianity in the making of the Americas even as it illumines how a particular coalescence of race, nation, and religion shaped the formation of the field in the United States. It is under contingent and contested conditions of contact that a host of New World theologies grew out of the cultural soils of the African American religious experience. Similarly, black theology as a scholarly endeavor was born amid the peculiar and particular circumstances of racial and cultural contact in the academy. In the following section, I move from advancing a hemispheric approach exclusively to outline a broader notion of contact as the context for black theology in the Americas more generally. Furthermore, my aim here is also to identify contact as a shared analytical referent for a set of related academic terms that have been employed as of late to interpret black life in the modern era. Then, before concluding, in a final section I sketch out a preliminary genealogy of contact within the field of black theology, including three trajectories of scholarship that are each animated by a concern with this category.

Black Theology in the Americas: Theorizing (Afro)Christianity in the Contact Zone

In recent years, a range of academic fields have attempted to cultivate analytical frameworks that better map the growing reality of the ever-increasing interconnectedness of societies around the world. To be clear, this phenomenon is about more than simply naming novel developments that have turned "globalization" into a dominant discourse. Indeed, the broader impulse here reflects an effort to account for the ways that social realities—in the present, but also in the past—are never entirely bounded by the modern contexts of particular nation-states. This scholarly concern is also often animated by a desire to decenter America in the work of knowledge production; an effort to counter an American (really, US) hegemony in the realm of ideas. Interestingly, there are a range of rubrics that name these theoretical approaches—including hemispheric, transnational, diaspora, and "Atlantic world" studies.[7] These developments have no doubt made significant inroads within the field of black theology, countering the field's dominant narrative of its North American emergence during the 1960s. If the coalescence (and crossing of the lines) of race and nation is foregrounded in such approaches, here primary attention is given to the role of religion in mediating relationships (and crossing borders) between state formations and racial regimes.

In this regard, black theology, then, has also taken up the task of reflecting upon how African American religious (primarily, Christian) practices have been cultivated betwixt and between the borders of various nation-states. Such an approach accounts for the ways in which an (Afro) Protestant hegemony has also worked in tandem with an equally privileged paradigm of the US nation-state. While there are specific subtleties attendant to the respective categories identified above (i.e., hemispheric, transnationalism, diaspora, Atlantic world), each of these terms can be connected by a shared sensibility that would locate black theology as emerging under novel conditions of contact within the context of the Americas. For instance, such an approach figures the story of African American religion(s) in the United States as part of a larger cultural, economic, and political order that emerged during the period of colonialism, conquest, and enslavement. Otherwise put, the forces and logics of colonialism helped to set in place structural arrangements between "North" and "South" in an emerging American hemisphere. And, more broadly, this historical moment—often generously bracketed as "modernity" or the "Age of Enlightenment"—witnessed the conjoining of Africa, Europe, and the Americas in the development of an Atlantic world established through transnational networks of what was the Atlantic slave trade. This trade facilitated the exchange of various material goods and services, as well as enabling (and requiring) new forms of contact between cultures, ideas, and peoples. Most precisely, for the field of black theology, the transatlantic slave trade's trafficking of black and brown bodies played a pivotal role in literally building the Americas even as those same bodies were simultaneously transformed into diasporic subjects.[8]

As indicative of the language of "trade," the Atlantic world emerged first and foremost as a marketplace, where ambitious nation-states competed with one another for a greater share of the resources of the new worlds that were the Americas. Various sorts of capital were never far from the motives of individual slaveholders and conquistadors, corporate entities and nation-states alike. However, in addition (and often attached) to such profits, the Atlantic world was also a space/place that allowed for vibrant interchanges in the realm of culture. For instance, languages, rituals, cosmologies, and agricultural acumen were just a few of the assets that came with the bodies of the enslaved when they were transported across the Atlantic to various regions of the American hemisphere. Long-standing economic and cultural practices—as well as the emerging discourses of religion, race, and nation previously foregrounded—were all vital ingredients to the novel cultures and economies that took root en route to and in the Americas. Each of these above terms helpfully captures the realities of movement and dislocation under the novel circumstances of contact subsequently named as modernity. Indeed, the complexities attendant to these multifold formations are perhaps most precisely captured by the idea of what Mary-Louise Pratt has termed "contact zones." In her now classic work on the cultural worlds of the colonial Americas, *Imperial Eyes: Travel Writing and Transculturation* (1992), Pratt writes that "contact zones" are

> social spaces where disparate cultures meet, clash and grapple with each other, often in *highly asymmetrical relations of domination and subordination* like colonialism, slavery, or their aftermaths as they are lived out across the globe today.[9]

In accounting for the dynamics of "contact zones" Pratt provides a framework that maps the multiple contexts in which colonialism and slavery were central to structural arrangements across the Americas. Such a perspective acknowledges the different sorts of societies that developed in light of the regional, national, and continental complex that was New World slavery, even as it identifies each of these iterations as interwoven in a shared imperial order and economic system. One might envision a host of more specific contact zones within a larger arrangement of space and place: the Contact Zone (i.e., the Americas). Thus, the black-white binary of the United States—which provided the specific social context for the birth of black theology as an academic project—was but one instantiation of a network of contact zones in which distinct cultures and ideas, and individuals and institutions, collided amid social conditions overdetermined by vast asymmetries of power.

Toward a Genealogy of Contact in Black Theology: Three Trajectories

One can begin to see more clearly the links between Christianity and colonialism that made for black theology as a discourse on (and of) the contact zone. Indeed, a theory of the Americas (or the Atlantic world, or African diaspora) ought always include an account of theology in the contact zone. Keeping in mind the long-standing histories and novel religious forms that converged and emerged in the Americas, it is also necessary to remember that Christianity has constituted what Charles Long has referred to as the "cultural categories of the American reality."[10] Or, to paraphrase Cornel West, Christianity has, in effect, functioned as the normative religious gaze in the West.[11] As such, in addition to spiritual resources, social power has always been attached to an embrace of Christianity. Conversely, a rejection of Christianity, or alignment with any other religious tradition, has always represented the risk of marginalization. This is the very nature of life in the contact zone. Religions are implicated in an "arena and field of power relationships," and in the context of the Americas Christianity has always amounted to an "ultimate" power play.[12] One way this normative power manifested itself was in establishment of black theology in the United States. In the final section of this essay, I will outline three trajectories that each carry out a critique of the manner in which religion, race, and nation coalesced in the formation of academic black theology as a North American Afro-Protestant project. Again, in delineating this preliminary genealogy, I will limit the narrative to academic theologians (with one exception) who have offered interpretations of African American religious life from a perspective that implicitly or explicitly embraces a broader notion of contact. To be clear, this genealogy in no way aspires to be comprehensive or claims to map an entire field. Nor does it fully capture the complexity of any single author's entire work. However, each of the works engaged here exemplifies an approach to black theology that foregrounds contact and which recognizes the flow of information and experience across the boundaries of particular nation-states—whether through a framework of the Americas, the African diaspora, or the Atlantic world.

By way of a first trajectory, it is important to note that adopting a theoretical perspective that is transnational in scope does not necessarily require turning one's analytical attention outside of the United States. In fact, one of the earliest challenges to the manner in which black theology took for granted its US context came in the form of a critique from at outsider of sorts, who turned his sights inward. Charles Long, while trained as a historian of religion, was deeply invested in the study of black religion in the United States. Shortly after the publication of James Cone's early work, Long challenged the dominance of a theological account of black religion, which in his estimation often led to the conflation of black religion with black churches. His critiques of the prominence of theology and the privileging of Christianity in scholarship on African American religious life are well known; and his arguments continue to influence current scholarship—both theological and humanistic—in this regard. Long's now classic essay "Perspectives for the Study of Afro-American Religion in the United States" begins with an effort to delineate how he understands the difference between religion and theology, and then proceeds to recommend three possibilities for thinking about religion in black culture on more expansive terms—that is, outside the categories of Christian theology.[13] It merits special noting that Long's arguments call equal attention both to questions of theory and method, and to the varieties of social phenomena that can be identified as comprising the black religious experience.

A number of recent studies of African American religion that emphasize what Charles Long once referred to as "extra-church orientations" (i.e., African-derived religious practices) are indebted to his seminal contributions in this regard.[14] While Long encouraged the field to move outside of a Christian norm and theological method, he nonetheless directed most of his own theoretical efforts to the United States, specifically, as "the classical example of the meaning of cultural contact." In this regard, Long's work is as much about inviting a theory and thicker description of the religious practices of black people in the United States as it is about unveiling the "dynamics of concealment and the creation of discourses of power." In this vein, he raised the question, "Are there any continuities between Hume the philosopher, Hume the historian, and Hume the colonial officer?" In other words, intellectual projects and politics were inextricably linked. For Long, one could examine black religion to discern "the meaning of cultural contact"; but one could also do so in "the history of European and American thought."[15] Moreover, America presented both as a historical reality and as a "hermeneutical situation," a logic apparent in the unfolding of American history, as well as in the field of history.[16] That is to say, the logics that mark African American religion and religion in America as distinct academic fields reflected the same asymmetries of power that have ordered the history of racial and cultural contact in the Americas.

While Charles Long put forward a theory of the Americas and a theology grounded in the history of contact within the United States, a second trajectory can be seen in the work of black theologians who have turned their attention to particular regions of the Atlantic world other than the United States, such as the Caribbean. For instance, Anthony Pinn's *Varieties of African American Religious Experience* (1998) offers a helpful theological introduction to various non-Christian practices, including voodoo and Santeria, which turn the field's attention outside of the United States. However, while Pinn no doubt intended to invite conversations about black theology outside of a North American context, his aims were more explicitly directed toward troubling a "narrow agenda and resource base" limited to "Christianity in ways that establish Christian doctrine and concerns as normative."[17] Here one notes the way in which a concern with decentering Christianity often overlaps with an effort to map black theology across a broader geography of the Americas. Before and since what

Pinn described as an "initial exploration of four underexplored traditions" (at least two of which tracked the transformation of religious practice from Africa to the New World), a number of other scholars have more explicitly advanced black theology from a Caribbean perspective. Noel Erskine's *Decolonizing Theology: A Caribbean Perspective* (1981) was one of the first to do so. At issue for Erskine was not so much the categories of Christian theology, as the cultural contexts through which these theologies were transmitted. For instance, he writes, "God as presented within the Caribbean Church was often not the symbol of freedom but, rather, the extension of the European and the North American church experience."[18] In Erskine's view, Christian theology as it was received in the Caribbean reflected the very same asymmetries of power that governed the structural and racial arrangements of colonialism in general. Thus, reminiscent of James Cone, Erskine sought to articulate a "Third World" perspective, which decolonized Caribbean Christianity of its white / European / North American past, through the framework of black liberation theology grounded in his own biographical context of Jamaica.[19]

Whereas Noel Erskine's early work aimed primarily to invert the colonial logics that figured Christianity's development in the Caribbean, later scholars (including Erskine himself) moved from examining Christian contexts in the Caribbean to also engaging other religious traditions as a resource for black theology.[20] Central here is the recognition of cultural contact across and between different religious traditions, even as those traditions traversed the boundaries of various nation-states. That is, colonialism facilitated the imposition of white supremacy via theological discourse and Christian practice, and novel spiritual forms that brought together African cosmologies, Christian doctrine, and ideas and practices indigenous to the Americas also emerged in these New Worlds. Black theologians working in this vein thus sought to identify, more specifically, the ways that various African-derived practices were formative in the development of religion and culture in the Caribbean.

One excellent example of this approach is found in the work of Dianne (Stewart) Diakité. In *Three Eyes for the Journey: African Dimensions of the Jamaican Religious Experience* (2005), Diakité argues that in the face of an overwhelming hegemony of "Eurocentric Christianity," there were also "coded Black religious institutions with ambiguous identities and practices yielding a surplus of seemingly contradictory meanings in their ritual uses of material from both African-based and Euro-Christian traditions."[21] Furthermore, Diakité resists framing indigenous Jamaican churches (i.e., Native Baptist, Revival, and Zion) as "unorthodox" or "Afro-Christian" derivatives of a "true" or "real" Christianity, as they are often understood.[22] Rather, she locates these indigenous "black churches" within a broader repertoire of African-derived religious traditions, including Obeah, Myal, and Kumina. Reversing the colonial logics of contact, for Diakité, requires refusing the impulse to comport religious practice in Jamaica to a Christian norm that then reinscribes a certain orthodoxy. Rather, she posits that these traditions are part of a "chain of remembering and linking African traditions from the past to the struggle for liberation." In this view, the task of "rethinking of black theology in the African Diaspora"—or decolonizing black theology, to borrow Erskine's term—involves more than divorcing Christianity in the Caribbean from a North American or European cultural context. It also insists that black theology acknowledge that the very categories employed to interpret these religious traditions bear the marks of a colonial past. Instead, Diakité embraces an "African counternarrative of religious presence" in which she then locates religion and culture in the Jamaican context.[23] In this way *Three Eyes for the Journey* both follows the evolution of religious practice across the Atlantic world (i.e., from Africa to Jamaica) and offers an account of spiritual agency in the Caribbean. That is to say, Diakité and others in this trajectory help readers to see that the transnational networks of religious practice cultivated across the African diaspora do not begin or end with colonial rule—be it via economic forces or theological discourse. While a history of asymmetric relations of power persists in ordering the terms of racial and cultural contact, black theology can account for the ways in which a Christian hegemony—via its own analytical categories—encounters and often overdetermines African-derived practices; but it can also document how such Caribbean traditions have actively resisted their own marginalization in the Americas.

A third trajectory could be aptly described as developing at the nexus of black theology (as it emerged in North America) and black British cultural studies. Following Paul Gilroy's critique of black studies, more generally, as a US-centered project, these scholars offer a theological interpretation of black life in Great Britain while also following the travel and transformations of religion and culture throughout the black Atlantic.[24] This approach to black theology very much tracks the flow and exchange between the former British Empire and its now postcolonial outposts. Two of the most prominent scholars working in this milieu have been Robert Beckford and Anthony Reddie. Beckford, who is typically credited as England's first tutor in black theology, has authored several monographs that place in conversation Afro-Pentecostalism in England and black popular cultures throughout the diaspora. Texts like *Jesus Is Dread: Black Theology and Black Culture in Great Britain* (1998), *Dread and Pentecostal: A Political Theology for the Black Church in Britain* (2000), and *God of the Rahtid: Redeeming Rage* (2003) established Beckford as a pioneering voice who synthesized black Atlantic religions and expressive cultures (i.e., Pentecostalism, Rastafarianism, reggae music) into a distinct black theology grounded in the British context.

Beckford's most recent book, *Jesus Dub: Theology, Music and Social Change* (2006), continued on this path but with a particular focus of the aesthetics of one musical form—namely, dub—that has received much mainstream attention in recent years.[25] Here Beckford begins his arguments with multiple appeals to a cultural context both for dub and black theology that confounds assumptions of any single national narrative. References to "African diasporan Christian traditions" and "African Caribbean Christian thought" signal a perspective not exclusively tied to the black churches in England that received much of his attention in earlier work. Still, Beckford clarifies that the dub music (and the larger genre of dancehall/reggae) that is his focus developed "within the highly charged political environments of Jamaica and inner city Britain."[26] Throughout the text Beckford moves conceptually back and forth from Jamaica to England, at the same time as he shifts from the "church hall" to the "dance hall" as sites and sources of black theology. In doing so, he weaves a story that resists a single national home even as he blurs what are often the accepted, or taken for granted, boundaries of religious practice and theological discourse (i.e., church/nightclub, sacred/secular). In each instance, Beckford's theology is fundamentally a diasporic form. Dub traverses the Atlantic world and is never the product of a single space or place. Further, a dub reading presents black theology as a cultural practice that emerged on the move across several political contexts, each of which imposed physical and legal constraints on the freedom to move of the people who created the aesthetic form. Indeed movement and migration (across and within multiple institutions and nation-states), and the novel identities and cultural forms such mobility occasions, might be identified as the central trope of black theology as put forward by Robert Beckford.

In a similar fashion, Beckford's black British contemporary, Anthony Reddie defines the task of black theology in terms of movement across institutions, as well as in its explicit articulation of practical commitments. Reddie puts the matter bluntly: "I am a practitioner of Black theology in Britain."[27] Here black theology is envisaged as a form of "Christian praxis" preoccupied with "social activism" rather than (and critical of) academic abstraction.[28] In addition to activist commitments, Reddie understands black theology to be a diasporic intellectual practice. As editor of *Black Theology: An International Journal,* Reddie resists linking black theology with any one particular nation-state in the very naming of the publication. Rather, *Black Theology* provides "a forum for the articulation and expression of issues faith coming Black people across the world... in relation to African, Caribbean, American, Antipodean or Asian origins and other contexts."[29] For Reddie, both black theology and religious practice reflect a transnational frame mapped out first via the routes of colonialism. Reversing that history, antiapartheid activism in South Africa, the modern civil rights movement in the United States, and Sam Sharpe—the Jamaican Baptist who helped lead a rebellion against slavery in 1831—are ready examples of the "black spirituality" that Reddie embraces as a resource for theological reflection. In doing so, he outlines and elevates a genealogy of religion in the black Atlantic world as the means for "re-affirming the movement of Black theology with the social activism of the left." While firmly grounded in his own liberal Protestant background—via the Methodist Church in England—Reddie, on one hand, confirms the Christian roots of academic black theology. Yet, on the other, he encourages a transatlantic dialogue concerning the roles that black churches have played in fostering social activism both in Great Britain and the Americas.

Each of the works in these first two trajectories helpfully carry out the aims of a hemispheric approach to black theology that moves across the boundaries of respective nation-states in the Atlantic world, as well as, and specifically, outside the borders of the United States. Some of these black theologians have also interrogated the ways that Christianity has worked to limit the object(s) of inquiry for black theology (i.e., black churches), as well as the methodologies employed therein. More recently, there are several examples of black theology that have followed the colonial logics of contact toward what Charles Long once referred to as "the classical example." In varying ways, works in this third and final trajectory have taken up both Long's critique of Christian theology and his larger theory of religion and contact as it applies to the United States.[30] For instance, Stephanie Mitchem's *African American Folk Healing* (2007) brings together theological and historical methods to examine how "non-Western sanctioned practices," Christian theology and "institutional biomedicine" existed coterminously and coalesced into a culture of healing practices present within black communities to this day. Indeed, Mitchem identifies African American communities in the United States as a contact zone (although not named as such) that gave rise to a holistic theology of healing, which she locates within a broader repertoire of "black mystical traditions."[31] Furthermore, through Mitchem's work one can see how the very term "folk" is itself a modern category produced by the forms of contact and exchange that are definitive of the particular history of race in the United States. Within this third trajectory, the most explicit effort to theorize the Americas toward the end of a hemispheric black theology can be found in the work of James Noel, who perhaps unsurprisingly explicitly identifies himself as a student of Charles Long. As Noel concedes, Long is quick to point out that he is not a theologian. Still, in following this chain of influence, one can begin to locate black theology within a set of theoretical investigations of black religious life in the Americas. Interestingly, in terms of theorizing the Americas as a site of contact, Long himself put the matter in theological terms. According to Charles Long, "The New World was intellectually and economically a matter of *ultimate concern*."[32]

As has already been noted, in recent years a number of scholars of African American religion and black theology have fruitfully extended critiques of black theology made earlier by Charles Long and others. However, James Noel's recent book, *Black Religion and the Imagination of Matter in the Atlantic World* (2009), is arguably the most ambitious effort to deploy Long's theoretical approach to the study of religion to advance the field of black theology. Where Mitchem appeals historical method (i.e., archival research) in her study, Noel weds Long's theory of black religion with historical studies of the emergence of the Atlantic world.[33] According to Noel, "Black religions in the New World were determined by new modes of exchange elaborated in the Atlantic World through the commodification of black bodies." "Modern" forms of contact and exchange facilitated by colonialism and enslavement were the very terms that gave rise to black religion as such. They also produced the very idea of blackness, in general, Noel explains. Not only is black theology a discourse on and of contact, bringing together multiple cultures and ideas amid all sorts of asymmetries of power. Contact in the Atlantic world also created the very idea of a "black people" as an outgrowth of a "complex system of contacts and exchanges that occurred between various African groups" prior to the development of the transatlantic trade.[34] Following Long, for James Noel conditions of "contact and exchange" are core features that comprise human existence, and religious experience, specifically. And the emergence of the Atlantic world—resulting from the intellectual and social advances ironically associated both with Enlightenment *and* the slave trade—occasioned a host of novel forms of contact. With this expansive notion of religion as contact, Noel proceeds to theorize black religion, in particular, by engaging what might be viewed as a set of case studies. Each case offers an instance of contact associated with black life in the United States, including slave insurrections, "mulatto" identity, African American visual art, and the aesthetics of black preaching. Each of the examples that Noel takes up come together to present a fresh vision of black theology that begins and ends with the conditions of contact and exchange in the Atlantic world.

Conclusion

My aims in this essay have been directed toward two related ends. First, I have outlined how the emergence of black theology as an academic field involved a coming together of discourses on religion, race, and nation. The convergence of these frames in the field's formation was effective to the point that to this day black theology continues to be presumed to be an African American Christian project grounded in and directed to black life within the borders of the United States. That said, the prevalence of this presumption continues despite a history of protest that dates back almost to the very founding of the field, as signaled by the publication of James Cone's first books and the reception they generated from his contemporaries. I have highlighted this particular North American history not to celebrate its prominence, but rather to then illustrate how over the several decades of black theology's history, scholars have pushed back against its dominant narratives both religious and national. In fact, challenges to black theology's Christian and US roots have gone hand in hand, such that efforts to engage "extra-church traditions" have also often directed attention to elsewhere in the Americas. A number of academic rubrics have been identified in efforts to do so, including what has been described herein primarily as a hemispheric approach to black theology. However, rather than adopting one exclusive approach to theorizing the ways in which experiences, identities, and practices are constituted within and across the boundaries of particular nation-states, I have argued that these varying terms each belie a concern with exploring the Americas as a novel site of contact that arose under the sign of modernity.

Following from this, the second goal I pursued in this essay was to provide a preliminary account of how the idea of contact—or what Mary-Louis Pratt has called "contact zones"—has been addressed over the history of the field of black theology. Shifting from a focus on traffic across national borders to an emphasis on contact between asymmetrically organized actors on an international stage has served the purpose of reminding us that a hemispheric approach (or diaspora, transnational, Atlantic world studies) is never simply about what is where, who is here and there, Christian or otherwise, black or white. Rather, relationships between religious practice in the Americas (North and South) and Africa (or the Caribbean) are always evolving and mutually influencing, and often involve active commitments to (or inheritances from) more than one of what are typically framed as independent and discrete religious traditions (i.e., Christian, etc.) or national identities. In short, Africa is here; and Christianity is there. Moreover, efforts to decenter the United States or unravel a Christian hegemony also often invite competing but equally limiting narratives of race, place, and orthodoxy. As Brian Axel puts it in his critique of diaspora studies: "This very common analytic posits that a homeland is originary and constitutive of a diaspora, and very often it supports an essentialization of origins and a fetishization of what is supposed to be found at the origin (e.g., tradition, religion, language, race)."[35] Thus, to tend to the contact zone is not to fetishize a source or site of origins, but rather to foreground the forms of religious practice and theological production that emerge in all sorts of social spaces (not just particular places). Even more, it tends to the fact that all such spaces and places, and various religious traditions, are overwhelmingly informed by asymmetries of power. Finally, it is important to note that the routes black theology has recently traveled, outside the constraints of a specific nation-state formulation, might in fact be more appropriately recognized as a reclaiming of the field's historic roots. For it is impossible to understand the formation of academic black theology in North America without locating it within the broader claims put forward by James Baldwin in 1962 in *The Fire Next Time* concerning "the historical role of Christianity in the realm of power."

NOTES

1. Henry Goldschmidt and Elizabeth McAlister, *Race, Nation and Religion in the Americas* (New York: Oxford University Press, 2005), 19.
2. Gustavo Gutiérrez, *A Theology of Liberation: History, Politics and Salvation*, trans. and ed. Sister Caridad Inda and John Eagleson (Maryknoll, NY: Orbis Books, 1973).
3. Eddie S. Glaude Jr., "Conclusion: 'Africa" in the Study of African American Religion," in *The African Diaspora in the Study of Religion* (New York: Palgrave Macmillan, 2007), 239–50.
4. Cecil Cone, *The Identity Crisis in Black Theology* (Nashville: AMEC Publishing House, 1975).
5. Henry Goldschmidt and Elizabeth McAlister, eds., *Race, Nation and Religion in the Americas* (New York: Oxford University Press, 2005).

6. Goldschmidt and McAlister, *Race, Nation and Religion.*
7. What follows are several texts that provide solid introductions to debates around each of these terms. On hemispheric approaches, see Caroline F. Levander and Robert S. Levine, *Hemispheric American Studies* (New Brunswick, NJ: Rutgers University Press, 2008). In Atlantic world studies, see John Thornton, *African and Africans in the Making of the Atlantic World, 1400–1800* (Cambridge: Cambridge University Press, 1998). As for diaspora, see Brent Hayes Edwards, *The Practice of Diaspora: Literature, Translation, and the Rise of Black Internationalism* (Cambridge: Harvard University Press, 2003); Paul Christopher Johnson, *Diaspora Conversions: Black Carib Religion and the Recovery of Africa* (Berkeley: University of California Press, 2007). In terms of transnationalism, see Winifried Fluck, Donald Pease, and John Carlos Rowe, eds., *Re-framing the Transnational Turn in American Studies* (Hanover, NH: Dartmouth University Press, 2011).
8. Thornton, *Africa and Africans*, 98–128; John Hope Franklin and Evelyn Brooks Higginbotham, *From Slavery to Freedom: A History of African Americans*, 9th ed. (New York: McGraw-Hill, 2011), 22–46.
9. Mary Louise Pratt, *Imperial Eyes: Travel Writing and Transculturation* (New York: Routledge, 2003), 4; italics mine.
10. Charles Long, *Significations: Sign, Symbols, and Images in the Interpretation of Religion* (Aurora, CO: Davies Group, 1986), 7.
11. Cornel West, *Prophesy Deliverance! An Afro-American Revolutionary Christianity* (Philadelphia: Westminster Press, 1982), 47–65. West's "Genealogy of Modern Racism" traces various historical forces "to show that the idea of white supremacy emerges partly because of the powers within the structure of modern discourse—powers to produce and prohibit, develop and delimit, forms of rationality, scientificity, and objectivity which set perimeters and draw boundaries for the intelligibility, availability, and legitimacy of certain ideas." Similarly, Protestant Christianity has played the role of the normative/hegemonic religious discourse, alongside of science and aesthetics. To operate outside of its parameters is to risk invisibility.
12. Long, *Significations*, 2–7.
13. Long, *Significations*, 187ff.
14. Long's impact on the field is quite significant and an article in the *Journal of the American Academy of Religion* makes a claim concerning the relevance of his work for the broader project of religious studies and American religious history. See Louis Benjamin Rolski, "Charles Long and the Re-orientation of American Religious History," *Journal of the American Academy of Religion* 80, no. 3 (September 2012): 1–25. For a short selection of works on African American religion that are influenced by Charles Long, see Yvonne Chireau, *Black Magic: The African American Conjuring Tradition* (Berkeley: University of California Press, 2003); Eddie S. Glaude Jr. *Exodus: Religion, Race and Nation in Early Nineteenth Century Black America* (Chicago: University of Chicago Press, 2000); Tracey Hucks, *Yoruba Traditions and African American Religious Nationalism* (Albuquerque: University of New Mexico Press, 2012); Anthony B. Pinn, *Terror and Triumph: The Nature of Black Religion* (Minneapolis: Fortress Press, 2003); Emilie Townes, *Womanist Ethics and the Cultural Production of Evil* (New York: Palgrave Macmillan, 2006).
15. Long, *Significations*, 141.
16. Long, *Significations*, 148–69.

17. Anthony B. Pinn, *Varieties of African American Religious Experience* (Minneapolis: Fortress Press, 1998), 1.
18. Noel Erskine, *Decolonizing Theology: A Caribbean Perspective* (Maryknoll, NY: Orbis Books, 1981), 1.
19. Erskine, *Decolonizing Theology*, 2–3.
20. Noel Erskine, *From Garvey to Marley: Rastafari Theology* (Gainesville: University Press of Florida, 2007).
21. Dianne Stewart Diakité, *Three Eyes for the Journey: African Dimensions of the Jamaican Religious Experience* (New York: Oxford University Press, 2005), xvi–xviii.
22. In this regard, Diakité highlights the ways in which claims of authenticity, normativity, and orthodoxy circulate in definitions of black theology and African American religion—as discourses on both race and religion—in a way that squares with current debates in religious studies, more generally. For a helpful analysis of such debates in religious studies, see Robert A. Orsi, *Between Heaven and Earth: The Religious Worlds People Make and the Scholars Who Study Them* (Princeton, NJ: Princeton University Press, 2006).
23. Stewart, *Three Eyes*, xvii.
24. Paul Gilroy, *The Black Atlantic: Modernity and Double-Consciousness* (Cambridge: Harvard University Press, 1993).
25. For a more extended treatment of this book, see my review: Josef Sorett, review of Robert Beckford, *Jesus Dub: Theology, Music, and Social Change* (New York: Routledge, 2006) in *Pneuma* 34 (2012): 431–78.
26. Beckford. *Jesus Dub*, 1–2.
27. Anthony G. Reddie, "The Quest for Liberation and Inclusivity," *Ecumenical Review (World Council of Churches)* (2012): 530.
28. Anthony G. Reddie, *Working Against the Grain: Re-imaging Black Theology in the 21st Century* (London: Equinox, 2008), 8.
29. See description of *Black Theology: An International Journal* at http://maneypublishing.com/index.php/journals/blt/.
30. Rolski, "Charles H. Long."
31. Stephanie Mitchem. *African American Folk Healing* (New York: New York University Press, 2007), 5–6.
32. Long, *Significations*, 110; italics mine. Pinn describes Long's work as situated between the historian of religion Mircea Eliade and the theologian Paul Tillich. See Anthony B. Pinn, "Black Theology," in *Liberation Theologies in the United States*, ed. Stacey M. Floyd-Thomas and Anthony B. Pinn (New York: New York University Press, 2010). Also see James Noel, *Black Religion and the Imagination of Matter in the Atlantic World* (New York: Palgrave Macmillan, 2009), 15–36.
33. Mitchem, *African American Folk Healing*, 11–24.
34. Noel, *Black Religion*, 4–7.
35. Brian Keith Axel, "The Diasporic Imaginary," *Public Culture* 14, no. 2 (Spring 2002): 411.

Selected Texts

Cone, Cecil. *The Identity Crisis in Black Theology*. Nashville: AMEC Publishing House, 1975.

Diakité, Dianne Stewart. *Three Eyes for the Journey: African Dimensions of the Jamaican Religious Experience*. New York: Oxford University Press, 2005.

Franklin, John Hope, and Evelyn Brooks Higginbotham. *From Slavery to Freedom: A History of African Americans*. 9th ed. New York: McGraw-Hill, 2011.

Gilroy, Paul. *The Black Atlantic: Modernity and Double-Consciousness*. Cambridge: Harvard University Press, 1993.

Goldschmidt, Henry, and Elizabeth McAlister. *Race, Nation and Religion in the Americas*. New York: Oxford University Press, 2005.

Levander, Caroline F., and Robert S. Levine. *Hemispheric American Studies*. New Brunswick, NJ: Rutgers University Press, 2008.

Long, Charles. *Significations: Sign, Symbols, and Images in the Interpretation of Religion*. Aurora, CO: Davies Group, 1986.

Noel, James. *Black Religion and the Imagination of Matter in the Atlantic World*. New York: Palgrave Macmillan, 2009.

Pratt, Mary Louise. *Imperial Eyes: Travel Writing and Transculturation*. New York: Routledge, 2003.

West, Cornel. *Prophesy Deliverance! An Afro-American Revolutionary Christianity*. Philadelp hia: Westminster, 1982.

CHAPTER 31

THE *AFRICAN* IN AFRICAN AMERICAN THEOLOGY

PETER J. PARIS

ANY inquiry into the relation between black theology and Africa must begin with a discussion about the traditional regard that Africans in North America have had for their ancestral homeland. From the middle of the twentieth century onward, several significant events occurred in North America and sub-Saharan Africa that greatly inspired African peoples on both sides of the Atlantic. The civil rights movement in America and the independence movements in Africa were expressive of a common impulse among oppressed peoples to take the initiative in confronting the established powers and demanding full participation in the various democracies that had abused them so greatly. The novel achievement of civil and political rights in North America and Africa respectively provided the motivation for the development of new theologies in each region. This essay constitutes a historical discussion of the ensuing complex relationships among those differing but related theologies.[1]

The emergence of black liberation theology[2] in the second half of the 1960s launched a new development in the North American theological academy. Though it was vigorously opposed by some,[3] many activist clergy in the civil rights movement including African American teachers and students in seminaries and divinity schools enthusiastically celebrated what appeared to be the dawn of a new era. Clearly, its enduring life many decades later is due to the resonance it continues to have for those who embrace the cultural ethos that was captured at that time in such symbols as *Black Power, black consciousness, black studies, Africentricity* to mention only a few.

Common Struggles among African Peoples

During the twentieth century African peoples on the continent and throughout the diaspora quickly discerned the many similarities between their common moral struggles against the Western world's historic embrace of the doctrines of white supremacy and black inferiority as natural endowments. Oppressed for centuries by Europeans and white Americans, African peoples utilized similar methods of resistance that ranged along a continuum of adaptation, deception, nonviolent protest, civil disobedience, and armed rebellion. As a racial minority in America their goal was first-class citizenship. By contrast, those on the African continent sought national sovereignty as their rightful dessert. Despite the immense suffering that each endured, they never doubted their full membership in the universal humanity of all peoples. Their firm grasp of that right constituted the bedrock for all their spiritual, political, and moral strivings.

The 1956 triumphal victory that ended the Montgomery Bus Boycott in the United States marked the beginning of the wider struggle against racial segregation throughout America. One year later, the political independence of Ghana signaled the beginning of the end of European colonialism in Africa. Clearly, African peoples on both sides of the Atlantic were mutually inspired by those separate though related achievements.

As a result of those radical social and political changes, two iconic leaders were catapulted onto the world stage: Martin Luther King Jr., who would eventually be honored posthumously with a national holiday and a permanent memorial site in the nation's capital; and Kwame Nkrumah, who gained world renown as the leader of the first African nation to gain independence from colonialism and head the first sovereign nation in sub-Saharan Africa. The two men met for the first time at Nkrumah's inauguration on March 6, 1957, in Accra, Ghana. King had been invited by Nkrumah as one of the state's official guests.

The Importance of Africa for African Americans

From the days of the transatlantic slave trade up to the present time African peoples in North America have longed for a symbiotic relationship with the peoples of their ancestral homeland. Yet the extent to which that desire was reciprocated by Africans on the continent continues to be unclear. A major signifier of that bond for Africans in

North America, however, has been the traditional pride they maintained for Liberia and Ethiopia as the only two countries in sub-Saharan Africa that escaped European colonization. The high esteem they had for Liberia was heightened in 1821 when the United States officially designated that country a colony for repatriated African slaves and again in 1847 when it became the first black republic in Africa.

Their delight in Africa was enhanced further in 1931 when Haile Selassie[4] was crowned emperor of Ethiopia and inherited a throne that dated back to the age of King Solomon.[5] The crowning glory for African Americans, however, was the six official visits of the emperor to the United States and most especially the visit in 1963 when President John F. Kennedy honored him with an official parade followed by a state dinner in Washington, DC.

Throughout the twentieth century African peoples in North America helped nurture various endeavors aimed at the independence of Africa from colonial rule. From 1900 to 1945 the series of pan-African conferences that were held periodically in London, Brussels, Lisbon, Manchester, and New York were organized largely by W. E. B. Du Bois, distinguished African American scholar and civil rights leader, in association with many of his international colleagues with blood ties to Africa. While the conferences facilitated the development of many personal relationships among Americans, Canadians, Caribbeans, and Africans from the continent, their main purpose was to share papers and promote conversations as foundational work for the eventual liberation of Africa from the oppression of European colonialism. Since the religion and theology of enslaved Africans in North America emerged under the severest conditions of slavery, we can rightly assume that the African influence in that process was veiled and oblique because the enslaved Africans were prohibited from practicing the religion they had brought with them from the continent or speaking their native languages. Nonetheless, a remnant of their religious orientation survived those horrific conditions and eventually expressed itself in various hybrid religions and cherished values that remained deeply embedded in their psyches, religious devotions, moral habits, leadership styles, music, and song. All of these helped to form their basic self-understanding and distinctive worldviews.

Further, the implicit influence of Africa on their cultural development is also discernible in the ways enslaved Africans gradually adapted Christianity to meet their needs through the art of syncretism, which resulted in a mixture of Christian and traditional African religious practices. Evidence of that process is seen in their music, dance, song, reverence for ancestors, and deep respect for the elderly, who were destined to join their ancestral spirits. Elements of Africa's influence can also be seen in the following features of their worldview: (*a*) the unity of the spiritual and physical realms of life, which enables harmony among all relationships while implying that all negative experiences result from the disharmony between those two dimensions of life and, hence, can be resolved only by appropriate ritual performances undertaken by traditional priests; (*b*) the integral relation between the family and the wider community that implies corresponding duties and responsibilities.[6]

Black Theology and Africa

Given this general overview of the enduring respect that African Americans have had for their ancestral homeland, we might have expected that James Cone's first book on black theology would have revealed a similar regard. Alas, only one or two indirect references to Africa occur in that text. The most obvious reason for its neglect undoubtedly reflects the spirit of theological education at that time, when white male scholars had produced an educational tradition that gave no substantive attention whatsoever to Africa or the sufferings of its peoples. Thus, it seemed natural that Cone, a recent Ph.D. graduate in systematic theology from a predominantly white seminary, would not have been disposed towards relating his scholarship to Africa in any direct way.[7] Having written a dissertation on the Swiss theologian Karl Barth's anthropology, it seemed likely that his first published book would reveal a strong Barthian influence, which did not go unnoticed by his critics. His endeavor to demonstrate the relationship of Christian theology to the African American experience of racial oppression clearly revealed a neo-Barthian perspective.

Prompted by a mixture of anger and grief over the assassination of Martin Luther King Jr., Cone spent several ensuing weeks tirelessly plunged in the process of writing his most important book, which launched a new era in theological education. As a result, a new generation of African American religious scholars was born.

The radical nature of Cone's work lay in his decision to take the most radical political symbol of the day, "Black Power," and make it the basis for his theological reflection. That first book, *Black Theology and Black Power*,[8] was a passionate, erudite, angry, independent, compelling response to racial injustice and a blatant condemnation of the hypocrisy of the European and American theological tradition. Thus, he wrote, "Since there was nothing in Euro-American theology that spoke directly to slavery, colonization, and poverty, why should I let white theologians tell me what the gospel is."[9]

In the absence of any academic role models for his novel academic endeavor, Cone's first conversational partners in the development of his thesis on black theology were the black clergy in the National Committee of Negro Clergymen (NCNC), later called the National Committee of Black Clergymen (NCBC), and the Black Methodists for Church Renewal (a black caucus within the United Methodist denomination). The prominent sociologist of religion C. Eric Lincoln was also one of his strongest supporters, who not only encouraged him in his work, but took the initiative in putting him in touch with his first publisher.[10]

The African American Debate about Black Theology

In 1970 the Society for the Study of Black Religion (SSBR)[11] was organized for the purpose of providing an independent space for black scholars to critique and encourage one another's academic work and assess the desired impact of black theology on the various disciplines in theological education. Most important, Cone's thought prompted a vigorous debate among the few black religious scholars teaching in seminaries at that time. The historian of religion Charles Long soon became black theology's major critic. He was supported by Gayraud S. Wilmore, a learned activist, church bureaucrat, and perceptive teacher who was interested primarily in the historical roots of black radicalism and its relation to black religion.[12] He was also the person who had introduced Cone earlier to the National Conference of Negro Clergymen and has remained one of his most beloved colleagues.

J. Deotis Roberts, professor of Systematic Theology at Howard University, was among the first to publish his appreciative critique of Cone's work under the title *Liberation and Reconciliation: A Black Theology*.[13] The title is altogether apt because it clearly reveals the argument of the book. While affirming Cone's theological treatise on liberation, Roberts argues then and thereafter that Cone's disconnection of liberation from reconciliation causes him to suspend his Christian faith. Thus, he declared, "James Cone is on the fence between the Christian faith and the religion of Black Power."[14] Roberts spend the rest of his career elaborating on his version of black theology, while Cone has insisted that he never fully understood Roberts's critique.

Long's critique, however, was the most radical of all the others because he viewed Western categories of thought as wholly inadequate for grasping the meaning of religious phenomena that had existed long before the development of the Western categories themselves. He claimed that in antiquity the language of "myth" was the only adequate descriptor of religion.[15] Thus, he regretted that it had been superseded by Western categories of thought, which, in his opinion, are not only inadequate descriptors of traditional African religion but distort and marginalize the substance of African religion itself.

Since most of the members of the SSBR had received their training in American seminaries, where they had had little or no exposure to the history of religions, the novelty of Long's arguments failed to persuade most of them. Yet the passion with which he expressed his concerns invariably gained the rapt attention of all who heard him.[16]

The Genesis of African Theology

It must be noted, however, that Cone's work in developing his own black theology was not in advance of similar efforts by African scholars on the continent. In fact, they had been pursuing a similar route long before Cone had entered seminary. As early as the mid-1950s, when Nigeria's independence from colonial rule was close at hand, the Christian Council of Nigeria published a book entitled *Christian Responsibility in an Independent Nigeria*[17] as a study guide for the churches. It implied first and foremost that as the nation sought independence from colonial rule, churches in Nigeria and elsewhere should also be preparing for their independence from the control of foreign missionaries. As a result, that council prepared study programs for churches throughout the country as tools for analyzing and assessing the various elements in their pre-Christian traditions that could be embraced by the churches in the forthcoming postcolonial era.[18]

In the Religious Studies Department of the University College of London, Ibadan (later named the University of Ibadan), the only university in Nigeria at that time, Professor E. Bolaji Idowu was busily at work completing his pioneering text, *Oludumare: God in Yoruba Belief*,[19] in which he laid the foundation for *the indigenization* of Christianity in Africa. That task was soon joined by the Kenyan theologian John S. Mbiti, whose foundational text *African Religions and Philosophy*[20] was also published in 1969, the same year as James Cone's *Black Theology and Black Power*.

In 1966 a conference was held in Ibadan under the auspices of the nascent All Africa Conference of Churches (AACC) that inquired into the Bible and African beliefs.[21] In fact, the essays of that conference were also published in 1969, the same year as Cone's first book.

Indeed, even earlier cultural productions in African Christianity had contributed to the development of an independent African theology. The African Independent Churches[22] (AICs), later known as the African Initiated Churches, emerged either by splitting off from the missionary churches in the late nineteenth century or founded by charismatic African leaders in the early decades of the twentieth century. Their desire for ecclesiastical independence implied the need for their own independent theologies and liturgical practices that were often described at the time by such conceptual signifiers as the *indigenization*, *inculturation*, or *Africanization* of the Christian gospel.

All of those endeavors gained worldwide visibility at the inaugural assembly of the All Africa Conference of Churches in 1963 when the participants called upon Christians in Africa to reject Western theology in favor of an authentic African theology, a term that Emmanuel Martey claims was used first by the beloved Francophone Franciscan theologian Father Placide Tempels as early as 1945 in his *La Philosophie Bantoue*.[23] Martey and many others attribute to him the honor of having been the first scholar to propose an African theology based on African philosophical understandings of spirituality, nature, anthropology, and time. Though a Belgium by birth and upbringing he spent a total of twenty-nine years in the Congo and became the founder of a significant group called Jamaa (translated, "the family") that flourished during the 1940s and 1950s. Most African theologians agree that Tempels was the first to grasp adequately the nature of African anthropology and its significance as the basic foundational element for any authentic African theology. Though many African theologians have offered critiques of his claim, all have praised his initial insistence that Africans must write their own theology from their own philosophical basis rather than that of the Western world. Accordingly, the contemporary catholic Malawian theologian Laurenti Magesa acknowledges Tempels's importance:

> Every human person, every individual is as it were one link in a chain of vital forces: a living link both exercising and receiving influence, a link that establishes the bond with previous generations and with the forces that support his own existence. The individual is necessarily an individual adhering to the clan.[24]

It is important to note, however, that Africans on the continent have not thought it necessary to agree on any particular form that such a theology should take. Rather, as they have experienced a plurality of African traditional religions, they are comfortable with a corresponding pluralism in theology. Yet most have assumed that any authentic African theology must comprise values, concepts, symbols, and liturgical practices rooted in the hybrid relation of traditional religious experience including the biblical witness. Nonetheless, there were others who argued that as Africa extricated itself from Western colonialism, it should also separate itself completely from the Christian religion and fully embrace once again its own traditional religious traditions. Such a move of seemingly "turning the clock backward" is not a real possibility.

Black Theology's Initiative toward Africa

In the 1960s African American theologians had little or no personal experience with African religious scholars on the continent, nor did the latter know much about them. Yet they desired conversation with their colleagues on the continent and readily seized the opportunity to make it possible. In my judgment they acted at first with many false assumptions about the status of theological discourse in Africa. In fact, their desire for a relationship was rooted in their painful loss of connection with their ancestral homeland. Naively, many believed that Africans on the continent had similar feelings toward them. Alas, they would soon discover that the peoples of Africa did not share such longings either for them or for their cultural productions.

Ironically, the Society for the Study of Black Religion had chosen the term "black religion" as part of its name rather than "black theology" because it would enable a more expansive inquiry than the latter implied. Further, the term corresponded more closely with Long's preference since he had little appreciation for theology. Prospectively, it is now a convenient term for many contemporary members of the organization who teach in religious studies departments where theology is not engaged. Then and now the term has resonated well with the academic discourse in Africa that centers on studies of traditional cultures as necessary starting points in the quest for an authentic African theology.

It is important to note also that black theologians in the United States were slow to perceive the seeming irrelevance of the racial term "black" in most African countries except for South Africa, where European racism expressed itself fully in the enactment of laws rooted in the ideology of racial apartheid. Though the psychological effects of racism on African peoples in North America was not the experience of those in either West or East Africa, the latter would later discover that colonialism had many similar effects on their peoples. Yet African American theologians only slowly realized the limits of racial analysis as an adequate explanatory tool for understanding the plight of Africans on the continent.

The Debate between Black Theology and African Theology

The first face-to-face encounter of black theologians from America with theologians in Africa took place in 1970 at the second assembly of the All Africa Conference of Churches in Abidjan, Côte d'Ivoire when two officers of the National Conference of Negro Churchmen (NCNC) participated as observers, namely, Metz Rollins, the executive director of the NCNC, and Gayraud S. Wilmore, chair of the NCNC's Theology Commission. Though the Americans and the Africans knew that they had endured similar injustices from Europeans, it would take some time for them to feel comfortable enough to share their painful memories and hopeful dreams with one another.

Eventually they were able to begin conversations that lay the foundation for more substantive discourse in the future. The relationships that began at those consultations were enhanced by various African theologians undertaking advanced study, teaching, and research at Union Theological Seminary, where Cone was teaching.[25] Professor John S. Mbiti accepted an invitation to serve as the Harry Emerson Fosdick

Visiting Professor for 1972–1973 and jointly taught a course with James Cone on African and black theologies. It is unfortunate that the two did not realize at the time the full nature of the disagreement that existed between them, which Emmanuel Martey has called the "inculturation-liberation tension."[26] Though many African theologians shared Mbiti's concerns about the differences between black and African theologies, his criticism of black theology was by far the most stringent while at the same time being honest, insightful, and gracious.

In brief, Mbiti argued that though he greatly admired the creativity, vitality, and relevance of black theology in addressing the historical situation of African Americans, it was unmistakably an American phenomenon that should remain in its own location and not seek to plant itself in Africa. Nonetheless, he saw much value in dialogical relations, where each side could learn about the other for the sake of mutual enrichment. Thus, he was convinced that each should develop its own independent theology. In fact, he also expressed the controversial claim that African theology had been born out of the joy of the Christian gospel while black theology originated from the misery and pain of suffering. Therein lay the basis for the immense chasm between the two scholars, as Mbiti states in the following:

> We (I) wish only for dialogue, fellowship, sharing of ideas and insights, and learning from one another as equal partners in the universal Body of Christ, even if we Africans may still speak the theological language of Christianity with a stammering voice, since most of us are so new to it. We appreciate what others are saying according to their peculiar circumstances and the inspiration of the Holy Spirit, but what they say reaches us only in whispers because they are speaking primarily to themselves and for themselves, just as we speak first and foremost to ourselves and for ourselves. We must recognize simultaneously our indebtedness to one another as fellow Christians and the dangers of encroaching upon one another's theological territories.
>
> Black Theology and African Theology have each a variety of theological concerns, talents and opportunities. Insofar as each contributes something new and old to Christian theology it will serve its immediate communities and also serve the universal Church.[27]

As stated above, the initiative for such conversations came from the African Americans themselves, who honestly believed at that time that their homegrown black theology would be helpful in the African struggles against colonialism and poverty. That presumption, however, was not embraced by their counterparts in West Africa, who by 1970 had achieved many victories in their anticolonial struggles including the following: (*a*) the joy of political independence for nearly two dozen sovereign nations; (*b*) the founding of the All Africa Conference of Churches (AACC) in 1963 as a continent-wide ecumenical association; and (*c*) the founding of the Organization for African Unity (OAU) now called the African Union

(AU). In short, Africans had greatly increased the membership list of the United Nations with many new democratic nations. Thus, it was more than a little presumptuous for African Americans to assume that African Americans had anything to offer the African continent in their struggles. Nonetheless, both sides soon realized that they did share many things in common even though the Africans clearly knew that the apparent commonalities of oppression were neither identical nor likely to lead to a common theology.[28] Undoubtedly, John S. Mbiti's 1974 article, "An African Views American Black Theology"[29] shocked James Cone and many of his colleagues because it leveled a devastating blow against the presumed ambitions of the black theology project for West Africa. Moreover, it came at a time when a developing coalition between the two regions appeared to be imminent. Alas, Mbiti squashed that prospect with his argument that the two theologies could never become one because they were developed in different historical contexts. Even though Cone felt that Mbiti had misrepresented his thought, Mbiti's critique[30] prompted a vigorous debate among African theologians in the eastern, western, and southern regions of the continent.[31]

If Mbiti misrepresented Cone's thought, as the latter claimed, Cone himself misunderstood the African theology of inculturation by viewing it as the nemesis of liberation. According to Cone's student, Emmanuel Martey, nothing could have been farther from the truth. Thus, he declares his agreement with the statement of the Second General Assembly of the Ecumenical Association of Third World Theologians (EATWOT) held in Oaxtepec, Mexico, in 1986, which claimed that Africans emphasize history as the fundamental methodological principle for any genuine theology, apart from which there can be no liberation. Thus the assembly declared:

> For Africans there is no liberation without their historical presence since they have been expelled from the field of history by their oppressors. Liberation if true, must be historical liberation; if not there is no liberation.[32]

In other words, inculturation must be a necessary precursor to liberation for all African theologians everywhere.

Similarities between Black and African Theologies

Surprisingly, it took a long while for black theologians in America to discern the similarity between the African theology of inculturation and black theology in the United States. In fact, black theologians should have been able to discern more readily than they did that their enslaved ancestors had done in America what the Africans were then striving to do at the time of independence, namely, inculturating the gospel into their lived cultural experience.[33] That activity was not only radical for their day but a constructive means for survival and the preservation of their humanity.

A similar process was also underway in the nascent black studies programs in American universities. In both contexts African and African American scholars were busily engaged in rejecting, revising, and rewriting the countless errors and distortions that their oppressors had inflicted on their respective cultural traditions. In all such activities their goal was to discern and implement principles of liberation in all their endeavors toward self-identity and self-determination. In fact, they viewed the hermeneutical principle of self-interpretation itself as a liberationist activity. Thus, writing one's own theology from outside the controlling grammar of Western thought processes signified a liberation process that EATWOT has called "historical rehabilitation."[34] Ironically, rewriting one's own history, as Africans and African Americans were doing, was an inculturating expression of liberation.

It soon became clear to African Americans, however, that black theology's challenge to racist America was more closely related to the antiapartheid struggle in South Africa than the struggle against colonialism in both West and East Africa because the politics of racism in both countries was unmistakably rooted in the doctrine of racial superiority. Similar to the concerns of the NCNC's Theological Commission, which had invited Cone to help them think theologically about Black Power, the South African Council of Churches found itself in need of an alternative theology that distinguished itself from the theology of the Dutch Reformed Church and the so-called Christian political establishment of apartheid. Thus, Desmond Tutu soon weighed in on the debate between Mbiti and Cone with his reconciling voice, which rendered support to both sides by declaring his embrace of both theologies (black theology and African inculturation theology) while admitting differences in their respective places of origin and the particular challenges their respective churches confronted. Thus, he summed up his argument accordingly:

> I myself believe I am an exponent of Black Theology coming as I do from South Africa. I also believe I am an exponent of African theology coming as I do from Africa. I contend that Black Theology has failed to produce a sufficiently sharp-cutting edge. It has indeed performed a good job by addressing the spirit in the African soul and yet it has by and large failed to speak meaningfully in the face of a plethora of contemporary problems which assail the modern African.... I believe this is where the abrasive Black Theology may have a few lessons for African theology. It may help to recall African theology to its vocation to be concerned for the poor and the oppressed, about men's need for liberation from all kinds of bondage to enter into an authentic personhood which is constantly undermined by a pathological religiosity and by political authority which has whittled away much personal freedom without much opposition from the church. In short, African theology will have to recover its prophetic calling.[35]

Undoubtedly, the interaction of black theology in America with African theologies[36] on the continent provided mutual enrichment to all sides of the controversy. Unfortunately, the paucity of financial support coupled with the gradual migration of many African theologians away from the academy have made it difficult for continuous interaction with one another. Nonetheless, much mutual enrichment has resulted from the interactions, chief among which being the hermeneutical concept of "anthropological poverty" that specifies a complex reality that has lent itself to considerable theological division among the theologies on the continent both north and south of the Zambezi River. That concept refers to the pauperization of African peoples along two distinct poles: the political-socioeconomic and the anthropological religio-cultural poles[37] This has led Emmanuel Martey to conclude that those on either side of the Zambesi who emphasize one pole over the other are indicative of a hermeneutical debate between two schools of thought, a debate deeply rooted in their different contextual situations.

In North America one often hears the criticism that apart from those churches that are manifestly Africentric, the rhetoric of black theology does not now or ever did represent the ethos of the black churches as a whole. In fact, many contemporary critics of contemporary black churches long for a return to the time when the widespread public struggles against racism in America were supported and inspired by the theologies of their respective churches. Clearly, from the late 1960s onwards James Cone and others were bent on sharpening and more poignantly articulating the mission of the black churches. Yet after the victories of the civil rights movement were won on the public stage, the black churches seem to have returned to their traditional functions of merely caring for the souls of their members through ministries of comfort and compassion in times of sickness and death; providing food and shelter for the needy; healing conflicts through acts of forgiveness and reconciliation; and proclaiming the graces of faith, hope, and love. As important as those ministries are, they have tended to bracket the prophetic dimension of black religion. No longer do the black churches appear to be on the vanguard of public unrest in pursuit of social justice.

While black liberation theology has an enduring life in the theological academies, some are beginning to acknowledge that the inculturation theologies are the most enduring because they arose from the spirituality of oppressed people themselves and are deeply rooted in their traditional self-expressions and understandings. In America that inculturation of the Christian gospel sprouted from the spiritual inclinations of the masses and cannot be specified by date, authorship, or place of origin. Rather, these theologies were constructed by the people under the severest conditions of slavery and racial segregation. From their souls burst forth spiritual works of beauty that have endured from generation to generation through the ritualistic practices of the black churches in the forms of celebrative spirituals and gospel songs alongside dynamic, rhythmic preaching and healing ministries that continue to inspire and empower countless numbers of their devotees.[38]

Most important, those two theological traditions (the pastoral and prophetic) were united during the mid-twentieth-century civil rights movement by a theology of freedom enunciated by Martin Luther King Jr. and his colleagues. The grace of nonviolent resistance inspired by Jesus's Sermon on the Mount pervaded the life and mission of that movement, which eventually came to be viewed as the prophetic voice of the black churches. The quality of that prophetic message did not differ from that of the pastoral ministry. Both were the bearers of healing, redemption, reconciliation, compassion, love, hope, and justice.

By contrast, however, black liberation theology is the systematic articulation of the black prophetic Christian tradition of resisting racial injustice. As such, its form is the product of the theological academy, while its content is deeply inspired by the black church tradition. Since its primary locus lies outside the daily life of the black churches, the latter have not been the bearers of its rhetorical message in the black community. Apart from some occasional preaching by black theologians in the black churches and displays of African art, black theology has contributed very little to the ritualized forms of worship through prayers, testimonies, litanies, songs, or music. Rather than enabling the churches to view black liberation theology as the prophetic side of their traditional survivalist pastoral ministries, black theologians have not contributed a great deal to that process. Hence, the novel name "black theology" makes it appear like a "new theology." Obviously, it has not yet succeeded in rooting itself deeply in the spiritual psyches of the people whom black theologians have sought to serve and empower.

Consequently, various endeavors continue to be organized as bridges of communication between the academy and the churches, such as the Kelly Miller Smith Institute on the Black Church at Vanderbilt University Divinity School, which was begun twenty-five years ago, and the Samuel DeWitt Proctor Conference,[39] which began in 2003 for the purpose of promoting education, advocacy, and activism in the service of social justice as it strives to liberate the most vulnerable from their distress.

The Theologies of Womanists and African Women

In the mid-1980s James Cone received a second shock. Several women students at Union Theological Seminary raised their voices of criticism against black theology's oversight of African American women's experience in religion. This concern was heightened by their discernment that the nascent white feminist theology also rendered black women invisible. Thus, they concluded that they should find their voices in the theological academy since they had a long history of exclusion, marginalization, and domination by black male leaders in the black churches and by white women in their respective organizations. Accordingly, inspired by the definition of the term *womanist*[40] provided by the novelist Alice Walker, they quickly decided to adopt that term as a fitting name for their own theological thought. In doing so they thought it necessary to separate themselves "temporarily" from both white feminists and black theologians in order to cultivate the academic terrain and form their own distinctive contribution to theological discourse. Walker's definition of the term *womanist* contained all the ingredients of inclusiveness that they desired for their mission, namely, rigorous analysis of race, gender, and class. Henceforth, *womanist* thought in any sphere of theology would be characterized by its inquiry into the functions of all three of those social indicators that have always disempowered black women.

Let me hasten to add that womanist theology is holistic in its aim to be inclusive of all peoples in all circumstances of life by emphasizing both a pastoral voice of love and compassion as well as a prophetic voice of criticism aimed at the call for and promotion of social justice for all.

During the past three decades the numbers of African American women entering all the degree programs in theological seminaries and divinity schools has multiplied exponentially in large part to the steady growth of black women theological scholars preserving, advancing, and promoting their womanist agenda in all the fields of theological education. Their work has been encouraged by James Cone himself, who considers womanist theology a necessary complement to black theology.

Prior to the birth of womanist theology in America, Professor Mercy Oduyoye[41] was teaching at the University of Ibadan in the 1970s when she declared that the male theologians in Africa spoke for only one half of Africa's population. The other half comprised women, who had always played important roles in religion and whose thought should be shared with one another. Oduyoye easily perceived a wide divide between men and women in both religious institutions and the academy because only the men were speaking and the women were silent by their absence. Thus, she and a small number of her women colleagues decided in 1989 to form the Circle of Concerned African Theologians, who would meet and work together in order to give public expression to their voices. Admittedly, only a few of them at that time were professional theologians or scholars-in-training, but those numbers would grow rapidly in the ensuing decades. Most important, like the womanist theologians in America, they were not interested in confrontation but in balancing the theological voices of men and women in order to effect greater wholeness and thus contribute to the reunion of God's divided humanity.

Oduyoye's many years of work in the World Student Christian Federation and the World Council of Churches and as guest lecturer at numerous events in various parts of the world afforded her access to many women from round the world whom she readily invited to join in the Circle's mission. Thus, Katie Cannon, one of the original mothers of womanist theology, attended the 1989 inaugural meeting of the organization as a member of the African diaspora and wrote the insightful foreword for the fourth printing of the book entitled *The Will to Arise: Women, Tradition, and the Church in Africa.*[42] Also, one of the Circle's strongest and most faithful supporters was the late Professor Letty Russell of Yale University Divinity School, who in addition to intellectual and moral support helped raised monies to support the organization.

Similar to black theology's relation to African theology, womanist theologians and African women theologians have striven to affirm and support one another. Both womanists and African women theologians carefully mine their respective cultural and religious traditions in order to discover and uncover the wisdom of their ancestral mothers that has been invisible to the wider public for such a long while. In both cases, the contemporary interaction with such wisdom enhances their understanding of the present-day world, and through criticism and constructive imagination they seek to renew the present with the wisdom of the ages. By raising criticisms about various practices of the past they lay the groundwork for transforming the church and the wider community with the hope of shaping a new world of wholeness: a world of enhanced moral value where there is no violence against women and all the rituals pertaining to the rites of passage are life-affirming; a world where the victims of the HIV/AIDS pandemic will receive the care, compassion, and respect owed to all who are sick and disabled; a world where men, women, and children are made whole in all the various circumstances of life and none are shunned, exploited, or disrespected. All of these values are correlated positively with the teachings of the churches and used to affirm, modify, or condemn various traditional practices that have prevented women from flourishing.

Clearly, the theology of African women appears to embrace a broader sense of community than womanist theologians have been able to do because they seek to do theology across the boundaries of gender, culture, religion, and nation. Further, Africa is a continent comprising scores of diverse nations and thousands of languages, while America is one nation with one official language. Consequently, the Circle of Concerned African Women Theologians presently has chapters in over thirteen countries and enjoys a wide international domain outside Africa. Yet both the womanists in America and the Circle of African Women Theologians have been strengthened by the encouragement, support, goodwill, knowledge, and wisdom that they share with one another.

Indicative of their love and concern for their people, the Circle of Concerned African Women Theologians changed the focus of their 2002 conference in Addis Ababa to that of the HIV/AIDS pandemic. That focus demonstrated more clearly than anything else their mission of addressing the most tragic social problem on the continent today, one that affects thousands of men, women, and children of diverse nationalities, religions, ethnicities, and social classes. The publicity generated by that endeavor has helped many churches and other religious groups to view the Circle as an ally rather than an enemy.

Conclusion

It now appears that the symbiotic relation that African Americans have desired with Africa throughout their many centuries of separation is slowly being developed. During the past several decades the wide physical divide and social alienation between America and Africa have been greatly reduced. This has been facilitated by a variety of programs that began in the late 1950s and early 1960s with Dr. James Robinson's Operation Crossroads Africa Program, the model for the US Peace Corps under President John F. Kennedy. Both of those programs have made it possible for increasing numbers of students and others to travel annually for study and work in various countries of Africa for short periods of time.

In addition, the global digitized revolution in communications, financial, and industrial markets coupled with numerous international conferences in Africa have resulted in increased contact between Africans on the continent and African peoples throughout the diaspora, including North America. Gradually, Africans on both sides of the Atlantic learned more about one another not only through personal contacts but also in African American and African studies programs that began developing in numerous universities and colleges during that same time period.

Further still, the various migration patterns of Africans emigrating from Africa to America and elsewhere were facilitated enormously by America's green card lottery program, which has attracted millions of applicants annually, resulting in thousands of African immigrants to this country. That program has made it easier for African Americans to develop deeper relationships with their African brothers and sisters. Presently African Americans are waging a vigorous battle in Congress against the threatened diminution of that program. Among other benefits, it has increased the number of Africans in religious studies and theological education in this country. Most important, the steady growth of program units pertaining to African religions in the American Academy of Religion and other learned societies have greatly enhanced the academic discourse between African and African American religious scholars.

Notes

1. Readers may be interested in knowing that I, the author of this essay, had returned to graduate school in the mid-1960s to pursue a Ph.D. in Ethics and Society at the University of Chicago Divinity School, where I was studying when black theology was born. Prior to that time I had spent three years (1961–1964) in Nigeria working as the national traveling secretary for the Student Christian Movement (SCM) of Nigeria through the Ecumenical Assistance Program of the World's Student Christian Federation, which brokered a

partnership between the SCMs of Canada and Nigeria. Dr. E. Bolaji Idowu (see below) was the chair of the National Board of the SCM of Nigeria and, hence, my boss. We worked very closely with the National Council of Churches using some of their materials as resources in the various SCM chapters throughout the country.

2. The following events are associated with the origins of black theology: (*a*) a full-page article in the *New York Times* on July 31, 1966, sponsored by a group of black clergy called the National Committee of Negro Clergy, offering theological support for the controversial symbol "Black Power" (*b*) the publication of James H. Cone's book, *Black Theology and Black Power* (New York: Seabury Press, 1969); (*c*) James Forman, "The Black Manifesto," i.
3. One of its greatest critics was Joseph H. Jackson, pastor of the Olivet Baptist Church in Chicago and then president of the National Baptist Convention, USA, the largest African American Christian organization in the world. The basic tenets of his argument are set forth in his address to that convention on September 3–8, 1971, under the title "The Basic Theological Position of the National Baptist Convention, U.S.A., Inc.," a reprinting of which is found in Gayraud S. Wilmore and James H. Cone, *Black Theology: A Documentary History, 1966–1979* (Maryknoll, NY, Orbis Books, 1979), 262–67.
4. See http://www.airspacemag.com/history-of-flight/The-Black-Eagle-of-Harlem.html?c=y&page=5 for a very informative discussion of two extraordinary African Americans, namely, Hubert Fauntroy Julian, known as the "Black Eagle of Harlem," and John Robinson, known as the "Brown Condor," each of whom established significant relationships with the emperor both before and after his accession to the throne.
5. It would be difficult to describe the psychological impact of His Imperial Majesty Haile Selasse's official title on African Americans: Emperor of Ethiopia, King of Kings, Conquering Lion of the Tribe of Judah, Elect of God.
6. This subject is more fully developed in Peter J. Paris, *The Spirituality of African Peoples: The Search for a Common Moral Discourse* (Minneapolis: Fortress Press, 1995).
7. The problem of racism in his graduate school and the absence of any black professors or African American subject matter in the curriculum is discussed at length by James Cone in his autobiography, *My Soul Looks Back: Journeys in Faith* (Nashville: Abingdon Press, 1982), chapter 1 and especially 36–38.
8. James H. Cone, *Black Theology and Black Power* (New York: Seabury Press, 1969).
9. Cone, *Black Theology and Black Power,* 43.
10. Cone, *Black Theology and Black Power,* 44.
11. At that time I was teaching at Howard University School of Divinity and was privileged to be a founding member of the SSBR, where I personally participated in the exciting discussions and debates in which we as black religious scholars were all deeply engaged as we struggled to discern the implications of black theology for our respective research and teaching.
12. See Gayraud S. Wilmore, *Black Religion and Black Radicalism* (New York: Doubleday, 1972).
13. J. Deotis Roberts, *Liberation and Reconciliation: A Black Theology* (Philadelphia: Westminster Press, 1971).
14. Roberts, *Liberation and Reconciliation,* 21.
15. The breadth and depth of this subject is outlined in Charles H. Long, *Significations: Signs, Symbols, and Images in the Interpretation of Religion* (Philadelphia: Fortress, 1986), 65–78.

16. It is interesting to note that several decades later many young contemporary black scholars have discovered Long's thought and are drawing upon its insights in their own works.
17. *Christian Responsibility in an Independent Africa* (Lagos: Nigeria Council of Churches, 1962).
18. In the early 1960s I was employed by the Student Christian Movement of Nigeria as its national traveling secretary and organized many conferences with church leaders and laypersons to help that process of studying traditional Nigerian cultures, religions, and moral teachings under the guidance of the National Nigerian SCM Board president, Professor E. Bolaji Idowu.
19. E. Bolaji Idowu, *Oludumare: God in Yoruba Belief* (London: Longmans, 1962); see also E. Bolaji Idowu, *Towards an Indigenous Church* (London: Oxford University Press, 1965);
20. John S. Mbiti, *African Religions and Philosophy* (New York: Doubleday, 1969).
21. See the publication of those papers in Kwesi Dickson and Paul Ellingworth, *Biblical Revelation and African Beliefs* (Maryknoll, NY: Orbis Books, 1969).
22. The following comprise some of the earliest academic studies of this phenomenon that was actively pursuing the goals sought later by black theology in the United States and by the ongoing work toward an African theology on the continent: Bengt Sundkler, *Bantu Prophets* (London: Oxford University Press, 1964); G. G. Baeta, *Prophetism in Ghana* (London: SCM Press, 1962); H. W. Turner, *African Independent Church*, 2 vols. (Oxford: Clarendon Press, 1967).
23. Placide Tempels, *La Philosophie Bantoue* (n.p.: Presence Africaine, 1945).
24. Laurenti Magesa, *Anatomy of Inculturation: Transforming the Church in Africa* (New York: Orbis Books, 2004), 162.
25. Among those African scholars who did research at Union Theological Seminary from the 1970s onward are the following: John S. Mbiti, Emmanuel Martey, Allan Boesak, Mercy Oduyoye, Gwinyai Musorewa, and Burgess Carr.
26. Emmanuel Martey, *Inculturation and Liberation* (New York: Orbis Books, 1993), 107.
27. John S. Mbiti, *Worldview* 17, no. 8 (August 1974): 44.
28. See Martey, *Inculturation and Liberation*, 107ff.
29. John S. Mbiti, "An African Views American Black Theology," *Worldview* 17, no. 8 (August 1974).
30. James Cone later responded to Mbiti's critique of black theology by offering his defense for a close working relationship between black theology in America and African theology on the continent by focusing on the liberation goal of solidarity with the oppressed and poor. See his argument in his essay "The Future of African Theology," in Wilmore and Cone, *Black Theology, 1966–1979*, 463–76.
31. Martey, *Inculturation and Liberation*, 108–9.
32. Martey, *Inculturation and Liberation*, 36.
33. James Cone himself was persuaded by his critics to find grounds for liberation theology in the black Christian tradition, which he did by studying the musical traditions of the so-called spirituals and blues. See the results of that inquiry in James H. Cone's *The Spirituals and the Blues* (New York: Seabury Press, 1972).
34. Cone, *Spirituals and the Blues*.
35. Desmond S. Tutu, "Black Theology / African Theology-Soul Mates or Antagonists," in Wilmore and Cone, *Black Theology, 1966–1979*, 490.

36. Some additional African theologians and philosophers who have contributed to this debate in various ways are the following: Gwinyai Muzorewa, Kofi Asare Opoku, Luke Mbefo, Paulin Hountondji, F. Eboussi Boulaga, V. Y. Mudimbe, Vincent Mulago, Charles Nyamiti, John Pobee, Itumeleng Musala, Jean Marc Ela, Engelbert Mveng, Buti Tihagale, Gabriel Setileone, Desmond Tutu, Alan Boesak, Aylward Shorter, Simon Maimela, N. K. Mugambi, Ogbu Kalu, Boganjalo Goba, Kwesi Dickson, Adeolu Adeg Bola, to mention only some of the most prominent.
37. See Martey, *Inculturation and Liberation*. See chapter 2 for a full discussion of this important topic.
38. A full description of this process is developed in Peter J. Paris, "When Feeling Like a Motherless Child," in *Lament: Reclaiming Practices in Pulpit, Pew, and Public Square*, ed. Sally A. Brown and Patrick D. Miller (Louisville, KY: Westminster John Knox Press, 2005), 111–20.
39. This organization was named after the deceased distinguished black theologian and preacher Samuel DeWitt Proctor, who sought in his ministry at the Abyssinian Baptist Church in New York City to unite the pastoral and prophetic dimensions of the black Christian faith.
40. See full definition of the term in Alice Walker, *In Search of our Mothers' Gardens* (New York: Harcourt Brace Jovanovich, 1983).
41. Mercy Amba Oduyoye's books include the following: *Hearing and Knowing: Theological Reflections on Christianity in Africa* (Maryknoll, NY: Orbis Books, 1986); *Daughters of Anowa: African Women and Patriarchy* (Maryknoll, NY: Orbis Books, 1995); with Musimbi R. A. Kanyoro, *The Will to Arise: Women, Tradition and the Church in Africa* (Maryknoll, NY: Orbis Books, 1992; *Beads and Strands: Reflections of an African Woman on Christianity in Africa* (Maryknoll, NY: Orbis Books, 2004).
42. Oduyoye and Kanyoro, *The Will to Arise*.

Selected Texts

Cone, James H. *The Spirituals and the Blues*. New York: Seabury Press, 1972.

Dickson, Kwesi, and Paul Ellingworth. *Biblical Revelation and African Beliefs*. Maryknoll, NY: Orbis Books, 1969.

Idowu, E. Bolaji. *Oludumare: God in Yoruba Belief*. London: Longmans, 1962.

Long, Charles H. *Significations: Signs, Symbols, and Images in the Interpretation of Religion*. Philadelphia: Fortress Press, 1986.

Martey, Emmanuel. *Inculturation and Liberation*. New York: Orbis Books, 1993.

Mbiti, John S. *African Religions and Philosophy*. New York: Doubleday, 1969.

Oduyoye, Mercy Amba, and Musimbi R. A. Kanyoro. *The Will to Arise: Women, Tradition, and the Church in Africa*. Maryknoll, NY: Orbis Books, 1992.

Paris, Peter J. *The Spirituality of African Peoples: The Search for a Common Moral Discourse*. Minneapolis: Fortress Press, 1995.

Roberts, J. Deotis. *Liberation and Reconciliation: A Black Theology*. Philadelphia: Westminst er, 1971.

Wilmore, Gayraud S. *Black Religion and Black Radicalism*. New York: Doubleday, 1972.

Wilmore, Gayraud S., and James H. Cone, *Black Theology: A Documentary History, 1966–1979*. New York: Orbis Books, 1979.

SECTION V

PROSPECTS FOR THE FUTURE

CHAPTER 32

PROSPERITY GOSPEL AND AFRICAN AMERICAN THEOLOGY

JONATHAN L. WALTON

MANY consider the prosperity gospel to be a practical spirituality—a theology concerned with emotional well-being, physical health, and material wealth. Academic theologians, for the most part, reject the prosperity gospel outright.[1] They are dismissive of its perceived callow ahistoricism, consumerist materialism, and crass individualism. Also known as the gospel of "health and wealth," it is most associated with the fast-talking, cosmetically altered faces of televangelists and the concupiscent indulges of what some have referred to as the "New Gilded Age" in the United States. As the share of total American income going to the top income earners rose from an already unequal 32 percent in 1970 to 44 percent by the end of the century and the top 0.1 percent of earners collected over 20 percent of all after-tax income gains in the final third of the century, it seemed many leading Christian evangelists followed this model of placing vast wealth on display.[2] Hence there is truth behind such crass characterizations of prominent Christian evangelists. Yet for many Christians that are desperately seeking spiritual strategies to address the deleterious effects of healthcare disparity and wealth inequality in the United States, prosperity-directed theologies seem to be a perennial option. So much so that prosperity theologies are principal forms of Protestant thought within American culture in general, and African American communities of faith in particular.

Definition

The term "prosperity gospel" is typically deployed as a broad appellation to describe a variety of Protestant traditions that emphasize mind-science, positive thinking, physical healing, and material rewards. These traditions include various strands of New Thought metaphysics, Evangelicalism, neo-Pentecostalism, and the Word of Faith movement.[3] The term "prosperity theology" is used here to describe varying conceptions of the divine and accompanying sacred teachings associated with these traditions. For this reason, any discussions of prosperity theology in America must be pluralized. It is better to say prosperity *theologies* in order to capture the multi-traditioned histories and conceive of competing theological frameworks. Moreover, the term "prosperity" must be contextualized and contrasted against its own use by different persons, groups, or movements. "Prosperity" is not a meta-theological category signifying the same meaning across space, time, and religious tradition. For some, prosperity has connoted community uplift and collective concern. For others prosperity refers to individual accomplishment and the accumulation of material goods on a personal level. And then there are others who reject the term "prosperity" altogether due to its negative connotations, yet embrace and model a lifestyle that signifies, if not glorifies, a divinely sanctioned life of luxury.[4] It is somewhat difficult, then, to make sustainable generalizations in assessing the relationship between liberatory themes and prosperity-inflected theologies. The historical context and religious carriers inform the prevailing tenets and telos of liberation. Liberation is not a static category. The way liberation is defined and ultimately achieved is ever-changing.

Nevertheless, there are three distinguishing characteristics that all prosperity theologies share: the materiality of ideas, the power of confession, and a commitment to spiritual, physical, and abundant material well-being. The first characteristic is grounded in New Thought metaphysics insofar as ideas (also referred to as both mind and spirit) underlie and animate everything in the universe. Matter is real as a form of experience. Put another way, "A chair is a chair as long as someone is sitting there." Yet it is the mind, or more importantly the ideas originated there, that actually constitutes the substance of life. A commonly referenced scripture is Proverbs 23:7, "For as he [*sic*] thinks in his heart, so is he." It is the articulation of ideas into existence through which the "real" substance of life is manifest. This is the second characteristic, the power of confession. Confession is neutral yet powerful, according to prosperity proponents. Reality as experienced is a collection of one's own ideas actualized. One can confess positively or negatively. This is why the often quoted "Death and life are in the power of the tongue," from Proverbs 18:21, underscores the importance of positive confession toward positive experience. Finally, prosperity theologies are unapologetic about the intended benefits of the faith. Whether it is physical healing or financial gain, prosperity advocates eschew puritanical asceticism and religiously induced material denial as an expression of spiritual discipline. Self-denial is not deemed a spiritual virtue. Health and wealth are the prosperous outcomes of creatively generated ideas and positive professions of faith, evidence that one is living a higher life consistent with God's will, whereas poverty and illness are manifestations of an impoverished and diseased mind and spirit. Thus prosperity gospel advocates commonly reference 3 John 1:2 in order to corroborate their theological claim, "Beloved, I pray that you may prosper in every way and be in health just as your soul prospers."

Prosperity Gospel Traditions

The Black Spiritual Movement

Since the inception of independent black congregations in the United States, there has been a dual concern for the spiritual and material well-being of African Americans. Black churches and independent denominations developed as religious and cultural responses to unfortunate American realities. This is not to suggest that these positive and productive religious spaces are merely reactive. But these people made spiritual choices in a larger unwelcoming context not of their own making—a context defined by racial, economic, political, and social disenfranchisement. Thus, on a spiritual level, African Americans sought answers to their particular predicament from "on high." What did their God have to say about black humanity and liberation in the context of a sinful and sick society that sought to dehumanize and enslave black bodies? And on a material level, the institutional aims were even more practical and pragmatic. Historically, black denominations emerged from, and grew alongside, mutual aid societies in the late eighteenth century. Community members invested resources to provide unemployment compensation, death benefits, and other necessities that provided quasi social safety nets. And other social services such as educational opportunities, job training and placement, and housing assistance remain staples of many congregations in the present moment.[5]

Due to this sort of theological accent on ascertaining and critical engagement with allaying the sources of black suffering and practical concern with securing *eudaimonia*, what the Greeks defined as "the good life," it makes sense that many African Americans have found spiritual solace in what scholars traditionally refer to as thaumaturgical-manipulationist orientations.[6] Such orientations, according to Hans Baer, "maintain that the most direct means of achieving socially desired objectives, such as financial prosperity, prestige, love and health, is to engage in various rituals to obtain esoteric knowledge and develop a positive attitude."[7] It is the "manipulation" of one's individual circumstances through varying rituals toward self-mastery over against social activism and cooperative community-based endeavors that tends to differentiate thaumaturgics from mutual aid societies of yesterday or religiously based community development corporations of the contemporary moment. The black Spiritual movement offers a quintessential example of the former.

Black Spiritual churches developed in the first quarter of the twentieth century among African Americans in religiously diverse cities such as New Orleans and Chicago. Religious diversity is central to the combinative aspects of black Spiritual theology. In a city like New Orleans, for instance, African, Caribbean, and Native American cultural practices intertwined with Afro-Protestantism, hoodoo, and Roman Catholicism in creative and constructive ways. Second-line music and early jazz rhythms animated the Carnival celebrations of Christian origins. African and Indian intermarriage and traditions of spirit worship and saint veneration were a distinct aspect of New Orleans culture.[8] And Christian rituals of Holy Communion and baptism were fused with voodoo/hoodoo rituals, spirit possessions, and other forms of divination and healing. In other words, as Claude Jacobs and Andrew Kaslow point out, "It was within the context of south Louisiana's diverse religious traditions, European and African, Catholic and Protestant, orthodox and unorthodox, institutionalized and popular, that the Spiritual churches came into being."[9]

This is not to suggest that the black Spiritual movement should be divorced from the tradition of Spiritualism in both Europe, the United States, and throughout the Caribbean. Spiritualism's rejection of a distinct supernatural realm divorced from everyday life, the power of the human mind, and ongoing growth and consciousness in the form of a spirit following physical death attracted those confronting the Civil War and high rates of diseases coupled with poor access to quality healthcare. The apparent ubiquity of death created the fertile cultural conditions for Spiritualism's growth among cross sections of the United States.[10] This was even more the case among black communities in the post-Reconstruction era. African Americans faced the challenges of racial apartheid, disproportionate levels of poverty, and the effects of mass migration in the first quarter of the twentieth century. Thus it seems safe to aver that many African Americans found black Spiritualism's conjuring form of Afro-Protestant Christianity an empowering and liberating alternative to the more traditional black denominations.

Current and future scholars must be careful, however, not to follow Baer and others down the overly reductionist and hyperracialized road of religion as class-based compensation. In his treatment of the black Spiritual movement, for instance, Baer contends that "the belief that events can be controlled by magical practices is found in all walks of life, but especially among the poor."[11] The author goes on to quote at length a 1962 article by Norman Whitten, who draws even a tighter connection between what he refers to as "occultism among Negroes in North Carolina" and religion as compensation. In describing the "proclivity of the American Negro to cope by magical means," Whitten states, "Due to his suppressed social position a Negro can find little satisfaction by coping directly with his frustrations and dissatisfactions. Misfortunes that befall him may have no real solution, though magical practices or the relegation of problems to magical causes may offer at least partial satisfaction by relieving some anxiety and tensions."[12] Perhaps this is the case for some. But American Spiritualism, like all of the leading prosperity gospel traditions in the United States, cut across racial identity and economic status, hence disrupting narratives that put the burden of belief in prosperity theologies solely on the backs of poor black people. And even when African Americans Spiritual assemblies sought to distinguish themselves from the larger Spiritualist movement, citing a distinction in musical style and with practices such as gris-gris (the use of amulets and other African retentions), the similarities in terms of conceptions of the sacred were largely the same. The spirit world plays a critical role in the personal affairs and social interactions of believers, and these spirits can be solicited and controlled by the power of one's belief. In fact, in the first quarter of the twentieth century, many Spiritual congregations were interracial, with a strong European immigrant presence.[13] This was the case of one of the earliest Spiritual congregations in New Orleans, led by Mother Leafy Anderson.[14]

Mother Leafy Anderson, founder of the Eternal Life Spiritualist Church Number 12, is considered among the first black Spiritual pastors in the country. Established in 1918 in an uptown section in New Orleans, Eternal Life offered spiritual "readings" (revealing unknown things to a person about her life that were not previously known), and training classes that taught aspiring leaders in Spiritualism. Anderson had honed her skills on the road, organizing missions in southern cities such as Memphis, Biloxi, and Houston, as well as in the northern urban center Chicago.[15] Like most Spiritual teachers, Anderson sold her services as well as products such as healing water and prayer oil at the church, collecting large sums of money. Anderson is described as having "dressed lavishly, favoring lace, sequins, expensive shoes and jots of jewelry."[16] Church services often incorporated jazz bands and dances associated with the nightclub scene such as the jitterbug and shimmy—a trend of incorporating popular culture in worship that remains a staple of black Spiritual life. And Anderson was also known for demonstrating various spirits, most notably Black Hawk (1776–1838), a deceased Indian chief. Black Hawk led the Sauk Indians in armed resistance against white settlers in what is now Illinois and Wisconsin. Though ultimately defeated by the US Army, and betrayed by rival Sauk leaders deemed more conciliatory to US expansionist policies, Black Hawk remains a legend for his fearlessness and bravery. It is this spirit of Black Hawk, as documented by anthropologist Jason Berry, that many Spiritualists channel during worship as a "watchman" who will "fight ya battles!"[17]

Spiritual churches like Eternal Life, then, offered what many considered a tangible religion to address real-world needs and concerns. According to Zora Neale Hurston, Spiritual ministers provided services comparable to obeah practitioners and "hoodoo doctors" throughout the Caribbean. Describing a New Orleans Spiritualist minister Mother Hyde, Hurston writes, "She burns candles as do the Catholics, sells the spirit oil, but gives a 'cake' to be used with the oil." Then Mother Hyde tells Hurston, "In case of trouble, arise at dawn and face the east. Take the vital of the spirit oil in one hand and the cake (in its box) in the other. Read the Twenty-Third Psalm and let that be your prayer. When you come to the part, 'Thou anointest my head with oil,' shake the bottle well and pour and anoint your head. Do this every time you want to conquer and accomplish."[18] These sorts of conjuring practices by Spiritual churches were used for everything from warding off evil spirits, to increasing an employment opportunity or even striking revenge on a former lover by causing disease.

To be sure, the hoodoo/conjuring labels are often considered pejorative descriptors that many Spiritual ministers resist. Surely this has to do with the negative connotations associated with hoodoo practice in Western culture in general, and the ways it was a favorite target of journalists in the late nineteenth century who sought to distinguish the "rational" religion of whites from the superstitious and hypersexual religious practices of blacks, in particular.[19] It may also have to do with the ways traditional conjuring forms such as root-working and folk healing have been integrated into Pentecostal-Charismatic practices to the extent of being wholly obscured or readily misrecognized. Nevertheless, such religious customs as divine healing surely inform strands of prosperity theology and practice today.

The Unity School of Christianity

By the turn of the century the New Thought movement—by then organized under the National New Thought Alliance—was both broad and ambiguous. Dating back to the teachings and writings of the nineteenth-century physician and mentalist Phineas Parker Quimby (1802–1866), within half a century New Thought was capturing the attention of many white conservative evangelicals, feminists, and middle-class progressive reformers of the era.[20] The message that through the power of one's mind persons could take charge of their religious lives and transform positively their individual circumstances was embedded into the American mainstream. Two of the more influential New Thought teachers of the era were a Kansas City couple, Charles and Myrtle Fillmore—the former a real estate developer with no formal educational background, and the latter a graduate of Oberlin College who descended from a family with a history of tuberculosis.[21] Myrtle experienced a healing of her disease in 1886 after hearing lectures from a former student of popular Christian Science teacher Emma Curtis Hopkins. Myrtle and Charles founded the magazine *Modern Thought* and by 1889 organized the Unity School of Christianity.[22]

The Unity School is similar to the larger New Thought tradition insofar as God is regarded as a ubiquitous spirit that inhabits everything and everybody. Moreover, the Fillmores emphasized the power of the mind as the creator and animator of reality and destiny. As stated in the Unity professions of faith, "Human beings create their experiences by the activity of their thinking. Everything in the manifest realm has its beginning in the thought."[23] Unity distinguished itself from the larger tradition of New Thought by embracing a Christocentric perspective, which aligned Unity in closer proximity to traditional Christian denominations. According to Charles Braden, the Fillmores demonstrated "a more warmly evangelical emphasis than most other forms of New Thought." But despite this traditional accent on Jesus Christ, Unity teachings framed Jesus as an impersonal, fluid deity. He is impersonal insofar as Christ is typically understood as an ideal or mindset rather than historical figure or as an "incarnate God." The Fillmores opted for the language of "the Christ in you" and "Christ-consciousness." And Jesus is fluid to the degree that, as an ideal or concept, Christ can become whatever a person needs this Christ-consciousness to be in a particular context. Thus there is great emphasis on believers tapping into a Christ potentiality, which professes a capacity for persons to attain unity with the higher self, as Jesus did, even to the point of immortality.

To be sure, African Americans were not religiously exempt or racially immune to New Thought's growing cultural influence at the outset of the twentieth century. In fact, New Thought's emphasis on personal transformation, positive thinking, and divinely sanctioned prosperity complimented popular self-help philosophies that were circulating within black communities and educational institutions. It is no wonder many black preachers combined aspects of New Thought philosophy with more traditional forms of thought and expression. Few in the first half of the twentieth century were more prominent than George Baker, better known as Major Father Jealous Divine (1876–1965).

Baker's first encounter with New Thought is unclear, though his biographer Jill Watts connects an early encounter to a 1906 visit to Los Angeles. While on the West Coast, the Maryland native both sought out New Thought proponents and literature and attended the Azusa Street Revival, which inaugurated modern American Pentecostalism. The city of Los Angeles was known for its large community of New Thought adherents and prominent "Metaphysical Library," which published periodicals and hosted New Thought lectures. But Baker also appreciated and participated in the spiritual expression of glossolalia, also known as "speaking in tongues."[24] These encounters reflect Baker's ongoing combinative spiritual approach. Back in Baltimore, Baker, along with three other spiritual interlocutors, turned their lodging accommodations into essentially a New Thought reading room known as Fairmount Avenue Ministry.[25] Here African American, largely working-class Baltimore residents, came to hear lectures and engage in spiritual discussions. Baker was particularly influenced by the Fillmores and Unity School teachings. According to Watts, "For Baker, much of the attractiveness of Unity School Theology rested in its implications. Fillmore's brand of New Thought provided a formula for the acceptance and inclusion of Americans without altering or threatening the structure of American society."[26] The message of economic uplift and prosperity through positive thinking and an indwelling God disrupted racial hierarchies. African Americans possessed the same God potential and capacity to tap into Christ consciousness as whites. African

Americans, then, can invariably transcend racial oppression and experience the perceived material benefits and cultural markers associated with the white upper classes. This theology provided the foundation from which Father Divine would erect his Peace Mission movement.

At his peak during the Great Depression, Divine attracted thousands, both black and white, to his Sayville, New York, mansion and numerous missions. From his Harlem headquarters he published *New Day* for his followers, those Divine referred to as "angels," and promoted communal living, shared responsibilities, and cooperative financial arrangements. These patterns led to financial prosperity among the movement—Divine acquired real estate holdings valued in the millions of dollars—and guaranteed lodging and labor for the most economically vulnerable members. But it was the exquisite meals served at what Divine referred to as his "Holy Communion" banquets where he articulated his prosperity teachings. Although Divine's sermons could be cryptic, they were anything but quixotic. He promoted what he considered practical principles that would cultivate the appropriate mindset for followers to move from poverty to prosperity.

In a 1937 message entitled "God's Words Are Materialized as Mankind Realizes the Materialization of Spiritual Things," Divine begins with an admonishment: "When one is lazy and expresses slothfulness and becomes a 'spiritual parasite,' he is deserving of remonstration that he might awaken to his individual obligations and be a true and worthy child of God." A devout proponent of America's capitalist system, Divine considered hard work a spiritual principle. Spiritual depth can never be divorced from human agency and purposeful intent. Divine referred to followers who felt they could live by Spirit alone as those "sitting on 'the stool of Do-Nothing,' by being impractical, unprofitable, and good for nothing." Yet hard work and a positive mindset necessitated a happy and healthy body. The lavish dinners and emphasis on material prosperity—hence, Divine's inverted formulation, "Man shall not live by Spirit alone"—created the necessary physical conditions for angels to repel sickness and slothfulness and attract further prosperity. "When you are robust and vigorous and filled with energy and courage, your physical fighting force will be powerful enough to fight off many diseases," Divine avers. Thus, he concludes, "Eat, drink and be merry, and enjoy the good of life; for as Solomon said on one occasion, if you do not enjoy these Blessings I say, 'They are all vanity, and will soon pass away.' "[27]

The Unity School also informed the ministry of Rev. Johnnie Colemon (192?–), founder of Christ Universal Temple Church (formerly Christ Unity Temple) in Chicago. Colemon was born in Mississippi and was a scholar-athlete at Wiley College in Texas. Around 1950 she migrated to Chicago to continue her teaching career, which had begun immediately following college. Not long after, according to her accounts, she was diagnosed with an "incurable" disease. Colemon testifies that during a visit to her mother, who was then a subscriber to Unity materials, she was introduced to the healing ministry of the Unity School of Practical Christianity. Her rise to national

New Thought prominence has become legend, which only adds to Colemon's highly gendered, racial, and religious mythology within the movement. She was soon cured of her disease, was the first African American to live and be ordained at the Unity Seminary campus in Missouri, and returned to Chicago to organize Christ Unity Temple in 1956. Within a decade, after serving on the board of trustees and as vice president, Colemon became the first African American president of the National Association of Unity Churches. Surely this had to do with the growth and stature of her congregation. This says something positive about the gender and racial openness of the movement at the time, as there were many other predominantly white denominations and organizations that would not have elevated any woman or an African American to such a prominent leadership position.

For the first two decades, Christ Unity Temple's theology focused more on the "health" than the "wealth" dimension of the prosperity message. In this regard, Colemon was a part of the larger trend of postwar healing revivalism flavored by metaphysical formulas. Unity mantras such as "You are the thinker that thinks the thought that makes the thing" appear throughout her sermons and writings. And, like her Unity mentors, Colemon applied these teachings to physical maladies. In her collection of teachings on healing, *Open Your Mind and Be Healed*, she writes, "The people at Unity had learned the Law, understood the Law, and applied the Law.... Thoughts of doom, negativity, jealousy, victimization and unworthiness were the root causes of disease. Thus disease was caused by wrong thoughts, beliefs and opinions."[28] But Colemon's particular genius came in her ability to integrate Unity theology with traditional revivalistic African American liturgy. She embraced the gospel rhythms of the city and a queenly yet charismatic homiletic style that made Christ Unity Temple a cultural mix of the Spiritualist tradition's ecstatic worship tempered by the Unity School's bourgeois aesthetic. Young professional African Americans attracted to Colemon's positive outlook and message of personal empowerment flocked to the church by the thousands. As Colemon told one Chicago reporter, "People come here because they're tired of being broke, tired of being sick, tired of being unhappy, tired of the old way of living."[29]

In 1979 Colemon broke ties with the Unity Association, citing fatigue over racial discrimination. Yet one might also cite Colemon's growing influence as an independent revivalist and expanding theological orientation. Colemon founded the Universal Foundation for Better Living (UFBL) in 1974, the Christ Universal congregation numbered over 3,000 Sunday attendees, and she had a growing media presence. Moreover, Colemon began accentuating the economic wealth dimensions of the healing and happiness message. Members referred to Colemon as the "jewelry box" due to her exquisite collection of gems, and she was unapologetic about her financially flamboyant lifestyle. "I go first class. Money is God in action. God is the source of my supply. I demonstrate the prosperity I teach about by having money in my pocket, money in my bank account, and material things."[30]

To be clear, for Colemon the term "prosperity" should never be reduced to money. She defines prosperity as "health, love, peace of mind, all that God is, all the good things of life."[31] And this seems to be the message that thousands of Christ Universal Temple members continue to gravitate toward even years after her retirement. But unlike Father Divine, whose missions catered to the economically vulnerable, Christ Universal Temple consecrated and thus legitimated the aspirations of many of Chicago's black bourgeoisie by offering a guilt-free theology of material luxuries and spiritual indulgences. This appeal to the black professional class and emphasis on wealth has caused some interpreters to confuse Colemon's Unity New Thought teachings with the Word of Faith movement. But as Stephanie Mitchem suggests, Colemon's success integrating the theology of Unity in a predominantly African American context without denying its New Thought sources, as well as her promotion of female clergy within the UFBL, separates her from the stridently charismatic Christian Word of Faith movement and its traditional masculinist hierarchies.[32]

Word of Faith

The Word of Faith movement developed in the second half of the twentieth century out of postwar healing revivals. Like the Unity School, it builds upon New Thought metaphysics, but adds a distinctively Pentecostal-Charismatic accent. The leading Faith preachers of the previous century all traced their ministry to Kenneth Hagin Sr. of Broken Arrow, Oklahoma. The former Assemblies of God minister developed a pedantic pedagogical approach to healing characterized by a methodical and meticulous presentation of the scriptures that was straightforward and thus accessible to the masses. This was in stark contrast to other white healing revivalists such as William Branham, Kathryn Kuhlman, and Oral Roberts, who were better known for their homiletic histrionics and theological sensationalism. Hagin's "teaching ministry" perused the Bible and presented scriptures that corroborated his message of divine health and material wealth in a seemingly systematic fashion. His ideas, however, were far from original. Many of Hagin's teachings were plagiarized from the writings of Essek William Kenyon, a Protestant preacher who integrated Higher Life teachings of the Keswick holiness movement with mind science. The former's perfectionist emphasis on the eradication of sin toward receiving the inward fullness of God resonated well with select mind science tenets. Human potentiality toward spiritual perfectibility allows believers to access all of the divine healing power of Christ with the power of one's thoughts.[33]

Kenneth Hagin used Kenyon's writings in the context of the neo-Pentecostal/ Charismatic turn toward financial prosperity in creative and constructive ways, while purposefully concealing New Thought philosophy. For believers to (*a*) know (believe in one's mind) who they are in Christ in order to live a higher life, (*b*) positively confess this knowledge insofar as they "name and claim" their divine entitlements, and (*c*) understand that they are obligated to financially contribute (sow) to a Word of Faith ministry because God is bound to return one's contribution at least tenfold (reap). Some of the largest (including *the* largest) Protestant congregations in the United States extend directly from Hagin's tutelage. They include the Lakewood Church (Houston), formerly led by the late John Osteen and now his son Joel Osteen; Eagle Mountain International Church (Fort Worth, TX), founded by Kenneth and Gloria Copeland; and Crenshaw Christian Center (Los Angeles), organized by Frederick K. Price, the earliest and for decades the most prominent African American Word of Faith pastor in the country.

Frederick Price entered the gospel ministry in 1955 and spent the next two decades trying to secure his ecclesial footing. He served several denominations, including both the African Methodist Episcopal and Baptist churches, and was attracted to Pentecostalism. In the early 1970s he came under the tutelage of Kenneth Hagin, was ordained into the Kenneth Hagin Ministries, and aligned his recently organized Ever Increasing Faith Ministries under the aegis of his "spiritual father." A distinct component of the Word of Faith movement in general, and Hagin's ministry in particular, is the emphasis placed on religious broadcasting. Hagin's *Faith Seminar of the Air* radio show and subsequent *Rhema* television ministry was more than a mere technological medium or proselytization tool. Word of Faith preachers consider religious broadcasting a central and constitutive element of their theological orientation. Radio, television, and publishing are morally neutral media that preachers sanctify and employ to fulfill the Great Commission of Jesus as set forth in Matthew 28:16–20. This approach has contributed to the immense success of Word of Faith congregations both in the United States and abroad. This was particularly true for Frederick Price and his *Ever Increasing Faith* television broadcast. By 1978 Price's sermons were airing in five major cities, and the local membership of his church, the Crenshaw Christian Center, exceeded 5,000. In 1981 his congregation purchased the former home of Pepperdine University, a thirty-two-acre campus, and by the end of the decade completed the 10,000-seat sanctuary known as the "FaithDome."

Price's ministry offers insight into the professed liberatory aims of Word of Faith theology, a theology that the ministry models in its financial practices and aesthetic representations. The first distinguishing theological tenet is the movement's approach to tithing, giving 10 percent of one's gross income to the church. Tithing itself is not particular to the Crenshaw Christian Center, as it is a common religious act. What is uncommon is the way Word of Faith teachers like Price emphasize the contractual nature of giving. Tithing is not regarded as an unqualified good or end in itself. Rather it is understood as a contractual obligation between believer and God where God is bound to give back at minimum tenfold of the original offering. In the words of sociologist Milmon Harrison, "It [the tithe] is according to the biblical 'law,' based upon the way God created the natural world to operate, that the one who 'sows' finances should expect to 'reap' a harvest of financial blessings in return."[34] Price refers to this "sowing and reaping" process as "God's financial plan," arguing that "tithes and offerings are God's methods through which He can bless His people financially and materially." Parishioners are taught that the way to attain financial security and material blessing is by "sowing" into a Faith ministry. "God has two purposes for prospering us financially and materially," according to Price. "First, to meet our own needs; second (and more importantly), to finance the proclamation of the Gospel."[35] Therefore, tithing is presented as a spiritual investment with guaranteed financial benefits for the believer.[36]

Directly tied to Price's second reason for prospering God's people (proclamation of the Gospel), the Faith message is dictated by the theological aims and material needs of the ministry.[37] The seed-faith concept actually originated with Oral Roberts as a fundraising tool to begin broadcasting on television in the 1950s.[38] And currently, consistent with the Faith movements' emphasis on religious broadcasting, Price's *Ever Increasing Faith* television broadcast airs each week in thirty states in the United States, multiple times per day. Therefore, there is a direct correlation between the associated costs of religious broadcasting and the need for persons to contribute financially, just as there is a relationship between increased giving and heightened promises of God's "contractual" obligation to "bless and multiply." This may come across to some readers as a theological Ponzi scheme. Evangelists collect money on behalf of a contractually bound Deity in order to offset the costs of religious broadcasting. But to many Christians who have felt a decrease in real wages or lost employment, savings, and retirement plans with the economic downturn in the United States, this contractually bound God seems as good a bet as any.

Finally, Word of Faith preachers are known for modeling diversity insofar as they disassociate the ministry from any racial (read: black) markers, particularly traditional black churches. Often white members or guests are seated down front and receive privileged camera time during television broadcasts. "International" is often a part of the church's name, a name that typically includes "Center," as opposed to a denominational affiliation. And traditional religious symbols such as stained glass windows, images of Jesus, or any representations of the sacred are conspicuously absent (this even includes a cross, since many Faith teachers associate the cross with suffering). Aside from international flags that often adorn sanctuaries, the royal blue carpet, elevated stage, and circular theater seating of the FaithDome are the Word of Faith sanctuary archetypè. In Harrison's words, "The complete lack of anthromorphic images of the deity, saints, or angels avoids any vision or conception of God in the image of any particular racial or ethnic group."[39]

To be sure, one cannot underestimate the ways many view these sorts of aesthetic representations as setting them free from what some perceive as the religious burdens of black religiosity. This is especially true among those who, for whatever reason, associate traditional black churches with struggle against racism, poverty, and other forms of social chaos. Word of Faith leaders, like many in the prosperity tradition, seem to understand that liberation for many African Americans means being freed from a past in order to claim a promise of divinely sanctioned prosperity in the here and now.

NOTES

1. Stephanie Y. Mitchem, *Name It and Claim It? Prosperity Preaching in the Black Church* (Cleveland: Pilgrim Press, 2007); Michael Scott Horton, *Christless Christianity: The Alternative Gospel of the American Church* (Grand Rapids, MI: Baker Books, 2008); Dwight N. Hopkins, *Heart and Head: Black Theology—Past, Present, and Future* (New York: Palgrave, 2002); Robert Michael Franklin, *Crisis in the Village: Restoring Hope in African American Communities* (Minneapolis: Fortress Press, 2007).
2. Jacob S. Hacker and Paul Pierson, *Winner-Take-All Politics: How Washington Made the Rich Richer—and Turned Its Back on the Middle Class* (New York: Simon & Schustser, 2010).
3. Milmon F. Harrison, *Righteous Riches: The Word of Faith Movement in Contemporary African American Religion* (New York: Oxford University Press, 2005); Darnise C. Martin, *Beyond Christianity: African Americans in a New Thought Church* (New York: New York University Press, 2005).
4. As an example, since Word of Faith theology regards prosperity as a result of a contractual agreement between the believer and God, many regard programs of social uplift and community concern as a fool's errand. Poverty represents a mindset, just as prosperity is a byproduct of positive thinking and fidelity toward God. On the other hand, there are evangelists such as Bishop T. D. Jakes of Dallas, Texas, who rejects the use of the term "prosperity." Yet he is unapologetic about flaunting his immense wealth as a cultural celebrity.
5. Andrew Billingsley, *Mighty Like a River: The Black Church and Social Reform* (New York: Oxford University Press, 1999); Anthony B. Pinn, *The Black Church in the Post-Civil Rights Era* (Maryknoll, NY: Orbis Books, 2002); Robert Michael Franklin, *Another Day's Journey: Black Churches Confronting the American Crisis* (Minneapolis: Fortress Press, 1997).
6. Hans A. Baer, *The Black Spiritual Movement: A Religious Response to Racism* (Knoxville: University of Tennessee Press, 1984), 167–69.
7. Hans Baer, "African American Religious Experience," in *Encyclopedia of Religion and Society*, ed. William H. Swatos Jr. (London: AltaMira Press, 1998), 10.
8. Claude F. Jacobs and Andrew Jonathan Kaslow, *The Spiritual Churches of New Orleans: Origins, Beliefs, and Rituals of an African-American Religion* (Knoxville: University of Tennessee Press, 1991), 30–37; Jason Berry, *The Spirit of Black Hawk: A Mystery of Africans and Indians* (Jackson: University Press of Mississippi, 1995), 104.
9. Jacobs and Kaslow, *Spiritual Churches*, 30.
10. Jacobs and Kaslow, *Spiritual Churches*, 76.
11. Baer, *Black Spiritual Movement*, 167.
12. Baer, *Black Spiritual Movement*, 168.
13. Jacobs and Kaslow, *Spiritual Churches*, 36.
14. Zora Neale Hurston, "Hoodoo in America," *Journal of American Folklore* 44, no. 174 (1931): 319.
15. Jacobs and Kaslow, *Spiritual Churches*, 33.
16. Jacobs and Kaslow, *Spiritual Churches*, 36.
17. Berry, *Spirit of Black Hawk*, 17.
18. Hurston, "Hoodoo in America," 320.
19. Carolyn Morrow Long, *A New Orleans Voudou Priestess: The Legend and Reality of Marie Laveau* (Gainesville: University Press of Florida, 2006), xxvii.

20. Catherine L. Albanese, *A Republic of Mind and Spirit: A Cultural History of American Metaphysical Religion* (New Haven: Yale University Press, 2007), 323; Beryl Satter, *Each Mind a Kingdom: American Women, Sexual Purity, and the New Thought Movement, 1875–1920* (Berkeley: University of California Press, 1999).
21. Charles Samuel Braden, *Spirits in Rebellion: The Rise and Development of New Thought* (Dallas: Southern Methodist University Press, 1963), 233.
22. Albanese, *Republic*, 431.
23. C. Alan Anderson and Debora G. Whitehouse, *New Thought: A Practical American Spirituality* (New York: Crossroads, 1995), 25.
24. Jill Watts, *God, Harlem U.S.A.: The Father Divine Story* (Berkeley: University of California Press, 1992), 25.
25. Watts, *God, Harlem U.S.A.*, 27–29.
26. Watts, *God, Harlem U.S.A.*, 24.
27. Father Divine, "God's Words Are Materialized as Mankind Realizes the Materialization of Spiritual Things," *New Day*, June 8, 1939.
28. Johnnie Colemon, *Open Your Mind and Be Healed* (Camarillo, CA: DeVorss Publications, 1997), 50–51.
29. Bruce Buursma, "Minister Practices What She Preaches; Her Gospel Is 'Success,'" *Chicago Tribune*, July 28, 1985.
30. Buursma, "Minister Practices."
31. Johnnie Colemon, *It Works If You Work It*, workbook (Chicago: Christ Universal Temple, n.d.), 11.
32. Mitchem, *Name It and Claim It?* 90; Martin, *Beyond Christianity*.
33. Harrison, *Righteous Riches*; Jonathan L. Walton, *Watch This! The Ethics and Aesthetics of Black Televangelism* (New York: New York University Press, 2009); Walton, "Stop Worrying and Start Sowing! A Phenomenological Account of the Ethics of Divine Investment," in *Pentecostalism and Prosperity: The Socio-economics of Global Charismatic Movement*, ed. Amos Yong and Katy Attanasi (New York: Palgrave Macmillan, 2012).
34. Harrison, *Righteous Riches*, 96.
35. Frederick K. C. Price, *Beware! The Lies of Satan* (Los Angeles: Faith One Publishing, 1999).
36. Walton, "Stop Worrying."
37. Harrison, *Righteous Riches*, 96.
38. Walton, *Watch This!* 64.
39. Harrison, *Righteous Riches*, 103.

Selected Texts

Albanese, Catherine L. *A Republic of Mind and Spirit: A Cultural History of American Metaphysical Religion*. New Haven: Yale University Press, 2007.

Anderson, C. Alan, and Debora G. Whitehouse. *New Thought: A Practical American Spirituality*. New York: Crossroads, 1995.

Baer, Hans A. "African American Religious Experience." In *Encyclopedia of Religion and Society*, ed. Jr. William H. Swatos, 7–11. London: AltaMira Press, 1998.

Baer, Hans A. *The Black Spiritual Movement: A Religious Response to Racism*. Knoxville: University of Tennessee Press, 1984.

Berry, Jason. *The Spirit of Black Hawk: A Mystery of Africans and Indians*. Jackson: University Press of Mississippi, 1995.

Billingsley, Andrew. *Mighty Like a River: The Black Church and Social Reform*. New York: Oxford University Press, 1999.

Braden, Charles Samuel. *Spirits in Rebellion: The Rise and Development of New Thought*. Dallas: Southern Methodist University Press, 1963.

Buursma, Bruce. "Minister Practices What She Preaches; Her Gospel Is 'Success.'" *Chicago Tribune*, July 28, 1985.

Colemon, Johnnie. *It Works If You Work It*. Workbook. Chicago: Christ Universal Temple, n.d.

Colemon, Johnnie. *Open Your Mind and Be Healed*. Camarillo, CA: DeVorss Publications, 1997.

Divine, Father. "God's Words Are Materialized as Mankind Realizes the Materialization of Spiritual Things." *New Day*, June 8, 1939, 15–18.

Franklin, Robert Michael. *Crisis in the Village: Restoring Hope in African American Communities*. Minneapolis: Fortress Press, 2007.

Franklin, Robert Michael. *Another Day's Journey: Black Churches Confronting the American Crisis*. Minneapolis: Fortress Press, 1997.

Hacker, Jacob S., and Paul Pierson. *Winner-Take-All Politics: How Washington Made the Rich Richer—and Turned Its Back on the Middle Class*. New York: Simon & Schustser, 2010.

Harrison, Milmon F. *Righteous Riches: The Word of Faith Movement in Contemporary African American Religion*. New York: Oxford University Press, 2005.

Hopkins, Dwight N. *Heart and Head: Black Theology—Past, Present, and Future*. New York: Palgrave, 2002.

Horton, Michael Scott. *Christless Christianity: The Alternative Gospel of the American Church*. Grand Rapids, MI: BakerBooks, 2008.

Hurston, Zora Neale. "Hoodoo in America." *Journal of American Folklore* 44, no. 174 (1931): 317–417.

Jacobs, Claude F., and Andrew Jonathan Kaslow. *The Spiritual Churches of New Orleans: Origins, Beliefs, and Rituals of an African-American Religion*. Knoxville: University of Tennessee Press, 1991.

Long, Carolyn Morrow. *A New Orleans Voudou Priestess: The Legend and Reality of Marie Laveau*. Gainesville: University Press of Florida, 2006.

Martin, Darnise C. *Beyond Christianity: African Americans in a New Thought Church*. New York: New York University Press, 2005.

Mitchem, Stephanie Y. *Name It and Claim It? Prosperity Preaching in the Black Church*. Cleveland: Pilgrim Press, 2007.

Pinn, Anthony B. *The Black Church in the Post-Civil Rights Era*. Maryknoll, NY: Orbis Books, 2002.

Price, Frederick K.C. *Beware! The Lies of Satan*. Los Angeles: Faith One Publishing, 1999.

Satter, Beryl. *Each Mind a Kingdom: American Women, Sexual Purity, and the New Thought Movement, 1875–1920*. Berkeley: University of California Press, 1999.

Walton, Jonathan L. "Stop Worrying and Start Sowing! A Phenomenological Account of the Ethics of Divine Investment." In *Pentecostalism and Prosperity: The Socio-economics of Global Charismatic Movement*, ed. Amos Yong and Katy Attanasi. New York: Palgrave Macmillan, 2012.

Walton, Jonathan L. *Watch This! The Ethics and Aesthetics of Black Televangelism*. New York: New York University Press, 2009.

Watts, Jill. *God, Harlem U.S.A.: The Father Divine Story*. Berkeley: University of California Press, 1992.

CHAPTER 33

AFRICAN AMERICAN THEOLOGY AND THE PUBLIC IMAGINARY

WILLIE JAMES JENNINGS

African American intellectuals have tried to name and then address a diaspora of people who were constituted a people because they were made a disapora. If diaspora connotes the spatial scattering of a people, then in the case of the scattering of African peoples we are not referring to the fragmentation of a people but a people formed by fragmentation. Some have looked at that fragmentation and tried to link those disaporic bodies in a common search, a common doing, and a shared agenda for prosperous life. African Americans inherited and also created a set of theologically conditioned imaginative frames through which they addressed a black public within a wider public or a wider public from within a black public consciousness. This essay delineates those frames, which together constitute an African American public imaginary.[1]

The Creation of a Public Black Body

The idea of a Western public begins for peoples of African descent with modern slavery. As they entered modern slavery, they entered the transformation of their bodies into commodities, and commodities are the quintessence of public existence. The bodies of these displaced peoples joined other objects of desire: weapons, gold and silver, alcohol, animals, and land. Together they formed the circuits of production and consumption through which flowed the lifeblood of New World colonies and Old World metropolises. These traumatic beginnings announce a public existence constituted precisely in the formation of the black body. Before we can detect the various senses of public that black peoples will envision as the centuries unfold, we must first capture the contours of public existence they will be forced to inhabit.[2]

The black body as commodity helped to generate public space in the emergence of the modern West and especially North America. It helped constitute the space within which the gestures of exchange and negotiation as well as forms of brutal utilitarian evaluation came to life. At every port of entry, every town square where buying and selling helped form the quotidian sensibilities of indigene, immigrant, and slave, the auctioning of black bodies gave rise to the ways in which peoples would view the world in its modern commodifying frame. The slave auction block is certainly not the only generative site of a New World sense of public. Nor am I suggesting the black body singularly created New World visions of public space and public existence.

The crucial point here is twofold: first, the bodies of Africans, positioned at the creative center of public life, facilitated the interaction and collaboration of a multiplicity of peoples within a wide theater of transactions that crisscrossed over, around, and through their bodies. The African body was made a public body. Second, the African's first sense of the modern public comes with an indelible sense of *being viewed*. Being viewed should not be equated with being watched. Black slaves and their children were of course watched, but being viewed has less to do with those active processes of surveillance symptomatic of colonialist cultures and more to do with their growing sense of being seen as racial objects by everyone.

Here a public comes into view precisely as it views the black body. The African enters a world in which she senses a public seeing her. This viewing did and does help constitute forms of racial identity, white, black, and everything in between. Yet equally significant is the way this viewing carries forward abiding angles of modern black publicity. Three viewing angles are important for us. *First, black bodies are in pain, but that pain may be ignored by the viewer.* Every forced gathering of terrified Africans on the continent's coasts, every unloading of melancholic human cargo, and every tear-filled and anguish-haunted slave auction demanded the same discipline: ignore their suffering and commodify them. Peoples have learned through centuries of training to view black bodies callously. I am not saying that each viewer is callous, always an emotionally unmoved viewer. I am naming a pedagogy embedded in public viewing of black bodies being tortured, impoverished, killed, bodies dying, sick, imprisoned, or simply mistreated or disrespected, that does not create the kinds of collective responses toward action one would anticipate from such viewing. Rather the suffering black body when viewed collapses back in on itself and invites viewers to explore the self-caused factors for that suffering. Much like Job's friends who gaze upon him in wonder about which self-defeating faults caused these calamities to come on him, modern viewing of black bodies facilitates a viewing public but rarely creates serious public responses.

Second, black bodies may be viewed as items of exchange. What is the effect of bodies seen for centuries as commodities? The commodity form comes to permeate the viewing of the body so that black bodies are viewed not only through a calculus of utility but also as fundamentally interchangeable. This utility and interchangeability mean that the viewing of black people loses social depth perception. We could think of this as a kind of stereotyping that is more than collapsing individual identity into group image. Rather this stereotyping constricts the narrative dimensions of existence through which people might be viewed and in turn maps onto them an overarching vision of use-value. This viewing angle thereby denies personhood in the precise moment when it imagines it sees a black person. This public viewing pivots on the sighting of productivity and binds the viewer to a hermeneutic of efficiency, utility, and proven worth. The viewing allows black people to be distinguishable and distinctive in the details of individual lives, but neither aspect of particularity is sufficient to break apart this commodifying process of stereotyping.

Third, black bodies are always to be publically evaluated. The evaluation of black bodies grew out of the comparative analytics that emerged with the subjugation of native peoples and the necessities of the slave market. Europeans drew comparisons of peoples with reference to their own bodies, thus setting the stage for hierarchical phenotypologies and the establishing of an ever-expanding racial aesthetic regime. The evaluation of black bodies became comprehensive, spanning space and time and capturing the analytical calculations of all colonial nations. In this way, it became ubiquitous and unrelenting. As I noted in another context, the bodies of these displaced Africans "underwent a new calculation—size, type, age, gender, tribal background, language, beauty, ugliness, strength, compliance, aggressiveness, viability—all geared to determine market potential."[3] On the one hand such unrelenting evaluation circumscribed black flesh in a distorted moral vision where the degrees of compliance, docility, and productivity inscribed character traits, while racialized physical features suggested human developmental capacities. On the other hand the cumulative effect of this operation was to instill the normalcy of the evaluation itself, marking this as a customary discursive practice embedded in white subjectivity and an element constitutive of the social performance of whiteness.

These viewing angles of the black body expose the complexity for Africans in the West of imagining "the public" or something called "public space." Their developments meant that slaves and their progeny had to swim in the rough currents of racial representation energized by the centuries-long textual operation of creating black people while at the same time trying to wrestle from white supremacists' hands modern black publicity. What they imagined as a public, black or white, and how they sought to address the public(s) can only be understood in relation to this epic struggle over commodification and its concomitant effect, racial representation. There was however, another overarching reality that profoundly affected the ways Africans in the West would imagine their publics: the rise of nationalist consciousness.

The Invention of Cultural Nationalism(s)

Africans, as did many other colonized subjects, looked out onto a world of peoples being made into national subjects, and they did so as those being formed inside of nationalist consciousness. This dual formation into national subjects and into seeing nationalities as natural states of racial and cultural existence were the achievements of modernity.[4] The formative process of nationalism owes much to the practices of accumulation fostered by capitalism through which slaves and indigenes were marked as possessions, and notions of ownership took on new symbolic forms that bound together people and land in sequestered spaces. It is precisely this possessive way of imagining people that resourced new configurations that tied the geographic boarders of nation-states to cultural boundaries. Nationalist visioning became a powerful new way of imagining collectivity, and from their many colonial sites Africans seized on its possibilities. A national subject was of course an imagined identity and an imagined global (spatial and conceptual) position that grew through the rise of vernacular space. Vernacular space came to exist at the intersection of the rise of printing technologies that expanded the reach of print media, the Protestant push for the vernacularization of the Bible, and the centralization and promotion of single languages (French, English, Dutch, German, Spanish, etc.) as the carriers of a people's cultural heritage in the cultivation of nationalist interests.[5] However, Africans as national subjects, especially in America, were a very thorny and contested reality.

Thinking of oneself nationalistically seemed almost unavoidable, but in America, Africans were barred from moving from national subject to citizen through the prohibition against slave literacy and the attempts to create an American self-image built from cultural fantasies of a white male confraternity. Yet Africans did think nationalistically along two general and well-established lines. First, they imagined themselves as frustrated citizens being denied the basic rights and freedoms of citizenship. A second nationalistic conceptuality marked Africans as a nation within a nation, that is, as a diaspora in search of a homeland, or needing to return to one, Africa. These two forms of nationalistic thinking were not mutually exclusive, so that anyone could imagine a public in either direction or both at the same moment.[6]

Theology of a (Black) Public

This reality of commoditized public existence and the rise of cultural nationalistic thinking together form the social womb within which African American voices will emerge, taking aim at the world they imagine to be capable of listening to them. If the African American public imaginary is born of the tumultuous social currents that constitute our public existence, then the primary site where we can see those chaotic currents is Christianity. Euro-American Christianity that became slaveholding Christianity that was and is racialized Christianity formed the poignant theater from which various visions of public existence have been performed and countless black intellectuals envisioned their theological existence. Theater is an apt metaphor here because Christianity in this regard *stages the public.* Christian practices of *ecclesia* (gathering), *didache* (teaching), *kerygma* (preaching), *liturgia* (worship), and *diakoneo* (service) form congregation and give sight of a public.

Africans from the origins of the colonial worlds forward found themselves participants in two constant moments of staging. On the one hand, they were invited into a Christian world in which Euro-Christians imagined them as insignificant players within the drama of redemption as either creatures of almost impenetrable sin or as carnal Christians in need of constant white tutelage, but almost never through deep spiritual-familial connection, and never as crucial contributors to understanding the nature of Christian faith. On the other hand, these Africans once inside a Christian narrative construal of life staged themselves as central actors in a drama of redemption that drew God to their plight, and made their multiple struggles a central divine concern. These struggles marked a reality called the "black church" that was never simple, monolithic, or culturally or socially uniform. The "black church" in this regard should be understood as the historically crucial site where black peoples generated visions of a public.

We could understand black church as a particular imagined public; however, I suggest we consider black church within a wider generative reality. In this regard, it forms a particular site within Western Christian life from which Africans of varying degrees of adherence to Christian faith or commitment to church life launched their imaginative work of address. Because of this history, there is an abiding theological character to African American and perhaps all black diasporic public imaginaries. It was precisely the missional orientation of colonial Christianity that produced imaginaries that *looked outward* into the world, envisioning connections between peoples and guiding peoples in the ways they would narrate those connections. There is thusly a theological character to an African American public imaginary.

An African American public imaginary is already a theological performance that gestures toward a black public theology. The remainder of my essay will offer a typology of African American public imaginaries. I contend that they carry the force of theological vision because they are infused with aspects of a Christian doctrine of salvation. This infusion of salvific elements means that what is envisioned is a public *able to become* something, even as it is imagined to exist as a public. What the public may become forms a crucial aspect of what the public is imagined to be. These imaginaries are also haunted by the specter of colonial imperialism because they are influenced by colonialism's desires to establish uniformity of thought and life as in some measure necessary to the transformation of space and the cultivation of peoples. My types are not ontologies and certainly not cosmologies, but rather reflective of various social positionalities that have been productive for creating social vision and possibly political action.

I will delineate these types around three points of reference. The first point of reference will be how they see the relation of racialized publics, white, black, and everything in between; second, what oppositional structures are at play; and third, how is agency generated and what actions are to be performed? The guiding image for each type will be the body, the public as body. This is certainly not a new idea, but here it will help us keep in view the racial calculus that is always operative in the ways individual addressers imagine not only their audience, but also who they imagine is or is not paying attention to them. The "body" metaphor also orientates us to the social character of black existence. The black body is fundamentally a socially constructed body formed over many centuries, spread out over vast geographic distances, encompassing multiple nation-states, and brutally binding together many different peoples under a white supremacist logic. This means that to imagine an individual black body is at the same moment to be inside a collective imagining, and to imagine the black body in private is already a public imagining. Of course, the same must be said about white bodies and all other bodies caught within the racial calculus. However, with the public black body we gain sight of the intricate mapping work that is part of the modern racial condition.

Whom would I associate with these types? These types do not reflect particular intellectuals or schools of thought (philosophical, religious, sociological, political, theological, artistic, etc.) so much as frames of social desire. With this sense at hand, I would associate them primarily with various social positions and particular angles of orientation toward peoples. I recognize that the descriptive vagueness that often comes along with typological abstraction may frustrate readers looking for precise categorization of particular scholars and theological positions. Yet I contend that the complexities of public existence for black peoples require a more synthetic account of the imaginaries at work in our modes of public address.

The Body in Need of Freedom

Africans from the colonial moment forward imagined their freedom from slavery. Imagining a public that was half enslaved and half free generated a very powerful moral vision that placed slaveholders and their supporters as the central target of address. Yet this vision of freedom drew black people into its circle as those who should demand and press for their emancipation. The oppositional structure envisioned here is at one level fairly straightforward: Slaveholders and slaveholding society stand against the freedom of the enslaved. At another level, enslavement itself generated a number of oppositional realities that thwarted the flourishing of black flesh such as torture, rape, brutal working conditions, the loss of loved ones through sale, the constant disinheriting of black people from any kind of ownership, their alienation from their labor and the products of their hands, and the canonizing of random acts of violence perpetrated on black bodies. Here enslavement's implications rippled across the black body, yielding a wider vision of what freedom meant beyond the immediate end of ownership. It also meant the reversal of the effects of enslavement. In this regard, the desired action to be performed began with slavery's end but moved on toward establishing the signatures of freedom in the lives of black people. Thus this imaginary lodges enslavement's historical effects yet rippling across the black body. Thus the body in need of freedom is a vision of a public where one yet sees the need to end the longitudinal effects of the historical formation of modern societies within slavery, and imagines the full effect of emancipation to remain unfulfilled.

The Body in Need of Discipline

The demand for freedom in no way denies claims for black agency in this first imaginary. The demand for freedom in fact exhibits black agency. Emphasis with the first view of a public falls on the reversal of the processes of commodification applied to flesh. This is one that pivots on captivity as a powerful image for public life, and therefore it focuses on what seems to be the lingering signs of enslavement's profound social trajectories. A second one imagines that what is necessary to sustain life after bondage is discipline. There is great irony to this imaginary in that it has its roots in the disciplinary regime that was pressed onto enslaved black bodies. Slavers and their supporters supposed that black people needed the disciplined life that slaveholding Christianity would provide. A body in need of discipline not only joins black bodies to all indigenes in the minds of slaveholding society, but also to those Europeans coming to the colonies from the Old World who have not yet become fully civilized. Discipline of body, mind, and soul was imagined not only as good for slaves, but was in truth ordained by God as the quintessential sign of God's providential care for them. The undisciplined (enslaved) black body gave way in this altered optic register to a vision of lack and deficiency born of slavery itself. An enslaved body is a body hampered by *induced* deficiencies, not only individually but also collectively.

This way of imagining a public takes shape through the discernment of various missing elements in the formation of a people who can effectively secure their own survival (e.g., lack of organization, mobilization, coordination of social, economic, or political power) or in the formation of individuals who lack proper cultivation. This vision is characterized by its unrelenting collapse of the social situation onto black people themselves. This imaginary does not ignore the wider material conditions of existence; they are simply not seen as decisive for this public. This public is primarily black people, and the point of opposition is found precisely in their own actions or inactions.

The Body in Need of Recognition

This imaginary attempts to draw attention to black bodies where it has been lacking, diverted, or episodic rather than constant. The relation of racialized publics here is certainly a "both/and." It is first a wider (white) public that must be made aware of the plight of black peoples, but it is also aimed at alerting or at least deepening the knowledge of black people to the precise challenges, dangers, or problems plaguing black communities. This vision carries the strong belief that the suffering of black flesh has yet to receive appropriate attention that leads to adequate public action. Ironically, that belief does not weaken the power of this imaginary and the hope that through careful data collection, analysis, and even rhetorical power, the presentation of attending problems will finally yield decisive positive responses. There are also those forces within this imagined public that seek to divert attention away from black communities or misdirect attention by drawing focus onto less substantial and less systemic matters. This opposition permeates this imagined public. The body in need of recognition also encompasses a vision of difference. Here the public is imagined as not yet sensitized to the multiple textures of human existence, especially the complex forms of life that constitute black life. Here the lives of black women especially come into view as fundamentally out of focus for this public. This public is characterized by what it does not see or understand and therefore the desired action is first simply to create enlightenment and then action.

The Body in Need of Integration

This way of envisioning a public has been captured by the nationalist imaginary and marks the public as a shared project of self-making. This imaginary focuses on the possibilities born of nation building for establishing a coherent narrative for social existence that might make sense of the collective horrors of the past. The formation of the nation on top of the suffering of the black body may be turned into the growing pains of a people toward self-awareness, civic and civil maturity, and deep appreciation of its common life in this vision. A public in need of integration is a public that needs to weave people's different and difficult stories of survival into one story of a people and allow that narrative to guide individual and collective action. So in America this imaginary fantasizes that the stories of slaves may join the stories of despised immigrants whose stories may join the stories of indigenous peoples that may join the stories of recent immigrants and together they will aim us toward the deepest possibilities of a new nation that houses the free spaces of democracy. Our social conflicts show us how we fail to weave our stories into a common narrative of a nation-forming. This public does not see its differences as life-giving strands that together form a living whole.

From education to business, cultural conflicts to poverty, the lack of integration helps explain in large measure the destructive behaviors of people, black, white, and everyone in between. This imaginary thusly locates the fundamental oppositional structure in the public itself in its failure to see how the many constitute the one and in its resistance to becoming the one. This imaginary seeks to orientate its public to a future of shared tasks in nation building, but that future moves in two contradictory directions. On the one hand, it has drawn forward the cultural logics of Western assimilation that press people into a white Western ideal type in speech, manner of dress and behavior, business practices, and educational form, among other things. Integration becomes fundamentally assimilation for the sake of survival of a people or of the nation itself. On the other hand, this imaginary suggests we work toward a multicultural integration through which peoples' differences are brought into various kinds of constructive relationships and/or minimized by being limited to a private sphere of cultural belonging. This means that this public imaginary envisions two very different kinds of becoming for this public.

The Body in Need of Authenticity

The black body had been inscribed in eternal blackness, formed into a slave, and made a commodity. Who then were these displaced peoples? Who are they in reality? And how would they find out? This imaginary pivots on sight of the real covered by the unreal. What is real in this regard circles around two nodes of knowledge, the real histories of various black peoples, and the real cultures of black peoples. The focus here is primarily on black peoples, and their need not simply for knowledge but to act on and move forward inside that knowledge. Moving forward is also moving away from forms of historical and cultural denial. What precisely constitutes historical and cultural denial is never easy to determine, but the perception of denial grows where there is denigration of black peoples and their cultures, ignorance of their histories, denial of their collective contributions to various societies, and most significantly the promotion of an aesthetic order that revolves around white bodies and European cultures as the fundamental anchors of the true, the good, and the beautiful.

This imaginary seeks to counter this white aesthetic not primarily with a black ideal type but with a multiplicity of cultural and social forms that all speak and celebrate black life. The oppositional structure is difficult to pin down because of the indeterminacy of historical or cultural denial. In one sense this denial is structural, having to do with, for example, educational processes that fundamentally discount the histories, contributions, or concerns of black peoples. Yet in another sense anyone who denies the real within this public may be an impediment to truth. The goal for this public is not simply enlightenment, but a kind of baptism in the real. A new people emerge from the waters of authenticity with a strong sense of their complex existence before the horrors of slavery and a direction that will always move them away from the collective habits of self-denigration and denial.

The Body in Need of Transformation

Black peoples are the subjects of endless social commentary. This grows out of the legacy of the objectifications of black flesh, but it is also due to the social position that black peoples most often inhabit as those who are the object of various gazes—medical, social, cultural, journalistic, and so on—and rarely in the position of those who form the objects of knowledge and control their dissemination. As such, black bodies are often presented as a field of flesh upon which we ascertain the status of various disciplinary knowledge(s) and the default site for making the latest pronouncements of the sciences. The real historical conditions that constitute the challenges of life for black peoples are in this imaginary transmuted into a constellation of pathologies that encircle the black body and from which the only hope is its full and complete transformation. It is not clear what black peoples would be transformed into in this imaginary, only what they would be transformed out of their current condition, which is somehow connected to their racial condition. Here we encounter a dilemma. If the pathologies are somehow bound to their being and not simply the effects of history or environment, then is transformation possible? This imaginary lives in this question and in fact generates the question.

So who is being addressed in this imaginary? The public imagined here exists in the dual position of object and gazer. The public who gazes is anyone who looks on the plight of the black body, including black peoples, yet the object is always only black peoples. This means that this imaginary posits the racialized publics it helps to create by constituting a white gaze onto black flesh that black peoples may participate in and thereby reify their own existence. The action suggested by this imaginary is ironically stupefying, because it points us toward aiding in the transformation of black bodies while recognizing that the condition of black peoples may be because they are black peoples. Who or what then is the point of opposition for this transformation? That opposition clearly falls back on the black body itself but also our lack of knowledge of its intricacies, which may in time be revealed through the latest advances in knowledge, which will again allow us to have a more precise view of the black body.

What follows is a graphic representation of this typology, moving from the black body to the white body. The types that are located near their primary racial target audience are also related to other potential audiences.

Black--------------(A Racialized World in between)---------------White

Discipline Authenticity Integration Transformation Recognition Freedom

Conclusion

Black peoples were forced to imagine the world through fragmentation. It is a great sign of hope that we tried to imagine a world at all. We imagine peoples of vastly different places and times of many hues joined by a common second skin not of our own choosing or making, but certainly of our remaking. African American public imaginaries are fundamentally about the remaking of a public, black, white, and everything in between, and this is profoundly a theological act born of Christianity and the church. Yet these imaginaries are born of trouble and strife, and so the most central question may not be which imaginary best serves the needs, interests, and concerns of black peoples, as opposed to which imaginaries are profoundly destructive. We could certainly entertain the question of whether we should move beyond all public imaginaries, but that seems to me to be quite unrealistic. The question pressed on us by this history might be if in fact we could imagine a public in ways that capture more powerfully the dreams of a God who has come to be with us, and invites everyone to share in God's own body. This God's dream was and is not simply to imagine a public, but to change it.

Notes

1. Charles Taylor, *Modern Social Imaginaries* (Durham, NC: Duke University Press, 2004); Michael Warner, *Publics and Counterpublics* (New York: Zone Books, 2005); Susan Buck-Morss, *Dreamworld and Catastrophe: The Passing of Mass Utopia in East and West* (Cambridge: MIT Press, 2000); Arjun Appadurai, *Modernity at Large: Cultural Dimensions of Globalization* (Minnesota: University of Minnesota Press, 1996).
2. Walter Johnson, *Soul by Soul: Life Inside the Antebellum Slave Market* (Cambridge: Harvard University Press, 1999); Frederic Bancroft, *Slave Trading in the Old South* (1931; Columbia: University of South Carolina Press, 1995); Anne C. Bailey, *African Voices of the Atlantic Slave Trade: Beyond the Silence and the Shame* (Boston: Beacon Press, 2005).
3. Willie James Jennings, *The Christian Imagination: Theology and the Origins of Race* (New Haven: Yale University Press, 2010), 176.
4. Walker Connor, *Ethnonationalism: The Quest for Understanding* (Princeton, NJ: Princeton University Press, 1994); Anthony D. Smith, *Myths and Memories of the Nation* (Oxford: Oxford University Press, 1999); Christopher L. Miller, *Nationalists and Nomads* (Chicago: University of Chicago Press, 1998).
5. Benedict Anderson, *Imagined Communities* (London: Verso, 1983); Partha Chatterjee, *The Nation and Its Fragments: Colonial and Postcolonial Histories* (Princeton, NJ: Princeton University Press, 1993).
6. Philip Dray, *Capitol Men* (Boston: Mariner Books, 2010); Patrick Rael, *Black Identity and Black Protest in the Antebellum North* (Chapel Hill: University of North Carolina Press, 2002); Michael C. Dawson, *Black Vision: The Roots of Contemporary African-American Political Ideologies* (Chicago: University of Chicago Press, 2001).

Selected Texts

Anderson, Benedict. *Imagined Communities*. London: Verso, 1983.

Appadurai, Arjun. *Modernity at Large: Cultural Dimensions of Globalization*. Minnesota: University of Minnesota Press, 1996.

Chatterjee, Partha. *The Nation and Its Fragments: Colonial and Postcolonial Histories*. Princeton: Princeton University Press, 1993.

Edwards, Brent Hayes. *The Practice of Diaspora: Literature, Translation, and the Rise of Black Internationalism*. Cambridge: Harvard University Press, 2003.

Hopkins, Dwight N., ed. *Black Faith and Public Talk: Critical Essays on James Cone's Black Theology and Black Power*. Waco, TX: Baylor University Press, 2007.

Johnson, Walter. *Soul by Soul: Life inside the Antebellum Slave Market*. Cambridge: Harvard University Press, 1999.

Miller, Christopher L. *Nationalists and Nomads*. Chicago: University of Chicago Press, 1998.

Mohanram, Radhika. *Black Body: Women, Colonialism, and Space*. Minneapolis: University of Minnesota Press, 1999.

Shelby, Tommie. *We Who Are Dark: The Philosophical Foundations of Black Solidarity*. Cambridge: Harvard University Press, 2005.

Taylor, Charles. *Modern Social Imaginaries*. Durham, NC: Duke University Press, 2004.

Warner, Michael. *Publics and Counterpublics*. New York: Zone Books, 2005.

CHAPTER 34

CULTURAL BOUNDARIES AND AFRICAN AMERICAN THEOLOGY

EMILIE M. TOWNES

This essay interrogates the ways in which black culture serves as a primary source for doing African America (black) theology. It considers the legitimization through which culture is defined and understood within African American theology, and which elements of this cultural production are used and why. Using both historical and contemporary perspectives, it both provides a broad overview and pauses to offer thick descriptions of how culture affects and informs African American theology.

With roots in the civil rights movement of the 1950s and 1960s and the Black Power movement of the 1960s and early 1970s, African American theology is shaped by theological categories like hope, eschatology, liberation, and salvation; black religious experiences and a history of systematic oppression from enslavement to the contemporary era; and culture. Like any racial group in the United States, blacks make meanings and develop survival skills in the larger US culture and the global arena. However, black folk have lived and continue to live within a panopticon[1] in which people who often demonstrate meticulous illiteracy about black lives watch them and judge them. Those who control the gaze of the panopticon refuse to acknowledge the impact of class, gender, and race on their observations and the ways in which illiteracy about black lives quickly morphs into stereotypes that damn and eviscerate black children, men, and women.

Black Culture as a Primary Source for Doing African American Theology

Living in a panopticon, or helping to maintain it, does not allow recognition of the richness of black cultures because it collapses black realities into postmodern minstrel shows that freeze-frame black life into a gross field of stereotypes and inaccuracies without recognizing our humanity or the rhythms and cadences of our living. Historical stereotypes of black folk as primitive, servile, and simple-minded have morphed into contemporary stereotypes of blacks as athletic, criminal, musically gifted, poor, and exceptionally religious. A list compiled by the class of a Teach For America corps member on stereotypes includes a sobering number of mostly degrading images: stupid, irresponsible, crack babies, teen pregnancy, dropouts, incarcerated, fathers leave their kids, love fried chicken and Kool-Aid, athletic, violent, live in the ghetto / the projects, wasted generation, loud, obnoxious, rude, nappy hair, bad attitudes, disrespectful, hoodlums, poor, obese, dirty, sex, drugs, porn, weed (marijuana), guns, low job expectations, speak different English.[2] These caricatures, which are largely negative, do not reflect the realities of a diverse group such as black folk in the United States.

In addition, they mask the often-grim realities of racism and other oppressions that black folk must deal with on a daily basis. For example, the phenomenon of "driving while black," in which African Americans are the subject of traffic stops in greater frequency than other racial groups, is a form of discretionary law enforcement harassment. This practice contributes to the fact that black males, in particular, acquire a criminal record more rapidly than whites. Further, there is a trickle-down effect in which black men have a greater chance of receiving a prison sentence and longer sentences than men in other racial ethnic groups, particularly white men.[3]

Negative black stereotypes are debilitating and make it difficult to develop healthy social, psychological, emotional, and theological outlooks. When black folk believe and also help reinforce black stereotypes, they become self-fulfilling prophecies. Hence, many of these brutalized and brutalizing images are internalized in black communities and in the individual lives of black children, men, and women when blacks accept them as accurate and true. One example of this dynamic is when a black person does not aspire to higher education because he or she believes that the stereotype that blacks are dumb and lazy is true and may go so far as to mock those who work hard in school for "trying to be white." This king of fatalism encourages far too many black folks to live their daily lives skipping rope with paralyzing demons, slipping into an endless spiral of horizontal violence without Martin King's dream, Malcolm X's nightmare, Alice Walker's color purple, or Mama Day's lightning powder.[4]

The Legitimization through Which Culture Is Defined and Understood within Black Theology

With a history and a present that include such vulgar spectacles as auction blocks, lynchings, and pedestals, it is ludicrous for African American theological reflection to advocate a methodology that ignores the powers that shape the world in which we live. Doing so precludes the possibility of developing more vibrant and accurate theological resources for all peoples and in our institutional households. Such work requires working with the blinding white-hot evils of racial, gender, and economic supremacies—at bare minimum—as theological categories as well as social categories. By expanding the traditional understanding of the theological, African American theology models for other theologies a more expansive understanding of God-talk and a more robust appreciation of the omnipresent nature of God.

To focus more specifically on the role of culture in the dynamics of African American Theology, we begin by turning to philosopher Paul Ricoeur. He notes, "When we discover that there are several cultures instead of just one and consequently at the time when we acknowledge the end of a sort of cultural monopoly, be it illusory or real, we are threatened with destruction by our own discovery. Suddenly it becomes possible that there are just *others*, that we ourselves are an 'other' among others."[5] This is an important reminder of the way in culture works, as there is not one acceptable culture be it high or low, but a plurality of them—each with its own audience

In a 1974 essay in the *Harvard Crimson*, Cornel West provides a rich definition of black culture:

> Black culture is the social adaptive apparatus which embodies and reflects the particular values, folkways, and mores of black people . . . [It] is dualistic; it has a functional dimension and an existential dimension. The functional dimension is characterized by the power-mastering capacity of blacks in the socioeconomic sphere. The existential dimension provides a defense against the culture's adversaries and propagates self-security within the culture. The functional and existential components of black culture are based on the historical experience of blacks, but the latter emphasizes the black ritual tradition. The ritual tradition of blacks is the inherited pattern of symbolic response to various societal phenomena.[6]

Ricoeur's prompt; West's rich definition that points to black culture as the values, folkways, and mores of black folk; and the history of African diasporic peoples in the United States provide the methodological linchpins for how culture is defined and understood within African American theology. Blacks created and nurtured a culture against the backdrop of racial, social, sexual, and economic exploitation and injustice. Black folk then became agents who responded to their varying situations as well as affecting these situations in crucial ways that are social, political, and theological. As noted earlier, although a part of the general American culture, Black culture has distinctive features that help maintain and shape the traditions of black communities as they struggle to survive in the midst of the panopticon of structural and persistent oppression. In this environment, common beliefs, value systems, and goals provide the framework for black culture and provide the grist for African American theology as it consciously integrates authentic black cultural realities in its theological musings to combat the gross stereotypes of black lives.

Hence, black culture becomes a key resource in combating discrimination and debunking a history of stereotypes that become reified into systems of oppression such as classism, sexism, and racism. Exploring the resources, histories, and worldviews found in genuine black culture provides a more accurate view of black peoples in the United States. For African American theology, this creates a rich resource for reflection on the nature of God-talk as it emerges in and through black lives. This combination of culture and theology produces a powerful testament to the ways in which black folk give credence to notions of the divine and the ways in which cultural productions can be a resource for all peoples engaged in theological reflection.

As a resource for doing African American theology, black culture is both distinct from and a part of US culture. When approximately 12 million Africans were shipped to the Americas during the transatlantic slave trade (1492–1888), they brought with them various cultures such as the Ashanti, Igbo, Bakongo, and Wolof ethnic groups of West Africa. Fearing slave uprisings, masters and mistresses forcibly intermingled Africans from different ethnic groups. This intermixing eventually created a new identity and culture that was composed of the different cultural elements from the various ethnic groups as well as some European cultural influences.

Therefore, black culture is made up of a variety of genres that people use for different purposes.[7] Building on West's definition, as a cultural production, the distinctive elements are art, clothing styles, foods, language, literature, music, and the ways in which these are produced by black folk. For example, music is an important cultural resource for African American theology. One form of music, jazz, is illustrative. Jazz has been a part of the US cultural landscape since the beginning of the twentieth century. In its birthplace in black communities in the South, Midwest, and North, it developed distinct regional differences. In New Orleans, it probably emerged from Congo Square, where black slaves performed music and chants from their African roots. As a music that blends Africa with Europe, blues, hymns, and spirituals, old French and Spanish music, it has a distinctive sound. Cornetists like Buddy Bolden, Freddie Keppard, and Louis Armstrong; pianists like Jelly Roll Morton; clarinetists like Jimmie Noone; and trombonists like George Lewis produced sounds that emerged from the souls of black folk. While they played, Sweet Emma Barret, Lizzie Miles, and Ann Cook sang the words that the music carried. Distinct from New York or Kansas City jazz, New Orleans jazz is meant for dancing, not listening because of its swinging, stomping, syncopated beat.

Emerging at the same time as jazz, New Orleans gospel music has its own unique sound. It began as the early three- and four-person quartets and choirs from storefront chapels and spirit-filled churches. It was always a cappella, although blacks in other parts of the South used tambourines, drums, trumpets, and saxophones. New Orleans gospel singers were slow to warm to using musical instruments, as religionists thought that too many instruments were the Devil's music. Eventually, jazz musicians began playing in churches in the 1920s and 1930s. They brought with them rich musical arrangements that paved the way for larger choirs of thirty to forty singers as well as the use of horns, drums, pianos, organs, and guitars. Nevertheless, a cappella and the minimal use of musical instruments remained strong through such groups as the Zion Harmonizers, the Moses Hogan Sisters, the Joyful Gospel Singer, and the Mighty Chariots of Fire. Individual singers like Jai Reed and Miss Emma were influential, as well as the queen of gospel music, contralto Mahalia Jackson, who died in 1972. A rich resource like music has had and continues to have an impact on the Christian churches in which it is heard; it is only one example of how black culture moves into the world of the religious to inform and engage a people and their religious worldviews.

Why Certain Elements of This Cultural Production Are Used

Given that black religions, themselves cultural markers, are key sources for African American theology, the strong cultural productions shaping religious institutions like the Christian Church are crucial to African American theology as well. These cultural productions not only help define a people, they also provide a defense for the systematic dehumanization black folk in the United States have faced historically and continue to negotiate today.

As Christianity became the dominant religion for enslaved Africans who brought their own religious beliefs and practices with them to the Americas, slave owners mounted an often brutal and always systematic campaign to de-Africanize slaves by stripping them of their animist or Muslim beliefs in favor of Christian religious dogmas. As slave owners emphasized obedience and piety instead of the equalizing and liberating elements of Christianity, enslaved peoples were attracted to the story of Moses leading the Israelites out of Egypt to the Promised Land and the Hebrew Bible's descriptions of a fierce warrior God who protected and avenged the chosen people.

The style of the Christian worship that emerged included elements of West African religions such as ring shouts, call-and-response, a belief in the supernatural, and the existence of the kalunga line (the unseen line beneath bodies of water where one could commune with the spirits of deceased ancestors). Many of these African influences survive today in black religious worship: the amen corner, praise shouts, "getting happy," gospel music, altered states of consciousness and speaking in tongues, and the ways in which the Jordan River figures in spirituals, liturgical imagery, and full immersion and river baptism.

Again, the importance of music emerges as a cultural production that carries the theological worldviews of believers. The language of Negro spirituals[8] contains messages of deliverance and endurance as well as expressions of faith. For African American theology, these are key cultural resources for theological reflection. For example, the spiritual "I Got Shoes," in which a key line is "Everybody talkin' 'bout heaving ain't goin' there," secretly mocked the hypocritical piety of slave owners. Slaves used shouts, praise songs, and hymns to warn about and to signal the time of escape. The spiritual "Steal Away" is an example of one of these songs. The lyrics in its chorus are

Steal away
Steal away
Steal away
Steal away to Jesus
Steal away
Steal away home
I haven't got long to stay here.

The spiritual "Swing Low, Sweet Chariot" was often used to refer to the Underground Railroad.[9]

Such cultural productions help ground African American theology and guard against theological abstractions based on false universals that often frame traditional and/or (neo)orthodox theologies. Rather than claim an objective stance (which is often extremely biased), African American theology intentionally grounds itself in black lives and the ways in which these lives make religious meanings out of the world around them. This kind of theological honesty is rare in historical and contemporary theologies in general, as the claim to represent universals and objectivity produces theologies that are usually grounded in the experiences of the people who do it with little reflection or pause to consider how much our experience (which is grounded in culture) plays into how we see the world, how we see others in that world, and how we conceive of the nature of the divine at work in that world.

Rather than commit the error of *mauvaise honte*, African American theology cultivates a conscious awareness that one's social location, history, and culture factor into one's religious expressions. This is the true grist for theological reflection. This is why African American theology often explores the ways in which enslaved

Africans managed to retain to some of their religious practices by integrating them into Christian worship in the hush harbors slaves created outside of the eye of their masters and mistresses. As a rich cultural resource for theological reflection, it holds theological musings accountable for gross integrations of materials that bear little resemblance to the realities of black religiosities. It is important that in doing so, African American theology does not fall victim to the temptation to romanticize these survivals or make more out of what did or did not survive slaveocracy.

African American theology builds on the practices of dance, shouts, African rhythms and movements, music, and singing as instructive cultural productions that are also religious resources for theological reflection. It also turns to folk traditions (beliefs, medicine, and tales) as well as jokes to understand how black folk create and sustain religious meaning. These are crucial for theological reflection within the panopticon because they help theologians provide a thick description of the theological universe of black folk in the United States and also provide a window into how, as a diasporic people, US blacks resonate or not with other black diasporic cultures in the Caribbean and South America.

The inclusion of culture in African American theology creates a space for health, healing, identity formation, resistance, celebration, and transformation. This space is where the "real lives" and the "real worlds" of peoples are found and not the media-driven images of black living that trick all members of US society into believing or living grotesque stereotypes of black life. It is the place where the realities of diversity, difference, disagreement, harmony, hope, and justice all exist. It shapes the radical differences within the lives of African American children, men, and women such that they are not a monolithic community, but an eclectic and diverse compendium of *communities* that provides the core resistance to devaluing oppressions.

The cultural production of African American theology is the space where we find Toni Morrison's dancing mind, Baldwin's room, Alice Walker's world in our eye, Wright's alarm clock, Sonia Sanchez's house of lions, Glave's song, and Edwidge Danticat's krik? krak![10] It is a place where black theological reflection yokes individual and communal accountability as it urges all of us to consider the ways in which we express our beliefs through our actions as embodied peoples. Rather than accept the stereotypes found in the panopticon as genuine representations of peoples lives, the astute use of culture encourages all of us to look more closely in the eyes, backs, hands, mouths, feet, shoulders, arms, necks, inside parts, lungs, life-holding wombs, life-giving private parts, hearts, spirits, and souls of black folk.[11]

Black theologians who make use of the importance of cultural productions in their work produce nuanced theological and moral reflections concerning how to live creatively in the tight circle of choices that are often given to those caught in the relentless gaze of the panopticon. Rather than allow the panopticon to continue the gaze that misshapes black lives, these theologians plot, scheme, and realize ways to craft the tight circle into a spiral of possibilities for the current generation and those that will follow.

For example, Lewis Baldwin explores the cultural underpinnings of the life and work of Martin Luther King Jr., and Katie G. Cannon uses the power of black women's literature and black women's experience—religious and social—to mine the deep richness of black communities. Monica A. Coleman uses cultural formulations to analyze globalization, religious pluralism, and sexual diversity. Rachel E. Harding plumbs the alternative space created by the Afro-Brazilian religion candomblé, which enabled enslaved blacks gain a sense of individual and collective identity. Dwight N. Hopkins often turns to slave narratives and folktales to explore the ways in which the diversity of black lives in the United States have a full and authentic and valued place in the larger sociocultural and political landscape of this country and globally. Anthony Pinn investigates the ways in which the body is of profound theological importance. Emilie M. Townes explores the ways in which evil as a cultural production has a peculiar place in black lives in the United States. The biblical scholars who contributed to *Stony the Road We Trod* and *Theorizing Scriptures* bring the ways in which black folk read and interpret sacred texts through their cultural perspectives.

These representative thinkers demonstrate the various ways that cultural production provides rigorous theological frameworks while addressing the gross iconization of black lives in the panopticon. Their work and the work of African American theology in general is placed in the context of a people who know emotional, physical, and theological violation, attempt to live their lives with dignity, and can shake with religious ecstasy or evince the calm of the mystical. Because it explores a rich and diverse peoples who are situated in a dynamic and ever-changing culture and society, African American theology crafts theological worldviews that both provide a refuge from the panopticon and critiques and seek to dismantle it by employing authentic black culture as the foundation for exploring the religious worldviews of black folk in the United States and beyond.

Notes

1. English philosopher and social theorist Jeremy Bentham designed the panopticon in 1785. It is a type of prison building designed to allow an observer to observe all prisoners without the incarcerated being able to tell whether they are being watched. See Jeremy Bentham, *Panopticon, or The Inspection-House, &C (Preface)*, in *The Panopticon Writings*, ed. Miran Božovič (London: Verso, 1995), 29–95.
2. http://beachflute.teachforus.org/2007/10/28/the-list-of-stereotypes/. Teach for Us is the independent blog network for members of Teach For America. Teach for America is a national corps of recent college graduates who commit to teaching in urban and rural public schools in an effort to eliminate educational inequality in these communities.
3. Bureau of Justice Statistics, *Prison Inmates at Midyear 2008—Statistical Tables*, March 2009, (revised April 8, 2009).
4. Martin Luther King Jr. "I Have a Dream," public speech, Civil Rights March, Washington, DC, August 28, 1963. Malcolm X's response to King's "I have a dream speech was: "Who ever heard of angry revolutionists all harmonizing 'We shall overcome . . . Suum Day . . .'

while tripping and swaying along arm-in-arm with the very people they were supposed to be angrily revolting against? Who ever heard of angry revolutionists swinging their bare feet together with their oppressor in lily-pad park pools, with gospels and guitars and 'I have a dream' speeches? And the black masses in America were—and still are—having a nightmare." Alice Walker, *The Color Purple* (New York: Pocket Books, 1985). Gloria Naylor, *Mama Day* (New York: Vintage, 1989).

5. Paul Ricoeur, *History and Truth* (Evanston, IL: Northwestern University Press, 1965), 278.
6. Cornel West, "Black Culture: The Golden Mean," *Harvard Crimson*, March 26, 1974.
7. Lawrence W. Levine, *Black Culture and Black Consciousness: Afro-American Folk Thought from Slavery to Freedom*, 30th anniversary ed. (New York: Oxford University Press, 2007), xxl.
8. Negro spirituals emerged during slavery as rural enslaved Africans gathered after the regular worship services that were controlled and monitored by their plantation slave owners. Spirituals allowed slaves to express their pain, joys, and hopes.
9. The lyrics are:

Chorus:
Swing low, sweet chariot,
Comin' for to carry me home;
Swing low, sweet chariot,
Comin' for to carry me home.
I looked over Jordan,
And what did I see,
Comin' for to carry me home,
A band of angels comin' after me,
Comin' for to carry me home.

Repeat chorus:
If you get there before I do,
Comin' for to carry me home,
Tell all my friends I'm comin' too,
Comin' for to carry me home.

10. Toni Morrison, *The Dancing Mind: Speech upon Acceptance of the National Book Foundation Medal for Distinguished Contribution to American Letters* (New York: John Knopf, 1996); James Baldwin, *Giovanni's Room* (New York: Dial Press, 1956); Alice Walker, "Beauty: When the Other Dancer Is the Self," in *In Search of Our Mothers' Gardens: Womanist Prose* (New York: Harcourt,1983); Richard Wright, *Native Son* (New York: Harper & Brothers, 1940); Sonia Sanchez, *Does Your House Have Lions?* (Boston: Beacon Press, 1998); Thomas Glave, *Whose Song? And Other Stories* (New York: City Lights Publishers, 2001); Edwidge Danticat, *Krik? Krak!* (New York: Vintage Books, 1996).
11. Toni Morrison, *Beloved* (New York: Alfred A. Knopf, 1987), 88–89.

Selected Texts

Baldwin, Lewis. *There Is a Balm in Gilead: The Cultural Roots of Martin Luther King, Jr.* Minneapolis: Fortress Press, 1991.

Baldwin, Lewis. *To Make the Wounded Whole: The Cultural Legacy of Martin Luther King, Jr.* Minneapolis: Fortress Press, 1992.

Cannon, Katie G. *Katie's Canon: Womanism and the Soul of the Black Community.* New York: Continuum, 1998.

Cannon, Katie G. *Black Womanist Ethics.* Atlanta: American Academy of Religion, 1988.

Coleman, Monica A. *Making a Way Out of No Way: A Womanist Theology.* Minneapolis: Fortress Press, 2008.

Felder, Cain Hope, ed. *Stony the Road We Trod: African American Biblical Interpretation.* Minneapolis: Augsburg Fortress, 1991.

Harding, Rachel E. *A Refuge of Thunder: Candomblé and Alternative Spaces of Blackness.* Bloomington: Indiana University Press, 2003.

Hopkins, Dwight N. *Being Human: Race, Culture, and Religion.* Minneapolis: Fortress Press, 2005.

Hopkins, Dwight N. *Down, Up, and Over: Slave Religion and Black Theology.* Minneapolis: Fortress Press, 1999.

Hopkins, Dwight N. *Shoes That Fit Our Feet: Sources for a Constructive Black Theology.* Maryknoll, NY: Orbis Books, 1993.

Pinn, Anthony B. *Embodiment and the New Shape of Black Theological Thought.* New York: New York University Press, 2010.

Townes, Emilie M. *Womanist Ethics and the Cultural Production of Evil.* New York: Palgrave Macmillan, 2006.

Wimbush, Vincent L., ed. *Theorizing Scriptures: New Critical Orientations to a Cultural Phenomenon.* Piscataway, NJ: Rutgers University Press, 2008.

Index

CPSIA information can be obtained
at www.ICGtesting.com
Printed in the USA
BVHW050256120222
628540BV00003B/10

9 780190 917845